INTRODUCING ECONOMIC SYSTEMS

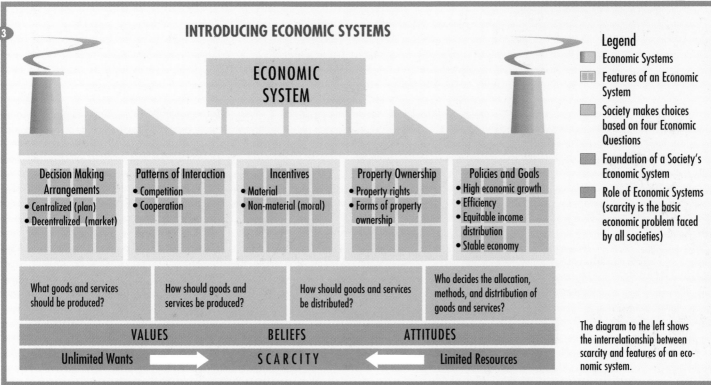

ECONOMIC SYSTEM

Decision Making Arrangements	Patterns of Interaction	Incentives	Property Ownership	Policies and Goals
• Centralized (plan) • Decentralized (market)	• Competition • Cooperation	• Material • Non-material (moral)	• Property rights • Forms of property ownership	• High economic growth • Efficiency • Equitable income distribution • Stable economy

What goods and services should be produced?	How should goods and services be produced?	How should goods and services be distributed?	Who decides the allocation, methods, and distrtibution of goods and services?

VALUES	BELIEFS	ATTITUDES

Unlimited Wants → SCARCITY ← Limited Resources

Legend

- Economic Systems
- Features of an Economic System
- Society makes choices based on four Economic Questions
- Foundation of a Society's Economic System
- Role of Economic Systems (scarcity is the basic economic problem faced by all societies)

The diagram to the left shows the interrelationship between scarcity and features of an economic system.

GLOBAL SYSTEMS CONCEPT MAP

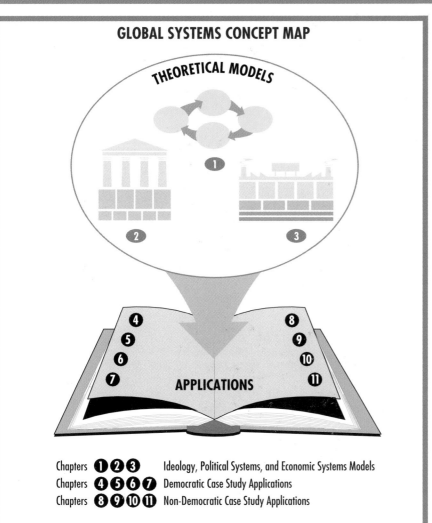

THEORETICAL MODELS

1

2   3

APPLICATIONS

4
5
6
7

8
9
10
11

ISSUE ICONS

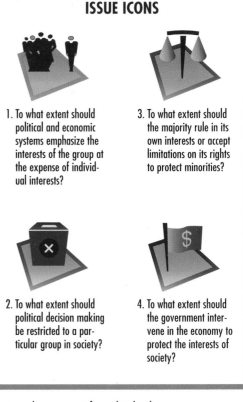

1. To what extent should political and economic systems emphasize the interests of the group at the expense of individual interests?

3. To what extent should the majority rule in its own interests or accept limitations on its rights to protect minorities?

2. To what extent should political decision making be restricted to a particular group in society?

4. To what extent should the government intervene in the economy to protect the interests of society?

The icons above represent four political and economic issues with which 20th century societies have been confronted.

The diagram to the left presents the conceptual design of this text book: the theoretical background and the models presented in Part I (Chapters 1–3) provide the foundation and organizational plan for the case study chapters of Part II (Chapters 4–11).

GLOBAL systems

BY DAVID J REES

WITH MICHAEL G JONES

ARNOLD
PUBLISHING LTD.

For more information or a catalogue contact:

Arnold Publishing Ltd.

11016–127 Street NW
Edmonton, Alberta, Canada T5M 0T2
Phone (780) 454-7477
            1-800-563-2665
Fax (780) 454-7463
E-mail orderdesk@arnold.ca
            info@arnold.ca
Website http://www.arnold.ca/

Author

David J. Rees with Michael G. Jones

Canadian Cataloguing in Publication Data

Rees, David John, 1955–
    Global Systems

Includes index.
ISBN 0-919913-74-1

1. Political science. 2. Comparative economics.
    3. World politics. I. Jones, Michael G., 1941–
    II.Title.
JC348.R43 1999   320.5   C98–911011–7

Arnold Publishing Project Team

Project Managers: Betty Gibbs, Karen Iversen
Project Coordinator: Judi McIntyre
Educational Editors: Phyllis A. Arnold,
    David Hardman
Editors: Betty Gibbs, Barbara Demers,
    Christina Barabash
Proofreader: Philippa Fairbairn
Design: Linda Tremblay, Marcey Andrews
Production: Linda Tremblay, Leslie Stewart,
    Judy Bauer, Anna Singkhone

Assisted by

Maps/Illustrations

Johnson Cartographics Inc., Wendy Johnson
Bidwell Design, Patrick Bidwell

Cover Design

Wayne Arthur Williams

Manufacturers

Creative Edge, Friesens

ACKNOWLEDGMENTS

This book would not have been possible without the support of a number of people. I extend a heartfelt thanks to Mike G. Jones for his good humour and conscientiousness. Thanks to Judi McIntyre for her dedication, Betty Gibbs for her editing, and Linda Tremblay, Leslie Stewart, Judy Bauer, and Anna Singkhone for their work on the book. Thanks to Karen Iversen for her insightful comments and guidance. Most of all, a special thanks to Phyllis Arnold for her unfailing support and commitment to this book.

Thanks to Robert J. Anderson, Marjorie, and Elizabeth in Victoria, BC; Kyril Holden, Tony Hollihan, David Kales (deceased), Waclaw Osadnik, and Anna Tulchinsky in Edmonton; Omill Omandi in Calgary; Natalya Djavrova in Ottawa.

Thanks also to: Vladimir I. Belikov, Mikhail V. Dmitriev, and Alexander P. Sergeev in Moscow, Russia; Igor Djavrov, Irina Shchegoleva, Tanya Skuba, Vasily V. Skuba, Sr. (deceased), Vasily V. Skuba, Jr., and Andrei A. Tatarinov in Sochi, Russia; Dwayne Weleschuk and Lena Sjoblom in Helsinki, Finland; Peter Svoboda in Vienna, Austria; and Gerry Magennis in Belfast, Northern Ireland.

Lastly, I would like to thank my mother Margaret Rees of Edmonton, Alberta; my father John Rees of Cultus Lake, BC; and colleague Lorraine Ross of Detroit, Michigan.

David J. Rees

I wish to thank David Rees for his professionalism and good humour, as well as Phyllis Arnold for providing me with this opportunity. I could not have sustained my effort without the support and guidance of Karen Iversen, who is a truly amazing person. Judi McIntyre worked very hard to make it easier for me in a cheerful and professional manner. Betty Gibbs provided thought-provoking ideas which were extremely valuable. I wish to thank all the other dedicated professionals at Arnold Publishing for their work. They are a great group of people. I wish also to thank my wife and son, Elva and David, whose love and support sustain my life.

Michael G. Jones.

The publisher gratefully acknowledges the following individuals for their invaluable contributions to this project.

Content Validators

Lawrence Aronsen
Associate Professor
University of Alberta
Department of History and Classics
Edmonton, Alberta

Satya Das
Columnist and Foreign Affairs Writer
Southam Newspapers
Edmonton, Alberta

Dr. Ryan Dunch
Assistant Professor
Department of History and Classics
University of Alberta
Edmonton, Alberta

J.C. Herbert Emery
Associate Professor
Department of Economics
University of Calgary
Calgary, Alberta

Masayuki Fukushima
Chairman of Pacific Rim Studies
Camosun College
Victoria, British Columbia

Dr. Bohdan Harasymiw
Professor
Department of Political Science
University of Calgary
Calgary, Alberta

Tom Keating
Professor
Department of Political Science
University of Alberta
Edmonton, Alberta

Dr. David R. Marples
Professor
Department of History and Classics
University of Alberta
Edmonton, Alberta

Dr. David Mills
Associate Professor of Canadian History
Department of History and Classics
University of Alberta
Edmonton, Alberta

Carl Widstrand, Ph. D.
Professor
Department of Technology, Society and Environment
Carleton University
Ottawa, Ontario

Sinh Vinh
Professor
Department of History and Classics
University of Alberta
Edmonton, Alberta

Tova Yedlin
Professor Emeritus
Department of Modern Languages and Cultural Studies
University of Alberta
Edmonton, Alberta

Educational Validators

Diane Blakelock
Humanities Teacher
John G. Diefenbaker High School
Calgary, Alberta

Diane Brayman
Social Studies Department Head
Paul Kane High School
St. Albert, Alberta

Kay Haslett
Social Studies Specialist
Calgary Board of Education
School, Student and Parent Services
Calgary, Alberta

Ian Kupchenko
Social Studies Teacher
Ross Sheppard High School
Edmonton, Alberta

Cordula Paletz
Social Studies Teacher
Henry Wise Wood High School
Calgary, Alberta

Dr. George Richardson
Social Studies Department Head and Advanced Placement Co-ordinator
Bev Facey Community School
Sherwood Park, Alberta

Errol B. Miller
Social Studies Teacher (Retired)

Teresa Saley
Social Studies Department Head
Queen Elizabeth Composite High School
Edmonton, Alberta

Bill Sommerfeld
Social Studies Department Head (Retired)

Dennis Theobald
Social Studies Teacher
Tofield School
Tofield, Alberta

Norma Thompson
Social Studies Teacher
David Thompson High School
Condor, Alberta

Lawrence F.C. Wearmouth
Curriculum Leader, Social Studies
James Fowler High School
Calgary, Alberta

Ron Windrim
Social Studies Teacher
National Sport School
Calgary, Alberta

Rick Winter
Department Head of Social Studies
St. Francis Xavier High School
Edmonton, Alberta

Bias Reviewers

James Maher
Social Studies Lead Teacher
Salisbury Composite High School
Sherwood Park, Alberta

Lois Westerlund
Social Studies Teacher
Strathcona Christian Academy
Sherwood Park, Alberta

Cover Photos

Phyllis A. Arnold

Jim Barabash

Judy Bauer,
    Arnold Publishing Ltd.

Corel Corporation
Ottawa, Ontario
This publication includes images from *Corel Professional Photos* CD-ROMs which are protected by the copyright laws of the US, Canada, and elsewhere. Used under license. The photographic images may not be copied and are only to be used for viewing purposes.

EROS Data Center
Sioux Falls, South Dakota, United
    States
Image courtesy of US Geological
    Survey

Graphics

Corel Corporation
Ottawa, Ontario
This publication includes images from Corel Gallery 2 which are protected by the copyright laws of the US, Canada, and elsewhere. Used under license.

Some of the images used herein were obtained from IMSI's Masterclips Collection, 1895 Francisco Blvd. East, San Rafael, California 94901–5506, United States.

One Mile Up, Inc.
Annandale, Virginia, United States

Logos

Courtesy of Bloc Québécois
Ottawa, Ontario, Canada

Courtesy of The Liberal Party of
    Canada
Ottawa, Ontario, Canada

Courtesy of New Democratic
    Party of Canada
Ottawa, Ontario, Canada

Courtesy of Progressive
    Conservative Party of Canada
Ottawa, Ontario, Canada
http://www.pcparty.ca

Courtesy of Reform Party of
    Canada
Calgary, Alberta, Canada

Special Thanks

Archive Photos
New York, New York, United
    States

Dr. Kamal Abdel-Malek
Assistant Professor
Department of Comparative
    Literature, Religion, Film and
    Media Studies
University of Alberta
Edmonton, Alberta, Canada

National Archives of Canada
Ottawa, Ontario

*United States Holocaust Memorial
    Museum*
Washington, District of
    Columbus, United States

Every effort has been made to identify and credit all sources. The publisher would appreciate notification of any omissions or errors so that they may be corrected.

We acknowledge the financial support of the Government of Canada through the Book Publishing Industry Development Program for our publishing activities.

Global Systems Homepage

Arnold Publishing invites you to visit our website at http://www.arnold.ca/ on the internet. For additional information, key in the **Global Systems** five number access code located on the inside front cover of this textbook. This will take you to Arnold Publishing's SKIMM™ (**Learning How to Learn**) web page.

TO THE STUDENT

Focus of *Global Systems*

To better understand today's world, it is important to critically examine the political and economic systems that have been created by 20th century societies. Understanding the origins and development of political and economic systems, their interrelationships, and their consequences for humankind will help you anticipate and make choices about issues that will affect our world in the 21st century.

This textbook provides opportunities for you to acquire the knowledge and skills necessary to

- analyse and compare underlying principles and features of political and economic systems
- assess why political and economic systems differ in theory and practice
- defend features of selected political and economic systems
- suggest changes that political and economic systems could incorporate to better serve the needs and interests of individuals and society.

The Global Issues

Global Systems examines four political and economic issues with which 20th century societies are confronted.

1. To what extent should political and economic systems emphasize the interests of the group at the expense of individual interests?

2. To what extent should political decision making be restricted to a particular group in society?

3. To what extent should the majority rule in its own interests or accept limitations on its rights to protect minorities?

4. To what extent should the government intervene in the economy to protect the interests of society?

These four political and economic issues are described in more detail on page 4 of *Global Systems*. The issue icons (which are printed in the front endsheet of the textbook for quick referral) are used throughout the book as part of the chapter organizer (e.g., pages 5, 127) and section organizers (e.g., pages 128, 164). Note that in some of the section organizers, one or more of the icons may appear in black and white while the others are in colour. The coloured icons indicate which issues are developed in that section.

Organization of *Global Systems*

Understanding how the textbook is organized will help you understand and learn the complex, interrelated subject matter. The textbook uses a number of strategies to help you learn. The ways the ideas are organized, the ways they are presented visually, and the special features of the book are all designed to contribute to effective learning.

Content Organization

The *Global Systems* Concept Map shown in the front endsheet of the book gives a visual summary of the organization of the content of the textbook.

Part I: Introduction to Political and Economic Systems

Part I traces the development of contemporary political and economic systems in theory, by first examining the values, beliefs, ideologies, and other thought upon which they are based, followed by a description of these systems, in theory, including features and comparative analyses.

The Part I Advance Organizer (page 3) introduces the chapter contents; the Part I Overview graphic organizer shows the relationship between values/ideologies and political and economic systems. (A graphic organizer is any kind of chart or diagram that visually represents the relationships between ideas. They are used throughout this textbook to aid understanding.)

The Models. The models used in the textbook have three purposes.

- They assist your understanding of the theory by showing the ideas in relationship in a visual form.
- They are used to organize the information in the case study chapters so that the case studies are readily comparable in all of the elements of the model.
- They provide a structure which you can use to relate new knowledge to what you already know in a way that it can be easily studied and remembered.

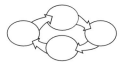 Chapter 1 (page 5) gives you a model for understanding the interrelationships between values, beliefs, and attitudes and the development of ideologies.

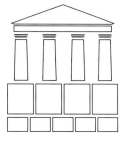 Chapter 2 (page 31) provides a model that organizes and explains the theory of political systems and relates it visually to the design of the Parthenon, a style often copied in government buildings.

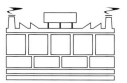 Chapter 3 (page 75) uses an image of a factory in a graphic organizer that organizes and explains the theory of economic systems.

Both the Parthenon and factory models are used in icon form within the chapter to relate the section or subsection being studied to the model. For example, on page 33 in the Advance Organizer for Features of a Political System, the columns of the Parthenon are highlighted. This refers to the four Features of Political Systems that appear on the columns of the model on page 31, as well as to the heading of the section. In the right margin of page 33, a Parthenon icon appears with the first column highlighted, referring to the first Feature on the Political Systems model and to the heading of the Government subsection.

Part II: Political and Economic Systems in Practice

Chapters 4 to 11 provide eight case studies of 20th century political and economic systems. The chapters apply the theory and the model for understanding political and economic systems to real-world case studies of different democratic and non-democratic systems.

The Part II Advance Organizer (page 125) introduces a model which is used in the chapters to relate ideology to the political system and economic system, and the political and economic systems to the political economy for each of the case studies.

The chapter Advance Organizers (e.g., page 127) provide a focussing quotation, an introduction, a list of key concepts, the four issue icons, and a chapter overview graphic organizer. The graphic organizer provides a topical outline of all of the sections of the chapter. The section Advance Organizers (e.g., page 128) repeat the icon from this model, listing the subsection headings.

Part III: Challenges of the 21st Century

The conclusion of the *Global Systems* study of political and economic systems is a brief section that focusses on six contemporary issues for you to consider for the 21st century.

The three theoretical models used in Global Systems are printed in the front endsheets of the textbook for quick reference as well as within the chapters.

Features of *Global Systems*

Focus On Critical Thinking

The textbook provides a variety of primary and secondary source material related to specific aspects of chapter content. The Focus On Critical Thinking pages are identified by their beige background colour. They present one or more points of view and provide opportunities to practise critical thinking skills (e.g., pages 112, 113, 146–147).

Margin Information

There are five types of notes found in the margins of chapter pages:
- model icons
- margin charts; both pie charts and numerical charts
- curriculum content related information (coloured backgrounds)
- additional information (coloured text)
- captions for photos and certain cartoons, charts, and maps (black text)

Titles

Titles are coded by size, type style, and colour so that the level of heading under which the content is organized is readily identifiable. A complete topical outline of the content of chapters can be created by following the hierarchy of headings. The level one headings are always in full capitals. These headings are summarized in the Chapter Overview and Section Overview advance organizers.

Review Pages

The review section at the end of each chapter includes a chapter summary and questions and activities to assist your learning. The questions are organized by section, using the corresponding headings. A final section helps you consolidate your learning through broader questions. These questions include continuing themes and cumulative activities that help you compare systems and draw general conclusions. The icons printed beside certain questions refer you to the Appendix on pages 454–463, entitled SKIMM™ (*Learning How to Learn*).

Ongoing Project

The Chapter Consolidations in Chapters 2 to 11 identify specific questions as ongoing projects. Your cumulative responses to the questions marked with the icon on the right will assist you in successfully preparing for possible essay questions on the four global issues (see page 4).

Endsheets

Inside the front and back covers are four pages of summary material for your quick reference. The front endsheets show the three models for learning about Values and Ideologies, Political Systems, and Economic Systems, as well as the *Global Systems* Concept Map, and the four Issues Icons. The back endsheets contain a world map with the case study countries highlighted, a database of comparative information about the eight case study countries and contemporary Germany, and the Evolving Systems model, which illustrates the general trends that have occurred in political and economic systems during the 20th century.

Appendix: SKIMM™ (*Learning How to Learn*)

SKIMM™ (*Learning How to Learn*), found on pages 454–463, provides extensive information about study skills, organizing effective notes, critical thinking (including bias, comparison, and thinking/writing from another's perspective), cartoon analysis, analysis of sources, essay writing, and answering multiple choice questions. A variety of charts and other graphic organizers are provided as examples of visual ways to organize and analyse information for effective learning. Each section of SKIMM™ is identified by an icon. These icons are used in the chapter questions to remind you to review this information for strategies to approach the question.

Global Systems Homepage

Arnold Publishing invites you to visit our website at http://www.arnold.ca/ on the internet. For additional information, key in the **Global Systems** five number access code located on the inside front cover of this textbook. This will take you to Arnold Publishing's SKIMM (**Learning How to Learn)**™ web page.

Study Skills

Organizing Effective Notes

Critical Thinking

Analysis of Cartoons

Analysis of Sources

Essay Writing

Multiple Choice Questions

TABLE OF CONTENTS

PART

I

INTRODUCTION TO POLITICAL AND ECONOMIC SYSTEMS

ADVANCE ORGANIZER

All societies create political and economic systems to satisfy human needs and wants. Political and economic systems organize, coordinate, and promote various human activities. The following three chapters examine values, ideologies, and characteristics of political and economic systems.

Chapter 1: Values and Ideologies

Values and ideologies are fundamental to political and economic systems. A value is a deeply held belief or conviction people hold about the nature of the world, their relationship to it, and the basic qualities of human beings. An ideology is a set of beliefs about human nature, society, and patterns of interaction between human beings. An ideology provides a believer with a picture of the world as it is and as it should be. It is an attempt to organize the complexities of the world into something that is simpler and more understandable.

Chapter 2: Introducing Political Systems

All societies are concerned with the problems of making decisions and selecting goals. Making decisions involves the use of power and authority. A political system provides a means of selecting societal goals, mobilizing resources for their attainment, and making societal decisions. A political system attempts to answer questions like

- By whom and by which criteria should leaders be chosen?
- How should the decision making process be structured, carried out, and enforced?
- What political institutions should be created? What functions and how much power should each have?
- How should the political process be structured?

Chapter 3: Introducing Economic Systems

All societies face the problems of scarcity and choice. The resources of a society are limited, whereas the demands of people are not. No society has unlimited supplies of the factors of production (land, labour, and capital). An economic system provides the means of solving these problems by selecting goals, mobilizing resources, and making decisions about production and distribution of wealth. An economic system attempts to answer questions like

- What goods and services should be produced?
- How should goods and services be produced?
- How should goods and services be distributed?
- Who should make the decisions about the allocation of resources, methods of production, and the distribution of goods and services?

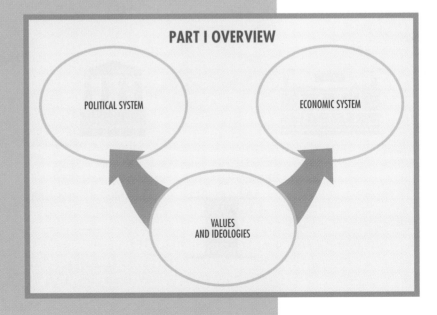

PART I OVERVIEW

POLITICAL SYSTEM

ECONOMIC SYSTEM

VALUES AND IDEOLOGIES

GLOBAL ISSUES

The world is a diverse place. Societies around the world vary considerably. They differ in the policies and goals they seek and also according to the cultural, historical, and geographical settings in which they function. At various times in the 20th century, societies have been confronted with the following four issues:

1. **To what extent should political and economic systems emphasize the interests of the group at the expense of individual interests?**

In the 20th century, many beliefs about individualism and collectivism have emerged. Some people called for organizing political and economic systems that emphasize individual interests. Other people argued for forming political and economic systems to serve the interests of the group. At the end of the 20th century, this issue of individualism and collectivism remains unresolved. In this book the issue of individualism and collectivism is represented by the accompanying icon.

2. **To what extent should political decision making be restricted to a particular group in society?**

Throughout the 20th century, societies have struggled to answer the question of who has the authority to rule in society's interest. Many believe that society's leaders should be chosen directly by the people, and that leaders should be accountable to the people for the policies they implement. Others argue that leaders should be chosen from a small elite distinguished from the rest of society by such factors as social background, personality, wealth, and education. The dilemma of who should rule is illustrated in this book by the ballot box icon.

3. **To what extent should the majority rule in its own interests or accept limitations on its rights to protect minorities?**

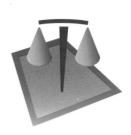

In the 20th century, many conflicts have been fought over the issue of the rights of the minority and their acceptance by the majority. Some people have argued that all members of society should have the same rights, regardless of race, culture, language, religion, and ethnicity. Others have claimed that minority groups should accept the views, ideas, and beliefs of the majority. The issue of minority rights and majority rights is represented in this book by the balance icon.

4. **To what extent should the government intervene in the economy to protect the interests of society?**

The growth of government and its increased involvement in the economy have provoked great debates among thinkers and political leaders in the 20th century. Some doubted the need for government involvement in the economy for any reason. Others believed passionately in government intervention in the economy for society's stability, prosperity, and welfare. The issue of economic control and freedom in society is represented in this book by the accompanying icon.

- the gov't should intervene when there's a market failure

VALUES AND IDEOLOGIES

"Very dangerous things, theories."
—Dorothy L. Sayers,
  *The Unpleasantness at the Bellona
  Club*, 1928.

Troops enter a provincial city, firing on supporters of an independence movement. Voters of a region cast their ballots in a referendum on establishing an independent country. Terrorists blow up a public building to begin their war on government, killing several hundred men, women, and children.

The Minister of Finance announces that the government will cut spending, raise taxes, and privatize crown corporations in order to balance the budget. County voters go to the polls and overwhelmingly reject a half-cent increase in the sales tax to bail their municipal government out of bankruptcy.

The previous events are examples of how people's ideologies (their ideas, beliefs, and attitudes, including their interpretation of available facts) affect their behaviour. Understanding various ideologies is necessary for understanding events in the world. Moreover, studying ideology can help us make sense of our own and other's values, beliefs, and attitudes, and our relationship with different peoples in our own or other countries and regions of the world.

Focus On Issue
Ideologies are sets of beliefs and ideas about human nature, society, and patterns of interaction between human beings. Ideologies are used to explain and justify the existence of political and economic systems. The following question will be answered differently by different people depending on the ideology they support:

- **To what extent should political
  and economic systems emphasize
  the interests of the group at the
  expense of individual interests?**

Chapter Overview: The diagram to the left shows the interrelationship between values, beliefs, and attitudes, and the diversity of choices made by ideology.

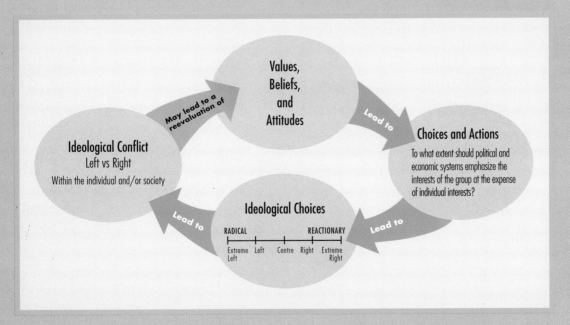

VALUES, BELIEFS, AND ATTITUDES

Advance Organizer

Our thoughts about the issues we face in life flow from our most basic values, beliefs, and attitudes. The individuals in a society develop values in response to a number of influences.

Key Concepts/Vocabulary
values
elitism

VALUES

Values are deeply held beliefs or convictions people hold about the nature of the world, their relationship to it, and the basic qualities of human beings. Values are our basic principles.

Influences on Individual Values		Influences on Societal Values	
• Family	• Workplace	• Historical Experiences	• Economic Development
• Peer Groups	• Government	• Culture, Traditions, Religion, and Language	• Social Structure
• Education	• Social Groups	• Geography	• Foreign Influences
• Mass Media	• Professions		
• Religion	• Aesthetics		

Individual Values (based on personal ideas, beliefs, and attitudes)

Societal Values (based on what is considered important to satisfy people's needs)

CHOICES

Both individuals and societies make choices about which values they believe are important.

Meaning and Origin

A value is generally defined as a deeply held belief or conviction people have about the nature of the world, their relationship to it, and the basic qualities of human beings. Values are our basic principles. They include beliefs and attitudes about ways of doing things, modes of thinking, and ideas about how people should interact with each other. These beliefs include preferences and ideals about personality, behaviour, politics, economics, and the nature of society. They provide us with meaning and purpose, as well as identifying means of satisfying basic human needs such as food, clothing, shelter, security, belonging, and friendship. Societal values are based on the values of individuals, plus generally held beliefs about what is important to satisfy the needs of people in the society.

Values have some of the following characteristics:

- Values are subjective and personal. In most cases, their correctness cannot be determined by ordinary observation or experiment. They are statements about what we think is desirable or believe ought to be desirable.

- Values affect choices in life and thus influence our behaviour. The choices we make in life depend on how strongly we hold our values. Though people in society may share universal values, it is the strength by which people hold certain values over others that distinguishes one society from another.

- Values provide us with standards by which we can judge actions and goals we want to achieve. They are basic to our preferences and our decisions, and give direction and meaning to all that we do. Values are crucial to a whole range of human activities.

- Values are not static; they evolve over time. As we become more informed, meet new people, travel to different places, and encounter new experiences, our values change. Over time, our views about what we consider to be important are tested, revised, and sometimes rejected and replaced by new ones. We ask ourselves questions such as those that follow on page 7.

What needs are important to me?

How can I satisfy these needs?

How should I relate to others?

How should I relate to the physical world?

How do I judge the actions of others?

By what criteria do I judge and evaluate my own actions?

What goals should I pursue for personal well-being and fulfilment?

Influences on Values

Societies share many universal values, but what distinguishes the value system of a particular society is the emphasis placed on values deemed most important. In addition to the personal sources of values listed on the graphic organizer on page 6, cultural anthropologists identify other sources for differences in value systems, including historical experiences; culture, traditions, religion, and language; geography; levels of economic development; social structure; and foreign influences.

Historical Experiences. War, power struggles, economic crises, social upheavals, and other historical events influence a society's outlook on the world and its relation to other societies and peoples. If a society's people believe that the world is a hostile and threatening place, then that society may be more inclined to hold values that emphasize self-discipline, duty, and the use of force. That society may also encourage group solidarity and social order.

Culture, Traditions, Religion, and Language. Societies strive to nurture a sense of identity by preserving their unique culture, traditions, religion, and language. For example, a society that values loyalty, community spirit, and belonging will be different from one more tolerant of outsiders, more open to outside ideas, more

accepting of different religions, and with a greater knowledge of other languages.

Geography. The presence of geographical features such as great spaces, mountains, rivers, deserts, and seas can hinder or enhance communication and interaction between societies and groups of people. Geographically isolated societies develop different ideas about the world than societies that are located close to and interact frequently with other societies. Societies that interact often with other societies have the opportunity to adopt more diverse outlooks, ways of doing things, and modes of thinking.

I want to be social & interactive.

Economic Development. The type of economic development within a society will greatly influence its values. A rural society based on agriculture may value tradition, authority, order, religion, and cooperation differently than will an urban society based on the production of technologically advanced goods and services. The urban industrial society may have different values about science, technology, progress, and education. In this type of society, technical progress may be perceived as beneficial, while in a rural agricultural society people may believe that certain types of technical progress will not necessarily bring them a better future.

Social Structure. All societies are not organized the same. In some societies, classes of rich landowners may impose their own values about power, success, and lifestyle on other social classes. In other societies, a large middle class of professional people, small business owners, managers, and government bureaucrats may influence the values of other classes. Societies that have large middle classes generally value hard work, personal initiative, individual responsibility, and competition. Societies composed of a small wealthy class and a large class of the working poor may have different values. In these societies, values such as tradition, duty, order, and stability may be generally stressed.

North America.

HK

> Every society has values that it believes are important in satisfying its needs.

Foreign Influences. The movement of goods, people, and ideas between societies can influence the ideologies a society adopts. Generally, societies do not accept foreign ideas without at some time modifying them to fit their own circumstances. Yet foreign influences have played a significant role in spreading ideologies from one society to another. As global markets expand and communication technology advances, foreign influences will likely become more significant in changing ideologies.

Value Conflicts

No matter where people live, they must make daily choices in order to solve problems and satisfy needs. Unfortunately, making choices and solving problems are complicated matters because they involve feelings, opinions, and perception of facts. Conflicts often arise when people have the same information but arrive at different conclusions.

Strongly held values have, in part, led countries and peoples to take up arms against others, believing that their values were superior. Intolerance, the unwillingness to accept differing values, and the inability to settle disputes based on conflicting values, has in the 20th century contributed to two world wars, the Cold War, hundreds of regional conflicts, and social strife within countries. The willingness to recognize and respect different values whether you agree with them or not and the ability to accommodate different values, or tolerance, is important for peace and a mutually beneficial exchange of ideas. Tolerance requires us to think critically—to be open-minded and aware of differing ideas and opinions.

In considering differing ideas and opinions, critical thinking requires us to understand, analyse, and evaluate the information provided. This also demands that we examine other sources of information and apply them to the issue or situation at hand. In so doing, we give ourselves the opportunity to clarify our values. By examining our own position in the light of new information, we may develop new ideas and approaches to issues.

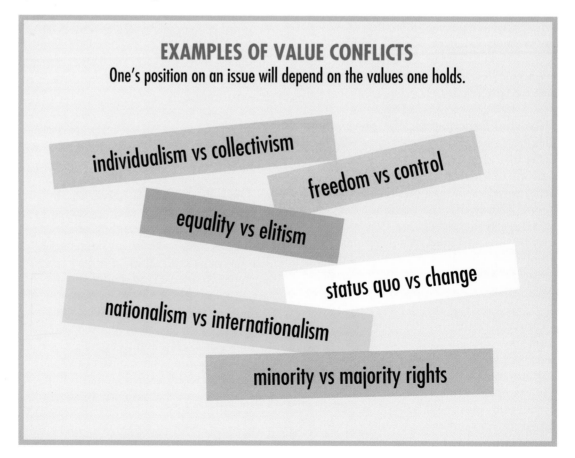

EXAMPLES OF VALUE CONFLICTS
One's position on an issue will depend on the values one holds.

individualism vs collectivism

freedom vs control

equality vs elitism

status quo vs change

nationalism vs internationalism

minority vs majority rights

IDEOLOGIES

Advance Organizer

The set of values, beliefs, and attitudes we hold about human nature, society, and ways people interact with each other make up our ideology. Ideology is an important factor in many of the choices we make in our daily lives. Theories and philosophical beliefs about society, institutions, and people form the base of ideologies.

Key Concepts/Vocabulary

ideology	collectivism
theory	individualism
philosophy	egalitarianism

Meaning and Origin

An ideology is a set of organized beliefs about the world that a group of people accept as true. The meaning of ideology continues to evoke lively debate, which stems in part from the fact that our values, beliefs, and attitudes are not consistent and are subject to influences of all kinds. At times we act consistently with our ideology, but at other times we may choose a contradictory stance. Since personal ideologies are based on our own ideas, beliefs, and attitudes, it may not be possible to find a broader ideology, such as communism or capitalism, with which we can totally agree.

We may accept parts of ideologies because we react positively or negatively to words that represent them. For example, before 1991 people growing up in the USSR were taught that communism was better than capitalism. In contrast, in countries like Canada and the United States people were taught that capitalism was better than communism. Even the term *ideology* can have powerful emotional connotations.

> Much of what we do every day is based in some way on our ideology.

IDEOLOGY

MEANING AND ORIGIN OF IDEOLOGY
A set of beliefs about human nature, society, and patterns of interaction between human beings.

AN INQUIRY INTO HUMAN NATURE
Ideologies possess sets of beliefs about human nature. Ideologies attempt to answer:
- What are the basic characteristics of human beings?
- What is the purpose of life?
- How do human beings relate to each other and society?

OTHER ASPECTS OF IDEOLOGIES
Ideologies can be distinguished by their
- language
- symbols
- leadership

JUSTIFICATION FOR POLITICAL AND ECONOMIC SYSTEMS
Ideologies include certain beliefs about what *ought* to be the nature and organization of political and economic systems.

The history of the concept of ideology is comparatively short. The term "ideology" was first used in France in 1796 by Antoine Destutt de Tracy to mean the science or study of the origin of ideas. Once the origin of ideas was understood, he argued, ideology could be used to form the foundation of a rational, progressive society.

Napoleon Bonaparte associated the term ideology with revolution and the destruction of established social institutions. Marx, Engels, and other socialists argued that ideology was abstract and false thought. However, by the early 20th century the term began to have fewer negative connotations and came to mean a set of closely related values, beliefs, and attitudes about the world.

Since 1945, political scientists have attempted to give ideology a more objective and value-free meaning. They define ideology as a set of beliefs about the way the world should be organized that people accept as true. This is the view put forward in this text.

Values, beliefs, and attitudes create the theoretical and philosophical base of an ideology, as outlined in the diagram below. The theoretical base of an ideology refers to a set of generalizations about a society. The philosophical base of an ideology

Canapress/Adrian Wyld

relates to a set of ideas on how society, institutions, and people *should* behave. These ideas are evaluative (normative); they cannot be measured or tested scientifically. Ideologies blend interpretation of fact and values with theory and philosophy.

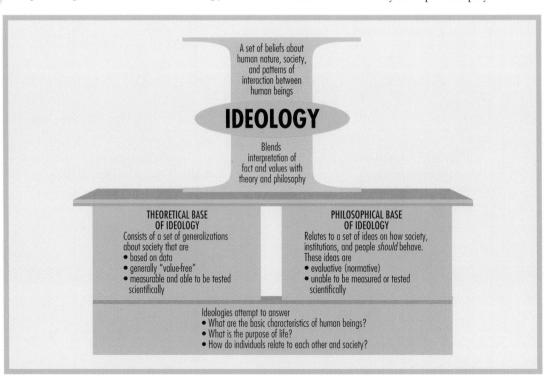

A set of beliefs about human nature, society, and patterns of interaction between human beings

IDEOLOGY

Blends interpretation of fact and values with theory and philosophy

THEORETICAL BASE OF IDEOLOGY
Consists of a set of generalizations about society that are
- based on data
- generally "value-free"
- measurable and able to be tested scientifically

PHILOSOPHICAL BASE OF IDEOLOGY
Relates to a set of ideas on how society, institutions, and people *should* behave. These ideas are
- evaluative (normative)
- unable to be measured or tested scientifically

Ideologies attempt to answer
- What are the basic characteristics of human beings?
- What is the purpose of life?
- How do individuals relate to each other and society?

© Mal Hancock

An Inquiry into Human Nature

Generally speaking, all ideologies include some fundamental ideas about human nature, the purpose of life, and the role of the individual in society.

Human Nature. There has been a long-standing debate on human nature. One viewpoint, assumed by some ideologies, is that human behaviour is determined by genetics. Human beings are good or bad, rational or irrational, cooperative or competitive by nature from birth. Changes in the environment and social conditions will not alter human nature.

Another viewpoint, accepted by other ideologies, is that human beings are shaped and nurtured by history, environment, and living conditions. Changes in the environment and social conditions will result in changes in human nature. There are other viewpoints as well.

Purpose of Life. Ideologies also include beliefs about the purpose of human life. Some ideologies are based on the belief that the purpose of life is to serve the community, while others emphasize individual accomplishment and fulfilment. Still others would include both ideas, giving them varying degrees of importance.

Role of Individuals in Society. Related to purpose of life is the role of individuals in society. All ideologies attempt to put forth a view of human interaction. Some people believe that human beings are

social creatures who form societies and work together for the common good. Others believe that people put personal or family interests first.

Many of the world's ideologies are based on the values of collectivism and individualism, which sometimes coexist and sometimes compete.

Collectivism is based on the following set of generalizations. If human beings are social creatures by nature, then they cannot realize their potential outside the group. They are part of the group like the cells of an organism, in which a close interdependence of the parts is necessary for the organism to function. Thus the group defines, prioritizes, and supports the actions of its members. In doing so, members of the group attain identity, a sense of belonging, and responsibilities. Society consists of an intricate web of interrelated parts and relationships among the parts.

The concept of the individual as a member of the collective society is an old one. In China, Confucius (551–479 BCE) formulated the concept that, as social beings, our actions and destiny are determined by our social roles and position. According to Confucius, human behaviour is regulated by a code of ethics that emphasizes duties and obligations prescribed by the roles individuals have in society. Social order is maintained when everyone fulfils his or her roles and duties.

Individualism is based on the generalization that we are independent beings with intrinsic worth. As such, we do not need the group to achieve personal fulfilment. According to this view, individuals create the society in which they live and can change it. All actions are an act of will based on consent and common effort with other individuals. Every individual has choices and is responsible for his or her own actions. Identity of the individual is determined by personal attributes such as talent, skill, and intelligence. In this case, society consists of a maze of overlapping, cooperating, and competing individuals and groups.

Major Components of Collectivism and Individualism

Cultural psychologists have conducted considerable research since 1980 to identify the main components (values) of individualism and collectivism. Some of their findings are reproduced in this chart.

Collectivism	Individualism
• The survival of the collective takes precedence over that of the individual.	• Individual self-worth; ultimate moral authority lies with the individual.
• Personal potential is attained through collective development.	• Personal potential is developed through individual effort.
• Uniformity and conformity are the ideal.	• Each person is unique.
• Collective identity is defined by group membership.	• A person's identity is defined by personal characteristics.
• Conformity to group norms, obedience, and harmony are expected.	• The individual makes independent decisions and judgments.
• The group is able and entitled to know what its members do and think in private.	• The person has the right to privacy; people should not interfere in what another person does and thinks.
• Collective responsibility is expected; the entire group is responsible for the actions of its members.	• The individual is morally and/or legally responsible for personal actions.
• Collective efforts are believed to be superior.	• Emphasis on individual initiative and personal achievement.
• Cooperation and conformity are the best way to achieve goals.	• Excellence attained and goals met through competition.
• The group assumes responsibility for the well-being of its members.	• The individual is responsible for personal well-being.
• Fulfilment of the group's obligations is important; actions are guided by group interests.	• Fulfilment of individual needs and interests; actions guided by self-interest.
• Sharing of wealth, egalitarianism, public or collective ownership are important.	• Material rewards and wealth are not shared; property is held privately.
• Rights of the group take precedence; individual rights are secondary.	• The individual's rights are paramount and protected by laws.

Adapted from David Yau-Fai Ho and Chi-Yue Chiu, "Component Ideas of Individualism, Collectivism, and Social Organization," in *Individualism and Collectivism: Theory, Method, and Applications*, edited by Uichol Kim *et al.* (Thousand Oaks: Sage Publications, 1994), pp. 139–141.

Justification for Political and Economic Systems

Ideologies include certain beliefs about what ought to be the nature and organization of political and economic systems, based on the ideas they espouse about human nature, the purpose of life, and the role of the individual in society.

Political Systems. The goals of any political ideology are to stir people to action, to unite people behind certain principles, and to provide people with information about their roles, positions, and rights in society. The ideology that a people accepts and the goals that they decide are worth achieving provide the justification for the development of a particular political system. Each political system includes ideas about the nature and role of

- leadership
- decision making
- political institutions
- the political process

The chart below outlines issues and questions that all ideologies attempt to answer to justify a certain political system.

Political Systems: Issues and Questions

Leadership
1. Should leaders be chosen by a select few or by the people?
2. According to what criteria should these leaders be chosen? For example, by personal attributes or social background?

Decision Making Process
1. Should political decisions be made by the few or by the many?
2. Should the decision making process be based on a set of written rules (a constitution) or an unwritten set of conventions?
3. How should the decisions be carried out and enforced?

Political Institutions
1. What institutions should be created to implement political decisions?
2. What functions should each institution have?
3. How much power should be given to each institution?

Political Process
1. What is the role of the individual in the political system?
2. To what extent should the individual participate in the political process?
3. What are the responsibilities of government toward the individual?
4. Should the government be a guarantor of personal freedoms?
5. Should the government restrict freedoms in the interests of society?
6. What rights and responsibilities does the individual have in the political system?

Economic Systems. Regardless of the ideology on which any economic system is based, its goals are to solve the problem of scarcity of human and material resources and to provide answers to the four basic economic questions listed below. The decisions made reflect the degree of freedom given to individuals in the society to produce and distribute goods and services. The type of economic system chosen is determined by how the society approaches the issue of scarcity and answers the basic economic questions.

There are two important related issues involving ideology and the economy:

- To what extent should individuals have the freedom to make decisions about production and distribution of goods and services?
- To what extent should society as a whole decide which goods and services should be produced and distributed to ensure the common good?

Each economic system relates to, and provides ideas about, production, distribution, and decision making. The chart below outlines the issues and questions that all economic systems attempt to answer.

Economic Systems: Issues and Questions

Production
1. What goods and services should the society produce?
2. How should these goods and services be produced?

Distribution
1. How should goods and services be distributed in the society?

Decision Making Process
1. Who should make the decisions about the allocation of resources, methods of production, and the distribution of goods and services?

Other Aspects of Ideologies

Besides possessing a set of beliefs about human nature and justifications for particular political and economic systems, ideologies can be distinguished by their language, symbols, and style of leadership.

Language. All ideologies have distinctive vocabularies of code words, phrases, and expressions that are used to communicate about issues. Expressions such as "class struggle," "dictatorship of the proletariat," "the invisible hand," and "the will of the people" have special significance and evoke different mental images.

Symbols. All ideologies claim to be unique. In this respect, symbols serve as important identification markers distinguishing one ideology from another. For example, the swastika is a symbol of national socialism, the bundle of rods of fascism, the clenched fist of anarchism, and the hammer and sickle of communism.

Leadership. Styles of leadership often distinguish one ideology from another. Some ideologies place great emphasis on the role of the leader and insist on loyalty and devotion to him or her. Other ideologies place less emphasis on loyalty and devotion to a leader.

20TH CENTURY IDEOLOGIES

Advance Organizer

Ideologies of today reflect a number of beliefs about the world. Over time beliefs and ideas about the world change. Therefore, it is logical that ideologies continually evolve.

There are different types of ideologies; some are more coherent and better articulated than others. The 20th century witnessed the continued growth and development of liberalism, conservatism, capitalism, socialism, and anarchism, as well as the emergence of communism and fascism.

The material in this section is intended to introduce various types of ideologies, most of which will be expanded on in later chapters.

Key Concepts

liberalism	Marxism
conservatism	communism
capitalism	fascism
socialism	anarchism

Ideologies Important to 20th Century Thought

Liberalism	John Locke John Stuart Mill
Conservatism	Edmund Burke
Capitalism	Adam Smith
Socialism	Karl Marx
Communism	Vladimir Lenin
Fascism	Benito Mussolini Adolf Hitler
Anarchism	Pëtr Kropotkin

Types of Ideologies

The following seven ideologies emerged in response to various political, economic, and social changes. The writings of Locke, Mill, Burke, Smith, Marx, Lenin, Mussolini, Hitler, and Kropotkin were attempts to understand changes and formulate new beliefs about the world.

Liberalism

Liberalism is an ideology that stresses individual rights and freedom of choice. Today it also includes the idea of an increased role for government to promote personal freedom and reduce inequities.

Two influential proponents of liberalism were John Locke and John Stuart Mill. Both philosophers believed that human beings are equal and independent. They argued that humans are endowed with certain inalienable rights, such as the right to life, liberty, equality, and ownership of property.

Based on Kneller, Godfrey/NATIONAL ARCHIVES OF CANADA/C-003717

John Locke (1632–1704)
Locke expressed the view that people are born free and equal. They agree among themselves to be governed in such a way as to allow them freedom and security. His philosophy of liberalism was expressed in the *Second Treatise of Civil Government*, written in 1690:

Men being . . . by Nature all free, equal, and independent, no one can be put out of this estate and subjected to the political power of another without his consent, which is done by agreeing with other men, to join and unite into a community for their comfortable, safe, and peaceable living, one amongst another, in a secure enjoyment of their properties, and a greater security against any that are not of it.

Several ideologies coexist within most societies, although one is usually dominant.

John Stuart Mill (1806–1873)

Mill accepted Locke's philosophy of liberalism and argued further that all individuals should have relatively unrestricted self-expression and independence. His later works supported reforms that would grant people greater freedom and opportunities in life. Many of these ideas were expressed in his work, *On Liberty* (1859).

> *No society in which these liberties are not . . . respected, is free, whatever may be its form of government; and none is completely free in which they do not exist absolute and unqualified. The only freedom which deserves the name, is that of pursuing our own good in our own way, so long as we do not attempt to deprive others of theirs, or impede their efforts to obtain it. Each is the proper guardian of his own health, whether bodily, or mental and spiritual.*

Conservatism

The leading philosopher of conservatism was Edmund Burke. He challenged many of Locke's beliefs about human beings, arguing that individuals and society have a moral responsibility to respect past traditions, customs, and habits. When individuals and society wish to make reforms, these must be slow and gradual, rather than violent and revolutionary. This is a conservative tradition that has been maintained to this day.

Edmund Burke (1729–1797)

Burke expressed his ideas about society in *Reflections on the Revolution in France* (1790).

> *Society is, indeed, a contract . . . . It is a partnership in all science; a partnership in all art; a partnership in every virtue, and in all perfection. As the ends of such a partnership cannot be obtained in many generations, it becomes a partnership not only between those who are living, but between those who are dead, and those who are to be born.*

Capitalism

Adam Smith is generally acknowledged to be the philosopher who first formulated the basic principles of economic freedom. In time, Smith's ideas on economic freedom were extended by others into what we today call capitalism.

Adam Smith (1723–1790)

In his major work, *An Inquiry into the Nature and Causes of the Wealth of Nations*, published in 1776, Smith argued for greater economic freedom for the individual. All individuals are guided by self-interest to improve their own personal welfare and in doing so improve the economic well-being of society without intending to do so. Smith noted this and wrote:

> *As every individual . . . necessarily labours to render the annual revenue of the society as great as he can. He generally, indeed, neither intends to promote the publick interest, nor knows how much he is promoting it . . . . [He] intends only his own security; and by directing that industry in such a manner as its produce may be of the greatest value, he intends only his own gain, and he is in this, as in many other cases, led by an invisible hand to promote an end which was no part of his intention.*

Socialism

The development of socialism is generally associated with the writings of the German philosopher Karl Marx. In his many works, Marx developed the concepts of class struggle, the working class (proletariat) as a revolutionary class, and revolution by the working class. These ideas of Marx, what he called scientific socialism, became known later in the 20th century as Marxism. However, many people rejected Marx's idea of revolution and instead focused on peaceful social change in the interest of the working class, developing the philosophy of democratic socialism or, as it is known in Europe, social democracy. This is the branch of socialism that remains strongest today.

Archive Photos

Karl Marx (1818–1883)
Marx's theoretical concepts of socialism were expressed in the celebrated pamphlet, *The Communist Manifesto*, written in 1848. In this pamphlet, Marx and his co-author Friedrich Engels (1820–1895) wrote:

The history of all hitherto existing society is the history of class struggles.

Of all the classes that stand face to face with the bourgeoisie today, the proletariat alone is a really revolutionary class. The other classes decay and finally disappear in the face of modern industry; the proletariat is its special and essential product.

The first step in the revolution by the working class, is to raise the proletariat to the position of ruling class . . . to wrest, by degrees, all capital from the bourgeoisie, to centralize all instruments of production in the hands of the state . . . and to increase the total of productive forces as rapidly as possible.

Communism

The development of communism owes much to the writings of Vladimir Lenin, who expanded on Marx's ideas and added his own about the nature and role of leadership for the purpose of carrying out revolution in Russia in the early years of the 20th century. Following the seizure of power by the Bolsheviks in November 1917, Lenin's adaptation of Marx's ideas to Russia became officially known as Marxism–Leninism.

Popperfoto/Archive Photos

Vladimir Lenin (1870–1924)
Born as Vladimir Ilyich Ulyanov, Lenin was a revolutionary who applied Marx's ideas to Russia. One of Lenin's many works on Marxism is a pamphlet, *The State and Revolution*, printed in August 1917. In this pamphlet, Lenin outlined the role of the state in the conquest of power by the working class and the dictatorship of the proletariat. He wrote:

The state is a special organisation of force: it is an organisation of violence for the suppression of some class. What class must the proletariat suppress? Naturally, only the exploiting class, i.e., the bourgeoisie. The working people need the state only to suppress the resistance of the exploiters, and only the proletariat can direct this suppression, can carry it out. For the proletariat is the only class that is consistently revolutionary, the only class that can unite all the working and exploited people in the struggle against the bourgeoisie, in completely removing it.

Fascism

The development of fascist ideology can be credited to Benito Mussolini and Adolf Hitler. Mussolini believed that true liberty of individuals involved service to the state. Hitler argued that all progress is a struggle for survival, leading to the dominance of the strongest. In general, fascism emphasized extreme nationalism, authoritarian leadership, use of violence, militarism, hostility to communism, and the subordination of the individual to the state.

Archive Photos

Benito Mussolini (1883–1945)
Mussolini's philosophy of fascism appeared in his book, *Doctrine of Fascism,* published in 1932. He wrote:
Fascism reaffirms the State as the true reality of the individual . . . . Therefore, for the Fascist, everything is in the State, and nothing human or spiritual exists . . . outside the State. In this sense Fascism is totalitarian, and the Fascist State, the synthesis and unity of all values, interprets, develops and gives strength to the whole life of the people.

Archive Photos

Adolf Hitler (1889–1945)
Many of Hitler's ideas about German National Socialism are revealed in his book, *Mein Kampf* (My Struggle), published in 1925–1926. In this book, Hitler outlined his beliefs about the state, national identity, and elitism. His ideas on these subjects were rooted in an extreme nationalism based on his view of race.
[National Socialist] philosophy finds the importance of mankind in its basic racial elements. In the state it sees in principle only a means to an end and construes its end as the preservation of the racial existence of man. Thus, it by no means believes in an equality of races, but along with their difference it recognises their higher or lesser value and feels itself obligated . . . to promote the victory of the better and stronger, and demand the subordination of the inferior and weaker in accordance with the eternal will that dominates this universe. . . . It sees not only the different value of the races, but also the different value of individuals.

Anarchism

Anarchism is an ideology that stresses the right of individuals to organize their own lives free from government domination. Anarchist thinkers have put forth views ranging from complete freedom for the individual to complete collectivism. Pëtr Kropotkin was a leading figure in the anarchist movement. His greatest contribution was the presentation of the anarchist cause in written form.

UPI/Corbis-Bettmann

Pëtr (Peter) Kropotkin (1842–1921)
In his first major work, *The Conquest of Bread,* published in 1888, Kropotkin disagreed with many of Marx's ideas about socialism. He argued that anarchism rested on economic and political liberty of individuals:
Anarchism . . . is the synthesis of the two ideals pursued by humanity throughout the ages—Economic and Political Liberty.
[Men] . . . attempt to free themselves from every form of government and to satisfy their need for organization by free contract between individuals and groups pursuing the same aim. The independence of each small territorial unit becomes a pressing need; mutual agreement replaces law, and everywhere regulates individual interests in view of a common object.

CLASSIFYING IDEOLOGIES

Advance Organizer

All ideologies have been influenced by historical traditions and have interacted and overlapped with a number of other ideologies. This makes the task of classifying ideologies very difficult. However, classifying ideologies helps us understand them. The most common methods of classification are

- the left–right continuum or spectrum[1]

LEFT-RIGHT CONTINUUM IN THE 20TH CENTURY

EXTREME LEFT	LEFT	CENTRE	RIGHT	EXTREME RIGHT
radicals	liberals	moderates	conservatives	reactionaries

- the political–economic grid or quadrant[1]

POLITICAL–ECONOMIC GRID

MAXIMUM POLITICAL FREEDOM

Democratic Socialism | Democratic Capitalism

MAXIMUM ECONOMIC CONTROL ← → MAXIMUM ECONOMIC FREEDOM

Communism | Fascism

MAXIMUM POLITICAL CONTROL

Key Concepts

left	liberal
right	moderate
centre	conservative
radical	reactionary

Left–Right Continuum

Roots of Left–Right Continuum

The idea of a left–right continuum in politics evolved during the French Revolution. At the first meeting of the National Assembly in 1789, the nobility and clergy sat on the King's right and the third estate, or bourgeoisie, sat on his left. Soon the seating of the deputies in the National Assembly came to signify their political attitudes about the King, where political authority should lie, and how power should be exercised. Deputies who supported a strong monarchy sat on the right, while those who advocated ending or limiting the power of the monarchy sat on the left. As the revolution changed and action taken became more extreme, there was a tendency for the more radical elements to sit to the left and more moderate members to sit to the right. This practice became the pattern for explaining left and right in politics.

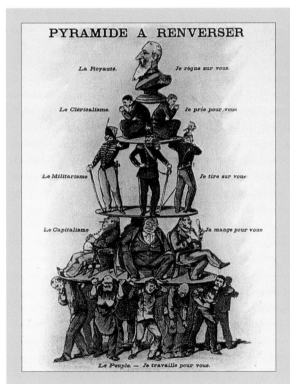

A French socialist poster, Pyramid to Overturn

Royalty—I rule over you
Clericalism—I pray for you
Militarism—I fire on you
Capitalism—I eat for you
The People—I work for you

Robert Philippe, *Political Graphics: Art As A Weapon.* Oxford: Phaidon Press Ltd., 1982, p.17.

[1] *Continuum* and *spectrum* are synonyms, as are *grid* and *quadrant.*

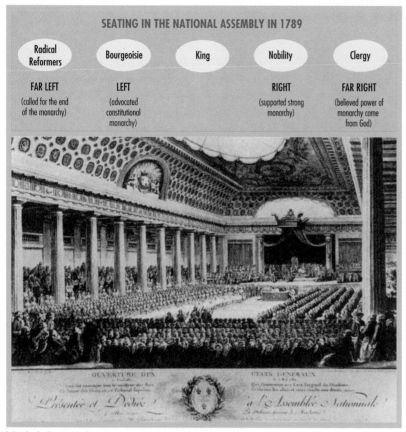

SEATING IN THE NATIONAL ASSEMBLY IN 1789

Radical Reformers	Bourgeoisie	King	Nobility	Clergy
FAR LEFT (called for the end of the monarchy)	**LEFT** (advocated constitutional monarchy)		**RIGHT** (supported strong monarchy)	**FAR RIGHT** (believed power of monarchy came from God)

Tackett, Timothy; *Becoming A Revolutionary: The Deputies of the French National Assembly and the Emergence of A Revolutionary Culture (1789–1790).* Copyright © 1996 by Princeton University Press. Reprinted by permission of Princeton University Press.

Left–Right in the 19th Century

Following the French Revolution, the left and the right came to represent attitudes about change and the status quo. As the chart below shows, those who demanded changes in the status quo—the radicals and the liberals—were grouped on the left. In the centre were moderates who generally supported the status quo and called for minor changes. On the right, conservatives

favoured maintaining the status quo, but reactionaries on the extreme right called for a return to the ways of the past. More importantly, the left–right classification revealed something about the values held by people on the left and right of the continuum. People on the left of the political continuum favoured human rights, equality (egalitarianism), personal liberty, and internationalism. People on the right revered property rights, elitism, authoritarianism, and nationalism.

Left–Right in the 20th Century

Today, these political 19th century labels—radical, liberal, moderate, conservative, and reactionary—carry considerable emotional weight. They evoke strong reactions in people's minds about what it is to be a radical, liberal, moderate, conservative, or reactionary. The following descriptions present theoretical viewpoints held by each of these groups.

Radicals are generally frustrated and impatient with the status quo and desire immediate, fundamental social change. Radicals feel that society prevents individuals from attaining their fullest potential as human beings, and its present structure alienates, exploits, and impoverishes individuals. Radicals on the extreme left advocate violence because they believe that society will not change voluntarily. Less extreme radicals restrict the use of violence to cases when peaceful methods fail to introduce change. Radicals generally are highly supportive of human rights, egalitarianism, freedom, and internationalism because their frustration with the existing social arrangement generally arises out of the restrictions, inequalities, limitations, and conflict that they see in society.

Liberals are less extreme than the radicals in their attitudes toward existing political and economic arrangements and the need for social change. The social change advocated by liberals is generally peaceful and accomplished by legal means. Liberals are optimistic about people's abilities to change society in a beneficial way. They believe that people are essentially good by nature and rational in their thinking and behaviour. Liberals basically believe in the

LEFT–RIGHT CONTINUUM IN THE 19TH CENTURY

EXTREME LEFT	LEFT	CENTRE	RIGHT	EXTREME RIGHT
radicals	liberals	moderates	conservatives	reactionaries
(favoured far-reaching changes)	(favoured some changes)	(favoured some minor changes)	(favoured maintaining the status quo)	(favoured returning to the way things were done in the past)

SUPPORTED VALUES OF

- human rights
- egalitarianism
- personal liberty
- internationalism

- property rights
- elitism
- authoritarianism
- nationalism

LEFT–RIGHT CONTINUUM IN THE 20TH CENTURY

EXTREME LEFT	LEFT	CENTRE	RIGHT	EXTREME RIGHT
radicals	liberals	moderates	conservatives	reactionaries
(favour immediate and fundamental social change; extreme radicals favour change through violence)	(favour change through peaceful and legal means; through government policy)	(favour gradual changes)	(usually content with status quo and maintaining existing traditions and social order)	(favour a return to the "good old days"; extreme reactionaries favour change through violence)

SUPPORT THE VALUES OF

• human rights • egalitarianism • freedom • internationalism	• human rights • personal liberty	• human rights with some limitations • personal liberty with some controls • equality with some inequality • international cooperation while defending national interests	• little government interference • few restrictions on personal freedoms • private property • law and order • some elitism	• authoritarian rule • inequality • private property • preservation and advancement of national interests

advancement of human rights and personal liberty. Some liberal principles about government have changed since the 17th and 18th centuries, when liberal thinkers believed government oppressed people. Contemporary liberals believe government should be used to improve life and guarantee human rights.

Moderates are more contented with society than liberals. They generally support gradual changes and minor reforms of the existing political and economic order. In occupying the centre of the political spectrum, moderates are supportive of human rights with some limitations, personal liberty with some controls, equality with some inequality, and international cooperation while defending national interests.

Conservatives are more content with the status quo than moderates. Most favour maintaining existing traditions and social order. They believe that changes in the status quo may not have beneficial effects. Conservatives are usually pessimistic about people's capacity to improve life, because they believe individuals by nature tend to be less than fully rational in their thinking and behaviour and easy to manipulate through emotional appeals and a forceful personality. Modern conservatives basically believe in small government, few government restrictions on personal freedoms,

private ownership of property, and political order. Most conservatives are not opposed to some elitism and authoritarian rule.

Reactionaries are generally frustrated with the status quo. This frustration is expressed in a desire to return to "the good old days" that existed before things were changed. They believe that present society is not an improvement on former social arrangements. Extreme reactionaries, like radicals, may advocate the use of violence to restore the old order. Most reactionaries are supportive of more authoritarian rule, inequality, private property, and foreign policy based on preserving and advancing national interests.

The rise of the socialist movement in the 19th century shifted people's political attitudes and added an economic dimension to the left–right spectrum. Being left or right began to signify people's attitudes about the role of government and personal freedoms in politics, and the role of inequality and private ownership of property in economics. These changes in political and economic attitudes were further emphasized by the growth of communism, fascism, and capitalism.

Political Attitudes. An important political issue of the 20th century has been what the nature of political authority should be. For example, to what extent should political authority maintain existing traditions, customs, and social order? Equally important has been the question of the extent of social change. For example, to what extent should society change existing conditions to promote greater personal freedom?

- **Anarchists** advocate revolutionary action to free all individuals from every form of organized government and from domination by any external force or institution.
- **Communists** believe in the necessity of revolution to make fundamental social change.
- **Socialists** believe in broadening power to all social groups and using controls to narrow social differences.
- **Liberals** argue for the government to intervene in society to resolve social and political inequities.

- **Conservatives** believe in maintaining authority and traditions. Some controls over individuals are thought necessary to preserve existing social order.
- **Fascists** believe that strong leaders, traditions, and authoritarian rule are necessary to preserve social order. They oppose the need for radical social change and the expansion of human rights advocated by communists and socialists, whom they arrest and imprison. Any social change is made in the direction of greater authoritarianism.

Economic Attitudes. The main economic issues of the 20th century have been concerned with the extent to which economic equality should be emphasized, and with how to achieve this goal: To what extent should wealth be distributed equally among all social groups by restricting or eliminating private ownership of property? Or, to what extent should all economic decisions be made in the market (the world of business and commerce), with varying degrees of government intervention?

- **Anarchists** argue that economic freedom can be achieved through mutual agreement, equality, and the pursuit of common interests.
- **Communists** believe that public ownership of the means of production and the restriction of private property would lead to equality of incomes in society.
- **Socialists** traditionally seek greater equality of incomes through public ownership of selected industries, management of the economy by the government, and expanded opportunities for the working classes.
- **Liberals** generally adopt a middle position, introducing some policies to eliminate some inequalities without changing the basic nature of the economy. Their economic policies favour the middle classes.
- **Conservatives** generally favour private ownership and support private efforts by volunteer organizations to reduce inequality among incomes.
- **Fascists** believe in private property, a state-directed economy, as well as income inequality being part of the natural order of things.

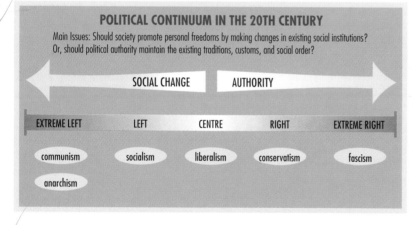

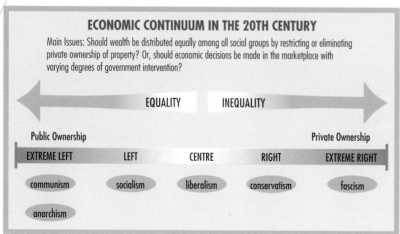

Critique of Left–Right Continuum

The left–right continuum helps us develop a basic understanding of political and economic systems. However, it has limitations. The 20th century has witnessed the formation of new systems that evolved to deal with the complexities of modern society. The relationships that exist between contemporary political and economic ideologies are often difficult to represent on the traditional left–right continuum.

In theory, communist ideology emphasized public ownership of the means of production, egalitarianism, and a collectivist approach to the organization of society. Therefore, communism was placed on the extreme left of the traditional left–right continuum. Fascist ideology emphasized private ownership of the means of production, elitism, and the subservience of the individual to the state. This placed fascism firmly on the extreme right of the traditional left–right continuum, as is shown in the diagram, "Communism and Fascism in Theory."

In practice, however, states based on both ideologies have established strong governments controlled by one political party and dominated by a strong leader who suppressed opponents, used terror and intimidation, and restricted individual rights. In order to more accurately place communism and fascism, the traditional left–right continuum has to be modified as shown in the diagram, "Communism and Fascism in Practice."

All ideologies include beliefs that explain and are used to justify political and economic systems. Sometimes these beliefs are contradictory. Many are impossible to categorize because of specific historical, cultural, economic, and geographic circumstances. The traditional left–right continuum is less suited to analysing these beliefs or the types of relationships that exist between political and economic systems. It was developed initially to rank only political beliefs; later in the 19th century economic beliefs were added.

Political and economic beliefs evolve as political and economic systems adapt to changing circumstances. In the 20th century, ideologies such as communism and socialism have been substantially revised in the face of differing views held by leaders, evolving economic conditions, and changing circumstances. Although fascism was defeated in 1945, several authoritarian strands continue to exist. Liberalism and conservatism today have many different versions. These realities are difficult to express on the traditional left–right continuum.

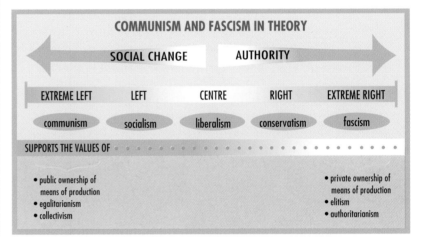

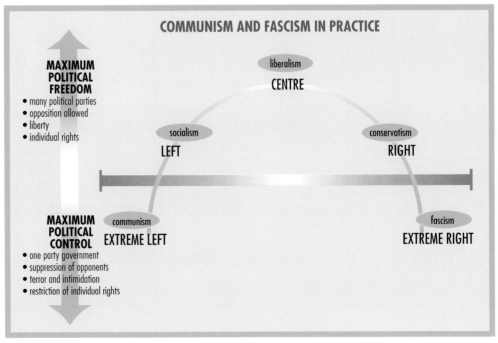

Political–Economic Grid

Although the traditional left–right continuum remains useful to describe basic political viewpoints, such as liberalism and conservatism, the political–economic grid is a more appropriate approach to representing political and economic ideologies in relation to one another. The grid below, based on degree of political and economic freedoms, allows for a more representative relative placement both of ideologies and the political and economic systems based on them.

The apparent contradiction within fascism posed by authoritarian political control and the apparent freedom to own property and make a profit can easily be expressed by showing political and economic beliefs in a grid format, as shown below. This format can also more effectively accommodate the evaluation of political and economic systems and changing political and economic policies of states. For example, the use of the grid called "Evolving Systems" on the back end-sheets of the textbook makes it easier to follow the remarkable political and economic changes that have occurred in China and Russia since 1990, as well as in Canada, Japan, and Sweden.

The grid below shows a relative placement of the main ideologies studied in this book. The grid on the back endsheets shows the relative placement of the countries covered in the case studies in this book and the political and economic changes in these countries over time.

Using the Grid

We must know what is meant by political and economic freedom or control before we can locate ideologies or countries on the political–economic grid.

Political Freedom/Control. Political freedom involves the ability of people to change their leaders peacefully, to elect individuals to represent their views, to speak what they think or feel, to decide what goals their leaders should pursue for them, and to have the opportunity to become leaders themselves. On the political–economic grid, only democratic socialism and democratic capitalism allow significant political freedom for people to express their own views and to make their own decisions. Under communist and fascist regimes, the freedom to choose political leaders, decide policies and goals, and express different views is reserved only for a select few. Participation by individuals in the political process is restricted. Individuals are expected to obey the orders and directives of their political leaders. People who express values, ideas, and views that do not conform to those of the political leadership may be arrested, exiled, imprisoned, or executed.

Economic Freedom/Control. Economic freedom involves the right to own private property, make individual decisions about what to produce and consume, and acquire wealth. Democratic capitalism allows people the greatest economic freedom to own private property and to make decisions that concern their own economic welfare and material needs. Under democratic socialism, there are some restrictions on private property. As well, the government regulates some economic activities and influences people's economic decisions. Under communism, private property is eliminated or subject to severe restrictions and the government controls many aspects of the economy and people's lives. Under fascism, people may own private property, but the government often restricts people's economic freedom in the interests of achieving national goals.

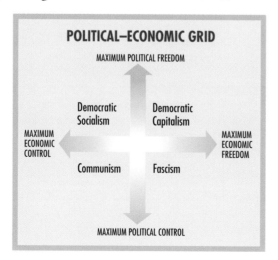

POLITICAL–ECONOMIC GRID

MAXIMUM POLITICAL FREEDOM

Democratic Socialism | Democratic Capitalism

MAXIMUM ECONOMIC CONTROL ← → MAXIMUM ECONOMIC FREEDOM

Communism | Fascism

MAXIMUM POLITICAL CONTROL

REVIEW

Summary

1. Values underlie a society's approach to making choices and solving problems. They are important because values provide people with approaches to live by. Dominant values vary from society to society because of different historical experiences, cultures, traditions, religions, languages, geography, level of economic development, social structures, and foreign influences.

2. Ideologies are sets of beliefs about human nature, society, and patterns of interaction between human beings. Political and economic systems are based on particular ideologies. Ideologies are further distinguished from each other by the specific language/terminology, symbols, and style of leadership each uses.

The major ideologies that have emerged or developed further in the 20th century are liberalism, conservatism, capitalism, socialism, communism, fascism, and anarchism. Each of these ideologies includes distinctive beliefs about human nature and suggests particular political and economic programs.

The traditional method of classifying ideologies is the left–right continuum, which appeared at the time of the French Revolution. By the 20th century, the greater complexity of political and economic life had complicated the traditional meaning of left and right. As a result, a political–economic grid has been developed to better describe the interaction between politics and economics in different societies.

Political–Economic Values Survey

1. Whether we are aware of them or not, values matter a great deal to how we perceive the world. The purpose of this questionnaire is to discover what values matter most to you. Read the following statements, then list the letters a) to x) in your notebook. Beside each statement you *agree* with, mark (A). There are no right or wrong answers to these statements. Check the glossary for any terms you do not understand.

a) People are basically good and concerned about the needs of others.

b) Private ownership and competition are more important than public ownership and cooperation.

c) A powerful leader should control the government and rule the nation with a strong hand.

d) All groups in society have the right to be treated equally and to participate in politics.

e) The best type of government is one led by workers.

f) The role of the government is to protect the rights of the individual to own property and operate a business.

g) The economy should be organized and controlled by groups of business people, professionals, and experts.

h) The rich should share some of their wealth with the poor.

i) People are often untrustworthy and out for themselves.

j) Profit, rent, and interest income should be banned.

k) Nationality is important to a country's development.

l) People should be allowed to make as much income as they want, though it may mean many others will receive little.

m) The government should own all industries and regulate the economy so that everyone can have the same standard of living.

n) Little government regulation of the economy is necessary for prosperity, high standards of living, and full employment.

o) The best economy is one which workers manage for the benefit of the many.

p) Personal initiative and competition are important features of success.

q) The government should provide social programs to help disadvantaged groups in society.

r) The future well-being of all peoples depends on establishing a classless society.

s) People who are not part of our culture can be dangerous to society.

t) A government elected by the people can solve social problems and create a more humane and compassionate society.

u) All people should work according to the principle of "From each according to his ability, to each according to his need."

v) At times the government must control the use of private property to make the country powerful.

w) A country must be self-sufficient and have a large army to dominate other countries.

x) Social programs are an important measure of a country's prosperity and well-being.

2. a) In your notebook, prepare a chart similar to the following:

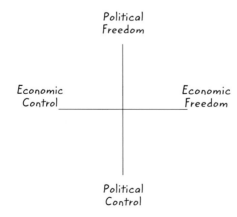

b) Place your *agree* (A) responses in the appropriate quadrant of your chart, following the key shown in the grid below. For example, if you agree with statement a), place the letter in the upper left quadrant of your chart. Complete this stage of the exercise before proceeding.

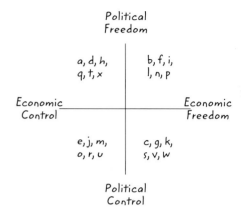

c) Label the quadrants of your chart: *democratic socialism* in the upper left, *democratic capitalism* in the upper right, *communism* in the lower left, and *fascism* in the lower right quadrant.

d) Notice which quadrant of your chart contains the most letters. This indicates which ideology you lean toward, based on your responses to the value statements. Your answers to this questionnaire only illustrate that you have personal preferences. Preferences change over time, and so may your preference for a particular ideology. People may disagree with your ideology, but they must also understand that the values that underlie your ideology are personal values.

e) What did the survey indicate about your own beliefs? In what ways do you agree or disagree with the results?

f) Why do you think there is a disparity between what you think and what the survey indicates?

Values, Beliefs, and Attitudes

1. Define values in your own words.
2. What impact do our values have on the decisions we make?
3. Explain how your values have been strengthened or changed during your life.
4. From the chart on page 6, list the three most important influences on your personal values. Briefly explain the reasons for your choices.
5. a) What is meant by critical thinking?

   b) How does critical thinking help solve value conflicts?
6. From what you have read, how and why might your values be different from those of someone who has recently moved here from another country?
7. Examine the examples of value conflicts on page 8. In a short paragraph, take and defend a position on two of the issues below. You may choose to agree, partially agree, partially disagree, or disagree with the question.
   a) Should individual rights always be placed ahead of the interests of society?
   b) Should people be free from any government control?
   c) Should the amount of influence a group in society has be based on their level of education and wealth?
   d) Should we encourage constant change in our society?
   e) Should we be concerned only about the well-being of our own country and let the world look after itself?
   f) Should minority rights be strongly protected in our society?
8. Outline your views on the following issue: Should people live by a particular set of values throughout their lives, or should people examine their values often and modify or change them if this seems appropriate?

9. Values are affected by crisis. How might the following affect your value choices?
   a) war
   b) economic recession/depression

Ideologies

1. What is the meaning of the term ideology as used in this text?
2. Why might your personal ideology be different from the general ideology that society accepts? What personal values are most likely to come into conflict with societal values?
3. a) Prepare notes for a discussion on what the text has to say about ideologies. Include ideas about human nature, the purpose of life, and the role of the individual in society.
   b) Two beliefs about human nature that affect ideology are that human nature is either basically good or basically bad, and that behaviour is either determined by genetics (nature) or environment (nurture). Indicate your beliefs about these two questions by placing a dot at an appropriate place in one of the quadrants of a grid such as the following.

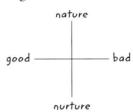

   c) Some ideologies are based on the belief that the purpose of life is to serve the community, while others emphasize individual accomplishment. Indicate your belief at the appropriate place on a continuum such as the following.

   serving the community ———————— individual accomplishment

   d) Some ideologies suggest that people should work together for the common good, while others suggest that people should put the needs of themselves and their family first. Indicate your belief on this issue at the appropriate place on a continuum such as the following.

common good ———————————— self and family first

4. In your own words, briefly explain the terms individualism and collectivism.

5. From the chart on page 12, choose three statements from each list that you think are the most important aspects of these two values. Explain each of your choices.

6. With which one of the following four statements do you *most* agree? Write two or three statements in your notebook explaining the reasons for your choice.
A. We should only be concerned with improving our own lives.
B. We need to contribute to society to some degree, but it is most important to look after ourselves first.
C. We need to take care of ourselves, but it is more important to contribute to society as a whole.
D. We should devote our lives to society, for in this way everyone will benefit.

7. Would you describe yourself as believing more in collectivism or more in individualism, as part of your personal ideology? Write a paragraph outlining your views and be prepared to discuss and defend your ideology with others. You may wish to use the continuum below to help you express your view on this question.

collectivism ———————————— individualism

8. a) What is a main goal of any political system?
b) What is a main goal of any economic system?

9. Review the charts on pages 13 and 14. Take careful note of the headings and write brief answers to all the questions, based on your values. This can be done individually or in a group setting. How do your values affect your answers?

20th Century Ideologies

1. a) Create a chart which summarizes the beliefs of each of the philosophers described under each type of ideology (pages 15–18).
b) Define the ideologies based on the beliefs of the philosophers.
c) From your chart, select ideas of each philosopher with which you agree and with which you disagree.
d) Explain each of your choices in 1(c).
e) Are your choices consistent with the ideology you expressed in Ideologies, question 7? Why or why not?

2. Review the chart on page 13. How might John Locke, Vladimir Lenin, Adolf Hitler, and Pëtr Kropotkin answer the following questions?
a) Should leaders be chosen by a select few or by the people?
b) Should political decisions be made by the few or the many?
c) What is the role of the individual in the political system?

3. Prepare a rebuttal from the point of view of one of the philosophers (pp. 15–18) to debate Kropotkin's view that government is unnecessary.

4. How would each of the thinkers describe the correct moral behaviour of a leader?

5. Which two thinkers do you think would hold the most opposite views? Why? You may wish to use the questions on page 13 as a guide.

6. From the perspective of Pëtr Kropotkin, present an argument against each of the ideologies on pages 15–18.

7. A communist and a fascist would disagree most about the role of the state in

A. the media
B. education
C. politics
D. economics

8. The following is a Soviet poster of a capitalist during the years 1918–1921, often reproduced throughout Europe.

"CAPITALISM" by Victor Deni 1919

a) Describe the artist's view of capitalism.
b) To what extent do you agree with the artist?
c) Which philosophers would most likely agree with the artist? Explain your choices.

9. Create a cartoon expressing the opinion of one or more of the thinkers on one of the following issues:

a) human rights
b) war
c) human nature

10. In small groups, discuss the apparent contradiction between actions sometimes advocated by radicals and the values they support.

Classifying Ideologies

1. The idea of left and right in politics has its roots in the French Revolution. On which side of the chamber did the most radical members sit? Where did the more moderate members sit?

2. What is the message of the poster on page 19? To what extent does this hold true today?

3. a) Describe how the left–right continuum developed during the 19th century.

b) Using the 19th century labels for political ideologies (p. 20), create a chart to answer the following questions for each group:
   • What is their reaction to the status quo?
   • What do they feel the role of government to be?
   • Where do they feel the use of violence is appropriate?
   • What are their views on human rights?

c) Examine the continuum on page 20. Keeping in mind that the continuum is based on the concept of change, and considering your own views, where would you place yourself on the continuum? Briefly explain your choice.

4. a) Discuss why the left–right continuum became more complicated in the 20th century.

b) How have the positions of or definitions for radicals, liberals, and others evolved in the 20th century?

5. What are the strengths and limitations of the traditional left–right continuum when used today?

6. What are the advantages and disadvantages of using the political–economic grid to better understand political and economic systems?

7. a) Using the information and chart on pages 20–21, write one slogan for each of a radical, liberal, moderate, conservative, and reactionary candidate on the issue: Should the government cut spending for health and education?

b) In small groups write a short election speech for either a radical, liberal, moderate, conservative, or reactionary candidate on the issue: Should the government cut spending for health and education? Present to the whole class for discussion.

8. Compare the diagrams on communism and fascism in theory and practice on page 23. What do these diagrams tell you about the difference between theory and practice? To what extent do these diagrams help you understand these two ideologies? Which diagram do you find most useful? Provide complete answers.

9. Using the chart and information on page 24, discuss the general trends shown on the grid on the back endsheet. Based on these trends, try to predict what the future may bring.

10. Create a left–right continuum and survey at least ten people as to where they would place themselves ideologically. What are their reasons for placing themselves as they did?

Chapter Consolidation

1. Review the chart on page 5. After studying this chapter, you should better understand the relationships between values, choices of ideology, and the reasons ideological conflicts occur within individuals and society. Ideological conflicts can lead to a reevaluation of values, leading to new choices, as the cycle repeats.

a) Record and discuss an example from your own experience where this has occurred.

b) Record and discuss an example where a government has made a change based on this process. For example, has our ideology regarding health care, education, or the role of government in business remained the same or changed in recent times?

2.   This chapter began with a quotation by Dorothy L. Sayers, "Very dangerous things, theories." Write a one-paragraph reaction to the quotation. You may agree, partly agree, partly disagree, or disagree. Provide some evidence from the text to support your point of view.

3. In small groups prepare a series of role plays of discussions among the various thinkers profiled on pages 15–18. Topics of discussion could include the following:

a) What is the purpose of government?

b) To what extent should citizens subordinate their own interests to those of the state?

c) What are the rights of the minority?

2 INTRODUCING POLITICAL SYSTEMS

> "The true forms of government . . . are those in which the one, or the few, or the many, govern with a view to the common interest; but governments which rule with a view to the private interest, whether of the one, or of the few, or of the many, are perversions."
> –Aristotle, *Politics*, 343 BCE

Every four years in November, American voters elect their head of state. Canadians recognize as their head of state a monarch who lives in another country and who accepts the advice of the Canadian government in appointing a representative to rule. This monarch is the head of state of Great Britain and of many other Commonwealth countries besides Canada. In Saudi Arabia, the head of state, the king, appoints a body of experts who advise him on policies of national importance. In Latin American, African, and Asian countries, military leaders have ruled and in some countries continue to rule in the name of law and order. Until recently, the countries of Eastern Europe and the former Soviet Union were ruled by a small group of people who formulated and implemented national policies.

There are many political systems in the world. The preceding paragraph lists examples of political systems in action. There are approximately 200 independent countries in the world. Within each country there are administrative units like states, provinces, counties, regions, and municipalities. All of these political systems serve to satisfy human needs.

Most political systems are established by people to bring order to society and to help them understand forces that confront them, issues they face, or changes that appear in their world. In this way, political systems organize, coordinate, regulate, and promote various human activities.

Focus On Issue

A political system provides an organized way of making decisions and resolving conflicts among the members of a society. Societies need to consider these important questions:

- **To what extent should decision making be restricted to a particular group in society?**
- **To what extent should the majority rule in its own interests or accept limitations on its rights to protect minorities?**

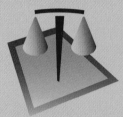

Chapter Overview: The diagram below shows the interrelationship between political culture and features of a political system.

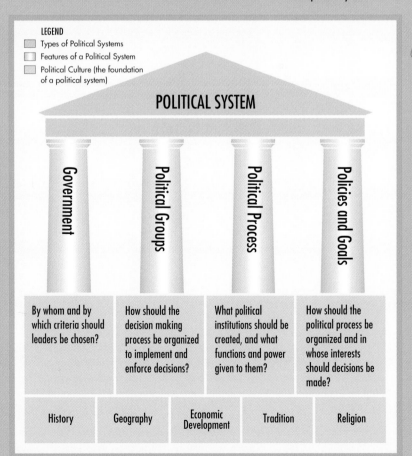

LEGEND
☐ Types of Political Systems
☐ Features of a Political System
☐ Political Culture (the foundation of a political system)

POLITICAL SYSTEM

Government	Political Groups	Political Process	Policies and Goals
By whom and by which criteria should leaders be chosen?	How should the decision making process be organized to implement and enforce decisions?	What political institutions should be created, and what functions and power given to them?	How should the political process be organized and in whose interests should decisions be made?

| History | Geography | Economic Development | Tradition | Religion |

ROLE OF POLITICAL SYSTEMS

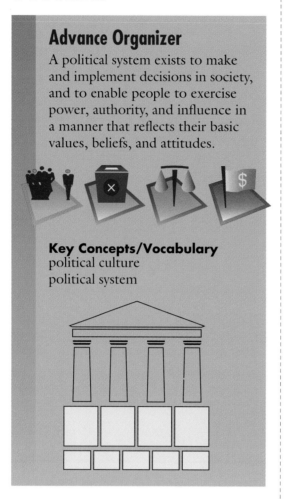

Advance Organizer

A political system exists to make and implement decisions in society, and to enable people to exercise power, authority, and influence in a manner that reflects their basic values, beliefs, and attitudes.

Key Concepts/Vocabulary
political culture
political system

A political system reflects a society's values and beliefs about power and decision making. These values and beliefs form part of a society's political culture.

Political Culture

Foundation

A political system reflects a society's values and beliefs about power and decision making. Beliefs about who should rule, what limits should be placed on the powers of leaders, what rights and freedoms individuals should have, and what goals should be pursued all form part of a society's political culture. In some societies, these beliefs are widely and deeply held, while in others the beliefs about who should rule and the rights of individuals are shared by some social groups but not by others.

History, geography, level and type of economic development, traditions, and religion shape a society's beliefs about power and attitudes to political issues, and cause society to reflect on and react to

issues in ways unique to itself. For example, in some cultures, geography has influenced policies about political isolation or alliance.

Although all of the factors influence political culture, variation in their importance determines how power is distributed and exercised in a society. For example, in some cultures religious power structures and religious beliefs may strongly influence law making and other aspects of the political system.

Political systems are composed of institutions that exercise power. Within the political system, society selects goals and implements policies to achieve them, then evaluates the results. The following questions are relevant to any political system:

- Who should choose the leadership and by which criteria?
- How should the decision making process be structured, carried out, and enforced?
- What political institutions should be created; what functions and how much power should each have?
- How should the political process be structured?

Whatever its characteristics, political culture is the foundation on which every society builds its political system.

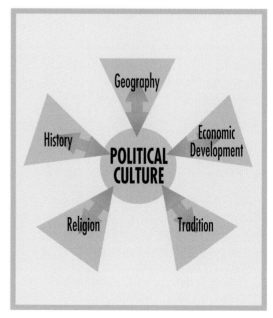

FEATURES OF A POLITICAL SYSTEM

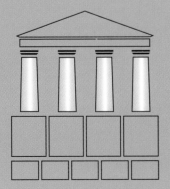
Government

Government is the largest component of a political system. All political systems have governments to allocate power and responsibility to leaders who choose goals, make and implement decisions, and evaluate the results of policies once they have been implemented. The organization and operation of government is often outlined in a body of rules and regulations called a constitution. The constitution may be written, unwritten, or include both written and unwritten elements.

Purpose of Government

Throughout history, philosophers have pondered the purpose of government and counselled leaders on the "art of government." Most have agreed that government was a necessity for both society and individuals but disagreed over how individuals should relate to government. Many existing societies have drawn on these ideas in creating their own systems of government. Other ideas important to the development of various forms of government will be discussed in later sections of this text.

Working with Information

As you read through the works of the philosophers, following on pages 34–38, think about how each philosopher would have responded to the following questions about the purpose of government:[1]

- How should leaders be chosen?
- How should political decisions be made, implemented, and enforced?
- What political institutions are necessary to carry out decisions made by leaders?
- How should the political process be organized?

[1]A blackline master to record this information is available in *Global Systems, Teacher Resource Package*.

Government is the largest political component of a political system and the first feature described in this book (pages 33–41).

- Purpose of Government
- Constitution

Popperfoto/Archive Photos

Confucius (551–479 BCE)

In *The Analects*, Confucius put forth the belief that society was based on a code of ethics. All individuals should strive to become persons of noble behaviour, guided by the inner virtues of humanity, integrity, righteousness, altruism, and loyalty, with an outward manner and dignity to match. Guidance by virtue, Confucius believed, could not be effective unless the ruler set a moral example for the people. He felt that the purpose of government was to promote the welfare of the common people. In doing so, a ruler promotes correct thinking, good moral behaviour, and harmony among the people.

The Master [Confucius] said, "Guide them by edicts, keep them in line with punishments, and the common people will stay out of trouble but will have no sense of shame. Guide them by virtue, keep them in line with the rites, and they will, besides having a sense of shame, reform themselves."

Chi K'ang Tzu [a student] asked Confucius about government. Confucius answered, "To govern is to correct. If you set an example by being correct, who would dare to remain incorrect?"

The Master said, "If a man manages to make himself correct, what difficulty will there be for him to take part in government? If he cannot make himself correct, what business has he with making others correct?"

Archive Photos

Plato (427–347 BCE)

In *The Republic*, Plato declared that society arises out of mutual need and differences in aptitude. No person is self-sufficient and good at all things. As society develops there will be a need for a ruling class of philosopher kings to govern in the interests of society. Training in philosophy, logic, mathematics, and ethics will prepare them for their task. Plato wrote:

Cities will have no respite from evil . . . nor will the human race, I think, unless philosophers rule as kings in the cities, or those whom we now call kings and rulers genuinely and adequately study philosophy. [Kings who do not study philosophy will be prevented from governing.]

Archive Photos

Aristotle (383–322 BCE)

In his book *Politics*, Aristotle criticized Plato for his desire to reform society and the state. Aristotle believed that government enabled individuals to become self-sufficient and to realize their potential. Society and government (state) were founded because human beings naturally seek political association with others. The purpose of government was to provide for a good life. The best form of government, Aristotle argued, was one in which there was a large middle class, reasonable

| 3500 BCE Sumerian civilization flourishes | 2500 BCE First Chinese dynasty | 2300 BCE Pharaohs rule in Egypt | 1000 BCE Greek civilization emerges | 753 BCE Founding of Rome | c.563 BCE Birth of Buddha and Buddhism | 300 BCE Collapse of Athenian Democracy | c.4 BCE Birth of Christ and Christianity |

Note: Timeline is not to scale

differences in wealth, and a constitution that moderated the treatment of its citizens.

Every state is a community of some kind, and every community is established with a view to some good; for mankind always act in order to obtain that which they think good. But, if all communities aim at some good, the state or political community, which is the highest of all, and which embraces all the rest, aims at good in a greater degree than any other, and at the highest good.

It is clear then both that the political partnership which operates through the middle class is best, and also that those cities have every chance of being well-governed in which the middle class is large, [and strong] . . . . For this reason it is a happy state of affairs when those who take part in the life of the state have a moderate but adequate amount of property; for where one set of people possesses a great deal and the other nothing, the result is either extreme democracy or unmixed oligarchy or a tyranny due to the excesses of the other two.

Saint Augustine (354–430)

Stock Montage, Inc.

Augustine wrote his major work, *City of God*, in response to the political and social upheaval in the Roman Empire. Saint Augustine wrote that peace and order were essential conditions for society.

The peace of the political community is an ordered harmony of authority and obedience between citizens . . . . Peace, in its final sense, is the calm that comes of order. Order is an arrangement of like and unlike things whereby each of them is disposed in its proper place.

Abu Nasr al-Fārābī (870–950)

Al-Fārābī, a philosopher and scientist known as the "Second Teacher," drew on the ideas of Aristotle and Plato then prevalent in Islamic philosophy. He argued in *Aphorisms of the Statesman* that a good king must rule and live by the highest ethical standards.

Rulership is of two kinds. (a) A rulership that establishes the voluntary actions, ways of life, and positive dispositions, with which to attain what is truly happiness. This is the virtuous rulership; the cities that submit to this rulership are the virtuous cities and nations. (b) A rulership that establishes in the cities the actions and states of character with which they [claim to attain happiness but do not]. This is ignorant rulership.

Nizām al-Mulk (1018–1092)

Al-Mulk's celebrated work, *The Book of Government*, advised the Sultan Malikshah of Persia on the virtues of a good leader. A virtuous king should be just, devout, fond of learning, alert, sound in judgment, and a steadfast defender of the faith.

The person most worthy for kingship is he whose heart is a repository of justice, whose house is a haven for wise and religious men, and whose . . . agents are discreet and God-fearing.

Images depicting Abu Nasr al-Fārābī and Nizām al-Mulk could not be located. The inscription of Abu Nasr al-Fārābī's name is in Arabic calligraphy and that of Nizām al-Mulk is in Farsi. Decorative use of calligraphy is common in Islamic art.

220 CE	313 CE	476 CE	500 CE	570 CE	633 CE	750 CE	962 CE	1095–1291 CE
Han dynasty falls in China	Christianity legalized in Rome	Collapse of Roman Empire	Mayan civilization flourishes	Birth of Muhummad and Islam	Establishment of Caliphate in Baghdad	Toltec civilization established in Mexico	Holy Roman Empire established	Christian Crusaders attempt to recapture Holy Land from Muslims

Archive Photos

Saint Thomas Aquinas (1225–1274)

Aquinas argued in his work *On Kingship* that society was natural to human beings and necessary for their normal development, and that government was needed for the maintenance of society. The best form of government was one that aimed for the common good. The purpose of the ruler was to seek the common good and avoid personal gain. He stated:

If . . . a multitude of free men is ordered by the ruler towards the common good of the multitude, that rulership will be right and just, as is suitable to free men. If, on the other hand, a rulership aims, not at the common good of the multitude, but at the private good of the ruler, it will be an unjust and perverted rulership.

Archive Photos

Niccolo Machiavelli (1469–1527)

In his major political work of the Italian Renaissance, Machiavelli outlined in *The Prince* policies and methods a ruler can use to acquire or maintain power. A ruler, wrote Machiavelli, should inspire fear but at the same time should be mindful of maintaining support of the people, if only to prevent foreign powers from encouraging rebellion by the people.

A prince ought to inspire fear in such a way that, if he does not win love, he avoids hatred; because he can endure very well being feared whilst he is not hated, which will always be as long as he abstains from the property of his citizens and subjects and from their women . . . but above all he must keep his hands off the property of others, because men more quickly forget the death of their father than the loss of their patrimony.

Archive Photos

Thomas Hobbes (1588–1679)

In 1651 in the aftermath of the English Civil War, Hobbes wrote in *Leviathan* that people lived with violence and depended on force and cunning to survive. This struggle for survival left no time for peaceful pursuits such as knowledge, industry, art, music, or culture. The only way to achieve peace was for people to choose a strong leader who would establish a government to ensure peace and common defence, and in return people would promise complete obedience. The leader would lose his position only if he failed to keep order. Government would have unlimited authority to grant freedom to those people who obeyed and punish those who did not. Without order and security, "the life of man [would be] solitary, poor, nasty, brutish, and short."

The final cause, end, or design of men (who naturally love liberty, and domination over others) in the introduction of that restraint upon themselves, in which we see them live in Commonwealths, is the foresight of their own preservation, and of a more contented life thereby; that is to say, of getting themselves out from that miserable condition of war . . . .

| 1215 Genghis Khan overruns China | 1236–1240 Mongols invade Russia | 1254–1273 Nobles dominant power in Holy Roman Empire | 1276 Kublai Khan founds China's Yuan dynasty | 1300 Ottoman dynasty begins in Turkey | 1325 Capital city in Mexico founded by Aztecs | 1368 Ming dynasty established in China | c.1400 Renaissance begins in Europe | 1453 Ottomans conquer Byzantine Empire | 1478 Spanish Inquisition | 1517 Martin Luther's 95 Theses spark beginning of Reformation | 1520 Spanish defeat Aztecs |

CE · 7 · 8

The only way to erect such a common power . . . is to confer all their power and strength upon one man, or upon one assembly of men, that may reduce all their wills, by plurality of voices, unto one will . . . in such manner as if every man should say to every man: I authorise and give up my right of governing myself to this man, or to this assembly of men, on this condition; that thou give thy right to him, and authorise all his actions in like manner.

Based on Kneller, Godfrey/NATIONAL ARCHIVES OF CANADA/C-003717

John Locke (1632–1704)

In 1690, two years after the Glorious Revolution in England resulted in the king becoming subordinate in power to the parliament, Locke wrote in *Two Treatises of Civil Government* that people were fundamentally reasonable and respectful of others. They created society because it fulfilled such human needs as security, belonging, identity, and prestige. People voluntarily created government to protect their property rights and liberties because every person was born free, with certain rights. Government could not rule over people without their consent and had to respect people's rights. Laws enacted by government had to reflect the will of the people and exist for the benefit of the many, not the few. When government failed to govern and lost people's trust, people had the right to rebel against it and change their leaders. As Locke noted:

Men being . . . by Nature all free, equal, and independent, no one can be put out of this estate and subjected to the political power of another without his own consent . . . .

The great end of men's entering into society [is] the enjoyment of their properties in peace and safety, and the great instrument and means of that [are] the laws established in that society; the first and fundamental . . . is the establishing of the legislative power, as the first and fundamental national law which is to govern the legislative. Itself is the preservation of the society and [the public good] of every person in it.

. . . whenever the legislators endeavor to take away and destroy the property of the people . . . they forfeit the power [to govern] . . . the people have a right to resist and defend themselves from injury.

Archive Photos

Charles Baron de Montesquieu (1689–1755)

In *Spirit of Laws* (1748), Montesquieu discussed forms of government, the nature of laws, and social institutions. He asserted that all human beings are born equal, but this equality disappears over time with the development of social institutions. The use of laws is the only way to recover equality of rights among individuals. The exercise of power, Montesquieu thought, often leads to abuses, which must be curbed through checks on power.

In the state of nature . . . all men are born equal, but they cannot continue in this equality. Society makes them lose it, and they recover it only by the protection of laws. . . .

So that one cannot abuse power, power must check power by the arrangement of things. A constitution can be such that no one will be constrained to do the things the law does not oblige him to do or be kept from doing the things the law permits him to do.

| 1529 Mughal dynasty founded in India | 1532 Spanish defeat Incan Empire | 1558–1603 The Elizabethan Age | 1600s– 1700s Age of Enlightenment | 1608 Champlain founds Quebec | 1618–48 Thirty Years War in Central Europe | 1620 Voyage of the Mayflower | 1642–47 Civil War in England | 1644 Manchus establish dynasty in China | 1682–1725 Reign of Peter the Great in Russia | 1688 The Glorious Revolution in England |

Archive Photos

Jean-Jacques Rousseau (1712–1778)

In *Social Contract*, Rousseau posed the question of how to establish a society that would promote the common good as well as maintain individual freedom. His solution was a social contract in which individuals voluntarily agreed to follow the general will. The general will would function in the interests of all and for the common good.

"The problem is to find a form of association which will defend and protect . . . the person and goods of each associate, and in which each, while uniting himself with all, may still obey himself alone, and remain as free as before." This is the fundamental problem of which the Social Contract *provides the solution. . . .*

Finally, each man, in giving himself to all, gives himself to nobody; and as there is no associate over which he does not acquire the same right as he yields others over himself, he gains an equivalent for everything he loses, and an increase of force for the preservation of what he has.

If then we discard from the social compact what is not of its essence, we shall find that it reduces itself to the following terms:

"Each of us puts his person and all his power in common under the supreme direction of the general will, and, in our corporate capacity, we receive each member as an indivisible part of the whole."

Summary

Whatever may be the philosophical bases of society and government, Confucius, Plato, Aristotle, Augustine, Aquinas, Machiavelli, Hobbes, Locke, Montesquieu, and Rousseau, among others, were concerned about the behaviour of rulers, their use of power, and what rights, if any, individuals have in society and in relations with their rulers. According to Confucius, political power was limited by a code of ethics and social position. To Plato and Aristotle the allocation of power evolved as the political needs of people changed in society. To al-Fārābī and Nizām al-Mulk, the leader had to possess ethical virtues. Augustine and Aquinas drew on the works of Plato and Aristotle to argue that political power should be directed to the common good. Machiavelli argued that the acquisition and exercise of power were important aspects of the nature of political power. Writing 200 years later, Hobbes, Locke, Montesquieu, and Rousseau called for some formal limitations on political power. In the 19th and 20th centuries, the basic ideas of these thinkers were carried forward and adapted by other political thinkers and practitioners such as Mill, Marx, Hitler, Lenin, Mao, and Gorbachev.

© Mal Hancock

CE   12

Constitution

In 1789, the United States of America became the first country to have a written constitution, followed by France in 1791. Canada received its constitution in 1867, when the British Parliament passed the British North America Act granting it internal self-government. Since then, constitutions, both written and unwritten, have become a key element in how power is allocated in a political system. Most contemporary constitutions allow for some allocation of power within the government, some organization and division of power between levels of government, and some rights and freedoms for individuals.

Allocation of Power. Most constitutions, written or unwritten, identify three branches of government—the executive, legislature, and judiciary. The executive branch of government is the oldest and the most widely adopted political institution. As early as 5000 years ago in the Middle East, the executive was generally a single person such as a chieftain, priest, or monarch. This leader was the focal point of political power and effective decision making. Today, the executive branch of government generally includes a leader and a group of advisors, commonly called the cabinet. In many systems the executive branch of government is considered to be the most powerful branch because it has access to a wide range of resources that are not generally available to other branches of government. These resources include information, organizations, and legitimacy. Access to these resources gives the executive considerable power over the other branches.

Because of their role as primary decision makers, leaders have unlimited access to information inside the country as well as internationally from other governments. They know how well or how badly things are going before most of us do. One significant source of information is the bureaucracy. Depending on the political system, most leaders exercise varying degrees of control over the civil service, military, and police. In some political systems, this degree of control is defined by law, whereas in other systems, the leader can exercise control as he or she wishes. All leaders exercise some control over their own political organizations. These organizations collect information for leaders, assist in policy making and drafting legislation, and help to disseminate information (leaders' views, policies, and decisions) among the people. This helps leaders to exercise their authority.

The functions of leaders vary according to a country's laws and political culture. Generally, the leader's roles include some of the following:

- acting as the head of state, the head of government, or both
- providing leadership
- making policy
- supervising the bureaucracy
- acting as the country's chief diplomatic representative
- appointing judges and ensuring that the courts enforce laws
- commanding the military

Based on Cooper, Robert/NATIONAL ARCHIVES OF CANADA/PA-141503

Compared with the executive branch of government, the legislature is a relatively modern branch. The oldest legislature to survive largely intact from earliest times is the British Parliament, which dates back to the 11th century. Since that time, the British Parliament has become the model for the modern legislature and has inspired many variations of elected or appointed assemblies in most political systems. The

> The organization and operation of government is often outlined in a constitution.

> Most constitutions allocate power within the government and identify three branches of government—the executive, legislature, and judiciary.

PHOTO: On April 17, 1982, Queen Elizabeth II, Canada's official head of state, signed into law the patriation of the Canadian constitution in the presence of Canada's then head of government, Prime Minister Pierre Trudeau.

type of political culture and political system determines the role and function of these assemblies. Nevertheless, most countries maintain legislatures either as an effective law making body or to provide symbolic support to the executive.

The judiciary has been an important institution of government since courts first appeared in Egypt in 2900 BCE. The Hebrews, Hindus, Chinese, Arabs, Greeks, Romans, Aztecs, Mayans, and Incas had elaborate court systems to administer justice. The common functions of the modern judiciary are to settle disputes, uphold the rule of law (the supremacy of law over arbitrary executive action), and interpret the constitution. From these functions, the judiciary, unlike the executive and legislative branches of government, is passive and does not initiate laws. In studying political systems, it is important to know to what extent a judiciary is free from interference by political leaders and the government.

Organization and Division of Power.
In addition to allocating powers within the government, a constitution may determine the organization of government. The government of a country can be organized as a unitary or a federal state. A unitary state is the most common form of government organization in the world today. They range in size and population—China is the largest unitary state and the Vatican the smallest. In a unitary state the central government possesses all authority. Any allocation of political power to regions, districts, or municipalities is largely made at the discretion of the central government and can generally be reduced, increased, or eliminated for any valid legal or constitutional reason. Policies initiated and decided on by the central government can be imposed on local governments, no matter how unpopular the decisions may be. Often the centralization of power makes political and social control easier for the government. In a unitary state, the central government is able to exercise full control over all areas of a country without having to be concerned about competition from other levels of government.

In a federal state, political power is allocated to or divided between levels of government. Today, more than 25 countries are formally organized as federal states, including countries such as Australia, Brazil, Canada, Germany, India, Russia, Switzerland, and the United States.

According to most constitutions of federal states, each level of government is assigned jurisdiction over certain areas of responsibility. The central government cannot reduce, increase, or eliminate the powers of regional or municipal governments unless it is constitutionally allowed to do so or unless agreement between the levels of government to change is reached.

Depending on the country's constitution, the central government may have jurisdiction over foreign affairs, national defence, and the economy. Provincial or state governments may have jurisdiction over health, social welfare, education, natural resources, and transport. This division of powers among the levels of government does not, however, stop provincial or state governments, or the central government, from attempting to expand their powers and areas of jurisdiction at the expense of the other. Competition for political power between the central (federal) government and regional levels of governments (usually called provinces or states) is common in federal states.

Most constitutions assign residual powers, new areas of jurisdiction arising after the constitution was written, to either the central or regional government.

> Most constitutions organize governments as unitary states or federal states.

Status of Selected Countries 1998

☐ Federal ☐ Unitary

Country	Local Government
Australia	State
Brazil	State
Canada	Province
China	Province, Region
Egypt	Governate
Germany	State
Great Britain	County, Region
India	State
Japan	Prefecture
Kenya	Province
Russia	Province, Republic
Singapore	—
Sweden	County
Switzerland	Canton
United States	State
Vatican	—

Compiled from *Political Handbook of the World, 1998*

Rights and Freedoms of Individuals. Most constitutions make some provision for extending rights and freedoms to individuals. However, the extent to which these are actually guaranteed and protected may vary considerably from society to society, depending on the political culture and system. The rights and freedoms granted to individuals include political rights and civil liberties.

Political rights enable people to participate freely in making political decisions. These rights include individuals' right to organize and participate freely in political parties, interest groups, and other political groups of their choice, the right to vote and elect government leaders and legislative representatives, and the right to run for office.

Civil liberties are the freedoms of individuals to develop values, views, and personal ideas independent of government. They include freedom of expression, worship, assembly, and demonstration, freedom of association in political parties and civic groups, equality under the law, protection from terror and unjustified imprisonment, and respect for personal property, gender, movement, and choice of residence. Other civil liberties that constitutions, explicitly or implicitly, grant to individuals are freedoms to join trade unions and professional organizations, to establish private businesses, and to be free from government corruption and indifference to their needs.

Most constitutions outline the people's political rights and civil liberties. These rights and freedoms vary from country to country.

The highlighted countries in the map below were selected from an annual survey of political rights and civil liberties published by Freedom House. Tabulated ratings for political rights and civil liberties are based on a seven-category scale, with 1 representing the most free and 7 the least free.

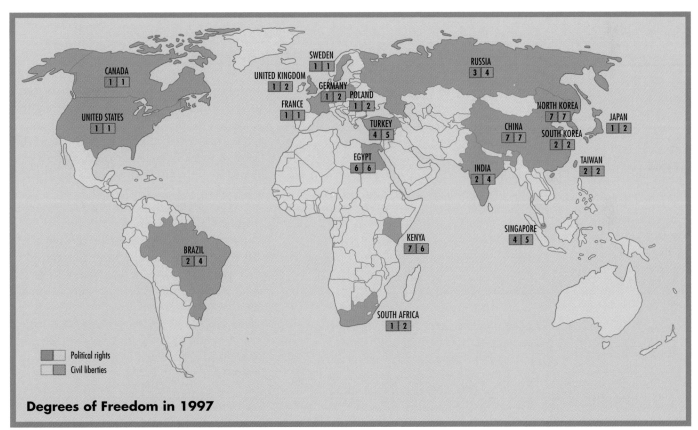

Degrees of Freedom in 1997

Legend:
- Political rights
- Civil liberties

CANADA 1 | 1
UNITED STATES 1 | 1
BRAZIL 2 | 4
SWEDEN 1 | 1
UNITED KINGDOM 1 | 2
GERMANY 1 | 2
FRANCE 1 | 1
POLAND 1 | 2
TURKEY 4 | 5
EGYPT 6 | 6
SOUTH AFRICA 1 | 2
KENYA 7 | 6
RUSSIA 3 | 4
NORTH KOREA 7 | 7
CHINA 7 | 7
SOUTH KOREA 2 | 2
JAPAN 1 | 2
TAIWAN 2 | 2
INDIA 2 | 4
SINGAPORE 4 | 5

Freedom House. *Freedom in the World: The Annual Survey of Political Rights and Civil Liberties, 1996–1997,* http://www.freedomhouse.org. (Note: Freedom House describes itself as a nonprofit, nonpartisan organization dedicated to promoting democracy around the world.)

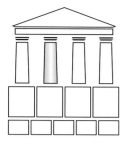

Political groups, the second political feature described in this book, exist to facilitate, influence, or control the policies and decisions of the government (pages 42–47).

Political groups consist of
• Political parties
• Interest groups
• Media

Political Groups

Political groups exist to facilitate, influence, or control the policies and decisions of the government. These groups include political parties, interest groups, and the media. Important questions that societies must address are what roles should these political groups perform in a political system and to what extent should the activities of political parties, interest groups, and the media be regulated. Many constitutions do not specifically mention political parties and interest groups. Yet, these groups are an important element of a country's political system and reveal another aspect of the distribution of power in a political system. The distribution of power among political parties and interest groups affects how decisions are made and whether these decisions will be accepted by all political groups in society.

Political Parties

Political parties are considered to be the most important political groups outside the government. They are generally defined as groups of people who come together voluntarily to represent certain views, including those on how to govern. Political parties vary greatly in their structure, goals, and the functions they perform in the political system. They often differ in the ideology that they support, in their acceptance of methods of gaining power, in the size of their membership, and in their bases of support.

Functions. The most significant function of political parties is their ability to act as a link between the people and the government. They attempt to educate, instruct and convince people to support their policies, and they stir the people to action. They seek to mobilize the population through their use of the media, local party organizations, and various social and economic organizations. The mobilization of support for the party may be furthered by mass rallies, uniforms, flags, and other symbols and displays of unity.

Recruiting political leaders is another important function of political parties in

all political systems, even when one political party dominates and is the only avenue to political power. Occasionally, political parties have been created or taken over by leaders as a means of taking power.

Besides widening popular participation and recruiting political leaders, political parties support or put forth a set of values for society to consider. All political parties have political ideologies, however vague or blurred or divorced they may be from the actual political behaviour of the party. For example, according to its 1925 program the National Socialist German Workers' Party held strongly left-wing political views, but when it was in power it instituted several right-wing policies that favoured big business. The ideology of the party may challenge prevailing ideologies and the political system, as when socialist parties appeared in Europe at the end of the 19th century to oppose existing liberal and conservative ideas among the political elites. The degree to which parties adhere to their ideological principles and goals is an important distinguishing feature of political systems. In some cases, political parties may behave in an entirely pragmatic fashion, whereas in other cases, parties behave in a manner consistent with their ideologies.

Most political parties generally try to limit conflict in society by being flexible and avoiding the polarization of opinion. Others, however, deliberately try to foster divisions within society to achieve their goals. One notable example of political division in the 20th century was the collapse of the Weimar Republic in Germany, which was hastened by the polarization of support between the National Socialist and Communist parties.

Structure. The structure of political parties is very closely related to the functions and methods they use to capture or retain political power. Parties which seek political power through peaceful means have different structures from those that attempt to gain power through revolution and violent seizures of power. The factors that determine party structure include the role of leadership, the degree to which power in the party is centralized, the power of the party bureaucracy, and the size of party membership.

The structure of parties that seek political power primarily through elections is generally composed of a parliamentary wing and an extra-parliamentary wing. The parliamentary wing consists of a caucus of elected party members. The extra-parliamentary wing consists of the party's central executive, committees, and various levels of party organization. The lowest level is the grassroots organization at the constituency level. At the constituency level, delegates are chosen for elections, party congresses, and party fundraising campaigns. However, distribution of power inside these political parties rests in the hands of its caucus of elected members, or parliamentary wing, with the leader generally having a great deal of power.

The structure of political parties dedicated to revolution and the seizure of power may be organized on the basis of cells or supported by para-military groups. Cells are generally organized in places of work and are geared to continual political activity, as was the case of the Communist Party in the Soviet Union and in China today. The cell structure is designed to ensure that the whole party structure will not be endangered by police infiltration or military attack. It is effective in countries where the party's political activities are illegal and forced to operate underground. Seeking political power through peaceful means is of secondary importance to cell-structured political parties. The organization of a para-military wing inside a party, such as the Blackshirts in the Italian Fascist Party and the Storm Troopers in the German National Socialist Party, was useful for intimidating rival political parties and preventing police infiltration of the party's organization and leadership. Power in these types of parties is typically concentrated in the hands of top leaders, with party members expected to obey decisions from the top. Other political parties dedicated to revolution and the seizure of power may be organized in different ways.

Classification. Political parties are most commonly classified as belonging to a one-party system, two-party system, or multi-party system. A one-party system is characterized by the existence of a single political party that controls the government and dominates the political process. In this system, party leaders are the leaders of the government and the country. Occasionally, the official party may authorize other parties, provided that these parties support the government and the official party, and operate within strict guidelines established by the government.

A two-party system is one in which political power and the control of the government may alternate between two major political parties. The two major parties dominate the political process. Smaller political parties may exist, but their chief function tends to be one of introducing new issues and different ways of looking at old issues, and of offering occasional support to one of the major parties.

A multi-party system exists where three or more parties have elected members in the legislature. In this party system, it may be necessary for several parties to join together and establish a government, which can be difficult to achieve because of ideological, personality, and political differences among the parties. A government composed and led by several parties in a multi-party system may also tend to be unstable when smaller parties of the government become unwilling to compromise their principles.

In the 1990s, Israel, Italy, and Japan were faced with the issue of an unstable multi-party government. On the other hand, some multi-party states such as Canada, Germany, and Sweden have been able to create stable governments.

Political parties are usually classified as belonging to a one-party, two-party, or multi-party system.

Interest Groups

Political parties are not the only political groups to influence decisions. Interest groups, commonly referred to as pressure groups, exist to influence government policies, and can be identified in all political systems. Some of these groups devote all or many of their activities to influencing government policy, while other groups rarely do. Interest groups in a political system include business associations, professional groups, religious organizations, educational groups, women's groups, farm groups, trade unions, the bureaucracy, single issue groups such as environmentalists, and in some countries the military. To influence key decision makers, interest groups may use both indirect and direct methods to get their message and interests across to policy makers. Indirect methods include lobbying and using influence; direct methods include demonstrations, strikes, and boycotts.

Indirect Methods. One widely used tactic of interest groups to influence decision makers is lobbying. The purpose of lobbying is to convince government leaders to alter policy or to introduce, pass, amend, or repeal laws. Special agents (called lobbyists), either from within or hired by the interest group, speak on its behalf at hearings, before legislative committees, or to influential government people in private.

In political systems where political power is concentrated in the executive branch of government, lobbyists may directly contact leaders and highly placed civil servants who have influence on the executive to seek special attention for their interest group's needs. In systems where individual members of the legislature have greater independence, they, too, are likely to be approached by lobbyists.

Another method used by interest groups to influence policy is the establishment of formal affiliations with political parties. Trade unions in many countries, including Canada, France, Spain, Great Britain, and Germany, are affiliated with socialist parties. These parties receive money, members, and organizational support from trade unions. Religious groups in Germany, Italy, and Latin America have historically maintained close ties with conservative parties. Business associations and professional organizations in many countries are closely allied with conservative and other parties that advocate pro-business policies.

In several countries the military is a powerful interest group because of the competence of its leaders and its role as a guardian of peace. For many people in these countries, joining the military is an important avenue to education, wealth, and prestigious careers. The capacity of the military to influence government policy arises largely from its ability to intervene directly into politics and remove government leaders should their policies threaten the military's power and prestige.

PHOTO: Lobbying is an important indirect method by which interest groups convince government leaders to change policies and laws.

Canapress/Andrew Vaughan

Direct Methods. When lobbying does not bring the desired results, interest groups may employ more direct methods to influence public opinion and exert pressure on leaders. These methods can include mass demonstrations, organized boycotts, letter writing campaigns, strikes, advertising, press conferences, and the publication of information in the media. The extent of the use of direct action will depend on the level of tolerance for these actions within the country's political culture.

Direct action is typically employed by interest groups when the issue has a more powerful ideological component. Groups involved in controversial issues that seek to dramatically change the status quo and the practices of established groups and the government tend to be more ideologically motivated. In these cases, the interest group is likely to use organized demonstrations and other confrontational methods to force the government to change policies.

The aims of the interest group, the nature and size of the membership, the amount of money available, and the nature of the leadership have an important bearing on the methods used. Regardless, many groups have at one time or another utilized local, national, and international advertising campaigns, personal contacts with people in government, strikes, boycotts, mass demonstrations, and civil disobedience in attempting to achieve their goals.

For example, doctors in Saskatchewan went on strike in 1962 to oppose the introduction of provincial medicare. In the early 1990s, environmentalist and native groups barricaded logging roads in British Columbia to protest the practice of clear cutting. Provincial teachers' associations present their views on education to the provincial government on an ongoing basis. Throughout Canada, numerous professional lobbyist groups arrange meetings between their clients and influential politicians.

Written and Unwritten Rules.
Depending on the political system, interest groups, just like political parties, are forced to operate according to various written and unwritten rules. In most political systems, the government has established laws to regulate the methods and practices by which interest groups may contact and influence political leaders. Many of these laws resulted from documented incidents of bribery involving government officials, and were intended to curb potential corruption. In other cases, the regulation of interest groups was necessary to ensure that no single interest group could dominate government policy and exclude other groups from contacting government leaders.

Generally, interest groups are less active in one-party systems, but occasionally their activities are tolerated and can lead to changes in government decisions. For example, during the 1980s, Soviet environmentalists were successful in convincing their government to reverse its plans to divert the flow of major Siberian rivers to the south for irrigation there.

Overall, interest groups have advantages and disadvantages for a political system. They are useful because they provide people and groups with access to government they would otherwise be denied regarding important issues. As well, they inform the public on important issues, albeit from their perspective only. On the other hand, the activities of interest groups often result in certain issues being given more attention than others that are equally important. Some groups, such as the homeless and unemployed, may have less influence than others who have a greater voice through lobbyists and interest groups.

Canapress/Tom Hanson

PHOTO: One form of direct action used by interest groups to force governments to change policies and laws is the strike.

Media

The media are an important component of 20th century political systems. The rise of the media as a force in political systems dates from the emergence of the first mass circulation newspapers in the late 18th century. Then, as now, the power of the press and that of television and radio (which appeared in the 20th century) arises from the ability to create images in people's minds about various issues, leaders, groups of individuals, and societies. For this reason, the media play several important roles in the political system.

The media are vehicles for the dissemination of information and views of all sorts, which they present in a variety of ways. The media can be used to enlighten and to stimulate discussion about the complexities of current issues and decisions of governments. The media also provide opportunities for people to express their views and enter into discussion with others, and sometimes with leading decision makers.

In cases where ownership and control of the media are concentrated in the hands of a few people, there is the danger that not all viewpoints will be expressed or objectively conveyed. Where dissenting viewpoints are absent, powerful voices may be able to influence the thoughts of large numbers of people. In this instance, society's interests may not be well served. It is important for society that people have broad access to information on a wide variety of issues and opinions if the public is to be well-informed.

There is a tendency for elements of the media to reduce important, often complex, messages to a superficial level—to what are commonly referred to as "sound bytes." Originally developed as quick summaries of events and issues for people who lead busy lives, sound bytes have become part of the established practice of the press, television, and radio. Critics of this practice claim that to rely on sound bytes exclusively for information is to ignore other available information sources that provide more substantial reporting and analysis. The result is a less well-informed public that forms judgements based on limited information. Defenders of sound bytes argue that short summaries of events do inform people who are less interested in detail but want to know the basic outlines of events and issues.

Critics believe that some elements of the media treat stories and events in a manner that can be described as sensational, seemingly for the purpose of maximizing exposure and profit with little regard for journalistic integrity and good taste. They suggest that the public is not so much interested in sensational stories but pays attention to them because they are available for entertainment or information. Defenders of the media argue that the public has a right to know and that it is the role of the media to satisfy this "demand" in a variety of ways.

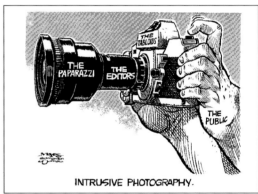

INTRUSIVE PHOTOGRAPHY.

© Malcolm Mayes, Edmonton Journal

The media today have tremendous influence on the political process, and media image is a crucial element of political success. Political strategy in the world of electronic communication normally includes a media plan, and at times professional media consultants are employed to maximize exposure. The debate over the role of media has expanded to include a discussion on whether laws need to be created to limit the use of political advertising, and limit the publication of the results of opinion polls in case the information affects voting patterns.

In societies where governments own or control them, the media often become instruments to indoctrinate and manipulate the population. The government uses the media to influence people's views about their leaders and to maintain or increase public support for the government. Information is reported selectively, always from the point of view of the government and with the aim of enhancing the prestige of the leaders. The result is a poorly informed public.

In spite of concerns about concentration of ownership, superficiality, and sensationalism, in most societies the roles the media play in political systems should not be underestimated. A free press is a precondition for a free society. In political systems where opposition is weak and disorganized the media sometimes act as an unofficial opposition. The media can inform the public about issues, expose misdeeds of public officials, and provide critiques of government policies. These efforts stimulate discussion among the people and allow them to speak out.

Since the early 1990s, electronic communication has grown at a spectacular rate. This is evident in the increased popularity of cell phones, fax machines, and electronic mail (e-mail). In the United States, Canada, and Western Europe (see chart below) the electronic medium of the internet offers free access to and exchange of information across national boundaries. This has created many new problems for societies, such as the spread of pornography, fraud, theft of intellectual property, and violations of personal privacy. Governments will need to understand the new technology and reassess present laws in order to regulate the internet.

Some countries are moving cautiously to resolve problems posed by the internet and others are introducing new laws to regulate the growth of on-line communication. In Germany, new laws have been introduced to prevent internet service providers from allowing public access to home pages, websites, and bulletin boards that post objectionable material such as pornography and neo-Nazi propaganda, which are illegal in Germany. In the United States, legal battles over the internet are being fought in the courts. In China and Singapore, the government is attempting to gain complete control over the internet by registering all personal computers and government-approved internet service providers. Most other governments remain undecided about how best to regulate the internet.

To some extent, this new medium is bypassing the traditional media of print, radio, and television, providing many new sources of information. More importantly, the internet is allowing people to communicate with each other more often and more easily.

Political parties, interest groups, and other groups or individuals increasingly use the internet to express their views, so people will need to be skilled at judging the validity of what they discover. Extreme views on public issues that otherwise receive little media attention are easily available on the internet. People need to be more prepared than ever to judge views carefully.

Most Electronically Wired Countries (1996–1997)

Personal Computers/1000 people		Internet Hosts/10 000 people	
Switzerland	408.5	Finland	653.61
United States	362.4	Norway	474.63
Australia	311.3	United States	442.11
Denmark	304.1	New Zealand	424.34
Norway	273.0	Australia	382.44
New Zealand	266.1	Sweden	321.48
Germany	233.2	Denmark	259.73
Netherlands	232.0	Canada	228.05
Singapore	216.8	Netherlands	219.01
Sweden	214.9	Switzerland	207.98
Canada	192.5	Singapore	196.30
United Kingdom	186.2	United Kingdom	149.06
Finland	182.1	Austria	108.25

World Bank. *World Development Indicators 1998.*

The political process, the third political feature described in this book, examines how political leaders are chosen. The political process focusses primarily on elections (pages 48–53).

Political Process

The political process is the interaction among political groups, conventionally called politics. Political parties, interest groups, voters, the media, and other groups in society represent interests, attitudes, and values in the political system and influence how political leaders and representatives are chosen. Most political systems have laws, rules, and customs that regulate political interaction as it applies to elections, representation, and voting. Some questions can be asked about elections: Do political groups come together to compete or strike deals? Are the rules written or unwritten? How do individuals become candidates for government office and how should they compete for office? How are candidates chosen for office?

Elections are one of the oldest social institutions. Anthropologists have traced the practice in the Middle East back nearly 5000 years, when people living along the Tigris and Euphrates rivers elected leaders.

Elections

Elections are a means of choosing represent-atives, but their purpose and importance vary from system to system. Elections allow voters to participate in choosing their repre-sentatives, but representatives often do not reflect the choices of voters. Voters may only be able to vote for or against a single candidate, or they may only be allowed to choose between candidates of a single party. In political systems where several political parties compete for power, the successful candidates may be the choice of a minority. Political parties sometimes have significant control over which candidates are presented to voters; in other instances, local residents may have a high degree of control. How a party selects its candidates and what opportunities voters have to influence that choice are crucial questions in all political systems.

Elections clearly determine which political party will form the government in one-party systems, where the outcome is known beforehand, and in most two-party systems. In a two-party system where small parties exist, or in a multi-party system, the party that becomes the government or the dominant party in a coalition following the election is usually decided by bargaining and negotiation.

The degree to which representatives can or do represent the actual wishes of constituents once they are elected varies a great deal. Much depends on the extent to which the representative is required to accept and support party policy. As well, all representatives are influenced by their own views and values. In one-party systems where party discipline is strong, representatives are less able to publicly represent their own views or those of their constituents. In two-party and multi-party systems where party discipline is strong, representatives are also encouraged to publicly support the view of the party. However, within the party they are free to express their own views or those of their constituents, as they attempt to influence the formation and direction of party policy.

Referenda and plebiscites are often used to allow voters to directly influence a specific issue, but they may not necessarily be binding on the government. It is possible for referendum campaigns to be dominated and manipulated by political parties and interest groups for their own purposes.

Corrupt election practices such as ballot stuffing, vote rigging, and gerrymandering distort people's choices, both in terms of which representative is elected and which political party takes power. Electoral manip-ulation by the ruling party can range from irregularities in enumerating voters to the control of the commission administering the elections and the counting of the votes. Many corrupt election practices have been reduced or eliminated because of stronger laws, improved enforcement, and greater judicial control over boundaries and regulations.

The choice and accountability of representatives are not the only functions of elections. Elections serve as a form of communication between political leaders and the people. They provide opportunity for political leaders to educate voters about issues. Voters have the opportunity to express their opinions and to discuss and debate issues important to them. Elections also serve to show the degree of public support for the government and its policies, as well as the degree of support for opposition parties and policies. In most elections, voters are given the opportunity to choose a new governing party or parties.

In countries with two-party and multi-party systems, elections often increase the intensity of the public mood. Parties distribute posters, pamphlets, brochures, and other items (such as flags, buttons, and hats) to promote the political party and appeal to voters to elect their candidates. Public rallies, personal appearances of party leaders, and televised debates of party leaders are organized to maximize the influence and power of each political party. Political parties also conduct public opinion polls to monitor the effectiveness of their campaign efforts and to determine the level of public support for them. The purpose of these efforts is to strengthen support among decided voters and to influence undecided voters.

In this atmosphere of excitement, the mass media play the important role of informing voters of the policies and activities of political parties and their leaders. In many cases they publish the results of public opinion polls in their attempts to inform the voter.

Tremendous sums of money raised from party members, the general public, businesses, and special interest groups are spent to ensure that voters will identify with a party's policies. In recent decades, the cost of elections has risen enormously, as political parties and candidates attempt to gain greater public support and exposure through the use of the mass media, especially television. This has effectively barred smaller parties from undertaking extensive campaigns. Consequently, governments of most societies have passed laws limiting the amount of individual contributions and requiring political parties and their candidates to publicly disclose the sources, amounts, and uses of campaign funds.

Campaigning by candidates is no less intense and demanding. Candidates travel throughout their constituencies, appearing at rallies, dinners, and benefits, greeting people in public places, participating in debates in local meeting halls, and canvassing door-to-door.

The length of the election campaign varies from country to country. In countries such as Canada, Germany, Great Britain, India, Israel, and Japan the electoral campaign is short (four to six weeks). In other countries such as Colombia, the United States, and Venezuela, presidential campaigns average 8–12 months in duration.

In contrast, in one-party systems, election campaigning differs in both form and content. Election campaigns tend to be conducted as shows of public support for the government and the ruling party. Public demonstrations and mass parades are carried out with considerable fanfare, complete with flags, banners, and speeches by top government leaders. Families with young children, students, pensioners, and workers are encouraged to participate in these rallies. The events often occur as a special holiday. Festivities such as carnivals, music concerts, and dances usually follow a public rally and give it an air more of celebration than of politics. The mass media report the rallies, parades, and demonstrations as conclusive evidence of widespread support for the government, describing them as "great victories." Speeches of prominent leaders are televised and printed in their entirety in the press the following day. Advertising in the media appears more in the form of urging the population to turn out in large numbers on election day and to vote massively for the official ruling party's candidates and leaders.

In spite of opportunities for electoral fraud and concerns about the expense of election campaigning, elections based on the broadest adult participation have become the single most important and influential political development of the 20th century. Never before has such a large mass of people gained the right to express their views in such a dramatic manner, simply by casting their ballot.

Voting and Suffrage

In many countries voting is compulsory. Belgium was the first country to adopt compulsory voting in 1893. Since that date other countries such as Australia, Italy, and Uruguay have made voting compulsory. Penalties for failing to vote in countries with compulsory voting laws range from a heavy fine to a public summons and a short prison term. In countries such as Canada, Great Britain, and the United States voting is not compulsory but regarded as a civic duty expected of every adult citizen.

Voting in most political systems is based on the principle of universal adult suffrage. Before 1900, suffrage was generally restricted, usually to men, often only to property owners.

PHOTO: The suffragette movement emerged as a political force in Canada, Great Britain, the United States, and other countries at the beginning of the 20th century. The movement campaigned for the right of women to vote. The woman in the photo is campaigning for British women's suffrage, or right to vote.

National Film Board of Canada/NATIONAL ARCHIVES OF CANADA/PA-143958

Women in Politics in Selected Countries

Country	Voting Rights Granted to Women
New Zealand	1893
Finland	1906
Norway	1913
Russia (USSR)	1917
Poland	1918
Canada (federal)[1]	1918
Germany	1919
Netherlands	1919
Sweden	1919
United States	1920
Great Britain	1928
Brazil	1932
Turkey	1934
France	1944
Japan	1945
China	1947

Country	First Woman Government Minister
Russia (USSR)	1917
Poland	1918
Finland	1926
Great Britain	1929
United States	1933
Norway	1945
Sweden	1947
New Zealand	1947
Netherlands	1956
Canada (federal)	1957
China	1957
Japan	1960
Germany	1961
Turkey	1971
France	1974
Brazil	1983

Country	First Woman Government Leader
Sri Lanka	1960
India	1966
Israel	1969
Argentina	1974
Great Britain	1979
Norway	1981
Philippines	1986
Pakistan	1988
Nicaragua	1990
Bangladesh	1991
France	1991
Canada (federal)	1993
Turkey	1993

Chronology of Women's History, 1994

[1] In 1916 Manitoba became the first Canadian province to give women the vote; Quebec was the last, in 1940. The Military Voters Act of 1917 enfranchised wives of men serving in the Canadian and British armed services.

New Zealand became the first country to grant women the right to vote in 1893. Finland followed in 1906, Norway in 1913, and Russia in 1917. After World War I, other countries such as Canada, Germany, Great Britain, Sweden, and the United States gave women the right to vote and participate in politics (see chart, page 50).

The extension of suffrage to women greatly expanded the size of the electorate, but more importantly it brought to the fore new concerns about equality, social welfare, the family, employment, and women's participation in government.

In the 1920s, women began to be elected to many legislatures and to become government ministers. The first woman to become a government minister was Aleksandra Kollontai, who became the Minister of Public Welfare following the Bolshevik seizure of power in Russia in November 1917. Though her term of office lasted only six months, it marked the beginning of women's participation in government (see chart, page 50). In 1957, Ellen Fairclough became Canada's Secretary of State and first woman federal cabinet minister.

In 1960, Sirimavo Bandaranaike became the first female head of government when she was elected Prime Minister of Sri Lanka. Since then, women have become Prime Ministers or Presidents in countries around the world, including Argentina, Bangladesh, Canada, France, Great Britain, India, Israel, Norway, Pakistan, and Turkey.

Sri Lanka High Commission, Canada

Electoral Systems

An electoral system is more than just the counting of ballots cast by the voters. It provides a system of political representation that includes such factors as who can vote, rules relating to candidates and parties, and regulations for administering elections. The method of casting the vote is part of an electoral system. The secret ballot, which came into general usage in the 20th century, is common to most political systems, but the size and shape of the constituency, riding, or electoral district often differ greatly. Aspects that generally distinguish electoral systems and representation are the methods of casting the vote, the ways in which votes are counted, and the representation of the votes in legislatures. The most common types of electoral systems used today are shown on the chart below and the one on page 52. The voting age in most countries today is 18 years (see chart below).

Secret ballot, done by marking a ballot in a voting booth, is the common form of voting.

PHOTO: Sirimavo Bandaranaike, the Prime Minister of Sri Lanka from 1960 to 1965 and from 1970 to 1977, was the world's first woman head of government.

Voting and Electoral Systems in Selected Countries

Electoral System	Country	Voting Age
Plurality	Bangladesh	18
	Canada (federal)	18
	Great Britain	18
	India	18
	United States	18
	Zambia	18
Second ballot	Egypt	18
	France	18
	Iran	15
Preferential	Australia	18
Proportional representation	Nicaragua	16
	Turkey	18
Proportional representation/plurality	Azerbaijan	21
	Germany	18
	Italy	18
	Japan	20
	Korea	20
	Russia	18
Proportional representation/second ballot	Ecuador	18
Proportional representation/preferential	Sweden	18

Compiled from *Inter-Parliamentary Union* http://www.ipu.org

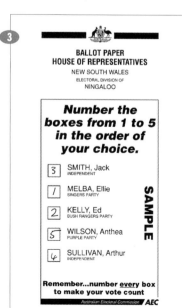

D O E, John	
•••••• Indépendant / Independent ••••••	◯
D O E, Sandra	
•• Appartenance politique / Political Affiliation ••	◯
NOM, Prénom Initiale	
•••••• Indépendant / Independent ••••••	◯
UNTEL, Anne	
•••••• Independent ••••••	◯
UNTEL, Pierre-Paul	
•• Appartenance politique / Political Affiliation ••	◯

Reprinted with permission from Elections Canada.

Reichspräsidentenwahl

Theodor Duesterberg	
Oberstleutnant a. D., Halle a. d. Saale	◯
Paul von Hindenburg	
Reichspräsident, Generalfeldmarschall, Berlin	◯
Adolf Hitler	
Regierungsrat im braunschweigischen Staatsdienst, München	◯
Ernst Thälmann	
Transportarbeiter, Hamburg	◯
Adolf Gustav Winter	
Betriebsanwalt, Großjena bei Naumburg a. d. Saale	◯

James K. Pollock. *The Government of Greater Germany.*
New York: Van Nostrand, 1940, p. 33.

**BALLOT PAPER
HOUSE OF REPRESENTATIVES**
NEW SOUTH WALES
ELECTORAL DIVISION OF
NINGALOO

Number the boxes from 1 to 5 in the order of your choice.

3	SMITH, Jack INDEPENDENT
1	MELBA, Ellie SINGERS PARTY
2	KELLY, Ed BUSH RANGERS PARTY
5	WILSON, Anthea PURPLE PARTY
4	SULLIVAN, Arthur INDEPENDENT

SAMPLE

Remember...number every box to make your vote count
Australian Electoral Commission AEC

Reprinted with permission from Australian Electoral Commission.

1 Single-member constituency and single vote

- "first past the post," simple plurality
- greatest number/plurality of votes wins
- winning party tends to be over-represented
- losing party under-represented
- common in Bangladesh, Canada, Great Britain, India, USA, and Zambia

2 Single-member constituency and second ballot

- must have a majority to win
- second election is used to find majority winner between two strongest candidates (usually one or two weeks later)
- other candidates removed from ballot and their supporters vote for remaining candidates
- system used in Egypt, France, and Iran; used in Germany in 1925 and 1932 to elect its president

3 Preferential Voting

- voter places candidates in order of preference
- if no majority, weaker candidates are dropped and vote redistributed according to preference
- continues until majority achieved
- used in Australia and Ireland

hier 1 Stimme
für die Wahl
einer Landesliste (Partei)
• maßgebende Stimme für die Verteilung der Sitze insgesamt auf die einzelnen Parteien •
Zweitstimme

◯	CDU	Christlich Demokratishe Union Deutschlands	1
◯	SPD	Sozialdemokratishce Partei Deutschlands	2
◯	GRÜNE	DIE GRÜNEN	3
◯	F.D.P.	Freie Demokratische Partei	4
◯	DIE GRAUEN	DIE GRAUEN Initiiert vom Senioren-Schultz-Bund "Graue Panther" e.V. ("SSB-GP")	5
◯	REP	DIE REPUBLIKANER	6
◯	NPD	Nationaldemokratische Partei Deutschlands	7
◯	ÖDP	Ökologisch-Demokratische Partei	8
◯	PDS/ Linke Liste	Partei des Demokratschen Sozialismus/Linke Liste	9

Adapted from sample ballot with the compliments of the Consulate General of the Federal Republic of Germany.

4 Proportional Representation

- allocates seats in proportion to votes received in multi-member constituencies
- most common is party list system in which people vote for a list of candidates
- seats allocated according to share of vote
- most common system in the world
- voter preferences are more accurately reflected

Canada's Electoral System

In the June 2, 1997, general election, the Liberals won a majority of the seats in the House of Commons with slightly less than 38% of the popular vote. The Reform Party won 20% of the seats with a 19.4% popular vote and the Bloc Québécois about 15% of the seats with less than 11% of the popular vote. The Conservatives and New Democrats received together about 30% of the vote but only 14.6% of the seats.

This is possible because in Canada's "first past the post" electoral system, the candidate with the most votes is elected. The result is that in Canada a political party can form a majority government with less than 50% of the popular vote. In the June 2, 1997, general election, about two-thirds of the 301 representatives were elected with less than 50% of the vote. When more political parties run, fewer votes are needed to elect a candidate. For example, in the Manitoba riding of Selkirk–Interlake, the Reform candidate won the seat with 28.3% of the vote, with the remaining 71.7% of the vote evenly divided among the Liberals, New Democrats, and Conservatives.

In Canada's first general election in 1867, distribution of seats between the Conservatives and Liberals in the House of Commons conformed more closely to the two parties' share of the popular vote. In that election, the Conservatives won 101 seats with 50.1% of the votes and Liberals won 80 seats with 49%.

In the general election of 1896, the Conservatives received a larger share of the vote (46.1%) than the Liberals (45.1%) but won 30 fewer seats than the Liberals (88 to 118) because two small parties, the Patrons of Industry and the Protestant Protective Association, received 8.8% of the popular vote and won seven seats. The two small parties drew enough votes from the Conservatives in certain ridings to deny them a majority of seats and the government.

In the May 1996 provincial election in British Columbia, the Liberals received 41.8% of the vote and the New Democrats 39.5% of the vote. However, the New Democrats formed a majority government with 39 seats and the Liberals became the official opposition with 33 seats. The other parties—Reform, Progressive Democratic Alliance, and Social Credit—split the remaining 18.7% of the vote and won only three seats in the 75-seat legislature.

Defenders of Canada's present system say that the "first past the post" system has worked well in Canada, Great Britain, and the United States since it was adopted. In Canada, it has provided government that is responsive to the public good, including the few times where election results have led to the creation of a minority government.

Critics of Canada's "first past the post" system argue that it is outdated for multi-party elections. Groups such as the Campaign for Electoral Reform argue for a proportional representation system similar to that used in Germany where people vote for party lists. Parties that win more than 5% of the vote would be allotted seats from the party lists. The results of the June 2, 1997, general election, calculated under this system, are depicted in the chart below. The Liberals would have won 119 seats, Reform 59 seats, Conservatives 60, New Democrats 33, and Bloc Québécois 30.

Recasting the June 2, 1997, General Election Results

	Share of Popular Vote (%)	"First Past the Post"		Under Proportional Representation
		Seats Won	Percentage of Seats	Seats Allocated
Liberals	37.9	155	51.5	119
Reform	19.4	60	19.9	59
Conservatives	18.9	20	6.6	60
New Democrats	11.0	21	7.0	33
Bloc Québécois	10.5	44	14.6	30
Others	2.3	1	0.4	0
TOTALS	100.0	301	100.0	301

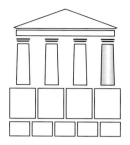

The fourth political feature of a political system, policies and goals of the government, is shown on page 54. It includes
• Equality and justice
• Self-government
• Stability
• Democratization

Policies and Goals

The policies and goals a government pursues vary from system to system and explain many of the differences in political approaches, procedures, and institutions among countries. Twentieth century political systems have been concerned with formulating and implementing broad political and social goals. Many of these goals have created tremendous political and social turbulence in the political systems. At other times, governments' policies and goals have been widely accepted and have helped to stabilize and strengthen their political systems.

Equality and Justice

Governments have enacted and revised countless laws to promote greater political equality among people and redress perceived injustices. In the 20th century, these included expanding the roles of women, achieving gender equality, and ending discrimination on the basis of race, religion, sexual orientation, and ethnicity. Many governments have made changes in laws to grant women full rights in matters concerning property, marriage, divorce, children, employment, and legal representation. Policies have been introduced to offer more opportunities for women to participate in society outside the traditional areas of family and home, including in education, business, science, and politics. The Charter of Rights and Freedoms was added to the Canadian constitution in 1982 to help all citizens achieve greater equality.

Self-government

Governments have modified constitutions to devolve, or delegate, power to regions, local governments, and ethnic groups. In the 20th century, this led to the creation of several federal states. In 1922, the Soviet Union was formed as a federal state composed of ethnically-based republics, in recognition of the country's multi-national makeup. In late 1991, the Soviet Union broke up peacefully into 15 separate countries. In 1980, residents of the Catalonia and Basque regions of Spain were granted local self-government following overwhelming approval in plebiscites. In September 1997, voters in Scotland and Wales voted for the establishment of local governments in Great Britain.

Stability

Governments at times have temporarily suspended individual rights of groups seeking to destabilize the political system using power and armed force. In October 1970, the Canadian government curtailed some individual rights when it invoked the War Measures Act to arrest and detain suspected members and sympathizers of the FLQ who had kidnapped a minister of the Quebec government. In the 1970s and 1980s in several Latin American and African countries, governments imposed emergency rule to suppress the activities of radical groups. In cases such as National Socialist Germany, the Soviet Union, and China, governments have controlled and restricted the activities of political parties, groups, and individuals in the interests of maintaining power.

Democratization

Governments have created political institutions to instil new values and ideas in the population, and at other times abolished long established political practices and organizations to promote greater participation of the people in political affairs. In the late 1980s, the Soviet government abolished single-candidate elections in favour of multi-candidate elections to promote greater accountability of the government to the people and to enhance its prestige in the eyes of the people. Elsewhere, governments have introduced more referenda and plebiscites as a way to better understand public desires. The government of Quebec has conducted two referenda (in 1980 and 1995) related to the future of that province in Canada.

TYPES OF POLITICAL SYSTEMS

Advance Organizer

Political scientists classify political systems according to how political power is acquired, organized, and used. Political systems may be organized as democratic systems and non-democratic systems. Democratic systems are characterized by free competition for political power, political equality for all, and rule by the many. Non-democratic systems are characterized by a lack of free political competition, absence of political equality, and rule by the few.

Key Concepts/Vocabulary

democracy	authoritarianism
direct democracy	indoctrination
majority rule	controlled participation
accountability	absolute monarchy
minority rights	autocracy
representative democracy	oligarchy
parliamentary democracy	military dictatorship
presidential democracy	minority tyranny
majority tyranny	apartheid
non-democratic system	totalitarianism

POLITICAL SYSTEMS

- Democratic Systems
- Non-Democratic Systems

Democratic Systems

Democratic systems are often called democracies, liberal democracies, or multi-party systems. Democratic systems take various forms, but most today are characterized by the use of majority rule, citizen participation, accountability of government to the people, respect for minority rights, guarantee of individual rights, acceptance of opposition, and many political parties. The main types of democratic systems are parliamentary democracy and presidential democracy.

Historical Overview

The word "democracy" originates from two ancient Greek words *demos* (people) and *kratia* (government): *democracy* thus means "rule by the people." In ancient Athens, democracy was reserved for male adult citizens, about 15–20% of the adult population. Women, slaves, and foreigners were not allowed to participate in politics or hold public offices. By today's standards of democracy, ancient Athens would not likely be considered democratic.

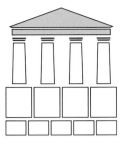

Democratic systems are characterized by free competition for political power, political equality, and rule by the many (pages 55–60).

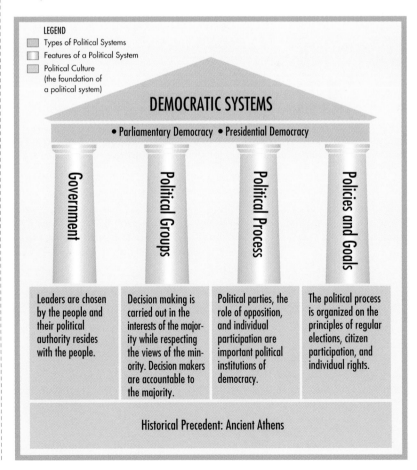

LEGEND
- Types of Political Systems
- Features of a Political System
- Political Culture (the foundation of a political system)

DEMOCRATIC SYSTEMS

- Parliamentary Democracy
- Presidential Democracy

Government	Political Groups	Political Process	Policies and Goals
Leaders are chosen by the people and their political authority resides with the people.	Decision making is carried out in the interests of the majority while respecting the views of the minority. Decision makers are accountable to the majority.	Political parties, the role of opposition, and individual participation are important political institutions of democracy.	The political process is organized on the principles of regular elections, citizen participation, and individual rights.

Historical Precedent: Ancient Athens

Athens was considered a direct democracy in that every eligible citizen had a moral responsibility and duty to participate in politics. Government posts were often filled by lottery. Public ostracism or even exile could result should a citizen decline his moral responsibility to serve.

Athenian democracy had its critics. Plato (427–347 BCE) criticized Athenian democracy for its instability and the ease with which people could be stirred up by leaders who played upon their fears and prejudices. As well, he thought democracy was best suited to small communities of not more than 5000 people.

Aristotle (383–322 BCE) argued that democracy could be easily undermined by leaders who placed their own interests above those of the whole community. When leaders ruled with their own interests in mind, general welfare was ignored and democracy became a tyranny, often of the majority against a minority.

Democracy ended by 300 BCE in Athens and did not reappear as a form of government for over 2000 years. In the 18th century, democracy re-emerged as a political ideal during the American and French Revolutions. Democracy has since become associated with concepts of representation, individual rights, and constitutional law.

Features of Democratic Systems

Though the institutions and procedures of democracy vary from country to country, all contemporary democracies have certain common features that must be present in order for the system to be judged democratic. The features are outlined below.

1. **Majority rule.** In a democracy, decision making resides with the people. The government is generally required to act according to the wishes of the majority, while respecting minority rights. This ensures that the will of the public is generally followed.

2. **Citizenship participation.** In a democracy, all adult citizens are the source of political authority. They have the right to participate in the political

Political power in a democracy is shared among all people in society.

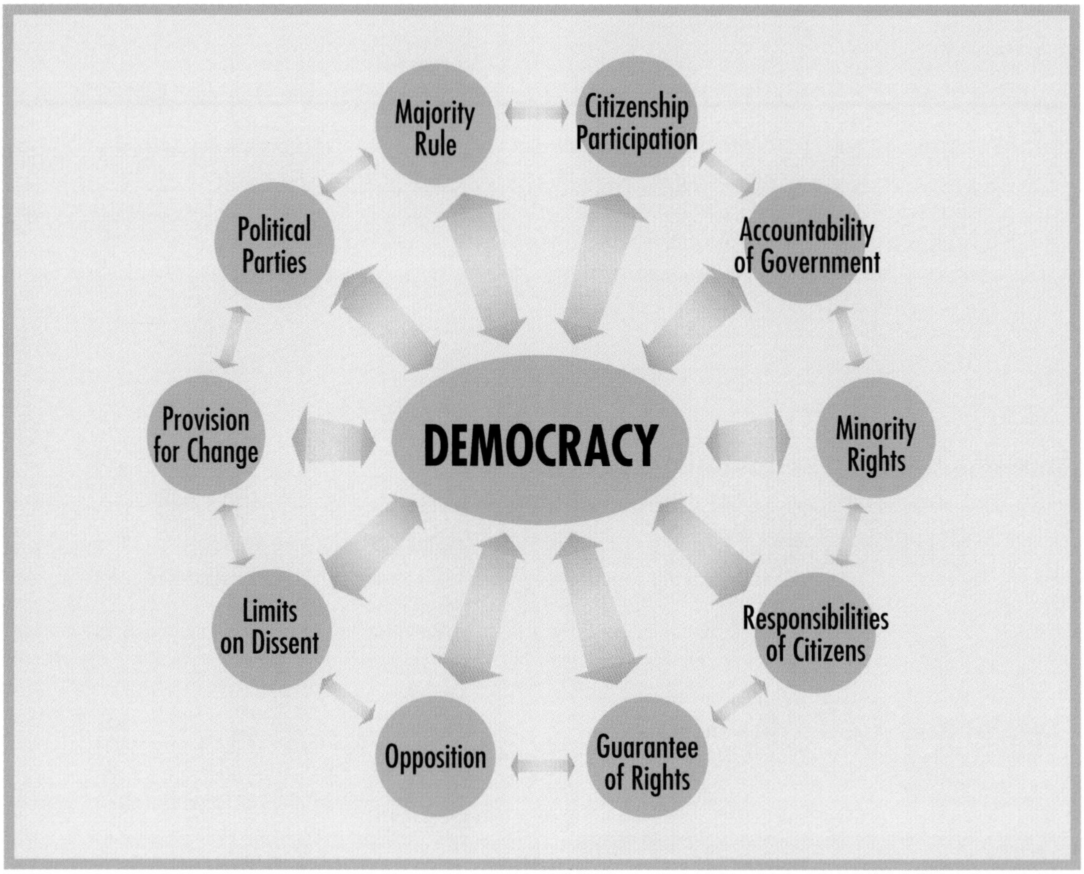

Majority Rule — Citizenship Participation

Political Parties

Accountability of Government

Provision for Change — **DEMOCRACY** — Minority Rights

Limits on Dissent

Responsibilities of Citizens

Opposition — Guarantee of Rights

decision making process. This ensures at least a minimum level of political equality. They have the right to choose their leaders on the basis of universal suffrage or "one person, one vote," using a secret ballot to ensure that they are free from political pressure.

3. **Accountability.** The powers and authority of government are limited by a written or unwritten constitution. Elected officials are required to justify their performance before the people, through regularly held elections. As well, in some political systems the executive branch of government must be accountable, virtually on a daily basis, to the legislature. Leaders who fail to maintain the support of the people or the legislature are required to step down and be replaced by others.

4. **Responsibilities of citizens.** In a democracy, citizens have important responsibilities. They are encouraged, expected, or required to vote in elections. They must accept the decisions of elected bodies and obey the law. They are allowed and encouraged to participate in the political process.

5. **Minority rights.** Minorities and people holding minority views have the right to challenge policies and opinions of the majority, and to propose alternative policies. The majority is required to consider the opinions and wishes of minorities, who have the same freedom of expression as the majority. The existence of effective opposition is generally regarded as the best defence of minority rights.

6. **Guarantee of individual rights and freedoms.** Governments are obligated by the constitution to protect each individual. All individuals are guaranteed political rights and civil liberties. Key among these are freedom of the press, freedom of expression, and freedom of association. These rights and civil liberties cannot normally be suspended by the government.

Individuals are equal before the law and have the right to challenge the power and authority of the government. The guarantee of individual rights and freedoms provides a powerful check on the arbitrary use of political power by the government. Even so, there may be occasions when rights and freedoms may be curtailed in the interests of society (such as national emergencies).

7. **Opposition.** All individuals have the right to question and propose alternatives to the policies of the government, generally without fear of retaliation, and they are encouraged to do so. Individuals and groups are allowed to express opposing viewpoints and ideas. The existence of an effective opposition ensures that full and open debate occurs on important issues.

8. **Limits on dissent.** Individuals and groups who disagree with the policies of the majority are nonetheless required to respect the wishes of the majority. However, limits on dissent generally apply only when a minority uses violence and force to oppose the wishes of the majority.

9. **Provision for changes to the system.** Changes to the political system are presented generally in the form of amendments to the constitution. They are accepted only after considerable debate in legislatures or review by an independent judiciary, free from political interference. Alternatively, change may occur by agreement between members of legislatures, generally involving debate and participation by the people.

10. **Political parties.** In a democracy, political parties and interest groups are allowed to exist, promote their activities, and compete openly for power. Their right to do so is based on freedom of association.

Types of Democratic Systems

Direct democracy of the type that existed in ancient Athens is rare today. It exists in some towns in New England, on Israeli kibbutzim, and in some Swiss cantons, where communities are small. It is generally unworkable in large communities because of the complexity of most issues or, for most people, the lack of time, interest, or access to adequate information.

The more common form of democracy in the world today is indirect or representative democracy, which appears in two basic types—parliamentary and presidential democracy.

Parliamentary Democracy. Parliamentary democracy is the most common form of representative democracy in the world. Parliaments first appeared in Western Europe during the Middle Ages as councils to assist and advise the monarch. Some important contemporary examples of parliamentary democracies are Australia, Canada, Germany, Great Britain, India, Japan, and Sweden.

The distinguishing feature of a parliamentary democracy is the relationship between the executive and legislative branches of government. The head of the government and cabinet must be members of the legislature and they are responsible to it.[1] For this reason, parliamentary democracy is often referred to as *responsible government* because the government is directly responsible and accountable for its actions to the legislature. This means that the government must present bills to the legislature for debate and approval. Important bills like the government budget must be approved by a majority vote in the legislature for the government to stay in power. The government is said to enjoy the confidence, or support, of the legislature.

Another feature of a parliamentary democracy is the division of the executive branch into a head of state and a head of government. In modern democracies head of state is largely a ceremonial position.

Political power is limited by custom or by a constitution. The head of state may be a president as in Germany, India, and Italy, or a monarch as in Canada, Great Britain, Japan, Netherlands, and Sweden. The head of government (usually called a prime minister, premier, or chancellor) is the leader of the elected government. He or she must receive support from, or enjoy the confidence of, a majority of the members of the legislature to stay in office.

In most parliamentary democracies the legislature is divided into two chambers, with an upper house representing special groups or regions and a lower house elected by the people. However, a few parliamentary democracies such as Sweden have only a lower house. The legislature is elected by voters for varying periods. In most parliamentary systems, the maximum duration of an elected legislature is five years, at which time it must be dissolved and voters allowed to elect a new one. Elections may occur at any time before then, announced by the head of state on the advice of the Prime Minister or Chancellor. Reasons for calling an election vary. For example, the government may call an election at a time of popularity. Also, if the government is defeated in the legislature following a vote on an important bill, an election must be called.

The judiciary is formally appointed by the head of state on the advice of the Prime Minister or Chancellor. Its main political task is to interpret the constitution when asked to do so. This is especially important in federal systems where decisions usually involve the division of powers between levels of government.

Defenders of parliamentary democracy claim that it is one of the most effective and efficient forms of government for initiating and passing legislation. As well, because the Prime Minister, cabinet, and government are part of and depend on the legislature for support, parliamentary democracy encourages the government to be accountable to the legislature.

Critics of parliamentary democracy claim that too much power is concentrated in the executive at the expense of the legislative and judicial branches of government.

---

[1] In Canada when a new leader of a party who does not have a seat in the legislature becomes the Prime Minister, by convention, the person has 90 days to become a member of the legislature, usually through by-election.

Furthermore, because the date of elections is not fixed, voters cannot easily influence their elected leaders to modify policies. As a result, some critics claim that parliamentary democracy is "an elected dictatorship." These and other aspects of parliamentary democracy will be discussed in chapters on Canada, Sweden, and Japan.

Presidential Democracy. The first presidential system of government was established in the United States in 1789, when George Washington was elected as President. Most contemporary presidential democracies are modeled after this system.

The separation of powers between the executive, legislative, and judicial branches of government, combined with a system of checks and balances, is a feature of a presidential democracy. Political power is more or less evenly distributed, or balanced, between the three branches, although each has its own distinct powers. As well, each branch has the power to stop (check) any abuse of power by the other branches in order to maintain democracy.

The executive branch combines the head of state and head of government in one position called a President. The President, who is directly elected by the voters, cannot be a member of the legislature, unlike the situation in a parliamentary democracy. The President appoints a cabinet to enforce and administer laws. Also, unlike in parliamentary democracy, he or she does not need the support of the legislature to remain in office. However, the President does need the support of the legislature to implement his or her legislative proposals. The President can propose legislation to the legislature and can usually veto any legislation passed by the legislature. The terms of office of the President and the legislature are generally fixed. In the United States, the President's term of office is four years and that of the legislature two years. In France, the President's term of office is seven years.

The legislature is elected directly by the voters and is usually divided into two chambers, an upper house (called the Senate in the United States) representing the regions and a lower house representing all the people (commonly called a House of Representatives). In the United States, these two chambers form the Congress. In France, the upper house is called the Senate and the lower house the National Assembly. Both chambers have the power to make laws. The two chambers of the legislature together can vote to override the veto of the President. All legislation passed by the legislature may be referred to the judiciary for constitutional review.

The judiciary, appointed by the President, interprets all legislation enacted by the legislature when asked to do so. In its capacity as interpreter of the constitution, the Court has the power to declare legislation unconstitutional and prevent its passage into law. New appointments by the President, or the legislature exercising its power to approve or deny the President's appointments, serve as checks on judicial power. Thus, the three branches share political power and prevent one branch of government from dominating the others.

Defenders of the presidential system of government claim that the greatest advantage of their system is that the people can directly elect the country's leader and government, whereas in a parliamentary democracy the leader of the party that holds most seats in the legislature becomes the leader of the government. Defenders of presidential democracy also argue that the system of checks and balances prevents one branch of government from becoming too powerful. Furthermore, many believe presidential democracy is superior to parliamentary democracy because it allows voters to pass judgement more quickly on government policies through regularly scheduled elections.

Critics of presidential democracy argue that this system is less efficient in passing legislation because of the system of checks and balances. This often leads to political deadlock between the branches of government. Critics also argue that the legislature cannot easily remove an unpopular president, except in the case of impeachment. These aspects of presidential democracy will be discussed in Chapter 5 on the United States.

Chart showing presidential democracy appears in Chapter 5 on USA, page 180.

In April–May 1995 Gallup asked over 16 000 people in 17 countries the following question: "How satisfied are you with the way democracy works in this country?"

Satisfaction with Democracy

	Satisfied (per cent)	Dissatisfied (per cent)
United States	64	27
Canada	62	24
Germany	55	27
Iceland	54	23
Thailand	54	27
Costa Rica	52	25
Chile	43	31
France	43	32
Dominican Republic	40	38
United Kingdom	40	43
Japan	35	32
India	32	43
Spain	31	30
Venezuela	28	59
Taiwan	25	18
Hungary	17	50
Mexico	17	67

Adapted from *The Gallup Poll Monthly*, June 1995.

Critique of Contemporary Democracy

As in ancient Athens, contemporary democracy has its critics, who cite some of the following concerns.

Majority tyranny. All democracies relying on majority rule have the potential to degenerate into a majority tyranny in which the political rights and civil liberties of minority groups and dissenters are not respected by the majority. The presence of a strong and effective opposition, a free press, and an independent judiciary are safeguards against majority tyranny.

Dominance of special interest groups. Vocal or economically powerful interest groups, by virtue of their organizational and financial resources, often are able to influence or set the political agenda with their own interests at the expense of the general interests of society.

Political apathy. Political apathy is a major threat to democracy. Most people focus on more immediate concerns of family, friends, and the necessity of making a living than on more abstract and distant political issues. Generally, democracy is strengthened by the broad participation of an informed and interested public.

Inefficiency and political deadlock. Because decision making in democracies generally requires considerable time for debate and discussion of issues, democracies often do not deal with serious issues quickly and efficiently. Many people must be consulted and their views considered before a decision is made. Only in situations of war or insurrections do democracies seem to react quickly.

Campaign donations and financing. There is the risk that wealthy special interests can influence the choice of candidates, the outcome of elections, and the legislative direction of the government. People of ordinary means may be prevented from running for office. In recent years, laws requiring disclosure of the source of donations to political parties and limits on the amount that can be donated have been passed, which has helped to resolve this problem.

Corruption. Political parties and interest groups may strike deals and make compromises that may lead to corruption among political leaders. A free press, a strong opposition, an independent judiciary, and an interested public can reduce corruption by exposing and punishing dishonest political leaders. In recent years, the exposure of corruption among certain political leaders has led to some dissatisfaction with democracy.

Defenders of democracy would point out that in spite of some concerns most democracies operate in the best interests of most people most of the time. An effective opposition and a free press are important. A well informed and politically active public whose individual rights and freedoms are protected must be recognized as important to the functioning of an effective democracy.

Non-Democratic Systems

Non-democratic systems are often called single-party systems and dictatorships. Although they take various forms, most non-democratic systems in the world today are characterized by concentration of power in the hands of the few, use of force, control of the media, restricted political competition, limits on dissent, and limited accountability of government. The main types of non-democratic systems are authoritarian government and totalitarianism.

Two Views

Just as democracy is an outgrowth of particular historical developments, so too are non-democratic systems the result of unique historical forces in a society's political culture. These forces create conditions for leaders to emerge and concentrate great power in their hands.

Archive Photos

Thomas Carlyle (1795–1881)

A British social critic and historian, Carlyle argued that the history of the world resulted from the activities of great leaders. In his lectures in 1840, *On Heroes, Hero-Worship, and the Heroic in History,* Carlyle stated:

For, as I take it, Universal History, the history of what man has accomplished in this world, is at bottom the History of the Great Men who have worked here. They were the leaders of men, these great ones; the modellers, patterners, and in a wide sense creators, of whatsoever the general mass of men contrived to do or to attain; all things that we see standing accomplished in the world are properly the outer material result, the practical realization and embodiment, of Thoughts that dwelt in the Great Men sent into the world: the soul of the whole world's history, it may justly be considered, were the history of these.

Carlyle's view of world history supported his belief that the growth of democracy was destroying important traditions and customs. He believed that a society which guaranteed community spirit and stability was superior to one which promoted individualism and individual liberty. Individualism, he argued, did not lead to liberty and freedom for the individual but to social upheaval.

Carlyle was not alone in distrusting democratic institutions. Many others in Great Britain and Europe also agreed that only traditions and customs could check the tendency of democracy for violence and cruelty of the kind that occurred in the French Revolution.

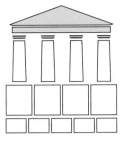

Non-democratic systems are characterized by a lack of free political competition, absence of political equality, and rule by the few (pages 61–68).

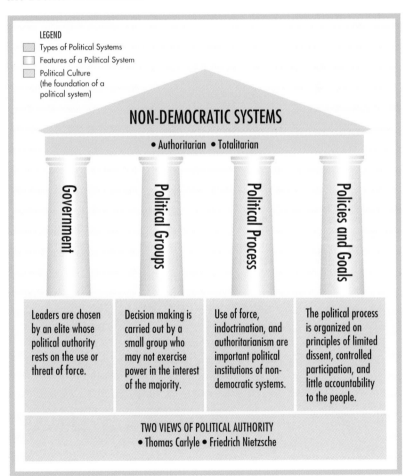

LEGEND
- Types of Political Systems
- Features of a Political System
- Political Culture (the foundation of a political system)

NON-DEMOCRATIC SYSTEMS

• Authoritarian • Totalitarian

Government	Political Groups	Political Process	Policies and Goals
Leaders are chosen by an elite whose political authority rests on the use or threat of force.	Decision making is carried out by a small group who may not exercise power in the interest of the majority.	Use of force, indoctrination, and authoritarianism are important political institutions of non-democratic systems.	The political process is organized on principles of limited dissent, controlled participation, and little accountability to the people.

TWO VIEWS OF POLITICAL AUTHORITY
• Thomas Carlyle • Friedrich Nietzsche

Archive Photos

Friedrich Nietzsche (1844–1900)

Friedrich Nietzsche believed that human beings were by nature a combination of "beast and the superbeast." As human beings develop their physical, psychological, and intellectual capabilities, Nietzsche argued, their capacity for doing good grows but so does their impulse to do great evil. As he noted in *The Will to Power* (1895):

With every degree of a man's growth towards greatness and loftiness, he also grows downwards into the depths and into the terrible . . . the more fundamentally we desire the one, the more completely we shall achieve the other.

Nietzsche condemned democrats and socialists for wanting to create free societies. In *Beyond Good and Evil* (1886), he wrote that democracy, by producing equality for all, created conditions for the rise of new and dangerous tyrants in the future:

The democratic movement is not only a form of the decay of political organization but a form of the decay, namely the diminution, of man, making him mediocre and lowering his value . . . .

The very same new conditions that will on the average lead to the [creation of] a useful, industrious, handy, multi-purpose herd animal—are likely . . . to give birth to exceptional human beings of the most dangerous and attractive quality.

I mean to say: the democratization of Europe [encourages] the cultivation of tyrants—taking that word in every sense, including the most spiritual.

Nietzsche did not provide justification for dictatorship; rather, he warned that by abandoning morality and creating more democratic societies and governments the result would be the creation of tyrannical government. His political vision was largely a critique of socialism and egalitarianism; he left it to others to draw from his philosophy what political conclusions they could.

Carlyle and Nietzsche are two thinkers supportive of non-democratic systems. Their ideas have often been adapted for use by some leaders, or used as justification for certain actions by those leaders.

Features of Non-Democratic Systems

Most contemporary non-democratic systems include the following distinctive features:

1. **Authoritarian rule.** Political power and authority are concentrated in the hands of one leader or a small group of people and exercised in a dictatorial manner. That is, power is exercised by a few. People are encouraged to identify with the leader rather than with the ideals or principles of a type of government. Where an official ideology is used to justify the leader's authority, it generally reflects the leader's personal views.

2. **Use of force.** A strong military and secret police exist to keep the government in power. From time to time the military is called on to intervene in political affairs to quell popular revolts, strikes, demonstrations, and other forms of rebellion against the authority of the leader. The secret police uses various methods to seek out and arrest suspected dissenters and enemies of the government.

3. **Indoctrination.** The media function to popularize the beliefs, viewpoints, and policies of the leader and the government. The media are either owned by the state or operate under strict rules of censorship to ensure that the leader and government are seen in a favourable light. Access to the internet, foreign publications, television, and radio is strictly controlled and monitored. Education is strictly controlled and monitored in an attempt to gain the support of youth and to teach ideas and values favoured by the government. Often government-sponsored youth groups exist to provide activities for youth, but also to encourage support for the government.

4. **Controlled participation.** Political participation is limited to involving people in activities such as elections

and referendums designed to demonstrate support for the government and its policies. These measures are meaningless because of the absence of real choice and serve only a symbolic purpose. Political competition is restricted or eliminated to ensure that all opposition to the government, even within the party, remains weak and divided.

5. **Limits on dissent.** Most non-democratic systems restrict dissent by closely monitoring people's views and activities and repressing opposition to the government. Other limits on dissent appear in the form of laws that emphasize the individual's responsibilities and duties to obey their leaders or the government. If individuals and interest groups support the government, then their activities go unhindered, but when they oppose the government, harassment, punishment, and imprisonment without trial are frequently employed to limit the dissent. More

extreme measures used to control dissent are exile, execution, and extermination.

6. **Limited accountability.** Decision making and political power are not conducted according to the rule of law. Leaders are not required to be accountable to the people for their policies and actions, although they may maintain that this is what they are doing. The exercise of power in a dictatorship often leads to widespread corruption, mismanagement, repression of civil liberties, loss of human life, and persecution of minorities.

7. **Few provisions for changes to the system.** Because of the concentration of political power in the hands of a leader or small elite, provisions allowing for peaceful transitions of power rarely exist. The death of the dictator is frequently followed by a violent power struggle.

Political power in a non-democratic system is concentrated in the hands of a small group of people.

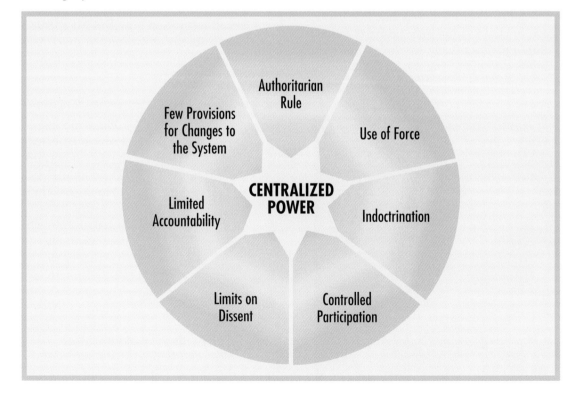

Types of Non-Democratic Systems

During the 20th century, two major types of non-democratic systems appeared. The first was the growth of authoritarian governments. The second was the development of totalitarianism.

Authoritarian Governments. Many different types of authoritarian governments have existed in the modern era. Today, authoritarian governments range from mildly repressive regimes that allow weak legislatures to exist, to profoundly repressive regimes where legislatures do not exist or exist only to support the leaders. There are five basic types of authoritarian government:

1. **Absolute Monarchy.** Absolute monarchies are autocratic governments led by a monarch from a traditional ruling family whose authority is based on tradition, religion, or divine right (believed to have been granted or ordained by God). Other political institutions may be permitted but they are very weak. Legislatures, if they exist, are likely elected on a franchise generally restricted to adult male property owners. Political parties usually are not allowed, but examples do exist. The monarch generally rules with the help of an appointed body

of experts. The Romanovs who ruled Russia from 1613 to 1917, the Bourbons who ruled pre-Revolutionary France, and the Hohenzollerns who ruled the German Empire from 1871 to 1918 are historic examples of absolute monarchies. At that time in Germany a parliament or *Reichstag* with limited powers did exist. Contemporary examples of absolute monarchies are Brunei, Qatar, and Saudi Arabia.

Canapress/Charles Dharapak

2. **One-person Autocratic Rule.** These governments are based on the personality of the leader. The leader is not a hereditary monarch and the regime is maintained by force. Political institutions may exist, but they are usually dominated and controlled by the leader. Before he was forced to give up power in May 1998, President Suharto's government in Indonesia was an example of one-person autocratic rule.

Archive France/Archive Photos

3. **Oligarchy.** Oligarchies are governments led by an elite group. The elite may be a family, an ethnic minority, or a social group such as landowners, merchants, or professionals. The elite rules in order to further its own interests at the expense of the majority. Most oligarchies offer limited civil liberties and political rights to the majority in order to maintain their domination and control of political institutions. Notable 20th century examples were Nicaragua under the Somoza family and Haiti under the Duvalier family.

Stock Montage, Inc.

4. Military Dictatorship. The most common form of authoritarian government in the world is military dictatorship. In such a system, military personnel control all key political positions through a military council, or *junta*, formed following the overthrow of a previous government. The junta controls all executive and legislative functions of government. Civilians are included in the government mostly as advisers in the formulation of government policies or to make the government appear to be legitimate. Direct military rule or "state of emergency" is the basis of authority in a military dictatorship. Military dictatorships are present in Iraq, Myanmar (Burma), and Nigeria. Elections are scheduled for February 1999 to replace the military dictatorship in Nigeria.

AP/Wide World Photos

Reuters/Mojahedin/Archive Photos

5. Minority Tyranny. This type of authoritarian government is led by a small minority that enjoys full political rights and restricts most political rights of the majority. The best known example of a minority tyranny in the 20th century was associated with the system of apartheid practised in South Africa. Under apartheid, black, mixed, and Asian South Africans were denied any rights to participate in formulating policies and choosing their leaders. Only white South Africans had full political rights. In 1994, apartheid was abolished in South Africa with the election of that country's first African leader, Nelson Mandela.

Lambert/Archive Photos

Canapress/Adil Bradlow

TOP LEFT: Barricades being removed by anti-riot police in Lagos, Nigeria

TOP RIGHT: Segregated beach during the apartheid era in South Africa

BOTTOM RIGHT: A civil rights activist, lawyer, and politician, Nelson Mandela campaigned against white minority rule in South Africa. Jailed in 1964 for his political beliefs and released in 1991, Mandela became South Africa's first black leader in 1994.

BOTTOM LEFT: Iranian National Liberation Army

Totalitarianism. Totalitarianism is a phenomenon of the 20th century. It is distinguished from authoritarian governments by the degree to which it attempts to control all aspects of life and society. Two noted political scientists, Carl Friedrich and Zbigniew Brzezinski, identified six key features of totalitarian dictatorship[1], summarized below:

1. Totalitarianism has an official ideology that espouses as its aim the creation of a new and perfect society in which the state controls all aspects of human life. The ideology rejects all existing societies and often seeks international domination.

2. A single mass political party is led by one person and a small group of members who are determined to implement policies based on the ideology. Party membership and recruitment is strictly controlled and limited to about 10% of the adult population. The party is highly organized and controls all social, political, and economic institutions.

3. A secret police employs modern technology and scientific methods to detect, monitor, control, and destroy all "enemies" of the system, real or imagined. Secret police are also used against the general population with the aim of ensuring mass compliance and loyalty to the party and its leaders.

4. All forms of mass media such as the press, radio, television, and cinema are controlled and used by the party and government to indoctrinate and educate the population about the goals of the party and government.

5. All military weapons are controlled by the government to prevent popular revolt and opposition to the party's leadership and the official ideology.

6. A centrally controlled economy is formed in which many activities and resources are planned by the state in accordance with the goals of the official ideology.

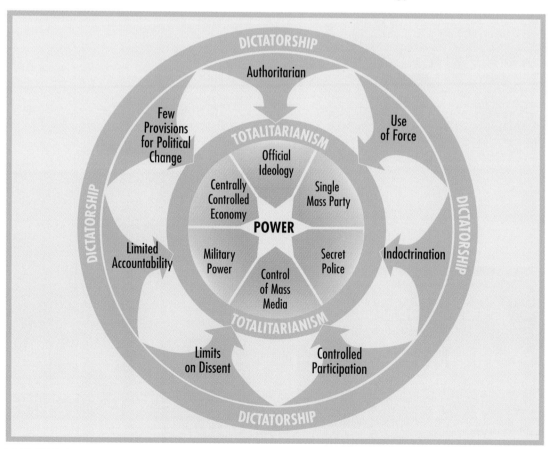

[1]For more information see Carl J. Friedrich and Zbigniew K. Brzezinski. *Totalitarianism, Dictatorship and Autocracy.* Cambridge: Harvard University Press, 1956.

66

Two models of totalitarian dictatorship that have appeared in the 20th century are communism and fascism.

1. **Communism.** First appearing in Russia following the October/November 1917 Bolshevik Revolution, communism spread to other parts of the world. In the communist political system, the Communist Party organized, controlled, and developed all aspects of society, government, and the economy according to the wishes of its leadership. Mass loyalty to the party was accomplished by using terror, indoctrination, propaganda, and by restricting personal freedoms. These features of totalitarian dictatorship under communism are further discussed in Chapter 9 on the Soviet Union and in Chapter 11 on China.

2. **Fascism.** Italian fascism under Benito Mussolini (1922–1945) and German National Socialism under Adolf Hitler (1933–1945) developed in the aftermath of World War I (1914–1918), out of political instability in Europe, fear of communism spreading from the Soviet Union, and economic collapse. Fascism was committed to establishing societies in which individuals worshipped the leader as a saviour of the nation, abandoned individualism in favour of collective identity, believed in the supremacy of the nation, and glorified the use of military force against communists and other enemies of the state. The government, much of the economy, and society were tightly controlled to advance the goals of the state; violence, the threat of violence, suppression of individual liberties and indoctrination were used to control the population. These aspects of totalitarian dictatorship under fascism are discussed in Chapter 8 on National Socialist Germany.

Mikhail Cheremnykh and Victor Deni 1920

David J. Rees

LEFT: A 1920 Soviet poster depicting Lenin sweeping away the capitalist order. The poster reads: "Comrade Lenin Sweeps the World Clean."

RIGHT: Emblem of the National Food Estate with motto "Blood and Soil."

Critique of Non-Democratic Systems

Contemporary non-democratic systems have their defenders and critics. Defenders argue that non-democratic systems can provide decisive leadership, political stability and social order, rapid mobilization of society's resources to accomplish national goals, and strong national defence. Defenders also contend that these strengths permit non-democratic systems to cope more easily with unrest and conflict than democratic systems.

Defenders of non-democratic systems have also argued that democracy can lead to considerable political instability, corruption, crime, and social chaos in societies that do not have strong democratic traditions. Since the collapse of Communist rule in Russia, many older Russians feel lost and confused about the change in their country. They long for the stability, control, and order that existed under communism, as the following quotes indicate:

"Under the Communists life was peaceful. There was law and order. There were few sudden changes; one knew what to expect."

"Our Communist leaders made decisions for the country without endless debate. They knew what the country needed and set about achieving it. They planned for the future development of the country. Now, our leaders think only about the present and themselves."

Critics of non-democratic systems cite some of the following weaknesses:

Lack of legitimacy. The political authority of the leader in most non-democratic systems rests largely on the threat or actual use of force to ensure continuation of the regime and obedience of the people.

Inefficiency and bureaucracy. Besides the military and public security agencies (secret police), most non-democratic systems rely on a bureaucracy to implement policies of top leadership. The bureaucracy is a source of employment and patronage for supporters of the system. Consequently, the bureaucracy becomes unwieldy and bloated with many meaningless positions. Often, this leads to competition and conflicts within the bureaucracy that can only be resolved by the top leaders. These conflicts often lead to a lack of direction for the system.

Unchecked corruption. The lack of accountability of the government to the people often results in unchecked corruption by political leaders. Because the legislature and judiciary are controlled by the government, political leaders and government officials have free rein to enrich themselves at the expense of the public treasury, knowing that their corrupt activities will not be exposed and punished.

Widespread apathy and cynicism. The suppression of dissent and government control of people's participation in the political process often lead to widespread apathy and cynicism among the people. People become passive toward the government and leaders and may believe that all policies of government exist to further the interests of the leaders. More importantly, this apathy and cynicism lead to a lack of critical thinking about the actions of the government. Intolerance to different ideas may develop.

Power struggles over succession. Because political authority rests in the hands of one person or a small group, little or no provision for succession of leadership is generally made. Following the death of the leader, power struggles among groups within the government often occur until one group is successful in consolidating its power over the others.

Elitism. While many non-democratic systems claim to rule in the best interests of society, most of these systems are based on some form of elitism. The reliance on a particular political group, social class, clan, or family group for support has led many times in the past to the adoption of policies that favoured these groups at the expense of the rest of society. This has more than once resulted in war, popular revolts, and the overthrow of the system.

REVIEW

Summary

A political system is an organized way of making decisions and resolving conflicts among the members of a society. How a society makes these decisions depends on its political culture and political system. The main features of a political system are government, political parties, interest groups, patterns of interaction, and policies of the government. Government is the most important organization in a political system because it allocates power to different bodies to choose goals and make decisions.

The organization and use of political power distinguish one political system from another. Two broad types of political system exist in the contemporary world—democratic and non-democratic systems. A democracy is a political system in which people are able to choose their leaders freely from competing groups and individuals. It is characterized by decentralized political power among branches of government. Also, individuals and groups may participate freely in formulating, promoting, and approving laws.

A non-democratic system, on the other hand, is a political system in which one person or a few people decide for the rest what goals should be set and decisions made. Non-democratic systems are generally characterized by a concentration of political power in the hands of one person or a small group of people and by control over who can participate in the political process. The main types of non-democratic systems in the world are authoritarian and totalitarian governments. Totalitarian and authoritarian governments are distinguished by the degree to which they attempt to control all aspects of the lives of the people.

Political Attitude Survey

1. Whether we are aware of it or not, we have beliefs about government and politics. The following survey is intended to help you discover what political beliefs matter most to you. Read the statements in the survey then list the letters a) to o) in your notebook. Beside each letter, mark whether you *agree* (A), *strongly agree* (SA), *disagree* (D), or *strongly disagree* (SD). There are no right or wrong responses to these statements.

   a) Every person has the right to demand an explanation from government leaders for the decisions they make.

   b) Opposition parties are necessary to ensure that the government enacts good laws, even if many opposition parties are most interested in criticizing the government.

   c) "One person, one vote" gives individuals power to influence policies and choose political leaders.

   d) Individual rights and liberties are more important than peace, order, and good government.

   e) Government has a moral responsibility to safeguard the rights of the individual against those of society.

   f) Frequent and regularly scheduled elections ensure that political leaders will enact laws and choose policies that benefit the people.

   g) A press that is able to criticize political leaders and reveal wrongdoing in government is necessary to guard against abuse of power.

   h) Every individual has a moral responsibility and duty to respect the opinions, customs, and traditions of others.

   i) The media can be trusted to report accurately and fairly on government policies and the actions of leaders.

   j) Political power should be distributed equally among all branches of government, even if this means that decisions take longer to make.

   k) Popular revolts, strikes, and demonstrations can be justified on the grounds that they will result in better government and more public participation in politics.

l) Political parties that call for social unrest and the overthrow of long-established institutions should be allowed to participate in the political process.

m) A good leader is one who is tolerant of dissenting views, compassionate toward the weak, and tries not to offend anyone.

n) Education, experience, and intelligence are the most important criteria in choosing political leaders.

o) The personal interests of individuals are more important than the interests of society as a whole.

2. Count all responses with which you *agree* (A) or *strongly agree* (SA). If you agree or strongly agree with most statements, you believe that public participation in decision making, accountability of leaders, the rule of law, and individual rights are important principles of democracy. If you *disagree* (D) or *strongly disagree* (SD) with most statements, you believe that strong leadership, social order, and stability are important goals for society.

Role of Political Systems

1. a) What do you understand by the term political culture?

b) Provide one piece of information from the history, geography, economic activity, and languages of our society that shape or have shaped our political culture. Be prepared to discuss your ideas with others.

c) What is the role of political culture in society?

2. a) In your society, to what extent are all members of the country involved in choosing political leaders, with opportunities to affect government decision making?

b) What values and beliefs have influenced these aspects of your political culture?

Features of a Political System

1. What do the textbook authors identify as the features of a political system? (See pages 33–54.) Create a chart in which to describe the features.

2. Most modern political systems are based at least in part on ideas about government that have been around for a long time. Ideas from a variety of cultures are outlined on pages 34–38.

a) Create a chart to summarize the main ideas expressed by the various philosophers.

b) From your chart, pick out three ideas that you agree should be part of a political system and three ideas with which you disagree.

c) Briefly explain your choices.

3.   Identify and provide examples of ideas expressed by the philosophers (pages 34–38) that you know are part of your political system.

4. a) Using the Working with Information questions on page 33, divide the thinkers (pages 34–38) into groups based on similarity of ideas.

b) What are the areas of greatest agreement?

c) What are the areas of greatest disagreement?

5. a) From the information provided in the text, which of the following statements would **most** likely be supported by Saint Augustine and Thomas Hobbes?

A. An effective leader is one who demands the obedience of the people.

B. People must have the right to make their own decisions.

C. People need to be able to live without feeling threatened.

D. A leader who is loved will be most effective.

b) Explain why you think your choice is correct and the other three are incorrect.

6. Most modern nations have a constitution which includes a set of principles and rules by which government operates. Depending on the nature of the political system, some constitutions are followed closely while others are not.
   a) What is the difference between written and unwritten constitutions? State which one you prefer and describe why.
   b) Identify the three branches of government to which constitutions may allocate power. Provide a brief description of their roles in government.
   c) Describe the difference between a unitary and a federal state.
   d) What are some of the rights and freedoms granted in most constitutions?

7. The map and caption on page 41 show one way to categorize political rights and civil liberties in the world.
   a) What trends does the map indicate?
   b) To what extent would the map influence someone's choice of where to live or take a holiday?
   c) What would you need to know to make a decision about the validity of the information on the map?
   d) What criteria would you use to determine the extent of political rights and civil liberties in a country?

8. a) What are the main functions of political parties?
   b) Briefly describe the main features of one-party, two-party, and multi-party political systems.
   c) What are the advantages and disadvantages of organized political parties?

9. a) What are the goals of interest groups?
   b) Describe both direct and indirect methods of action. Discuss which methods you find acceptable and unacceptable.
   c) In considering the advantages and disadvantages of interest groups, what limits, if any, would you place on their activities?

10. The cartoon on page 46 takes a position on who is responsible for intrusive photography. To what extent do you agree with the cartoonist's position?

11. The media play an important role in any political system, whether they are completely free to express their views or whether they exist only to support the government. Write a paragraph in which you take and defend a position on one the following issues:
    a) Should there be any restrictions on the way the media report or comment on political events or the lives of politicians?
    b) To what extent may the concentration of ownership of the media in the hands of a few people result in a poorly informed public?
    c) Should there be controls on free expression on the internet?

12. How has modern technology changed the political process? To what extent are these changes for the better?

13. The political process is characterized by interaction that is particularly intense during elections (pages 48–49).
    a) What are some of the purposes of elections?
    b) Choose three examples that demonstrate the variety of election practices.

c) What purposes do referenda and plebiscites serve? Give an example of the use of a referendum or plebiscite. What was the result? Why do you think politicians both like and dislike these practices?

d) How do elections in one-party states differ from those in two-party or multi-party states?

14. Prepare notes for an essay or discussion in which you take and defend a position on the following issues on the subject of elections:

a) Should elected representatives speak more for the voters or their political party?

b) Should constituency organizations have more control over who runs for office in their community than national party officials?

c) Should political parties have to inform the public as to the source of all donations for their campaigns?

15. a) 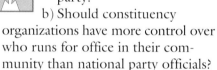 In the 20th century, women gained the right to vote in most countries. Examine the chart on page 50. What general statement can be made about the progress of women in politics in Canada compared to other countries?

b) 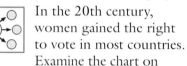 Take and defend a position on the issue: Should the voting age in Canada be dropped to age 16?

16. As demonstrated by the chart on page 52, Canada's electoral system is characterized by single-member constituencies and a "first past the post" system (simple plurality). From the information provided, which do you think would be the most effective system? Give reasons for your choice.

17. Examine the article Canada's Electoral System and the chart on page 53.

a) What are the apparent weaknesses in this electoral system? Provide one or two examples.

b) In the 1997 election, which party would have benefited the most and which the least under proportional representation?

18. Write a one-page editorial criticizing the Canadian electoral system, and propose improvements to its structure.

19. Which do you feel is the most important goal discussed on page 54? Should the other goals be sacrificed to protect this goal? Be prepared to defend your position.

Types of Political Systems

1. a) What were the strengths and weaknesses of Athenian democracy?

b) What features of Athenian democracy exist in our system of government today?

2. In ancient Athens, participation in political life was both a moral responsibility and a duty. To what extent would you agree with this statement?

3. Read Features of Democratic Systems on pages 56 and 57. Prepare notes to support a defence of your views on these issues:

a) To what extent are the rights of minorities as important as the rights of the majority?

b) To what extent should citizens assume responsibility in the political process?

c) Should the public be able to remove a leader from office between elections if they feel the leader is not being accountable to them?

d) To what extent should governments be able to suspend rights and freedoms in the interests of society?

e) To what extent is democracy weakened if there is little or no effective opposition?

f) To what extent should governments place limits on dissent?

g) Should any group of people have the right to form their own political party?

4. What are the strengths and weaknesses of direct democracy? In what situations might it be used today?

5. The two main types of representative (indirect) democracy are parliamentary democracy and presidential democracy.

a) Construct a chart comparing the main features of the three branches of government in these two types.

b) Consider the remarks made by defenders and by critics of parliamentary and presidential democracy. Prepare arguments to defend the system that you think can provide better government.

6. Suggest ways by which citizens and political groups can reduce or eliminate the problems discussed in Critique of Contemporary Democracy on page 60.

7. What do you feel is the most critical weakness of democratic systems?

8. What do you consider to be the most important feature that separates democratic from non-democratic systems?

9. What concerns did Thomas Carlyle and Friedrich Nietzsche, writing in the 19th century, express about democracy? Be careful to note the major difference in their views. To what extent do you agree with their specific concerns?

10. Read Features of Non-Democratic Systems (pages 62–63) and answer the following questions.

a) To what degree are these features present in democratic systems?

b) Consider the education that you have received over recent years. To what extent do you believe that one purpose of all educational systems is to indoctrinate students to certain political, economic, or other points of view?

c) How do you think your life would be different if you lived under a non-democratic system of government?

11. Create a chart showing the features of the types of non-democratic systems described on pages 64 and 65. What features do they have in common? How are they different?

12. Read Totalitarianism on page 66 and answer the following questions.

a) What characterizes a totalitarian system?

b) What is meant by the statement "all totalitarian regimes are dictatorships but not all dictatorships are totalitarian."

13. Compare the role of the media in democratic and non-democratic systems.

14. Non-democratic systems based on the ideologies of communism and fascism emerged during the 20th century. Give examples from the text indicating how these systems are both similar and different.

15. Review the examples given on pages 64–65. What conditions might lead to the creation and public acceptance of authoritarian governments?

16. Read Critique of Non-Democratic Systems on page 68 and answer the following questions. Be prepared to discuss your ideas with others.

a) What do you think is the most serious criticism of non-democratic systems?

b) Are there circumstances which might justify a non-democratic system?

Chapter Consolidation

1. Identify the types of lobby groups that would be most effective in each type of political system. Provide reasons for your choices.

2. How do individual political systems use controlled participation to validate their policies and actions?

3. This chapter began with a quotation by Aristotle from Politics. He wrote that "[T]he true forms of government . . . are those in which the one, or the few, or the many, govern with a view to the common interest; but governments which rule with a view to the private interest, whether of the one, or of the few, or of the many, are perversions."

a) Was Aristotle more concerned about the type of government or its purpose?

b) To what extent do you agree with Aristotle?

4. Based on what you have learned in this chapter, write a short essay in which you take and defend a position on each of the following questions:

 a) To what extent should political decision making be restricted to a small group in society?

 b) To what extent should political systems emphasize the good of society at the expense of individual interests?

c) To what extent should minority rights be protected in society? Should there be limits on the rights of the majority?

3

INTRODUCING ECONOMIC SYSTEMS

"Under capitalism man exploits man; under socialism the reverse is true."
—Polish anecdote (1980s)

A large railway company announces that it is reducing its workforce by 10 000 people to cut costs and increase profits. A small Canadian mining company discovers a large nickel deposit in Labrador and the price of its shares skyrocket as people rush to buy them, hoping to make a fortune. Meanwhile, the price of nickel suddenly drops after the announcement of the discovery. Prices of personal computers tumble by 15% on reports of increased production in South Korea. Unemployment among people in Canada between ages 18 and 25 reaches its highest level ever, forcing more young people to obtain increased training and education to get their first job. The French government announces that it will sell several state-owned banks to private individuals. Industrial production in Russia continues to decline, having plunged more than 50% since 1990. The Mexican government takes over several privately-owned banks on the verge of collapse to prevent financial chaos. These are examples of economies in action.

Societies regard economic issues differently based on how strongly they hold certain values about economics. Consider the following statements. Privately-owned businesses are better managed than government-owned ones. Some goods and services can best be

obtained from governments, not from private businesses and individuals. Education, skills, and intelligence matter more for a country's future prosperity than the natural resources it may possess. Technological change is an important source of economic growth. Governments have a responsibility to provide support for less advantaged members of society. Such economic statements reveal societal values.

Focus On Issue

All economic systems attempt to satisfy human wants and include ways by which people make decisions about production, consumption, and distribution of goods and services. All societies need to face this major issue:

- **To what extent should the government intervene in the economy to protect the interests of society?**

The response to this question has varied widely from one society to another and over time.

Refer to page 4 for explanation of icon.

Chapter Overview: The diagram below shows the interrelationship between scarcity and features of an economic system.

The role of govt to meet

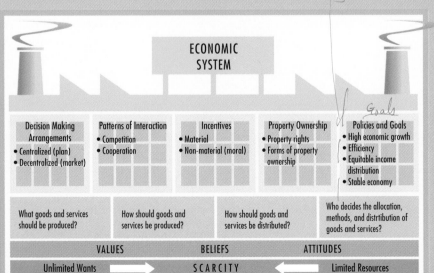

ECONOMIC SYSTEM

Decision Making Arrangements	Patterns of Interaction	Incentives	Property Ownership	Policies and Goals
• Centralized (plan) • Decentralized (market)	• Competition • Cooperation	• Material • Non-material (moral)	• Property rights • Forms of property ownership	• High economic growth • Efficiency • Equitable income distribution • Stable economy

Goals

What goods and services should be produced?	How should goods and services be produced?	How should goods and services be distributed?	Who decides the allocation, methods, and distribution of goods and services?

VALUES	BELIEFS	ATTITUDES

Unlimited Wants →	SCARCITY	← Limited Resources

Legend
- Economic Systems
- Features of an Economic System
- Society makes choices based on four Economic Questions
- Foundation of a Society's Economic System
- Role of Economic Systems (scarcity is the basic economic problem faced by all societies)

ROLE OF ECONOMIC SYSTEMS

An economic system is a set of institutions that attempt to solve the problem of allocating society's scarce resources in the face of unlimited demands.

Advance Organizer

An economic system exists in order to satisfy human needs and wants. How a society's economic system develops is determined by how it uses and manages its basic economic resources of land (natural resources), labour (people), and capital (equipment, buildings, money). No society has unlimited quantities of these resources and so cannot produce unlimited quantities of goods and services. As a result, demand for resources will always be greater than the supply of them. This scarcity of resources is the basic economic problem faced by all societies. All societies approach this issue in unique ways as they attempt to satisfy their peoples' demands for goods and services.

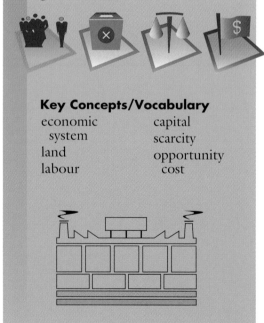

Key Concepts/Vocabulary

economic system	capital
land	scarcity
labour	opportunity cost

An economic system reflects a society's values and beliefs about production, wealth, ownership, and exchange.

Economic Culture

Foundation

Making Economic Choices. Because resources are scarce, a society is compelled to make choices (decisions) about what goods and services it should produce, how they should be produced, how they should be distributed, and who should decide about resource allocation, methods of production, and distribution of the goods and services. In making these choices, society must be aware of opportunity cost. Opportunity cost arises when a decision to have more of one thing involves having less of another thing.

These decisions about how to deal with the issue of scarce resources are based on values, attitudes, and ideas that have evolved and continue to evolve over time. The foundation of a society's economic system is formed from values, attitudes, and ideas relating to production, wealth, ownership, and exchange of goods and services. As a society's values, attitudes, and ideas about production, ownership, and exchange of goods and services evolve, changes are made in the economic system. For example, during most of the 20th century there was widespread support for an increased role in the economy for government. More recently, there has been a trend toward a reduced role in the economy for government.

Economists define an economic system as a way of doing things that attempts to solve the problem of allocating society's scarce resources in the face of unlimited demands.

CHOICES ARISING FROM SCARCITY

Advance Organizer

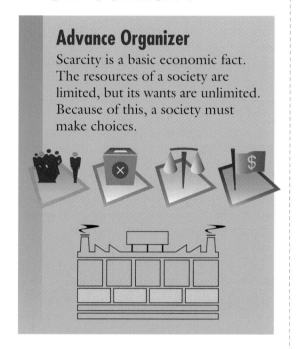

Scarcity is a basic economic fact. The resources of a society are limited, but its wants are unlimited. Because of this, a society must make choices.

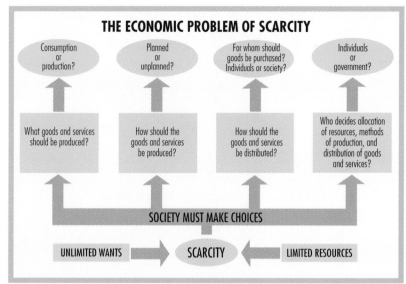

THE ECONOMIC PROBLEM OF SCARCITY

Consumption or production? | Planned or unplanned? | For whom should goods be purchased? Individuals or society? | Individuals or government?

What goods and services should be produced? | How should the goods and services be produced? | How should the goods and services be distributed? | Who decides allocation of resources, methods of production, and distribution of goods and services?

SOCIETY MUST MAKE CHOICES

UNLIMITED WANTS → SCARCITY ← LIMITED RESOURCES

Four Economic Questions

The basic economic problem of scarcity leads societies to make decisions on economic questions. A society's basic values, beliefs, and attitudes provide the foundation for the development of an economic ideology. This ideology will direct or influence the choices a society makes about what features it chooses to include in its economic system. The features chosen will influence the answers to the four basic economic questions.

1. What goods and services should be produced? Should the goods and services be produced to satisfy society's needs or an individual's needs? When more goods such as weapons are produced because this supports a particular society's belief system, fewer goods such as cars are likely to be produced for individual needs. Production is the making of goods or the providing of services. Consumption is the using of goods and services produced to satisfy human needs and wants. Should more goods and services be produced as investment for future production and consumption (buildings, equipment, machinery) or present consumption (food, clothing, cars)?

2. How should goods and services be produced? Should the goods be produced according to a government plan or should individuals decide? Should goods and services be produced in order to make a profit for the producer or to fulfil society's basic needs? What proportions of land, labour, and capital should be used to produce goods and services? For example, should emphasis be placed on using as much labour as possible in order to provide jobs for everyone, or should there be emphasis on using machinery and technology in order to modernize and reduce labour costs? Should land be used for agriculture, industry, or housing?

3. How should the goods and services be distributed? Should people be free to make their own decisions about what goods and services they wish to purchase, based on price and their income? Or, should society make decisions about the distribution of goods and services to people, based on what is deemed to be in their best interests?

4. Who decides on the allocation of resources, methods of production, and distribution of goods and services? Should governments or individuals make decisions about the allocation of resources and the production and distribution of goods and services? Should people in society have a voice in how these decisions are made?

Society must make choices based on four economic questions.

FEATURES OF AN ECONOMIC SYSTEM

Advance Organizer

Economic systems possess five main features. They are a set of decision making arrangements, patterns of interaction, a system of incentives, property ownership, and policies and goals. Each of these five characteristics shapes the operation of an economic system. They are coloured tan on the model on page 75.

Key Concepts/Vocabulary

plan	incentives
market	profit
demand	property rights
supply	private ownership
equilibrium	public ownership
competition	
monopoly	collective property
oligopoly	

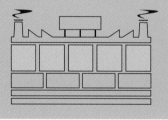

Decision Making Arrangements

Decisions about the production and distribution of goods and services are made in all economic systems. In this process, people and groups collect information, set goals, and make assumptions about how to earn income, produce goods, and spend money. These arrangements in an economic system will reflect the emphasis a society places on the role of the individual or the group. An economic system is a complex social organization. Within it, decisions are made about how a society's resources (land, labour, and capital) will be allocated for production and consumption. How these decisions are made vary from system to system. Should individuals make most decisions or should groups and various institutions, including the government, be responsible for the decisions? A distinguishing characteristic of an economic system is who makes the decisions about production, consumption, and distribution.

Decision making in an economic system can be done in a centralized or in a decentralized manner. Typically, centralized decision making appears in the form of a plan developed by institutions of the government, while decentralized economic decision making occurs through the mechanism of the market. Most economic systems have a mixture of decision making arrangements that varies according to a society's needs, values, and economic goals.

Centralized Decision Making

A plan is a conscious effort by a person or group to set goals, assess the availability of resources, organize and implement activities, and evaluate results. The first step in compiling a plan is to collect information about what has been done in the past and is happening presently. This information is used to develop goals for the future. Once goals have been determined, information about available resources of land, labour, and capital is collected and analyzed, and decisions can be made about whether or not the goals can be accomplished with the resources on hand. Decisions are then made to allocate resources needed to achieve the goal. Decisions are implemented, and after some time results are evaluated. If the results do not match expectations, the plans are either modified or abandoned. Families, households, and various organizations such as schools, banks, corporations, and government departments make plans to implement their decisions. Countries prepare plans to realize national goals such as industrialization, mass education, health care, and military preparedness.

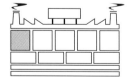

Decision making is the first economic feature described in this book (pages 78–79).

Should individuals or should groups and various institutions, including government, be responsible for decisions about production and distribution of goods and services?

Decentralized Decision Making

Unlike the plan, the market is a mechanism for decentralized decision making. In a market, individuals decide for themselves what goods and services to produce and consume. Their decisions about production and distribution are formulated on the basis of information about demand and supply. Demand is the quantity of goods and services people are willing to buy at a given price. Supply is the quantity of goods and services available for sale at a given price. The interaction of supply and demand results in a price acceptable to both buyers and sellers (equilibrium price).

On the graph below, the point of equilibrium (Z) represents the price (P) at which buyers and sellers agree. Q is the quantity bought and sold. If quantity demanded is greater than quantity available for sale (for example, at a price of $3), then a shortage appears and price rises. If quantity demanded is less than quantity available for sale at a price of $7, then a surplus occurs and the price falls. When quantity demanded and available for sale is in equilibrium, or in balance (for example, at a price of $5), then the price does not change.

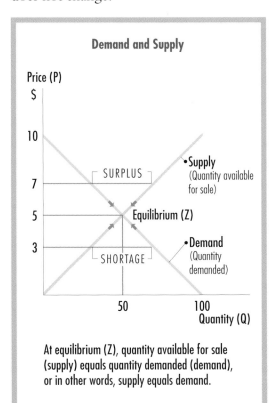

Demand and Supply

Price (P)
$

10

7 — SURPLUS

• Supply
(Quantity available for sale)

5 — Equilibrium (Z)

3

SHORTAGE

• Demand
(Quantity demanded)

50   100
Quantity (Q)

At equilibrium (Z), quantity available for sale (supply) equals quantity demanded (demand), or in other words, supply equals demand.

Patterns of Interaction

Patterns of interaction among decision makers in an economic system are determined by sets of rules, written or unwritten. For example, to what extent should people compete or cooperate among themselves to make decisions about production and distribution of goods and services? The main patterns of interaction will depend on decision making arrangements in the economic system. An economic system that is dominated by markets and allows individuals to make most decisions about production, consumption, and distribution will emphasize competition. When many decisions about production and distribution are centralized in the hands of a group of people and formalized in plans, cooperative activity is emphasized. In the real world, most economic systems include features of both patterns of interaction.

Competition

Competition is generally associated with markets and few restrictions on the activities of individual decision makers. People who favour competition believe that it serves both the individual and society well, and that the interests of the individual are generally more important than those of the group. Competition results from individuals vying with one another to gain recognition for their achievements or to secure customers for their products. In a competitive system, it is believed that no group of persons should be allowed to dominate or control the production and distribution of goods and services.

Cooperation

Cooperation occurs when individuals agree to work together to realize goals that have been mutually agreed upon. Individual interests are subordinated to those of the group. The group believes that cooperation will result in greater gains for society than those obtained from competition. Some gains that may arise from cooperation are the provision of goods and services necessary for community life, such as national defence, parks, roads, mass transit, TV and radio broadcasts, and internal order.

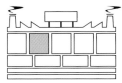

Patterns of Interaction, the second economic feature described in this book, are determined by sets of rules (pages 79–80).
• Competition
• Cooperation

To what extent should people compete among themselves, or should they cooperate to make decisions about production and distribution of goods and services?

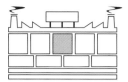

Incentives, the third economic feature described in this book, are used to influence individuals and organizations (pages 80–81).
- Material incentives
- Non-material moral incentives

What types of incentives should be used to motivate people and to what extent should individual initiative be rewarded or contribution to the well-being of the group be emphasized?

These gains are shared by consumers in society. In theory, gains from cooperation in production are jointly shared by workers and employers. It is believed that workers will acquire skills and experience that will provide them with higher incomes. Employers will benefit as their workers become more skilled and experienced, resulting in greater production and efficiency. Fewer mistakes, accidents, and other inefficiencies will occur, leading to lower costs of production, higher production levels, and higher profits.

Monopoly and Oligopoly

The domination or control of production and distribution of goods and services can appear as a monopoly or in the form of an oligopoly.

A monopoly occurs when there is only one seller or producer of a good or service in an industry. Monopolies exist when there are significant legal, technological, or financial barriers that prevent other producers from continuing in or entering the industry and competing effectively with the dominant producer. Consequently, the consumer is faced with absence of choice in the marketplace. Some types of monopolies allowed to exist in Canada and elsewhere are providers of basic services such as water, electricity, natural gas, telephone, public transit, and cable television. Some of the companies granted monopolies are publicly owned while others are privately owned. In both cases, the activities of these companies are heavily regulated and controlled by a government body.

An oligopoly exists when a few producers control an industry. In this type of industry, the number of producers is small enough that each producer must consider the reaction of other producers when it changes its price. Oligopolies often exist when the high cost of technology and the need for considerable capital in an industry prevent all but the largest companies from starting up and operating. Automobiles, beer, tobacco, steel, and banking are some industries in Canada dominated by a small number of producers.

Incentives

Incentives are an important element of all economic systems. They are necessary to motivate individuals and businesses to carry out decisions and fulfil commitments made to others. Incentives also motivate individuals and organizations to perform certain activities and to carry out decisions made at higher levels. It is important to consider what types of incentives should be used to motivate people and to what extent individual initiative should be rewarded or contribution to the well-being of the group should be stressed. Incentives generally take two forms—material and non-material.

Material Incentives

Individual initiative is encouraged and rewarded by the promise of material incentives. Income, most often in the form of profits made or wages earned, is the most common type of material incentive. Other material incentives may be free trips, clothing, cars, and special discounts on purchases.

Incentive plans are also used to reward an individual or group for increasing production. One kind of incentive plan is the piecework payment system, in which the individual or group is paid according to the amount of goods produced or services provided. Another kind pays bonuses to individuals for reaching stipulated levels of production. Profit-sharing is an incentive plan that pays a portion of profits to individuals or the group as wages. In the Soviet Union and National Socialist Germany, piecework and bonuses were the most common incentives paid to individuals for increasing production. Piecework is the most common incentive system used for increasing the production of goods in many countries, including Bangladesh, China, India, and Russia. In places where profit-sharing plans have been introduced, such as Canada, the United States, Japan, and many Western European countries, they have become an effective means of encouraging people to increase sales, reduce costs, and increase profits.

Non-Material or Moral Incentives

Non-material or moral incentives are used to motivate people to think and act in ways that consider group interests. A kind word from a co-worker or employer, a plaque or trophy that recognizes a particular accomplishment, publicity, personal loyalty, the belief in doing a job well, and the desire to improve the general welfare of others are all examples of non-material incentives. Non-material incentives do not benefit a person with tangible things like money and goods. The benefits obtained from non-material incentives are strictly personal and internal. A person may feel happy because of what he or she did and how this activity benefited others.

One important type of non-material incentive employed in the Soviet Union and National Socialist Germany was the awarding of special medals to individuals for exemplary service to the state. For example, in the Soviet Union, workers who produced high quality goods or performed exemplary service were celebrated as "Heroes of Labour." In National Socialist Germany, government officials drew public attention to the exemplary efforts of workers and called on all other workers to strive for greater service to the state and "fatherland."

Property Ownership

Ownership of property is a fundamental characteristic of economic systems. Property includes both real property (land, buildings) and other items of value, including intellectual property (ideas, writings, art). The questions of how and by whom property is owned, and what rights are accorded to property owners, influence all decisions about production, consumption, income, and exchange of goods and services. Property ownership has a dramatic impact on the answers to the basic economic questions about production and distribution.

Property Rights

Ownership is more than the physical possession of an object. Economists define ownership as a collection of rights an individual has over objects. This collection of property rights includes the right of use, the right of disposal, and the right to income.

Right of Use. The right of use is the freedom to use an object in whatever way the owner considers appropriate. Only the owner has the right to use the property and can exclude others from using it. However, the owner may not use the property in a way that damages the property of others or interferes with the rights of other owners to use their property. For example, a person may operate a small business based in his or her home; however, if it generates considerable noise and activity, nearby homeowners may complain about the noise and request that the home-based business be shut down or moved to another location so that they can enjoy the use of their property in peace and quiet.

Right of Disposal. The right of disposal is the freedom to dispose of the property, or transfer the title of it to another owner. This can be done by gift or sale. In either case, the owner transfers the ownership to another person, group, or institution. The property now belongs to another.

Right to Income. The right to income is the freedom to use the property to earn an income. The income can arise from the sale of the property for a financial gain, or from leases and rents. In the case of leases and rents, the owner grants the right of use to another person for a fixed sum of money over a specified period of time. For example, a homeowner can rent a room to a person for a sum of money.

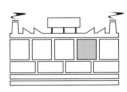

Property Ownership is the fourth economic feature discussed (pages 81–82).
• Property rights
• Forms of property ownership

To what extent should property be owned by the state or held in private hands?

Forms of Property Ownership

In an economic system, there are two forms of property ownership—private and public.

Under private ownership, all three property rights belong to the individual. The individual can use, dispose of, and generate income from the property. Under public ownership, the three property rights belong to the state. The state may choose to delegate some rights of ownership to a group of individuals or collective.

The collective farm was one prominent example of public ownership where the state retained the rights of ownership but delegated some of these rights. Collective farms were first established in the late 1920s in the Soviet Union. Each farm was owned and worked by a collective. Each member of the collective had the right to use a private plot, but with some restrictions. The farmer could keep all income from the private plot but could not sell the land. The farmer could bequeath the right of use to heirs, but the right of disposal belonged to the collective. The farmer could not use hired help to work the private plot.

Policies and Goals

All economic systems have a set of policies and goals. These policies and goals reflect the values, beliefs, and attitudes of society. The goals that are pursued will determine the direction and performance of the economic system. Important questions to consider are which policies and goals should be pursued and who should make decisions about them. The choice of these goals depends on the availability of resources. The necessity of choosing to pursue some goals at the expense of others results from the fundamental scarcity of resources, which prevents every economic system from producing unlimited quantities of goods and services. Some of the economic goals pursued in the 20th century have been high economic growth, efficiency, equitable income distribution, and a stable economy.

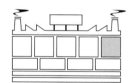

The last economic feature, Policies and Goals, reflects the values, beliefs, and attitudes of society (pages 82–83).
- High economic growth
- Efficiency
- Equitable income distribution
- Stable economy

Which policies and goals should be pursued and who should make decisions about them?

High Economic Growth

High economic growth has been a widely pursued economic goal in the 20th century. A high economic growth rate is equated with rapid increases in the value of output and improvements in the living standards of the population. A high economic growth rate has also been associated with the rapid depletion of resources, environmental degradation, urbanization, and overcrowding.

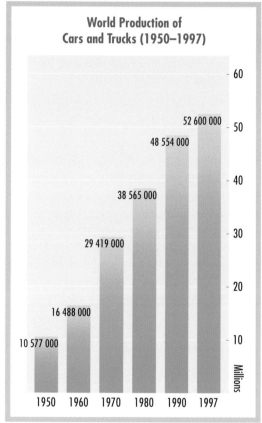

World Production of Cars and Trucks (1950–1997)

- 1950: 10 577 000
- 1960: 16 488 000
- 1970: 29 419 000
- 1980: 38 565 000
- 1990: 48 554 000
- 1997: 52 600 000

(Millions)

American Automobile Manufacturers Association

Efficiency

As an economic goal, efficiency is often related to technological progress and innovation. Efficiency refers to the effectiveness with which an economic system utilizes its available resources. A highly efficient economic system is characterized by high economic growth and a cost-effective use of scarce resources. The application of new technologies has made production more efficient but has often led to unemployment, leading to the need to retrain the affected workforce.

Equitable Income Distribution

Achieving a more equitable distribution of wealth and income has been an important economic goal of most societies and economic systems in the 20th century. There has been an attempt to have all individuals in society benefit to some degree from economic activity. Some governments have instituted taxes to reduce differences in wealth and have redistributed income via social programs. The goal has been to reduce poverty and equalize income of all citizens. Other governments have owned, controlled, and regulated the factors of production in an effort to redistribute wealth so that people have equal access to sufficient income.

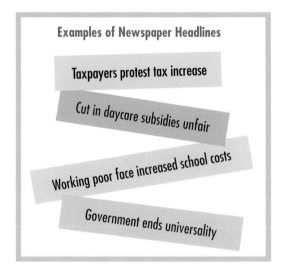

Examples of Newspaper Headlines

Taxpayers protest tax increase

Cut in daycare subsidies unfair

Working poor face increased school costs

Government ends universality

Stable Economy

Another economic goal pursued by societies in the 20th century has been the effort to stabilize levels of economic activity; that is, to reduce fluctuations in economic growth, maintain low rates of unemployment, and avoid high inflation. Economic stability is desirable because an unstable economy adversely affects various segments of the population by creating hardship and may lead to losses in potential output. For example, pensioners living on fixed incomes are hurt by high inflation, while unskilled workers are hurt by high unemployment. Losses in potential output are difficult to measure, but can include underemployment, little technological innovation, and fewer improvements in living standards.

Summary

The economic goals a society wishes to pursue have important consequences for the functions of the state or government and its level of involvement in the economic system. For much of the 20th century, most governments have pursued two broad policy objectives: promoting economic growth, efficiency, and stability, and improving income equity. The chart below summarizes how the functions of the state vary according to its economic goals and its level of involvement in the economy.

Summary: Policies and Goals		
	Promoting Economic Growth, Efficiency, and Stability	**Improving Income Equity**
Minimum involvement	Defence Law and order Currency Public health	Anti-poverty programs Disaster relief
Intermediate involvement	Basic education Environmental protection Utility regulation Anti-trust policy Financial regulation Consumer protection Health insurance	Pensions Family allowances Unemployment insurance
Maximum involvement	Industrial development Promoting markets	Redistribution of wealth and incomes Public ownership of means of production

Adapted from *World Development Report 1997: The Evolving Role of the State*. Table 1.1, p. 27.

TYPES OF ECONOMIC SYSTEMS

Advance Organizer

Economists identify two basic economic systems organized according to the principles of private enterprise and public enterprise. A private enterprise or market economy is based on individual initiative, competition, and private ownership of property. A public enterprise or centrally planned economy is based on central planning, cooperation, and public ownership of property.

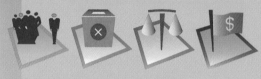

Key Concepts/Vocabulary

private
  enterprise
mercantilism
physiocrats

laissez-faire
invisible hand
classical
  economics

Social
  Darwinism
consumer
  sovereignty
public enterprise
centrally planned
  economy
utopian
  socialism

class struggle
bourgeoisie
proletariat
dictatorship of
  the proletariat
capitalism
surplus value
quota

ECONOMIC SYSTEMS

Private Enterprise Economy

Public Enterprise Economy

EVOLUTION OF ECONOMIC THOUGHT

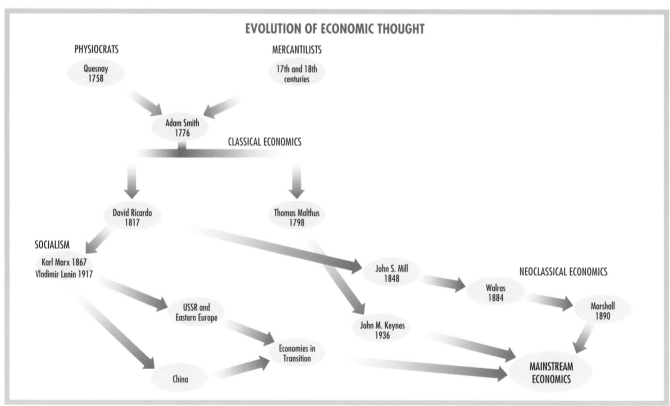

PHYSIOCRATS — Quesnay 1758

MERCANTILISTS — 17th and 18th centuries

Adam Smith 1776

CLASSICAL ECONOMICS

David Ricardo 1817

Thomas Malthus 1798

SOCIALISM — Karl Marx 1867 / Vladimir Lenin 1917

USSR and Eastern Europe

China

Economies in Transition

John S. Mill 1848

John M. Keynes 1936

Walras 1884

Marshall 1890

NEOCLASSICAL ECONOMICS

MAINSTREAM ECONOMICS

Adapted from Paul A. Samuelson and William D. Nordhaus. *Economics.* Fourteenth edition. New York: McGraw-Hill Inc., 1992. Reprinted with permission of The McGraw-Hill Companies.

Private Enterprise Economy

A private enterprise economy is also referred to as a market economy, free enterprise economy, price system, or capitalist economy. Although they may take quite different forms, most economic systems in the world today incorporate the main features of private enterprise or are based on its principles.

© West Edmonton Mall

Foundations

Mercantilism. From the 15th to about the end of the 18th century the most common economic system in Europe was mercantilism. This economic system was associated with world exploration, the colonialization of other lands, and the protection of the home economy. The principles of mercantilism can be summarized as follows:

- A nation's wealth is based on the amount of gold and silver it possesses.
- A nation increases its wealth by selling more goods to other countries than it buys from them.
- Government regulation of foreign trade is necessary to promote exports and to restrict imports so that more gold and silver enters the country than leaves it.
- High taxes on imported goods and privileges to a home country's industry are necessary to expand manufacturing and develop sources of cheap raw materials.
- Rapid population growth and a large labour force are necessary to keep wages low and increase exports.

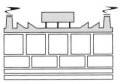

Private enterprise economies are characterized by individual initiative, competition, and private ownership of property. Private enterprise economies are examined on pages 85–93.

Mercantilism is a school of thought that believes in promoting exports and limiting imports as the means for a nation to accumulate wealth.

PHOTO: A privately-owned shopping mall in Canada sells goods and provides services to individuals.

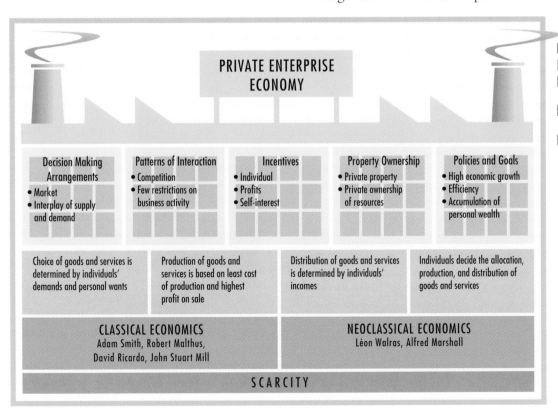

PRIVATE ENTERPRISE ECONOMY

Decision Making Arrangements
- Market
- Interplay of supply and demand

Patterns of Interaction
- Competition
- Few restrictions on business activity

Incentives
- Individual
- Profits
- Self-interest

Property Ownership
- Private property
- Private ownership of resources

Policies and Goals
- High economic growth
- Efficiency
- Accumulation of personal wealth

Choice of goods and services is determined by individuals' demands and personal wants

Production of goods and services is based on least cost of production and highest profit on sale

Distribution of goods and services is determined by individuals' incomes

Individuals decide the allocation, production, and distribution of goods and services

CLASSICAL ECONOMICS
Adam Smith, Robert Malthus, David Ricardo, John Stuart Mill

NEOCLASSICAL ECONOMICS
Léon Walras, Alfred Marshall

SCARCITY

Legend
- Type of Economic System
- Features of Economic System
- Society makes choices based on four Economic Questions
- Foundation of a Society's Economic System
- Role of Economic Systems (scarcity is the basic economic problem faced by all societies)

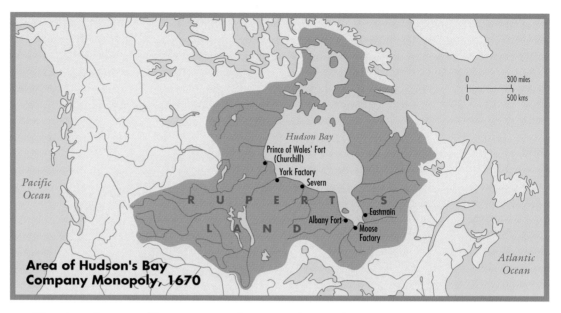

Area of Hudson's Bay Company Monopoly, 1670

The aim of mercantilism was to make the nation as wealthy as possible, often at the expense of other nations. National wealth was measured in the amount of gold and silver a nation accumulated from trading with other nations and its colonies. To accumulate gold and silver from trade, the government controlled economic activities, especially foreign trade, and established colonies as sources of cheap raw materials and new markets. The purchase of foreign-made manufactured goods and the sale of domestic raw materials were restricted or prohibited. Generally, only essential foodstuffs and raw materials unavailable domestically could be brought in from other countries. Skilled workers were not allowed to emigrate to other countries. To expand the sale abroad of domestically-produced manufactured goods, subsidies and special privileges were granted to producers. Government-supported voyages of exploration were undertaken to locate and exploit new lands rich in precious metals and exportable commodities.

The granting of royal charters (licenses) by the monarch to merchants, friends, and relatives created many monopolies in which one producer dominated the production of a good. This permitted the holders of the royal charter to make large profits from their protected business. A business that still exists today which was created by royal charter is the Hudson's Bay Company in Canada. Established in 1670 by a charter from the King of England, the Hudson's Bay Company was given the right to trade furs, minerals, and other goods on the waters and lands bordering Hudson Bay. The original owners of the Hudson's Bay Company included a cousin of the King of England.

As an economic policy, mercantilism has not entirely disappeared. Several countries today continue to pursue policies that promote exports and restrict imports, with the aim of generating surpluses in the country's trading account.

Physiocrats. Mercantilism had its many critics. In France, these critics called themselves physiocrats. Their leader was François Quesnay.

Corbis-Bettmann

François Quesnay (1694–1774) Quesnay was a court physician to Louis XV. Quesnay disagreed with the mercantilist assumption that the wealth of a nation originated in industry and trade. He argued that agriculture was the most important sector of the economy and the sole source of new wealth.

According to Quesnay and other physiocrats, industry and the export of goods were economic activities that did not create national wealth but merely handled the wealth produced by agriculture. He criticized government control and regulation of industry because it hindered the flow of income and goods throughout the economy. He called for free trade and the end of all government restrictions on economic activity, popularizing government inspector Vincent de Gournay's slogan "*Laissez-nous faire*" (Leave us alone), later shortened to *laissez-faire.*

Adam Smith. In Great Britain, the best known critic of mercantilism was Adam Smith, a Scottish economist and philosopher. In 1765–1766, Smith visited Paris and met Quesnay and other physiocrats. In these meetings with Quesnay, Smith found support for his belief in economic freedom and his criticism of mercantilism. However, he disagreed with Quesnay and other physiocrats that agriculture was the sole source of wealth in an economy. Following his return to Great Britain in 1766, Smith wrote *An Inquiry into the Nature and Causes of the Wealth of Nations* (*Wealth of Nations,* for short), which was published in 1776.

The publication of *Wealth of Nations* popularized Smith's criticism of mercantilism. A set of economic beliefs began to develop that later became known as capitalism. According to Smith, the nature of all human beings is to barter and exchange one thing for another. He wrote that human beings interact with each other to pursue their own interests and satisfy their own wants:

Give me that which I want, and you shall have this which you want, is the meaning of every such offer; and it is in this manner that we obtain from one another the far greater part of those [things] which we stand in need of. It is not from the benevolence of the butcher, the brewer, or the baker, that we expect our dinner, but from their regard to their interest.

Smith condemned mercantilism because of government interference in the economy. He argued for more economic freedom for individuals, noting the following:

- A nation's wealth is not measured by the amount of gold and silver it has, but by the sum total of its production of all goods.
- Increasing a nation's wealth is achieved by educating its people, encouraging them to do what they want, and allowing them to compete among themselves.
- Encouraging people to trade freely among themselves without government regulation leads to greater national wealth, less exploitation, and fewer conflicts.
- Mercantilism neglects consumers and favours producers. This affects economic growth because producers manipulate the government into granting them special privileges, which concentrates wealth in the hands of a privileged few.
- A large labour force is not necessary to keep wages low and increase exports. It is better for a nation to have a population that earns high wages for their skills and resourcefulness than a nation that tries to keep the wages of its people low to increase exports.

In his critique of mercantilism, Smith argued that a country's economic progress can be enhanced if the activities of its government were limited to providing national defence, justice, and public works (roads, bridges, waterways, and public education). Smith's key insight was that the needs of society as a whole could best be met by allowing each individual to pursue his or her own interests in an unregulated economic environment. The pursuit of profits, Smith argued, would act like "an invisible hand" guiding individuals to look after their own best interests. In this way they would contribute to meeting the needs of the people living around them without deliberately setting out to do so.

Classical Economics. In the 19th century, a number of writers refined Smith's ideas on economic freedom. The underlying assumptions of *laissez-faire*—individual initiative, economic freedom, and a self-adjusting economy—were necessary for economic and social progress. These assumptions formed the basis of what has become known as classical economics or classical economic liberalism.

Archive Photos

Thomas Robert Malthus (1766–1834)

In 1798, Malthus wrote in his book *Essay on the Principle of Population* that poverty was a consequence of rapid population growth. He argued that the poor were responsible for their own fate and their only way to escape from poverty was to have fewer children. Malthus believed that assistance to the poor would not eliminate poverty because it would only encourage them to have more children. For any major improvement in living standards, production, especially of food, had to increase faster than population.

Archive Photos

David Ricardo (1772–1823)

In 1817, Ricardo published *Principles of Political Economy and Taxation*, in which he called for the end of all government restrictions on businesses. His argument was that the economy, if left alone, would achieve the highest growth possible because businesses would be able to maximize profits and, in doing so, accumulate the maximum amount of capital needed for expanding production. This led Ricardo to demand the repeal of all tariffs on imported grain because these taxes raised the cost of wages, lowered profits, and slowed the accumulation of capital and economic growth.

Archive Photos

John Stuart Mill (1806–1873)

Mill's views on *laissez-faire* were influenced by his father James Mill and Jeremy Bentham, who believed that people made decisions on the basis of pursuing personal happiness. In 1848, in his book *Principles of Political Economy*, John Stuart Mill argued that individual self-interest was natural, rational, and desirable and that government should not restrict the freedom of the individual. In other publications, Mill supported public education, the creation of trade unions, cooperatives, and profit-sharing as ways to make the private enterprise system operate in the interests of more people, in what Bentham had termed, "the greatest good for the greatest number."

BELOW: The growth of industry in the 19th century laid the foundation of capitalism and the development of the private enterprise economy in the 20th century.

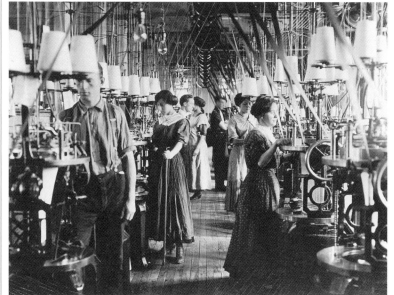

City of Toronto Archives/SC 244-137

Social Darwinism. Two sociologists put forth views that supported the ideas of classical economists and added to the body of thinking about society and the role of individuals in it. They were Herbert Spencer and William Graham Sumner.

Archive Photos

Herbert Spencer (1820–1903)

An evolutionist before Darwin, Spencer wrote in his book *Social Statics* (1850) that all social systems develop as individuals pursued their own interests and personal welfare. Development occurs as a result of competition among individuals and where government does not interfere with individual welfare. According to Spencer, the "survival of the fittest" was the source of economic and social progress. The ideas of Spencer and others about humanity were reinforced by Darwin's writings in biology, which led Spencer and others to call their views "Social Darwinism."

Archive Photos

William Graham Sumner (1840–1910)

Spencer's ideas on individualism were popularized in the United States by William Graham Sumner. Sumner argued in his major work *Folkways* (1907) that persons with ability, intelligence, and drive would rise to prominence by competing with all others. Sumner's ideas provided justification for the rise of the "robber barons" and giant corporations led by men such as Andrew Carnegie, John D. Rockefeller, and John P. Morgan.

Neoclassical Economics. From 1870 to 1900 the ideas of classical economists were modified to form a new view of capitalism called neoclassical economics. This new school of economic thought viewed a private enterprise economy as one that produced what consumers wanted, distributed products efficiently, and normally operated with little unemployment. This view of capitalism represented a modernization of Adam Smith's model of capitalism with a philosophy of individualism and newer ideas about scientific method. Prominent among these economists were Léon Walras and Alfred Marshall.

Mark Blaug, *Great Economists before Keynes*. Brighton UK: Wheatsheaf Books Ltd., 1986.

Léon Walras (1834–1910)

Writing in his book *Elements of Pure Economics* (1884), Walras argued that economic decisions made in a private enterprise economy were mainly tied to the spending decisions of consumers. All prices and production were determined by changes in consumer purchases. The whole economy automatically adjusts to match production to demand.

Stock Montage, Inc.

Alfred Marshall (1842–1924)

In 1890, Marshall published *Principles of Economics.* One important conclusion he reached was that production was determined by decisions of individual consumers. Marshall argued that a system of free markets tended to maximize individual benefits and that the whole economic system revolved around individual consumers and their needs.

Economic Questions Answered

In the private enterprise economy, the basic economic questions are answered primarily by individuals, according to classical economists like Smith, Malthus, and Mill, social philosophers like Spencer and Sumner, and neoclassical economists such as Walras and Marshall. People make their own decisions about production, consumption, and distribution through the pursuit of their own interests.

1. What goods and services should be produced? In a private enterprise economy, people decide which goods and services should be produced and offer them for sale. Consumers demand goods and services to satisfy their needs and wants. What they can purchase is limited by the amount of money and income they have and by the availability of goods and services for sale. Consumers are forced to make choices about which goods and services they can buy. These choices or trade-offs are based on the concept of opportunity cost, which is the cost of giving up one good to have another. Producers supply goods and services that consumers want with a view to earning a profit.

2. How should goods and services be produced? In a private enterprise economy all resources in society—land, labour, and capital—are limited. Individuals are motivated to engage in profitable activities out of self-interest. Producers must decide how to use scarce and expensive land, labour, and capital in the most cost-effective manner to produce goods and services for consumers. The most efficient and least expensive methods of making goods and providing services are chosen, permitting producers to earn the highest possible profits from the sale of goods and services to consumers.

3. How should goods and services be distributed? In a private enterprise economy the distribution of goods and services is determined largely by people's incomes and their ability to buy the goods and services produced. Producers sell goods and services to anyone who can buy them. A person with a high income can buy more goods and services than a person with a low income. A person's income is determined by the market for the skills, labour, and capital that he or she is able to supply.

4. Who should make decisions about resource allocation, production methods, and distribution of goods and services? People who produce goods and provide services decide what should be produced. By their purchases, consumers determine whether or not these goods and services will continue to be produced. Producers make decisions about how goods and services will be produced based on the most cost-effective use of available scarce resources. Decisions about how goods are distributed are made by consumers based on their available income. In a private enterprise economy, government's role in making these decisions is very small, except as a provider of some services and as a consumer of goods and services.

PHOTO: People make their own decisions about what to produce, consume, and distribute in a private enterprise economy.

Judy Bauer/Arnold Publishing Ltd.

Features of Private Enterprise

By the early 20th century, a market or private enterprise economy was well developed and common over much of the globe. The following features are characteristic of a private enterprise system:

1 Decision Making Arrangements.
The interplay of supply and demand through the market is one of the prominent features of a private enterprise economy. In a market, buyers and sellers meet to exchange goods and services. Supply and demand determine the prices of all goods and services. When the demand for goods and services is greater than the available quantity, the prices of the goods and services increase. When the demand for goods and services is less than the supply of goods and services, prices fall.

The market benefits both consumers and producers. Consumers benefit because they can move from seller to seller trying to get the best product or service at the lowest price. Producers benefit in that the market provides them with the opportunity to supply goods and services to consumers. Producers discover in the market which products and services are in demand among consumers. They specialize in producing only those goods and services demanded.

The concept of consumer sovereignty underlies all markets. This means that consumers ultimately decide what goods and services will be produced simply because producers will provide only goods and services consumers are willing to buy. This is also called dollar voting. Consumers express a preference for how the economic resources of society will be used by choosing the goods and services they want to consume.

2 Patterns of Interaction.
Competition is a critical feature of a private enterprise economy. Competition assures that economic resources are used effectively and efficiently. People are encouraged to specialize in activities where they receive the greatest rewards for their efforts. Competition provides important benefits for consumers and producers.

Features of Private Enterprise
1. Interplay of supply and demand through the market
2. Competition
3. Profit-driven incentives; individual self-interest
4. Private ownership of property
5. High economic growth, efficiency, and productivity

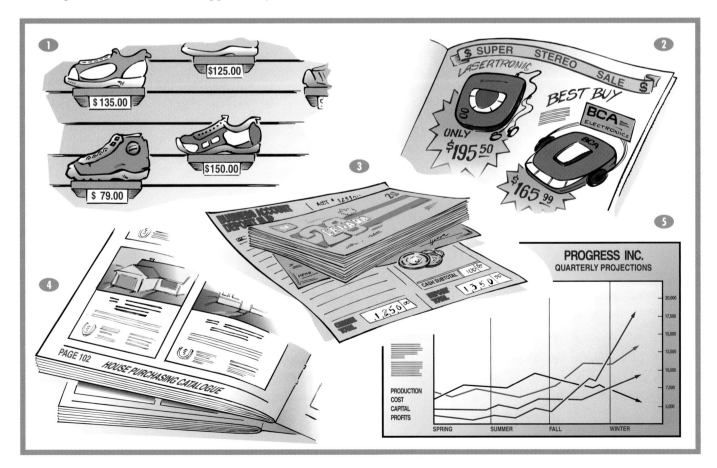

Consumers benefit from competition in the following ways. When the number of firms selling goods is large, prices of goods and services are generally lower. The selection of goods available to consumers is typically larger. Other benefits are higher quality goods, faster delivery, and better customer service. When there are few competitors, prices of goods are generally higher, because producers are not compelled to keep prices low and provide better quality goods, faster delivery, and better customer service in order to keep or increase their market share.

Producers also benefit from competition. When the number of firms supplying materials for use in production is large, the costs of them are generally lower, the supply better, and the selection wider. When there is a single supplier, the cost of goods sold to producers is often higher. These higher costs of production faced by producers will be passed on to consumers in the form of higher prices for finished goods.

Because competition is a crucial feature of a private enterprise economy, it is believed that it is necessary at times for the government to intervene in the economy to prevent monopolies from being formed and control other efforts by producers to lessen competition. It is felt that government intervention in the economy should be limited to implementing legislation to promote free and unrestricted competition. This role of government is based on the belief that competition provides consumers and producers with the greatest degree of economic freedom and choice.

3 **Incentives.** Incentives in a private enterprise economy are based on individual self-interest and the profit motive. Individual self-interest means that people will undertake those activities that make them better off personally. Material incentives motivate people to pursue their individual self-interests.

Consumers have an incentive to seek out the highest quality products at the lowest possible prices. Producers have an incentive to produce and sell those products.

Those firms that produce the goods and services that meet the needs of consumers, and that consumers will buy, are rewarded in the form of profits. Firms that fail to respond to their prospective customers' needs will not generate profit and may even go out of business.

4 **Property Ownership.** Private property is an essential feature of a private enterprise economy. It is a prerequisite to the existence of markets, competition, and the profit motive. Private ownership is a fundamental requirement for people to exchange goods and services among themselves. People cannot sell goods and services if they do not have the right of ownership allowing them to dispose of them and transfer ownership to others. Private ownership is important to competition because it encourages people to use their property effectively and efficiently. Private ownership is essential to individual self-interest and the profit motive because ownership allows people to use their property to earn income by either selling it or renting the use of it to other people.

All of this explains why most natural resources, factories, equipment, and other means of production in a private economy are owned by individuals or groups of individuals. This is one reason why many economists call an economy based on private ownership a private enterprise economy.

5 **Policies and Goals.** High economic growth, efficiency, and productivity are important economic goals in a private enterprise economy. The most important economic goal for producers of goods and services is the maximization of profits. For consumers, the main economic goal is to obtain the highest degree of satisfaction at the lowest possible cost. One important factor in the attainment of these economic goals is the accumulation of capital (both physical and human), which has given the private enterprise economy its more common label of capitalism.

Critique of Private Enterprise

Obvious advantages of a private enterprise economy are competition, high quality goods, a wide selection of goods and services, efficient production, and high productivity. Competition is an important advantage because it compels people to be creative and to use their training and opportunities to the fullest. High quality and a wide choice of goods and services arise from competition among producers to satisfy the wants of consumers. This leads to an efficient use of scarce resources in production, because inefficiency costs money and lowers profits. New types of machinery, equipment, and technology are constantly developed to improve production methods and to reduce production costs. All of this leads to high productivity, in which producers are able to sell to consumers the largest possible quantity of goods and services at various levels of quality and price.

Private enterprise also places decision making in the hands of the consumer. A society's resources will be used in the manner thought most appropriate by consumers living in that society. Because of decentralized decision making, private enterprise can adjust quickly to changing consumer demands.

However, a private enterprise economy has some important disadvantages. An uneven distribution of incomes, economic booms and busts, unemployment, and inflation can all be factors. In a private enterprise economy, individuals decide most economic questions and are expected to make the best use of their own opportunities. Because people's skills and training differ, differences in incomes and employment opportunities appear. These differences in incomes are often intensified by the fact that this type of economy experiences periods of booms (economic expansion) and busts (economic contraction). During periods of economic expansion, production and demand for goods and services are high. Opportunities for earning high incomes become widespread. Employment rises and people are able to find work. However, when demand for goods and services drops, accompanied by a drop in production, opportunities for continued high incomes become fewer. Many people become unemployed and have difficulty finding work.

Since consumer decisions drive the private enterprise economy, some question the economy's ability to use resources in the most socially responsible and efficient manner. Much of the production in contemporary private enterprise economies is directed to meeting what might be regarded as frivolous needs, and it may impose costs, such as pollution and resource depletion, on society as a whole. Called externalities, these costs are not borne directly by those involved in producing or consuming goods and services. The costs are borne by all of society.

Advantages and Disadvantages of a Private Enterprise (Market) Economy

Advantages
1. Competition promotes high quality goods and low prices.
2. A wide selection of goods and services is available to consumers.
3. Pursuit of profits leads to an efficient and productive use of resources.
4. Technological change and innovation take place rapidly.
5. Consumers influence the production of goods and services through consumer sovereignty.
6. The economy is flexible and can respond quickly to changing consumer demand.

Disadvantages
1. Income and wealth may be unevenly distributed, resulting in great differences between the rich and the poor.
2. The economy experiences periods of boom and bust.
3. Unemployment and underemployment may occur frequently.
4. Consumers can be manipulated by producers through advertising.
5. Producers can influence prices through the creation of monopolies and cartels.
6. Not all resources are used efficiently or effectively, and externalities (costs borne by society) can be created.

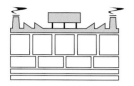

Public enterprise economies are characterized by central planning, cooperation, and public ownership of property. Public enterprise economies are discussed on pages 94–101.

PHOTO: This state-owned factory in China produces goods for the benefit of society rather than for the individual.

Public Enterprise Economy

A public enterprise economy, often called a command economy, centrally-planned economy, or state enterprise economy, is based on some of the ideas of 19th century utopian socialists, but mostly on the ideas of Karl Marx. Emphasis is placed on the collective good over that of individual interests, in the belief that if the interests of all people are served then each person will benefit.

Glen BonBernard

Foundations

Utopian Socialism. In the early 19th century, utopian socialists expressed their ideas as a protest against inequalities of wealth in Europe. Influential among these were Charles Fourier (1772–1837), Robert Owen (1771–1858), and Louis Blanc (1811–1882). They hoped to find some solution to the inequalities of wealth created by the Industrial Revolution and the growing capitalist economy in Western Europe. In France, Charles Fourier envisioned an efficiently-run communal society where members would share in the profits of their work according to their contribution. In Scotland, Robert Owen improved wages and living and working conditions, ended the worst abuses of child labour, and provided basic practical education for people working in his textile mills in New Lanark. He demonstrated that profits would rise when workers were well treated. His attempts to establish a similar community in the United States at New Harmony, Indiana, failed. Louis Blanc in France put forth the idea of government-financed social workshops that would be managed and operated by

Legend

▨ Type of Economic System

▨ Features of Economic System

▨ Society makes choices based on four Economic Questions

▨ Foundation of a Society's Economic System

▨ Role of Economic Systems (scarcity is the basic economic problem faced by all societies)

PUBLIC ENTERPRISE ECONOMY

Decision Making Arrangements	Patterns of Interaction	Incentives	Property Ownership	Policies and Goals
• Plan • Political leaders decide economic goals	• Cooperation • Campaigns to promote cooperation • Egalitarianism	• Promotion of group identity • Collectivism	• Public property • Public ownership of resources	• High economic growth • Equitable distribution of income • Economic development

Choice of goods and services is determined by economic plans for satisfying needs of society.	Production of goods and services is based on planned levels set out in production quotas.	Distribution of goods and services is determined by the state on the basis of social need.	The state acting on behalf of society decides the allocation, production, and distribution of goods and services.

UTOPIAN SOCIALISM Charles Fourier, Robert Owen, Louis Blanc	SOCIALISM Karl Marx, Vladimir Lenin

SCARCITY

workers for their own benefit. Most of these social experiments eventually failed, but not before the socialist movement emerged as a politically influential force.

Socialism. One of the founders of the socialist movement was Karl Marx. In 1848, Marx and Friedrich Engels (1820–1895), a German factory owner, published a call to action, *The Communist Manifesto.*

Archive Photos

Karl Marx (1818–1883) In *The Communist Manifesto,* Marx and Engels rejected the idea of peacefully creating a utopian society in favour of creating a more equitable society through revolution. They advanced four basic ideas:

1. An interpretation of human history as a history of class struggle.

History of all hitherto existing society is the history of class struggles. . . . Freeman and slave, patrician and plebeian, lord and serf, guild-master and journeyman, in a word, oppressor and oppressed, stood in constant opposition to one another, carried on an uninterrupted, now hidden, now open fight, a fight that each time ended, either in a revolutionary reconstitution of society at large, or in the common ruin of the contending classes.

2. The bourgeoisie and proletariat are products of changes in the modes of production and of exchange.

We see, therefore, how the modern bourgeoisie is itself the product of a long course of development, of a series of revolutions in the modes of production and of exchange. . . . In proportion as the bourgeoisie, i.e., capital, is developed, in the same proportion is the proletariat, the modern working class, developed—a class of laborers, who live only so long as they find work, and who find work only so long as their labor increases capital. These laborers, who must sell them-

selves piecemeal, are a commodity, like every other article of commerce, and are consequently exposed to all the vicissitudes of competition, to all the fluctuations of the market . . . .

Modern industry has converted the little workshop of the patriarchal master into the great factory of the industrial capitalist. Masses of laborers, crowded into the factory, are organized like soldiers. As privates of the industrial army they are placed under the command of a perfect hierarchy of officers and sergeants. Not only are they slaves of the bourgeois class, and of the bourgeois state; they are daily and hourly enslaved by the machine, by the overlooker, and above all, by the individual bourgeois manufacturer himself.

3. Inevitable victory of the proletariat over the bourgeoisie.

But not only has the bourgeoisie forged the weapons that bring death to itself; it has also called into existence the men who are to wield those weapons—the modern working class— the proletariat. . . . The development of modern industry cuts from under its feet the very foundation on which the bourgeoisie produces and appropriates products. What the bourgeoisie therefore produces, above all, are its own gravediggers. Its fall and the victory of the proletariat are equally inevitable.

4. The victory of the proletariat would lead to a workers' government and centralization of economic power in the hands of the state.

The proletariat will use its political supremacy to wrest, by degrees, all capital from the bourgeoisie to centralize all instruments of production in the hands of the state, i.e., of the proletariat organized as the ruling class; and to increase the total of productive forces as rapidly as possible.

The centralization of power in the hands of the proletariat (called the dictatorship of the proletariat) would be achieved with the implementation of the following measures:

- Abolition of private ownership of land
- A heavy progressive or graduated tax on incomes
- Abolition of all right of inheritance

- Confiscation of the property of all emigrants and rebels
- Centralization of credit in the hands of the state
- Centralization of communication and transport in the hands of the state
- Nationalization of factories and means of production
- Equal obligation of all to work; establishment of industrial armies, especially for agriculture
- Gradual abolition of differences between town and country
- Free education for all children in public schools

Marx's Critique of Capitalism. In 1867, with financial assistance from Friedrich Engels, Marx published the first volume of *Das Kapital* (Capital), in which he criticized 19th century capitalism for its exploitation of the proletariat. Capitalism, Marx believed, was a most efficient and productive economic system. However, he was more concerned about the human condition. He argued that capitalism forced people to work for subsistence wages, below the value of what their labour produced, and concentrated wealth in the hands of a few factory owners who were driven by the need to maximize profits (surplus value). Factory owners increased their profits by replacing workers with machines, which lowered the costs of production and wages. The resulting pool of unemployed workers competed for whatever wages the factory owners were willing to pay. These wages were barely sufficient for human survival. Increasing impoverishment compelled the proletariat to rise up against the bourgeoisie.

The revolt of the proletariat against the bourgeoisie was inevitable because capitalism was inherently unstable and subject to overproduction. In the resulting final crisis and collapse of capitalism, the proletariat would carry out a revolution, which would be violent because the bourgeoisie would never agree to the disappearance of capitalism. While the revolution would be violent in Germany, Marx believed that in Great Britain and the United States the revolution would be achieved by parliamentary means.

Following the revolution a dictatorship of the proletariat would be established. It would be an intermediary stage between the onset of the revolution and the final stage, the creation of a classless society. This stage would be reached only when all elements of bourgeois capitalist society were eliminated. Eventually, the state itself would cease to exist. As Marx put it, "the state would wither away."

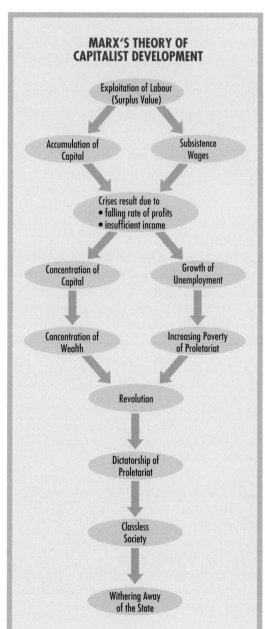

MARX'S THEORY OF CAPITALIST DEVELOPMENT

Exploitation of Labour (Surplus Value)

Accumulation of Capital

Subsistence Wages

Crises result due to
• falling rate of profits
• insufficient income

Concentration of Capital

Growth of Unemployment

Concentration of Wealth

Increasing Poverty of Proletariat

Revolution

Dictatorship of Proletariat

Classless Society

Withering Away of the State

Adapted from Daniel R. Fusfeld, *The Age of the Economist*, p. 65.

Imperialism—Highest Stage of Capitalism. Though Marx foresaw the emergence of giant businesses and great concentrations of capital in the hands of a few, it was Vladimir Lenin who extended Marx's theory of capitalist development to include the growth of the international economy.

In 1916, Lenin wrote *Imperialism, the Highest Stage of Capitalism.* In this pamphlet, he argued that the concentration of capital and growth of banks were leading to the formation of monopolies and international corporations (trusts). Imperialism, he noted, is not only the territorial division of the world among capitalist powers, but also its domination by large industrial and banking enterprises. Imperialism is the highest stage of capitalism.

Imperialism is capitalism in that stage of development in which the dominance of monopolies and finance capital has established itself; in which the export of capital has acquired pronounced importance; in which the division of the world among the international trusts has begun; in which the division of all territories of the globe among the biggest capitalist powers has been completed.

The division of the world among capitalist powers and giant monopolies, Lenin remarked, will invariably lead to wars among nations striving for economic domination. These wars will reveal internal weaknesses of capitalism and hasten its collapse. He thought that this collapse would occur first in Russia.

Sovfoto

Four Basic Economic Questions Answered

According to Marx and Lenin, in an economic system based on public enterprise, the basic economic questions are answered primarily by the state or government. Through the use of plans, cooperative behaviour, group incentives, and public ownership and control of scarce resources, the state controls all economic activities.

1. What goods and services should be produced? In a public enterprise economy the production of goods and services are determined by economic plans. Political leaders provide planners with a set of economic goals that they wish the economy to fulfil. After assessing the availability of scarce economic resources, planners determine what goods and services can be produced in the economy. The plan gives priority to the needs of society rather than to those of individual consumers.

2. How should goods and services be produced? All important decisions about methods of production are specified in the plan. However, the plan does not necessarily specify the most cost-effective method of production. What matters more in the plan and to producers is the quantity of goods and services to be produced.

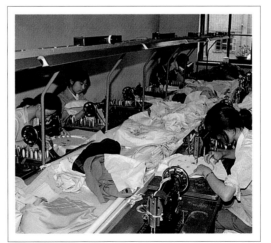

Phyllis A. Arnold

In a public enterprise economy, the state, on behalf of society, answers the four basic economic questions about consumption, production, distribution, and allocation.

LEFT: Lenin called on Russian workers to overthrow the capitalist economy and establish in its place an economic system which would benefit all society.

RIGHT: Factory workers in a government-owned clothing factory in China produce garments for internal sale and external trade.

3. How should goods and services be distributed? All goods and services produced in the economy are distributed on the basis of "social need." In the plan, social needs shape the economic goals that determine where, to whom, and to which sectors of the economy goods and services go. Political leaders, acting in the interests of society, decide how to distribute and allocate goods and services. For example, consumer goods are distributed in such a way as to ensure that citizens have equal access to basic goods and services such as milk, bread, housing, and public transportation.

PHOTO: In China, official ideology emphasizes the importance of state control over the distribution of goods and services and the allocation of resources for the common good, as in this state-owned oil storage facility.

Phyllis A. Arnold

4. Who should make decisions about resource allocation, production methods, and distribution of goods and services? A small group of people, planners, and political leaders decide what should be produced, what methods of production will be used, and to whom and how goods and services will be distributed.

Features of Public Enterprise

Marx and Engels did not develop a clear picture of what a public enterprise economy based on "scientific socialist principles" would look like. The task of creating this type of economic system was left to Vladimir Lenin and Joseph Stalin in the 20th century in the Soviet Union (see Chapter 9). The model they developed of a public enterprise economy was based on central planning, cooperation, group incentives, and public property. The following features are characteristic of a public enterprise system:

① Decision Making Arrangements. The use of a central plan for the whole economy is the most well-known characteristic of a public enterprise economy. The plan is a program of economic goals; it specifies the methods by which these goals can be achieved and how the production of goods and services will be allocated in the economy. The plan concentrates all decisions about production and distribution of goods and services in the economy in the hands of a few people. It replaces what Marx called, "the anarchy of the market" (the interplay of supply and demand) with a decision making process that considers the best interests of all society.

Political leaders establish economic goals and instruct a central planning authority to develop an economic plan based on these goals. To do this, planners analyse the types and extent of society's economic resources and then determine what goods and services can be produced. Planners examine the projected supply of each good and the projected demand for that good, with the view of balancing all available inputs needed for production with the distribution of goods produced within society. Planners also analyse the needs of different industries and regions, current consumption and future investment needs, household income and consumption, labour demand and supply, and imports and exports. Other tasks undertaken by the central planning authority include making sure that sufficient labour, natural resources, and

finances are available. Once all these decisions have been made, a plan is formulated and given to producers in the form of quotas or production targets. The gathering of all this information is very difficult and costly.

These production targets are legally binding on producers. Farms are required to produce a certain number of tonnes of grain. Factories must produce so many units of goods. Mines must produce so many tonnes of ore.

Consumers under central planning do not have the freedom to demand the goods and services they want. They must buy the products made by producers at prices set by the plan.

❷ Patterns of Interaction.
Competition in a public enterprise economy is replaced by the belief that cooperation leads to better decisions in production and distribution, both for society and individuals. Through cooperation, scarce resources will be used to produce goods and services that will

benefit society. This aspect of a public enterprise economy finds its inspiration in Marx's maxim "from each according to his abilities, to each according to his needs."

Cooperation in a public enterprise economy is promoted by campaigns and official declarations. These campaigns and declarations appeal to people's emotions and sense of community to encourage them to produce more for the good of the society. People are persuaded to believe that in producing more for the common good, as defined by political leaders, everyone will be better off. This supports the belief, arising from the value of egalitarianism, that each person should be the economic equal of every other person.

❸ Incentives.
Non-material incentives, like appeals to duty and responsibility for the common good, are important examples of group incentives in a public enterprise economy. Group incentives are given out in the form of special pins, prizes, medals, and awards by top government officials. Their function is to promote the

Features of Public Enterprise

1. Centrally planned economy
2. Cooperation
3. Non-material and group incentives
4. Public ownership of property
5. High economic growth, equitable distribution of income and wealth, stability, and economic development

identification of the individual with the group and to instil a spirit of cooperation among individuals. Self-interest and profit, which may motivate people in a private enterprise economy, are considered to be harmful because they promote conflict and the exploitation of people by others.

However, material incentives like money and goods, which are commonly used to motivate people in a private enterprise economy, are also used in a public enterprise economy to reward people, above and beyond their wages, for their ability and performance. However, these incentives are generally given out to people who have performed in an exemplary way on behalf of society.

4 **Property Ownership.** In a public enterprise economy, public ownership is the dominant form of property ownership. Under public ownership, all rights of ownership belong to the government or state. Public ownership and control of the factors of production are necessary for central planning, cooperation, and group incentives to function effectively.

To ensure that producers supply all goods and services dictated in the plan, the state must possess all rights of ownership. Through its ownership and control of the factors of production, the state can use these resources to fulfil the objectives of the plan. Public ownership also enables the state to use resources to expand production, or in activities deemed socially beneficial, such as social welfare, health care, education, and national defence. Public ownership also ensures that producers follow the plan, because producers cannot dispose of assets without official permission.

Public ownership and control of resources are important for promoting cooperation and using group incentives. In owning and controlling most factors of production, the state can compel people to cooperate with each other by denying goods and services to those who are uncooperative. Competition among people is restricted because the state owns most of society's resources and prevents people from using property for their own purposes.

Public ownership prevents self-interest and personal profit because people do not have the right to use property to earn income, either by selling or renting it to other people.

All of this explains why most natural resources, factories, equipment, and other goods in a public enterprise economy are owned and controlled by the state. An economy based on public enterprise is generally an economic system in which collective interests are more important than the interests of the individual. In order for collective interests to be satisfied, the state must control most property rights.

5 **Policies and Goals.** By instilling in people the values of egalitarianism, the importance of cooperation, group solidarity, and public (collective) property, the public enterprise economy promotes collectivism—the importance of the group. In so doing, the public enterprise economy aims to pursue economic goals such as high economic growth, equitable distribution of income and wealth, stability, and economic development. The underlying assumption of these economic goals is the belief that all individuals should work for the public good.

In the 1950s and 1960s, the principles of public enterprise were widely adopted outside the Soviet Union as an alternative model of economic development. In China, Vietnam, and Eastern Europe, Communist governments developed public enterprise economies. As many countries in Asia and Africa received their independence from colonial rule, they accepted central planning, cooperation, group incentives, and public ownership and control of the factors of production as measures to promote rapid industrialization and raise people's living standards. In Latin America and Western Europe, national plans and public ownership of some factors of production were used to increase economic growth, stabilize the economy, and promote more equitable distribution of income and wealth.

Critique of Public Enterprise

Some important advantages of a public enterprise economy are a more equitable distribution of income and wealth, little unemployment, economic stability, and a high rate of investment in production.

In a public enterprise economy there is an attempt to ensure that all individuals have the same opportunities to work and acquire goods and services for personal consumption. Individuals have the right to work and do not suffer from unemployment. This makes a public enterprise economy more stable than a private enterprise economy. This stability is further enhanced by a high rate of investment in the production of goods. A public enterprise economy is committed to continual annual increases in the production of basic goods and services so that no one will suffer from want. Production of goods and services is planned to meet social needs so that all individuals are provided with the basic necessities of life.

However, a public enterprise economy has several important disadvantages. There is little technological change, production may be inefficient, productivity low, and waste widespread.

Because producers are required to meet production quotas, they are not encouraged to stop production and switch to producing new kinds of goods to satisfy consumer demand. Production quotas also discourage producers from introducing modern equipment and new production methods. The time required for installation and retooling means that producers might fail to meet their quotas and be penalized for this failure. Consequently, producers may maintain existing production methods, which over time become obsolete and inefficient. This affects productivity and product quality. The planned economy becomes unresponsive to changing economic conditions. This leads to widespread waste of scarce resources, which would not occur if the economy were more flexible and responsive to needs for efficient production. More importantly, because workers receive fixed wages and are rewarded only for meeting production quotas, they lack motivation and incentive to be careful in their work. Low worker productivity contributes to the problem of "hidden unemployment" or "underemployment" of people.

Since the plan drives the public enterprise economy, consumer desires are considered to be less important. Consequently, consumers are not offered a wide selection of goods and services. This leads to the emergence of black markets or a "second economy" to provide consumers with goods and services they want.

Advantages and Disadvantages of a Public Enterprise (Command) Economy

Advantages
1. Income and wealth are more evenly distributed.
2. There is little unemployment.
3. The economy experiences few booms and busts.
4. Profits are used for expanding production.
5. Production of goods and services is planned to meet society's needs.
6. Consumers receive basic necessities of life.

Disadvantages
1. Technological change and innovation are discouraged by the need to meet production quotas.
2. Because of lack of incentives, low-quality goods are often produced.
3. Because of planning, the economy is inflexible and slow to respond to economic changes.
4. Inefficiency and widespread waste of scarce resources occur in production.
5. Incomes and wealth are controlled by the state.
6. Consumers are not offered a wide selection of goods and services, which leads to the emergence of black markets or a "second economy."

ECONOMIC SYSTEMS IN PRACTICE

Advance Organizer

Beginning in the 1930s, but most dramatically since 1945, many societies have modified their economic systems to achieve various additional economic goals because of changing circumstances. The result of these actions has been the creation of mixed economies. In recent years, some societies have abandoned one type of economic system and are adopting another.

Key Concepts/Vocabulary

mixed economy	social democracy
New Deal	social welfare
Keynesian economics	welfare capitalism
inflation	stagflation
fiscal policy	neoconservatism
monetary policy	supply-side economics
business cycle	Thatcherism
depression	Reaganomics
recession	market socialism
monetarism	transitional economy
demand-side economics	

Historical Overview

Between 1945 and 1980, governments of countries with economic systems based on private enterprise, like France, Germany, Great Britain, the Netherlands, and Sweden, as well as Canada and the United States, introduced policies to implement some features of public enterprise, some economic control, and some emphasis on the collective good, for the purposes of achieving a more equitable distribution of income and wealth. Attempts have also been made to reduce unemployment and the negative effects of booms and busts in the economy. In the 1970s and 1980s, public enterprise economies such as China, the Soviet Union, Hungary, and Poland introduced policies to encourage more private enterprise, economic freedom, and individualism to improve productivity, end shortages, and raise living standards.

Since 1990, the governments of Germany, Great Britain, Sweden, Canada, and the United States, among others, have retreated from their previous level of involvement in the economy and are placing renewed emphasis on economic freedom and individualism. This has been accomplished by reducing government regulation, public ownership of business, and spending on social programs. In China, policies emphasizing private enterprise have brought rapid economic growth and rising living standards. In Hungary, Poland, and the newly independent states of the former Soviet Union, a radical transformation of the public

This diagram is intended only to illustrate general changes in economic systems since 1945.

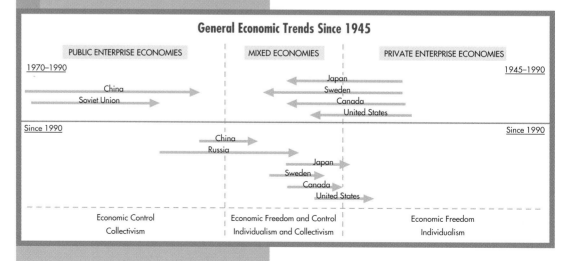

General Economic Trends Since 1945

enterprise economy into one based on private enterprise has created transitional economies.

From Private Enterprise to Mixed Economy

The origins of government intervention into the private enterprise economy after 1945 lie in the years of the Great Depression and the writings of the British economist John Maynard Keynes. The Great Depression dramatically altered people's attitudes about the role of government in the economy. Keynes's belief that a private enterprise economy may not adjust itself to economic crises without government intervention revolutionized economic theory and its application to the real world.

The Great Depression

For a period of ten years (1929–1939) the world economy experienced unstable economic growth, widespread unemployment, mass poverty, and great disparities in income and wealth. Before 1930, whenever the economy experienced periods of declining production and rising unemployment, the economic policy of the day was to keep government intervention in the economy as small as possible and allow the economy to correct itself. The charts below show that during the Great Depression the economy did not self-correct after the October 1929 stock market crash. Industrial production in Germany, Great Britain, and Sweden did not exceed 1929 levels until 1936. Production in the United States and Canada did not exceed 1929 levels until 1937. Unemployment remained stubbornly high in all countries at the end of 1938, except for Germany, with its program of rapid military rearmament.

New Deal (1933–1939). The first prominent attempt by government to lessen the effects of the Great Depression and provide relief, economic recovery, and reform was the New Deal, launched in March 1933 by newly-elected US President Franklin D. Roosevelt. The specific objectives of the New Deal were to raise personal incomes, boost private consumption and investment, and provide work for millions of unemployed in order to bring about economic recovery. To achieve these objectives, the US federal government raised spending sharply, introduced controls on the banking system, provided subsidies for agriculture, and enacted social reform measures such as unemployment insurance, old-age security, old-age pensions, and welfare, aimed at reducing poverty. These

> The evolution of economic systems based on private enterprise to a mixed economy occurred largely after 1945. The inspiration for the growth of government in the economy came from the writings of John Maynard Keynes and his critique of classical economic theory.

Great Depression in Selected Countries (1929–1938)

Industrial Production (1929=100)

	1929	1930	1931	1932	1933	1934	1935	1936	1937	1938
United States	100.0	81.9	67.3	51.8	61.8	67.3	77.6	94.6	102.8	79.1
Canada	100.0	90.7	78.8	66.7	66.7	78.5	86.7	94.8	107.4	99.5
Germany	100.0	86.6	72.5	59.8	67.7	86.8	99.5	108.7	117.7	127.3
Great Britain	100.0	91.0	82.2	82.2	88.0	99.9	107.6	118.7	127.4	117.3
Sweden	100.0	102.2	98.3	93.2	97.3	116.5	128.4	138.0	151.7	154.0

Unemployment (% of labour force)

	1929	1930	1931	1932	1933	1934	1935	1936	1937	1938
United States	8.2	14.5	19.1	23.8	24.3	20.9	18.5	13.3	10.5	16.8
Canada	5.7	11.1	16.8	22.0	22.3	18.2	15.4	13.2	10.8	13.0
Germany	9.9	16.1	23.7	30.1	25.8	14.5	11.6	8.1	4.5	3.7
Great Britain	8.2	11.8	16.7	17.6	16.4	13.9	13.1	11.2	9.4	10.5
Sweden	10.7	12.2	17.2	22.8	23.7	18.9	16.1	13.6	11.6	14.7

Statistical Yearbook of the League of Nations

measures did not end the Great Depression in the United States, but they did place the economy on a better financial foundation, provide some relief, and encourage better use of the country's natural resources.

Keynesian Economics

Keynesian economics argues that government spending can be used to stabilize the economy.

Popperfoto/Archive Photos

John Maynard Keynes (1883–1946)
British economist John Maynard Keynes published *The General Theory of Employment, Interest and Money* in 1936. His book represented an important turning point in the discipline of economics. Keynes began with a strong criticism of the basic assumptions of classical economic theory and *laissez-faire* policies that developed from it:

I have called this book the General Theory of Employment, Interest, and Money, placing the emphasis on the prefix general. The object of such a title is to contrast the character of my arguments and conclusions with those of the classical theory of the subject . . . which dominates the economic thought . . . of the governing and academic classes of this generation, as it has for a hundred years past. . . . Moreover, the characteristics of . . . classical theory happen not to be those of the economic society in which we actually live, with [the] result that its teaching is misleading and disastrous if we attempt to apply it to the facts of experience.

Classical Economic Theory. Classical economists argued that a private enterprise economy is characterized by the following assumptions:

- People produce only to exchange their products for other goods they need and want. Production thus creates its own demand. Economic crises such as gluts and overproduction are temporary and do not affect the demand for all other goods. Business cycles, when they arise, are brief in duration and mild in severity.
- Perfect competition characterizes the economy. Prices and wages react immediately to changes in supply and demand.
- Full employment is the normal state of the economy. All individuals who want to work are able to find employment and receive a wage that reflects their productivity. Due to competition in labour markets, if unemployment occurs, wages fall to such an extent that unemployed labour is rehired at the lower wage.
- All savings of the population are always invested by businesses to increase production. The cost of borrowing for businesses is lower than the expected rate of return on investment in increased production.
- Money has no real effect on production and distribution of goods and services in the economy; it is just a medium of exchange.

To Keynes, the preceding assumptions more appropriately described a largely rural agricultural economy, in which small shopkeepers, farmers, and skilled artisans determined the production and distribution of goods and services. In such an economy, producers supplied goods and services largely for local consumption. Few producers exported their goods to countries abroad.

By 1930, this type of economy had given way to an urban industrial economy in which large-scale factories, big banks, trade unions, and extensive transportation networks dominated the production and distribution of goods and services. Producers not only supplied goods and services for domestic consumption, but also exported a large share of their production to other countries.

Critique of Classical Economic Theory.
Keynes criticized classical economic theory because it failed to recognize certain problems. His critique was based on the following arguments:

- It is not the case that everything that is produced will be in demand. Effective demand (the actual amounts consumers plan to spend and businesses plan to spend and invest) determines the level of production. Should economic crises cause consumer and business spending to decline, incomes will fall and lead to further decreases in demand and in incomes. As a result, the economy may not quickly self-adjust.
- Prices and wage rates do not adjust immediately to changes in supply and demand.
- Full employment may be a special case that is rarely achieved. The general case may be one in which the economy operates at less than full employment. Because wages do not adjust quickly to economic conditions, businesses may be discouraged from employing all those who want to work.
- Savings are not always invested by businesses to increase production. Businesses may choose not to borrow money at low rates of interest because the expected rate of return on new investment may be lower than the cost of borrowing.
- When people lose confidence in the economy they tend to spend less, hence demand for goods and services drops. This leads to declines in the production of goods and services.

Effective Demand. The centrepiece of Keynes's theory is the concept of effective demand—total planned spending on consumption and investment (see chart). Consumer spending, Keynes argued, moves up or down as people's incomes rise and fall. This relationship between consumption and income is defined by how much income households spend on goods and services. Business investment goes up and down depending on whether interest rates go up or down, and also on expected returns on new investments. If businesses and consumers believe that the economy is improving, they may increase their spending, raising effective demand (total planned spending by consumers and businesses) and, in turn, total output and employment. However, Keynes believed, increases in spending by consumers and businesses may not occur in the short run because of feelings of pessimism and fear of future crises. He argued that the government can stimulate effective demand by increasing its purchases of goods and services, thereby expressing confidence in the economy.

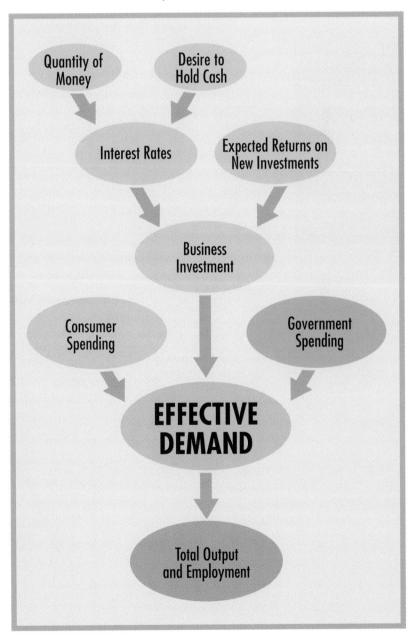

Adapted from Daniel R. Fusfeld: *The Age of the Economist*, p. 120.

Fiscal and Monetary Policies. Stimulating effective demand through government purchases of goods and services was not the only means for the government to intervene in the economy. Keynes believed that the government should also actively attempt to reduce inequities in the distribution of wealth and income. In the final chapter of his book, Keynes identified the main faults of a private enterprise economy:

The outstanding faults of the economic society in which we live are its failure to provide for full employment and its arbitrary and inequitable distribution of wealth and income.

Keynes argued that the government required new policies to deal with the problems of unemployment and inequitable distribution of income. One way was to raise or lower levels of taxation and government spending. Another was to control the amount of money available for business investment and consumer spending. Together these would help to maintain economic stability and promote economic growth. Keynes believed that economic activity could be managed by government in the interest of society as a whole, while leaving the economy to respond freely to the decisions of individual consumers and producers. In so doing, individual freedom and social order would be preserved and prosperity would be available for all.

Fiscal policy has to do with the effects of government spending and taxation on the economy. The main features of fiscal policy are changes in government spending on goods and services and changes in tax rates on incomes and profits. According to Keynes, through these measures government could influence total spending on goods and services in the economy. These measures could be

useful in moderating economic fluctuations that arise because of the business cycle.

For example, when economic conditions are difficult, consumers and businesses tend to be pessimistic about the economy and reduce their spending. By increasing its spending on goods and services and reducing taxes on incomes and profits, the government would stimulate demand for goods and services to ensure that total output in the economy would not fall too sharply and unemployment not rise too high. These actions are used to "prime the (economic) pump." A typical example of this is increased government spending on public works like buildings, bridges, and roads. When a government does this, it would most likely have a budget deficit, spending more than it receives in taxes.

When economic conditions appear more favourable, encouraging consumers and businesses to be optimistic about the economy and increase their spending, the government should reduce its spending on goods and services, and increase taxes on incomes and profits. These actions would prevent total output in the economy from rising too quickly and cause price increases or inflation. In this situation, the

> Economists define a recession as a mild decline in production and employment that is expected to last for a short period of time.

> Depressions are defined by economists as sharp declines in production and employment.

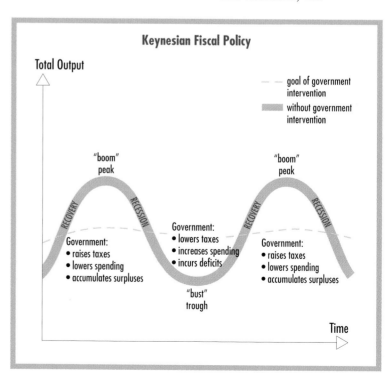

Keynesian Fiscal Policy

Total Output

- - - goal of government intervention

▬▬ without government intervention

"boom" peak

"boom" peak

RECOVERY RECESSION RECOVERY RECESSION

Government:
• raises taxes
• lowers spending
• accumulates surpluses

Government:
• lowers taxes
• increases spending
• incurs deficits

Government:
• raises taxes
• lowers spending
• accumulates surpluses

"bust" trough

Time

government would have a budget surplus that can be used to reduce government debt incurred during times of economic difficulty.

The overall objective of Keynes's fiscal policy was to moderate the variability of total economic output in order to maintain economic stability. In other words, if the economy falters, governments should implement policies to stimulate it and if the economy grows too rapidly, governments should implement policies to slow its advance. Such policies are said to run counter to the economic trend or business cycle and are called countercyclical (see chart on previous page).

Monetary policy is concerned with measures to control the supply of money and credit in the economy. Primary responsibility for the formulation of monetary policy is assigned to the central bank, which in Canada is the Bank of Canada, founded in 1935. Keynes argued that in some situations monetary policy is less effective than fiscal policy. When the economy is in a depression or recession, changes in money supply and interest rates may not lead to increases in output. In a recession and in a depression, he noted, businesses generally do not want to invest because returns on new investments are low. Interest rates may fall to very low rates, but this may not encourage businesses to borrow money for investment if the interest rate charged on the loan is higher than what businesses think will be the return on the new investment. Keynes also noted that in times of recession and depression, people want to hold cash, out of fear of unemployment and possible bank collapses. The main roles of the Keynesian monetary policy are to regulate the financial system to prevent bank collapses and to help governments finance their budget deficits without too much disruption to the overall economy.

Monetarism. In the 1960s and 1970s, Keynesian monetary policy came under sharp attack by Milton Friedman and a number of other economists, who argued that growing government deficits were increasing the demand for money, as

governments borrowed to cover their deficits. This government action did not lead to an increase in production of goods and services. Instead, it increased demand for goods and services because people had more money to spend. This resulted from government spending on social programs. The increased demand led to rapidly rising prices. Friedman and others called for a policy of monetarism. Monetarism is when the central bank actively adjusts money supply and interest rates to stabilize the amount of money available to finance purchases of goods and services, and the ability of the economy to produce these goods and services.

Under a monetarist policy, when consumers and businesses are pessimistic about the economy and plan to reduce their spending and borrowing, the central bank increases the money supply, thereby lowering interest rates. These lower interest rates encourage consumers to borrow and spend money on goods and services. It also makes it easier for businesses to borrow money to expand their production and purchase more goods and services. This borrowing for purchases and business expansion has the effect of increasing overall production. When consumers and businesses are optimistic about the economy and plan to increase their spending and borrowing (which increases the danger of overexpansion of production and a rise in prices or inflation) the central bank decreases the money supply and raises interest rates. The higher interest rates discourage consumers and businesses from borrowing money to spend on goods and services. This leads to less spending, less demand for goods and services, and less inflationary pressure on the prices of goods and services. The overall objective of a monetarist policy is to keep inflation low. Monetarists rely on competition in the marketplace to maintain economic growth and stability.

Monetarism is the belief that the control of the money supply is the most important tool for administering economic policy and preventing inflation.

Government Intervention

After 1946, Keynes's ideas were further refined and developed into a major body of economic thought known as Keynesian economics, also known as "demand-side economics." Keynesian economics became the rationale for the economic policies of next few decades of the 20th century in Western Europe and North America. There it led to the further development or creation of mixed economies. Most mixed economies are based on either social democracy or welfare capitalism.

Social Democracy. Keynes's ideas about the economic role of government were readily accepted in Western Europe at the end of World War II. One factor was the existence of a large social democratic movement in Western Europe. This movement had emerged in the 1890s and was dedicated to the belief that social and economic change should be accomplished through peaceful and democratic means. The movement accepted the importance of private enterprise, and worked toward creating greater social equality and a fairer distribution of income and wealth by nationalizing selected industries and establishing a social welfare system financed by progressive income taxes. Social democrats supported the idea that government should manage the economy in the interests of all. Keynes provided a justification for their views and a foundation on which to build. In 1945, social democratic policies were implemented in Great Britain by the newly elected Labour Party and in Sweden by the Social Democratic government.

Another factor encouraging greater government intervention in the economy was the fear of a new postwar depression, similar to the Great Depression. Many people feared that radical political movements such as communism would benefit from economic instability, as had the fascists in Italy and Germany in the 1920s and early 1930s. By developing programs that would increase economic stability, address social inequity, and redistribute wealth, governments hoped to preserve social and political stability. The result was the formation of the social welfare economy, which retained many features of a private enterprise economy.

Decisions about production and distribution were left mainly to individuals, with the government providing some planning through its fiscal and monetary policies, strategic forecasts of the economy, and its regulation of banking, transportation, utilities, and communications. Competition was encouraged by the government as a motivating factor to produce high quality goods and services at the lowest price, while the government provided some social services. Governments encouraged cooperation between business and labour organizations, with a view to encouraging greater social harmony. Though profit remained the main incentive for the production of goods and services, social programs were developed and paid for through progressive income taxes, which generally required people whose incomes were higher to pay higher taxes. The purpose of progressive income taxes is to promote greater income equality. Public ownership was confined mainly to natural resources, transportation, utilities, and some key industries such as chemicals, steel, and aircraft making. Chapter 6 discusses further aspects of social democracy as they developed in Sweden.

Welfare Capitalism. In North America, Keynes's ideas about the role of government in the economy led to the creation of a mixed economy, termed welfare capitalism. Keynesian policies were accepted as a means of reforming private enterprise so that it could provide opportunities for people to have a better economic life. In the 1930s, Canada and the United States experienced mass unemployment that did not disappear until the beginning of World War II. By 1935 in Canada, the Conservative government of R.B. Bennett established some basic relief programs to reduce the effects of the Depression. During World War II, Canada's social democratic movement, which favoured extensive social welfare legislation, grew rapidly. The Cooperative Commonwealth Federation

(CCF) became the official opposition in Ontario in 1943 and the government in Saskatchewan in 1944. The CCF convinced the federal Liberal government of the importance of government participation in the economy. In the United States, the popularity of the New Deal in the 1930s persuaded the governing Democrats to continue their policy of active government intervention.

After 1945, both countries moved toward economies in which a welfare system aided the poor, the sick, the disabled, the disadvantaged, and the aged, while still relying largely on private enterprise. In the United States, additional programs such as affirmative action were later instituted to correct serious social and racial inequities. The purpose of affirmative action programs was to allow minorities and women equal access to opportunities in employment and business. In Canada, an extensive system of social programs, including health care, welfare, old-age security, and income support, was developed based on the principles of universal and equal access.

Through spending and taxation policies, Canadian and American governments attempted to stabilize economic growth by encouraging high rates of investment and production in the private sector. In the United States, government spending on military armaments promoted the development of a large military-industrial complex, employing millions of citizens in production, distribution, research, and design. In Canada, the government supported private industry through myriad regional development programs, subsidies, grants, and tax incentives.

Government involvement in the economy appeared also in the form of regulation of private business, including competition or anti-trust legislation to prevent the formation of monopolies and cartels, end unfair business practices, and improve working conditions. In the 1970s, many of these regulations centred on protecting the environment, consumer rights, and pensions.

Public ownership was confined to sectors of the economy where private businesses were reluctant to invest because of the likelihood of low profits. Public ownership in Canada has been more extensive than in the United States, and at one point the Canadian government was heavily involved in natural resources, transportation, communications, utilities, broadcasting, aircraft making, and petrochemicals. Further aspects of welfare capitalism as it has been practised in Canada and the United States will be discussed in Chapters 4 and 5 respectively.

Whether the economic system of a country traces its origins to social democracy or welfare capitalism, the differences between them today are largely a matter of degree. In most countries today, governments play an important role in managing the economy and provide a range of social welfare programs, some more universal and general than others.

Results of Keynesian Policies. From 1945 to the early 1970s, economic policies based on Keynesian economics were highly successful. The much feared postwar economic depression never materialized. Instead, North America, Western Europe, and Japan entered a period of unprecedented economic prosperity. Personal incomes grew rapidly, while unemployment and inflation remained relatively low. When the economy did enter a period of weak growth and rising unemployment, government spending on goods and services was increased to lessen the effects on the business cycle and to hasten economic recovery. The introduction of various social programs, subsidies, and income supports for the poor, and progressive taxes on high income earners helped to narrow the difference between low and high income groups. These economic successes quickly disappeared after oil prices increased dramatically in 1973 and a worldwide recession occurred in 1974–1976.

Critique of Government Intervention

The huge increase in oil prices worldwide in the 1970s affected all goods produced from petroleum, ranging from gasoline to fertilizer to eyeglass frames. As prices rose sharply, consumption, and thus production, dropped, creating the twin problems of inflation and unemployment, which became known as stagflation. This combination of economic stagnation and inflation proved difficult to solve by applying Keynesian methods like increased government spending and deficit financing.

The inability of Keynesian methods to resolve the problem of stagflation did not lie in Keynes's basic idea that government fiscal policy can counteract the effects of the business cycle on production and employment. On the contrary, it was politicians' desire to continue maintaining high government spending to meet the demands of voters for more government services that contradicted the principle of fiscally responsible government postulated by Keynes. During periods of prosperity, according to Keynes, government should increase taxes and reduce spending to generate surpluses in its budget. These surpluses would act to dampen down inflation and be used to pay for debts previously incurred when the economy was in a recession, or for higher government spending during future recessions. In the long run, the deficits and surpluses should cancel each other, and government debt should not rise to destabilize the economy and impair its continued growth. Keynes's fiscal advice was ignored, as governments ran deficits during periods of both prosperity and recession, amassing huge public debts in the process. By the late 1970s, mounting public debt and budget deficits were creating inflation, low economic growth, and higher unemployment.

In this climate of economic difficulty, a new belief about government intervention called neoconservatism emerged. Practitioners of this belief rejected Keynesian economic principles in favour of classical economic ideas about the need for government to avoid undue interference in the economy. Neoconservatives or "supply-siders" believed that government spending on social welfare programs, taxation, regulation of private businesses, public ownership, public sector deficits, and government fiscal policy were restricting the economy's productive capacity to meet demand. They argued that the large size of government was destabilizing the economy and preventing optimal levels of production from being reached.

The basic outlines of the neoconservative argument are summarized in the chart on the next page. Generally speaking, supporters of supply-side economics believe in reductions in all kinds of taxation. This leaves more money in the hands of business to invest in increased production and more money in the hands of consumers to purchase more goods and services. This, combined with privatization of state-owned companies and reduction in social spending, results in a more productive economy, a smaller, less intrusive government, a more self-reliant population, and greater freedom for individuals to make decisions.

"DON'T WORRY, WE'LL FIND A WAY TO PAY OFF THAT BUDGET DEFICIT SOMEHOW!"

© Harley Schwadron

Fiscal Policy

1. Creates economic instability by distorting the operation of supply and demand
2. Promotes high levels of spending on social programs
3. Leads to high levels of taxation
4. Encourages politicians to run budget deficits

Public Sector Deficits

1. Contribute to a rising tax burden
2. Reduce private investment through high interest rates

High Social Spending

1. Stifles individual incentive to find work
2. Promotes dependency on government handouts
3. Discourages individual creativity and personal betterment
4. Encourages government interference in personal lives

High Taxes

1. Stifle individual incentive to earn higher incomes
2. Discourage investment by reducing profits and returns on new investments
3. Lower people's savings by reducing disposable incomes
4. Distort the operation of supply and demand
5. Raise the prices of goods and services to consumers

Excessive Regulation

1. Raises production costs
2. Discourages the establishment of new businesses
3. Promotes the formation of monopolies
4. Reduces competition among producers

Public Ownership

1. Creates unfair competition with private businesses
2. Leads to waste of scarce resources and inefficiencies
3. Offers little variety of goods and services to consumers.

Two Schools of Neoconservatism

Two schools of neoconservative thought emerged in the 1980s—"Thatcherism" in Great Britain and "Reaganomics" in the United States.

Canapress

Thatcherism. The Conservative government of Prime Minister Margaret Thatcher (1979–1990) in Great Britain adopted new beliefs about the role of government in the economy. Labelled "Thatcherism," the government's economic policies called for the deregulation of the economy, the sale of government-owned enterprises, and the decentralization of government departments to various regions of the country. On May 15, 1979, in her first speech as Prime Minister of Great Britain, Thatcher noted:

By reducing the burden of direct taxation and restricting the claims of the public sector on the nation's resources, [fiscal and monetary policies] *will start to restore incentives, encourage efficiency and create a climate in which commerce and industry can flourish. In this way,* [fiscal and monetary policies] *will lay a secure basis for investment, productivity and increased employment in all parts of the United Kingdom.*

The Conservative government initiated several programs aimed at reducing unemployment and budget deficits. Large government-owned companies such as British Telecom, British Steel, British Airways, British Coal, and electrical companies were privatized, as well as smaller, municipally-owned utilities and public transit systems. Millions of ordinary British citizens bought shares in these companies in hope of making profits. As well, thousands of government-owned houses were sold to their tenants. However, reductions in government spending on social programs left many people vulnerable and unable to adapt to these economic changes. Higher rather than lower unemployment resulted from these changes. However, the foundation for a stronger, more competitive British economy was laid, even as many people found life more difficult because of government cutbacks. In November 1990, Margaret Thatcher resigned as Prime Minister after high interest rates provoked a financial crisis.

focus on
CRITICAL THINKING

The Thatcher Record

(Excerpts) *The Economist*, November 24, 1990, p. 17. ©1990 The Economist Newspaper Group, Inc. Reprinted with permission. Further reproduction prohibited. www.economist.com

She was Britain's longest lasting prime minister this century; the wartime Churchill apart, its most successful one and its most admired; without rival, its most innovative and its most detested.

. . . [It was her] conviction that good housekeeping, the basis of a sound and prosperous economy, was best guaranteed by commercial self-interest.

The other side of that belief, in the long term one that mattered even more, was to get private enterprise flourishing where the state could not. And success must be won in the market: no more featherbeds, no cushions for those who fell. The state might give a helping hand at first—as in inner-city renewal or the promotion of small business—but then the market must take over. The state, at most, should help those who helped themselves, not those who failed, or did not try.

Money making, correspondingly, was to be rewarded, not penalised. Mrs. Thatcher was barely in office before the 83% top rate of tax on earned income (plus 15% on investment income) was cut to 60% and later to 40%. Capital gains tax was eased, as was the tax bite on small businesses.

The statistics of company formation, private share-ownership, productivity, and a thousand other measures will prompt different verdicts on her success. But the old presumption that Britain's mixed economy could only be endlessly ratcheted to the left has been demolished, just as she intended.

Courtesy Ronald Reagan Library

Reaganomics. United States President Ronald Reagan (1981–1989) set about reducing government spending and cutting taxes. Known as "supply-side economics" and also called "Reaganomics," these policies placed emphasis on production. By reducing personal income taxes, more money would be left in people's hands to enable them to consume more goods and services. Lower corporate and other business taxes would leave firms with more money to invest in greater production. Fewer social programs would encourage more people to seek work. With more people working, government revenues would increase even with lower tax rates. Similarly, as production and profits rose, corporate tax revenues would be increased even with lower tax rates. This, combined with reduced social spending, would lead to increased revenues for the government, lower budget deficits, and less public debt. As Reagan remarked in his inaugural speech on January 20, 1981:

Those who do work are denied a fair return for their labor by a tax system which penalizes successful achievement and keeps us from maintaining full productivity. . . . But great as our tax burden is, it has not kept pace with public spending. For decades we have piled deficit upon deficit, mortgaging our future and our children's future for the temporary convenience of the present. To continue this long trend is to guarantee tremendous social, cultural, political, and economic upheavals.

Under Reagan, taxes were lowered and government spending on social programs was cut or frozen. However, Reagan increased military spending, which led to mounting budget deficits and public debt. In the eight years of his presidency the public debt of the federal government increased from less than one trillion dollars in 1981 to almost three trillion dollars in 1989.

The New Quarterback

(Excerpts) *The Economist*, January 21, 1989, pp. 13–14. ©1989 The Economist Newspaper Group, Inc. Reprinted with permission. Further reproduction prohibited. www.economist.com

Every Japanese emperor gets his own era; it comes with the job. American presidents have to earn an era, and most don't. But who can doubt that the 1980s will be remembered as the Reagan era in America? They have been times of prosperity, peace and renewed respect for America and its values. Ronald Reagan is the first president since Eisenhower to complete two terms, and he has dominated the nation's life in a way Eisenhower never did. He leaves the White House more popular than when he entered it—the only president to do so alive since polling began. . . .

If restoring Americans' confidence in themselves and their leadership was Mr. Reagan's biggest success, it came about partly because of his biggest failure. Despite his early rhetoric about balanced budgets and personal thrift, he persuaded many Americans that their country could increase its spending by 3½% every year even though it was increasing its production by only 3% a year. True, for a while, perhaps for a long while; but not for ever. His genial charm aside, one secret of Mr. Reagan's popularity—the essence of his magic—was his penchant for the good news: he told few difficult truths, made few painful demands. As a result, he leaves Mr. Bush a society not just economically spendthrift but spiritually flaccid, less prepared than a superpower should be to make the sacrifices needed to preserve its prosperity and freedom.

Mr. Reagan is an ideologue, but he never let ideology stand in the way of popularity. Unlike another national leader who certainly has earned herself an era, Mr. Reagan can make no serious claim to an -ism as well, and these days gets an -omics [as in Reaganomics] only from his critics. Mrs. Margaret Thatcher entered office promising a revolution in British life and delivered one, however painfully. Mr. Reagan promised a revolution and delivered a dinner party. He did not reduce the federal government's share of national income (and he cannot blame Congress for that: the budgets he got were barely larger than the budgets he asked for). He did not increase private saving and investment; quite the reverse. Instead, he presided over a boom in public and private consumption financed by borrowing.

For short-term popularity, he was right: a dinner party, not a revolution, is what Americans really wanted. There is no serious constituency for smaller government in America, if that means smaller government-benefits for me. There is a large constituency for not paying the bill. The only economic sacrifice that Mr. Reagan's America endured was the recession of 1981–82, while inflation was being slashed. That slashing was the biggest economic achievement of the Reagan years, but it owed more to the determination and independence of Mr. Paul Volcker's Fed [Federal Reserve System] than to the administration.

Sacrifice for the sake of it is not good economics. Nor, though, is an endless budget deficit. Whether that deficit, and the foreign debt it has spawned, will cause a financial crunch is not something that can be predicted with certainty. But a wise president would not wish to find out. . . .

Ronald Reagan in his own words:

August 1980
. . . , I believe it is clear our federal government is overgrown and overweight. Indeed, it is time our government should go on a diet.

January 1981
In this present crisis, government is not the solution to our problem; government is *the problem.*

January 1985
Let us make it unconstitutional for the federal government to spend more than the federal government takes in.

February 1986
The federal government cannot provide prosperity or generate economic growth; it can only encourage private initiative, innovation, and entrepreneurial activity that produces economic opportunities.

January 11, 1989
The way I see it, there were two triumphs, two things that I'm proudest of. One is the economic recovery in which the people of America created—and filled—19 million new jobs. The other is the recovery of our morale: America is respected again in the world, and looked to for leadership.

Further details about Reagan's neoconservative economic policies will be discussed in Chapter 5.

From Public Enterprise to Mixed Economy

The first attempts to reform a public enterprise economy were made in the 1960s in Yugoslavia and Hungary. Both countries attempted to add several features of private enterprise to their planned economies; in the process, a mixed economy called market socialism emerged.

Market Socialism

Market socialism emerged largely as a result of economic reforms in central planning to redress shortages, low productivity, and widespread waste. Under market socialism, supply and demand were expected to determine the prices of goods such as consumer products and imported goods. Basic goods and services like food, rent, electricity, water, and fuel would, however, remain fixed by central planners. Central planners would make major decisions about production and distribution for key sectors of the economy like heavy industry, finance, transportation, and communication. Under market socialism, individuals would make most decisions about the production and distribution of consumer goods. The Communist Party would continue to determine policies and goals for the national economy.

Competition among producers of consumer goods and in industries the Communist Party did not consider important to national interests would be permitted. Producers would be allowed to keep profits earned from the sale of consumer goods and services. In the key sectors of the economy, profits would be reinvested into production, and performance would be rewarded on the basis of fulfilment of production quotas set by central planners. However, all means of production would continue to be owned and controlled by the government.

Canapress/Dave Buston

Perestroika (**Restructuring**). In April 1985, Mikhail Gorbachev, the new leader of the Soviet Union, announced an economic policy called *perestroika*, which was expected to improve the performance of the Soviet economy. The objectives of *perestroika* were to increase labour productivity, introduce better production methods, improve central planning, and increase production of goods and services for consumers. Initially, *perestroika* did not advocate major changes in how goods and services were produced and distributed. *Perestroika* was gradually expanded, with the issuing of new laws legalizing small private businesses and the sale of goods and services produced by private individuals. State-owned enterprises were given more independence to make decisions about production and distribution. Gorbachev's attempts to introduce market socialism into the Soviet economy are discussed in Chapter 10.

Canapress/Mark Avery

The Four Modernizations. In China, economic reform began in 1978: Deng Xiaoping, as China's new leader of the Communist Party, announced a new policy called "The Four Modernizations." The objectives of this policy were to revitalize the Chinese economy, open up the country to the outside world, and quadruple the size of the economy by the year 2000 by modernizing industry, agriculture, the military, and science and technology. After 1983, the policy became known as "building socialism with Chinese characteristics." The policy abolished all commremes and allowed peasants to farm the land as they wished. Peasants were permitted to invest the profits from the sale of their grain to the government in village enterprises and private businesses.

Price controls on agricultural products were gradually removed. In some cities, special economic zones were established to produce consumer goods for export abroad. Deng's policies are discussed in Chapter 11.

Advantages and Disadvantages of Market Socialism

Elements of a private enterprise economy introduced into a public enterprise economy create a mixed economy known as market socialism.

Advantages

1. **Reduced planning complexity.** Economies were becoming larger and more complicated; planning was more difficult because of the need to collect more information. Economic reforms aimed to reduce the workload on central planners, who were finding it increasingly difficult to plan for national needs, by giving people greater economic freedom to make their own decisions about production and distribution.

2. **Wider selection of goods.** Once private businesses were allowed to operate, they began to provide goods and services demanded by consumers. The result was higher production of goods, a wider assortment, and an end to shortages.

3. **More technological progress.** For many years central planning discouraged state-owned enterprises from using modern technology because of the need to fulfil production quotas. Economic reforms gave state-owned enterprises more independence to make decisions about investing in new equipment and adopting more efficient production methods.

4. **More balanced economy.** Central planning had promoted the expansion of heavy industry at the expense of light industry, and unbalanced the economy. Reforms allowing private businesses to produce consumer goods were intended to create an economy that was more balanced and oriented to the consumer.

Disadvantages

1. **Income inequality.** As economic reforms allowed the creation of private businesses, income inequality appeared. The more skilled and enterprising people left state-owned enterprises to go into private business where incomes were higher. This created shortages of skilled personnel in many state-owned enterprises. Also, economic reforms gave rise to a growing disparity of incomes between cities and villages. Private businesses in the cities and coastal regions were better situated to export their production abroad and to have foreign investors. In the villages, most private businesses faced higher production costs, shortages of capital, lower sales, and difficulties with local authorities.

2. **Inflation.** When economic reforms allowed prices to fluctuate according to demand and supply, it led to inflation. Prices of most goods and services had been controlled for many years and no longer reflected the actual cost of production. Once the controls were lifted, prices often rose dramatically to levels where demand and supply were in balance.

3. **Unemployment.** Under central planning, state-owned enterprises were encouraged to have large workforces. As state-owned enterprises received more freedom to make decisions about production, they began to change their production and hiring methods. Some state-owned enterprises reduced their workforces, while others stopped hiring new workers. Together, this led to the growth of unemployment, especially among young people.

Transitional Economies

Since 1991, with the collapse of communism and the Soviet Union, a new group of economic systems has appeared. The World Bank, an international financial organization, calls these economic systems transitional economies or economies in transition. A transitional economy is a public enterprise economy that is transforming itself into a private enterprise economy. The main features are undeveloped markets, weak competition, extremes of profit, and mass privatization. A transitional economy is unique because of the scale of transformation. A more detailed discussion of the process as it applies to Russia appears in Chapter 10.

Undeveloped Markets. Under central planning, markets for goods and services were determined by planners and the government. In the transitional economies of the countries of the former Soviet Union, markets are weak and unstable. Consumers and producers are unfamiliar with how a market works and how to establish markets for goods and services that never before existed under central planning. Producers now must learn to answer important economic questions such as what kinds of goods and services should they supply, how many goods and services should be supplied, and at what price these goods and services should be sold to consumers. Consumers now must learn to make spending decisions based on their income. Together, producers and consumers must learn that scarcity and making choices are important aspects of demand and supply.

Weak Competition. Under central planning, the production of goods in many industries was dominated by one or two large producers. Many of these large producers, especially in heavy industry, long relied on the government for subsidies and protection from competitors. In the transitional economies of the former Soviet Union, the idea of competition remains an unfamiliar concept to many producers, who produced goods for years according to production targets. Many newly formed private businesses are discovering that a small number of producers can easily influence prices by withholding goods and services from the market. Business laws and regulations to stop this practice are slow to be introduced by governments.

Extremes of Profit. Under central planning, the government ensured that incomes among occupations did not vary too widely. People were told that profit was the exploitation of one person by another, one person taking advantage of another. In the transitional economies, people are now learning how to sell things for a profit. For some people, selling goods is difficult and has generated little profit and low income; for others, selling goods has brought huge profits and high income. Some people discover that they can earn high profits through the sale of illegal goods and participation in criminal activities. Other people can earn immense profits through connections in the government and from the sale of newly privatized state property.

Mass Privatization. Under central planning, all means of production were owned or controlled by the government. In transitional economies, mass privatization of state property has been complicated by undeveloped markets, weak competition, little information, and capital shortages. The sell-off of state property also requires the development of an entire legal system, business laws, and privately-owned banks. Clear and enforceable laws on property rights are needed. Can private property be protected from theft? Can people trust the courts to protect their ownership of property?

Authorized by Galeria Autorska Andrzeja Mleczki. 31—018 Kraków. Ul. Św. Jana 14.

REVIEW

Summary

Economic systems exist to solve the basic economic problem of scarcity and to make decisions about what goods and services to produce, how to produce them, and how to distribute the goods and services among the people. The main decision makers in an economic system are consumers, producers, and government.

Economic systems are distinguished by how they solve the problem of scarcity and how people make economic decisions about production and distribution. Two broad types of economic systems exist: private enterprise and public enterprise. A private enterprise economy is characterized by markets, competition, profits, and private property. In a private enterprise economy, private individuals make most of the economic decisions about what, how, and for whom to produce.

A public enterprise economy, on the other hand, is characterized by central planning, cooperation, group incentives, and public property. In a public enterprise economy, the government answers most of the economic questions of what to produce, how much to produce, and what to distribute among the people. Consumers and private enterprises have little say in the decision making process.

Many economies combine features of both a private enterprise economy and a public enterprise economy. In a mixed economy, the basic economic questions are decided by consumers and producers, and to some extent by government, which regulates some aspects of production.

An economic system does not exist in isolation in the world. It interacts with the world around it and changes over time. Since 1980, many economies have changed substantially, especially in Eastern Europe, the former Soviet Union, Latin America, and Asia.

Economic Attitude Survey

1. The purpose of this questionnaire is to discover what economic values matter most to you. Read the following statements, then list the letters a) to r) in your notebook. Beside the letter for each statement you *agree* with, mark an (A). There are no right or wrong answers to these statements.

   a) No one should be allowed to possess great wealth when many in society have so little.

   b) The right to compete freely in business is essential for personal well-being and the common good of society.

   c) Every individual has a duty to help the poor, disabled, and disadvantaged in the interests of all society.

   d) Health care and education are better provided by government than by private organizations and individuals.

   e) Taxes on business profits are too high and should be reduced to create more employment and production of goods.

   f) All human beings have the same rights to employment, housing, and the basics of life.

   g) Government regulation of some business activities is necessary to eliminate pollution and protect consumers from unfair treatment.

   h) Cooperation with and concern for the group are the highest aims a person can hope to achieve.

   i) Public ownership of utilities and natural resources is to the benefit both of individuals and all of society.

   j) Private property provides the greatest amount of freedom for individual action.

   k) Every individual should pay his or her fair share of taxes so that society can help those less fortunate.

   l) Personal initiative, drive, and intelligence are essential to success and well-being.

   m) Private property is theft and should be abolished for the common good.

n) Government should introduce policies that promote more employment and reduce inequalities of all kinds.

o) Labour, business, and government have a responsibility to work together for the betterment, prosperity, and stability of society.

p) Privately owned businesses are more efficient and provide a greater variety of goods and services for consumers than government-owned ones.

q) Rapid economic growth and rising living standards can best be achieved through the use of government plans.

r) Education, skills, and intelligence matter more for a country's future prosperity than the natural resources it possesses.

2. In your notebook, draw a continuum similar to the following:

Public Enterprise Economy   Mixed Economy   Private Enterprise Economy

Statements a), c), f), h), m), and q) in the survey refer to a public enterprise economy. Statements b), e), j), l), p), and r) refer to a private enterprise economy. Statements d), g), i), k), n), and o) refer to a mixed economy. Place the letter of each statement with which you *agree* (A) in the appropriate place on the continuum. What conclusions can you make about your economic attitudes?

Role of Economic Systems

1. Describe the change in the role of government in the economic culture in the 20th century. Provide examples from your own knowledge to demonstrate these changes.

2. a) Do you think that the current trend of government involvement in the economy will continue or will the trend revert to what it was earlier in the 20th century?
b) Which trend do you favour? Why?

Choices Arising from Scarcity

1. Define the term scarcity as it applies to economics. Do you think that the issue of scarcity is the same for every country? Provide examples from your own knowledge.

2. Read page 77 and note the four economic questions. Prepare notes for a one-page essay where you take and defend a position on the following issue: To what extent do you think that individuals should be free to make all economic decisions? Be prepared to discuss or debate your position.

Features of an Economic System

1. 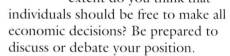 Explain the difference between centralized and decentralized decision making. Provide examples.

2. On a graph, plot the data in the table below. Label the y-axis "price" and the x-axis "quantity," as shown on the diagram on page 79.
a) When are demand and supply in equilibrium?
b) What generalizations can you make about demand and supply?

Price $	Quantity Demanded	Quantity Supplied
10	0	100
9	10	90
8	20	80
7	30	70
6	40	60
5	50	50
4	60	40
3	70	30
2	80	20
1	90	10
0	100	0

3. In economic terms, to what extent do you favour competition or cooperation? Are there situations when you think that your least favourite pattern might be best? Provide illustrative examples.

4. What do you understand to be the meaning of the terms monopoly and oligarchy?

5. To what extent are material incentives the most important type of incentive? Have there been times when non-material incentives were important to you? How important do you think non-material incentives are in society?

6. a) Explain the difference between private and public property rights.

b) How important are property rights in our society?

7. In what ways might each of the four economic goals affect you?

8. How would a person who believes in cooperation and a big role for government in the economy react to each of the newspaper headlines on page 83.

9. Review the cartoon on page 83.
a) What does the roller coaster represent?
b) In economic terms, what is about to happen in the cartoon?
c) Explain the significance of the caption.

Types of Economic Systems

1. a) Read the statements below. Choose which statement you think is correct, then write why you think it is correct and the others are incorrect.

A. John M. Keynes is the most important economist of the 20th century.

B. Economies in Eastern Europe will continue to be based on socialism.

C. All economic systems are increasingly based on the same economic thought.

D. The ideas of Adam Smith and Thomas Malthus are dominant in modern economics.

2. What conclusion can you draw about the evolution of economic thought from the diagram on page 84?

3. Describe the level of government involvement in the economy under the system of mercantilism.

4. What were the objections or criticisms that François Quesnay and the Physiocrats had about mercantilism?

5. Summarize in your notes the ideas of Adam Smith. Give examples of his ideas that we see today.

6. The ideas of other philosophers who contributed to the development of private enterprise are outlined on pages 88 and 89.

a) Create a chart and summarize in your own words the main ideas expressed by these philosophers. Include their views on what the role of the government should be in the economy.

b) From your chart, pick out three ideas with which you agree and three with which you disagree. In one or two lines explain the reasons for your choice.

c) In chart form identify what you think might be the advantages and disadvantages for you personally, and for society in general, of following an economic policy based on Social Darwinism?

7. In a private enterprise system, who provides the answers to the four basic economic questions?

8. a) Summarize the Features of Private Enterprise in chart form under the headings Decision Making Arrangements, Patterns of Interaction, Individual Incentives, Property Ownership, and Policies and Goals.

b) What does the concept of consumer sovereignty suggest about your importance to a private enterprise system?

c) How does competition benefit you as both a consumer and producer?

d) Why is profit important in a private enterprise system?

e) Could a private enterprise system operate without a system of private ownership?

f) What aspects of private enterprise ideology do you agree and disagree with? Be prepared to discuss or debate your ideas.

9. What do you think are the single most important advantage and most important disadvantage of private enterprise?

10. What is the central belief underlying public enterprise economies?

11. What was the main concern of the utopian socialists? In your view, how realistic were their goals?

12. a) Summarize in your own words the ideas of Karl Marx. Include his views on what the role of government in the economy should be.

b) Which social class created the proletariat? How is it that the interests of these two groups are opposed?

c) What were Marx's criticisms of capitalism?

d) With which ideas of Marx do you agree and disagree? Be prepared to discuss or debate your ideas.

13. Identify the strengths and weaknesses of Marx's Theory of Capitalist Development (page 96).

14. How does a public enterprise system answer the four basic economic questions?

15. a) Summarize in point form in a chart the Features of Public Enterprise under the headings Decision Making Arrangements, Patterns of Interaction, Group Incentives, Property Ownership, and Policies and Goals.

b) What features of public enterprise ideology do you agree and disagree with? Be prepared to discuss or debate your ideas.

16. Examine the chart on page 101. What do you think is the most important advantage and the most important disadvantage of public enterprise? Be prepared to discuss your views.

Economic Systems in Practice

1. Examine the chart and text on page 102.

a) How would you describe the general economic trend since 1945? Provide evidence from the information given to support your answer.

2. a) For what reasons did governments begin to intervene in the economy to a greater extent in the early 1930s? Why was this intervention believed to be necessary?

b) What other factors besides increased government intervention might account for the slight improvement in the economy after the mid-1930s shown on the diagram on page 103?

3. a) What were the objectives of the New Deal?

b) What methods were used by the government of Franklin Roosevelt to deal with the Great Depression in America?

c) Did these policies move the American economy towards emphasizing individual initiative or the collective good of society? Explain your answer.

4. In *The General Theory of Employment, Interest, and Money* (1936), John Maynard Keynes strongly attacked classical economic theory and suggested a new role for government in the economy.

a) Briefly summarize classical economic theory in your notes.
b) What were Keynes's criticisms of the classical theory?
c) Explain his concept of effective demand and what actions can be taken by government to increase effective demand when necessary.
d) Explain why his policies can be called demand-side economics.

5. a) What were Keynes's main criticisms of private enterprise economies?
b) What is fiscal policy? Explain the significance of the phrase "prime the pump" as part of your answer.
c) Examine the diagram on page 106. Describe Keynes's ideas of how government use of fiscal policy can reduce the peaks and troughs of the business cycle.
d) What advice would Keynes give to a government about how to finance its intervention in the economy and maintain a balanced budget in the long term?
e) What was the overall goal of Keynes's ideas on the use of fiscal policy?

6. In the 1970s, Keynesian economics came under attack from monetarists such as Milton Friedman.
a) What was the basis of their criticism?
b) What is the difference between monetary policy and fiscal policy?
c) Briefly explain the monetarist approach to dealing with economic problems.
d) Would Milton Friedman suggest more government intervention in the economy than John Maynard Keynes, or less? Explain your answer.

7. a) How is the life of the man sitting in the chair in the cartoon on page 110 about to change?
b) To what extent would someone who believes in free enterprise support the action about to be taken in the cartoon?

8. a) How did stagflation and government misuse of Keynesian economics result in massive debt?
b) Explain the neoconservative, or supply-side, economics approach to government intervention in the economy.
c) What criticisms do supply-siders have of the Keynesian, or demand-side, approach to government intervention in the economy?
d) According to supply-siders, should the government play a larger or smaller role in the economic life of the nation?

9. Read the Focus On Critical Thinking articles on pages 112–113.
a) How were the policies of Margaret Thatcher and Ronald Reagan similar and different?
b) What policy of Reagan's seemed to nullify any gains that might have been achieved by "Reaganomics" and, in fact, worsened the problem of government debt?
c) Explain the contradiction posed by "The New Quarterback" and the quotes from Ronald Reagan on the side of page 113?
d) From which perspective or ideological position do you think each of these articles is written? Explain your answer.

10. a) Would you favour Keynesian or supply-side economics, in theory, to achieve the goals of full employment and economic stability? Provide reasons for your choice.
b) What have been the benefits and drawbacks of both Keynesian and supply-side economics in practice?

11. What do you think is the most valid and least valid neoconservative criticism of government intervention? Provide evidence to support your view.

12. Choose what you think is the right answer to the question below, then write why you think it is correct and the others incorrect.

The statement "the business of government is not business" would **most likely** have been said by a person who believes that
A. the ideal economy should be a mix of public and private enterprise
B. private enterprise can provide all the services that society needs
C. government should plan the economy in the interests of society
D. government should reduce disparities in income

13. a) Briefly describe market socialism in general terms.

b) To what extent are *perestroika* and the Four Modernizations similar in their goals?

14. Examine the advantages and disadvantages of market socialism. What criticism would be made of market socialism by someone who is a Marxist?

15. If you were a factory worker living in a country with a transitional economy, how would your life be affected by the changes described?

Chapter Consolidation

1.   This chapter began with a Polish anecdote from the 1980s: "Under capitalism man exploits man; under socialism, the reverse is true."

a) What is the main point this humorous anecdote makes?
b) To what extent do you agree with the point being made?
c) How significant is the time period of the anecdote? What was happening in Poland and nearby countries during that decade that would influence the writer's view?

2. Explain the message in the cartoon on page 116. What segment of society does the man symbolize?

3. The early part of the 20th century was characterized by a trend towards more socialist, government interventionist, or communist ideologies. How would you characterize the closing of the 20th century? Which trend would you prefer to prevail in the 21st century?

4.   Based on what you have learned in this chapter, write a short essay in which you take and defend a position on the following issues:
a) To what extent should economic systems emphasize the collective good at the expense of individual interests?
b) Should the government intervene in the economic system to protect the interests of society?

Symbology

Global language uses visual symbols relating to abstractions such as ideologies. Symbols are used to convey information, express a message or viewpoint, or reveal an issue. What is the usual association made with each of the following?

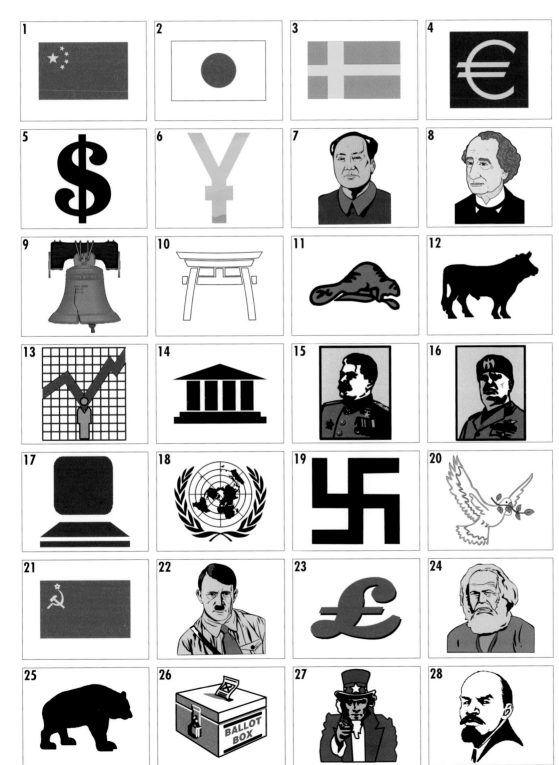

PART

II

POLITICAL AND ECONOMIC SYSTEMS IN PRACTICE

ADVANCE ORGANIZER

Political and economic systems continually adapt to changing circumstances in society and interact with each other. This interaction is often referred to as political economy. Chapters 1 to 3 develop a model for understanding political and economic systems which is applied in the following eight chapters to examine the political and economic systems of Canada, United States, Sweden, Japan, National Socialist Germany, Soviet Union, Russian Federation, and China.

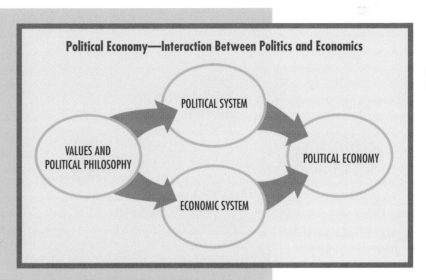

Political Economy—Interaction Between Politics and Economics

Chapter 4: Canada

A parliamentary democracy since 1867, Canada has experienced many political and economic changes in the 20th century. Two of the most significant were the development of a political system based on broad public participation and, since World War II, the growth of a mixed economy with considerable government intervention designed to reduce social and economic inequalities. Since the early 1980s, Canadians have become increasingly concerned about the growth in the power of government to intervene in their daily lives.

Chapter 5: United States

In the 20th century, the United States witnessed several far-reaching political and economic changes in its society. Most of the political changes in the country's presidential system of government resulted from popular demands and the recognition of people's needs and aspirations for greater participation in government and politics. During the 20th century, the American economic system evolved from one based on unrestricted personal freedom to one in which the government became a greater participant in ensuring high

economic growth, stability, and prosperity. In the last 20 years of the 20th century, the American people have actively debated the need for government to intervene in their daily lives, and the nature of its role.

Chapter 6: Sweden

During the 20th century, Sweden emerged as a parliamentary democracy based on social democratic principles of respect for human rights, broad public participation, and accountability of all public officials to the people. Its economic system was modified, giving a larger role for government in ensuring greater equality of income, economic stability, and high living standards. In the last 20 years of the 20th century, Swedish citizens have changed their view about the role of government in the economy and have opted for greater economic and political integration with the rest of Europe.

Chapter 7: Japan

During the 20th century, Japanese political and economic systems have experienced profound changes. Before World War II, the country's parliamentary system accorded significant power to the Emperor and the military. In 1947, American occupation authorities reorganized the country's political system on the principles of individualism, broad public participation, and accountability of the government to the people. Japan began to industrialize after 1868, and has developed into a global industrial power since World War II. Its economic system emerged as a model for other countries seeking to industrialize through the promotion of exports. In the last years of the 20th century, the country's political and economic systems have experienced difficulties adapting to rapidly changing circumstances at home and abroad.

Chapter 8: Nazi Germany

From 1933 to 1945, German politics and economics were heavily influenced by the ideology of National Socialism (fascism) developed by Adolf Hitler. Under Hitler, the political and economic systems were modified to satisfy national interests. A totalitarian regime was created based on one-party rule, control over all aspects of German society, and the subordination of the economy to national interests. The defeat of National Socialism in 1945 led to the division of Germany into two countries, democratic West Germany and communist East Germany. They were reunited in 1990, following the collapse of communism in East Germany and Eastern Europe.

Chapter 9: Soviet Union

From 1917 to 1985, Soviet politics and economics were based on the principles of communism developed by Vladimir Lenin and extended by Josef Stalin. A totalitarian regime was established that emphasized the undisputed rule of the Communist Party, controlled political participation, and created a centrally planned economy. Following Stalin's death, the political leadership attempted to make the Soviet system more flexible to meet the needs of a more educated, urban, and industrial society.

Chapter 10: Russian Federation

In 1985, Mikhail Gorbachev launched a series of social, political, and economic reforms to modernize the Soviet system. These reforms destabilized the Soviet Union and led to its collapse in 1991, after which 15 new states emerged, the largest being the Russian Federation. Today, the Russian Federation is attempting to develop a stable democratic system based on the rule of law, parliamentary procedure, and respect for individual freedoms. Its economic system is an example of a transition economy, shifting from one based on public enterprise to one based on private enterprise. These far-reaching changes are dramatically altering how Russians relate to one another and their neighbouring newly independent states.

Chapter 11: China

From 1949 to 1976, the political and economic system of China was based on the principles of communism developed by Mao Zedong. Following Zedong's death in 1976, Deng Xiaoping introduced economic reforms in a bid to rapidly develop the Chinese economy, while at the same time preserving the political authority of the Communist Party. These economic reforms are bringing fundamental changes to Chinese society and the country's political institutions. Since Deng's death in 1997, Chinese leaders have declared their intention to continue to reform the Chinese economy and society.

CHAPTER

4

CANADA

"What a government does with scarce resources shows what its values are."
—Paul Martin, Minister of Finance, budget speech, February 18, 1997

With the exception of a few small island nations in the Caribbean, Canada is the only major parliamentary democracy in the Western Hemisphere. The Canadian political system is built on the parliamentary principle of a government responsible to an elected legislature. Political parties are an integral part of Canadian parliamentary democracy and determine who will govern the country and who will become its head of government. As a result, Canada has developed its own social and political institutions, distinct from most other countries in the world.

Though the Canadian economy is closely integrated with the American economy, it has developed unique economic institutions. Governments have been willing to intervene directly in the economy to promote various social and economic goals. A comprehensive social welfare system funded by various contributions and taxes

provides workers and businesses with a degree of economic stability in an economy that remains highly dependent on world prices for natural resources and foreign trade.

In the 1990s, Canadian political and economic institutions underwent considerable change. Some of these changes were political responses to the growth of government and concerns about the high level of government debt.

Key Concepts/Vocabulary

constitutional
  monarchy
Governor-General
Prime Minister
cabinet
parliament
Senate
House of
  Commons
responsible
  government

party whip
backbencher
ministerial
  responsibility
sovereignty-
  association
sole proprietorship
partnership
corporation

Focus On Issues

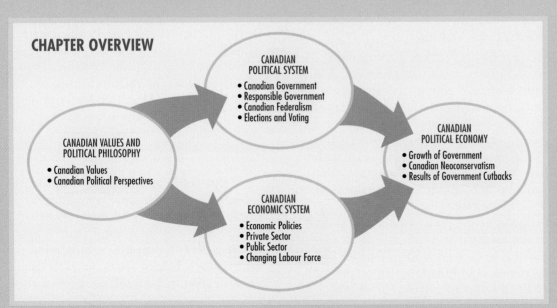

CHAPTER OVERVIEW

CANADIAN VALUES AND POLITICAL PHILOSOPHY
- Canadian Values
- Canadian Political Perspectives

CANADIAN POLITICAL SYSTEM
- Canadian Government
- Responsible Government
- Canadian Federalism
- Elections and Voting

CANADIAN ECONOMIC SYSTEM
- Economic Policies
- Private Sector
- Public Sector
- Changing Labour Force

CANADIAN POLITICAL ECONOMY
- Growth of Government
- Canadian Neoconservatism
- Results of Government Cutbacks

CANADIAN VALUES AND POLITICAL PHILOSOPHY

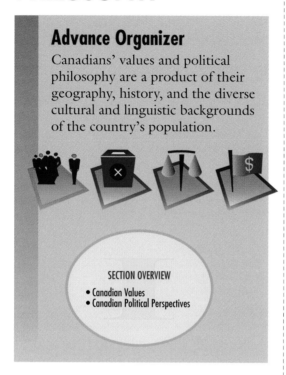

Advance Organizer

Canadians' values and political philosophy are a product of their geography, history, and the diverse cultural and linguistic backgrounds of the country's population.

SECTION OVERVIEW
- Canadian Values
- Canadian Political Perspectives

Canadian Values

Since the last half of the 18th century, a distinctive set of Canadian values has evolved as a result of geography, history, ethnic diversity, and linguistic differences. Values held by Canadians encourage individualism but they also promote a collective spirit among the people.

Sources of Values

Geographically, Canada is the world's second largest country. Extremes of climate, from long cold winters to short hot summers, have provided both challenges and opportunities for Canadians. Climate has also influenced human settlement. Over 90% of the total population resides within 250 km of the southern Canada–United States border. This geography has impressed upon Canadians the necessity of having strong ties with close neighbours, a sense of community that is often local or regional in outlook, and an attitude of cooperation and sharing with others—all essential values for survival in what is

sometimes a harsh environment. These conditions have also contributed to the development of a strong sense of individualism and a recognition that struggle is necessary to overcome difficult conditions.

Historically, human settlement of Canada began with the First Peoples many millennia ago. The first permanent European settlements were established at Port Royal in Nova Scotia in 1605 and at Québec City in 1608. These settlements relied on agriculture to a degree but largely on the fur trade with neighbouring Huron and Iroquois peoples. In later centuries, European settlements based on agriculture and the exploitation of natural resources were established. Settlement gradually spread to the far western and northern reaches of the country. In the 20th century, Canada became heavily urbanized and industrialized. The greatest concentration of population is found in central Canada.

Canadian society has been culturally and ethnically diverse since its earliest history. Before the arrival of Europeans, over 50 different nationalities lived in Canada. Groups ranged in size from a few thousand to tens of thousands. In 1605–1608, French settlements were established in Eastern Canada. By the end of the 17th century these settlements had grown and English settlements had appeared in Newfoundland. In the mid-18th century, British settlements were established in Nova Scotia, and later in New Brunswick and Ontario. In the 19th century, Canada welcomed thousands of emigrants from Britain. Except for its First Peoples, the country was largely a land of two cultures—British and French. In the 20th century, the arrival of several million Europeans, Asians, and Latin Americans dramatically altered the ethnic composition of the country and impressed on Canadians the need for tolerance and acceptance of all cultures.

From 1605 until the 1770s, Canada was largely a French-speaking country. After the American Revolution, about 40 000 British subjects, the United Empire Loyalists, fled to British North America from the new United States. In 1791, the British Parliament created the provinces of

Upper Canada (Ontario) and Lower Canada (Québec) to accommodate the cultural, linguistic, and political aspirations of these groups. Upper Canada adopted British institutions based on the English language, common law, and the British monarchy. Lower Canada was also granted British institutions but retained its distinctive institutions based on the French language, Roman law, and the Catholic faith. In 1867, Ontario, Québec, New Brunswick, and Nova Scotia agreed to form Canada as a self-governing federal state with a strong central government and recognition of the founding provinces' distinctive social, political, and economic institutions.

Core Values

Canadians' views about their society and the role of the individual in it are many and varied. In 1995, the Canadian Policy Research Network identified seven core values.[1]

Self-reliance. Most Canadians consider self-reliance to be an important value. Individual effort and responsibility for one's actions, as well as personal sacrifices made to avoid depending on or continuing to depend on government assistance, are generally valued by Canadians.

Compassion and collective responsibility. While Canadians strive to be self-reliant, they recognize that circumstances are not always favourable for individual effort. They believe that society has a collective responsibility to help the less fortunate—those who, through no fault of their own, are faced with various obstacles to personal achievement and may require some temporary government assistance in the form of a social security safety net.

Education. The importance of education is a deeply held value for most Canadians. Children are seen as the future of the country, and their education is the most important investment society can make, ensuring that every child realizes his or her full potential. Supporting families to achieve the realization of a child's potential is also valued.

Democracy. Canadians are deeply attached to the principles of democracy. They regard majority rule as an important aspect of democracy, in that the views of the majority should take precedence, but they also recognize that the views of minorities should be heard and differences settled peacefully and democratically. As well, Canadians believe in accountability from their politicians, public servants, and citizens.

Freedom and tolerance. Canadians value freedom of speech and choice. Most believe that multiculturalism enriches Canada and they support a society where people of different races and cultures can live and work together in harmony. Canadians perceive their country to be one that's highly tolerant of people from different ethnic or religious groups. Most agree that laws should promote tolerance and discourage racism.

Equality. Equality of opportunity and equality of treatment are deeply held values. Most Canadians believe that equality of opportunity can be achieved through education, ability, and experience. Canadians believe that most groups in society in most situations should be treated equally, but that groups in special situations deserve different treatment. There is strong support in most of the country for the political equality of provinces and regions and for the political equality of people.

Fiscal responsibility. Most Canadians want government to assist them in times of personal need, but they stress the importance of greater accountability and efficiency in government. They are concerned about the cost, abuse, and overuse of government services. They do not necessarily want less government, but more efficient government.

Canadian political culture reflects the country's values, beliefs, and attitudes.

[1]Suzanne Peters, *Exploring Canadian Values: Foundations for Well-Being.* CPRN Study No. F–01. Revised edition. Ottawa: Canadian Policy Research Networks Inc., 1995.

Canadian Political Perspectives

Diverse political views and perspectives are a distinguishing feature of Canadian political culture.

For most of the 20th century, Canadian politics at the national level was dominated by two political parties, the Liberal Party and the Progressive Conservative Party. The Liberal Party held power for most of the time. Except for brief periods in power, the Progressive Conservatives were the official opposition party. This political alignment was shattered in 1993, with the successful emergence of regional parties in Western Canada and Québec and the demise of the Progressive Conservative Party at the national level.

Canadian political views have shifted noticeably since 1945. Between 1945 and 1984, the country's major political parties agreed on the need for government to intervene in society and the economy to reduce social and economic inequities. The New Democratic Party was most insistent on an expanded role for government. Since 1984, the policies of the country's main parties have shifted toward the right, which favours reducing government involvement and promoting greater individualism. The Liberal Party continues to dominate the centre, while the right is now occupied by the Progressive Conservative Party and the Reform Party. The New Democratic Party and the nationalist Bloc Québécois dominate the left.

The Centre

Liberal Party. The political centre in Canada is held by the Liberal Party. In the 19th century and early 20th century, the Liberal Party was the voice of Canadian liberalism, which held the view that the purpose of government was to promote the happiness of individuals by moving away from traditions such as close ties with Great Britain and encouraging greater participation by more people in politics. The Liberal Party advocated democracy, freer trade, and little government involvement in the economy.

After 1945, the Liberal Party emphasized the need for government to assist the poor and disadvantaged groups in society so that they could exercise their civil liberties more effectively. The party called for the establishment of a social welfare system, more government regulation of the economy, and a larger role for the federal government in promoting national unity. Since 1990, the Liberal Party has adopted policies which call for less government regulation and more self-reliance by individuals. According to Elections Canada, support for the Liberal Party is strong among urban, well-educated, and ethnic voters, and in Ontario, Québec, Atlantic Canada, and British Columbia.

The Right

Progressive Conservative Party. Until the 1993 federal election, the Progressive Conservative Party was the main federal political party of the Canadian right. In the 19th century, the Conservative Party was the chief voice of Canadian

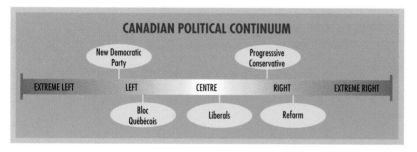

CANADIAN POLITICAL CONTINUUM

EXTREME LEFT — LEFT — CENTRE — RIGHT — EXTREME RIGHT

New Democratic Party · Progresssive Conservative · Bloc Québécois · Liberals · Reform

Prime Ministers of Canada and Canadian Political Parties in Power Since 1867

Conservative Party[1]		Liberal Party	
Sir John A. Macdonald	1867–1873	Richard B. Bennett	1930–1935
Alexander Mackenzie	1873–1878	William L. Mackenzie King	1935–1948
Sir John A. Macdonald	1878–1891	Louis St. Laurent	1948–1957
Sir John J. C. Abbott	1891–1892	John G. Diefenbaker	1957–1963
Sir John S. D. Thompson	1892–1894	Lester B. Pearson	1963–1968
Sir Mackenzie Bowell	1894–1896	Pierre E. Trudeau	1968–1979
Sir Charles Tupper	1896	Joseph Clark	1979–1980
Sir Wilfrid Laurier	1896–1911	Pierre E. Trudeau	1980–1984
Sir Robert L. Borden	1911–1920	John Turner	1984
Arthur Meighen	1920–1921	Brian Mulroney	1984–1993
William L. Mackenzie King	1921–1926	Kim Campbell	1993
Arthur Meighen	1926	Jean Chrétien	1993–
William L. Mackenzie King	1926–1930		

[1] called the Progressive Conservative Party after 1942

conservatism, which believed that institutions and customs are important elements of society and that a society without a strong social and moral framework cannot preserve freedom. The Conservative Party believed in national unity, close ties with Great Britain, the protection of national industries from foreign competition, and Canadian control over all lands north of the 49th parallel. "Peace, order, and good government" has been the motto of Canadian conservatism. In the 20th century, especially after 1945, the Conservative Party (renamed Progressive Conservative Party in 1942) became more supportive of establishing a social welfare system based on the individual's right to freedom of choice. In the early 1980s, the Progressive Conservative Party sought to reduce government involvement in all aspects of society and supported free trade and closer ties with the United States. Support for the Progressive Conservative Party today is strongest in Ontario, in parts of Québec, and in Atlantic Canada.

Reform Party. In the 1980s, dissatisfaction with the Progressive Conservative Party grew, and in 1987 a new right-wing party called the Reform Party was formed. The Reform Party calls for a significant reduction in the size and role of government in Canadian society. Its members believe that Canadians should not rely on government for their personal welfare, but rather should be more self-reliant, competitive, and individualistic. They support balanced government budgets, elimination of government debt, and the equality of all provinces. Support for the Reform Party is strongest among small business owners, farmers, professionals, and skilled workers. The Reform Party's support today is strongest in Western Canada and weakest in Central and Eastern Canada.

☐ The Left

New Democratic Party. The New Democratic Party (NDP) is the main political party of the Canadian left. Formed in 1961, the NDP had its origins in the Cooperative Commonwealth Federation (CCF), which

was founded in Calgary in 1932 as the voice of Canadian socialism. Some of its early leaders were motivated by Christian principles to serve their fellow human beings. Socialism emerged in Canada in the early 20th century with the arrival of millions of European emigrants, principally British emigrants who brought to the country a version of socialism called social democracy. Social democracy considers socialism to be an extension of democracy from the political sphere into the social and economic sphere. Under this type of socialism, society would be collectively organized for the general good by the state, acting on behalf of an enfranchised people. Hard work and persuasion rather than class war would lead society to socialism. The NDP favours the preservation of a comprehensive social welfare system and some government regulation of the economy. Support for the NDP is strongest among intellectuals, working poor, and unionized labour. Historically, support for the NDP was strongest in Western Canada and Ontario. In recent years, the NDP has become a strong political voice for discontent in Atlantic Canada over changes to social welfare policies.

Bloc Québécois. Formed in 1990 as the political voice of Québec nationalism in the Canadian parliament, the Bloc Québécois advances the cause of a sovereign independent Québec. Besides this goal, the Bloc Québécois remains a strong supporter of an extensive social welfare program. Support for the Bloc Québécois is concentrated among Francophone Québécois.

Other parties registered with Elections Canada during the 1997 general election were the Natural Law Party, Green Party, Marxist–Leninist Party, Canadian Action Party, and Christian Heritage Party.

CANADIAN POLITICAL SYSTEM

Advance Organizer

The Canadian political system is organized as a parliamentary democracy. Established in 1867, Canada is a constitutional monarchy based on the principles of responsible government and federalism. Political parties are important to the effective operation of government and compete with one another for power during periodic elections.

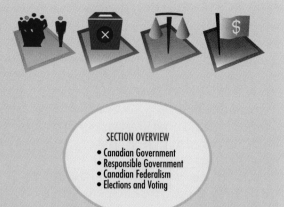

SECTION OVERVIEW
- Canadian Government
- Responsible Government
- Canadian Federalism
- Elections and Voting

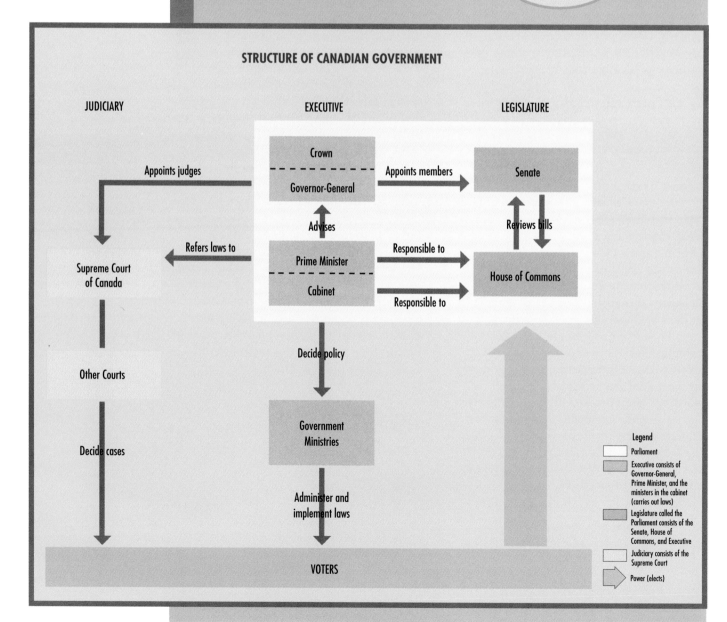

STRUCTURE OF CANADIAN GOVERNMENT

JUDICIARY   EXECUTIVE   LEGISLATURE

Crown

Governor-General — Appoints members → Senate

Appoints judges

Advises

Reviews bills

Refers laws to

Prime Minister — Responsible to → House of Commons

Cabinet — Responsible to →

Supreme Court of Canada

Other Courts

Decide cases

Decide policy

Government Ministries

Administer and implement laws

VOTERS

Legend
- Parliament
- Executive consists of Governor-General, Prime Minister, and the ministers in the cabinet (carries out laws)
- Legislature called the Parliament consists of the Senate, House of Commons, and Executive
- Judiciary consists of the Supreme Court
- Power (elects)

Canadian Government

The Canadian constitution establishes three branches of government—an executive headed by a Governor-General acting in the name of the British monarch, a national legislature comprised of an elected House of Commons and an appointed Senate, and a judiciary consisting of a system of courts and Supreme Court (see chart on the previous page).

Executive Power

Canada is a constitutional monarchy. According to the constitution, executive power is vested in the British monarch, represented in Canada by a Governor-General acting as the head of state. The general duties of the Governor-General include the following:

- appointing representatives (lieutenant-governors) in the provinces
- appointing and summoning members of the Privy Council
- appointing judges of the Supreme Court
- appointing members of the Senate
- summoning and calling together the House of Commons and Senate
- dissolving the House of Commons for elections
- signing into law legislation passed by the House of Commons
- acting as commander-in-chief of the country's armed forces in the name of the British monarch.

The Governor-General is assisted in carrying out his or her duties for Canada by a council of advisors called the Privy Council. The Privy Council is appointed and summoned by the Governor-General. In practice, the Council is the cabinet and the Prime Minister. Formally, anyone who has ever been a member of cabinet retains the title of privy councillor after leaving government, but only those who are active members of the government have real power.

Formal executive power in Canada lies with the Governor-General, but real executive power is held by the Prime Minister and cabinet, who are appointed to office by the Governor-General. The constitution makes no provision for the office of the Prime Minister. However, according to parliamentary convention, it is understood that the person who heads the political party that can command a majority of votes in the House of Commons, generally the largest party, is the Prime Minister. He or she has the power to decide the following:

- who will be appointed to or removed from cabinet
- when a new election will be held
- the administrative structure and decision making process of government
- what policies will be introduced in the House of Commons
- who will be selected for new appointments as senators, judges, members of government agencies, directors of Crown corporations, and ambassadors.

These powers make the Prime Minister the most powerful member of the Canadian government. The Prime Minister and each member of the cabinet are individually accountable or responsible to the House of Commons for the actions of their departments. The entire cabinet is collectively accountable or responsible to the House of Commons for government policy. Consequently, the Prime Minister as the head of government is held personally responsible by other parties in the House of Commons and also by the media outside for the overall performance of government and its policies.

photography by/photographie par KARSH

Canadian government is organized into three branches: executive, legislative, and judicial.

The annual salary of the Governor-General in 1997 was $97 375.

In 1997 as a member of Parliament, Prime Minister Jean Chrétien received a salary of $64 400, plus a tax-free expense allowance of $21 300, and a salary of $69 920 as the head of the cabinet, for a total of $155 620.

LEFT: Jeanne Sauvé was Canada's first woman Governor-General. She served from 1984 to 1990.

Legislative Power

According to the Canadian constitution, legislative power resides in a parliament that consists of the Crown (represented by the Governor-General), the Senate, and the House of Commons (see chart on page 132).

Senate. The Senate is the upper house of the parliament and is said to act as a chamber of "sober second thought." Members of the Senate are appointed by the Governor-General on the advice of and as selected by the Prime Minister. The views of key members of the Prime Minister's party in the province are considered during the selection process. A senator must be at least 30 years old, a citizen of Canada, and have a net worth of at least $4000. The senator is required to retire at 75 years of age but can be dismissed if he or she misses two consecutive sessions of Parliament, commits treason or theft, or declares personal bankruptcy.

The map on page 135 shows representation in the House of Commons and Senate as of April 1, 1999, when the Senate will have a total of 105 seats.[1] Representation in the Senate is based on regions. Four main regions (Atlantic, Québec, Ontario, and Western Canada) are represented with each having 24 seats. Newfoundland has six seats and one seat each is held by Yukon, Northwest Territories, and Nunavut. The constitution sets the maximum number of seats in the Senate at 112. To gain a Progressive Conservative majority in order to pass legislation creating the Goods and Services Tax (GST), the government of Brian Mulroney temporarily raised the number of Senators from 104 to 112 in 1990.

In the 1980s and early 1990s, various proposals called for the election of senators and the allocation of more Senate seats to women and First Nations peoples. One prominent proposal of Senate reform was the concept of "Triple E," which was officially endorsed in May 1985 by the Alberta legislature. The "Triple E" concept called for a reformed Senate directly elected by the people of Canada, with equal provincial representation, and with powers that would allow it to be effective. Proponents of "Triple E" claimed that only a directly elected Senate would have significant political and legislative authority to make a more valuable contribution to the Canadian Parliament. Equal representation by province would make all provinces equal partners in Confederation and check the power of the federal government. As an effective legislative body, the Senate would have the power to initiate any legislation except a money or taxation bill. Critics of "Triple E" stated that the concept did not accept the historical fact that Confederation was based on two founding cultures—English and French. The Québec government rejected "Triple E" on this basis.

In 1989, the province of Alberta took the unprecedented step of holding a province-wide election to choose a candidate to fill a vacant Senate seat. Prime Minister Mulroney announced that he would not be bound by this result because it was his responsibility to make the appointment, not the people of Alberta. However, he appointed Stan Waters, who had been chosen by the people of Alberta, invoking his right to decide while not wanting to alienate Alberta voters. In late 1998, Alberta voters elected two senate candidates (called senators-in-waiting) to fill future senate vacancies. Prime Minister Chrétien's immediate response was that he would make the choice.

From time to time, the suggestion to abolish the Senate is raised. Those in favour point out that it is against the principles of democracy to have an appointed body involved in the legislation process because it is not accountable to anyone. Though there are some exceptions, most senators are appointed because they have been of service to their political party. Supporters of the Senate say that only senators can defend the interests of their region or province because members of the House of Commons represent their constituents or the interests of their political party.

[1]On April 1, 1999, Nunavut Territory separates from the Northwest Territories.

House of Commons. The House of Commons is the elected lower house of parliament and is modelled after the British House of Commons. The House of Commons is responsible for most of the legislation introduced in parliament. The number of seats in the House of Commons is not restricted by the constitution. Currently the House of Commons has 301 members who are directly elected in constituencies or ridings that are supposedly equal in population. In reality, representation by population is not very equal in the House of Commons. The chart below shows that the average population of a constituency can vary from less than 35 000 in Prince Edward Island, Yukon, Nunavut, and Northwest Territories to over 103 000 in Ontario, Alberta, and British Columbia. Compared to the national average of 95 900 people per House of Commons seat, the provinces of Atlantic Canada, Manitoba, and Saskatchewan are overrepresented while the provinces of Alberta, British Columbia, and Ontario are underrepresented. Within provinces it is generally true that rural ridings have fewer people and are thus similarly overrepresented.

The unequal representation of the provinces in the House of Commons is the result of special constitutional rules. One rule is that Québec cannot have fewer than 75 seats in the House of Commons. Another is the "Senate floor" rule, which states that a province cannot have fewer House of Commons seats than the senators representing it (see chart below). This rule was instituted in 1915 to protect the provinces of Atlantic Canada from losing representation in the House of Commons as a result of falling population. In 1985, the constitution was amended to ensure that no province could have fewer seats than it had in 1976. This rule protects the representation of Manitoba and Saskatchewan in the House.

Legislative power within the House of Commons is divided between the governing political party and other parties. The party with the greatest number of seats in the House of Commons usually has the right to form a government. If the party has a majority of the members of the House it forms a majority government. A minority government occurs when the largest political party does not have a majority of the members of the House and is forced to rely on support from members of other parties to form a government. A situation can arise where no party is large enough to form a government and has to join with other parties to form a coalition government. From 1917 to 1920, Canada had a coalition Union government composed of Liberals and Conservatives, which governed the country during the last years of World War I.

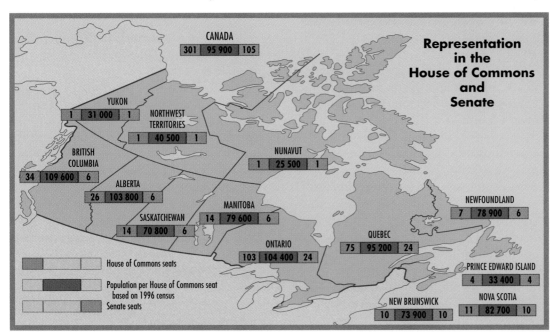

Representation in the House of Commons and Senate

CANADA: 301 | 95 900 | 105

YUKON: 1 | 31 000 | 1

NORTHWEST TERRITORIES: 1 | 40 500 | 1

NUNAVUT: 1 | 25 500 | 1

BRITISH COLUMBIA: 34 | 109 600 | 6

ALBERTA: 26 | 103 800 | 6

SASKATCHEWAN: 14 | 70 800 | 6

MANITOBA: 14 | 79 600 | 6

ONTARIO: 103 | 104 400 | 24

QUEBEC: 75 | 95 200 | 24

NEWFOUNDLAND: 7 | 78 900 | 6

PRINCE EDWARD ISLAND: 4 | 33 400 | 4

NOVA SCOTIA: 11 | 82 700 | 10

NEW BRUNSWICK: 10 | 73 900 | 10

House of Commons seats

Population per House of Commons seat based on 1996 census

Senate seats

135

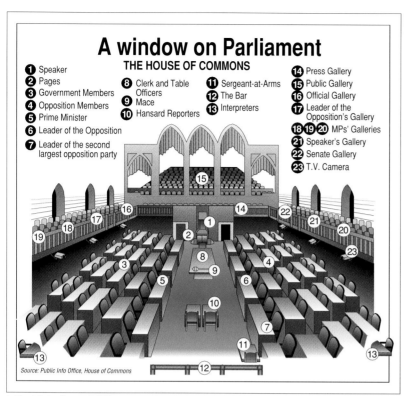

A window on Parliament
THE HOUSE OF COMMONS

1 Speaker
2 Pages
3 Government Members
4 Opposition Members
5 Prime Minister
6 Leader of the Opposition
7 Leader of the second largest opposition party
8 Clerk and Table Officers
9 Mace
10 Hansard Reporters
11 Sergeant-at-Arms
12 The Bar
13 Interpreters
14 Press Gallery
15 Public Gallery
16 Official Gallery
17 Leader of the Opposition's Gallery
18 19 20 MPs' Galleries
21 Speaker's Gallery
22 Senate Gallery
23 T.V. Camera

Source: Public Info Office, House of Commons

Paul Perrault/Southam Newspapers © 1996

In the past, politicians who have been seen to interfere with judicial independence have been rebuked and some have been removed from cabinet.

© Library of Parliament. Photographer: Stephen Fenn.

This relationship of power between the government and the opposition within the House of Commons is reflected in the physical layout of the chamber. The House of Commons is a rectangular room divided by a central aisle. The government sits on the Speaker's right and the opposition parties on the left (see diagram). On the government side about halfway down the aisle, the Prime Minister sits in the front row, flanked by cabinet members. The leader of the Official Opposition sits directly opposite the Prime Minister, surrounded by the senior members of his or her party. Leaders of smaller opposition parties sit farther away from the Speaker.

Independents, who are not members of a political party, sit farthest away.

Judicial Power

The constitution gives the parliament the authority to create courts. In 1875, this authority was used to establish the Supreme Court of Canada, although the final authority remained in Great Britain. Since 1949, the Supreme Court has been the country's highest court of appeal. The constitution assigns to the provinces responsibility for the administration of justice and for law enforcement. However, the constitution says very little about the relationship between the judiciary and the other branches of government. The fundamental principles underlying the role of the judiciary in Canada are judicial independence and separation of powers.

In the Canadian political system efforts are made to guarantee that the judiciary is free from political interference in its decision making. Judicial independence is enhanced by the fact that judges' salaries and conditions of service are established by law. Judges are appointed by the Prime Minister or a provincial legislature, with the advice of federal or provincial law societies. Once appointed to their office, judges are expected to maintain "good behaviour" and to refrain from any activity that may compromise their work. Judges can be removed by resolutions of the House of Commons or a provincial legislature.

The judiciary's role as interpreter of the constitution underlies the principle of separation of powers in the government. Since 1875, judicial opinion has altered the Canadian constitution, making the power of the federal government less general and more specific. Amendments to the Constitution in 1982 led the Supreme Court of Canada and provincial courts to become deeply involved in interpreting the Charter of Rights and Freedoms. Various groups and individuals have undertaken legal action in the courts to protect their rights. In the process of deciding these cases, the courts have struck down laws and practices on the grounds that they contravened the Charter's guarantees of rights and freedoms.

Responsible Government

Responsible government is the foundation of Canadian parliamentary democracy. All important legislation introduced by the government must be voted on by members of the House of Commons. The government must defend its policies in debates and accept criticism from members of the House of Commons. Every policy and bill the government introduces must receive the support of the House, indicated by a simple majority vote. In this way the government is held accountable to the House of Commons for its policies and actions. Aspects of responsible government include majority voting, ministerial responsibility, and the supremacy of parliament to make laws.

Majority Votes

In order to govern, the Prime Minister and cabinet must have the confidence of a majority of the members of the House of Commons. This confidence is expressed through majority votes on important pieces of legislation such as the budgets, important money bills, or on formal motions of non-confidence put forth by opposition parties. Voting in the House of Commons is by roll call whereby each member of parliament is required to openly express his or her vote for or against the motion. If a majority of the members of the House of Commons express no confidence in the government, it is defeated and must resign. The consequences of this are either the calling of a general election or the Opposition parties are given an opportunity to form a government. In the 20th century, governments were defeated several times by a vote in the House. These occurred when a minority government was in power and did not have a majority of the seats in the House, needing to rely on support from other parties. Generally, party discipline prevents majority governments from being defeated.

Party discipline, the tendency of parties to expect and enforce support from their elected members, is strong in Canada and enforced in the House of Commons by the presence of party whips. The primary task of a party whip is to ensure that all party members of parliament are present for important votes and that the party votes as a bloc. When party members break with party discipline and vote independently they are usually reprimanded, often severely. If the vote was important enough to the party, they are generally forced to leave the party and sit as independents or join other parties. In the case of government members of parliament, this means sitting on the Opposition side of the House.

Opposition members have also been known to join the government when forced to leave their party. However, party discipline does generally discourage party members from "crossing the floor" from the government to the opposition or from the opposition to the government side.

Critics of Canadian parliamentary democracy claim that strong party discipline undermines the legislature's control over the government by restricting the ability of members of parliament, especially of backbenchers, to publicly represent the views of their constituents. Generally speaking, government members are less free to speak than members of the Opposition. Critics argue that parliamentary procedure in the House of Commons should be modified to allow for more free votes, where members of parliament may vote as they choose in accordance with the wishes of their constituents. In the absence of a free vote, members of parliament are expected to adhere to and defend the party line and wishes of the party leader.

Defenders of party discipline point out that in the private and closed meetings of elected members, the party caucus, people are free to voice their opinions, convince others, and engage in free and open discussion about party policy. Elected members of parliament spend a great deal of time gathering information from their constituents, all of which is passed on to the political party. Defenders also point out that membership in all political parties is open and all members can play a role in developing party policy at provincial and national conventions and policy meetings.

Political parties are an integral part of Canadian parliamentary democracy and help to determine who will form the government and govern the country.

The Canadian political system is built on the parliamentary principle of government being responsible to an elected legislature.

Ministerial Responsibility

Ministerial responsibility is another important aspect of responsible government. Members of the cabinet, usually called ministers, are expected to explain and defend policies and actions carried out in their names. A cabinet minister is selected by the Prime Minister to be responsible for the administration of a particular government ministry or department.

The Prime Minister takes a number of factors into account when choosing a cabinet. Administrative competence is important but so is the need to ensure that all regions of Canada are represented if possible. Ideally the cabinet should also include people from a broad range of occupations, represent the country's cultural diversity, and attempt some level of gender balance. As a rule, cabinet members are members of the House of Commons, but this has not prevented the Prime Minister from appointing a senator or two to the cabinet to give the government representation from a region or province where the government party has elected few or no members. In recent years, the federal cabinet has varied between 35 and 40 members, depending on need and political circumstances. The country's first cabinet in 1867 consisted of 13 members, of which 5 were senators.

Cabinet ministers remain in office as long as the Prime Minister wants them. The Prime Minister chooses them and recommends their appointment to the Governor-General. It is also the Prime Minister who recommends to the Governor-General that a minister's resignation be accepted. For various reasons, the Prime Minister also periodically changes the size and composition of the cabinet through promotion and shuffling of cabinet ministers.

Ministers in the cabinet are generally divided into two groups: those with department responsibilities and those without, called ministers without portfolio. Ministers with department responsibilities are the largest group in the cabinet. These individuals are the political heads of departments and ministries, such as the Ministers of Finance, Agriculture, Transport, and Health and Welfare. Ministers are responsible for the activities of their respective department or ministry and must be willing to answer for any shortcomings of their subordinates, having the final word in all important decisions. When a serious failing is discovered, the minister is obliged to resign. However, this rule of ministerial responsibility is not always observed. There have been many cases where a minister has not resigned, having demonstrated that he or she was not aware of the situation or had implemented steps to correct the shortcoming.

Although ministers are individually responsible for their own performance, they are also collectively responsible for cabinet performance. Ministers who disagree with the cabinet's policies must either withdraw their objections and publicly support the cabinet decision or resign. This principle is known as cabinet solidarity. The cabinet's collective responsibility is the essence of the system of responsible government. If the House displays no confidence in the cabinet, the cabinet must resign. Generally, the defeat of a money bill in the House is interpreted as a vote of non-confidence.

PHOTO: The Honourable Christine Stewart, a new member of the cabinet being sworn in; each cabinet minister swears allegiance to the Crown and promises to faithfully carry out the duties of office.

Jean-Marc Carisse, Office of the Prime Minister

When the government has a majority in the House of Commons, the backing of the government party's backbenchers (generally members who are not cabinet ministers) enables the Prime Minister and the cabinet to push their legislative agenda through Parliament without serious difficulty. This can change when the government party is in a minority and must continually seek the support of the members of other parties by changing and making compromises in policies. This is often done before an important vote in the House of Commons to avoid a motion of non-confidence.

Supremacy of Parliament

The Canadian constitution gives the parliament (House of Commons and Senate) the supreme power to make laws. Both chambers have substantially the same legislative powers, but the House of Commons, as the elected body, carries greater authority than the Senate, an appointed body. For a bill to become law, it must first be introduced in either the Senate or the House of Commons. Only the House of Commons can introduce bills that require spending of public money. A bill must pass through various stages in each chamber, after which it must receive royal assent before it becomes a law.

The sources of legislation in both chambers are public bills and private bills. Public bills are so described because they are proposals that will affect a large number of Canadians. They are almost always introduced by cabinet ministers, though any member of the House of Commons can introduce public bills, which are known as Public Bills. Public bills constitute the largest part of all legislation considered and passed in the House of Commons. No distinction is made on the basis of who introduces a bill in the Senate.

Private bills are more limited in scope than public bills. Generally, they concern an individual or a group of individuals, often involving a company, nonprofit organization, or professional association. Private bills are not the same as Public Bills. Private bills are based on petition and follow a different procedure of passage through the two chambers. Most private bills are introduced in the Senate.

Most legislation originates with the cabinet. The cabinet formulates the legislation program by making choices, setting priorities, and then deciding which policies it wants to introduce. Once the cabinet concludes that a particular policy measure is required in a particular area, the minister responsible ensures that the bill drafted by department officials is acceptable to the whole cabinet. Once cabinet has approved the bill, it is ready for introduction into the House of Commons or Senate. Because few ministers responsible for departments sit in the Senate, most bills are introduced in the House of Commons.

PHOTO: Most legislation in Canada originates with the cabinet. Members of the cabinet meet regularly to discuss and formulate government policy.

Canapress/Fred Chartrand

Law Making

Making Laws in Canada. Once a bill has been drafted, it begins a fairly lengthy process of passage from one chamber to the other. The chart below illustrates in a simplified way the process of creating a law in Canada.

HOUSE OF COMMONS

First Reading

↓

Second Reading

↓

Committee Stage

↓

Report Stage

↓

Third Reading

↓

SENATE

↓

Royal Assent

↓

LAW

First Reading. The bill is introduced into the House of Commons. A motion is made to read the bill for the first time and have it printed. The bill receives an order number and is recorded either as a government order, if sponsored by a cabinet minister, or as private members' business, if sponsored by a private member of the House.

Second Reading. The motion for second reading asks that the bill be read a second time and referred to a committee for consideration. The principles of the bill are debated. A vote is then taken to accept or reject the bill in principle. If the bill is approved in principle, it goes to a committee.

Committee Stage. In this stage, a committee submits the bill to a detailed examination, studying it clause by clause. The committee summons witnesses and experts whom it believes are important for improving the bill. The committee debates, studies, revises, and modifies the bill. Once all changes to the bill are approved by the committee, it is sent back to the House of Commons.

Report Stage. Once the committee has made its report on the bill to the House, debate begins on whether to accept the committee report or to make further amendments to the bill. Members of the opposition may propose changes, and the government may also wish to make changes to the bill. However, the underlying principle of the bill must not be altered from that which was approved by the House at second reading. Amendments to the bill are debated and voted on in the House.

Third Reading. The bill is read again and undergoes further debate. Additional amendments are proposed, debated, and voted on. The bill is put to another vote. If the House of Commons approves the bill, it is sent to the Senate to be approved.

Senate. The bill is introduced in the Senate where the process of a bill's examination follows a similar series of readings and debates as in the House of Commons. However, the Senate examines the bill for small defects, weaknesses, poor wording, or technical errors that may have been missed in the House. Once the Senate approves the bill, the bill is ready for Royal Assent.

Royal Assent. After the bill has been passed by the House of Commons and the Senate, members of the House are summoned to the Senate, where the Governor-General, acting as the representative of the monarch, signs the bill into law.

Adapted from *Canadian Parliament.* http://www.parl.gc.ca

Critique of Canadian Law Making

The process of making laws in Canada has both advantages and disadvantages.

Advantages

1 Ease of debate and amendment. At each stage of the legislative process in the Canadian parliament, a bill undergoes considerable debate and modification. A bill must receive approval from both the House of Commons and the Senate before it is signed into law. Members of the House of Commons may debate a bill. As long as the original principle of a bill is not significantly altered in the process, members of the House of Commons can propose changes to it. Members of the Senate examine the bill for technical errors, poor wording, and other defects before the bill can be passed into law.

2 Quick passage. One important goal for the government is to get its legislation passed without undue delay. Through the cabinet, the government sets the legislative agenda. It has control over the parliamentary timetable and can determine how much time should be allotted for debate of a bill, usually with the consent of other political parties in the House of Commons. The government relies on its backbenchers to remain loyal in order to secure passage of its legislative proposals. This is accomplished by the party whip who ensures that party members will support government bills.

3 Public accountability. An important feature of the Canadian legislative process is the daily question period. Members of the House of Commons and Senate are allowed to ask questions about the government's policies. In the House of Commons, cabinet ministers and the Prime Minister usually are present for the question period. Members of the opposition parties ask questions of cabinet ministers and the Prime Minister. The intent of the questioning is to expose government weaknesses, criticize controversial policies, and probe possible scandals. Ministers and the Prime Minister, for their part, will defend their actions and policies and reject the claims of the questioners. Question Period is televised and also reported in daily newspapers.

The Committee stage is also important because lobbyists and other members of the public have input into the shaping of legislation.

4 Independent judiciary. The judicial process helps refine and clarify laws passed by parliament.

Disadvantages

1 Closure. Because the government controls the legislative agenda of the House of Commons, it can determine without the consent of other parties the time allotted to debate a bill. One measure used to control debate on a bill is closure. Closure occurs when the government ends debate on a bill by imposing limits on opposition party members' time to speak. In recent years, the government has used closure to pass very controversial legislation. In early 1989, the Conservative government used closure to pass the Canada–United States Free Trade Agreement, and again in 1990 for the Goods and Service Tax.

2 Patronage. To ensure quick passage of its legislative proposals and to promote party discipline, the government has engaged in patronage. Notable examples of patronage include appointments to the Senate, the judiciary, Royal Commissions, and government-appointed boards, such as parole and immigration boards.

3 Lack of accountability. Critics claim that party discipline does not allow elected members of the House, especially backbenchers, to vote according to the wishes of their constituents, but rather requires them to vote according to party policies. The resolution to this problem, critics claim, is to have more free votes. However, more free votes may not be considered possible if the government must rely on party discipline to stay in power.

Lobbying by special interest groups puts great power in the hands of unelected and well-financed organizations.

Canadian Federalism

The Canadian constitution establishes Canada as a federal state. Canada's federal structure of government was a compromise. Many of the Fathers of Confederation were not very enthusiastic about federalism. Most Anglophone politicians in Ontario and Québec favoured a unitary government under which all power would be concentrated in the hands of the new parliament in Ottawa. They were opposed by Francophone politicians in Québec and the Anglophone political leaders of New Brunswick and Nova Scotia. Québec Francophones insisted on protecting their linguistic and cultural identity through a federation. In New Brunswick and Nova Scotia, politicians feared a unitary government would reduce local autonomy and identities. In spite of these great differences, the Fathers of Confederation agreed to form a union in which legislative powers would be divided between the federal state and the provinces, with the most significant powers residing with the federal government.

Confederation (1867)

In 1867, the British North America Act (now called the Constitution Act 1867) established Canada as a confederation of four provinces—Ontario, Québec, New Brunswick, and Nova Scotia. The Act specified the powers of the federal government and provincial governments.

Under the Act the federal government received exclusive powers over areas such as trade and commerce, postal service, national defence, currency, interest rates, copyrights, and census (see chart below).

Provincial governments were organized in similar fashion to the federal government, although today there are some important exceptions. For example, no province has had an upper house or Senate since 1968, when Québec abolished its upper house. The Lieutenant-Governor is appointed by the Prime Minister, which, in an earlier age, gave the federal government some influence in the province. As well, the division of powers in the constitution clearly grants powers of a more local nature to the province. The provinces were granted exclusive powers over areas such as health and welfare, municipalities, natural resources, education, and language. The federal government could not interfere in provincial jurisdictions without invitation of the provinces. Since 1867, the allocation of powers between the federal government and the provinces has changed little. However, as the cost of meeting those responsibilities has risen dramatically a constant demand by the provinces for more money to meet their obligations has resulted. The chart below summarizes the major jurisdictions and powers of the two levels of government. Except in the areas of immigration and agriculture, there are few areas in which the two levels of government share jurisdiction.

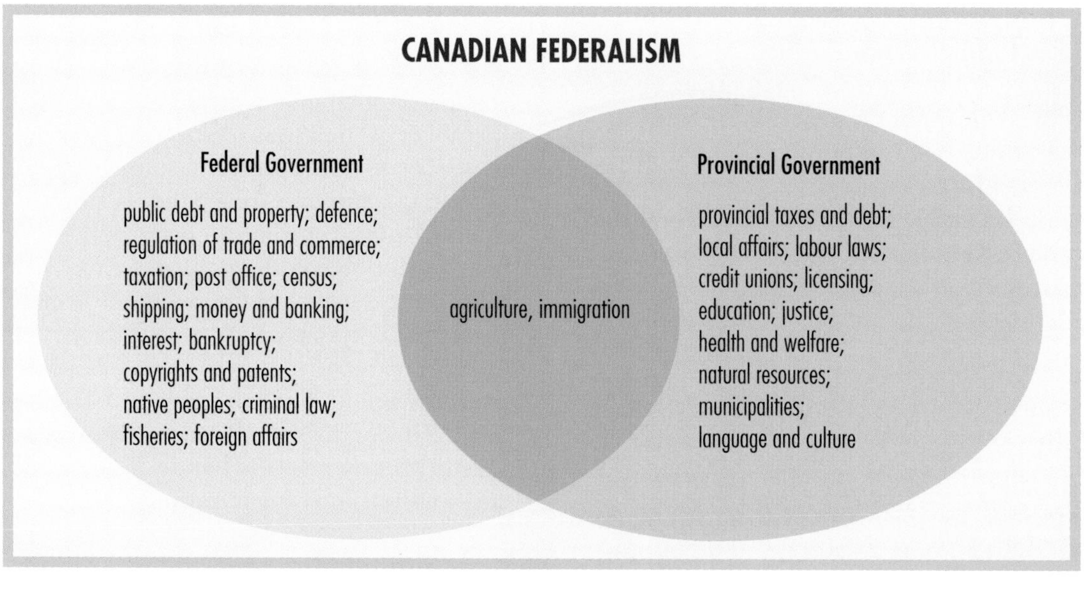

CANADIAN FEDERALISM

Federal Government

public debt and property; defence; regulation of trade and commerce; taxation; post office; census; shipping; money and banking; interest; bankruptcy; copyrights and patents; native peoples; criminal law; fisheries; foreign affairs

agriculture, immigration

Provincial Government

provincial taxes and debt; local affairs; labour laws; credit unions; licensing; education; justice; health and welfare; natural resources; municipalities; language and culture

Constitutional Change

Recent efforts to modify Canadian federalism have focussed on amending the Canadian constitution to grant more powers to the provinces. The Québec government has long argued that Confederation is a partnership between French and English Canada. Other provinces maintain that Confederation is a union of provinces, each having the same rights, under a strong central government.

Québec Referendum (1980). In November 1976, Québec voters elected a Parti Québécois government dedicated to establishing Québec as an independent state with a close economic association with Canada. On May 20, 1980, Québec voters participated in a referendum on whether to give the Québec government the power to negotiate sovereignty-association with Ottawa and the rest of Canada. The referendum was defeated, with 59.5% against and 40.5% in favour.

Patriation of the Constitution (1982). Following the May 1980 Québec referendum, the federal government and the provinces began the process of patriating the constitution from Great Britain, where it had been held since 1867. The patriation took place April 1982, adding several new provisions, including a charter of rights, recognition of Canada's multicultural heritage, the concept of equalization payments, and an amendment procedure. The Québec government refused to accept the patriation of the constitution because it did not recognize Québec's special status in Confederation.

Meech Lake Accord (1987). In April 1987 at Meech Lake, the Prime Minister and Premiers of the provinces agreed in principle to recognize Québec's cultural distinctiveness. The Meech Lake Accord proposed a formula for constitutional change, an expanded role for the Supreme Court, and senate reform. A unanimous vote of the House of Commons, Senate, and all provincial legislatures was required for the Accord to take effect. When Elijah Harper, a First Nations member of the Manitoba legislature, remained silent, the vote on the Accord failed. Harper claimed that the Accord recognized only Québec's distinctiveness and not that of Canada's First Peoples.

Charlottetown Accord (1992). The failure of the Meech Lake Accord sparked a constitutional crisis and led to several proposals to determine Québec's special status in Canada. In 1992, the Prime Minister and provincial Premiers met at Charlottetown and endorsed a new constitutional accord, which proposed to recognize Québec's distinctiveness, protect Native people's rights, create an elected senate, reform the House of Commons, and establish a charter for social programs. In a national referendum in October, over 54% of Canadian voters rejected the Charlottetown Accord, including 55% of Québec voters and 70% of Western Canadian voters. Voters in Ontario and Atlantic Canada narrowly approved it.

Québec Referendum (1995). The defeat of the Charlottetown Accord was followed by the election in 1994 of a Parti Québécois government led by Jacques Parizeau, who was committed to establishing Québec as a sovereign and independent state with an economic association with Canada. On October 30, 1995, Québec voters narrowly defeated (50.5% against and 49.5% in favour) a referendum to give the Québec government the right to declare the province's independence from Canada should negotiations to create a new relationship with Canada fail.

Supreme Court Decision (1998). In August 1998, at the request of the Federal government, the Supreme Court issued a statement on the constitutionality of Québec's right to secede from Canada. The Court ruled that Québec did not have the right to declare independence from Canada without negotiations with other provinces. The Court also declared that the other provinces had a moral responsibility to negotiate with the Québec government if a clear majority of the province's population voted in favour of independence.

Elections and Voting

Through elections, Canadians are given the opportunity to judge the performance of the government and to decide whether to keep it in power. In recent years, general elections have revealed significant changes in Canadian voting patterns.

Electoral Campaigns

General elections take place when the Prime Minister calls on the Governor-General to dissolve the House of Commons. The constitution requires that an election of representatives to the House of Commons and provincial legislatures must be held every five years. Within this time period, the Prime Minister or Premier can call an election at any time, generally when his or her party is seen to have the best chance of being returned to power. The Prime Minister or Premier, in consultation with the cabinet and important party advisors, determines the most favourable period for an election, usually on the basis of public

opinion polls. With opinion polls showing high levels of support for the Liberal Party in April 1997, Prime Minister Jean Chrétien called a general election to be held on June 2, 1997. During the course of the electoral campaign, public support for the Liberal Party began to decline but remained high enough for the party to win a slim majority of seats in the House of Commons on June 2, 1997.

Canadian electoral campaigns generally last no more than six weeks. The 1997 general election was the first to be held under new rules that shortened the length of campaigning from eight to six weeks. Electoral campaigns for provincial legislatures usually last three to four weeks. In all of these electoral campaigns, candidates and political parties compete vigorously for voters' support, canvassing local neighbourhoods, holding public rallies, distributing political literature, and participating in candidate debating forums. In recent years, political advertising on television has become one of the main ways of persuading voters to elect members of a political party to form the next government.

In recent years, electoral campaigns, both nationally and provincially, have become increasingly expensive for political parties. The Elections Expenses Act was passed in 1974 to control campaign spending. Among other measures, candidates running for election in a House of Commons seat are required to disclose publicly the sources and uses of funds received. Maximum campaign expenses in a constituency in the 1993 general election were set at $60 000. The Act also provides for a partial reimbursement of a candidate's expenses if he or she receives at least 15% of the popular vote. These spending limits do not apply to advertising by special interest groups, lobbies, and private organizations promoting issues that may also be supported by a party.

An important change in election campaigns, especially since 1980, has been the growing involvement, participation, and success of women in politics. In the 1997 general elections, 24.4% of all candidates and 18.3% of elected members were women (see chart, left).

Women in Politics (1980–1997)

	1980	1984	1988	1993	1997
Registered parties	9	11	12	14	10
Candidates	1504	1449	1575	2155	1672
Women candidates	216	210	300	476	408
As percentage	14.4%	14.5%	19.1%	22.1%	24.4%
Elected members	282	282	295	295	301
Women elected	14	27	39	53	62
As percentage	5.0%	9.6%	13.2%	18.0%	18.3%

Office of the Chief Electoral Officer

Voting

General elections are always held on a Monday, unless that day is a statutory holiday, in which case the elections are held the following day. All Canadian citizens aged 18 and older are permitted to vote in the riding in which they live. The right to vote is guaranteed by the Canadian Charter of Rights and Freedoms. However, universal suffrage was not always the case. Women obtained the right to vote in federal elections in 1918 and to run as candidates in 1919. Chinese and South Asian Canadians were enfranchised in 1947, Inuit and Japanese Canadians in 1949, and First Nations peoples living on reserves in 1960. In 1992, prison inmates were given the right to vote in federal elections.

Voting by secret ballot has a long history in Canada. The general election of 1878 was the first conducted by secret ballot. In the first Canadian general election of 1867, representatives to the House of Commons had been elected by voters stating their choice of a platform. This system of voting had suffered from corruption, patronage, and the buying of votes.

The system of electing candidates in Canada today is plurality voting, commonly called "first past the post." Under this electoral system, the candidate who receives the greatest number of votes wins. In most Canadian elections, owing to the presence of several political parties, candidates have been elected with significantly less than 50% of the popular vote.

For most of the 20th century, Canadian politics have been dominated by two large parties. This has not prevented the emergence of other parties. The 1993 general elections fundamentally changed Canadian politics. The New Democratic Party lost many seats, the Progressive Conservative Party collapsed utterly, and two new regional parties emerged, Reform and Bloc Québécois (see chart). The 1997 general elections confirmed this political realignment. By number of seats in the House of Commons, the main political parties were the Liberal Party, Reform Party, Bloc Québécois, New Democratic Party, and Progressive Conservative Party.

Voter turnout in Canadian elections since 1945 has averaged 70–75% for national and provincial elections. Voter turnout in the 1993 and 1997 federal elections was below 70%, owing in part to voter dissatisfaction and disinterest in campaign issues (see chart below). The highest voter turnout ever recorded in Canada occurred on October 30, 1995, when almost 95% of all eligible voters in Québec cast ballots in a referendum on whether the province should negotiate sovereignty-association with Canada.

The Wartime Elections Act gave women the right to vote.

Seven Members of Parliament younger than 30 years old were elected to the House of Commons in the June 2, 1997, general election. Four of them belonged to the Bloc Québécois and three Members elected in Alberta belonged to the Reform Party.

Federal Election Results (1980–1997)

	1980 Vote	1980 Seats	1984 Vote	1984 Seats	1988 Vote	1988 Seats	1993 Vote	1993 Seats	1997 Vote	1997 Seats
Liberal Party	44.4%	147	28.0%	40	31.9%	82	41.3%	177	37.9%	155
Conservatives	32.5	103	50.0	211	43.0	170	16.0	2	18.9	20
New Democrats	19.8	32	18.8	30	20.4	43	6.9	9	11.0	21
Bloc Québécois	—	—	—	—	—	—	13.5	54	10.5	44
Reform Party	—	—	—	—	2.1	—	18.7	52	19.4	60
Others	3.3	—	3.2	1	2.6	—	3.6	1	2.3	1
Total	100.0%	282	100.0%	282	100.0%	295	100.0%	295	100.0%	301
Voter turnout	69.3%		75.3%		75.3%		69.6%		67.5%	

Office of the Chief Electoral Officer

When reading the following two articles, consider these issues: To what extent is Canadian decision making affected by particular groups in society? To what extent does the majority limit its rights to protect the rights of the minority?

B.C. voters remember, and recall

The Globe and Mail, December 10, 1997. Reprinted with permission from The Globe and Mail.

For the first time in Canadian history, voters are being given the opportunity to turf out their representatives between elections. The site of this experiment is British Columbia, where two New Democratic MLAs face the possibility of being recalled by their constituents. As a result, Glen Clark's government, which now holds the upper hand by a mere three seats, could fall. That could make for another first: a majority government forced to go to the polls early.

Here's how B.C.'s voter recall law works: If, in the space of 60 days, 40 percent of the voters registered for the last election sign a petition demanding the removal of their representative, that MLA loses his or her seat. A by-election would then have to be called—a by-election in which the recalled member would be free to run, and might even win. At least one of the B.C. races could turn out that way.

B.C.'s NDP government is these days increasingly unpopular, above all because it clearly deceived voters as to the state of the province's finances in the 1996 election. A lawsuit has even been launched against the government, alleging that the NDP, by distorting the truth, came to power by fraud. The courts have been asked to order new elections.

We do not believe that the courts are the proper forum to decide the question of who deserves to govern—but the court of public opinion is another matter. There are those who argue that recall laws are a mistake, and that they undermine the parliamentary system's careful balance between democracy and stability. In the parliamentary system, the leash upon representatives is not yanked continuously, but it is always there, and come election time, and only at election time, voters may pass judgment and withdraw their support. In normal circumstances, that is as it should be.

There are, however, exceptional circumstances where a particular member or perhaps an entire government have become overwhelmingly unpopular, for whatever reason. Perhaps they are accused of stealing an election, perhaps their policies are simply not liked: whatever the reason, whether it is Sheila Copps's promise-breaking on the GST or Jag Bhaduria's résumé embellishment, voters have to have some mechanism of separating themselves from a representative whom a substantial majority of them cannot support.

There are those who argue that the recall law is a recipe for chaos, that it guarantees nothing but instability and endless by-elections. If the hurdle is set too low—if recall can be triggered by just, say, a few hundred signatures—such concerns are hardly misplaced. In the case of the B.C. law, which the NDP introduced after nearly 80 per cent of voters expressed support for the concept in 1991, the possibilities appear to be a bit more constrained. Two-fifths of registered voters must put their names, addresses and signatures to a petition, a fairly high bar.

That said, the way the B.C. law plays out bears watching. The two MLAs under the gun, Helmut Giesbrecht of Skeena and Education Minister Paul Ramsey from Prince George North, both took only 40 per cent of the vote in 1996. The number of signatures needed to unseat Mr. Ramsey is 8908, which is only a couple of hundred more than the number of people in [Prince George] who voted for someone other than him in 1996. In Mr. Giesbrecht's riding, the situation is even more startling: more people voted against him than are needed to recall him.

The principle of recall, as an *in-extremis* tool of popular sovereignty, is sound. It must, however, be structured so that its use does not become an abuse, and so that it is employed successfully only in cases where public indignation has been deeply and widely justified.

Recall campaign succeeds. In April 1998, Elections BC issued a petition to start a recall campaign against Paul Reitsma, MLA for the Vancouver Island riding of Parksville–Qualicum. The MLA admitted to writing fake letters praising himself while criticizing unfairly other BC MLAs. When the recall campaign ended in June, enough signatures of registered voters had been collected to force Reitsma to resign his seat. Reitsma resigned two weeks later before he was required to do so under the Recall and Initiative Act.

One of the basic principles of a democratic system is that the judiciary operates independently from the legislative branch of government. When reading the following article, consider this issue: Should the judicial branch continue to operate independently from the legislative branch of government?

Sopinka: On telling the majority it is wrong

(Excerpts) *The Globe and Mail*, November 28, 1997.

On Monday, Mr. Justice John Sopinka of the Supreme Court of Canada died after a short illness. In his eulogy, Chief Justice Antonio Lamer described him as a "marvellous colleague" and "a formidable and prolific judge." Last month, at the Ukrainian–Canadian Conference on Judicial Independence and Authority in Kiev, Ukraine, Judge Sopinka delivered an address from which the following is excerpted:

To insist that the courts must be independent of the political arms of government is to insist that law is and must be separate from politics. It is to believe that a decision can be *legally* correct even though it is *politically* insupportable.

Shielding the judiciary from inappropriate influences means, first and foremost, shielding it from other branches of government—because it is in these branches of government where political interests are most powerfully felt. Politics, power, and interests are the lifeblood of a legislature, a cabinet, a constituent assembly, or a presidency.

Their halls are filled with people who would love to be able to determine the outcome of legal disputes. Indeed, such people, especially if they represent a majority, would prefer that all disputes be political, rather than legal, because politics lets the powerful win. Only the law allows the weak to win against the strong. . . .

Recent changes in our Constitution and in the dynamics of society have made it more difficult for judges to maintain the appearance of impartiality. Until 1982 the role of judges in relation to legislation was to interpret the law. In addition, because we are a federation in which the power to pass legislation is divided between the federal government on the one hand and the provinces on the other, the courts were empowered to decide whether legislation was properly within the sphere of the branch of government that passed it.

In 1982, all that changed. With the adoption of a Charter of Rights and Freedoms, there are areas in which neither the federal Parliament nor the provinces can legislate. As well, all government action can be subjected to judicial scrutiny. These new powers have brought the court into the political arena. By way of example, our court struck down legislation in our Criminal Code, a federal statute, which prohibited abortion except under certain stringent terms; struck down federal legislation prohibiting all federal civil servants from engaging in partisan political activity; and passed upon the validity of a federal government order-in-council which authorized the testing of cruise missiles by the United States on Canadian soil.

. . . The paradox created by the Charter is that it was adopted by means of a democratic process to protect the individual against an abuse of power by the majority, but many feel that it is undemocratic for unelected judges to overrule the majority. The majority does not like to be told it is wrong.

The unfortunate fact is that the Charter has turned the court into the messenger who is likely to get shot for bringing bad news. By enacting the Charter, the legislative branch of government enacted a permanent invitation to the judiciary to tell the majority that it is wrong—that it cannot do what it wants to do, or at least that it cannot do it in a way it wants to do it. If the majority is in a particularly surly mood, bringing this kind of bad news can be a singularly unpleasant business.

How does this relate to the topic of judicial independence? In a very direct way. The Charter is a law. It is the supreme law of the land. It is the duty of courts to apply the law. In order to apply the Charter, courts must be willing to declare laws enacted by elected representatives unconstitutional—to say, in effect, that the majority is breaking the law.

Now if the courts are subject to effective political pressure, whether that be through public criticism aimed at shaming judges into changing their rulings, or through the threat of disciplinary proceedings at the instigation of the executive branch, then the judicial system will be less capable of telling the majority that it is wrong. They will be less able to apply the Charter in an effective manner. And this means the end of the rule of law.

CANADIAN ECONOMIC SYSTEM

Advance Organizer

The Canadian economic system generally combines elements of private enterprise and public enterprise. Many aspects of public enterprise, most notably the development of an extensive social welfare system to redress social and economic inequities, were adopted after 1945.

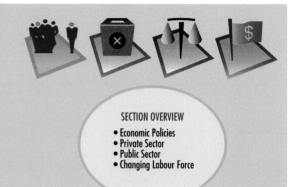

SECTION OVERVIEW
- Economic Policies
- Private Sector
- Public Sector
- Changing Labour Force

CANADIAN ECONOMY IN ACTION

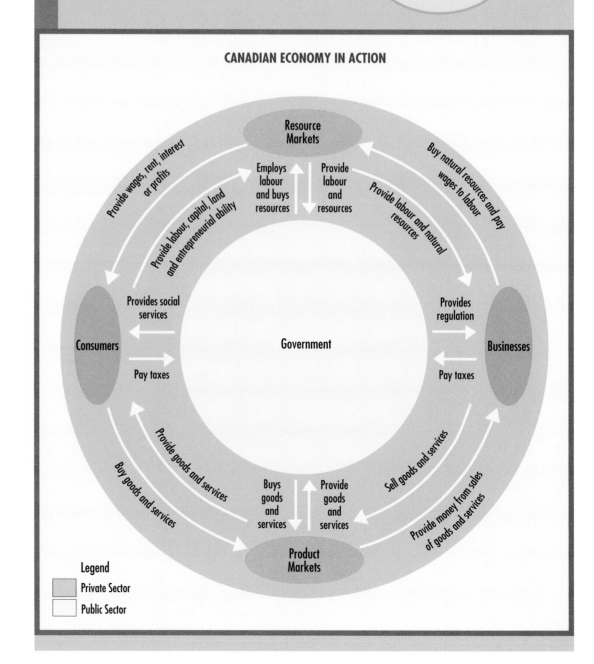

Resource Markets

Provide wages, rent, interest or profits

Buy natural resources and pay wages to labour

Employs labour and buys resources

Provide labour and resources

Provide labour and natural resources

Provide labour, capital, land and entrepreneurial ability

Provides social services

Provides regulation

Consumers

Government

Businesses

Pay taxes

Pay taxes

Provide goods and services

Sell goods and services

Buy goods and services

Buys goods and services

Provide goods and services

Provide money from sales of goods and services

Product Markets

Legend
Private Sector
Public Sector

Economic Policies

The economic policies of Canadian governments have undergone significant shifts in the 20th century. In the years preceding the Great Depression, governments pursued a policy of limited intervention in the economy. In the wake of the Great Depression and World War II, in pursuit of high economic growth, full employment, and a more equitable distribution of income and wealth, governments intervened extensively. More recently, governments have reduced levels of intervention and are reemphasizing the roles of private enterprise and the individual.

Limited Intervention (to 1929)

In the first 30 years of the 20th century, government intervention was confined largely to maintaining public order, ensuring national defence, implementing laws to promote business activity, protecting the national currency, and providing some public works such as roads and public education. Where government intervention in the economy occurred, it was justified on the grounds that it was necessary to serve the national interest. For example, to promote the war effort, the federal government became involved in managing the economy during World War I.

After World War I ended, the federal government began to reduce its involvement in the economy, but the economy had changed considerably during the war. In 1919 the government created Canadian National Railways from several bankrupt railways. Between 1921 and 1929, the federal government increased its financial support of provincial old-age pension plans and unemployment relief. Generally, political and business leaders of the day viewed all other forms of government intervention in the economy as unnecessary and potentially harmful.

Great Depression (1929–1939)

During the Great Depression the economy experienced its widest fluctuations in production and employment, demonstrating to the government how unstable the Canadian private enterprise had become. Before 1929, the economy had experienced periods of boom and bust, but the economy always seemed to self-adjust and resume its course of growth. However, between 1929 and 1933 the economy experienced a pronounced decline in production and employment. Industrial production plummeted by 33% and unemployment rose dramatically, at one point in 1933 affecting over 22% of the labour force.

Initially, the Conservative government of Richard B. Bennett declared that the economy would correct itself and prosperity return. In the meantime, Bennett proposed to cut spending and raise tariffs to balance the budget and protect Canadian industry from foreign competition. By 1933, the long expected economic turnaround had still not materialized, and Bennett's government was compelled to institute a temporary program of public relief and public works to provide work for the unemployed.

In a series of radio broadcasts in early 1935, Bennett outlined a "New Deal for Canada. His proposals included a more progressive taxation system, a minimum wage, more regulation of working conditions, unemployment insurance, health and accident insurance, an improved old-age pension, and support for agriculture. In October 1935, Canadian voters elected the Liberals led by William Lyon Mackenzie King to power. King's government introduced many of the measures that Bennett had announced earlier.

> The economic system reflects Canadian values, attitudes, and ideas.

> Private enterprise has been the underlying principle of the Canadian economy since the 19th century.

| 1914–1918 World War I | 1919 Canadian National Railways created | October 1929 Stock market crash | 1933 Unemployment reaches 22% of labour force; federal government announces temporary program of public relief and assistance for unemployed | 1934 Bank of Canada created | 1935 Canadian Wheat Board established | 1936 Canadian Broadcasting Corporation set up | 1937 Trans-Canada Airlines (Air Canada) created |

Limited Intervention—To 1929　　　　　　　　　　**Great Depression 1929–1939**

Note: Timeline is not to scale

Development of Mixed Economy (1939–1975)

The entry of Canada into World War II in 1939 marked the beginning of a period of unprecedented government intervention in the economy. Many of the ideas behind the government's management of the economy came from British economist John Maynard Keynes. Keynes argued in 1936 that, through its fiscal policy, government can reduce fluctuations in production and employment, and eliminate some inequalities in income.

After 1945, government intervention focussed on maintaining high economic growth, full employment, and stable incomes. A social welfare program was established to provide financial assistance to the unemployed, children, and families, pensions for workers, and a health insurance scheme for the general population. An additional aspect of government fiscal policy during the postwar period was a set of measures to stabilize fluctuations in production and employment resulting from the business cycle (see chart below). These measures focussed on stimulating the economy through government spending on goods and services during bad economic times. When the economy was growing quickly, government spending on goods and services were to be reduced and budget surpluses saved for bad economic times, when they would be needed to stabilize production and employment. However, as it happened, governments increased their spending in good economic times as well as in bad economic times, resulting in continuing budget deficits.

Retreat of Government from the Economy (Since 1975)

Beginning with the increase in world oil prices in 1973–1974, inflation and increasing government deficits made the economy more unstable. To stabilize the economy and control the rise in prices, a different set of economic policies was introduced. These policies focussed on controlling the rate of growth of the money supply. Before 1973, the money supply grew as a result of rapid growth in production and inflation.

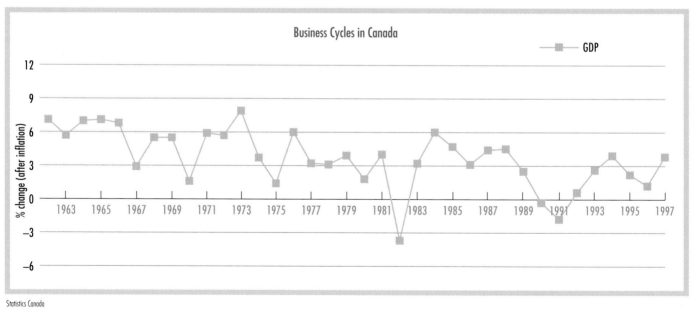

Business Cycles in Canada

Statistics Canada

| 1939–1945 World War II | 1940 Unemployment Insurance Act passed | 1945 Family allowances introduced | 1946 Canada Mortgage and Housing Corporation created | 1947 Saskatchewan universal insurance plan set up | 1949 BC hospital insurance plan established | 1956 Federal Hospital Insurance Act passed | 1962 Saskatchewan universal medical care insurance established | 1966 Canada Pension Plan and Québec Pension Plan created | 1968 National medical care insurance introduced | 1971 Unemployment insurance plan expanded to all workers | 1973–1974 First world oil price rise |

Development of Mixed Economy 1939–1975

This did not appear to be a serious concern of the Canadian government and people. After 1973, the growth of the money supply resulted less from increases in production and more from government deficits. Prominent economists of the day argued that the rate of growth of the money supply in an economy determined the rate of growth of prices. The faster the money supply grew, the higher prices rose. To control the rate of growth of the money supply, these economists argued, the government must reduce its spending on goods and services, reduce regulations on business activities to encourage more investment and growth in production, and allow the value of the national currency to fluctuate freely on world currency markets.

These monetarist views found ready acceptance in the newly emerging school of neoconservative thought. In Canada, neoconservatives took their inspiration from the policies of Margaret Thatcher in Great Britain and Ronald Reagan in the United States. Neoconservative thought in Canada entered mainstream politics in 1987, with the formation of the Reform Party headed by Preston Manning. In the late 1980s and early 1990s, the Reform Party called for sharp reductions in government spending, taxes, and debt. In the provinces, especially Alberta and Ontario, newly elected Progressive Conservative governments dramatically cut government spending in attempts to lower budget deficits, which were subsequently largely eliminated.

Federal Budget Speech (excerpt), Feb. 27, 1995.

This government came into office *because* it believes that the nation's priority must be jobs and growth. And it is because of that, not in *spite* of that, that we must act now to restore the nation's finances to health. As the Prime Minister [Jean Chrétien] has said: "The time to reduce deficits is when the economy is growing. So now is the time."

Not to act now to put our fiscal house in order would be to abandon the purposes for which our Party exists and this government stands—competence, compassion, reform, and hope. The debt and deficit are not inventions of ideology. They are facts of arithmetic. The quicksand of compound interest is *real*. The *last* thing Canadians *need* is another lecture on the dangers of the deficit. The *only* thing Canadians *want* is clear action.

Canapress/Jonathan Hayward

PHOTO: Paul Martin, Canadian Minister of Finance since November 1993.

Retreat of Government from the Economy—Since 1975

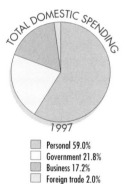

1997

Personal 59.0%
Government 21.8%
Business 17.2%
Foreign trade 2.0%

1997

Wages and salaries 70.3%
Business profits 13.6%
Interest and investment 7.4%
Self-employment 8.4%
Farming income 0.3%

Statistics Canada

PHOTO: Consumers
influence the economy
through their spending on
goods and services.

Private Sector

Private enterprise has been the underlying principle of the Canadian economy since the 19th century. Today, apart from government, the main decision makers in the economy are consumers and business enterprises. These two groups together form what is called the private sector.

Consumers

Consumers are the main decision makers in the Canadian economy. They consist of households, individuals, and families. Businesses are also consumers, buying goods and services needed for production. Consumers decide which goods and services to buy to satisfy such needs and wants as food, clothing, shelter, protection, travel, and entertainment.

Through their spending decisions, consumers influence the production of goods and services. Personal spending on goods and services accounts annually for about 60% of all spending in the Canadian economy (see chart "Total Domestic Spending"). Wages and salaries are the main source of income in Canada, accounting for over 70% of total domestic income. Other types of income are business profits (13.6%), interest and investment (7.4%), self-employment (8.4%), and farming (0.3%) (see chart "Total Domestic Income").

Judy Bauer/Arnold Publishing ltd.

Business Enterprises

The main activities of business enterprises are the production and distribution of goods and services to consumers in Canada and abroad. Canadian business enterprises are organized as sole proprietorships, partnerships, or corporations.

Sole Proprietorship. A sole proprietorship is the simplest and most common form of business enterprise in Canada. It is owned and operated by one individual. Most small businesses and family businesses in Canada are sole proprietorships. Examples are businesses run by doctors, dentists, store owners, insurance agents, restaurateurs, painters, and other self-employed people. An estimated 1.1 million sole proprietorships employ about one-quarter of the Canadian labour force.

The advantages of a sole proprietorship are that it is easy to set up, and all income earned goes to the owner. Some disadvantages are that the owner is liable for all debts and many have to use personal assets to pay expenses of the business, such as wages to employees and purchases of goods.

Partnership. A partnership is owned and operated by two or more individuals. Examples of partnerships are some professional practices of accountants and lawyers. Some advantages are the pooling of skills and financial resources and the sharing of risk. Some disadvantages are the legal liability for all debts, and difficulties in making decisions acceptable to all partners. There are about 150 000 partnerships in Canada.

Corporation. A corporation is created in Canada only with permission of either the federal or a provincial government, both of which have the legal authority to grant charters to corporations. An estimated one million corporations operate in Canada.

A corporation can sell shares to private individuals or to the general public. The owners of the corporation are referred to as the shareholders. A corporation owned by private individuals is referred to as a privately controlled company. A corporation that sells shares to the general public who can trade these shares on a stock exchange is called a publicly listed company. The main stock exchanges in Canada are the Toronto Stock Exchange (TSE), Montreal Stock Exchange (MSE), Vancouver Stock Exchange (VSE), and Alberta Stock Exchange (ASE). The MSE is the country's oldest stock exchange, founded in 1874, but the TSE is the largest.

A corporation has many advantages. A corporation can usually acquire larger amounts of money more easily than a sole proprietorship or partnership. Shareholders or owners of a corporation are not personally liable for the corporation's debts. The life of a corporation does not end with the death of a shareholder, as it would in the case of a sole proprietorship or partnership.

Limited liability is the most important advantage of a corporation. Unlike sole proprietorships and partnerships, where owners are exposed to many risks, including all debts and expenses of the business, in a corporation the owner is exposed to fewer risks and debts of the business. If the corporation fails, then the owner loses only the amount of money he or she invested in the business, and does not have to use personal assets to pay all debts of the business, as would be the case in a sole proprietorship or partnership.

The main disadvantage of a corporation lies in the rules and regulations that it has to follow. The corporate form of business enterprise can also be costly to set up and maintain. Depending on the corporation's profits, the level of taxation on profits can be high, although not as high as for a sole proprietorship.

Generally, most corporations in Canada are owned by private individuals and companies, but governments can also own corporations, known as Crown corporations. A Crown corporation is usually set up by an act of Parliament or a provincial legislature for a specific purpose, some of which have included regional development, economic stabilization, provision of essential services, and accrual of income for the government.

Competition

Most Canadian markets are characterized by strong competition among many firms. This competition is stimulated by the fact that any person who has the necessary capital, motivation, knowledge, and an idea can set up a business to produce or distribute goods and services for sale to consumers. There are few restrictions preventing individuals from going into business and competing with others. Retail stores, fast-food restaurants, hair salons, delivery services, and farming are sectors of the economy where there are many firms and strong competition. In these sectors, price is determined by the interplay of supply and demand.

Several industries, however, are dominated by a few large businesses. Telecommunications, motor vehicle production, and gas retailing are examples of industries that have few producers. In recent years, the federal government used its anticombine legislation to investigate price fixing and other means by which large companies limited competition.

Incentives

Profits are an important feature of Canadian business and are one of the main reasons thousands of Canadians decide to own a business. In Canada in 1997, profits from the production and sale of goods and services were the second-largest source of income after wages and salaries, amounting to an estimated $116.4 billion. Some of the most profitable companies in Canada were in banking, publishing, automobile production, oil and gas production, and entertainment (see chart on page 154, "Canada's Top Corporations").

Corporate Canada

The largest Canadian corporations are listed below. These corporations dominate industries such as telecommunications, motor vehicle production, entertainment, mining, oil and gas extraction, pipelines, food retailing, and high technology. Of these 15 largest corporations, 12 are listed on stock exchanges and 3 (General Motors, Ford Motor, and Chrysler Canada) are private subsidiaries of large American corporations. The total sales of these 15

large corporations account for about 28% of the total value of Canadian gross domestic product (GDP), but they only employ about 4% of the total labour force. In 1997, these corporations collectively earned more than $6.03 billion in profits, prompting many Canadians to complain about the power and influence of these corporations on competition.

Another aspect of the domination of Canadian industry by large corporations is the high level of foreign ownership. More

Canada's Top Corporations (1997)
(in millions of C$)

	Industry	Sales	Profits	Employees	Foreign Ownership
General Motors of Canada	Motor vehicles and parts	$33 600	n.a.	29 000	100.0%
BCE Inc.	Telecommunications	33 191	$(1536)	122 000	—
Ford Motor	Motor vehicles and parts	27 900	685	24 402	100.0
Seagram Company	Entertainment	17 161	686	30 000	—
Chrysler Canada	Motor vehicles and parts	16 688	115	16 000	100.0
TransCanada Pipelines	Pipelines	14 242	457	3042	—
George Weston	Food/merchandising	13 921	244	83 000	—
Thomson Corporation	Publishing and printing	12 137	762	50 000	—
Onex Corporation	Conglomerate	11 212	54	43 000	—
Alcan Aluminium	Mining and smelting	10 768	648	33 000	—
Imasco	Tobacco/financial services	10 008	790	27 000	42.4
Canadian Pacific	Transport/oil and gas	9560	1255	33 600	—
Imperial Oil	Oil and gas	9512	847	7000	69.8
Bombardier Inc.	High technology	8508	420	47 000	—
Magna International	Motor vehicles and parts	7691	603	36 000	—

Losses appear in brackets.

Compiled from annual company reports and *Globe and Mail Report on Business*

Canada's Top Banks (October 1997)
(in millions of C$)

	Assets	Sales	Profits	Employees
Royal Bank of Canada	$244 774	$9311	$1679	50 719
Canadian Imperial Bank of Commerce	237 989	8621	1551	42 446
Bank of Montreal	207 838	7167	1305	34 286
Bank of Nova Scotia	195 153	6365	1514	38 648
Toronto Dominion Bank	163 852	5472	1088	28 001
National Bank of Canada	66 235	2375	342	13 327
Hongkong Bank of Canada	23 910	733	138	4015
Laurentian Bank of Canada	13 422	464	60	3384

Compiled from annual company reports and *Globe and Mail Report on Business*

than 50% of Canadian industry is owned and controlled by foreign companies, mainly American corporations. Over 15% of all American investment abroad is located in Canada. This has contributed significantly to close corporate ties between Canada and the United States, to the extent that over 80% of all Canadian exports are shipped to the United States.

In terms of assets, sales, and employees, Canadian banks are very large corporations (see chart on page 154, "Canada's Top Banks"). The six largest banks control $1.12 trillion in assets and about 90% of all deposits held by Canadians. All but the Hongkong Bank of Canada, which is foreign-owned, have their shares listed on the stock exchange. In 1997, these banks earned almost $7.7 billion in profits, which provoked a public outcry over the power of the Canadian banks and a demand for greater government regulation of bank profits for the good of consumers. In 1998, the creation of two superbanks, each with over $400 billion in assets, was proposed. The proposed merger of the Royal Bank of Canada and Bank of Montreal was followed by a similar proposal from the Toronto Dominion Bank and Canadian Imperial Bank of Commerce.

Crown Corporations

Role in the Canadian Economy.

Throughout the 20th century Crown corporations have played a major role in the Canadian economy. Before 1945, they were largely associated with nation-building and forging communication links between Canadians living in different regions. In 1919, Canadian National Railways was created to provide an important second rail link, while Trans-Canada Airlines (later Air Canada) was created in 1937 to provide air service to all regions of Canada. The Canadian Broadcasting Corporation (CBC) was set up in 1936 to provide national radio and television broadcasting as well as regional and local programming throughout the country. CBC radio has been viewed by some as an important link between Canadians, contributing significantly to the development of the Canadian nation and identity.

In addition to their historical contribution to nation building, Crown corporations are active in the production of goods and services. They are especially active in the generation of electricity, urban transport, the sale and distribution of alcoholic beverages, postal service, and sale of lottery tickets (see chart). Though these Crown corporations are owned by

A Crown corporation, owned by the federal or a provincial government, is established to carry out regulatory, advisory, administrative, or financial services, or to provide goods and services.

Largest Crown Corporations (1997) (in millions of C$)				
	Industry	Sales	Profits	Employees
Ontario Hydro	Electricity	$8925	$(6326)	21 130
Hydro-Québec	Electricity	8287	786	17 164
Canadian Wheat Board	Agriculture	6111	n.a.	574
Canada Post Corporation	Postal services	5086	113	63 529
Loto-Québec	Lotteries	2619	982	5000
BC Hydro	Electricity	2403	339	5819
Ontario Lottery Corporation	Lotteries	2067	652	750
Liquor Control Board of Ontario	Liquor sales	1997	701	2828
CSST	Insurance	1722	215	3042
Société des alcools du Québec	Liquor sales	1077	372	1974
New Brunswick Power	Electricity	1037	(19)	2626
Manitoba Hydro	Electricity	1025	101	3021
EPCOR Utilities	Electricity	930	116	1360
Saskatchewan Power	Electricity	915	132	2000
Canadian Commercial Corporation	General services	905	1	90

Losses appear in brackets.

Compiled from *Financial Post 500*, June 1998 and *Globe and Mail Report on Business*

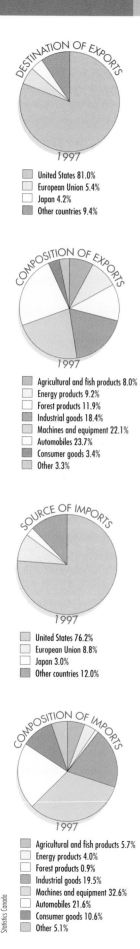

DESTINATION OF EXPORTS

1997

- United States 81.0%
- European Union 5.4%
- Japan 4.2%
- Other countries 9.4%

COMPOSITION OF EXPORTS

1997

- Agricultural and fish products 8.0%
- Energy products 9.2%
- Forest products 11.9%
- Industrial goods 18.4%
- Machines and equipment 22.1%
- Automobiles 23.7%
- Consumer goods 3.4%
- Other 3.3%

SOURCE OF IMPORTS

1997

- United States 76.2%
- European Union 8.8%
- Japan 3.0%
- Other countries 12.0%

COMPOSITION OF IMPORTS

1997

- Agricultural and fish products 5.7%
- Energy products 4.0%
- Forest products 0.9%
- Industrial goods 19.5%
- Machines and equipment 32.6%
- Automobiles 21.6%
- Consumer goods 10.6%
- Other 5.1%

Statistics Canada

government and should be considered part of the government or public sector of the economy, in recent years governments have insisted that their Crown corporations act more as independent profit making business enterprises that are less dependent on government financial support.

Marketing Boards. Other important Crown corporations operating in the Canadian economy are marketing boards. In the 1930s, provincial and federal governments established various boards, commissions, and agencies to control the marketing of agricultural crops and help stabilize farming incomes. Currently, over 100 marketing boards oversee the production of cereal grains, dairy products, eggs, turkeys, and chickens in every province.

The most important and largest marketing board is the Canadian Wheat Board. Established in 1935 by the federal government, the Canadian Wheat Board is charged with the orderly marketing of western grains. It is the sole seller in export markets of prairie wheat, barley, and oats. However, in recent years several farmers have challenged in court the authority of the Canadian Wheat Board to sell their grain. The courts have decided in favour of the Canadian Wheat Board.

Other marketing boards, such as those for dairy products, eggs, turkeys, and chickens, control production through quotas. These quotas control the entry of new producers and the amount of the product produced or marketed. Through these measures, the boards are able to determine prices. Critics argue that marketing boards have contributed to increased food prices and less choice, while defenders contend that the boards have stabilized food prices and increased producers' incomes.

Foreign Trade

Canada's private sector and several of the country's Crown corporations depend heavily on foreign trade. At least one in three jobs in the private sector depends directly on the export or import of goods. Since 1945, the Canadian economy has become more closely integrated with the neighbouring American economy.

Exports and Imports. Canada is one of the largest trading nations in the world. In 1997, Canadian companies exported over $301 billion and imported almost $280 billion in goods. The main market for Canadian goods was the United States, which purchased 81% of all exports, while the European Union and Japan purchased much smaller shares, as the chart "Destination of Exports" indicates.

The main products exported in 1997, as indicated in the chart "Composition of Exports," were automobiles (23.7%), machines and equipment (22.1%), and industrial goods (18.4%). Historically, Canada was noted for its exports of forest products, energy, and foodstuffs, which accounted for 29.1% of total exports in 1997.

The main source of imports into Canada in 1997 was the United States, accounting for 76.2% of all imports, followed by the European Union and Japan (see chart "Sources of Imports").

As the chart "Composition of Imports" indicates, the main goods imported into Canada in 1997 were machines and equipment (32.6%), automobiles (21.6%), and industrial goods (19.5%). Consumer goods, foodstuffs, energy, and forest products accounted for 21.2% of total imports.

Trade Agreements. Many attempts were made in the 20th century to expand free trade between Canada and the United States. Most failed to obtain approval in the Canadian parliament or from voters. In 1947, Canada became a signatory nation of the General Agreement on Tariffs and Trade (GATT) and carried out negotiations with the United States on reducing some tariffs and other barriers to trade between the two countries. The discussions led to a number of trade initiatives being implemented over the years.

One important initiative to expand trading ties between Canada and the United States was the Canada–US Automotive Products Agreement (known as the Auto-Pact) signed in 1965. The basic objectives of the Auto-Pact were to create a broader market for the sale and manufacture of motor vehicles, enable both countries to trade on an equitable basis, and develop conditions which would permit more efficient patterns of investment, production, and trade. The Auto-Pact created a single North American market for passenger cars, trucks, buses, tires, and automotive parts. Under the agreement, manufacturers of automotive vehicles and parts were committed to producing goods with 60% Canadian content. For many years, the Auto-Pact protected Canadian and American automotive producers from foreign competition, mainly Japanese, by imposing tariffs and quotas on imported automotive goods that did not have at least 60% North American content. During negotiations over free trade in 1987, Canada and the United States resolved to keep the Auto-Pact.

In 1988, the Canadian and American governments signed the Canada–US Free Trade Agreement (FTA). The FTA recognized the fact that the countries were each other's largest customer, Canada buying over 25% of all American exports and the United States buying over 80% of all Canadian exports. The main objectives of the FTA were to end all tariffs on all goods and services exchanged between the two countries by 1999, remove other restrictions to trade and investment flow, and set up a trade-dispute settlement mechanism.

The Free Trade Agreement became the main issue in the 1988 Canadian general elections. Defenders of FTA, mainly supporters of the Progressive Conservatives and directors of large corporations, claimed that the agreement guaranteed Canadian businesses access to the large American market and that this would lead to enhanced opportunities for employment, and economic growth in Canada. Defenders of FTA noted that, although industries like textiles, furniture, food processing, and consumer goods would be forced to lay off several thousand workers to become more competitive, the agreement would create more jobs overall in Canada. Critics of FTA, largely supporters of the Liberals and New Democrats, countered, saying that free trade would eventually make the economy more dependent on the United States, increase unemployment, and expose

Canadian small businesses to unfair competition from American businesses, which could produce greater quantities of goods at much lower cost.

Also, critics of FTA argued that the agreement would allow more American influence over Canadian affairs and sovereignty. However, two weeks after the Progressive Conservative government was reelected in December 1988, legislation on the free trade agreement was passed in the House of Commons and came into effect on January 1, 1989.

In 1994, the Canada–US Free Trade Agreement was expanded to include Mexico and became known as the North American Free Trade Agreement (NAFTA). NAFTA proposed to eliminate tariffs and quotas on imported goods in North America within five years. Defenders of NAFTA claimed that extending free trade to Mexico would provide new export markets for Canadian goods as well as political stability in Mexico. Opponents to NAFTA, particularly trade unions, feared that many businesses would invest their money in Mexico where wages and other costs of production were significantly lower.

The many claims that free trade would either bring great prosperity or destroy domestic industry have not been realized. Free trade has brought both benefits and losses to Canadians. Many subsidiaries of American firms that had located primarily in Ontario and Québec to manufacture consumer goods for the Canadian market in earlier years have closed, throwing many thousands out of work. However, at the same time, foreign investment has continued to flow into Canada, establishing new companies and creating high-paying skilled jobs in advanced technology, computer software, and aerospace. Many Canadian firms, assured of markets in the United States, have expanded domestic manufacturing operations to produce for the United States. The predicted drain of investment capital from Canada to Mexico has not occurred. Since 1996, some Canadian firms have discovered that it is easier to produce goods in Canada because there are more skilled workers, less corruption, and fewer regulations.

FEDERAL GOVERNMENT SPENDING

1997

- ☐ Goods and services 21.9%
- ☐ Transfers to individuals 32.6%
- ■ Transfers to businesses 1.6%
- ☐ Transfers to non-residents 1.7%
- ☐ Transfers to other governments 15.4%
- ☐ Interest on public debt 26.8%

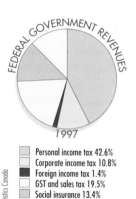

FEDERAL GOVERNMENT REVENUES

1997

- ☐ Personal income tax 42.6%
- ☐ Corporate income tax 10.8%
- ■ Foreign income tax 1.4%
- ☐ GST and sales tax 19.5%
- ☐ Social insurance 13.4%
- ☐ Investments and other 12.3%

Statistics Canada

Personal Income Tax Rates (1997)

Personal		
Income <	$29 590	17%
Income	$29 591–59 180	26%
Income >	$59 181	29%
Business		
Basic rate		38%

Revenue Canada

Public Sector

Since Confederation, the public sector has played an important role in the development of the Canadian economy. Today, the main economic activities of the public sector are conducted through its fiscal policy, monetary policy, and a comprehensive social welfare system.

Fiscal Policy

The main functions of Canadian fiscal policy are expenditures on goods and services, taxation, and regulation. All these functions are outlined in the government's budget.

Expenditure. The main objective of government expenditures on goods, services, and capital investments is to influence the activities of the private sector and stimulate the economy. Consumer spending on goods and services is influenced by the government mainly through transfers of cash payments to consumers, such as employment insurance, pensions, and welfare. Transfer payments are one of the most effective government methods of equalizing incomes. Government purchases of goods (such as paper, furniture, books, military hardware) and services (such as consulting, advertising, and printing) influence the production and distribution decisions of many businesses. The chart "Federal Government Spending" shows that in 1997 the main expenditures of the federal government were for goods and services, transfers to individuals, businesses, non-residents, and other governments, and interest on public debt. These expenditures are mainly funded by taxation.

Taxation. Taxes, the main source of revenue for governments, can influence consumer and business spending. When consumers pay taxes, they have less money left to buy goods and services and for savings. Taxes also affect what products businesses produce and distribute. In recent years, taxation on personal incomes and on the sale of all goods and services has grown. The chart "Federal Government Revenues" shows that the main sources of revenues for the federal

government in 1997 were personal income taxes, corporate income taxes, sales taxes, social insurance contributions (mainly employment insurance contributions), and investments.

Personal income taxes are by far the largest source of revenue for the federal government, followed by income from sales taxes. The percentage of total federal government revenues belonging to corporate income taxes has fallen over the years, but the amount of money the federal government receives in corporate income taxes is the highest in history.

Regulation. Though in recent years governments have considerably reduced regulation of the private sector, regulation remains a powerful function of government fiscal policy. Most current government regulation aims to eliminate business activities that are harmful to the environment and to protect consumers from unscrupulous business practices. Other regulations establish criteria for the setting of prices of services such as telephone, electricity, and water; and establish and enforce safety and health standards in the workplace and in the manufacturing of goods.

Monetary Policy

Since the late 1970s, the monetary policy of the Bank of Canada has become more important than fiscal policy as a mechanism to stabilize and encourage economic growth. Established in 1934, the Bank of Canada is responsible for regulating the supply of money in the economy through regular adjustments in credit and interest rates. Its objectives for the Canadian economy are to

- maintain a high and stable level of employment
- promote stable prices and prevent high inflation
- encourage a high rate of economic growth
- stabilize the value of the Canadian dollar
- ensure a fairer distribution of economic benefits among Canadians.

Interest Rates. The Bank of Canada regulates the money supply in Canada through changes in its bank rate, the interest rate it charges Canadian banks to borrow money. The setting of the bank rate is achieved through the sale of government bonds to banks and investors. During the 1980s, the Bank of Canada pursued a policy of "tight money" by raising its bank rate, causing Canadian banks to raise interest rates on all types of credit in order to slow down the growth of the money supply and rate of inflation. Throughout most of the 1980s, the bank rate rarely fell below 8.4%, provoking numerous demands from businesses and consumers for the government to lower interest rates (see chart below).

Canadian Dollar. In the 1980s, the Bank of Canada's policy of raising interest rates to reduce the rate of inflation was used to protect the value of the Canadian dollar. The Bank realized that a stable Canadian dollar was important for maintaining the country's international competitiveness as a trading nation. In spite of high interest rates, the average value of the Canadian dollar dropped from US$1.014 in 1976 to US$0.685 in 1998 (see chart "Changes in Value of Canadian Dollar"). A lower value for the Canadian dollar makes the cost of foreign travel and imported goods more expensive but Canadian exports cheaper and more competitive in foreign markets.

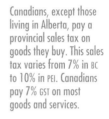

A $100 investment earning an annual return of 10% will be worth almost $200 after seven years if one does not withdraw any interest earned during that time. At an annual return of 5% and with no withdrawal, a $100 investment will double in value after 14 years.

Canadians, except those living in Alberta, pay a provincial sales tax on goods they buy. This sales tax varies from 7% in BC to 10% in PEI. Canadians pay 7% GST on most goods and services.

Businesses in Canada pay a provincial and a federal tax on profits. Provincial corporate taxes vary from 5.5% in Alberta to 17% in Manitoba. Federal corporate tax is 38% on annual profits above $200 000.

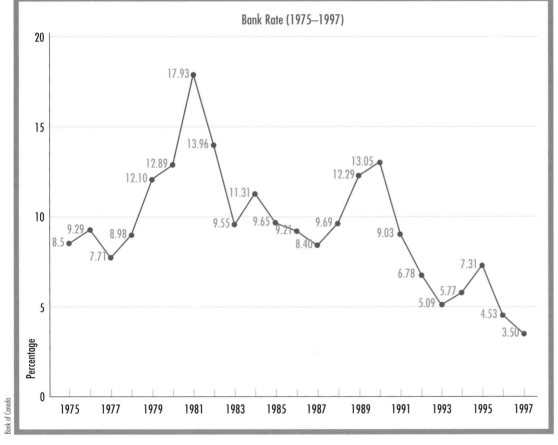

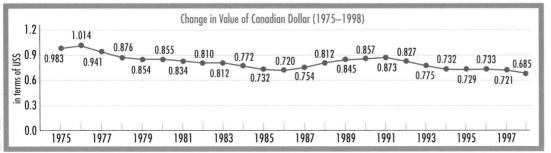

Bank of Canada

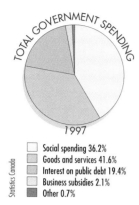

TOTAL GOVERNMENT SPENDING

1997

Statistics Canada

- ☐ Social spending 36.2%
- ☐ Goods and services 41.6%
- ☐ Interest on public debt 19.4%
- ☐ Business subsidies 2.1%
- ■ Other 0.7%

Canadian Social Welfare

Spending on various social welfare programs is a major component of the public sector in Canada. About 36% of expenditures by all levels of government is related in some way to providing social programs. The historical emphasis of Canadian social programs has been on solving individual problems and addressing regional inequalities.

Historical Background. Before 1940, the federal government provided little social assistance to less advantaged groups, including poor, sick, elderly, and young people, and women. The few social programs that existed were set up mainly to lessen social unrest and disorder caused by unemployment and poverty.

In the 1940s, the foundations of modern Canadian social welfare institutions were created. A series of government inquiries were established to determine general objectives for Canadian social welfare policy. In 1940, the federal government passed the Unemployment Insurance Act to provide limited benefits for unemployed workers. In 1945, it introduced the universal Family Allowances program to give some financial support to families with children. In 1946, it created the Canada Mortgage and Housing Corporation to provide low-interest loans for house construction. At the provincial level, in 1947 Saskatchewan introduced a universal hospital insurance plan, followed by British Columbia in 1949. In 1956, the federal government passed the Hospital Insurance Act to provide financial support for provincial hospital insurance programs.

In the 1960s, the federal government undertook to develop the country's social welfare institutions. In 1966, it created Canada Pension Plan to provide retirement and disability benefits. Québec established its own pension plan. In 1968, the federal government enacted universal medical care insurance, which had been implemented provincially in Saskatchewan in 1962.

In the 1970s, all levels of government further expanded the social welfare system. In 1971, the federal government extended unemployment insurance coverage to more groups and included sickness and maternity leave. At the provincial level social services were expanded. Various initiatives were undertaken to coordinate social programs with municipalities and private charities.

In the 1980s and the 1990s, Canadian social welfare institutions came under considerable financial pressure. In 1984, the Canada Health Act was passed to stop the growing practice of extra-billing from affecting universal medical care. In the early 1990s, governments at all levels introduced numerous changes to social welfare programs in an attempt to control the rising costs of social services. Education and health care were particularly affected, resulting in strong public reaction in some areas of Canada.

Principles. Since its establishment, the Canadian social welfare system has been based on the principles of equal access, social equality, and universality. To ensure that all regions of the country can provide social programs, the federal government provides financial support to provincial and local governments. The purpose of this financial support is to ensure that everyone in the country has access to a similar level of social welfare benefits.

Social equality through income support is another principle of the social welfare system. The objectives of these programs are to promote equality of opportunity and greater access to government services.

All basic social welfare programs in Canada are based on the concept of universality. This means that every Canadian, regardless of income, is entitled to them. A Canadian citizen must not be denied the use of these social services or charged extra fees for using them. More recently, this principle has been eroded by the increasing implementation of user fees.

Social Welfare System

The main components of the Canadian social welfare system today are a national health insurance plan (popularly called medicare), old-age security (OAS) and retirement plans, and an employment insurance program.

Medicare. Medicare is made up of 12 interlocking provincial and territorial health insurance plans governed by the Canada Health Act. These health insurance plans provide Canadians with free hospital insurance and doctor services, though most provinces do levy an annual insurance premium. When Canadians need medical care they go to the doctor of their choice, who in turn bills the provincial government according to a fee schedule negotiated between the provincial medical association and the provincial government. All health services are under provincial jurisdiction, though the federal government makes financial contributions toward each provincial plan. These contributions are governed by the Canada Health Act, which penalizes provinces that allow extra-billing by doctors or hospital user fees for insured health services.

Old-Age Security and Retirement. Security for seniors is provided by three different plans. The first is old-age security, a universal benefit paid by the federal government to Canadians aged 65 and over who meet minimum residency requirements. The OAS is supplemented by the Guaranteed Income Supplement (GIS) and Spouse's Allowance payments for recipients with little or no other income.

The second type of retirement plan is the Canada Pension Plan/Québec Pension Plan. The Canada Pension Plan covers workers outside Québec and is administered by the federal government. The Québec Pension Plan covers workers in Québec and is administered by the Province of Québec. The two pension plans enforce compulsory participation by most employed and self-employed individuals between the ages of 18 and 70. The plans are financed through employer, employee, and self-employed contributions. Employees and self-employed pay 3% of their earnings, and employers match this contribution through a payroll tax.

The third type of retirement plan includes private pension plans funded through employee and employer contributions. Less than half of the total labour force belongs to private pension plans. The federal government provides tax incentives to encourage people to contribute to registered retirement savings plans (RRSP). The contribution any person can make to an RRSP is set by the government annually and depends on income. Payment of tax on income placed in an RRSP can be deferred until retirement when income may be lower.

Employment Insurance. Employment insurance is a major component of the Canadian social welfare system. The program provides income insurance in the event of job loss to Canadians who receive a salary or an hourly wage. In addition to regular benefits, recipients may qualify for training, maternity leave, sickness, or fishing benefits. The program is financed by contributions from employers and employees. Employees contribute 2.7% of their earnings and employers match this contribution through a payroll tax of 3.78%. In the early 1990s, the federal government imposed new conditions on the eligibility and payment of employment insurance benefits. In 1996, the Unemployment Insurance Commission, reorganized as the Employment Income Commission, reduced benefits to seasonal workers, a highly unpopular measure in many small rural communities in Atlantic Canada where seasonal work is common.

Canadians contributed over $20 billion to their RRSPs in 1998.

The monthly old-age security (OAS) payment to seniors in 1998 was $407.15. The maximum monthly Guaranteed Income Supplement (GIS) payment a senior could receive in 1998 was $483.17.

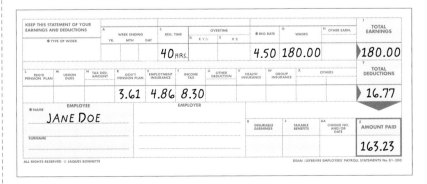

161

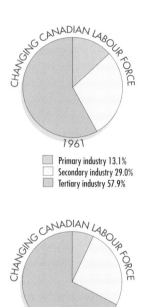

Changing Labour Force

At the same time as social welfare programs were expanding, the Canadian labour force underwent two significant structural changes. They were the growth of the service sector and greater numbers of women entering the labour force.

Growth of the Service Sector

In 1961, 42.1% of the Canadian labour force was employed in primary industry (agriculture, mining, and forestry) and in secondary industry (manufacturing and construction). The remaining 57.9% were employed in tertiary industry (services). By 1980, the percentage of people employed in primary and secondary industries had declined to 32.7% and that of people working in tertiary industry had risen to 67.3%. In 1997, about 73.9% of the total labour force was employed in tertiary industry while 5.1% worked in primary industry and 21% in secondary industry. The three "Changing Canadian Labour Force" charts illustrate this growth of the service sector.

One main factor explaining the growth of employment in the service sector was an unprecedented expansion of public sector employment between 1961 and 1980. In 1961, 18.2% of the labour force was employed in the public sector, providing instruction in schools, providing medical services in hospitals, and administering

government programs. By 1980, the share of the labour force working in the public sector had increased to 24.6%. This growth in public sector employment occurred as governments at all levels increased their spending on social welfare, health care, and education. All of these government services were very labour intensive. Employment in the public sector continued to grow throughout the 1980s, though the overall percentage of the labour force working in the public sector declined.

In 1992, employment in the public sector peaked. Since then all three levels of government have laid off thousands of public servants as one means of reducing budget deficits. Total employment in the public sector in 1997 was reduced by over 10% from 1992 levels and its share of the labour force fell to about 22%.

Women in the Labour Force

The number of women employed in the labour force has expanded dramatically, from 1 764 000 in 1961 to 6 292 000 in 1997. The percentage of women workers in the Canadian labour force rose from 27.3% in 1961 to 45.1% in 1997 (see chart "Employment by Gender"). This indicates that more women in their adult years are participating in the labour force.

Just as more women have been employed outside the home, so have more women become unemployed and are

Employment by Gender (1961–1997)			
	1961	1980	1997
Employment Share:			
Women	27.3%	40.4%	45.1%
Men	72.7	59.6	54.9
Both sexes	100.0	100.0	100.0
Unemployment Rate:			
Women	3.7%	8.9%	9.2%
Men	7.8	6.7	9.2
Both sexes	7.1	7.5	9.2
Youth (15–24)	4.3	13.5	16.7

Statistics Canada

162

looking for work. The rate of unemployment among women rose from 3.7% in 1961 to 9.2% in 1997, a rate similar to that among men. In contrast, the rate of unemployment among young people (ages 15–24) has grown sharply over the years owing to changes in the state of the economy, from 4.3% in 1961, to 13.5% in 1980, to 16.7% in 1997 (see chart on page 162 "Employment by Gender"). In 1961 the economy was growing rapidly, but in 1980 it was entering a recession. In 1997 the economy was beginning to recover from a sharp recession.

Most women who have entered the labour force since 1961 found employment in the service sector. In 1961, the most common occupations women pursued were clerical, sales, and the professions (primarily teaching and nursing). The main occupational areas for men were in manufacturing, agriculture, mining, and transportation. Almost forty years later, in 1997, professions like nursing and teaching, and clerical and sales jobs continued to be common occupations of women, though increasing numbers of women were finding work in once male-dominated occupations such as construction, management, and transportation. After almost 40 years, manufacturing and transportation were still common occupations of men, though many men were working in management, sales, and clerical positions (see chart below, "Occupations by Gender").

Women in Business

As women enter the labour force, growing numbers of women are owning or operating businesses. Today, Canadian women own or operate over 730 000 firms that employ some 1.7 million people. A 1997 report from the Bank of Montreal noted that over 30% of all firms in Canada are owned or operated by women, ranging from 23.5% of firms in Newfoundland to 33.2% of firms in Alberta (see chart "Share of Women-Led Firms by Province.")

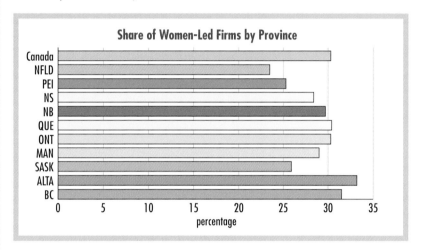

Women-led firms are represented in all industries throughout Canada. More women have set up businesses in non-traditional industries such as agriculture, mining, communications, wholesale trade, finance, and business services, and some traditional industries have fewer women-led businesses (see chart "Distribution of Women-Led Firms by Industry").

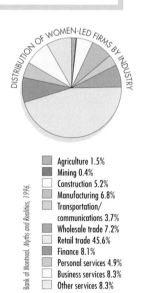

Bank of Montreal. *Myths and Realities*, 1996.

- Agriculture 1.5%
- Mining 0.4%
- Construction 5.2%
- Manufacturing 6.8%
- Transportation/ communications 3.7%
- Wholesale trade 7.2%
- Retail trade 45.6%
- Finance 8.1%
- Personal services 4.9%
- Business services 8.3%
- Other services 8.3%

Occupations By Gender (1961–1997)				
	Women		Men	
	1961	1997	1961	1997
Farming, fishing, mining	4.4%	3.0%	16.4%	7.4%
Transportation	2.3	4.4	10.0	10.3
Manufacturing	11.4	9.6	26.1	20.0
Construction	—	1.3	7.3	8.7
Services				
• sales	23.2	17.0	8.7	17.2
• managerial	3.0	6.4	9.9	12.6
• professional	15.9	27.0	7.9	8.5
• clerical	29.3	23.5	6.9	10.8
• financial	10.5	7.8	6.8	4.5
Totals	100.0	100.0	100.0	100.0

Statistics Canada

CANADIAN POLITICAL ECONOMY

Advance Organizer

For much of the postwar period in Canada, government expanded to meet the public demand for more social spending, regulation of the private sector, and employment. All of this assumed that the growth of government was a positive development and would have little impact on the overall economy. Many politicians believed that it was possible to expand government indefinitely because government was not affected by the same economic forces that influenced the decisions of the private sector. In the late 1970s, a few politicians and economists began to question the assumptions about unrestrained government spending, budget deficits, and debts. By 1990, the financial situation of governments had become serious and, in the view of many economists and analysts, threatened to destabilize the economy.

CANADIAN POLITICAL ECONOMY

• Growth of Government
• Canadian Neoconservatism
• Results of Government Cutbacks

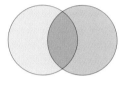

☐ Canadian Political System
☐ Canadian Economic System
☐ Canadian Political Economy

Growth of Government

The chart below illustrates the unprecedented growth in the size of all levels of government from 1945 to 1997. In 1945, government spending accounted for 40.6% of the gross domestic product (GDP), but by 1991 it was over 50% of GDP. This growth of government spending was accompanied by higher taxes, and after 1975 by mounting budget deficits. Taxes as a percentage of GDP rose from 26.7% in 1945 to 46.3% in 1997. From 1975 to 1997, government budget deficits rose from 0.4% of GDP in 1975 to a high of 6.8% in 1992–1993 and then to a small surplus in 1997, the first in 23 years. From 1975 to 1997, net government debt rose from 21.3% of GDP in 1975 to 93.0% in 1997.

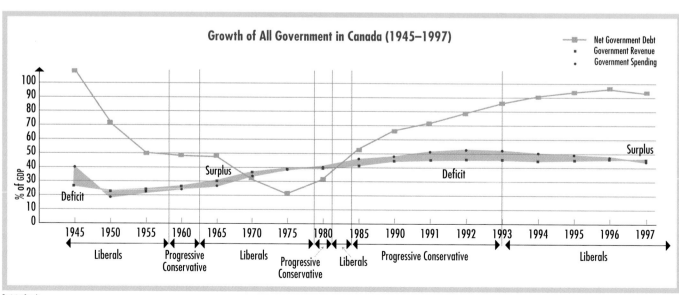

Growth of All Government in Canada (1945–1997)

Statistics Canada

Canadian Neoconservatism

The rapid snowballing of governmental debt produced a surge of support among many voters in the early 1990s for tough measures to reduce government spending, taxes, and budget deficits. At the provincial level, this widespread discontent with big government brought to power a new administration in Alberta and a new government in Ontario dedicated to cutting government spending and reorganizing the social welfare system. Both governments drew on the neoconservatist philosophy of smaller, less intrusive government that had appeared in the 1980s in Great Britain under Margaret Thatcher and in the United States under Ronald Reagan.

Alberta

people's wants ↔ gov't values & ↔ economic ideology policies have an impact through election.

LE V DE LA VICTOIRE...

GARNOTTE

LE DEVOIR, MONTRÉAL, MARCH 13, 1997.

"The Alberta Advantage."

In June 1993, the Progressive Conservative Party led by Ralph Klein was reelected to power in Alberta. Klein promised to deal decisively with the province's large $3.5 billion budget deficit. Under Premier Don Getty (1985–1992), the provincial government had spent over $2.2 billion to support private businesses in the hope that this would lessen the province's dependence on oil and gas production. In February 1994, Klein's government unveiled its first budget, promising deep cuts in all spending and a balanced budget in three years, without raising taxes. Cuts in spending on education, social services, and health care were ordered. These measures included centralizing the province's hospitals, merging school boards, and keeping greater control over municipal finances. Other policies implemented were cuts in social assistance and the end of social benefits to single, employable people. As well, the budget called for the privatization of government-owned liquor stores and government services such as car registration, and the deregulation of business. In April 1994, Klein touted these policies as part of "The Alberta Advantage," which was described as low taxes, a balanced budget, debt-free government, deregulation, and the creation of a climate in which businesses would grow and prosper. In early 1996, the government revealed that a budget surplus had been recorded and was being used to reduce provincial debt. The surplus resulted more from an unexpected rise in oil and gas prices than from spending cuts. In March 1997, Ralph Klein, riding a wave of popularity, called a provincial election and was reelected with an increased majority. Subsequently, he set up a plan for increasing spending on health care and education.

PHOTO: Production from Alberta's tar sands accounts for over 25% of Canada's total oil ouptut. Annually, oil produced from the tar sands contributes several hundred millions of dollars in royalties to the provincial government.

© Syncrude Canada

Ontario

"The Common Sense Revolution."

In June 1995, Ontario voters rejected the NDP government of Premier Bob Rae (1990–1995) and elected to power the Progressive Conservatives led by Michael Harris. His platform was "The Common Sense Revolution," which called for a 20% cut in government spending, a 30% cut in provincial income tax rates, the elimination of regulation of business, a balanced budget by 2000, slashed welfare benefits and implementation of workfare, and the creation of 725 000 new jobs over five years. In the first year of office, Harris's government implemented $8.2 billion in cuts in spending on education, health care, municipal grants, and social assistance. Legislation was enacted to change labour laws, reorganize hospital boards, abolish local governments, scrap environmental laws, deregulate electricity, and privatize government-owned liquor stores, Ontario Hydro, and social housing.

In June 1996, the government launched a workfare program, whereby welfare recipients would earn their benefits by working on local community projects. At the same time, an additional $3.5 billion in spending cuts on education, social assistance, and health care were announced. Unlike Klein in Alberta, who met with weak but sometimes vocal public resistance, Harris faced strong opposition from organized labour, public servants,

and community groups. These groups staged "Days of Action" throughout the province to protest Harris's sharp cuts in social spending and his government's corporate agenda favouring big business over ordinary people. In 1997, public servants and teachers staged several strikes against the government policies to cut public services.

In spite of these protests, Harris announced in the provincial budget in early May 1998 that due to a growing economy the Ontario government expected to reduce its budget deficit by $1 billion. The budget also announced a modest program of spending on health care and education. The budget stated that a provincial income tax cut will come into effect July 1, six months ahead of schedule. Cuts in business taxes were also outlined.

Ontario Hydro Corporate Archives/NEG#91.0271-3

RIGHT: The Otto Holden Hydraulic Generating Station is one of Ontario Hydro's many stations that produce electric power for the province's growing industries and population.

BELOW: To protest Premier Harris's cuts in social spending and his government's pro-business policy, organized labour, public servants, and community groups have staged "Days of Action" like this one in St. Catherines on May 1, 1998.

Canapress/JT Lewis

Neoconservative Influence

Neoconservative thought was not implemented solely in the provinces of Alberta and Ontario. Demands for balanced budgets, reduced spending on social services, greater efficiency in government, less regulation of business, and the privatization of Crown corporations were heard by governments of various political stripes.

Federal Government. One promise Brian Mulroney and his Progressive Conservative Party made when they formed a government in September 1984 was to cut federal government spending and balance the budget. Under Mulroney's leadership, the federal government was unable to balance the budget (see chart below). When the Liberals led by Jean Chrétien took power in October 1993, the state of government finances demanded action. In February 1994, Finance Minister Paul Martin warned Canadians to expect deep cuts in the future. In February 1995, he announced dramatic measures to improve government finances and prevent a downgrading of the country's international credit rating. An article appearing in the *Wall Street Journal* a month earlier had asserted that Canada had "now become an honorary member of the Third World in the unmanageability of its debt problem." Martin announced:

- a cut in spending of more than $25 billion over three years
- cuts in government transfer payments to the provinces
- the end of many business subsidies
- the elimination of 45 000 positions in the federal civil service
- privatization of Crown corporations and agencies
- elimination of transportation subsidy for Western grain
- an increase of $3.7 billion in taxes.

As a result of Martin's reductions in government spending and an improving economy, the deficit of $32.6 billion in 1993 became a surplus of $7.2 billion in 1997 (see chart below).

© Graham Harrop

Saskatchewan. When Roy Romanow and the NDP took power in 1991, Saskatchewan adopted a different approach to balance its budget deficit. Through a combination of lower spending on social services, government decentralization, higher taxes, and increased utility rates, the province announced in 1995 that it had balanced its budget. Like neighbouring Alberta and Manitoba, Saskatchewan introduced legislation requiring the government to balance its budget every year.

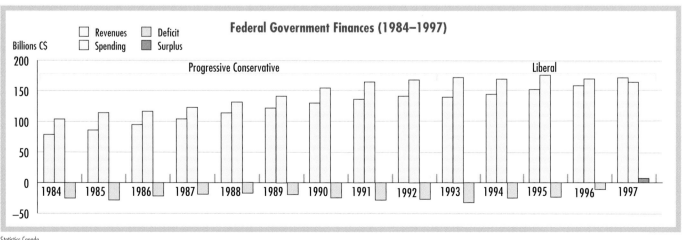

Statistics Canada

Results of Government Cutbacks

Since 1993, governments have followed policies of reduced spending and cutbacks to government services. The effects on the individual and the common good are at the centre of much on-going debate.

1. Privatization

Since 1984, governments have privatized more than 100 Crown corporations and government agencies, for an estimated $18.5 billion in revenue. The largest Crown corporations privatized were Canadian National Railways, Petro-Canada, Alberta Government Telephones, and Navigation Canada. As the chart below demonstrates, the federal government has carried out some of the largest privatizations. Despite the claims of government, privatization has not necessarily brought lower prices, increased competition, and more employment. The privatization of Petro-Canada, Canadian National Railways, and Air Canada led to the loss of more than 20 000 jobs. Many of these job losses were absorbed through early retirement, and others through layoffs. Several small privatized Crown corporations went bankrupt after a few years of private ownership. However, from the point of view of governments, privatization stimulated the growth of competitive free enterprise while bringing to an end the investment of public money into businesses, some of which were not economically viable.

2. Deficit Reduction

In 1997, the public sector as a whole registered a budget surplus. The federal government saw its budget deficit of $11.0 billion in 1996 become a surplus of $7.2 billion in 1997. At the provincial level, a budget surplus of $3.52 billion was recorded in 1997, though Ontario and Québec continued to have budget deficits. Local governments recorded more surpluses, but they were faced with having to fund more social services that their provincial governments had once financially supported.

Though supporters of less government have claimed credit for deficit reduction, critics noted that the improved financial situation of most governments was due more to a stronger economy and lower interest rates on government debt than to cuts in government spending. Though it seemed that budget deficits had been eliminated, financial analysts remained concerned about the size of debts of the federal and provincial governments, and how these governments would ever repay them. Some economists have noted that as the population ages and more people retire, the burden of repaying the public debt will fall on younger generations in the form of even higher taxes and fewer government services.

> ○ Ricardian equivalent thm. ⎤ macro.
> ○ Overlapping generation. ⎦ policy

Biggest Privatizations in Canada (1985–1997)			
Year	Crown Corporation/agency	Government	Amount (000)
1997	Manitoba Telephones	Manitoba	$ 755
1996	Navigation Canada	Federal	1500
1995	Canadian National Railways	Federal	2440
1992	Nova Scotia Power	Nova Scotia	851
1991–96	Cameco Corporation	Saskatchewan/Federal	958
1991–96	Petro-Canada	Federal	1520
1990–91	Alberta Government Telephones	Alberta	1751
1990	Alberta Home Mortgage Corporation	Alberta	612
1989–91	Potash Corporation	Saskatchewan	470
1988	Canadian National assets	Federal	870
1988–89	Air Canada	Federal	718
1988	BC Hydro natural gas assets	BC	741
1987	Teleglobe Canada	Federal	607
1986–89	Saskatchewan Oil and Gas Corporation	Saskatchewan	728
1985–87	Canada Development Corporation	Federal	361

Compiled from Robert Bernier and James I. Gow, *Un état réduit? [A Shrunken State?]*, pp. 212–213 and *Globe and Mail Report on Business*

3. Income Distribution

Many critics of government cutbacks have claimed that most of the cutbacks in government services since 1990 fell disproportionately on the poorest 20% of the population while the richest 20% of the population benefited from lower taxes and reduced government spending on social programs. The chart indicates that the poorest 20% of the population maintained its relative share of income and the top 20% increased its share of income. The middle 60% of the population, who see themselves as middle class, experienced a decline in standard of living.

The widening of income inequities is a socioeconomic phenomenon observed in every major industrial country. Though the widening of income inequities in Canada has not been as great as many people claimed, the trend is worrisome for two reasons.

① First, some groups are not adjusting quickly to rapid technological change and face diminished job prospects in the future. This is the case for many young people who have not finished secondary education. Job prospects for these young people are bleak. Another group affected by rapid technological change is the older worker aged between 50 and 65. Many in this group face longterm unemployment or forced retirement from the labour force because of lack of advanced technical training. Many of these people entered the labour force 30–35 years ago as unskilled workers in manufacturing and service industries.

② Second, reductions in government spending on education have forced many educational institutions to increase tuition fees and introduce fees for various services such as computer and book rentals. Students today are expected to pay a greater share of the cost of their education, especially at the university and college level. All of this prevents many students from low-income and middle-income families from attending higher education institutions, a situation that can create future social instability.

Income Distribution in Canada (1965–1995)

Income Group	1965	1975	1985	1995
Top 20%	41.4%	42.6%	43.0%	44.1%
Second 20%	24.5	25.1	24.9	24.5
Middle 20%	18.0	17.6	17.0	16.4
Fourth 20%	11.8	10.6	10.4	10.2
Lowest 20%	4.4	4.0	4.6	4.7
Totals	100.0	100.0	100.0	100.0

Statistics Canada

4. Social Responsibility

Government cutbacks in social welfare and health care have added a new dimension to Canadian social policy. Daniel Drache, social policy analyst, commented in an article on social welfare that the cutbacks in social spending may not have positive results for Canadian society. The removal of a social safety net in the hopes of compelling individuals to take responsibility for themselves may not help individuals become self-reliant. Instead, less spending on social welfare may only aggravate existing social inequities, create deep divisions in Canadian society, and undermine what sense of social responsibility Canadians may feel toward their fellow citizens.

What is being lost is any viable notion of social responsibility—the institutional capacity for the achievement of a more equitable society. Those who want training will have to pay for it. Those who want a better education will have to finance it. Those who want child care will have to ante up. Those who receive welfare will have to accept workfare. What is novel is that society will no longer pay for these entitlements through taxes. The rationalization is that as governments tax corporations less, the former will have less to spend on society-reinforcing programs and on social policy in particular. Should this trend become permanent, it is the end of social welfare programs as we have known them.[1]

---

[1] Daniel Drache, "The Eye of the Hurricane: Globalization and Social Policy Reform" in *Warm Heart, Cold Country*. Ottawa: Caledon Institute of Social Policy, 1995, p. 46.

REVIEW

Summary

Canadians have long believed in the importance of goals and policies that enhance the roles of both the individual and groups in society and promote the common good. Canadian political and economic systems reflect these beliefs about the individual and the common good.

The Canadian parliamentary system is organized as a constitutional monarchy and is based on the principle of responsible government. Canadian parliamentary democracy gives considerable power to individuals to choose their leaders and influence decision making. Canadian democracy also recognizes, for the most part, the need to limit the rights of the majority in order to protect the rights of minorities.

The Canadian economy is a mixed economy, combining features of private enterprise and public enterprise. In the Canadian economy, consumers and businesses are the main decision makers. Since 1945, Canadians have generally accepted the importance of government intervention in the economy to protect the interests of society. Governments pursued various fiscal and monetary policies and created a comprehensive social welfare system to promote high standards of living, prosperity, and the common good.

In the 1980s and 1990s, many Canadians became increasingly critical about the cost and effectiveness of their governments. They also became alarmed about the effects on the economy of higher taxes, growing public debt and budget deficits, and greater government regulation of business. Yet, Canadians still generally believed in a social welfare system which could provide people with health care, assistance in time of need, and pensions when retired.

Canadian Values and Political Philosophy

1. To what extent has Canada been culturally and ethnically diverse from earliest times?

2. To what extent do you support the core values of Canadians as outlined on page 129?

3. Read the descriptions of Canada's political parties on pages 130–131, keeping in mind the seven core values from page 129.

   a) Which political party most closely supports the same core values you hold?

   b) To what extent do you feel you could vote for each party?

4. Choose what you think is the right answer to the question below, then explain why you think it is correct and the other three are incorrect.

   From the information provided in the text on page 131, which of the following concerns most likely led to the formation of the Reform Party?

   A. "Governments are not providing enough social assistance to people."

   B. "The public worry too much about growing government deficits."

   C. "Governments interfere too much with people's right to make their own decision."

   D. "Atlantic (Eastern) Canada is largely ignored by the federal government."

Canadian Political System

1. a) If we define "democratic means" as "chosen directly by the people through a free and fair voting procedure," which of the following do **not** achieve their positions in the Canadian government by democratic means?

   Monarch, Prime Minister, Member of Parliament, Senator, Governor-General, Cabinet Ministers, Judges

b) If we define "democratic means" as chosen directly or indirectly by the people (e.g., appointed by elected representative) following a free and fair voting procedure, what changes would you make in your answer?

c) What are possible consequences, both positive and negative, of electing people to positions that are currently appointed by elected officials? Be prepared to discuss or debate your ideas.

2. Study the map on page 135. Explain the reasons behind the following breakdown of representation:

a) Ontario has 103 MPs, Alberta 26, and Prince Edward Island 4.

b) Each MP in British Columbia represents 109 600 people, and the MP for the Yukon represents 31 000.

c) Ontario is represented by 24 Senators, British Columbia by 6.

3. Explain the concepts of judicial independence and separation of powers. Why are these important?

4. a) Explain what the concept of responsible government means.

b) What role does a non-confidence vote in the House of Commons play in ensuring that the government is responsible?

5. A cabinet minister could lose his or her appointment for all of the following reasons except one. Choose the **exception**.

A. The Governor-General believed that he or she was not responsible.

B. The Prime Minister had lost confidence in his or her ability.

C. A serious problem occurred in his or her department.

D. He or she lost his or her seat in an election.

6. Which one of the following gives opposition parties the best opportunity to influence the content of government bills? Give a reason for your choice.

A. closure

B. patronage

C. Parliamentary committees

D. party whips

7. a) Explain the differences in the roles of the House of Commons and the Senate in introducing and passing legislation.

b) Why is it important that the House of Commons has more power than the Senate? Include the concept of responsible government in your answer.

8. Explain how each of the following helps to protect the public interest:

a) Question Period

b) coverage of parliamentary debates by the media

c) Senate examination of bills

9. Read over the Critique of Canadian Law Making (page 141). To what extent do you think the advantages outweigh the disadvantages?

10. Because Canada has a federal system, citizens have a loyalty to their country and also to their province or territory. As you can see on page 143, this has made amending the Canadian constitution difficult.

a) Which constitutional change was attempted by negotiation between the federal and provincial cabinets? Which by having votes in the federal and provincial legislatures? Which through a national referendum?

b) In your view, is any one of these approaches to change more democratic than the others? Explain.

11. What obstacles prevent many Canadian citizens from being elected?

12. Under the Canadian constitution, the Prime Minister can call an election anytime within five years. In some countries, the government is elected for a set period (e.g. four years), at the end of which an election is held. What are some advantages and disadvantages of the Canadian system?

13. What are the advantages and disadvantages of regional parties taking part in a national government?

14. Read the article, "B.C. voters remember, and recall" on page 146 as a basis for the following activities.

a) Chart the advantages and disadvantages to the recall process.

b) Prepare a debate on the recall process using the information you have gathered.

15. Read the article, "Sopinka: On telling the majority it is wrong" on page 147 to answer the following questions.

a) Do you agree that what is "legally correct" can be considered "politically unsupportable"?

b) Is it acceptable that a minority can dictate what is correct for a majority? Be prepared to defend your position in a discussion or debate.

Canadian Economic System

1. 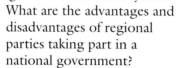 Create a chart outlining the changes that have taken place in the Canadian economy since the beginning of the 20th century.

2. a) With which of the following reasons for government intervention in the Canadian economy would you agree and with which disagree?

A. stimulate the economy during periods of high unemployment (depression)

B. give a stimulus to a particular region that is experiencing economic difficulty (Atlantic fisheries)

C. build a transportation system that will aid the private sector in developing resources and earning profits (government-built roads and railways)

D. create a government monopoly in order to ensure that the public is well-served and prices are kept low (Ontario Hydro)

b) Write a paragraph in which you explain the principle on which a government should base its decision for intervention.

3. Examine the graph on page 150.

a) In what years did industrial production experience the greatest changes?

b) When there are changes in industrial production, there are corresponding changes in GDP, unemployment, and incomes. What problems are created for wage-earning Canadians when these drastic changes occur?

4. Entrepreneurs and workers are both involved in producing and consuming goods and services.

a) How are the entrepreneurs rewarded for setting up and operating their businesses?

b) How are the workers rewarded for the labour and skills that they provide?

c) What risks do entrepreneurs undertake when they set up a business?

d) What are the risks of being a wage-earner?

5. The following are some ways in which the government intervenes in the private sector between the business person and the worker.

a) In your opinion, which of these interventions are justified and which are not? Give reasons for your choices.

A. setting a minimum wage
B. enforcing labour laws
C. regulating hours of work, overtime, and working conditions
D. enacting laws making unions legal if workers want them
E. establishing a worker's compensation board to which employers must contribute to help workers who are injured on the job

b) Would you recommend more or less intervention?

6. What harm to the economy and to consumers would result from one company having a monopoly over the production and sale of gasoline?

7. In the past, Canada Post was a department of the federal government, but it always operated with a deficit. The government decided to make it a Crown corporation, and the directors were told that it would no longer be able to operate at a deficit. Take and defend a position on the issue: Should Crown corporations be required to operate at a profit?

8. Free trade agreements such as the Canada–US Free Trade Agreement and NAFTA are being entered into by the Canadian government.
a) What are the advantages and disadvantages of free trade?
b) The values of Canada's trading partners are likely to be somewhat different than those of Canadians (review pages 128–129). Which values would you most want to protect when these treaties are being negotiated? Be prepared to defend your view.

9. "When the US economy sneezes, the Canadian economy catches a cold." As the statistics on page 156 show, the Canadian economy is closely tied to that of the United States.
a) Give at least five reasons why the economies are closely linked.

b) What are the advantages and disadvantages of this situation for Canadians?

10. Explain the difference between fiscal policy and monetary policy.

11. Parties on the left in the political continuum generally believe that profits should be taxed at a high rate, because they consider profits to be excess earnings. Parties on the right generally believe that profits should not be taxed at a high rate because companies reinvest profits in the economy.
a) What would the adverse effects of increasing the taxes on profits (corporate income tax) be for owners and employees?
b) What would the beneficial effects of decreasing the taxes on profits be for owners and employees?
c) If the corporate income tax was reduced, taxes on personal incomes might have to be increased (Federal Government Revenues, page 158). What would you advise the government to do?

12. The Canadian government uses a progressive income tax. That is, as a person's income increases so does the rate at which he/she is taxed (Personal Income Tax Rates, 1997, page 158).
a) In what ways is this a fair means of taxation?
b) In what ways is this an unfair means of taxation?

13. Supporters of universality argue that this is the best way to ensure that all Canadians have at least a minimum standard of living.
a) What programs are universal today?

b) When the principle of universality is not applied, how should the government decide who should be entitled to receive the benefits?

14. More women are involved in the business world today as employees and employers (pages 162–163). There are also more women involved in politics and government today (pages 144–145). Do you think that there is a connection between the two trends? Explain.

Canadian Political Economy

1. a) What does the term "neoconservatism" mean?

   b) What evidence did the neoconservatives give to support a change to a new economic philosophy?

   c) It appears that the majority of voters in Alberta and Ontario supported the neoconservative policies. Which minority groups might have opposed these policies? Why would they have opposed them?

2. a) Place neoconservatism on a continuum between collective good and individual interests.

   b) Place the philosophies supporting "Limited Intervention (to 1929)" and the "Development of Mixed Economy (1939–1975)" (pages 149–150) on the same continuum.

   c) On the basis of this comparison explain why economic philosophies change over time.

3. a) Explain the difference between government deficit and government debt.

   b) Under what conditions, if any, should governments run budget deficits?

4. a) Brainstorm in small groups or as a class the options that governments have for reducing deficits and debt.

   b) Which of these do you think would have the least impact on Canada's welfare system?

   c) Which would have the greatest negative effect on Canada's welfare system?

Chapter Consolidation

1. This chapter began with a quotation from Paul Martin, "What a government does with scarce resources shows what its values are."

   a) Explain what Paul Martin means by this statement.

   b) To what extent does what is happening in our political and economic systems today reflect the core Canadian values described on page 129.

2. a) On what values were the political and economic systems of Canada based?

    b) Whose ideas were influential in the development of the political and economic systems of Canada? Briefly explain the ideas and how they were applied in Canada.

    c) Create a chart, identifying the type of political system and economic system in Canada and the strengths and weaknesses of those systems.

5 UNITED STATES

"We must do what America does best: offer more opportunity to all and demand more responsibility from all. It is time to break the bad habit of expecting something for nothing from our government or from each other. Let us take more responsibility for not only ourselves and our families but for our communities and our country."
—Bill Clinton, inaugural speech in Washington, January 20, 1993

Since the early years of the 20th century, the United States has had the strongest and most influential economy on the globe, and since 1945 it has arguably had the world's most powerful military. This economic and military might and the resulting political power and influence of the United States have been based on its own distinctive values and beliefs about politics and economics, and its perception of the international balance of power.

Since its independence from Great Britain in 1776, the United States has had a presidential form of government in which the legislative, executive, and judicial branches have been assigned distinct powers and roles by the constitution. The President of the United States is elected by the people and is one of the most influential politicians in the world.

Although the American economy today is generally regarded as mixed, throughout most of the 20th century it was seen as a private enterprise economy in action. At times the federal government has intervened in the economy to achieve some national goal.

Key Concepts/Vocabulary

republic
electoral college
Congress
filibuster
presidential veto

pork barrelling
primary
military-industrial
  complex
affirmative action

Focus On Issues

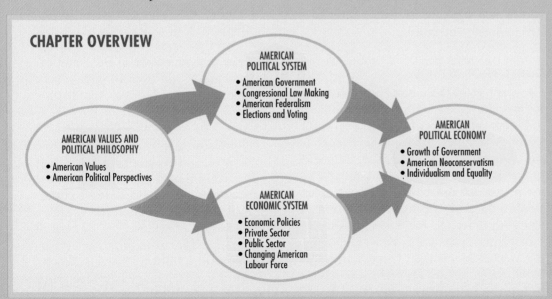

CHAPTER OVERVIEW

AMERICAN VALUES AND POLITICAL PHILOSOPHY
• American Values
• American Political Perspectives

AMERICAN POLITICAL SYSTEM
• American Government
• Congressional Law Making
• American Federalism
• Elections and Voting

AMERICAN ECONOMIC SYSTEM
• Economic Policies
• Private Sector
• Public Sector
• Changing American Labour Force

AMERICAN POLITICAL ECONOMY
• Growth of Government
• American Neoconservatism
• Individualism and Equality

AMERICAN VALUES AND POLITICAL PHILOSOPHY

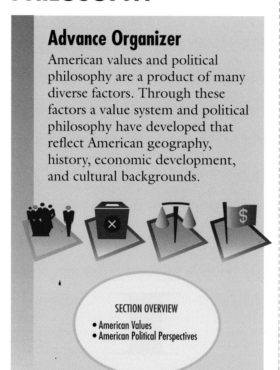

Advance Organizer

American values and political philosophy are a product of many diverse factors. Through these factors a value system and political philosophy have developed that reflect American geography, history, economic development, and cultural backgrounds.

SECTION OVERVIEW
- American Values
- American Political Perspectives

American Values

Americans care deeply about the rights of the individual and the individual's personal goals and objectives. The sources of this strong belief in individualism lie in the country's geography, history, economic development, and culture.

Sources of Values

Geographically, the United States is one of the world's largest countries, extending for 3500 km across North America. Much of this large landmass has a suitable climate and sufficient arable land to support intensive human settlement. For several millennia the region was inhabited by First Peoples. Prior to the arrival of Europeans in the 16th and 17th centuries, there was an estimated First Nations population of six million living in what is now the United States. By 1998, the population of the United States had grown to over 265 million. As the world's third most populous nation, the United States is known for its diversity, its achievements in many spheres, and its belief in progress.

The earliest permanent European settlements appeared in Florida in 1565 and Virginia in 1607. From 1607 to 1776, western Europeans escaping religious persecution and rigid social conventions found a safer and freer life. This fostered a belief in individual freedom and private enterprise, and a distrust of government. These beliefs were tested in the 19th century over the issues of conflict with the First Peoples, and whether or not to abolish slavery and grant freedom to African-Americans. Slavery was abolished in 1863, but not before the country was plunged into a brutal civil war between northern and southern states.

Following the end of the Civil War in 1865, the United States entered a period of unprecedented economic development, territorial expansion, and European settlement of lands in the west occupied by First Peoples. This westward advance reinforced beliefs in individual freedom, personal achievement, equality of opportunity, private enterprise, and democracy. By the 20th century, these beliefs and values coalesced into what became known as "the American dream," a belief that combined "rugged individualism" with the view that material prosperity was available to everyone who worked hard. The "American dream" remains a compelling belief for most Americans today.

In the 20th century, the United States became known as the "land of opportunity" for over 40 million people emigrating from Europe, Asia, Latin America, and the South Pacific. The result today is an American society that is multicultural, but emphasizes individual freedom, initiative, and achievement more than the preservation of linguistic and ethnic differences from heritage cultures. In this respect, the United States is considered by some to be a "melting pot," where all immigrants are expected to assimilate, more than a "mosaic," which allows customs and language of ethnic groups to be maintained. Many Americans claim the mixing of cultures reinforces freedom and individualism. The reality is, however, that many people retain their language and culture. Where their numbers are large, their way of life predominates over the dominant American culture.

Core Values

In the past 30 years, numerous studies of American values have appeared. An examination of contemporary American values by Lamar Alexander and Chester E. Finn in 1995 identified individual freedom and responsibility, personal achievement and success, equality of opportunity, belief in progress, democracy, private enterprise, limited government, and humanitarianism as core values of American society.[1]

Individual freedom and responsibility. Americans strongly believe that the individual is the unique centre of power and value in society. To this end, all individuals must have the greatest possible freedom to enhance their personal dignity, purpose in life, and the pursuit of happiness. In the United States, the pursuit of personal happiness is constitutionally guaranteed as a right of every individual.

Personal achievement and success. Personal achievement and success are believed to be essential to the individual, with education and hard work forming the bases of personal success and recognition. The accumulation of wealth is valued as part of a good life and is considered an indicator of personal achievement and success.

Equality of opportunity. Equal opportunity to pursue one's own interests is felt to be important for personal freedom and achievement. Americans believe that every person is created equal and has the same right to be successful and acquire wealth.

Belief in progress. To Americans, the belief in progress means the belief in a better future. This optimism expresses itself in the belief that there is no problem that cannot be solved. Every generation is expected to be better off materially and socially than the previous one.

Democracy. Americans believe that democracy is the political system most appropriate to preserving individual freedom, liberty, and self-expression. Individuals are assumed to be equal before the law and have the right to due process. It is expected that all government officials should be elected and held accountable to the people for their actions. As the American constitution states, democracy is "government of the people, by the people, and for the people."

Private enterprise. Private enterprise is considered important because it is believed that private enterprise encourages people to be creative, inventive, and successful. As well, it provides the least amount of infringement on individual freedom. Competition in the production and distribution of goods and services is believed to be necessary to prevent the emergence of powerful monopolies. The value of consumer choice in the US justifies the limited government involvement in its citizens' affairs. Personal gain and profit are thought to ensure high efficiency and productivity in the production and distribution of goods and services.

Limited government. In the United States, the government is believed to exist to protect the constitutional rights of individuals to freedom of speech, assembly, and worship; freedom to participate in government; and freedom to bear arms. Most Americans believe government intervention should be limited to providing justice, national defence, and public order. They feel that a small government that does not intrude in people's lives is preferable to a large one that interferes a great deal.

Humanitarianism. Most Americans believe that private charity, not public charity, is the basis of humanitarianism, a belief in helping less fortunate individuals. Humanitarianism is often accompanied by a powerful commitment to a religion and faith in a supreme being.

American political culture is based on a strong commitment to the individual.

In 1995 over 38% of young people between 18 and 24 years old volunteered their time to help others. The average number of hours volunteered per week by 18–24 year olds was 2.8 hours. Almost one-half of the total population worked as volunteers in 1995.

[1]Lamar Alexander and Chester E. Finn, Jr. (eds.) *The New Promise of American Life*. Indianapolis: Hudson Institute, 1995.

American Political Perspectives

Politics in the United States in the 20th century has been dominated by two political parties of roughly equal strength—the Democratic Party and the Republican Party. The two parties have alternated in power (see chart "American Administrations Since 1900"). Efforts by individuals and other parties to change this two-party system have been unsuccessful.

American political views have shifted considerably in the 20th century. Before 1933, the Republican Party was the main political choice of most American voters. After 1933, the Democratic Party emerged as the stronger political party with a platform calling for increased social spending and government regulation of business. In the 1980s, the Republicans, led by Ronald Reagan, called for smaller and less intrusive government, except in the area of defence spending.

The presence of two political parties of roughly equal strength, the Democrats and the Republicans, is a distinguishing feature of American political culture.

AMERICAN CONTEMPORARY CONTINUUM

EXTREME LEFT — LEFT — CENTRE — RIGHT — EXTREME RIGHT

Socialist Party — Democratic Party — Republican Party

American Administrations Since 1900

Republican Party ☐   Democratic Party ☐

1901–1909	Theodore Roosevelt	1961–1963	John F. Kennedy
1909–1913	William H. Taft	1963–1969	Lyndon B. Johnson
1913–1921	Woodrow Wilson	1969–1974	Richard M. Nixon
1921–1923	Warren C. Harding	1974–1977	Gerald R. Ford
1923–1929	Calvin Coolidge	1977–1981	Jimmy Carter
1929–1933	Herbert C. Hoover	1981–1989	Ronald Reagan
1933–1945	Franklin D. Roosevelt	1989–1993	George Bush
1945–1953	Harry S. Truman	1993–	Bill Clinton
1953–1961	Dwight D. Eisenhower		

☐ The Centre

Democratic Party. The Democratic Party is considered to be the party of the centre and the voice of American liberalism. In the 19th century, the Democratic Party supported farmers, workers, and small businesses by calling for the end of privileges to special groups such as plantation owners and large factory owners, and for the protection of industry from foreign competition. The issue of slavery split the Democrats in the 1850s. In 1860, this split resulted in the newly formed Republican Party being elected to power. After the Civil War, support for the Democrats was limited to European–American voters in the southern states and in northern cities such as New York and Chicago. In the 1920s, electoral support for the Democrats was confined mainly to the southern states. In the 1930s under Franklin D. Roosevelt's leadership, the Democrats broadened their support among African–Americans, organized labour, ethnic voters, and urban residents. Following the 1932 presidential election of Franklin D. Roosevelt, the Democratic Party became the political party of the poor, disadvantaged, and powerless, and organized labour. In the 1960s under John F. Kennedy and Lyndon Johnson, the Democrats introduced programs for minorities, social assistance, and government regulation of business to promote greater equality of opportunity and to redress some social injustices. In the 1980s and 1990s, the Democrats retreated from their earlier program of social action because of the growing popularity of the Republican Party. Many African–Americans and women are strong supporters of the Democratic Party.

1776–1783 War of Independence	**1787** American Constitution signed	**1829** Democratic Party formed	**1850** Great debate on slavery begins	**1854** Republican Party formed	**1860** Republican Abraham Lincoln becomes President; abolishes slavery; southern states secede from the US	**1860–1865** American Civil War; North defeats South	**1865** President Lincoln assassinated

Note: Timeline is not to scale

The Right

Republican Party. Today, the Republican Party is regarded as the political party of the right and the voice of American conservatism. When the party was formed in 1854 to end slavery in the country, the membership held many liberal beliefs. In 1860 under Abraham Lincoln's leadership, the Republican Party was elected to power; in 1863 it abolished slavery, granting African–Americans the same civil liberties as European–Americans. After the Civil War (1860–1865), the Republicans stressed patriotism, national expansion, limited government involvement in the economy, high tariffs, neutrality, and noninvolvement in foreign politics. These beliefs helped to make the Republicans the dominant political party between 1860 and 1932. Voter support for the Republicans was strong throughout the country, except in the southern states where it was confined to African–Americans. After 1932, the Republican Party began to emphasize the importance of traditional values about the family, local community, and religion. Conservative beliefs, such as a stricter interpretation of the American constitution and individual rights, including the right to bear arms, the right to liberty, and the right to a fair trial by jury came to dominate the Party more. In the 1980s under Ronald Reagan, the Republican Party emphasized the importance of religion, morality, smaller government, and lower taxes. In the 1990s, the Republican Party came to be perceived as the party focussed on national security and law and order, the party of various groups that believed religion and morality should be part of government. Many professionals, business people, and skilled workers have been strong supporters of the Republican Party.

The Left

Socialist Party. Prior to 1880, socialist ideas of collectivism and government intervention were not accepted by American society, which regarded individualism to be more important. In 1901, the Socialist Party was officially formed through the combination of two small parties. It received its greatest electoral support in 1912, with 6% of the popular vote. The rise of communism in the Soviet Union and the radicalism of the very small American Communist Party in the early 1920s turned many Americans away from supporting the Socialist Party. After 1945, the spread of communism in Eastern Europe and the growth of the military might of the Soviet Union convinced many Americans that communism posed a serious threat to their country. Since 1945, the left has had little influence in the overall American political spectrum. However, in 1990 a socialist congressman was elected by voters in Vermont to represent them in Washington.

Independents

One unique feature of the American political scene is the presence of a large bloc of voters who claim to be independent, supporting neither the Democrats nor Republicans. This bloc, estimated to be one-third of all voters, has occasionally inspired individuals to run as independent candidates in presidential elections. The most recent attempt by an independent candidate to challenge the domination of the political process by the Democrats and Republicans was Ross Perot, a Texan billionaire businessman, in the 1992 and 1996 presidential elections. He did not win but received 19.4% of the popular vote in 1992 and 8.1% in 1996.

The donkey was adopted by the Democratic Party during the 1828 presidential election. In the 1870s the donkey was popularized as the symbol of the Democratic Party. Democrats see the donkey as humble, smart, courageous, and lovable.

The elephant became the symbol of the Republican Party during the 1860 presidential election. Political cartoonists popularized the elephant as the symbol of the Republican Party in the 1870s. Republicans see the elephant as loyal, logical, clever, and committed to principles.

1901	1917–1918	1921	1932	1933	1941–1945	1945	1961	1963	1974	1981–1988	1992	1996
Socialist Party formed	US enters World War I; Revolution in Russia	Communist Party of the United States formed	Democrat Franklin D. Roosevelt elected President	Roosevelt announces New Deal	US enters World War II	President Roosevelt dies; Vice President Harry S. Truman takes over	Democrat John F. Kennedy becomes youngest President	President Kennedy assassinated; Vice President Lyndon Johnson becomes President; announces policy to reduce poverty and social inequalities	Republican President Richard Nixon resigns to avoid impeachment	Republican President Ronald Reagan introduces program to cut government spending and build up military power	Democrat Bill Clinton elected President; independent Ross Perot receives large protest vote	President Clinton reelected

AMERICAN POLITICAL SYSTEM

Advance Organizer

The United States has a presidential system of government. It is also a republic that combines the head of government and head of state into one office, the President. It is a federal state with power divided between the central government and state governments. Political parties play a secondary role in American government.

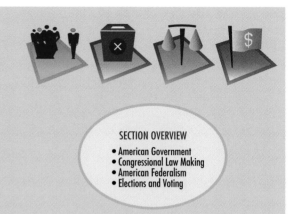

SECTION OVERVIEW
- American Government
- Congressional Law Making
- American Federalism
- Elections and Voting

STRUCTURE OF AMERICAN GOVERNMENT

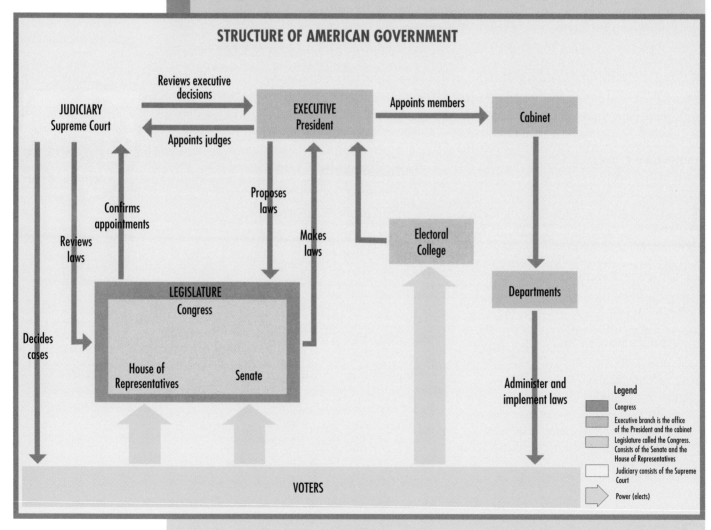

JUDICIARY
Supreme Court

Reviews executive decisions →

EXECUTIVE
President

Appoints members →

Cabinet

Appoints judges

Confirms appointments

Reviews laws

Proposes laws

Makes laws

Electoral College

Departments

Decides cases

LEGISLATURE
Congress

House of Representatives   Senate

Administer and implement laws

Legend

Congress

Executive branch is the office of the President and the cabinet

Legislature called the Congress. Consists of the Senate and the House of Representatives

Judiciary consists of the Supreme Court

Power (elects)

VOTERS

American Government

The organization of American government is outlined in the country's constitution and its amendments. The most distinctive feature of the presidential system is the separation of powers among the executive, legislative, and judicial branches of government. This separation of powers is supported by an elaborate system of checks and balances that prevents any branch of government from dominating the other two branches.

Executive Power

Office of the President. Executive power in the American presidential system is vested in the Office of the President (see chart on page 180). A person can be elected to the Office of the President for only two terms of four years. Unlike the Prime Minister in the Canadian parliamentary system, the President is directly elected by the people and confirmed by an electoral college of 538 members. To qualify for the office, a presidential candidate must be a "natural-born" citizen and be at least 35 years of age. If a President is removed from office, dies, resigns, or is incapable of performing the duties of the office, the presidency is assumed by the Vice President.

According to the constitution, the President is both the head of state and the head of government. The duties of the President as head of state include

- greeting foreign dignitaries as the representative of the United States
- concluding foreign treaties and international agreements
- making the annual State of the Union address
- acting as commander-in-chief of the country's armed forces
- calling special sessions of the Congress
- performing ceremonial functions such as the proclamation of holidays.

The President's duties as head of government include

- appointing the cabinet and numerous high-ranking bureaucrats in the government (with approval from the Senate)
- signing into law bills passed by the legislative branch

- proposing policies for approval by the Congress.

In contrast to the Canadian parliamentary system, in the American government the President cannot be a member of the legislative branch or appear in the legislature to introduce a bill.

Legislative Power

The United States has an elected bicameral or two-chamber national legislature called the Congress. The Congress is divided into a 435-member House of Representatives and a 100-member Senate (see chart on page 180).

Senate. The Senate is the Congress's elected upper chamber. The Senate was designed in 1787 to give each state equal representation. Every state, no matter its population, is represented today by two senators. The state of California, with a population of over 30 million people, elects the same number of senators as the state of Wyoming, with fewer than 500 000 people. Originally, the state legislatures appointed senators, but a constitutional amendment in 1913 made the Senate an elected upper house of the Congress.

A senator is elected to a six-year term. There is no limit on the number of terms a senator can serve. Every two years one-third of all Senate seats come up for election. To qualify for election to the Senate, a senator must be at least 30 years of age. A senator enjoys considerable privileges, including the right of unlimited debate (called filibuster), which members of the House of Representatives do not have.

The Senate has the power to initiate legislation and modify or reject legislation passed in the House of Representatives. Presidential appointments of the cabinet, ambassadors, and judges to the Supreme Court must be confirmed by the Senate. Foreign treaties made by the President must be ratified by the Senate. The Senate has the power to remove the President from office through the process of impeachment. This power can be seen as a strength when used as a check on a perceived abuse

President Andrew Johnson was the only President to be judged at an impeachment trial. The trial, held by the Senate in May 1868, failed by one vote—35 for to 19 against. It would have sentenced Johnson for treason and other high crimes of state.

of power by the President, or as an obstacle when used to block approval of a presidential policy.

House of Representatives. The House of Representatives is the Congress's elected lower chamber. Representation in the House of Representatives is assigned to the states mainly on the basis of population. Each state is entitled to at least one representative. Electoral law ensures that every seat in the House of Representatives represents a roughly equal population.

Members of the House of Representatives are elected to two-year terms. There is no limit on the number of terms a member can serve. A member of the House of Representatives must be at least 25 years of age. A representative enjoys numerous advantages of office and also receives extra income from speeches and lectures to various interest groups. Because of the short term of office, a representative is required to spend considerable time and money campaigning for reelection.

The constitution grants the House of Representatives three powers in addition to its power to initiate all legislation. They include

- the exclusive right to initiate money bills
- the power to elect the President when no candidate receives a majority of votes in the electoral college
- the right to impeach the President and other federal officials.

Members of the House of Representatives are seated in a semicircle facing the rostrum of the Speaker of the House. The Speaker is elected by a simple majority of representatives and is generally a member of the political party with the most seats. The Speaker presides over the House and represents the majority party to the President and the general public.

Judicial Power

Judicial power in the American presidential system of government resides in a decentralized system of courts that extends from the Supreme Court of the United States in Washington to state supreme courts, district courts, and local courts.

Supreme Court. The Supreme Court of the United States is the highest court in the land. It hears cases on appeal from lower courts, each year hearing 100–150 cases in which it hands down full opinions. The Court's most important political function is to review challenges to legislation brought before it and decide whether the legislation is constitutional (see chart on page 180).

The Supreme Court sits as a tribunal of nine judges appointed by the President and approved by the Senate. Because judges serve for life, appointments can influence the direction of the Supreme Court on legal and constitutional matters for decades. For this reason, Senate hearings on the confirmation of Supreme Court appointments have in recent years become dramatic power struggles between liberals and conservatives, as they attempt to tip the balance in the Supreme Court in their favour.

The most widely publicized case in the 1990s was the nomination and confirmation of Clarence Thomas to the Supreme Court in June 1991. Thomas's nomination was attacked by liberals on the grounds that he was too conservative on social issues and that his confirmation would further strengthen the court's conservative majority. As well, because he had faced accusations of sexual harassment, many people considered him unfit for high office. Clarence Thomas was confirmed by the Senate 52 to 48, the closest Supreme Court confirmation vote in recent years.

Congressional Law Making

In the interests of permitting the broadest possible discussion of a bill, the legislative process in the Congress follows a complicated, and at times slow, path. Other times, by mutual agreement among members of Congress, a bill may be put on a "fast track" to passage when urgent treatment is warranted on matters of national importance. The following chart illustrates in a simplified manner the process through which a bill must pass in the Congress before it becomes law. A bill begins as a similar proposal in the House of Representatives or the Senate, though money bills are always introduced in the House of Representatives.

Steps for a Bill to Become a Law

Introduction. Any member of the Senate and the House of Representatives may introduce a bill. Once done, the bill is numbered, referred to a committee, labeled with the sponsor's name, and sent for printing so that copies can be made for study and action. Presidential bills are introduced by a senior member of the President's party in the Senate or House of Representatives.

Committee Action. With few exceptions, bills are referred to a full committee for approval or rejection. Representation on this committee corresponds to the relative party strength in the Senate or House.

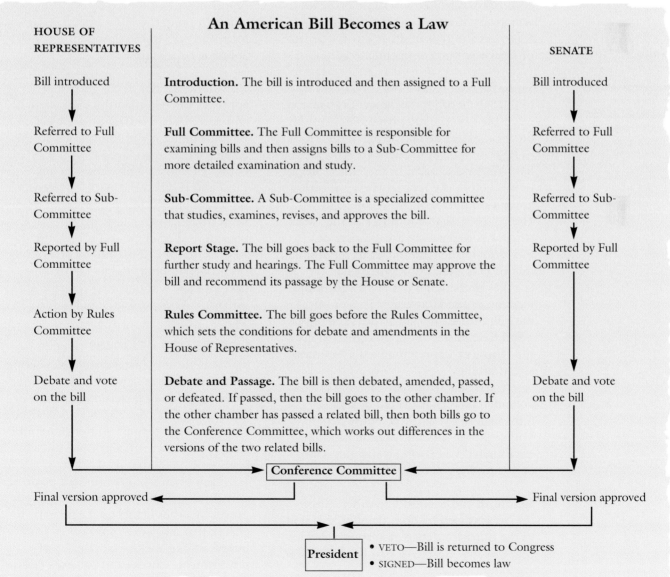

An American Bill Becomes a Law

HOUSE OF REPRESENTATIVES

Bill introduced

Referred to Full Committee

Referred to Sub-Committee

Reported by Full Committee

Action by Rules Committee

Debate and vote on the bill

SENATE

Bill introduced

Referred to Full Committee

Referred to Sub-Committee

Reported by Full Committee

Debate and vote on the bill

Introduction. The bill is introduced and then assigned to a Full Committee.

Full Committee. The Full Committee is responsible for examining bills and then assigns bills to a Sub-Committee for more detailed examination and study.

Sub-Committee. A Sub-Committee is a specialized committee that studies, examines, revises, and approves the bill.

Report Stage. The bill goes back to the Full Committee for further study and hearings. The Full Committee may approve the bill and recommend its passage by the House or Senate.

Rules Committee. The bill goes before the Rules Committee, which sets the conditions for debate and amendments in the House of Representatives.

Debate and Passage. The bill is then debated, amended, passed, or defeated. If passed, then the bill goes to the other chamber. If the other chamber has passed a related bill, then both bills go to the Conference Committee, which works out differences in the versions of the two related bills.

Conference Committee

Final version approved

Final version approved

President
- VETO—Bill is returned to Congress
- SIGNED—Bill becomes law

Adapted from *Congressional Quarterly.* http://www.cq.com

When a bill is referred to a Full Committee, it is placed on that committee's calendar. Members of the committee choose from the calendar bills they want to consider. The failure of the committee to consider a bill is equivalent to killing it.

Once a bill is chosen by the Full Committee, it is sent to a Sub-Committee. Members of the Sub-Committee investigate the purposes of the bill, determine its value, and may amend it. The Sub-Committee requests comments on the bill from interested government agencies and experts. After considering these views, the Sub-Committee prepares a report on the bill and presents it to the Full Committee.

After the Sub-Committee's report is read, the Full Committee votes on whether to recommend the bill to the chamber that originated it, Senate or House of Representatives. Most of the time the bill is approved and reported back to the Senate or House with recommendations.

Floor Action. After a bill is reported back to the Senate or House where it originated, it is placed on the calendar for debate. The duration of debate on the bill in the House of Representatives depends on whether the bill is under discussion by the House proper, or it is before the House when it is sitting as the Committee of the Whole. The House sits as the Committee of the Whole when it considers any tax measure or money bill. The Committee of the Whole cannot pass a bill but reports whatever changes to the bill it has approved. A full meeting of the House may pass or reject the bill, or occasionally it refers the bill to a Full Committee. Voting on the bill in the House of Representatives is recorded electronically.

In the Senate, debate on a bill is unlimited but can be halted by a three-fifths majority vote of the entire Senate. Voting on the bill can take the form of an untabulated voice vote, a standing vote, or a recorded roll call.

Action in the Second Chamber. After the bill is passed by one chamber, it is sent to the other for debate and approval. This chamber may decide to pass the bill as it is, send it to committee for study, reject it, or ignore the bill submitted while it prepares its own version of the proposed legislation. The second chamber may make only minor changes to the bill or it may approve a version of the bill that differs greatly from the version passed in the other chamber. When this occurs, the bill is "sent to conference."

Conference Action. In Conference, senior members of Senate's and the House of Representatives' Full Committees meet to reconcile differences in the bill's versions. Occasionally, the differences result in deadlock and the bills approved in both chambers die. When the Conference reaches agreement on the version of the bill, a report is submitted to each chamber. The report must be adopted by both chambers, at which point the bill is passed in identical form and sent to the President for final approval or rejection.

Presidential Veto. If the President approves the bill, then the bill is signed and dated. The President may reject a bill by not signing it and returning it to the chamber that introduced it with an explanation of refusal. This action by the President is called the veto. To override the President's veto, supporters of the bill must obtain a two-thirds majority of those present in the Senate and the House of Representatives. If the President's veto is overridden in both chambers, the bill becomes law without the President's signature. Otherwise, the bill is dead.

Checks and Balances

The American political system is based on a strict separation of powers among the three branches of government. The President, Congress, and Supreme Court all have clearly defined and separate functions. As well, a member of one branch cannot be a member of another.

Each branch of government possesses constitutional checks on the exercise of power by other branches. These exist to ensure that a balance of power is maintained among the three branches of government. Checks and balances ensure

Between 1789 and 1996, American Presidents vetoed about 2500 bills passed by Congress. Congress overrode presidential vetoes about 100 times.

that no branch can dominate or behave in a tyrannical manner.

For example, the President can veto legislation passed by the Congress. The Congress can pass legislation despite a presidential veto with a two-thirds majority vote in both chambers. The Supreme Court can declare legislation that has been passed by the Congress and approved by the President to be unconstitutional. The President can change the composition of the Supreme Court by filling a vacancy with a person with compatible values, subject to confirmation by the Senate.

Critique of Law Making

The legislative process in the American Congressional system has important advantages and disadvantages.

Advantages

1 Ease of debate and amendment. At each stage of the legislative process, a bill undergoes considerable debate and modification. The requirement that a bill must be passed by both chambers of the Congress provides politicians in both chambers with opportunities to debate and propose amendments before a bill is approved.

2 Freedom of action. The committees investigating legislation and special matters allow members of Congress considerable freedom of action to determine the value and merits of various bills under consideration. This freedom of action is strengthened by the separation of the executive and legislative branches of government. It is further enhanced by the absence of strong party discipline. Individual members are free to act for their own reasons. As well, the President does not necessarily need to rely on the support of a particular political party for the passage of presidential bills.

3 Presidential check on bad legislation. An effective check on the passage of poor legislation by the Congress is the President's veto. By refusing to sign a bill, the President sends it back to Congress for reconsideration. In this

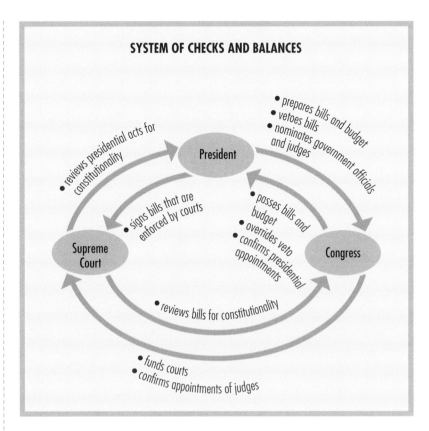

SYSTEM OF CHECKS AND BALANCES

- reviews presidential acts for constitutionality
- prepares bills and budget
- vetoes bills
- nominates government officials and judges
- signs bills that are enforced by courts
- passes bills and budget
- overrides veto
- confirms presidential appointments
- reviews bills for constitutionality
- funds courts
- confirms appointments of judges

President — Supreme Court — Congress

way, the President can stop legislation from becoming law.

Disadvantages

1 "Logrolling" and "pork barrelling." The ability of politicians to influence the debate and passage of legislation in Congress has allowed politicians to engage in practices such as "logrolling" and "pork barrelling." "Logrolling" occurs when politicians agree to support each other's bill. A politician may also add amendments to a bill to attract another politician's support. "Logrolling" invariably gives rise to "pork barrelling," the appropriation of money or the passage of bills that benefit a politician's electoral district. At times, decisions about such matters as the location of military bases and public housing projects have been made more on the basis of a politician's negotiating skills than on other factors.

Between 1789 and 1996, the Supreme Court declared about 150 bills passed by the Congress to be unconstitutional.

The longest recorded filibuster occurred in 1957, when one senator from South Carolina talked for 24 hours, 27 minutes, in an attempt to stop the passage of the Civil Rights Act.

2 Cumbersome and slow. Because all bills must be passed by both chambers of Congress, the legislative process often is cumbersome and slow. A bill may be quickly passed by one chamber only to meet delay or death through inaction or numerous amendments in the other. The right of unlimited debate (called filibuster) has been used in the past by senators to delay the passage of important bills.

3 Misuse of presidential vote. Because the President is not responsible to Congress, the President is not constrained in rejecting legislation. The President's misuse of the veto may be stimulated when the chance of veto override in both chambers of Congress is low. President George Bush (1989–1993) was so skilful at stopping legislation with vetoes that some critics called his administration "government by veto."

American Federalism

The allocation of powers between the federal and state governments is an important feature of the American political system.

One of the primary objectives set out by the authors of the United States constitution in the 18th century was to allocate powers between the federal and state governments within a federal structure. At that time, the idea of creating a federal state was an innovative approach to government. However, it was consistent with the unique historical development of the region, and the desire of each of the 13 colonies to preserve a level of local self-government, which they had enjoyed up to that time.

United States of America

Following the Declaration of Independence in 1776, the British colonies of America convened a Continental Congress in 1777 to draft the Articles of Confederation. These Articles proposed to create a "voluntary union of states." The Articles of Confederation were redrafted in 1787, after consultation with the states. In 1788, a majority of states ratified these articles, which became the Constitution of the United States of America.

The constitution outlines the organization of government and the powers of the federal government clearly. Article I of the constitution gives the federal government exclusive jurisdiction and power over foreign trade, immigration, national currency, foreign affairs, post office, and national defence (see diagram below). As well, the federal government has the responsibility of guaranteeing the rights and powers of the states. In the 20th century, the power of the federal government grew as it began to provide funds to the states for highways, schools, and public housing. Its original jurisdictions also grew in importance.

AMERICAN FEDERALISM

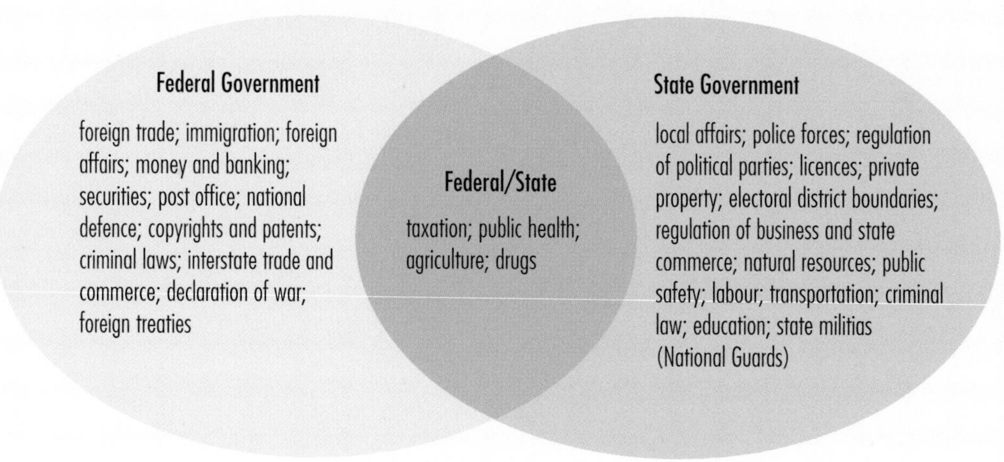

Federal Government
foreign trade; immigration; foreign affairs; money and banking; securities; post office; national defence; copyrights and patents; criminal laws; interstate trade and commerce; declaration of war; foreign treaties
Federal/State
taxation; public health; agriculture; drugs
State Government
local affairs; police forces; regulation of political parties; licences; private property; electoral district boundaries; regulation of business and state commerce; natural resources; public safety; labour; transportation; criminal law; education; state militias (National Guards)

Unlike the Canadian constitution, which defines clearly the powers of provincial governments, the American constitution is unclear about the powers and jurisdictions of state governments. It forbids state governments from intruding on federal jurisdictions, while granting all other jurisdictions to state governments. In the 20th century, state governments have strengthened their jurisdiction and power over local affairs, the regulation of business, public safety, and education (see diagram, page 186).

Since 1787, the Supreme Court of the United States has adjudicated cases on conflict of jurisdiction between the states and the federal government. The Supreme Court has sometimes ruled in favour of the states and sometimes for the federal government.

Constitutional Change

Constitutional change in the United States has been infrequent because amending the constitution is not an easy process. It requires a two-thirds majority of both the House of Representatives and Senate (357 of 535) as well as the ratification by three-quarters of the 50 states (38 of 50). As a result of this, only 27 amendments have been made to the constitution since 1788.

Most amendments to the constitution since 1788 have been significant adaptations of government to new social circumstances (see chart, right). The first ten amendments were adopted in 1791 to address concerns about civil liberties. These ten amendments are known today as the "Bill of Rights." The Second Amendment grants Americans the right to bear arms, and remains controversial to this day. It was passed in the first decade after the conclusion of the War of Independence and seemed to be intended to remind Americans of the importance of everyone's contribution to national defence. Today, however, it is seen as an inalienable right, accounts in large measure for the widespread ownership of weapons, and is an important expression of American political culture.

In the 19th century, five amendments were enacted, of which three (13th, 14th, and 15th) outlawed slavery, defined the privileges of citizenship, and granted the right to vote to men, regardless of race, colour, or past servitude. In the 20th century, the constitution has been amended 12 times. The most important of these amendments were the introduction of income taxes (1913), the modification of the Senate into an elected upper chamber of the Congress (1913), the granting of voting rights to women (1920), limitation on the number of terms of office the President can hold (1951), and lowering of the voting age to 18 years (1971). The latest amendment to the Constitution (the 27th Amendment) was approved in May 1992, limiting compensation paid to elected representatives in the Congress.

An inalienable right is a right that cannot be given away or taken away.

Constitutional Amendments Since 1788

1st–10th Amendments (December 15, 1791)	• Bill of Rights
11th Amendment (January 8, 1798)	• Protection of judicial rights of Americans
12th Amendment (September 25, 1804)	• Conditions governing the election of the President and the Vice President
13th Amendment (December 18, 1865)	• Abolition of slavery in the United States
14th Amendment (July 28, 1868)	• Definition of citizenship privileges
15th Amendment (March 30, 1870)	• Granting of the right to vote to men, regardless of race, colour, or past servitude
16th Amendment (February 25, 1913)	• Introduction of income taxes
17th Amendment (May 31, 1913)	• Modification of the Senate into an elected upper house of the Congress, with each state having two senators elected for six-year terms
18th Amendment (January 29, 1919)	• Introduction of Prohibition
19th Amendment (August 26, 1920)	• Granting of voting rights to women
20th Amendment (February 6, 1933)	• Fixing of the inauguration date of the term of President
21st Amendment (December 5, 1933)	• Ending of Prohibition
22nd Amendment (February 26, 1951)	• Limitation on the office of the President to two consecutive terms for a total of eight years
23rd Amendment (April 3, 1961)	• Granting of representatives to the District of Columbia
24th Amendment (January 23, 1964)	• Prohibition of voting restrictions arising out of failure to pay taxes
25th Amendment (February 10, 1967)	• Naming of successor to the President in the case of death, resignation, or impeachment
26th Amendment (June 30, 1971)	• Lowering of voting age to 18 years
27th Amendment (May 18, 1992)	• Limitations on perks of elected office

Elections and Voting

American voters participate in regularly scheduled elections of officials and representatives to their national, regional, and local assemblies. These events are an important feature of the American political scene.

Electoral Campaigns

American electoral campaigns are long and expensive undertakings for most candidates. In these campaigns, candidates and their supporters devote considerable energy and money to a wide range of activities. Candidates must get their supporters to register them on the ballot in each state, a process which all but prevents most candidates who do not belong to the two main registered parties from mounting effective national campaigns.

Presidential Campaigns. Every four years, there is a presidential election. This electoral campaign generally lasts about ten months. Elections called primaries are held from March to June for registered Democratic and Republican voters to choose delegates to attend a national party convention to support the presidential candidate of their choice. In recent years, the primary has become a contest of image and personality. The elected delegates meet at a convention, held usually in the July or August prior to the election, and choose the party's candidate for President.

The electoral campaign for President begins after the first Monday in September and lasts until election day in early November. During this two-month period, presidential candidates present their policies to the voters and debate with other candidates. Supporters of the candidates (interest groups, lobby organizations, and political action committees) canvass voters, organize public rallies, and distribute literature to the voters. Political advertising on television is one of the most effective ways to publicize a candidate's policies. In recent years, much political advertising on television has taken the form of "attack ads" slurring the reputation of the candidate's main political opponent.

Since 1976, the major parties' presidential election campaigns have been financed by the federal government. Limits on campaign spending were introduced. In the 1996 presidential election, campaign spending limits for the Democrats and Republicans were set at about $120 million each. Independent candidate Perot declined to accept any campaign funds from the federal government.

Congressional Campaigns. Every two years the terms of all members of the House of Representatives and one-third of all Senate members expire and new elections are required. Congressional elections for the House of Representatives and the Senate are exhausting and expensive affairs for candidates. Candidates are expected to maintain close contact with local district groups, attend important local events, make public speeches, give lectures to students, and organize fundraising activities. Many fundraising activities are organized by special interest groups and political action committees (PACs). Many PACs are powerful groups which can help or hinder a candidate's chances of election to the Congress.

In the 1996 congressional elections, the average campaign expenditure of the winning candidate for the Senate was $4.5 million, of which roughly 40% came from PACs. The winning candidate for a seat in the House of Representatives in 1996 spent an average of $500 000, with one-third of it coming from PACs.

Voting

Election day for Congress in the United States is fixed on the first Tuesday in November in years divisible by four. All registered voters can go to the polls to cast a secret ballot for the candidate of their choice. Successful candidates are elected by simple plurality—a system of "first past the post." Under this electoral system, the candidate who receives the greatest number of votes wins. Because of the dominance of the Democratic and Republican parties, the winning candidate generally obtains more than 50% of all votes cast in a district.

When Americans vote for their presidential candidate, they indirectly elect delegates to a 538-member electoral college, which chooses the President. The objective of most presidential campaigns is not just to win the most votes overall in the country, but also to win the most votes in those states that have the greatest number of delegates in the electoral college. The more populous states have more delegates. Democrat Bill Clinton's reelection as President in 1996 was accomplished by obtaining the greatest number of votes cast in populous states such as California, New York, and Florida. Overall popular vote for his candidacy was 49.2% (see chart below). His opponent from the Republican Party, Bob Dole, won only Texas. His electoral support was 40.7% of all votes cast. Other presidential candidates received 10.1% of all votes cast.

Voter Turnout. Average voter turnout in American elections is one of the lowest for a major democracy. Turnout in most municipal, state, and congressional elections is usually less than 50%. Voter turnout for the 1996 presidential elections dropped below 50% for the first time, to 49.1% (see chart below).

In congressional elections, the Democratic and Republican parties are the dominant political parties. In the 1920s and 1930s, third parties such as the Socialists, Farmer-Labour, and Progressives tried to overturn the domination of American politics by the Republicans and Democrats. In 1990, the first socialist was elected to the House of Representatives.

Women Voters. The greatest change in 20th century American federal politics was granting of voting and political rights to women in 1920. Before 1900, women had voting rights in several western states such as Colorado, Montana, Idaho, and Wyoming. In 1916, before women's suffrage, Jeanette Rankin, a Republican from Montana, became the first woman elected to the House of Representatives. Rankin did not seek reelection in 1918, choosing instead to run unsuccessfully for a seat in the Senate. In 1931, Hattie Caraway, a Democrat from Arkansas, became the first woman elected to the Senate. A record 56 women representatives and 9 women senators were elected in the 1998 congressional elections.

In a presidential system, voters elect their leader to be both head of state and head of the government, whereas in a parliamentary democracy voters elect a political party that forms a government if it has majority support in the Parliament. In a parliamentary democracy, the leader of the political party then becomes the head of government. The position of head of state may be held by a monarch or a person chosen by Parliament.

American Election Results (1980–1998)

Presidential Elections	1980 Popular Vote	1980 Electoral Delegates	1984 Popular Vote	1984 Electoral Delegates	1988 Popular Vote	1988 Electoral Delegates	1992 Popular Vote	1992 Electoral Delegates	1996 Popular Vote	1996 Electoral Delegates
Republican Party	50.8%	489	58.8%	525	53.4%	426	37.4%	168	40.7%	159
Democratic Party	41.0	49	40.6	13	45.7	112	43.0	370	49.2	379
Others	8.2	0	0.6	0	0.9	0	19.6	0	10.1	0
Total	100.0	538	100.0	538	100.0	538	100.0	538	100.0	538
Voter Turnout	53.2%		53.3%		50.2%		55.0%		49.1%	

Congressional Elections House of Representatives	1980	1982	1984	1986	1988	1990	1992	1994	1996	1998
Republican Party	192	166	182	177	175	167	175	230	227	223
Democratic Party	243	269	253	258	260	267	259	204	207	211
Independents	0	0	0	0	0	1	1	1	1	1
Total Seats	435	435	435	435	435	435	435	435	435	435
Women representatives	19	21	22	23	25	28	47	47	51	56

Senate	1980	1982	1984	1986	1988	1990	1992	1994	1996	1998
Republican Party	53	54	53	45	45	44	43	53	55	55
Democratic Party	47	46	47	55	55	56	57	47	45	45
Total Seats	100	100	100	100	100	100	100	100	100	100
Women senators	2	2	2	2	2	2	6	8	9	9

Compiled from *Congressional Quarterly* and *Center for the American Women and Politics*

AMERICAN ECONOMIC SYSTEM

Advance Organizer

Until recently, the role of government in the economy expanded to reduce fluctuations in the business cycle and social inequities. The United States has a mixed economy, but one firmly rooted in the principles of private enterprise. Basic features of the contemporary American economy are markets, competition, profit making, and private ownership of the means of production.

SECTION OVERVIEW
- Economic Policies
- Private Sector
- Public Sector
- Changing American Labour Force

AMERICAN ECONOMY IN ACTION

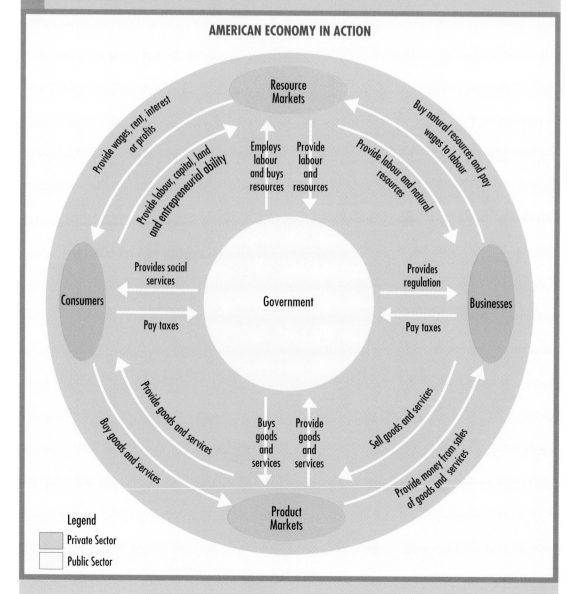

Resource Markets

Provide wages, rent, interest or profits

Provide labour, capital, land and entrepreneurial ability

Employs labour and buys resources

Provide labour and resources

Buy natural resources and pay wages to labour

Provide labour and natural resources

Provides social services

Consumers

Pay taxes

Government

Provides regulation

Businesses

Pay taxes

Provide goods and services

Buy goods and services

Buys goods and services

Provide goods and services

Sell goods and services

Provide money from sales of goods and services

Product Markets

Legend
- Private Sector
- Public Sector

Economic Policies

Economic policies of American governments have undergone several changes in the 20th century. From 1900 to 1933, the government favoured a policy of little intervention, except during World War I when the government intervened to mobilize the country for war with Germany. Beginning in 1933, the American government began a policy of greater involvement in the economy, based on higher taxes and higher spending, which would last until 1981. Since 1981, the government has retreated from its previous level of intervention and allowed private enterprise to function with fewer restrictions.

Limited Intervention (to 1929)

From before 1900 until 1929, American governments intervened little in the economy, as a matter of economic policy. The main tasks of government activity in the economy were to maintain public order; to develop laws and a court system to promote competition (antitrust legislation), protect business activity, and safeguard private property; to protect the national currency; and to provide some public works (roads and public education). The government did enact some legislation on child labour, employment, health care, and worker safety. However, President Calvin Coolidge (1923–1929) described his government's economic policy as "More business in government, less government in business." In the 1920s, government spending was kept small, taxes low, and the budget balanced. Budget surpluses were used to reduce government debt.

Though American governments from 1900 to 1933 believed in limited spending and low public debt, governments were not averse to introducing measures that restricted the movement of people, goods, and capital into the United States. In 1921, the Republican-controlled Congress passed legislation that set the annual number of immigrants entering the country at 357 000. The annual limit was lowered to 150 000 immigrants in 1924. These immigration laws favoured immigrants from northern and western Europe over people from southern and eastern Europe, Africa, and East Asia.

In May 1921, the Congress passed laws that raised duties and tariff rates on imported agricultural goods. Primarily intended to protect American farmers, the high tariffs still did not alleviate the plight of small American farmers in the 1920s.

Great Depression (1929–1939)

On Tuesday, October 29, 1929, the excitement and optimism that gave the decade of 1920–1929 the name "Roaring Twenties," ended abruptly with a financial panic on the New York Stock Exchange. From the spring of 1926 to the autumn of 1929, millions of Americans had borrowed billions of dollars to buy stocks of companies such as Ford Motors, General Motors, US Steel, Westinghouse, and General Electric in the hopes of becoming rich. The lucky few who sold their stocks before October 1929 made large profits, but for millions of others the sudden plunge in the value of their stocks in October forced them to sell to repay their loans. Many went bankrupt. The effects of the October 29 stock market crash reverberated throughout the American economy. Consumers reacted to the financial crash by sharply curtailing their

| 1913 | 1914–1918 | 1917 | 1921 | 1926–1929 |
| Federal Reserve System established | World War I | United States enters World War I | Limits on immigration introduced; tariffs on imported agricultural goods raised | Speculation and boom in the stock market |

Limited Intervention—To 1929

Note: Timeline is not to scale

spending. As sales of goods and services fell, businesses reacted by laying off workers. By 1933, the value of all production had fallen almost 50%. The unemployment rate rose from 3.2% in 1929 to 24.9% in 1933.

In 1930, Congress passed the Smoot–Haley tariff on all goods entering the United States as a measure to protect domestic business from foreign competition and save jobs. Later that year, President Herbert Hoover (1929–1933) introduced a program of relief and government assistance for the country's growing number of unemployed. The economic package represented only a partial retreat from the Republican Party's traditional economic policy of *laissez-faire*. Hoover believed that prosperity was around the corner, with jobs for all.

Hoover's expected economic recovery was dealt a severe blow in 1931 when a banking crisis in Europe cut short a gradual recovery in the American economy. Unemployment began to rise and some American banks collapsed. In 1932, Franklin D. Roosevelt, the Democratic presidential candidate campaigning on a program of "Relief, Recovery, Reform," argued that government intervention was necessary to save the economy from collapse. Roosevelt pledged to seek "a new deal for the American people."

New Deal (1933–1939). Following his inauguration as President in March 1933, Roosevelt called the Congress to meet in a special session to enact legislation on the economy. The special session met from March 9 to June 16. During these Hundred Days, the Congress enacted a comprehensive body of legislation which formed the core of Roosevelt's New Deal.

The objectives of the New Deal were to alleviate the economic crisis created by the Great Depression. The legislation of the Hundred Days was aimed primarily at relief and recovery. Among the pieces of legislation enacted during the Hundred Days were the Emergency Banking Relief Act to stabilize the banking system, the Tennessee Valley Authority Act to promote the economic development of the Tennessee Valley region, and the National Industrial Recovery Act to reduce unemployment through public works projects (see chart, page 193).

In January 1935, Roosevelt outlined a program of social reform. Among the legislation enacted were acts to create a social security system (unemployment insurance, old-age security, old-age pensions, and welfare); to recognize labour unions and their right to collective bargaining; and to create a national housing authority to provide low-interest loans to local governments for slum clearance and housing projects. Another major initiative in April 1935 was establishment of the Works Progress Administration (WPA) to administer a national works program for the unemployed, which one year later employed more than 3.4 million persons. While most WPA projects were created to employ manual labour, provision was made for projects employing musicians, writers, actors, and artists.

The New Deal did not end the Great Depression in the United States, though it did moderate some of its effects. The economic demands of World War II (1939–1945) were largely responsible for the return to prosperity in the country. The New Deal, however, encouraged better use of the country's natural resources

October 1929
Stock market crash

1930
Smoot–Haley tariff on all imported goods passed; temporary program of public relief and assistance for unemployed introduced

1931
Banking crisis in Europe cuts short economic recovery in the US

1932
Democratic presidential candidate Franklin D. Roosevelt announces programs of "new deal for the American people"

Great Depression 1929–1939

192

and contributed to the development of the conservation movement. The New Deal also extended federal government authority to many fields, notably banking, agriculture, social security, and public welfare. Its labour legislation benefited organized labour and small businesses. African–Americans and women benefited indirectly, with the establishment of minimum standards for wages, working hours, relief, and security. Opposition to the New Deal came from conservatives in the Democratic and Republican parties, who attacked government programs as state interference in private business.

Stock Montage, Inc.

Major Legislation of the Hundred Days

Emergency Banking Relief Act (March 9, 1933)

- to protect the banking system from collapse

Civilian Conservation Corps Act (March 31, 1933)

- to provide work for 250 000 jobless youth in reforestation, road construction, soil erosion prevention, national parks, and flood control

Agricultural Adjustment Act (May 12, 1933)

- to control surplus agricultural production through price supports and subsidies

Tennessee Valley Authority Act (May 18, 1933)

- to establish a government agency to construct dams and power plants and to promote the economic development of the Tennessee Valley region

Federal Securities Act (May 27, 1933)

- to compel full disclosure to investors of information relating to new securities issues

National Employment System Act (June 6, 1933)

- to establish a national employment system

Home Owners Refinancing Act (June 13, 1933)

- to provide loans and mortgages to homeowners

Glass–Steagall Act (June 16, 1933)

- to regulate the banking industry and to guarantee people's savings during bank failures

Farm Credit Act (June 16, 1933)

- to provide short-term and medium-term loans to farmers for production and marketing

National Industrial Recovery Act (June 16, 1933)

- to revive industrial activity and reduce unemployment through government regulation and to establish the Public Works Administration for the construction of roads, public buildings, and other projects

America Between Two World Wars, pp. 342–346

PHOTO: Formerly called the Boulder Dam, the Hoover Dam was one of many public works projects begun under the New Deal. The dam was completed in 1936 and is used for flood control, electric power, and irrigation.

1933
Unemployment reaches 24.9% of the labour force

March–June 1933
"Hundred Days" legislation marks the beginning of the New Deal

1935
Program of social reform and welfare announced

Mixed Economy in America (1939–1975)

The entry of the United States into World War II in 1941 marked the beginning of unprecedented government intervention in the economy. After 1945, the government continued many of the New Deal's roadbuilding, dam, and housing projects and its regulation of banking, insurance, and foreign exchange trading. However, under the influence of ideas from John Maynard Keynes, the scope of government fiscal policy was expanded. In the 1930s, Keynes had examined the effects of the Great Depression on a private enterprise economy and the role of government in stabilizing the economy. At Cambridge University, Keynes taught his economic theory to his students, many of whom were Canadian. During World War II, several of these students found employment in American government agencies.

After 1945, the American government adopted many of Keynes's fiscal policy instruments, seeking to provide stability to the economy and even out the fluctuations in production and employment caused by the business cycle. It was hoped that government spending on goods and services, as well as its transfers of income to the poor, would stabilize the economy. The government also hoped that it could counteract the effects of the business cycle on employment and production by adopting a countercyclical fiscal policy. In bad economic times, the government increased its spending on goods and services and lowered taxes to stimulate the economy. In good economic times, the government attempted to reduce its spending on goods and services and increase taxes to slow the economy.

From 1945 to 1970, American government fiscal and economic policies based on Keynesian principles promoted high economic growth, full employment, and stable incomes (see timeline below). However, by 1970, American expenditure and involvement in a war in Vietnam began to increase prices. In late 1973, the price of world oil rose sharply and pushed the American economy into a deep recession in 1974–1975. Industrial production and economic growth fell sharply and unemployment rose (see chart, page 195).

PHOTO: The oil price rise in late 1979 brought long line-ups at most American gas stations.

Lambert/Archive Photos

1939–1945	1948	1950–1953	1965	1965–1973	1973–1974	1974–1975
World War II	General Agreement on Tariffs and Trade (GATT) signed	Korean War; military-industrial complex in US begins	Medicare and Medicaid established	Increased military spending; active military involvement in Vietnam	First world oil price rise	First major postwar recession in US

Mixed Economy in America 1939–1975

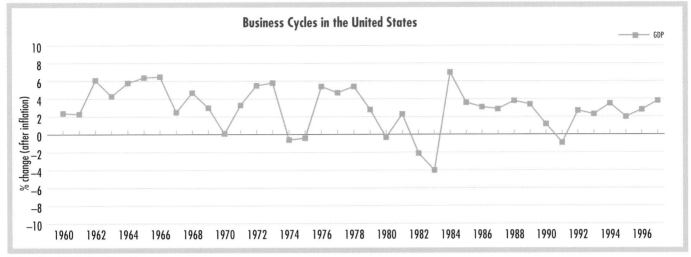

Business Cycles in the United States

% change (after inflation)

U.S. Bureau of Economic Analysis. *Survey of Current Business*

Retreat of Government from the Economy (since 1975)

In the mid-1970s, economist Milton Friedman, among others, called for smaller government. To stabilize the economy and control the rise of prices after 1975, economic policies focussing on the money supply were given greater emphasis. Interest rates were allowed to rise sharply to limit the demand for money by the government, which wanted to finance mounting budget deficits and control the rise in prices. As interest rates rose, businesses began to cut back their investment plans. Consumers reduced spending, forcing businesses to cut production and lay off workers. The economy went into a deep recession in 1981–1982.

In 1981, newly-elected President Ronald Reagan announced an economic policy that would return the country to

prosperity. The policy, later known as "supply-side economics" or "Reaganomics," called for lower government spending on social welfare programs, lower personal and corporate income taxes, less regulation of business activities, and lower increases in the growth of the money supply. Under Reagan's administration, income taxes were lowered, regulations on business reduced, the money supply tightly controlled, and some government spending on social programs cut. However, because Reagan increased military spending, his government was unable to reduce its budget deficits, which compelled his successor George Bush to raise taxes in the early 1990s.

After 1993, President Clinton struggled to balance the government budget. A growing economy and higher employment in the late 1990s helped to all but eliminate government budget deficits.

1979–1981	1981–1982	1988	1989	1990	1994	1995	1997
Second world oil price rise; Federal Reserve interest rates raised to curb inflation	Recession in US; Reagan's new economic policy announced	Free Trade Agreement with Canada signed	Agency to close bankrupt banks established	End of Cold War; miltary spending lowered; many bases closed	NAFTA with Canada and Mexico established	GATT becomes World Trade Organization (WTO)	Clinton approves cuts to social welfare

Retreat of Government from the Economy—Since 1975

Americans spent their income in 1997 on the following:

Food	14.0%
Clothing	5.3
Housing	32.4
Transportation	18.6
Recreation	5.5
Medicine	5.4
Education	1.5
Other	17.3

Bureau of Labor Statistics

Young people between 15 and 24 years old account for about 20% of all spending on movies, fast food, travel, clothing and CDs.

TOTAL DOMESTIC SPENDING

1997

- ☐ Personal 66.5%
- ☐ Government 14.6%
- ☐ Business 18.9%

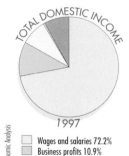

TOTAL DOMESTIC INCOME

1997

Bureau of Economic Analysis

- ☐ Wages and salaries 72.2%
- ☐ Business profits 10.9%
- ☐ Interest and investment 8.4%
- ☐ Farming income 0.7%
- ☐ Self-employment 7.8%

PHOTO: Women entrepreneurs are a growing force in American business.

Private Sector

The main decision makers in the American economy are consumers and business enterprises. Together, these two groups account for about 70% of all economic activity in the United States.

Consumers

Consumers are the largest group of decision makers in the American economy. They account for almost two-thirds of all spending on goods and services. Annually, some 66.5% of total domestic spending in the United States is made by consumers (see chart "Total Domestic Spending"). Spending by government and by businesses accounts for 14.6% and 18.9% respectively. Wages and salaries from employment in businesses are the main sources of income, accounting for 72.2% of total domestic income. Other types of income in the chart "Total Domestic Income" are business profits (10.9%), interest and investment (8.4%), and self-employment (7.8%).

Business Enterprises

The main activities of American businesses are the production and sale of goods and services to consumers. American businesses are generally organized as sole proprietorships, partnerships, or corporations.

Sole Proprietorship. Most small businesses in the United States are sole proprietorships, owned and operated by one person. As in Canada, the owner of a sole proprietorship is responsible for its success or failure. Profits in a sole proprietorship go directly to the owner, and losses are the responsibility of the owner as well. By law, a sole proprietorship pays fewer taxes at a lower rate than other types of business enterprises.

The economic contributions of a sole proprietorship are many. The sole proprietorship is often the starting point for development of a new product or service. If the new product or service is successful, then the business grows or the product is acquired by a larger firm. The sole proprietorship is well suited to meet local needs and to provide individualized products and services for customers. Customers tend to believe that the familiar owner of a sole proprietorship will do a good job. The Internal Revenue Service (IRS) reported that in 1997 there were over 13.5 million sole proprietorships in the United States. Of these about five million were owned and operated by women. The vast majority of sole proprietorships have annual sales of less than $100 000.

Sole proprietorships account for about 90% of all small businesses in the United States. The small business sector employs about 55% of the labour force, generates 44% of all sales, and produces 38% of the nation's gross domestic product (GDP).

Judy Bauer/Arnold Publishing Ltd.

Partnership. In 1997, an estimated 1.85 million partnerships operated in the United States. Partnerships are regulated by laws of the state where they are formed and by a legal agreement among co-owners. Most partnerships are established when a sole proprietor wishes to expand his or her business. As in Canada, the owners of a partnership share in its profits, have the right to participate in its management, and are responsible for its losses and debts. Partnerships in the United States are the most common form of business arrangement in the professions of law, medicine, and accounting.

Corporation. In the United States, a corporation is a specific legal form of organization of persons and resources chartered by 1 of the 50 states for the purpose of conducting business. A corporation may own property, sue or be sued in court, and make contracts. A corporation is well suited to conduct business through small and large enterprises. In 1997, an estimated four million corporations operated in the United States.

Although most of the estimated four million corporations in the United States are small and have few shareholders, about 100 000 have issued shares to the general public. Many of these corporations are listed on the country's ten stock exchanges. The largest of these stock exchanges are the New York Stock Exchange (NYSE) and the National Association of Securities Dealers Automated Quotations (NASDAQ).

The NYSE is located on Wall Street in Manhattan, New York City. It is the country's oldest stock exchange, founded officially in 1817, when fewer than 100 shares were traded daily. Today, the average daily volume of shares traded exceeds 600 million. Over 11 000 corporations are listed on the NYSE. In terms of dollar value of shares traded, the NYSE is the world's largest stock market. In recent years, many Japanese, European, and Canadian companies have listed their shares on the NYSE to raise new investment capital. During the 1990s, the prices of shares on the NYSE rose markedly.

The NASDAQ, founded in 1971, uses computers and high technology telecommunications to trade and monitor the trading of about 600 million shares daily. Over 5000 corporations are listed on the NASDAQ.

An estimated 60 million Americans, or 25% of the country's population, own shares of large corporations.

A bull market occurs when investors are optimistic about the economy. In a bull market, prices of shares rise more often than they fall.

A bear market occurs when investors are pessimistic about the economy. In a bear market, prices of shares fall more often than they rise.

Canapress/Adam Nadel

PHOTO: The trading floor of the New York Stock Exchange (NYSE), the world's largest stock exchange.

Corporate America

Some 500 major corporations occupy an important role in the American economy. These corporations had sales of almost $5.52 trillion and profits of $324.1 billion in 1997. Most of these corporations operate worldwide, including in Canada. All of these corporations have their shares listed on the NYSE or NASDAQ.

These large corporations are present in every major industry in the United States. They are major producers of automobiles, electronics, computers, petroleum, and consumer goods, as well as services such as telecommunications and retailing. The chart "Top American Corporations" lists the 20 largest corporations in the United States. Collectively, these large corporations had sales of $1.358 trillion and profits of $76.3 billion in 1997. They employed over 4.36 million people.

In terms of assets, sales, profits, and employees, American banks are also very large corporations (see chart "Top American Banks"). The ten largest American banks controlled over $2.08 trillion in assets but less than 25% of all deposits held by Americans. These banks in 1997 had sales of $187.5 billion, profits of $21.8 billion, and employed over 520 000 people. However, the American banking system is dominated by many small banks.

There are over 9000 banks in the United States. The vast majority operate as small local banks with one or two branches, while in Canada banks may have branches across the country. Federal and state laws do not allow banks to operate across state lines, though they may be allowed to operate subsidiaries in other states. These laws were introduced in the 19th century on the assumption that small banks are more responsive to local needs than big banks. However, small banks have less capital to survive unfavourable economic conditions. Every year several small banks fail and are taken over by the government to protect people's savings.

Total corporate profits exceeded $800 billion in 1997.

Top American Corporations (1997)
(in millions of US$)

	Industry	Sales	Profits	Employees
General Motors	Automobiles	$178 174	$ 6698	608 000
Ford Motor	Automobiles	153 627	6920	363 692
Exxon	Petroleum	122 379	8460	80 000
Wal-Mart Stores	Retailing	119 299	3526	825 000
General Electric	Electronics	90 840	8203	276 000
IBM	Computers	78 508	6093	269 465
Chrysler	Automobiles	61 147	2805	121 000
Mobil	Petroleum	59 978	3272	42 700
Philip Morris	Consumer goods	56 114	6310	152 000
AT & T	Telecommunications	53 261	4638	128 000
Boeing	Aerospace	45 800	(178)	239 000
Texaco	Petroleum	45 187	2664	29 313
Hewlett Packard	Computers	42 895	3119	121 900
Du Pont de Nemours	Chemicals	41 304	2405	98 396
Sears Roebuck	Retailing	41 296	1188	296 000
Chevron	Petroleum	36 376	3256	39 362
Procter & Gamble	Consumer goods	35 764	3415	106 000
Amoco	Petroleum	32 836	2720	43 451
K-Mart	Retailing	32 183	249	258 000
JC Penny	Retailing	30 546	566	260 000

Losses appear in brackets

Compiled from *Fortune 500*, April 27, 1998

Top American Banks (1997)
(in millions of US$)

	Assets	Sales	Profits	Employees
Chase Manhattan	$365 521	$30 381	$3708	69 033
Citicorp	310 897	34 697	3591	93 700
Nationsbank (1)	264 562	21 734	3077	80 360
JP Morgan & Co.	262 159	17 701	1465	16 943
Bankamerica Corp. (1)	260 159	23 585	3210	77 000
First Union Corp.	157 274	14 329	1896	43 933
Bankers Trust New York	140 102	12 176	866	18 286
Banc One Corp. (2)	115 901	13 219	1306	56 600
First Chicago NBD Bank (2)	114 096	10 098	1525	33 962
Wells Fargo & Co.	97 456	9608	1155	33 100

(1) Nationsbank and Bankamerica agreed to merge in April 1998.
(2) Banc One and First Chicago NBD agreed to merge in April 1998.

Compiled from *Fortune 500*, April 27, 1998

American Foreign Trade and Investment

The impact of America's massive corporations and banks is not limited solely to sales, profits, and employees. Since the beginning of the 20th century, they have also influenced the country's foreign trade and foreign investment policies.

Foreign Trade. American foreign trade policy after 1945 has emphasized the need to promote freer trade among nations, a goal that the country's major corporations viewed as important to their continued growth and expansion outside the United States. To this end, the United States initiated the General Agreement on Tariffs and Trade (GATT) in 1948, which was signed by 22 nations, including Canada. The purpose of the GATT was to reduce trade barriers such as tariffs and subsidies, and to provide a means for resolving trade disputes among member states. Several rounds of trade negotiations have been held since 1948. The most recent was the Uruguay Round, held to further reduce tariffs and government subsidies to agriculture. After many years of negotiation, on January 1, 1995, GATT became the World Trade Organization (WTO).

In 1994, the Free Trade Agreement between Canada and the United States was expanded to include Mexico and became known as the North American Free Trade Agreement (NAFTA). NAFTA proposed to eliminate tariffs and quotas on imported goods within five years.

Many American economists believed that the three countries under NAFTA would enjoy higher economic growth and greater prosperity. NAFTA has increased trade among the three countries. Today, Canada and Mexico collectively account for 32.1% of American exports and 29.2% of imports (see pie graphs, top right). The total value of American exports in 1997 was $689 billion and imports $886 billion.

Foreign Investment. Since the beginning of the 20th century, American corporations have been active investors outside the United States. Before 1939, much of American investment abroad was concentrated in Latin America and Canada. Since 1945, American investment has grown considerably and spread to many parts of East Asia, Europe, and Africa, as well as Latin America and Canada. From 1980, American investment outside the United States has grown from $215.4 billion to $796.5 billion in 1996 (see chart "US Investment Abroad").

Glen BonBernard

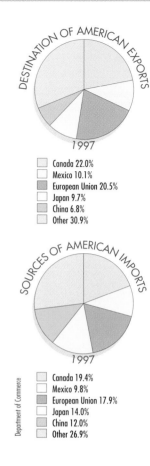

DESTINATION OF AMERICAN EXPORTS
1997

- Canada 22.0%
- Mexico 10.1%
- European Union 20.5%
- Japan 9.7%
- China 6.8%
- Other 30.9%

SOURCES OF AMERICAN IMPORTS
1997

- Canada 19.4%
- Mexico 9.8%
- European Union 17.9%
- Japan 14.0%
- China 12.0%
- Other 26.9%

Department of Commerce

PHOTO: The United States exerts great influence on international trade, both as the world's largest buyer of imported goods and largest seller of goods to the rest of the world.

Cooperation among nation-states is achieved through diplomacy, alliances, treaties, international law, international organizations, and economic interdependence.

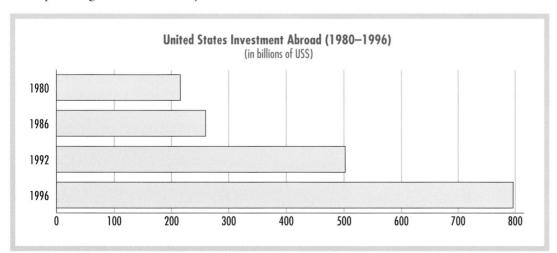

United States Investment Abroad (1980–1996)
(in billions of US$)

Year	
1980	~215
1986	~260
1992	~500
1996	~796

0   100   200   300   400   500   600   700   800

Bureau of Economic Analysis

Public Sector

The public sector accounts for one-third of the American economy. Its main activities are conducted through fiscal policy, monetary policy, and various social programs.

Fiscal Policy

The main functions of American fiscal policy are expenditures on goods and services, taxation, and the regulation of business activities.

Expenditures. Over 60% of all spending by the federal government in 1997 was transfers to individuals, businesses, and other governments (see graphs, left). Almost one-quarter of total federal government spending was on goods and services. The federal government is the largest single purchaser of goods and services in the country. Every year, its purchase of goods and services accounts for about 5% of all production. Defence spending contributed $270 billion directly to the national economy in 1997.

Since 1950, high defence spending has created a large military-industrial complex in the United States. In the 1980s, it employed more than five million people directly and indirectly in the production of jet fighters, ships, missiles, rockets, tanks, and guns. General Motors, Ford Motors, General Electric, Chrysler, Du Pont, and Motorola, among other large corporations, owe their growth over the years in part to military contracts.

The ending of the Cold War and arms race between the United States and the Soviet Union in 1990 brought an end to the growth of the American military–industrial complex. In 1991–1992, the federal government sharply cut its orders for new armaments. With fewer military contracts, many defence firms laid off thousands of workers and closed plants. Though the military–industrial complex has shrunk in size, it still influences the economies of California, Illinois, New York, Ohio, Texas, and Virginia, where many defence plants continue to operate.

Taxation. The addition of the 16th Amendment to the Constitution in 1913 allowed governments to levy taxes on personal incomes, and income taxes have become the single largest source of revenue for the federal and state governments. In 1997, the main sources of revenue from the federal government were personal income tax (44.7%), social insurance contributions (35.6%), and corporate income tax (11.7%), shown in the graphs. Sales taxes levied on the purchases of goods were a minor source of revenue for the federal government.

Regulation. Although in recent years governments have reduced their regulation of private businesses, regulation remains an important facet of government economic policy, especially for the federal government. Through more than 100 agencies, the government regulates banks, insurance companies, brokerage houses, interstate trade, communications, nuclear power, product safety, employment, and environmental protection.

One of the first attempts at regulation of private business was the Sherman Antitrust Act, passed in 1890. The Act made it illegal for any person or business to monopolize trade or restrict trade. The Act was originally used to break up large corporations in order to promote competition, and it continues to be used as a measure to prevent large corporations from dominating various industries. In 1998 Microsoft was investigated and charged under the Act for achieving monopoly control over the production and sale of computer software programs. Supporters of antitrust legislation argue that competition is essential to the American values of individual freedom and personal initiative.

Other important federal regulatory agencies are the Equal Employment Opportunity Commission, which scrutinizes the hiring of minorities, the Occupational Safety and Health Administration, which examines working conditions, and the Environmental Protection Agency, which seeks to control and reduce air and water pollution.

FEDERAL GOVERNMENT SPENDING 1997

- Goods and services 22.5%
- Transfers to individuals 48.0%
- Transfers to businesses 5.3%
- Other governments 9.4%
- Interest on public debt 14.8%

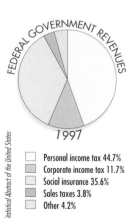

FEDERAL GOVERNMENT REVENUES 1997

- Personal income tax 44.7%
- Corporate income tax 11.7%
- Social insurance 35.6%
- Sales taxes 3.8%
- Other 4.2%

Statistical Abstract of the United States

Monetary Policy

Monetary policy in the United States is regulated by the Federal Reserve System. Its most important function is to manage the country's supply of money and credit, and maintain stability in the country's financial system.

Federal Reserve System. The Federal Reserve System was created by Congress in 1913 to strengthen the supervision of the country's banking system and prevent periodic bank panics, such as occurred in the 19th century. The Federal Reserve today consists of 12 regional Federal Reserve banks. Most commercial banks are members of the Federal Reserve System.

The Federal Reserve System is administered by a Board of Governors who are appointed by the President for 14-year terms. Although the Federal Reserve is directly responsible to Congress, by law the governors are independent of political pressure from Congress and the President. The Federal Reserve does not rely on Congress for funding but pays all of its operating expenses from investment income and fees for its services. However, the Federal Reserve is expected to coordinate its policies with those of the President's administration.

Since its establishment, the policies and operations of the Federal Reserve have evolved in response to major events. During the Great Depression of the 1930s, the Federal Reserve developed measures to regulate the banking system. During World War II, it lowered interest rates to allow the federal government to borrow large sums of money for investment in the war effort. From 1951 to 1979, the Federal Reserve focussed its policies on promoting economic growth, price stability, and full employment. In 1979, mounting inflation forced it to adopt a policy aimed at controlling the money supply. This policy of "tight money" slowed the growth of the money supply, limited credit, and raised interest rates. It brought down the inflation rate, but also pushed the economy into a recession in 1980 and in 1981–1982.

Since 1982, the Federal Reserve has pursued a policy of monitoring the money supply so as to keep the inflation rate from rising too rapidly. It accomplishes this objective through changes in its discount rate, which is the interest rate it charges commercial banks to borrow money. Changes in the discount rate lead commercial banks to alter the interest rates they charge their customers. The setting of the discount rate is achieved through the sale of government securities and bonds to banks, which affects the demand and supply of money. However, Federal Reserve policies on money supply take some time to affect the direction of the economy.

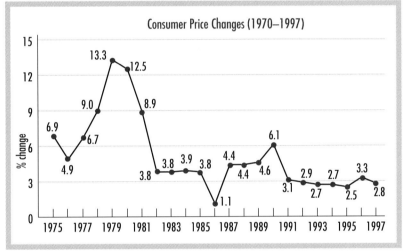

Consumer Price Changes (1970–1997)

Bureau of Labor Statistics

Financial Rescue. Another aspect of monetary policy is to maintain stability in the country's banking sector. In 1989, Congress and the President approved the Financial Institution Reform, Recovery, and Enforcement Act (FIRREA) to provide government funds for closing several hundred bankrupt savings banks. A special government agency called Resolution Trust Corporation was established to sell the assets of these failed savings banks in order to pay back depositors. Federal government estimates suggest that the total cost of liquidating these failed savings institutions will eventually reach $500 billion. In Canada, the Canada Deposit Insurance Corporation (CDIC) insures all savings deposits up to $60 000 Canadian, in the event of a failure of a bank or trust company.

Social Security

The American social security system was established as part of the New Deal when the Social Security Act was signed into law by Franklin D. Roosevelt in August 1935. It created a federal system of old-age benefits for retired workers and a federal–state system of unemployment insurance. Over the years, the system was broadened with the addition of disability insurance, Medicare, and Medicaid for retired people and low income groups, and special programs for military veterans and low income earners.

Old-Age Security. Old-age security was originally designed to provide compulsory coverage to all workers upon retirement at age 65. Benefits are paid out to eligible persons who have worked for at least 10 years in a job. Old-age security is designed to benefit low income workers. People in high income brackets generally receive a lower percentage of their earnings when they collect benefits. In 1997, 46 million people collected old-age security.

Unemployment Insurance. Unemployment insurance is administered by state governments, with some support from the federal government. To be eligible for unemployment insurance benefits, workers must be ready, able, and willing to work, and must be registered at a state public employment office. A worker's benefit is based on his or her previous employment and earnings. Employees pay a payroll tax of 6.2% for unemployment insurance premiums.

Medicare and Medicaid. There is no universal government-funded health care program in the United States, such as there is in Canada. Health care insurance is provided by privately owned insurance companies that charge customers for coverage. Many people do not have any private coverage because they cannot afford to pay the premiums. Others who may not have any private health insurance coverage are young people, people between jobs, and small business employees. The federal government estimated in 1997 that over 40 million Americans were not covered by health insurance. A limited government-funded health care insurance, in the form of Medicare and Medicaid, is available to low income earners and people who are on old-age security. Medicare was established in 1965 and provides assistance for medical expenses for the aged and disabled. The program consists of hospital insurance to cover the costs of hospitalization and a supplementary medical insurance which provides coverage for doctor's services, medical tests, home care, and prescriptions. A small premium is charged for this medical insurance.

Medicaid, established in 1965, provides medical benefits for low income persons. It is funded largely by the federal government and administered by state governments. Medicaid is limited to persons who receive welfare payments. Persons eligible for Medicaid include the visually impaired, disabled, and single parent families.

In the 1992 presidential campaign, Bill Clinton campaigned hard on the issue of health care reform, promising that once elected President, he would take steps to ensure that every American had basic medical coverage. He noted that the United States was the only industrialized country to not have a comprehensive national health insurance program for its citizens. In 1993, he appointed Hillary Clinton to head a committee on national health care. Private health insurance companies and Republicans attacked the committee's proposal for a national health plan as too bureaucratic and "socialistic." The idea of establishing a national health plan was shelved.

Special Programs. War veterans are eligible for a wide range of services and benefits from the Department of Veteran Affairs. Other special programs are housing subsidies for lower income households, food stamps, supplemental security income support for needy aged, and aid to families with children.

Changing American Labour Force

The growth of social security and government since 1960 has brought significant structural changes in the American labour force. The most important changes were the growth of the service sector and the entry of large numbers of women into the labour force.

Growth of the Service Sector

In 1960, about 43.8% of the American labour force was employed in primary industries (agriculture, mining, and forestry) and in secondary industry (manufacturing and construction), while 56.2% of the labour force was employed in tertiary industry (services). By 1997, about 26.9% of the labour force worked in primary and secondary industries (see chart "Changing American Labour Force").

Changing American Labour Force (1960–1997)

	1960	1980	1997
Primary industry	8.5%	3.6%	2.9%
Secondary industry	35.3	30.5	24.0
Tertiary industry	56.2	65.9	73.1
Totals	100.0	100.0	100.0

Department of Labor

Women in the Labour Force

Since 1960, the number of women in the labour force has more than doubled, from 23 268 000 in 1960 to 62 866 000 in 1997. Thus, the percentage of women employed in the American labour force rose from 32.5% in 1960 to 46.2% in 1997. The number of men in the labour force grew less rapidly, from 48 221 000 in 1960 to 73 232 000 in 1997. The rate of unemployment for men and women has changed little since 1960. Unemployment among young people (ages 16–24) has remained high over the years, above 10% (see chart "Employment by Gender").

Most of the women entering the labour force since 1960 have found employment in the service sector. In 1960, the most common occupations of women were clerical, catering, and professional work, whereas for men they were in the fields of manufacturing, management, professional, and agriculture. In 1997, the professions, clerical, and catering remained the main occupations of women, but increasing numbers were finding work in management and sales (see chart "Women in Selected Executive and Professional Ranks"). For men in 1997, the most common occupations were manufacturing, the professions, management, and sales (see chart "Occupations by Gender").

Today, more than one-third of all firms in the United States are owned or operated by women. Women-led businesses are active in all industries, from agriculture, construction, and manufacturing to retail trade, finance, consulting, and services.

Employment by Gender (1960–1997)

Employment Share:	1960	1980	1997
Women	32.5%	42.0%	46.2%
Men	67.5	58.0	53.8
Both sexes	100.0	100.0	100.0
Unemployment Rate:			
Women	5.9%	7.4%	5.2%
Men	5.2	6.8	5.0
Both sexes	5.4	7.0	5.1
Youth (16–24)	11.2	13.9	11.5

Department of Labor

About 40% of all young people between 16 and 19 years old had a job in 1998.

Women in Selected Executive and Professional Ranks (% of share)

Medical Managers	75.3%
Psychologists	61.4
Accountants	56.0
Editors/Reporters	55.7
Economists	54.4
Authors	54.1
Financial Managers	54.0
Personnel	51.6
Administrators	47.7
Purchasing Managers	45.7
Teachers, University	43.5
Management analysts	41.1
Marketing	37.8
Musicians	34.2
Mathematicians	30.6
Lawyers	29.5
Scientists	29.3
Physicians	26.4
Architects	16.7
Dentists	13.7
Engineers	8.5

Bureau of Labor Statistics

Occupations by Gender (1960–1997)

	Women		Men	
	1960	1997	1960	1997
Farming, fishing, mining	4.4%	1.3%	9.6%	4.6%
Transportation	0.3	0.8	5.7	6.9
Manufacturing	16.3	8.9	40.9	31.9
Services				
• sales	7.7	13.2	5.8	11.1
• managerial	5.0	13.7	13.6	14.4
• professional	12.4	20.1	10.8	15.2
• clerical	30.2	24.2	7.1	5.5
• catering	23.7	17.8	6.5	10.4
Totals	100.0	100.0	100.0	100.0

Department of Labor

AMERICAN POLITICAL ECONOMY

Advance Organizer

For much of the postwar period in the United States, all levels of government expanded to meet the public demand for more spending on social security, regulation of the private sector, and spending on defence to counter the military threat of the Soviet Union. There arose a public belief among the people and many politicians that the growth of government could continue indefinitely so long as the national economy grew faster. However, in the late 1970s, as the economy entered a severe recession, several economists and some politicians began to question the assumptions behind spending on social security and regulation of business. This questioning of the principles of social security and regulation initiated a public debate over the role of government in American society, a debate which continues as the United States enters the 21st century.

SECTION OVERVIEW
- Growth of Government
- American Neoconservatism
- Individualism and Equality

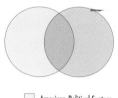

American Political System
American Economic System
American Political Economy

Growth of Government

The growth of government (federal, state, and local) has been the single most important issue shaping American politics and economics since 1945. After 1950, the share of government spending in the national economy grew from 21.2% of GDP in 1950 to 32.0% of GDP in 1997 (see chart below). This unprecedented growth in government spending was accompanied by higher taxes, increasingly higher budget deficits, and government debt. Taxes as a percentage of GDP rose from 23.9% in 1945 to 32.0% in 1997. Budget deficits grew from 2.1% of GDP in 1970 to 4.9% in 1992 and then fell to 0.8% in 1997, while government debt as a percentage of GDP, after falling for 35 years, rose from 32.7% in 1980 to 67.5% in 1997.

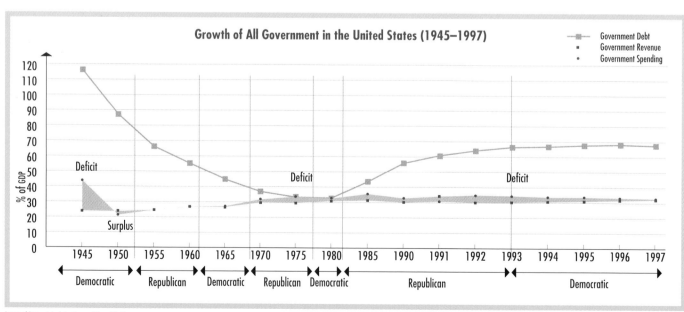

Growth of All Government in the United States (1945–1997)

Bureau of Economic Analysis, *Survey of Current Business*

American Neoconservatism

In the mid-1970s, several conservative economists began to draw attention to the rapid increase in the level of government spending and taxation, and their effects on the national economy. Prominent among these economists were Milton Friedman and Arthur Laffer.

Conservative Economists

Milton Friedman. An economist at the University of Chicago, Friedman received the Nobel Prize in economics in 1976 for his work on monetary theory and monetarism. His book *Free to Choose*, published in 1979, outlined his belief in smaller government. Friedman was critical of the impact of controls imposed on the economy by government but hopeful because he believed that Americans were rediscovering the importance of freedom:

. . .The economic controls that have proliferated in the United States in recent decades have not only restricted our freedom to use our economic resources, they have also affected our freedom of speech, of press, and of religion. . . .

Fortunately, we are waking up. We are again recognizing the dangers of an over-governed society, coming to understand that good objectives can be perverted by bad means, that reliance on the freedom of people to control their own lives in accordance with their own values is the surest way to achieve the full potential of a great society.

Fortunately, also, we are as a people still free to choose which way we should go—whether to continue along the road we have been following to ever bigger government, or to call a halt and change direction.

Arthur Laffer. The idea that a smaller government, providing fewer services and collecting lower taxes, would solve many economic ills took specific form when Arthur Laffer in 1974 drew a graph on a restaurant napkin to demonstrate to a member of President Gerald Ford's staff the possible effects of a tax cut (see graph, right). The simple drawing, later called the "Laffer Curve," attempted to show that if tax rates were increased, the amount of tax

Government Efficiency Report

1970's — Six games of solitaire per hour

1990's — Seventeen games of solitaire per hour

WHOA! TIME TO GET BACK TO SHUFFLING E-MAIL!

Since the 1970s, a neoconservative view has arisen among Americans that their government is inefficient, wasteful, bureaucratic, and intrusive into their lives.

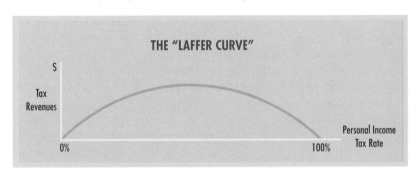

THE "LAFFER CURVE"

$ Tax Revenues

Personal Income Tax Rate

0%   100%

revenues would begin to drop. This would result because people working and operating businesses would be discouraged or would attempt to work without declaring their income to the government. The "Laffer Curve" was popularized by several journalists, notably Jude Wanniski of the influential business newspaper *Wall Street Journal*. Laffer and other advocates of tax cuts could not say what the ideal tax rate ought to be, but the idea of cutting taxes had considerable popular appeal.

In June 1978, voters in California approved Proposition 13 by a margin of 65% to 35%. It called for cutting property taxes by 60% and placed limits on the ability of local governments to increase taxes or introduce new ones. By sharply cutting the main source of revenue for local governments, Proposition 13 set into motion widespread cuts in local school, hospital, police, and fire services. The success of Proposition 13 inspired Ronald Reagan to declare tax reduction to be one of the main planks of his presidential campaign in 1980.

According to monetarist theory, the rate of growth of the money supply in an economy determines the rate of growth of prices. The greater the increase in money supply, the greater the increase in prices.

Ronald Reagan (1981–1989)

Courtesy Ronald Reagan Library

Friedman's views on economic freedom and Laffer's arguments about the potential benefits of tax cuts were incorporated into Reagan's budget and economic policies. Two months after his inauguration as President, Reagan announced his economic program in March 1981.

First, we must cut the growth of government spending. Second, we must cut tax rates so that once again work will be rewarded and saving encouraged. Third, we must carefully remove the tentacles of excessive government regulation which are strangling our economy. Fourth, while recognizing the independence of the institution, we must work with the Federal Reserve Board to develop a monetary policy that will rationally control the money supply. Fifth, we must move, surely and predictably, toward a balanced budget.

Economic Program. The Reagan administration's economic program between 1981 and 1988 was more than a single program to cut taxes and reduce social spending: it was a plan for sweeping change in the role of the federal government. It made some groups winners and others losers. For the rich, Reagan's economic program cut taxes on high incomes, gifts, and inheritances. It did not materially reduce taxes for the middle class. For low income groups, the minimum wage was frozen and public housing subsidies were reduced. For the very poor and recipients of social security, benefits were cut and limitations on eligibility imposed. Some felt that these cutbacks imposed financial hardship on lower income groups.

Reagan's Economic Program (1981–1988)

- Taxes on high incomes were cut by $749 billion; taxes on gifts and inheritances were sharply reduced.

- Social spending, especially social assistance, was cut by $112 billion.

- Compulsory workfare (welfare in return for work) for heads of single-parent families was introduced.

- Housing subsidies were reduced, the construction of low-income housing halted, and rents for public housing increased.

- Legal aid for the poor was reduced by 33%.

- Investigation of each social program was accompanied by a campaign against alleged abuses by recipients.

- Community groups helping the disadvantaged, women, and immigrants were denied federal funding.

- Spending on Medicaid was cut by $5.1 billion.

- The minimum wage was frozen.

Compiled from Frédéric Lesemann. *La politique sociale américaine: les années Reagan* [*American Social Policy: The Reagan Years*], Paris, 1988.

The Reagan Record

Conservative historians and politicians claim that Reaganomics restored the vitality of the American economy. Other scholars are not so certain. Some consequences of Reaganomics are certain—a dramatic increase in government deficits and overall debt, mounting trade deficits, greater income disparity, high interest rates, and deregulation.

Government Finances. A glance at the chart "Federal Government Finances," page 207, shows clearly that none of the objectives of lower government spending, fewer taxes, and a balanced budget were accomplished during Reagan's two terms of office. Except for 1983, taxes continued to rise, and by the end of his second term in 1989 taxes were more than 75% higher, from $517.1 billion in 1980 to $909.0 billion in 1988. Government spending on social security, national defence, and other items increased by more than 80%, from $590.0 billion in 1980 to $1064.1 billion in 1988. The largest increases in government spending occurred in national defence, which more than doubled, from $134.0 billion in 1980 to $290.4 billion in 1988, more than one-quarter of total spending. Other expenses, mainly interest on public debt, rose by two-thirds, from $143.5 billion in 1980 to $240.3 billion in 1988. All of this meant that after 1980 the federal government faced ever-rising budget deficits, which rarely fell below $150 billion throughout the Reagan years. When George Bush became President in 1989, the financial condition of the federal government forced him to introduce new taxes and reduce government spending in an effort to balance the budget.

Trade Deficits. For much of the 20th century, the United States enjoyed a trade surplus, exporting more goods than it imported. This situation changed in the mid-1970s and became progressively worse under Reagan. Americans, flush with cash from a booming economy, spurred on in large measure by lower taxes and huge increases in defence spending, were buying more goods. In cooperation with other foreign governments, in September 1985, the Reagan administration initiated a policy to lower the value of the US dollar in the hope of making American goods more attractive abroad and boosting exports. Between September 1985 and February 1987, the dollar dropped 40% against other major currencies. At first, the rapid decline in the dollar increased the trade deficit, which reached $152 billion in 1986 and 1987. It also created uncertainty in financial markets that led to a sudden crash on the New York Stock Market on Monday, October 19, 1987. As well, in the 1980s a large trade deficit had emerged in American trade with Japan and threatened to destabilize trading relations between the two countries.

Federal Government Finances (1980–1989)
(in billions of US$)

Year	Total Revenues	Total Spending	Social Security	National Defence	Other Expenses	Budget Deficits
1980	$ 517.1	$ 590.0	$ 313.4	$ 134.0	$ 143.5	$(73.8)
1981	599.3	678.2	362.0	157.5	158.7	(79.0)
1982	617.8	745.8	388.7	185.3	171.8	(128.0)
1983	600.6	808.4	426.0	209.9	172.5	(207.8)
1984	666.5	851.8	432.0	227.4	192.4	(185.4)
1985	734.1	946.4	471.8	252.7	221.9	(212.3)
1986	769.1	990.3	481.6	273.4	235.3	(221.2)
1987	854.2	1003.9	502.2	282.0	219.7	(149.8)
1988	909.0	1064.1	533.4	290.4	240.3	(155.2)
1989	990.7	1153.2	568.7	303.6	280.9	(152.5)

Losses appear in brackets.

Statistical Abstract of the United States

United States Foreign Trade (1980–1989)
(in billions of US$)

	1980	1981	1982	1983	1984	1985	1986	1987	1988	1989
Exports	$220.6	$233.7	$212.3	$200.5	$217.9	$213.1	$217.3	$254.1	$322.4	$363.8
Imports	244.9	261.0	244.0	258.0	325.7	345.3	370.0	406.2	441.0	473.4
Deficit	(24.2)	(27.3)	(31.8)	(57.5)	(107.9)	(132.1)	(152.7)	(152.1)	(118.6)	(109.6)

Losses appear in brackets.

Statistical Abstract of the United States

Income Distribution. The assumption underlying Reaganomics, or "supply-side economics," was that by reducing social spending and taxes, economic activity would be stimulated and these benefits would trickle down from the high income groups to the lower income groups. The high income groups would benefit first from lower taxes. With more disposable income, they would invest this money in new business ventures and employ people. The middle class would benefit, not from lower taxes but from more opportunities for high paying jobs. As more people become employed, more goods and services would be demanded, further expanding the economy. Economic expansion would eventually benefit the lower income groups, who would find better paying jobs, which would lift many of them out of poverty. Unfortunately, reality proved to be somewhat different.

The disproof of the "trickle down theory" lies in the distribution of income among population groups. The richest fifth of American families were the main beneficiaries during the Reagan years. Their share of national income rose from 42.1% in 1976 to 46.1% in 1986 and to 49% in 1996. All other income groups were worse off. Their shares of national income declined throughout the 1980s and continued to do so in the 1990s. Middle income groups fared the worst,

dropping from a total share of 53.8% in 1976 to 50.2% in 1986 and to 47.3% in 1996 (see chart "Income Distribution"). Although the figures below include only cash income and exclude taxes, as well as noncash benefits such as food stamps and Medicaid, the trend in the income distribution in the United States since 1976 has been toward greater concentration of income and wealth among the top fifth of the population.

High Interest Rates. The monetary policy of "tight money" pursued by the Federal Reserve, beginning in 1979, and strongly supported by the Reagan administration, made the 1980s a decade of high bank interest rates (see chart below). High interest rates were a consequence of the rising government demand for money to finance its growing budget deficits; rates rarely fell below 8.2%. High interest rates became necessary to attract foreign money into the country to buy the bonds and securities the federal government issued to pay for its budget deficits, and which fewer Americans were buying. This also pushed up the value of the dollar and made American exports more expensive and less competitive abroad, worsening the trade deficit.

Deregulation. Measures to deregulate various industries in the early years of the Reagan administration were welcomed by the private sector. More importantly, antitrust legislation on mergers among large corporations was softened. The stock market reacted favourably to this development by bidding up share prices and encouraging a huge wave of mergers among large corporations. Long-established companies such as Gulf Oil, Telex, Sperry, Nabisco, and Kraft were taken over by larger corporations.

Income Distribution (1976–1996)			
	1976	1986	1996
Top 20%	42.1%	46.1%	49.0%
Fourth 20%	25.1	24.3	23.2
Third 20%	18.3	16.2	15.2
Second 20%	10.4	9.7	8.9
Bottom 20%	4.1	3.8	3.7

Bureau of the Census

Bank Interest Rates (1980–1989)

interest rates in %

1980: 15.3
1981: 18.9
1982: 14.9
1983: 10.8
1984: 12.0
1985: 9.9
1986: 8.3
1987: 8.2
1988: 9.3
1989: 10.9

Federal Reserve Bulletin

Individualism and Equality

The neoconservative movement was not only interested in reducing the influence of government in American society. It also challenged the assumptions that such social measures as affirmative action provided greater opportunities for the country's African–Americans, Hispanics, and women. However, negative attitudes and stereotypes continued to frustrate the aspirations of African–Americans and other minorities to share in the "American dream."

Affirmative Action

Affirmative action was enacted into law by the Congress in 1964, with the aim that government and its agencies would not "use race, sex, color, ethnicity or national origin as a criterion for either discriminating against or granting preferential treatment to any individual or group." The law banned all forms of discrimination against African–Americans, Hispanics, and women. The general objective of affirmative action was to promote equality of access and opportunity for members of social groups who, for reasons of background, education, and race, did not have the same chances for advancement as Americans of European origin. A government agency, the Equal Employment Opportunity Commission, was set up to administer affirmative action programs.

Though the law banned discrimination, it allowed the use of preferences and quotas to encourage greater access for African–Americans, Hispanics, women, and other disadvantaged groups to jobs and education. Government agencies were required to award a certain percentage of all government contracts to companies owned and operated by minorities and women. Publicly funded colleges and universities were required to admit a certain number of members of these groups in order to get government money.

The banning of discrimination on grounds of race, colour, religion, or national origin produced great changes in the lives of many African–Americans. Schools were ordered to end segregation of students by race. Businesses were required to change employment practices that placed African–Americans in low-paying positions and denied them opportunities for advancement if the businesses wanted to receive or continue getting government contracts. Federal and state courts mandated quotas on the basis of race and sex in the hiring practices of many local and state governments, as well mandating more desegregation of schools. Voter registration was made easier and safer, which enabled African–Americans to vote in large numbers, so more African–American legislators might be elected at the municipal, state, and national level.

Supporters of affirmative action challenged traditional occupational roles of men and women. Major legal cases led to strong requirements for recruiting women for skilled manual and mechanical work. Congress mandated the entry of women into all branches of the armed forces except those directly involved in combat. The federal government required local police and fire forces to hire women police officers and fire fighters. All kinds of examinations and tests for employment were ordered to be changed, to avoid bias according to sex for specific jobs.

Critique of Affirmative Action

By the early 1990s, a reaction against affirmative action had begun to appear. It appeared first in California, where several individuals legally challenged the quota system for admission and employment standards in higher educational institutions. Their legal challenge was based on the argument that instead of providing equal access for all to education and employment, affirmative action programs evaluated the individual on the basis of race or ethnic group and not on the basis of ability and achievement.

It was further argued by critics of affirmative action that it created a new form of discrimination called "reverse discrimination." Under this form of discrimination, the disadvantaged groups were not African–Americans, Hispanics, and women, but often well-qualified white men who were passed over for promotion or hiring. This form of discrimination, they argued, was as unjust as previous discrimination based on race, ethnicity, religion, and national origin. It denied opportunities to individuals for no other reason than their race and sex. More importantly, critics of affirmative action stated that affirmative action marked a serious infringement on personal freedom and an attack on individualism because it did not reward personal initiative and recognize personal achievement.

Supporters of affirmative action countered with the argument that it was still necessary because African–Americans, Hispanics, women, and other disadvantaged groups were not yet fully represented in higher education, professions, and business. Until representation of these groups was more equitable in these areas, quotas and special treatment through affirmative action should continue.

In November 1996, California voters narrowly approved Proposition 209, which proposed to end all forms of affirmative action in the state's educational institutions and government departments. The criteria for admission to the state's educational institutions and for employment in government departments were to be personal ability and achievement. Since California voters approved Proposition 209, other state governments have considered cancelling their affirmative action programs.

Affirmative action remains a controversial issue in American society. Race will become an even more important issue in the next 30 years. Government estimates suggest that by the year 2020 over 40% of the country's population will be non-European in origin, and that by the year 2050 the majority of the population will be African–American, or Hispanic–American, Asian–American, or others, and Americans of European origin will be a minority (see chart, left).

United States Population By Race (1990–2050)

	1990	2000	2020	2050
European–American	71.3%	66.2%	58.7%	48.9%
African–American	12.1	13.1	14.1	14.0
Hispanic–American	9.0	12.7	18.6	28.1
Asian–American	2.9	3.1	3.5	3.8
Other	4.7	4.9	5.1	5.2
Totals	100.0	100.0	100.0	100.0

Bureau of the Census

HENRY PAYNE reprinted by permission of United Feature Syndicate, Inc.

"Racial Preferences Are Outdated"[1]

(Excerpts) Wallace Terry, *Parade Magazine*, May 31, 1998, pp. 4–5.

'We can continue perpetuating the outdated premise on which race and gender preferences are based," said Ward Connerly, "that blacks, women and other minorities are incapable of competing without a handicap. Or we can resume the journey to a fair and inclusive society. I wouldn't accept a job or college admission based on color. I would not want the stigma, the cloud hanging over me. There could be no greater insult."

Connerly, 58, led the campaign to ban affirmative action at the University of California in 1995. Then, a year later, he headed the Proposition 209 ballot initiative to end the practice in all California state and local government programs. Those victories thrust him into national leadership as the most active opponent of racial and gender preferences.

Proposition 209 was passed at a time when courts were paring down affirmative action and President Clinton was pleading to "mend it, don't end it." Last year Connerly formed the non-profit American Civil Rights Institute to urge Congress and states to support need-based programs only. And this year he organized a group of mostly conservative scholars and politicians to serve as an alternative panel to Clinton's race initiative.

I met Connerly at his offices in a handsome mansion in Sacramento. He is a cordial man. Until the summer of 1995, he was a behind-the-scenes political operative and land-use consultant. Now he travels across the country speaking about his vision of a color-blind America.

"Thirty years ago, we agreed that racism was morally wrong and we embraced affirmative action to remedy the harm done to black people," Connerly told me. "But somewhere along the line, we became addicted to government and its occupation of our lives."

Under affirmative action, 42% of the blacks at the University of California at Berkeley dropped out in the years 1988–91, as opposed to only 15% of the whites, said Connerly. "Most students will perform in the range that their entering academic credentials suggest," he added.

The first impact of Proposition 209 was felt this spring, when California's prestigious public universities announced huge drops in the admission of black, Hispanic, and Native American students. Of 8034 students accepted at Berkeley, for example, only 191 were black—a 66% drop from last year. Connerly said he felt vindicated by the news.

"No one can look at the sharp decline in non-Asian minority admissions and not feel saddened," he said, "but I see plenty that is positive." He pointed to the sharp increase in minority admissions to less-competitive universities. "And those blacks who will enter Berkeley today," he explained, "can say with pride that they were admitted on their own."

Connerly, who is black, has been the target of the vitriol the black community once reserved for the Ku Klux Klan. Even some relatives have tried to undermine his credibility with reporters. But Connerly holds fast to his convictions and has no regrets. "I would do it again," he said, "in a heartbeat."

Wardell Anthony Connerly was born on June 15, 1939, in Leesville, La. Before Ward turned 2, his father, Roy, a handyman, abandoned the family. When Ward was 4, his mother, Grace, died from a brain tumor. Mary Soniea, Ward's maternal grandmother, gained custody of him. She sent Ward to live with her daughter Bertha and son-in-law Hames Louis in Sacramento.

James and Bertha taught Ward about the value of work. He ran errands, helped a carpenter, and sold sodas. Ward's grandmother eventually moved to Sacramento, built a two-bedroom house and, in 1951, reclaimed Ward. But her funds soon were spent, and they were on welfare for a few months. "Those were desperate times," Connerly recalled. He worked 27 hours a week as a stock boy for 65 cents an hour to help pay the mortgage and buy food.

Connerly went to nearby American River Junior College because it was all he could afford. He transferred to Sacramento State University—where, he said, the teachers (all white) recognized his leadership potential and encouraged his intellectual growth. He became the first black vice president and then president of the nearly all-white student body, But he never thought of himself as a "first."

After graduating from college in 1962, Connerly wed a white fellow student. Presently he is under attack in the black community for having a white wife, in part because of his views on affirmative action. "What can be more fundamental to the pursuit of happiness than the freedom to marry whomever you want?" Connerly asked. They have two grown children, a son and a daughter.

Two days after graduation, Connerly took a job at a development agency in Sacramento. In 1966 he joined the California Department of Housing and Community Development, becoming its liaison to the Legislature. In 1968, Connerly met Assemblyman Pete Wilson, who hired him as his chief consultant. Connerly registered with the GOP, and Wilson became his mentor and close friend. "He is the reason I'm a success," said Connerly.

In 1973, he opened Connerly & Associates in a 100-square-foot office with his wife, Ilene, as his partner and a single contract of $4000 a month. "I had two children to support," he said. "It was scary." But the business grew rapidly. Today the company helps private interests and local governments comply with state land-use laws, guides businesses through the housing and building regulations Connerly helped to devise, and manages the assets of building trade associations. The staff now totals 15 full-time employees.

In 1993, Pete Wilson—who has been governor since 1991—was under pressure to appoint a nonwhite to the University of California board of Regents. He offered Connerly a 12-year term that paid no fee. Connerly

accepted to give something back to his adopted state. In his first months, he was applauded by students and professors for spending time on campus. "I was ready to ask tough questions of the administration," he said.

In 1994, Connerly met a white couple from La Jolla, Jerry and Ellen Cook, whose son had been rejected by the medical school in San Diego despite grades so good that he got into Harvard. They showed Connerly statistics suggesting that whites were being passed over for admission in favor of blacks and Latinos with lesser academic records and test scores. Connerly also learned that colleges were advertising jobs by race. "I had never seen this kind of racial engineering," he said. "it was preference, pure and simple."

Connerly talked with Governor Wilson, who had been a longtime supporter of affirmative action, about the need to end preferences. Wilson agreed to back Connerly's efforts. On July 20, 1995, the Board of Regents voted to end its 29-year policy of preferences for minorities and women in admissions, jobs, and contracting.

The new policy's impact was first felt at Berkeley's law school. Only 14 blacks were among 792 accepted, a drop of 81%, and none of them chose to enter. "It shows we have a long way to go," Connerly said. But he is pushing for preferences based on economic need. "It makes sense to give extra consideration to a [qualified] student who is poor," Connerly added. Meanwhile, the regents are sending tutors to low-performing schools to help minority students become more competitive academically.

The affirmative action vote led to Connerly's leadership of Proposition 209, to prohibit the State of California and local governments from discriminating or gaining preferential treatment on the basic of race, gender, color, ethnicity or national origin in public education, employment and contracting. He traveled across the state, pleading for support. In 1996, Californians voted 54% to 46% to pass Proposition 209. Among blacks, 29% voted for it.

To counter Connerly's national efforts, Martin Luther King III, a son of the slain civil-rights leader, has organized a coalition of groups called Americans United for Affirmative Action. "Civil rights in the '90s is about getting decent-paying jobs and competing in corporate America," King said. Anita Perez Ferguson, the president of the National Women's Political Caucus, has joined King.

Ward Connerly believes the future of black America lies in assimilating into mainstream organizations like the Chamber of Commerce. "It's not white culture," he noted. "It's *our* culture." And how does he want to be remembered? "As an ordinary American who saw something he considered wrong and had the conviction to pursue a solution," Connerly replied. "You don't have to be an elected official to make a difference. That's democracy."

REVIEW

Summary

Americans have long believed in the importance of the value of individualism over that of collectivism. Their political and economic systems reflect these values and beliefs about the individual.

The American presidential system is characterized by a separation of political power between a directly elected President, an elected Congress, and an appointed Supreme Court, with a system of checks and balances to prevent any one branch of government dominating another. Americans believe this system of checks and balances allows all groups in society to participate in choosing their leaders and determining policies, and it means individuals have a say in political decision making. The majority are expected to accept some limitations on their rights to protect the rights of minorities.

The American economy is a mixed economy based fundamentally on private enterprise. In the American economy, consumers and businesses are the most important decision makers. From 1945 to 1990, the role and size of government grew appreciably. Government intervention took the form of fiscal and monetary policy, regulation, the provision of some social programs, and the use of an affirmative action program to protect the interests of less advantaged groups. The growth in the size of government was also accompanied by increased spending on the military and the emergence of a powerful military-industrial complex that provided millions with jobs in privately owned firms.

In the 1980s and 1990s, Americans became increasingly concerned about the economic problems of higher taxes, growing budget deficits, and mounting public debt created by the growth of government. They also became less willing to accept government regulation of the economy as a means to improve their lives. They wanted greater freedom for the individual and more accountability from their political leaders.

American Values and Political Philosophy

1. What American value was Bill Clinton addressing in his 1993 inaugural speech? (See page 175)
   A. patriotism
   B. equal opportunity
   C. community welfare
   D. individual responsibility

2. Lamar Alexander and Chester E. Finn identified eight core American values. With which one would you most agree, and with which one would you most disagree? Provide reasons for your choices.

3. Most democracies have multi-party political systems. Why do you think Americans have remained committed to a two-party system?

4. Since their beginnings, the Democratic and Republican parties have undergone significant philosophical changes. The Democrats have abandoned their conservative roots and become the modern liberals, while the Republicans have become the conservative party of the right. In relation to a political continuum such as that shown on page 178, what has been the general direction of both parties since the 1980s? Does this mean that people can look to government for help to a greater or lesser degree?

5. Using the chart on page 21 as a guide, create your own chart on the philosophy of the Democratic and Republican parties.

6. The ideas of many philosophers and leaders are outlined on pages 15–18 and 34–38. Identify those with which the Democrats would likely agree and those with which the Republicans would likely agree.

American Political System

1. Why did the writers of the American Constitution separate powers among the executive, legislative and judicial branches of government?

2. What are two of the restrictions identified for the office of the President? To what extent do you agree with these? Provide reasons for your decisions.

3. The American Constitution grants executive power to the President. Examine the powers of the American President (page 181) and the Canadian Prime Minister (page 133).

   a) To what extent are the powers similar?

   b) List at least three examples of the power of each office.

   c) Which office do you think possesses more power within the leader's own country? Provide evidence for your choice.

   d) Identify one strength and one weakness of the operation of the executive branch in each country.

4. 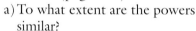 The American Congress has similar functions to the Canadian House of Commons and Senate.

   a) What are the two Houses of Congress called, and how are the members chosen for each House?

   b) What are the powers of the Senate? Identify those that provide a check on the office of the President.

   c) Why do you think each state, no matter its size or population, was given equal (2) representation in the senate?

   d) Why do you think that one-third of all Senators are up for reelection every two years, rather than all 100 every six years?

   e) What does the Electoral Law ensure for the House of Representatives?

   f) What is the length of the term of office in the House of Representatives?

   g) What are the powers of the House of Representatives?

5. What is the most important political function of the Supreme Court?

6. a) In small groups, list reasons why the Supreme Court should be appointed and reasons why the Supreme Court should be elected.

   b) Take and defend a position on the issue: Should US Supreme Court justices be elected?

7. Briefly describe the importance of the veto and override process to the American system of checks and balances.

8. Modern democracies all have mechanisms to prevent the abuse of power by government. The American system is characterized by a system of checks and balances.

   a) The division of powers within the United States government were based on the ideas of Montesquieu (page 37) which greatly influenced the framers of the US Constitution. To what extent do you agree with Montesquieu's view of power? Give examples to support your position.

   b) Compare the American system of checks and balances to prevent abuse of power with that of another democracy you have studied, focussing on the differences between the two systems.

9. What would you say are the two main advantages and disadvantages of the American system of law making? Give reasons for your choices.

10. Identify the main principles of American federalism.

11. a) Examine the powers of the Federal and State governments on the chart

on page 186. How do you think it was decided to give certain powers to each level of government?

b) To what extent is this division of powers similar to the division of powers between Federal and Provincial governments in Canada?

12. In what areas have the power and responsibility of the federal government grown over the years?

13. Both the Canadian and American constitutions are difficult to change. Do you think it should be possible to change constitutions more easily? Explain the reasons for your view.

14. The right to bear arms is entrenched in the Second Amendment and has become increasingly controversial. To what extent should Americans have the "right to bear arms"? Be prepared to defend your position.

15. Using the chart on page 187, choose what you think are the five most significant amendments to the American Constitution since 1788. Provide reasons for your choices.

16. What are the reasons it is difficult for third party candidates to run in American elections?

17. List the important steps in a presidential election campaign.

18. Winners in American elections are decided by a simple plurality, or what is referred to as "first past the post".

a) What do these phrases mean?

b) Because there are usually only two candidates (Democrat and Republican) running, the winner usually receives over 50% of the vote. This is often claimed to be a strength of the two-party, compared to the multi-party system, where winning candidates often receive less than 50% of the vote. To what extent do you agree with this claim? Be prepared to defend your position.

19. What would be the advantages and disadvantages of having election dates set, compared to the Canadian or any other system that allows election dates to be decided by government leaders?

20. Some people believe voter turnout is a problem for democracy in the USA. What evidence could be used to support this view?

American Economic System

1. Examine the chart on page 190.

a) What are the roles of consumers, government, and businesses in the American economy?

b) How might the activities of government and businesses change if consumers reduce their spending?

2. Up to 1929, the American government followed a policy of limited government intervention in the economy.

a) What were seen as the main tasks of government?

b) How did the limits on immigration conflict with the economic policy?

3. a) Using a web, describe the impact of the 1929 stock market crash in the USA.

b) In the long term, what effect do you think the Smoot–Haley tariffs had on consumers in America?

4. a) Using the text and chart on pages 192 and 193, summarize Roosevelt's New Deal in your notes. Include his slogans, programs, and the overall changes the New Deal brought to the American economy.

b) What core American values appear to be contradicted by Roosevelt's New Deal?

5. Adopting the policies of John Maynard Keynes, the American government increased its intervention in the economy from 1945 to 1975.
   a) What was the main purpose of this policy?
   b) What was the countercyclical fiscal policy to do in bad and good times to achieve this purpose?
   c) What was the overall effect of these policies on the American economy from 1945 to 1970?

6. President Ronald Reagan is identified with reduced government in the economy.
   a) What is "Reaganomics" also called?
   b) Create a chart identifying "Reagan-omics" policy points and what the policy actually achieved.

7. Analyse the chart Business Cycles in the United States, on page 195, focussing on the rise and fall of GDP. From this, develop arguments to support a position on the statement "Reaganomics was a great success for the American economy."

8. a) The section on page 196 on consumers, including text, graphs, and charts, supports the view that the main focus of a government's economic policy should be
   A. job creation
   B. reduced taxes for corporations
   C. support for small business
   D. increased government spending
   b) Identify the evidence used to support the view.

9. The Private Sector section (pages 196–199) provides information specifically detailing how the American economy is largely privately owned and run by individuals.
   a) Identify five points of information that show the extent to which the American economy is dominated by private enterprise.

   b) Using figures from the chart on page 198, calculate the proportion of sales and profits earned by the top ten of the top 500 American corporations. To what extent do you agree or disagree that this represents an overconcentration of wealth and power, and that government should reduce the size of some of these corporations?

   c) Based on the information provided about banks in the US and Canada, develop arguments defending the banking policy you think is the more effective.

10. America's major corporations have pursued freer trade since 1945.
    a) Explain why American corporations would be in favour of free trade.
    b) How might you use the margin graphs on exports and imports (page 199) to indicate Canada's importance to a skeptical American?

11. a) For what portion of the economy does the public sector account?
    b) What are the three elements of the public sector in the American economy?

12. In 1997, defence spending contributed $270 billion to the American economy. In chart form, identify the advantages and disadvantages of a high level of defence spending.

13. Personal income tax was first levied in the United States in 1913. By 1997, it constituted 44.7% of government revenues, while corporation taxes were 11.7%. Should corporations pay a larger portion of tax revenue? Be prepared to defend your position.

14. Take and defend a position on the issue: To what extent should government regulate a free enterprise economy? Use the following questions on regula-tions in the United States to help support your position.

a) How many regulatory agencies are there?

b) What is the Sherman Antitrust Act, and when and why was it passed?

c) Why was Microsoft investigated?

d) What is the argument used to support antitrust legislation?

e) What other regulatory agencies are there?

15. Modern governments all attempt to manage their economies through the use of fiscal and monetary policies.

a) Explain how the United States manages its economy through the use of these two policies.

b) In a private enterprise economy, where individuals are expected to be primarily responsible for their own welfare, should government provide financial rescue? (See page 201) Be prepared to defend your position.

16. The United States is often characterized as a nation that doesn't care about its less fortunate, yet it has a number of social security programs. To what extent is the United States a country that cares for the less fortunate? Use the following questions as a guide. Be prepared to defend your view.

a) What social security programs exist, and when did they begin?

b) What are some of the key features of the programs?

c) Why was Bill Clinton's universal medical plan shelved?

17. Using the information on page 203, take and defend a position on the issue: To what extent are women treated fairly in the American economy?

American Political Economy

1. From the position of an American neoconservative, write a short article advocating a reduction in the size and scope of the American government. Use the following questions as a guide.

a) What five pieces of data from page 204 could be used to support the position that government has grown too large, inefficient, and unresponsive to individual needs in the United States?

b) What are the two main areas of neoconservative concern?

c) How does Milton Friedman think the United States will best achieve its potential as a great society?

d) What does Arthur Laffer attempt to show by his "Laffer Curve"?

e) What was Proposition 13, and what was its effect?

2. a) On what stereotype did the cartoonist draw in order to portray a neoconservative issue?

 b) Do you think Milton Friedman would agree or disagree with the cartoonist's viewpoint?

3. The election of Ronald Reagan represented a shift to the neoconservative right in American society. Reagan believed that a reduction of the size of government and a reduction in taxes would stimulate the economy and benefit everyone.

a) Critics often claim that Reaganomics benefited the rich and was an attack on the poor and middle class. To what extent does the information on page 206 support this view?

b) What values would a neoconservative supporter of Reagan hold?

4. Summarize the positive and negative aspects of Reaganomics. Use government finances, trade deficits, income distribution, interest rates, and deregulation as suggested categories.

5. Affirmative Action was enacted to equalize opportunity in the United States, particularly for certain disadvantaged groups. Take and defend a position on the issue: Should government enact and preserve affirmative action programs? Read pages 209–212, and use the following questions as a guide.

a) When was affirmative action enacted, and at what specific groups was it aimed?

b) How were preferences and quotas used to achieve the objectives of affirmative action?

c) What are four ways the government has attempted to improve the lives of African–Americans through the affirmative action program?

d) How did the government program change traditional male and female occupational roles?

e) California has successfully challenged affirmative action with Proposition 209. What did Proposition 209 propose? Instead of quotas, what were to be the new criteria?

f) Create a chart outlining the arguments for and against affirmative action. Add your own arguments to the list.

Chapter Consolidation

1. This chapter began with a quotation from a speech given by President Clinton. Having studied the political and economic system of the United States, to what extent do you think it is possible for individuals and families in the United States to look after their own best interests without the intervention of government?

2.

a) On what values were the political and economic systems of the United States based?

b) Whose ideas were influential in the development of the political and economic systems of the United States? Briefly explain the ideas and how they were applied in the United States.

c) Create a chart, identifying the type of political system and economic system in the United States and the strengths and weaknesses of those systems.

SWEDEN

"I believe in the welfare state. It is one of the great inventions of our time. All citizens should be given equal chances in life. They have a right to equal access to education, health care and the provision of other basic needs. . . . Because social equity, a well educated population and an active labour market policy represent investment in human capital, the welfare state can be a source of competitive advantage."
—Swedish Minister of Finance (1991–1994) Anne Wibble, speech at Harvard University, 1992

Sweden is a parliamentary democracy based on the principles of social democracy. Unlike the Canadian parliamentary democracy, which is based on opposing views, Swedish democracy is based on developing broad agreements among political parties, interest groups, and the government on important issues. In keeping with this aspect of Swedish politics, Swedish voters elect their political leaders on the basis of popular vote.

Private enterprise is the basis of the Swedish economic system, but the large role of government in business charac-terizes the economy as a mixed economy. Since 1945, government has used some central

planning, encouraged labour–business cooperation, and established a comprehensive social security system.

For much of the 20th century, Sweden has avoided involvement in European politics. However, in 1994 Sweden's political and economic relations with Europe changed dramatically, when it agreed to join the European Union. Today, Sweden is deeply involved with other countries in establishing greater political and economic unity in Europe.

Key Concepts/Vocabulary

social democracy
welfare state
Riksdag
ombudsperson
consensus
party list

indicative planning
collective
 bargaining
co-determination
cooperative

Focus On Issues

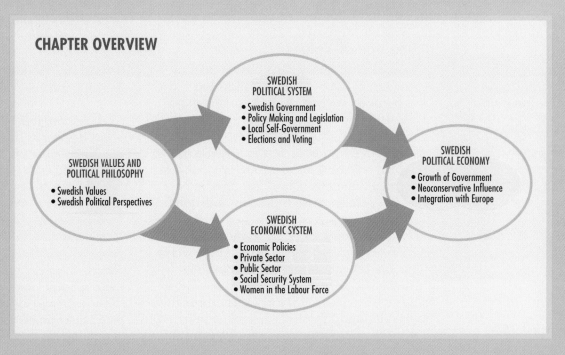

CHAPTER OVERVIEW

SWEDISH VALUES AND POLITICAL PHILOSOPHY
• Swedish Values
• Swedish Political Perspectives

SWEDISH POLITICAL SYSTEM
• Swedish Government
• Policy Making and Legislation
• Local Self-Government
• Elections and Voting

SWEDISH ECONOMIC SYSTEM
• Economic Policies
• Private Sector
• Public Sector
• Social Security System
• Women in the Labour Force

SWEDISH POLITICAL ECONOMY
• Growth of Government
• Neoconservative Influence
• Integration with Europe

SWEDISH VALUES AND POLITICAL PHILOSOPHY

Advance Organizer

Contemporary Swedish values and political philosophy are strongly rooted in social democratic values and a belief that society should help its citizens to realize their potential.

SECTION OVERVIEW
- Swedish Values
- Swedish Political Perspectives

Swedish Values

During the 20th century, the establishment and growth of the social democratic movement promoted the development of a distinctive set of values in Sweden.

Source of Values

Social Democracy. This unique political tradition, composed of socialism and liberalism, is a product of a division in the socialist movement between those who wanted to realize socialist ideals peacefully and those who believed that socialist ideals could only be realized through violent class struggle and revolution. The division became permanent with the consolidation of Communist power in Russia in 1918–1919 and the formation of the Communist International in March 1919. Those who wanted to transform society peacefully became known as social democrats. Those who wanted to transform society through revolution and violence became known as communists. The chart "Social Democratic and Communist Theory" on page 221 compares the values of these two groups.

> Social democracy is a variant of socialist thought that does not believe in armed struggle by the workers. It promotes peaceful change in the social conditions of workers.

> In North America social democracy is referred to as democratic socialism.

Social democracy in Europe appeared at the end of the 19th century when the socialist movement adopted new ideas about politics and economics. In Great Britain, a view of socialism as an extension of democracy into the social and economic sphere was developed by the Fabian Society, which was founded in 1883 and led by Beatrice Webb, Sidney Webb, and George Bernard Shaw. Unaffiliated to any existing party, the Fabians played a unique political role by issuing numerous papers on public finance, local government, factory conditions, poverty, and housing, all of which greatly influenced the Labour Party after its formation in 1906.

In Sweden and elsewhere in continental Europe, as the reform wing of the socialist movement grew stronger, social democracy emerged, calling for greater democratization of authoritarian governments, universal adult suffrage, and the creation of a welfare state to remedy economic and social inequalities caused by industrial growth and urbanization. As some of their political and social policies were implemented, social democratic parties became more moderate in their socialist views.

Core Values

Political scientist Henry Milner[1] notes that since 1945 social democracy in Sweden has been characterized by a commitment to compassion and collective responsibility, democracy, freedom and tolerance, social equality, and collective social action.

Compassion and collective responsibility. Social democrats strongly believe in helping disadvantaged groups in society. This belief is associated with the view that all individuals in society have a moral and collective responsibility to help others in need.

Democracy. Social democrats believe that people should be encouraged to participate actively in government and freely express their political views. Regular elections allow people to express political preferences and to choose leaders.

[1] Henry Milner, *Sweden: Social Democracy in Practice.* Oxford: Oxford University Press, 1989.

Social Democratic and Communist Theory

Values	Social Democrats	Communists
Personal freedom	Important for the development of the individual and society	Less important; limits on personal freedom determined by the group
Individualism	Individual interests are important and directed to benefit society overall	Individual interests subordinated to group interests
Equality	Basic human rights and political equality important for social peace and harmony; acceptance of other social classes	Important for the development of society; achieved through class struggle; abolition of all social classes except the proletariat
Collectivism	Important for creating political equality and social peace; a degree of political equality achieved through some sharing of wealth	Group interests more important than individual interests; the needs of the state are most important
Democracy	Parliamentary government with frequent elections, political parties, and universal voting to allow for personal preferences	Government led by workers (called the dictatorship of the proletariat), with the centralization of political power in the hands of one political party
Social welfare	Social welfare policies necessary to reduce inequalities and enhance the dignity of the individual	Social welfare necessary for promoting worker solidarity and the common good
Private ownership	Private ownership of the means of production necessary for economic development and prosperity	Abolition of private ownership of the means of production; private property permitted only for personal possessions
Public ownership	Not necessary, except in certain cases where society can benefit; nationalization with compensation	Public ownership of means of production necessary for rapid economic development; nationalization without compensation
Central planning	Not necessary, though government can provide some overall direction to the economy	Necessary to mobilize society's economic resources for rapid industrialization and establishment of a socialist society

Freedom and tolerance. Social democrats regard personal freedom and tolerance as important values for attaining social peace and harmony. By encouraging individuals to express themselves peacefully and pursue their own interests, society benefits and develops more diverse forms of social and political expression.

Social equality. Social democrats believe in promoting equality among all social groups. This means all citizens have equal and universal access to social programs, paid for by a system of progressive income tax, which redistributes the wealth of society to reduce income differences between people. No person can be denied access to social programs on the basis of income. Another aspect of social equality is the use of heavy taxes on high incomes to reduce differences among incomes and personal wealth. Social democrats believe that social equality is promoted through these measures.

Social democrats are committed to establishing a mixed economy in which government management and control of some aspects of the economy are combined with private enterprise to promote stable economic growth. Social democrats accept the importance of private enterprise, but believe that the private sector cannot produce stable economic growth on its own. The public sector can help the private sector with plans and regulation. Social democrats believe these measures promote stable economic growth and higher living standards. However, social democrats believe work and personal initiative remain important factors for economic prosperity.

Collective social action (welfare state). Social democrats are committed to creating a welfare state in which government-funded social programs raise people's living standards and quality of life. They believe that all people in society, regardless of social background, should be allowed opportunities to reach their personal potential. Collective social action and universal social programs that eliminate social problems such as unemployment, poverty, crime, and illiteracy are used to promote the development of personal potential of all citizens.

Swedish Political Perspectives

For most of the 20th century, Swedish politics has been remarkably stable. Except for two brief periods in the 1970s and early 1990s, the country's largest political party, the Social Democrats, has held power since 1932 (see chart "Swedish Governments Since 1926"). Since 1945, Swedish politics have been dominated by two evenly matched political groupings. The chart "Swedish Political Continuum" shows the positions of the parties in relation to each other on the left-right continuum. However, in Swedish political discourse they are often referred to as the "socialist" and "nonsocialist" blocs. As well, there are two parties that claim to belong to neither bloc, which are referred to as "other parties."

Socialist Bloc

Socialism has been a powerful political force in Swedish politics since the 1890s. The main political parties of the socialist bloc are the Social Democratic Party and the Left Party. (See chart "Swedish Political Continuum.") There has never been any formal cooperation between these two socialist parties. Often they have disagreed over policies, but on many important issues the Social Democrats have been supported by the Left Party.

Social Democratic Party. The Social Democratic Party formed in 1889, advocating reforms and peaceful change. Social Democrats believed that once they gained political power they would be able to transform Swedish society. From 1932 to 1976, the Social Democrats formed a government committed to promoting social justice, full employment, and a fair distribution of incomes.

In 1976, the Social Democrats were defeated by a coalition of nonsocialist parties (see chart "Swedish Government Since 1926"). They returned to office in 1982 and remained in power until 1991, when they were defeated in national elections because of their economic policies. In 1994, the Social Democrats formed a government on the promise that they would reduce unemployment, cut government spending, and lower the government's growing budget deficit.

Left Party. This party was founded as the Swedish Communist Party in 1921 by left-wing Social Democrats. In 1967, the party adopted the name Left Party Communists. In 1990, following the collapse of communism in Eastern Europe, they dropped the word communist from their name. Communist beliefs about revolution, violent class struggle, and nationalization of the economy remain unpopular among Swedish voters. Support for the Left Party is found mainly among intellectuals and in universities. The Left Party supports many policies of the Social Democrats.

Swedish Governments Since 1926

	Socialist Bloc		Nonsocialist Bloc		Other Parties

1926–1928	Liberals
1928–1930	Conservatives
1930–1932	Liberals
1932–1976	Social Democrats
1976–1982	Coalition (Centre Party/Liberals/Moderates)
1982–1991	Social Democrats
1991–1994	Coalition (Moderates/ Liberals/Centre Party/ Christian Democrats)
1994–	Social Democrats

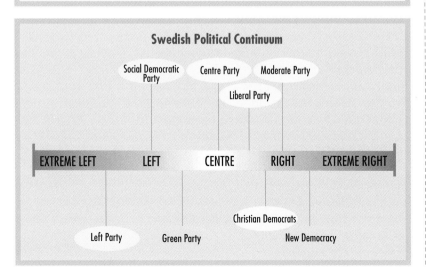

Swedish Political Continuum

Social Democratic Party · Centre Party · Moderate Party

Liberal Party

EXTREME LEFT — LEFT — CENTRE — RIGHT — EXTREME RIGHT

Left Party · Green Party · Christian Democrats · New Democracy

Swedish Government

As in Canada and other parliamentary democracies, Swedish parliamentary democracy was the product of many constitutional reforms that began in the early 19th century and continued in the 20th century. The country's first modern constitution, adopted in 1809, established Sweden as a constitutional democracy with a bicameral parliament (Riksdag). The upper chamber was abolished in 1971, and the Swedish parliament became a unicameral body.

Executive Power

The Swedish constitution confirms the monarch as the head of state but without any formal power. The power to govern the country resides in the cabinet, headed by the Prime Minister and accountable to the Parliament.

Monarch. The current head of state is Carl XVI Gustav, whose main role is to represent the country. According to the constitution, he is forbidden to participate in political affairs or be a member of the government.

Courtesy of the Swedish Institute. Photographer: Hans Hammarskiöld

Prime Minister. The Prime Minister is the head of government and accountable to the Riksdag. The Speaker of the Riksdag, chosen by secret ballot, has the power to select a Prime Minister after consultations with the leaders of political parties. The choice of a new Prime Minister must receive a majority vote in Parliament, then be appointed by the Speaker. As in Canada, the Swedish Prime Minister is the head of government and must have the support of the majority of members of the Riksdag. Similarly, the Prime Minister can

- appoint and dismiss a cabinet
- appoint various government officials and judges
- determine government policies and submit them as proposals to Parliament.

Swedish Prime Ministers Since 1932

Felix Hamrin	1932	Ola Ullsten	1978–1979
Per Albin Hansson	1932–1936	Thorbjörn Fälldin	1979–1982
Axel Pehrsson-Bramstorp	1936	Olof Palme	1982–1986
Per Albin Hansson	1936–1946	Ingvar Carlsson	1986–1991
Tage Erlander	1946–1969	Carl Bildt	1991–1994
Olof Palme	1969–1976	Ingvar Carlsson	1994–1996
Thorbjörn Fälldin	1976–1978	Göran Persson	1996–

Legislative Power

The constitution allocates all legislative power to the 349-member unicameral Riksdag, which is elected every four years.

Riksdag. The Riksdag is responsible for all legislation enacted in the country. Legislative power within the Riksdag is based on majority votes. The political party that can attract support from other parties in the chamber to command a majority has the right to form a government. This party remains in power between elections as long as it continues to enjoy majority support in the Riksdag. If the Prime Minister and cabinet do not have the support of the Parliament, the Speaker asks the leaders of other political

Swedish government is organized into three branches—an executive consisting of a monarch and Prime Minister, a unicameral legislature called the Riksdag, and an independent judiciary with power to review legislation.

Swedish monarchs of the 20th century:

Oskar II
1872–1907

Gustav V
1907–1950

Gustav VI Adolf
1950–1973

Carl XVI Gustav
1973–

PHOTO: Sweden is a constitutional democracy with a monarch as head of state. The country's current monarch is King Carl XVI Gustav, photographed here with his wife Queen Silvia.

parties to form a government. For much of the 20th century, Swedish governments have been coalition governments with several political parties sharing power and having members in the cabinet.

One feature of the Riksdag is the Parliamentary Ombudsperson. The position was established in 1809. The Ombudsperson is appointed by Parliament to monitor the performance of the civil service and protect the interests of individuals against arbitrary treatment by the civil service or bureaucracy. Individuals who have complaints can submit them to the Parliamentary Ombudsperson, who can choose to mediate or undertake legal action against the civil service on behalf of the individual. There are also ombudspersons for consumer affairs, competition, equal opportunities, the press, and against ethnic discrimination. The system is regarded as an important part of Swedish democracy.

The Swedish ombudsperson system has spread to other countries. The first ombudspersons in Canada were appointed by the provincial governments of Alberta and New Brunswick in 1967. The other Canadian provincial governments soon followed. The Canadian federal government has yet to create an office of the ombudsperson but it has established commissioners to investigate public complaints about the civil service as needed from time to time.

Judicial Power

The Supreme Court is the highest court in Sweden. It hears important cases involving legal principles in civil and criminal law. The five members of the Supreme Court are appointed by the government and serve until they reach age 65, resign, or are removed for neglect of office. Over time, the Supreme Court has acquired the right to determine if laws are constitutional.

Policy Making and Legislation

Unlike in Canada and the United States, policy making in Sweden involves an extensive "prelegislative" process before a bill is presented to Parliament. In the Parliament, a bill undergoes further analysis, debate, and finally passage. All of this is valued as an important contribution to informed public debate and to responsible government.

Policy Making

Swedish policy making is characterized by the extensive use of commissions of inquiry, participation by interest groups, and consensus building efforts.

Commissions of Inquiry. Each new piece of legislation is thoroughly investigated by a commission of inquiry. Every year, ministries set up commissions to study various policy matters and prepare draft bills for the government.

When a policy is highly controversial, Parliament sets up a parliamentary commission of inquiry to study the matter and make recommendations on it. Representatives of parties, ministries, and interest groups sit on these commissions.

Interest Groups. Interest groups have considerable influence in Swedish policy making. They study and make recommendations on government proposals. Most interest groups are closely tied to the country's main political parties. Labour unions have close ties with the Social Democratic Party, while business groups work closely with the Moderates and Liberals. Farmers' groups cooperate with the Centre Party and environmentalists with the Green Party.

Consensus. Consensus is an important feature of Swedish policy making because the country's largest political parties often do not have a majority of the seats in the Riksdag and must seek support from smaller political parties. This reality compels all parties to work together to resolve differences, and it sometimes leads to coalition governments in which cabinet posts are shared among different political parties.

Legislative Process

The sources of legislation in the Riksdag are private members' proposals and government bills. Most private members' proposals are amendments to government bills. The most important government bill is the budget.

Once a government bill is tabled in the Riksdag, it is sent to a committee for study. As in Canada, the committee prepares a report on the bill, which is then debated in Parliament. Cabinet ministers are called to answer questions from members of opposition parties on government bills prepared by their respective ministries.

When debate is concluded, the chamber votes on the bill. A majority vote is necessary for passage. Party discipline is maintained by ensuring that only the most loyal party members enter Parliament on the party list, rather than by party whips as in Canada (see page 52).

GOVERNMENT BILL

↓

RIKSDAG

↓

Tabling

↓

(Standing) Committee Stage

↓

Debate

↓

Enactment

↓

LAW

Adapted from *Sveriges Riksdag [Swedish Parliament]* http://www.riksdagen.se

Local Self-Government

Local self-government is an important principle of Swedish democracy. Although Sweden is organized as a unitary state, the country is divided into county councils and municipalities with powers and responsibilities delegated to them by Parliament. County councils and municipalities are the basic units of local government in Sweden. These local governments are elected every four years. They are considered important for local self-government.

The central government in Stockholm determines the responsibilities and activities of local governments. It is also directly responsible for public law and order, national defence, higher education, roads, labour, housing, economic affairs, communications, and energy (see diagram below).

County councils and municipalities are responsible for administering national programs such as health services, social insurance, education, housing, and environmental protection. They receive grants from the central government to enable them to fulfil the objectives of national legislation.

Though Sweden is organized as a unitary state, the central government and Parliament grant local governments considerable power to administer national programs.

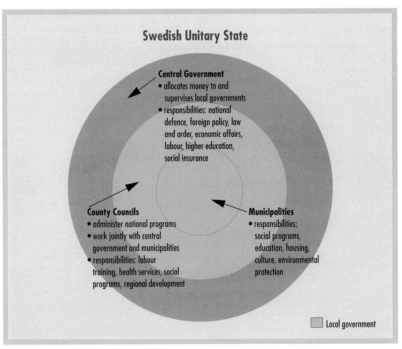

Swedish Unitary State

Central Government
- allocates money to and supervises local governments
- responsibilities: national defence, foreign policy, law and order, economic affairs, labour, higher education, social insurance

County Councils
- administer national programs
- work jointly with central government and municipalities
- responsibilities: labour training, health services, social programs, regional development

Municipalities
- responsibilities: social programs, education, housing, culture, environmental protection

Local government

Adapted from Agne Gustafsson. *Local Government in Sweden*, 1988

Elections and Voting

Elections are important events in Swedish politics. They allow Swedes to voice their concerns and choose their leaders. In recent years, Swedish elections have become emotionally charged and lively.

Electoral Campaigning

Because Swedish election campaigns last no more than six weeks, all political parties advertise heavily on television and radio, distribute party pamphlets, posters, and other literature, and hold public rallies to attract the voting public. Issues are generally more important than personalities in Swedish electoral campaigns. This is reinforced by the country's system of proportional representation that stresses political parties rather than individual candidates.

Electoral System

The current electoral system in Sweden is a mixture of proportional representation and preferential voting.

Proportional Representation. Sweden is divided into 29 multi-member constituencies that send 310 members to Parliament. Another 39 seats are allocated strictly on the basis of popular vote.

Every party publishes a list of candidates for each constituency and for the country as a whole. Swedish voters cast a ballot for a political party. A party wins seats in a multi-member constituency based on the popular vote it receives. The minimum popular vote needed for a party to get a candidate elected in a constituency is 12%. For a party to obtain some of the 39 seats, it must obtain at least 4% of all votes cast throughout the country.

Preferential Voting. Swedish voters can also rank candidates on the party list according to preference. By entering a mark beside the name of a candidate, the voter can cast a personal vote. A voter must choose only one candidate. If a voter chooses more than one, the ballot becomes invalid and is considered spoiled. More than 2% of all ballots cast in the September 1998 elections were spoiled. To be elected on the basis of personal votes, the candidate must receive at least 8% of all votes cast for the party in the constituency.

By-elections. Under the Swedish system of proportional representation and party lists, there are no by-elections to fill vacancies as in Canada and the United States. When a seat in Parliament becomes vacant due to a resignation or death, a substitute member on the party list fills the vacancy. When people vote for the party list, they also choose substitute members.

Voting. In 1994, a new election law changed the holding of elections to every four years. Elections are held on the third Sunday in September. On this day, municipal and county elections are also held. The voter is given different coloured ballot papers in the form of party lists. Plain white ballots are for municipal elections, blue ballots for county council elections, and yellow ballots for national elections. The voter selects the party list of his or her choice, seals it in a coloured envelope, and then hands the envelope to the election officer for immediate placement in the ballot box. The colour of the envelope matches the appropriate slot in the ballot box—yellow for Riksdag, white for municipal, and blue for county.

Pål Sommelius/Pressens Bild

Referenda

In the 20th century, Swedish voters have decided some controversial issues by referenda. The first was in 1922 over the prohibition of alcohol. Prohibition was narrowly defeated, 49.0% in favour to 51.0% against. In 1957, voters were asked to choose between three different pension plans put forth by the main parties. None of the plans obtained a majority. In 1960, after a bitter debate, the pension question was settled when the Parliament passed a law on state-financed pensions.

The referendum held in 1980 over nuclear power seriously divided the main parties and created a parliamentary crisis. Voters were asked to choose between dismantling all nuclear power plants, building new nuclear reactors, or maintaining existing nuclear reactors. None of the three options obtained a majority.

In November 1994, voters approved the country's admission into the European Union by a majority of 52.3% Yes to 46.8% No.

Voting Patterns

Since 1985, Swedish voters have become more inclined to change their votes. In the 1988 general election the Green Party became the first new political party to be elected to the parliament in 70 years, receiving over 4% of the popular vote. In the 1991 general election two political parties, the Christian Democratic Alliance, a centrist party, and the New Democracy Party, a right-wing party, were elected to the Riksdag. The popular vote of the Social Democrats fell to 37.7% and that of the four main nonsocialist parties rose, giving them enough seats to form a coalition government. In the 1994 general election, the Social Democrats increased their popular vote and formed a minority government.

The 1998 general elections produced several surprises. Support for the Left Party and Christian Democrats doubled. The Social Democrats saw their support fall to the lowest level since 1920 after campaigning on a platform of improvements to welfare and continued repayments of public debt. Voter turnout was 81.4% (see chart below).

The number of women deputies elected to the Riksdag has risen considerably since the 1982 general elections. Women's increasing role in politics has led to greater numbers of women being included on the party lists (see chart below).

Over the years, Swedish voters have decided important national issues in referenda.

In recent years, voters have become more inclined to support new political parties.

Riksdag Election Results (1985–1998)

| | Popular Vote | | | | | Number of Seats | | | | |
	1985	1988	1991	1994	1998	1985	1988	1991	1994	1998
Socialist Bloc	50.1%	49.0%	42.2%	51.5%	48.6%	178	177	154	183	174
Social Democrats	44.7	43.2	37.7	45.3	36.4	159	156	138	161	131
Left Party (Communists)	5.4	5.8	4.5	6.2	12.0	19	21	16	22	43
Nonsocialist Bloc	47.9%	44.7%	46.6%	41.4%	44.3%	171	152	170	148	159
Moderates (Conservatives)	21.3	18.3	21.9	22.4	22.9	76	66	80	80	82
Centre Party	12.4	11.3	8.5	7.7	5.1	44	42	31	27	18
Liberal Party	14.2	12.2	9.1	7.2	4.7	51	44	33	26	17
Christian Democrats	–	2.9	7.1	4.1	11.8	0	0	26	15	42
Other Parties	2.0%	6.3%	11.2%	7.1%	7.1%	0	20	25	18	16
Green Party	1.5	5.5	3.4	5.0	4.5	0	20	0	18	16
New Democracy	–	–	6.7	1.2	0.2	0	0	25	0	0
Others	0.5	0.8	1.1	0.9	2.4	0	0	0	0	0
TOTALS	100.0%	100.0%	100.0%	100.0%	100.0%	349	349	349	349	349
Voter Turnout	89.9%	86.0%	86.7%	86.8%	81.4%					
Women deputies						108	130	115	141	149
As percent of total						31.0	37.2	33.0	40.4	42.7

Compiled from *Statistisk årsbok* (*Statistical Yearbook of Sweden*) and *Riksdagsvalet 1998* [*Parliamentary Elections 1998*].

SWEDISH ECONOMIC SYSTEM

Advance Organizer

The Swedish economic system is classified as a mixed economy. Before World War II, the economy was based on private enterprise. After 1945, Sweden adopted many aspects of public enterprise, establishing a comprehensive social welfare system, collective bargaining, and indicative planning in order to promote social justice, full employment, income equality, and high living standards.

SWEDISH
ECONOMIC SYSTEM

- Economic Policies
- Private Sector
- Public Sector
- Social Security System
- Women in the Labour Force

SWEDISH ECONOMY IN ACTION

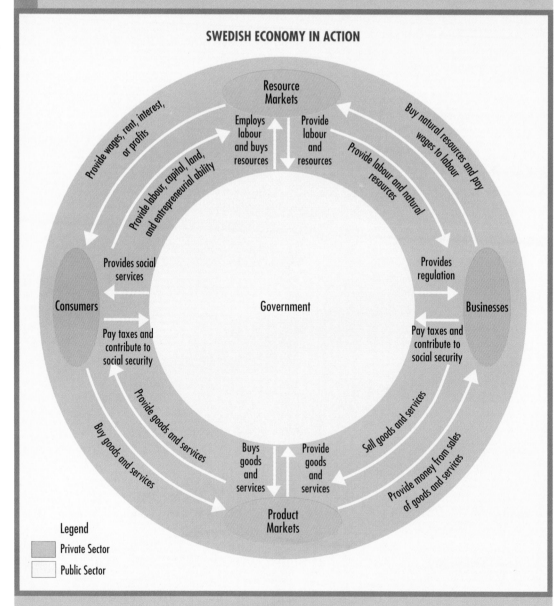

Resource Markets

Provide wages, rent, interest, or profits

Employs labour and buys resources

Provide labour and resources

Buy natural resources and pay wages to labour

Provide labour, capital, land, and entrepreneurial ability

Provide labour and natural resources

Provides social services

Provides regulation

Consumers

Government

Businesses

Pay taxes and contribute to social security

Pay taxes and contribute to social security

Provide goods and services

Sell goods and services

Buy goods and services

Buys goods and services

Provide goods and services

Provide money from sales of goods and services

Product Markets

Legend
- Private Sector
- Public Sector

Economic Policies

In the 20th century, Swedish governments have pursued two broad economic policies. Before 1944, the government followed a policy of limited intervention in the economy. After 1944, government intervention took the form of increased regulation of private business, social assistance plans, and labour–business agreements.

Limited Intervention (to 1944)

Before World War I (1914–1918) Swedish industrial development was stimulated by exports of manufactured goods. Many Swedish companies became internationally known for their high quality products. However, this reliance on foreign trade made the economy very sensitive to changes in world trade.

In 1930, the Swedish economy was greatly affected by the American government's decision to raise tariffs on all goods entering the United States. For Sweden, this resulted in falling export sales and rising unemployment.

In 1932, the Social Democratic Party took power and raised government spending to reduce unemployment and stabilize the economy. By 1939, unemployment had fallen to 11% from 23% in 1932, and industrial production had risen by 60%, mainly on the strength of booming exports of industrial equipment, iron ore, and manufactured goods to Germany, which was rapidly rearming itself.

Building Social Democracy (1944–1975)

Although Sweden remained neutral during World War II, the war affected the economy and required the government to impose price controls and production quotas. In 1944, the Social Democrats unveiled a comprehensive program to build a socialist society in Sweden.

The program proposed to create a universal social welfare system in which everyone would receive a pension, sick pay, and free medical care as needed. Under this social security plan, everyone would be treated equally. Taxes on higher incomes would be increased to achieve greater income equality.

The program also called for increased spending for housing, government-funded schools, higher education and research, and assistance to agriculture. Housing construction was to be supported by government loans and subsidies. Public schooling was expanded and available free of charge. The government established research foundations in higher education. Subsidies and price supports were set by the government and farmers' groups as assistance to agriculture.

In the 1950s and 1960s, the Swedish economy grew rapidly, fuelled by rising demand for its industrial goods and cheap imported oil. In 1973–1974, the rapid rise in international oil prices seriously affected the economy. Demand for Swedish goods fell as Europe and North America fell into a recession. At the same time, Swedish industry faced higher production costs because of the new higher prices for imported oil. As a result, unemployment in Sweden began to rise.

Swedish economic policies during the 20th century became increasingly focussed on creating a comprehensive social welfare system, especially after 1945.

October 1929
Stock market crash in New York

1930
American tariffs affect Swedish imported goods

1932
Unemployment reaches 23% of labour force

1933
Social Democrats introduce public relief for the unemployed

1914–1918
World War I; Sweden neutral

1938
Basic Agreement between employers and organized labour signed; nationwide collective bargaining established

Great Depression 1929–1939

Limited Intervention—To 1944

1939–1945
World War II; Sweden neutral

1944
Social Democrat social welfare system program introduced

1946
System of indicative planning introduced

1955
National health insurance put into effect

1958
European Economic Community established

1960
General supplementary pension plan introduced; Sweden becomes member of European Free Trade Association

1973–1974
First world oil price rise

1975–1976
First postwar recession in Sweden

Building Social Democracy 1944–1975

Note: Timeline is not to scale

Economic Crisis and Change (1976–1990)

In 1976, a nonsocialist coalition took power, promising to improve the economy. From the beginning, the new government faced problems related to the country's recession, which had begun in late 1975. By late 1981, the government introduced a program to combat the country's economic problems, including some reduction in government spending and a 10% devaluation of the currency, the krona, which would make Swedish goods cheaper in foreign markets.

In 1982, the Social Democrats led by Olof Palme returned to power on a program of making Sweden save and work its way out of the economic crisis. The government immediately devalued the krona by 16% to stimulate exports and industrial employment. Government spending was tightened and some taxes increased. Interest rates were raised to attract more capital into the country to help finance the country's balance of payments deficit and keep wage and price increases from rising too rapidly.

By mid-1983, these policies led to a strong economic recovery supported by exports and industrial investment. In spite of this, growth rates were less than those achieved before 1970 (see chart "Business Cycle in Sweden").

The leadership of the Social Democrats changed when Olof Palme was assassinated in 1986. In the late 1980s, led by Ingvar Carlsson, the Social Democrats began to consider changes in taxation policies. In Great Britain, Prime Minister Margaret Thatcher had reduced income tax rates on high income groups, while in the United States, President Ronald Reagan embarked on tax reform. In 1990, the Swedish government announced a major tax reform, with the aim of reducing tax rates on high incomes from 45% to 35%.

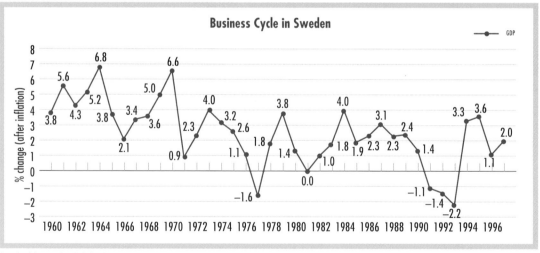

Business Cycle in Sweden

Statistisk årsbok (Statistical Yearbook of Sweden)

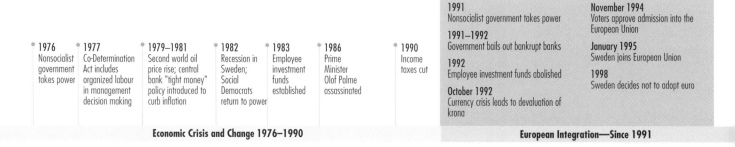

1976 Nonsocialist government takes power

1977 Co-Determination Act includes organized labour in management decision making

1979–1981 Second world oil price rise; central bank "tight money" policy introduced to curb inflation

1982 Recession in Sweden; Social Democrats return to power

1983 Employee investment funds established

1986 Prime Minister Olof Palme assassinated

1990 Income taxes cut

1991 Nonsocialist government takes power

1991–1992 Government bails out bankrupt banks

1992 Employee investment funds abolished

October 1992 Currency crisis leads to devaluation of krona

November 1994 Voters approve admission into the European Union

January 1995 Sweden joins European Union

1998 Sweden decides not to adopt euro

Economic Crisis and Change 1976–1990

European Integration—Since 1991

European Integration (since 1991)

As a small economy heavily dependent on foreign trade, Sweden's postwar prosperity rested on free trade. In 1960, Sweden joined with Austria, Denmark, Great Britain, Norway, Portugal, and Switzerland to form the European Free Trade Association (EFTA) to promote free trade among its members. EFTA aimed to remove all tariffs and other kinds of barriers to the free movement of goods. In 1973, EFTA was seriously weakened when Denmark and Great Britain joined the European Economic Community (EEC).

Sweden's policy of neutrality prevented it from joining the EEC in the 1970s and 1980s because the EEC was a political organization as well as a trading bloc. All its members except for Ireland belonged to NATO and had strong military ties with the United States. For Sweden, membership in the EEC was not desirable if the country also had to become a member of the North Atlantic Treaty Organization (NATO).

In late 1990, Sweden experienced the beginning of a severe economic recession that forced the country to reconsider its economic policies. A feeling emerged among economists and government experts that the economy could not support further growth of the public sector, and argued that the country's future economic prosperity rested on expanding trading and investment ties with the rest of Europe.

In early 1991, the Social Democrat government of Ingvar Carlsson began negotiations with the European Community for membership. The campaign leading up to the vote on European membership was an emotional, sometimes bitter one.

Opponents of European membership argued that decisions made by bureaucrats in Brussels would undermine the sovereignty of the Riksdag and over time threaten the stability of the country's social security system. They also pointed out that the country would no longer be able to remain neutral if it joined the European Union.

Supporters of European membership cited the following reasons for joining the European Union:

- access to a larger market for Swedish goods
- freer movement of people and goods
- protection for Swedish manufacturing jobs
- higher incomes and lower taxes
- more economic prosperity
- greater peace in Europe
- greater Swedish influence and a voice in European decision making.

Furthermore, supporters felt that the European Union is an important organization whose aim is to create prosperity, peace, and stability in Europe, and therefore Sweden should join it. In a November 1994 referendum, after three years of negotiations, Swedish voters narrowly approved the country's admission into the European Union.

For much of the 20th century Sweden pursued a policy of neutrality and free trade. Since the early 1990s, the country's leaders have come to realize that Sweden's future economic prosperity lies in being a member of the European Union.

PHOTO: The flag of the European Union has a star for each member country—15 in 1998.

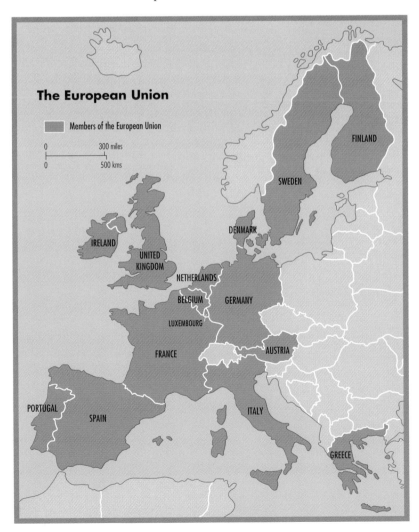

The European Union

Members of the European Union

0 — 300 miles
0 — 500 kms

FINLAND
SWEDEN
IRELAND
UNITED KINGDOM
DENMARK
NETHERLANDS
BELGIUM
GERMANY
LUXEMBOURG
AUSTRIA
FRANCE
PORTUGAL
SPAIN
ITALY
GREECE

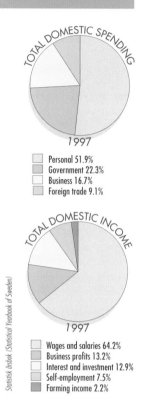

Statistisk årsbok (Statistical Yearbook of Sweden)

Consumers and businesses are the main decision makers in the Swedish economy.

TOTAL DOMESTIC SPENDING

1997

- ☐ Personal 51.9%
- ☐ Government 22.3%
- ☐ Business 16.7%
- ☐ Foreign trade 9.1%

TOTAL DOMESTIC INCOME

1997

- ☐ Wages and salaries 64.2%
- ☐ Business profits 13.2%
- ☐ Interest and investment 12.9%
- ☐ Self-employment 7.5%
- ☐ Farming income 2.2%

PHOTO: Ikea is one of many Swedish corporations that have expanded and set up operations outside Sweden.

Private Sector

The Swedish economy is influenced by the decisions of consumers and producers as well as by government spending and intervention.

Consumers

In terms of total spending on goods and services, consumers are the largest and most influential group of decision makers in the Swedish economy. In 1997, they accounted for 51.9% of total domestic spending on goods and services. In contrast, government purchases of goods and services accounted for 22.3% of all domestic spending. Spending by business was 16.7% of total domestic spending in 1997, consisting primarily of purchases of equipment and machinery, the construction of new buildings and factories, and payment for financial services. Spending on foreign trade accounted for 9.1% of domestic spending in 1997 (see chart "Total Domestic Spending").

Wages and salaries are the main sources of income, accounting for 64.2% of total domestic income in 1997. Other sources of domestic income (see chart "Total Domestic Income") came from business profits (13.2%), income from interest on savings and gains and dividends from investments (12.9%), self-employment (7.5%), and farming (2.2%).

Business Enterprises

Business enterprises in Sweden are organized mainly as family businesses, partnerships, or corporations. Other types of business enterprises are cooperatives.

Family Businesses. Like sole proprietorships in Canada and the United States, these businesses are owned and operated by family members and generally employ family members. They are most common in farming, retail trade, insurance, construction, and trucking.

Partnerships. As in Canada and the United States, members of Swedish partnerships are personally responsible for the business's debts and they share in the profits and management. The most common areas for partnerships are retail and wholesale trade, consulting, insurance, and real estate services.

Corporations. Corporations, called joint stock companies in Sweden, are separate legal entities. They are allowed to issue shares to people, hire employees and managers, buy supplies, and undertake production. In Sweden, corporations are the most common form of business enterprise in mining, manufacturing, retail trade, banking, and business services. Over 210 000 corporations operate in the country, but only a few hundred have their shares trade on the Stockholm Stock Exchange.

Cooperatives. Up to one-third of Swedes are members of cooperatives. Swedish cooperatives are based on the principles of self-help, cooperation, and public spirit. The cooperative movement is represented by the two million member Swedish Cooperative Union and Wholesale Society (KF). The KF is the country's third largest employer and its retail stores account for about 25% of all sales. It also owns companies that produce food and consumer goods for sale, and also provide insurance and banking services. Other cooperatives build houses and sell heating oil and gasoline.

Jonas Ekströmer/Pressens Bild

Corporate Sweden

Private initiative and inventiveness have long been hallmarks of Swedish industry. In the late 19th and early 20th century, many powerful international companies were founded to produce products based on Swedish inventions. Sweden's best known industrialist of those years was Alfred Nobel, the inventor of dynamite. In later years, the wealth that Alfred Nobel accumulated from the sale of dynamite was used to establish the Nobel Prize fund, which recognizes personal achievements in science, the humanities, and literature. Other important Swedish inventions were the power generator, industrial ball bearings, and the safety match.

In terms of sales, profits, and employment, Sweden's largest companies dominate the domestic economy and have extensive international operations. About 40% of the labour force in manufacturing is employed by the country's largest companies. Over 80% of total sales of the companies listed in the chart "Sweden's Top Companies" come from the export of goods and services abroad, mainly to the European Union. ABB GROUP, a major producer of electrical goods and electronics in Europe, is the country's largest industrial company, with sales of US$31.27 billion. Volvo, Sweden's second largest industrial company, is Europe's ninth largest producer of cars and trucks, with sales of US$24.04 billion.

L.M. Ericsson is Europe's fifth largest producer of telecommunication equipment. Electrolux is Europe's fifth largest manufacturer of household appliances. Other large Swedish companies are SCA-Svenska Cellulosa, Skanska, Astra, Stora Group, Scania, SAS Airlines, and SKF Group.

Since the early 1990s, Sweden's top companies have become more integrated into the European economy through mergers with other European firms. These mergers were undertaken to improve competitiveness and efficiency, as well as to develop new markets. In 1994, ABB Group was established as a joint Swedish–Swiss corporation serving all of Europe. In 1995, Volvo and the French firm Renault negotiated a merger to create a joint Swedish–French carmaker.

Swedish banks are large profitable businesses. The country's four largest banks have over US$386.4 billion in assets and 85% of all domestic savings deposits. In 1997, the Swedish banking industry experienced several mergers, and the last banks which the government had taken over in 1991–1992 to protect people's savings were privatized. In 1992, the government was forced to provide extensive financial support to Swedish banks to prevent the banking sector from collapse in a crisis caused by real estate speculation and deregulation of banks in the late 1980s.

> Sweden's largest companies dominate the domestic economy and have extensive global operations.

Sweden's Top Companies (1997)
(in thousands of US$)

	Industry	Sales	Profits	Employees
ABB Group	Electrical and electronics	$31 265 000	$568 000	213 100
Volvo Group	Automobiles	24 035 100	1 355 900	65 900
L.M. Ericsson	Electrical and electronics	21 955 800	1 563 000	95 600
Electrolux	Household appliances	14 790 800	46 100	106 000
SCA-Svenska Cellulosa	Forest products	7 675 000	361 000	33 400
Skanska	Construction	7 184 000	983 000	37 200
Astra	Personal care	5 881 000	1 336 000	21 000
Stora Group	Forest products	5 824 000	207 000	20 400
Scania	Automobiles	5 202 000	260 000	23 000
SAS Airlines	Airlines	5 099 000	215 000	25 100
SKF Group	Industrial products	4 836 000	204 000	41 900

Compiled from *Fortune*, August 3, 1998, and *Forbes*, July 27, 1998

See page 158 for comparable rates in Canada.

GOVERNMENT SPENDING
1997

- [ ] Goods and services 39.7%
- [ ] Transfers to individuals 35.1%
- [ ] Transfers to other governments 11.0%
- [ ] Interest on public debt 10.5%
- [ ] Other 3.7%

GOVERNMENT REVENUES
1997

- [ ] Personal income tax 36.0%
- [ ] Corporate income tax 5.3%
- [ ] Social security fees 22.9%
- [ ] Sales taxes 21.9%
- [ ] Investment income 7.6%
- [ ] Other 6.3%

Ministry of Finance

Public Sector

Since 1945, the public sector has played a major role in the development of Swedish social democracy. Today, the main activities of the public sector are carried out through the government's fiscal policy and monetary policy. The government has used planning, collective bargaining, and social programs to promote various policies.

Fiscal Policy

Up to 1990, the main purpose of Swedish fiscal policy was to maintain full employment and redistribute wealth among the population. To keep unemployment low the government provided social services, subsidies, and income supports to maintain people's incomes. To achieve greater equality among incomes, the government introduced a progressive income tax system under which the rate of tax paid increases as personal income increases.

Government spending and taxation policies since 1990 have become less important ways of influencing the direction of the economy, but they continue to be utilized. The main expenditures of government in 1997 were purchases of goods and services, payments to individuals and other governments, and interest on public debt (see chart "Government Spending"). The main sources of revenue for the government in 1997 were personal income taxes, social security fees, sales taxes, and investment income (see chart "Government Revenues").

Monetary Policy

Since the 1980s, the monetary policy of Sweden's central bank, the Riksbank, has become more important than the fiscal policy as a means of stabilizing and encouraging economic growth. As well, the Riksbank has various measures to reduce inflation and stabilize the value of the national currency, the krona.

The most effective measure used by the Riksbank to influence economic growth has been interest rates. During the 1980s, like the Bank of Canada, the Riksbank followed a policy of "tight money" by raising its bank rate, which in turn caused Swedish banks to raise interest rates on all types of credit to slow down the growth of the money supply and rate of inflation. Throughout most of the 1980s, the bank rate rarely fell below 9%. In the early 1990s it rose rapidly (to over 16% in 1992) because of speculation against the krona (see chart "Average Bank Rate").

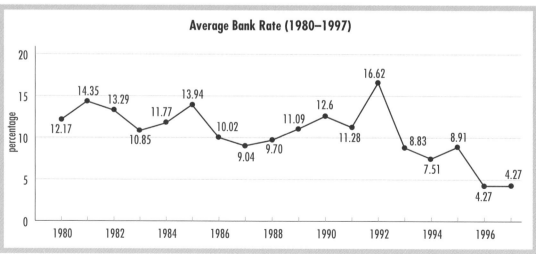

Average Bank Rate (1980–1997)

Riksbank (Bank of Sweden)

In the early 1980s, the government allowed the krona to fall sharply against the American dollar as a way of improving the country's international competitiveness as a trading nation. The value of the krona dropped to US$0.116 in 1985 and then rose to US$0.172 in 1992, when the central bank tried to protect the value of the currency by raising interest rates. The policy failed but not before short-term interest rates briefly reached 350% in late October 1992. Since then, the value of the krona has stabilized between US$0.128 and US$0.149 (see chart "Average Value of Krona").

Indicative Planning

In 1946, the Social Democrats introduced a system of planning called indicative planning. Under this system, members from trade unions, professional groups, and business organizations met frequently to discuss economic goals for the country. They established committees to study specialized economic problems. With information collected from government, labour, and the private sector, these committees prepared reports and made recommendations that were passed to various planning groups for use in economic forecasts.

These economic forecasts provided production targets and guidelines for various sectors of the economy. Targets were not legally binding on private companies and businesses because many companies sold their products abroad and the government could not control these sales. The main objective of economic forecasts was to identify the direction the economy was moving and identify potential economic problems.

Once the economic forecasts identified trends in the economy and future population needs, the government used them to adjust its fiscal and monetary policies to meet the expected changes. The government used the forecasts to allocate subsidies to low income groups and increase funding for public housing, transportation, and electricity generation. The government also used the economic forecasts to develop incentives to promote regional economic development and encourage

businesses to modernize their factories. On the basis of economic forecasts, the government also introduced changes in interest rates to influence private investment and personal spending on goods and services.

Since 1977, many planning activities of the central government have been delegated to local governments. Today, various public planning bodies exist at central, regional, and local levels of government for every form of activity, or for sectors such as education, energy, and care of the elderly. Surveys about what is needed are taken and budgets are drawn up to meet the need. Each municipality also prepares plans for the overall use of its land and water for meeting residential, commercial, and recreational needs. Long-range plans covering a five-year period are prepared and updated annually to take into consideration changes in population, the tax base, and investments.

Indicative planning in Sweden is used by government to allocate subsidies to and investment in the public sector and to encourage private business to cooperate with government to solve potential economic problems.

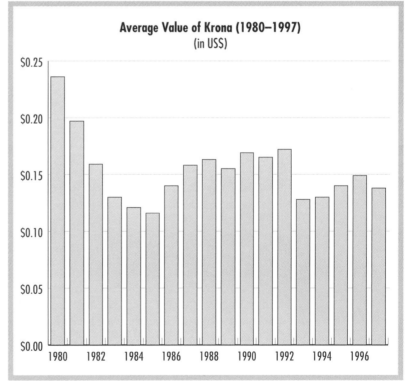

Average Value of Krona (1980–1997)
(in US$)

Riksbank [Bank of Sweden]

Collective Bargaining

Another important feature of government policy in Sweden until 1990 was the use of collective bargaining in nationwide negotiations between employers and trade unions over wage levels and working conditions. Collective bargaining originated in the 1930s, when relations between employers and labour were stormy. In 1934, the Social Democratic government requested that leaders from the country's major labour and business groups meet to discuss their differences. Representatives of the two groups met at the seaside resort of Saltsjöbaden outside Stockholm, and in 1938 they signed the Basic Agreement.

Basic Agreement. Under the Basic Agreement labour and business agreed to undertake nationwide negotiations every two or three years. The agreements were then applied to all member organizations. (In Canada, negotiations take place between individual companies and unions.) One result of Sweden's Basic Agreement was that the government did not pass many laws on wages and working conditions; labour and business decided these issues among themselves. Labour peace, which the government needed for economic growth and the development of the social welfare system, was a result of the Basic Agreement. Labour peace also led to higher profits for business. For labour, the main benefits of cooperation were better working conditions and higher wages.

Over time, business and labour developed a cooperative system of studying economic conditions in Sweden, and evaluating the ability of Swedish industry to compete successfully with foreign producers. Business leaders became sensitive to labour issues such as working conditions and wage levels. Labour leaders began to understand the importance of productivity, efficiency, and profitability and they discussed these issues with their trade union members in preparation for upcoming negotiations. As a result of these discussions and subsequent agreements, profitable companies began to offer high wages and good working conditions in exchange for high productivity and efficiency from their workers. Less profitable companies or companies that did not want to pay high wages were forced out of business.

Labour and Business Groups. The system of nationwide negotiations between employers and trade unions was made possible by the presence of two powerful groups—the Swedish Trade Union Confederation (LO) and the Swedish Employers' Confederation (SAF). In 1997, the Swedish Trade Union Confederation had 2.2 million members or 85% of all blue collar workers in the country. The Swedish Employers' Confederation had a membership of 43 000 companies employing about 1.3 million workers in 1997.

Besides these two groups there were two other labour organizations which also participated in nationwide collective bargaining. They were the Central Government Organization of Salaried Employees (TCO) and the Swedish Confederation of Professional Associations (SACO). About 1.7 million white collar and professional workers belonged to these two labour groups in 1997.

Decline of Collective Bargaining. Until the late 1980s, nationwide collective bargaining worked very well and became known as the "Swedish model." As long as the economy grew rapidly and companies earned high profits, workers received large annual increases in their wages. The situation became very different in the 1990s, when the economy grew much more slowly. This compelled many companies to negotiate directly with their own trade unions over wages and layoffs in order to control production costs and increase productivity. Nationwide collective bargaining continues today, but plays a less important role in determining wage rates and working conditions than formerly.

Co-Determination and Collective Ownership

During the 1970s, nationwide collective bargaining was a successful element of the economic system of Sweden. In 1971, the Swedish Trade Union Confederation asked the government and parliament to approve policies to limit the power of employers at workplaces. Initially, the Social Democrat government of Olof Palme was receptive to the request. They appointed various commissions of inquiry to study changes in the rules governing the labour market. The Swedish Trade Union Confederation (LO) did not believe that collective bargaining would give trade unions greater say in the making of business decisions that affected employment and investment. The LO hoped that if the government enacted legislation that allowed greater union participation in the factory, then a form of economic democracy in business decision making would prevail. Swedish businesses were initially against the idea of greater union participation in management. In 1976, Parliament passed the Co-Determination Act, which went into effect on January 1, 1977.

Co-Determination Act. The purpose of the Co-Determination Act was to enable employees to have greater influence on personnel and management issues. The Act allowed trade union representatives to participate in decision making at the factory level and to sit on the company's board of directors. The Act ordered all major industrial companies to sign co-determination agreements with their trade unions. Although the Act did not have a major impact on decision making at the board of directors level in most large Swedish businesses, it did have some influence on business decisions made at the factory level.

In large companies such as Volvo, Electrolux, and Ericsson, co-determination agreements allowed trade unions to participate with company officials in designing better working practices and conditions. In the case of Volvo, the country's largest carmaker, assembly line work was replaced by production teams that performed many stages of assembly and became responsible for quality control. Instead of performing routine and monotonous jobs, workers became involved in all stages of car assembly. Productivity increased as workers became more active in the design and production of cars. Also, workers became aware of the need to build high quality products that could compete successfully in foreign markets. Since 1980, carmakers in Europe and North America have adopted many of the innovative production practices established at Volvo under co-determination.

Employee Investment Funds. Besides co-determination, the Swedish Trade Union Confederation also wanted the government to enact legislation that would promote greater employee ownership of businesses. In the late 1970s and early 1980s, employee investment funds became a hotly debated issue in Swedish politics. Opponents of the funds, mostly employer and business groups, believed that the proposed funds would fundamentally change the country's economic system; supporters, mainly trade unions, argued that workers had a right to own a share of the businesses in which they worked. Despite fierce opposition from entrepreneurs and big business, Parliament passed a bill to establish employee investment funds in December 1983.

The government stated that the purpose of the employee investment funds was to maintain employment and increase employee influence on companies. Profits from the new funds would go into the pension fund system to increase the value of future pensions. Employers continued to criticize the funds as an unwelcomed intrusion by government and labour into business. In early 1992, the nonsocialist government of Carl Bildt passed a bill that abolished employee investment funds.

In the 1970s and 1980s, labour groups called for greater worker participation in business. Two controversial proposals were co-determination and employee investment funds.

Social Security System

The establishment of a universal social security system was a major goal of the Social Democrats' program for Swedish society after 1944. The objective of the social security system was to achieve important social goals such as public health, income stability, and social equality.

National Insurance Act

The features of the social welfare system—national health insurance, a basic pension plan, and a general supplementary pension plan—evolved gradually after 1945. National health insurance became operative in 1955. The basic pension plan for retired people had been introduced before World War II, but after 1945 benefits under this plan were raised substantially. An inconclusive referendum on pensions was held in 1957, then the general supplementary pension plan was introduced in 1960. In 1963, the three social security plans were united under the National Insurance Act. All these social security benefits are paid partly by the government from taxation and partly by direct contributions from employers and workers.

National Health Insurance. National health insurance, as in Canada, gives universal coverage to all citizens and people with foreign resident status. Swedish national health insurance provides more services than Medicare in Canada. It includes

- free medical care, including doctor and dentist fees, medicine, hospital care, and necessary travel
- a daily sickness allowance
- family allowances.

Basic Pension. Similar to the Canadian old-age security program, the basic pension is available to all Swedish citizens. It is financed by contributions from employers, the central government, and municipalities. The employers' contribution is calculated as a tax on payroll. The main benefits of the basic pension plan include

- general old-age pension at age 65
- disability pension
- wife's supplement (which is subject to an income test)
- widow's pension
- children's pension if one or both parents are dead
- benefits for housing and special care.

General Supplementary Pension. The general supplementary pension plan covers all employed individuals. The plan provides an old-age pension at the age of 65, a disability pension, and a widow's and children's pension. The plan is financed by contributions from employers and self-employed persons. This pension plan is similar to private company pension plans in Canada.

Other Social Benefits

By legislation, Swedish workers are ensured various social benefits besides those under the National Insurance Act. The most important of these are occupational injury insurance, workers' protection insurance, unemployment insurance, child allowances, and rent subsidies. All of these benefits are provided by the government.

PHOTO: Home care is a basic benefit provided under Sweden's National Insurance Act.

Lars Nyman/Pressens Bild

240

Neoconservative Influence

For decades, most Swedish voters willingly accepted the role of government in their lives. Their support for social democratic ideas about social equality and social welfare was based on the belief that a major portion of their high taxes would come back to them in the form of free education, heavily subsidized health care, and other government-paid benefits. In the late 1980s, many Swedes began to question the value of the government-paid benefits they received and their heavy tax burden. As the economy began to deteriorate, many accepted neoconservative ideas about the need to improve the economy through smaller and less intrusive government. In 1991, voters elected a nonsocialist coalition committed to cutting government spending, deregulating the economy, and privatizing state-owned enterprises.

Cutting Government Spending

When the nonsocialist parties took power in 1991, their first measure was to cut spending on social security to reduce the budget deficit. The measure was unsuccessful, as economic growth dropped and unemployment rose sharply. An additional problem arose in 1992–1993, when the government was forced to save the country's banking sector from collapse resulting from loans taken out in the 1980s for real estate speculation. The cost of the government bailout was estimated at 112 billion krona (US$20 billion). The deficit was the highest among industrial nations in 1993, at 12.2% of GDP.

In September 1994, the Social Democrats returned to power and immediately moved to raise taxes and social security contributions and reduce most social security benefits. Social security benefits that were lowered included child allowances, disability pensions, sick pay, and parental insurance benefits. As in Canada, the government defended these cutbacks by stating that to save the social security system, parts of it had to be dismantled. The government also stated that universality, the basic feature of the social security system, would be preserved. The budget deficit has been reduced through the measures of raising social security fees and lowering social benefits.

Deregulation

When the nonsocialists took power from the Social Democrats in 1991, they introduced several new laws to deregulate the economy. The role of the government in the economy was to be reduced in favour of giving more choice to individuals. The health insurance plan was modified to allow for private medical clinics. Government regulation of the railroads and electricity was sharply reduced. Prices for electricity, which had earlier been set by government boards, were now allowed to fluctuate according to supply and demand.

Since the late 1980s, consumer prices in Sweden have generally risen faster than in other industrial countries. Since 1988, consumer prices in Sweden have risen at an average annual rate of 4.7%, compared to 2.8% in Canada, 3.5% in the United States, and 2.8% in Germany, the country's largest trading partner (see chart below).

> Public support for less government spending, deregulation of business, and the privatization of state-owned enterprises has grown in recent years in response to a weak economy.

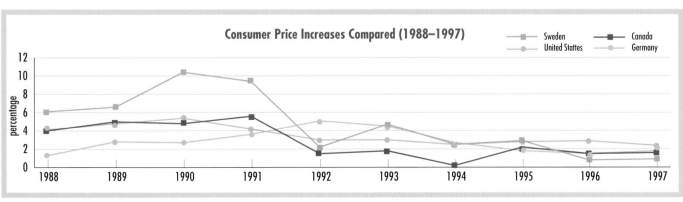

Consumer Price Increases Compared (1988–1997)

Compiled from Organization for Economic Cooperation and Development

This higher inflation rate affected Swedish companies' ability to sell their products abroad, as Swedish goods became more expensive. Exports account for almost 40% of the country's total production of goods and services. In 1992, the country was forced to devalue the krona by 30% to make Swedish exports more competitive.

For many years Sweden had been known for its very low unemployment rate. In the late 1980s, unemployment averaged less than 2%. In Canada the unemployment rate did not fall below 7%, and it was 5% in the United States and Germany (see chart "Unemployment Rates Compared"). Since 1991, the rate of unemployment in Sweden has risen sharply and remains high. Many economists have blamed high social security costs, high wage rates, and strong labour unions for increasing production costs and discouraging many firms from hiring new workers.

Privatization

Historically, government ownership of companies has been limited in Sweden. Under the Social Democrats the government rarely nationalized private companies and it was done only to save jobs. In 1992, the nonsocialist government took control of three insolvent banks that threatened the savings of thousands of people. Since 1992, the government has sold several companies to reduce its budget deficits. When the Social Democrats returned to power in 1994, they pledged to privatize several more state enterprises, including the railroads and utilities. Presently, the government owns the postal services, some railroads, television stations, telecommunications companies, and utilities, and it is a major player in radio broadcasting. Like most Canadian provinces, the Swedish government controls the sale of alcoholic beverages through government-owned stores.

Integration with Europe

Throughout the 20th century, Sweden has followed a policy of neutrality towards its neighbours and an economic policy of free trade. In the 1990s, Sweden began to reconsider these long-held beliefs about its place in the world. The end of the Cold War in 1990 and the collapse of the Soviet Union in 1991 made it clear to Sweden's political leaders that the country could not continue its policy of strict neutrality and nonparticipation in the political affairs of Europe.

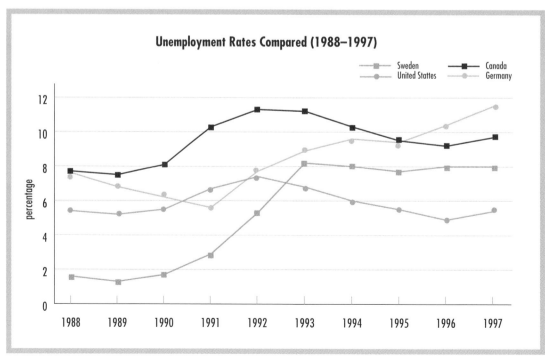

Unemployment Rates Compared (1988–1997)

Compiled from Organization for Economic Cooperation and Development

Membership in the European Union (EU)

On November 13, 1994, Swedish voters went to the polls to cast their ballots in a referendum to decide if Sweden should join the European Union (EU). The vote was close, with 52.3% of voters approving Sweden's membership in the EU and 46.8% rejecting membership. Over 83% of eligible Swedish voters turned out to cast a ballot. On January 1, 1995, Sweden became the 15th member country of the European Union.

Entry into the EU has required the Swedish government to introduce new laws and amend existing ones to conform to the laws of the European Union. This has meant changes in some labour regulation, the sale of agricultural produce, subsidies to farmers, production of various industrial goods, and tariffs on goods imported from non-EU countries. For example, the European Union has required Sweden to make changes in policies regarding the advertising of chocolate, which in Sweden is made without milk. Swedish manufacturers were told that they could no longer label their product as milk chocolate. Other examples of changes required by EU policies affected the size of strawberries and the shape of cucumbers available for sale.

These changes in national laws have made many Swedes less supportive of their country's membership in the EU. In Swedish opinion polls taken since 1995, public support for the EU has declined. A majority of the Swedes believe that the EU has not benefited them (see chart "Swedish Views on the EU").

Swedish youth who were polled on what the EU meant to them personally, viewed the EU favourably. They saw it as a way for people to travel freely throughout Europe, a source of jobs, a better future for young people, and a guarantee of lasting peace in Europe. At the same time, many believed the EU created a lot of bureaucracy (see chart "Swedish Youth and Europe").

Membership in the European Union has brought changes in many Swedish laws and ways of doing things. EU membership remains a controversial issue for many Swedes, though Swedish youth view membership favourably.

Swedish Views on the European Union

Support for the EU	Autumn 1995	Spring 1996	Autumn 1996	Spring 1997	Autumn 1997	Spring 1998
A good thing	32%	29%	27%	27%	31%	32%
A bad thing	36	42	45	41	46	38
Neither good nor bad	28	25	23	26	20	25
Do not know	4	4	5	5	3	5
Results of EU membership						
Benefited	19%	17%	18%	17%	21%	20%
Not benefited	54	56	56	54	61	55
Do not know	27	27	26	29	18	25

Compiled from *Eurobarometer*

Swedish Youth and Europe

"Which of the following statements best describe(s) what the European Union means to you personally?"

The ability to go wherever I want in Europe	44%
A lot of bureaucracy, a waste of time and money	38
A way to create jobs	35
A way to create a better future for young people	30
Guaranteed lasting peace in Europe	24
A means of improving the economic situation in Europe	24
A European government	20
The risk of losing our cultural diversity	15
Just a dream, a Utopian idea	13
A way to protect the rights of citizens	6
Don't know	2
Other	1

Eurobarometer, No. 47 (Spring 1997), pp. B76–77

© European Communities, 1995–1998
(Source: www.europa.eu.int)

Over 85% of all Swedish
foreign trade is with
countries of the European
Union.

Economic and Monetary Union

A far-reaching step in establishing greater economic and monetary integration in Europe was the signing of the Maastricht Treaty in December 1991. The Treaty proposed an economic union in which all members of the European Union would coordinate their economic policies and monitor their fiscal policies to prevent large budget deficits. The Treaty also proposed a monetary union, in which a single currency called the euro would begin to replace national currencies on January 1, 1999 (see chart "Euro Countdown"). For this to occur, the Treaty required each member country to meet the following economic criteria:

- Annual budget deficits must not exceed 3% of GDP.
- Government debt must not exceed 60% of GDP.

Sweden in 1997 did not meet all these criteria. Although its annual budget deficit was lower than 3% of GDP, its government debt was higher than 60% of GDP. However, many people in Sweden believe that their country will have no choice but to join the monetary union, if not in 1999 then a few years later, because of the country's close trading ties with other members of the European Union, especially with Germany, which publicly stated that it would join the monetary union in 1999.

Euro Countdown	
December 31, 1998	Conversion rates into euro fixed
January 1, 1999	Economic and monetary union begins; all electronic and non-cash bank transactions done in euros
January 1, 2002	Euro notes and coins introduced alongside national notes and coins
July 1, 2002	National notes and coins no longer accepted and withdrawn from circulation

In 1997, the Social Democrat government of Göran Persson publicly declared that Sweden would not join the monetary union nor replace the krona with the euro in 1999. Public opinion since spring 1996 has been strongly against adopting the euro (see chart "Support for the Euro in Sweden").

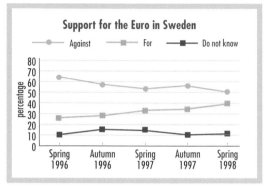

Compiled from *Eurobarometer*

Support for the euro among citizens in other European Union member countries has not declined greatly since spring 1996 (see chart "Support for the Euro in the European Union"). In spring 1998, a majority of citizens surveyed in Denmark and Great Britain disapproved of replacing their national currencies with the euro. However, support for the euro was strong among a majority of citizens in Austria, Belgium, Finland, France, Germany, Greece, Ireland, Italy, Luxembourg, Netherlands, Portugal, and Spain. Overall, in spring 1998, 60% of citizens in the European Union supported the adoption of the euro.

Support for the euro is strongest among young people, people with higher education, and individuals who have professional and managerial positions. Support for the euro is weakest among people aged 55 or older, people with secondary education, and manual workers.

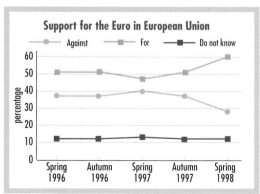

Compiled from *Eurobarometer*

Swedish Views on the EU

Although Sweden entered the European Union in 1995, Swedish political parties have been split over the European Union and the country's future membership in the economic and monetary union (EMU). The following viewpoints are taken from the official platforms of the country's main political parties, as found on their internet websites.

Left Party

We are working against the EU and oppose Swedish membership. The European Union is based on the superiority of free movement of market forces over social and environmental targets. The national self-determination of members is largely annulled in favour of an undemocratic and bureaucratic power structure in Brussels. The creation of the EU is directed by transnational companies' needs for growth.

Green Party of Sweden

The Green Party is opposed to Swedish membership in the EU. Sweden may not accept the convergence criteria of the EMU as a goal for Swedish economic policy and may not join the third stage of the EMU (i.e., a common central bank and a common European currency). The Green Party of Sweden works for a decrease in EU's protectionism vis-a-vis the rest of the world. However, trade rules should be bound to harsh environmental and social protection clauses against deleterious effects of uncurbed free trade.

The Green Party will support critical and open reports about EU activities and their effect upon Swedish society. We encourage the Swedish people to take part

actively in the ongoing process and we are urging a new referendum to leave the European Union, which should take place after the Intergovernmental Conference which started in 1996.

As a member of the European Union, Sweden has lost its economic and national independence. Many of the decisions affecting our country are made behind closed doors in Brussels.

Centre Party

Our participation in the integration of Europe must be conditional on our being able to assert our independence and our fundamental values of democracy, environmental quality, social security, and regional development. Sweden's participation must be shaped in response to developments in the EU and in Europe generally. The limits to our participation in European integration are dictated by Sweden's independent foreign policy and neutrality, and by the continuing assertion of our basic values.

Social Democratic Party of Sweden

The EU is becoming important in many different areas, not least in areas high on Sweden's agenda: employment, the environment, equality between men and women. Sweden will give priority to these questions during its presidency of the EU in 2001. The supranational decision making of the EU is needed, but it must be limited to those questions which require supra-nationality. In other cases, the gap between people and the elected representatives will be too great to bridge. The model must be one of inter-state cooperation. We maintain that the cooperation within the EU must

aim at strengthening the national democracies—not weakening them.

Liberal Party

This generation has the historic opportunity to see both a free, united Europe and a Europe at peace. We do not see the EU as an end in itself, but as Europe's best means for securing freedom and peace. A healthy environment and an effective fight against crime require cooperation. The most important task of the EU is to broaden cooperation and allow membership of Baltic and Central European countries.

The EU should focus on transnational issues. It should not be involved in issues which are best solved by member states individually. EU support for farmers and many EU regional policies should be phased out.

European monetary union is needed for the creation of a stable financial environment for small companies and reduced unemployment. Sweden should join the EMU as soon as possible.

Moderate Party

The Moderate Party has since 1961 been at the forefront of the debate on Sweden's integration in Europe.

The Moderate Party has always stressed the inseparable link between freedom and peace. Only when individuals and nations are given their freedom, can a durable and stable order of peace and security be built. Accordingly, the Moderate Party has never accepted the then socialist dictatorships of Central and Eastern Europe.

We regard the European Union as the core and engine of cooperation in Europe as a whole.

REVIEW

Summary

The Swedish political system is a parliamentary democracy in which the Riksdag (Parliament) is the highest law making body in the country. Consensus is the basis on which most important decisions are made. Interest groups play an important role in the decision making process. In keeping with these aspects of law making, Swedish voters elect their political leaders on the basis of proportional representation.

Though the Swedish economy is based on private enterprise, government intervention in the economy has been extensive. This intervention over the years has taken the form of indicative planning, a system of collective bargaining, and an extensive social security system. The objective of government intervention was to improve public health, promote income stability, and achieve social equality.

For much of the 20th century, the Swedish political and economic systems developed according to the principles of social democracy. Since 1990, the country has been forced to adjust to changes in international politics caused by the collapse of the Soviet Union and of communism in Eastern Europe. The country now faces the challenge of becoming more integrated in the European economy.

Swedish Values and Political Philosophy

1. Henry Milner has identified five core Swedish values. Which one would you most likely support, and which one would you be least likely to support? Provide reasons for your choice.

2. Examine the chart on page 221.
   a) What do communists consider to be more important than individual freedom?
   b) What are the major differences in the values of socialism and communism?

3. The name that a Swedish political party chooses can be very important to its success.
   a) Why do you think the Communist Left Party changed its name to the Left Party?
   b) What advantages might the name Christian Democratic have in attracting votes?
   c) Which voters would be less likely to be influenced by party names?

4. a) What characteristics distinguish the Centre Parties (Liberal, Centre, Christian Democrat, and Green) from the Social Democratic Party?

   b) Why do the Centre Parties sometimes align themselves with the Social Democrats, and sometimes with the Moderate Party?

Swedish Political System

1. Compare Sweden's unicameral legislature with a bicameral legislature of another country that you have studied. What are the advantages and disadvantages of each?

2. Sweden is a constitutional monarchy. Why is the monarch not allowed to have real political power?

3. a) What is a coalition government?

   b) Under what conditions would the speaker of the Riksdag ask the Prime Minister and cabinet to resign and ask other political parties to form a coalition government?

4. Why is the ombudsperson important to Swedish democracy?

5. a) Explain how decision making by consensus is different from decision making by majority vote.

b) What advantages are there to making decisions by consensus?

c) For each pair of interest groups listed below, give at least two issues on which it would be difficult for them to reach a consensus with each other.
A. labour unions, business associations
B. environmentalists, pulp and paper mill owners
C. social welfare organizations, the very wealthy

6. Which interest groups would you expect to support and which to oppose free post-secondary education?

7. Which of the three levels of government in Sweden has the most influence in policy making? Provide evidence to support your choice.

8. Examine the chart on page 229. In 1982, 48.6% of the votes for the nonsocialist parties was not enough to allow them to form a coalition government. However, their 46.6% of the vote in 1991 enabled them to put the socialist parties out of power and form a coalition.
a) What factor made the difference in the two elections?
b) To what extent do you agree that proportional representation is more democratic than the system of plurality voting? (Refer to Chapter 2.)

9. Based on the Swedish experience, do you think that referenda are a better way of making laws than by elected representatives?

Swedish Economic System

1. a) List examples of government intervention in the economy prior to 1991.
b) How successful were the attempts to solve the economic problems of these years?

c) Examine the business cycle chart on page 232. What words would you use to describe the state of the economy between 1960–1996?

2. Using the pie charts on page 234, explain why a high rate of unemployment would be a concern in the economy.

3. Using the text and the chart on page 235, write three generalizations describing the Swedish economy.

4. a) What is meant by the term progressive income tax?
b) To what extent is the progressive income tax system consistent with the core values of Sweden?
c) To what extent would someone who is an individualist support this system of taxation?

5. When the bank rate increases, interest rates on loans and savings for companies and individuals also increase; the reverse is true when the bank rate decreases. Examine the Average Bank Rate graph on page 236, and answer the following questions.
a) In the period 1987–1990, what would you expect to have happened to the amount of money people put into savings accounts? What might have happened to the willingness of companies to expand their businesses?
b) What do you think would be the effect on unemployment when the bank rate is increased?

6. How successful were the manipulations of the bank rate in stabilizing the krona? Provide evidence from the text and the graphs on pages 236 and 237 to support your conclusions.

7. a) Define indicative planning as practised in Sweden.

b) Chart the advantages and disadvantages of indicative planning for
A. the government
B. individual sectors of the economy
C. the national economy

8. What means did the government use to encourage the private sector to follow its forecasts?

9. a) Has government legislation been successful in reducing strikes in Sweden?

b) To what extent is government legislative interference in the collective bargaining process consistent with Sweden's core values?

10. a) What is the purpose of the Co-Determination Act?
b) What rights and responsibilities do employees have under the act?
c) What advantages could there be for a business under this act?

Swedish Political Economy

1. John Maynard Keynes wrote that in prosperous times governments should cut spending, raise taxes and build up a surplus; in bad economic times they should increase spending and decrease taxes. To what extent has the Swedish government followed this theory? Give examples from the 1980s and 1990s to support your answer.

2. In 1991, a nonsocialist coalition was voted into office. In 1994, the Social Democrats were voted back into office. Use the graphs on pages 242–244 to explain why the voters may have made their decisions based on economic conditions.

3. Read the Focus On Critical Thinking on page 247, and answer the following questions.

a) Briefly summarize the position of each political party on membership in the EU.

b) Are the parties of the right or the left more supportive of membership in the EU?

c) Considering all the views presented, how would you summarize Sweden's views on membership in the EU?

Chapter Consolidation

1. This chapter began with a quotation from a speech given by Anne Wibble, a former Swedish Finance Minister. How successful has Sweden been in meeting the promises given in the quotation?

2. a) On what values are the political and economic systems of Sweden based?

b) Whose ideas were influential in the development of the political and economic systems in Sweden? Briefly explain the ideas and how they were applied in Sweden.

c) Create a chart, identifying the type of political system and economic system in Sweden and the strengths and weaknesses of those systems.

JAPAN

"The power of Japan Inc. may owe something to the abilities of its bureaucrats, but the real reason for the country's economic development lies in the support of the people, who sacrifice their own comfort for the sake of Japan Inc."
—Masao Miyamoto, *Straitjacket Society*, 1994

Since Japan was forced to open up the country to the world after American ships sailed into Tokyo Bay in 1853, Japan has endeavoured to become a major global power to protect itself from foreign domination. From 1890 to 1945, Japan used its military force to assert its influence on the international stage. These expansion efforts led to World War II in the Pacific and Japan's defeat and occupation by the United States. Since 1945, Japan has channelled its energies into making itself a global economic power. Today, the country has the world's largest economy after the United States. Japan is one of

Asia's few parliamentary democracies and constitutional monarchies. Since the end of World War II, its democratic institutions have given the country stable and competent political leadership. As well, the government has provided the country with policies that promote exports and international trade. These policies have helped transform the country from one devastated by war into a major industrial power. In the 1990s, after many years of prosperity, Japan experienced economic setbacks that have led to some questioning about the future.

Key Concepts/Vocabulary

Emperor
Diet
House of
  Councillors
House of
  Representatives
zaibatsu
keiretsu

lifetime
  employment
seniority-based
  wages
company union
administrative
  guidance
iron triangle

Focus On Issues

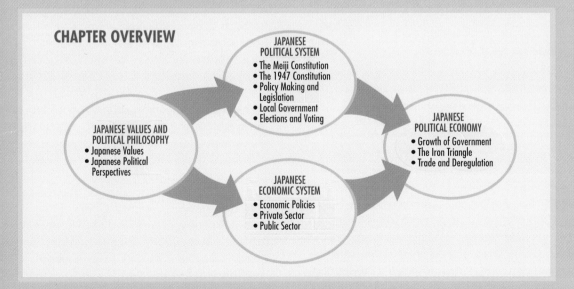

CHAPTER OVERVIEW

JAPANESE VALUES AND POLITICAL PHILOSOPHY
• Japanese Values
• Japanese Political Perspectives

JAPANESE POLITICAL SYSTEM
• The Meiji Constitution
• The 1947 Constitution
• Policy Making and Legislation
• Local Government
• Elections and Voting

JAPANESE ECONOMIC SYSTEM
• Economic Policies
• Private Sector
• Public Sector

JAPANESE POLITICAL ECONOMY
• Growth of Government
• The Iron Triangle
• Trade and Deregulation

JAPANESE VALUES AND POLITICAL PHILOSOPHY

Contemporary Japanese values and political philosophy have been influenced by the country's geography (an island archipelago), long history of human settlement, unique culture, and rapid industrialization in the 20th century.

Advance Organizer

Over the centuries Japan has developed a distinctive culture and values, at times drawing on outside influences and at other times protecting its unique cultural identity in the face of enormous pressure to adopt foreign ideas.

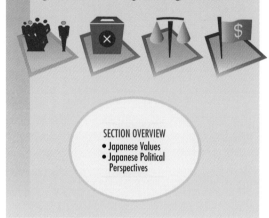

SECTION OVERVIEW
- Japanese Values
- Japanese Political Perspectives

Japanese Values

Group affiliation and identity, allegiance, and harmony are traditional Japanese values. To these have been added basic democratic values. Contemporary Japanese values are a product of the country's geography, history, and economic development.

Sources of Values

Geographically, Japan is a chain of islands, stretching almost 3000 kilometres from northeast of Hokkaido to southwest of Okinawa. At its nearest point to the Asian mainland, Japan is 200 kilometres from Korea. Except for a brief period after World War II, from 1945 to 1952, the country experienced no real occupation by outsiders. In the 13th century, unfavourable weather conditions prevented two Mongol attempts to invade and occupy Japan. The country long enjoyed a degree of isolation from the outside world, which fostered a view among its citizens that they were unique and blessed with divine protection.

The earliest historical accounts of the Japanese people are found in Chinese chronicles from the years AD 200–300. They tell of a country of 100 kingdoms, some of which sent emissaries to China. In the 6th century, Japan came under Chinese influence, with the arrival of Buddhism, Confucian beliefs, and the Chinese written script. The country modelled its government and cultural institutions on those of the Chinese. During the next 500 years, Chinese influence left deep impressions in the country's law, administration, religion, architecture, art, and literature.

Towards the end of the 12th century, Chinese influence declined as Japan developed its own form of feudalism and a code of ethics called *bushido* (way of the warrior) based on discipline and self-sacrifice. The country entered a period of internal strife in the early 16th century. The first European explorers and missionaries arrived in Japan in the middle of the 16th century. In the early 17th century, a new government under the Tokugawa *Shogun* (warrior prince) was established at Edo (present-day Tokyo). It banished all foreign contacts, and Japan remained in a state of self-imposed seclusion for the next 200 years. In 1853, US Commodore Perry arrived in Tokyo Bay and forced Japan to open its ports to foreign contact.

In 1868, the Meiji Emperor was restored to the throne, ending rule by the *samurai* (warrior) class and ushering in a new era. Japan embarked on a rapid program of economic and political modernization. A government based on constitutional law was established. Modern European technology was used in the first factories. By the end of World War I (1914–1918), Japanese society was undergoing rapid social and economic change as its population moved into the cities to work in factories. In the 1920s and 1930s, the country increasingly began to assert its power and nationalistic spirit on the world stage by aggression against China. The nationalist spirit eventually led the country into a war with Great Britain and the United States in 1941, and subsequently to military defeat in 1945.

Following Japan's surrender in August 1945, the country experienced many political and economic reforms at once. Under American occupation (1945–1952), a new constitution was written for Japan which made the country a democracy and gave equal rights to men and women. The American authorities reorganized the Japanese economy and encouraged the country to export goods to the United States. After 1953, the country developed quickly into a major industrial power. Becoming the world's second largest industrial power has been a source of pride to Japanese society.

Core Values

A cultural study of Japanese values and society done by anthropologist Joy Hendry,[1] has identified group affiliation, loyalty, harmony, consensus, egalitarianism, self-development, and democracy as core values. These values make Japanese society more collectivist in outlook than most Western democracies.

Group affiliation. Japanese society is highly structured and organized into groups. Much of an individual's identity is expressed through membership in groups like the family, work unit, and social clubs. The group provides its members with purpose, honour, pride, a code of conduct, and a view of the world. Group membership stimulates personal development, while at the same time offering security and protection from external forces.

Loyalty. Loyalty and obligation are deeply held values and important to developing and maintaining long-term relationships. Close family ties are maintained through respect and loyalty given to older family members and family ancestors. Relationships are important sources of moral and financial support in times of need and as aids to attaining personal success, particularly in politics and government. Much business is conducted on the basis of friendships and relationships with trusted associates.

Harmony. Harmony is highly regarded by most Japanese. One is expected to try at all times to establish and maintain peace in social relations and to avoid disputes. This means that one should understand another's situation before acting. Harmony is also maintained by recognizing and understanding the social and moral responsibilities of one's social status.

Consensus. Most Japanese believe that consensus should be achieved in decision making. By considering all opinions, views, and ideas of the interested parties, a broad agreement among concerned participants is achieved. This promotes cooperation, trust, and a spirit of commitment, avoids confrontation, and strengthens group solidarity.

Egalitarianism. Most Japanese view wide disparities of income and wealth as sources of social instability and threats to harmony. They recognize that individuals have different abilities and talents, but they also believe that these differences should be channelled toward group benefit. Competition and individual initiative, though important, should not be encouraged if they lead to confrontation and disruption of social harmony.

Self-development. The overall goal of self-development is to think for oneself and understand oneself in order to understand others. Through education, hard work, and self-sacrifice, the individual develops qualities such as perseverance, attention to detail, discipline, reliability, self-reliance, and personal responsibility.

Democracy. Since 1945, the Japanese have accepted democracy as their country's preferred political system. They regard it as a means by which individuals can pursue personal interests and achievements while also being reminded of the need to fulfil their obligations to others.

---

[1]An extensive study of Japanese society appears in Joy Hendry, *Understanding Japanese Society*, second edition, London: Routledge, 1996.

Japanese Political Perspectives

Politics in Japan since 1945 have been influenced by particular a set of beliefs about authority, government, and political change. From 1955 to 1993, Japanese politics were dominated by two main political parties, with the Liberal Democrats as the party of government and the Socialists as the main opposition party. The July 1993 general elections shattered this political arrangement and gave rise to several new parties. Since then, Japanese politics have been characterized by considerable change and shifting allegiance to new political parties.

In August 1993, a coalition government led by a group of reform-minded politicians of the Renewal Party took power. The Renewal Party, formed in June 1993 by former Liberal Democrats, joined with other parties to establish the New Frontier Party, a centrist reform-minded party, in late 1994. It was renamed the Liberal Party in 1998.

Until 1993 Japanese politics were dominated by two large political parties—the Liberal Democrats and Socialists.

Japanese Governments Since 1945

Right	Left	Centre

1945–1952	American Occupation Administration
1952–1955	Liberals/Democratic Party
1955–1993	Liberal Democratic Party
1993–1994	Coalition government led by Renewal Party
1994–1996	Coalition government led by Social Democratic Party
1996–	Liberal Democratic Party

Japanese Political Continuum

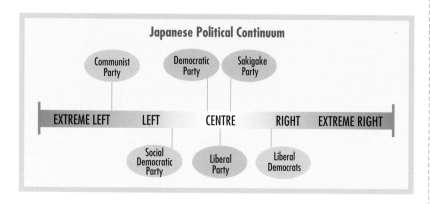

The Right

Liberal Democratic Party. The Liberal Democratic Party has been the dominant political party in Japanese politics since its formation in November 1955 from a merger of the prewar Liberal and Democratic parties. From 1955 to 1993, the Liberal Democrats formed the government and guided the country to its present status as the world's second largest industrial power. In July 1993, voters removed the party from power, after a series of public scandals revealed widespread corruption among top party leaders. Voters wanted political and economic reforms. In 1994, the Liberal Democrats formed a coalition government with the Social Democrats. In the October 1996 general elections, voters returned the Liberal Democrats with sufficient members to form a minority government. The party's support is strongest in rural districts and small urban centres, and weakest in the large cities. Business people, government officials, and farmers are strong supporters of the Liberal Democratic principles of liberalism, democracy, and a market economy.

The Left

The Japanese left has declined in popular support since 1990. In the 1996 general elections, the Communist Party replaced the Social Democratic Party (formerly called the Socialist Party) as the main party of the Japanese left.

Communist Party. The Communist Party is the main political party of the Japanese left today. Its historical roots lie in the prewar Communist Party formed in July 1922 and disbanded in 1942. The party, officially reestablished in October 1945, claims to be the only true opposition party to the Liberal Democrats. Its support is concentrated in the large cities and among urban professionals, skilled workers, and intellectuals.

Social Democratic Party. In 1993, the Social Democratic Party became the new name of the Socialist Party. The Socialist Party was established in November 1945 by various prewar socialist groups that had appeared in the 1920s and 1930s. From 1945 to 1993, the Socialist Party was the main opposition party, but internal divisions prevented it from becoming a serious challenger to the Liberal Democratic Party. In the 1996 general elections, the party suffered a serious decline in its traditional support among organized labour.

The Centre

Since 1993, the centre of the Japanese political spectrum has become occupied by many new parties, several of which are off-shoots from the Liberal Democratic Party and the Social Democratic Party.

Liberal Party. Formed in December 1994 as the New Frontier Party from the merger of four parties, it included some former Liberal Democrats, young conservatives, moderate socialists, and groups with ties to militant Buddhism. The New Frontier Party emerged as the main opposition party to the Liberal Democratic Party after the October 1996 general elections. In early 1998, the New Frontier Party became the Liberal Party. Several of its members joined the Democratic Party, while others left the party to sit as independents. The program of the Liberal Party calls for reform of parliamentary procedures, deregulation of the economy, the end of subsidies to agriculture, reform of the bureaucracy, and a more active foreign policy for Japan.

Democratic Party. Formed in 1996 by reform-minded members of the Liberal Democratic Party and the Social Democratic Party, the Democratic Party calls for tax reform, improvements in social security, greater democratization of politics, more local self-government, education reform, and an end to government regulation of the economy. In the October 1996 general elections, they emerged as the third largest party.

Sakigake Party. The Sakigake, formed in 1993 by a small group of reformers who left the Liberal Democrats, joined the first coalition government after the 1993 general elections to prevent the Liberal Democrats from returning to power. In 1996, the party became a member of a coalition government led by the Social Democrats and Liberal Democrats. The Sakigake calls for greater accountability of politicians to their voters, less power for bureaucrats to make policy, and less government regulation of the economy.

Roger Dahl—The Japan Times

JAPANESE POLITICAL SYSTEM

Advance Organizer

The contemporary Japanese political system is the product of the Meiji Constitution of 1889 and the Constitution of Japan, drafted in 1946 by American authorities and enacted in 1947. The Meiji Constitution was proclaimed as a gift from the Emperor, who voluntarily gave up a small measure of his powers to allow the people a say in the administration of national affairs. The 1947 Constitution borrowed many ideas from the American Constitution and declared that sovereignty resided with the people.

This constitution also renounced war and military force. The 1947 Constitution remains in force today.

The Japanese political system has undergone two major reforms. The first was the Meiji Constitution, which restored the power of the monarchy in Japan. The second was the 1947 Constitution, which made Japan a democratic state.

SECTION OVERVIEW
- The Meiji Constitution
- The 1947 Constitution
- Policy Making and Legislation
- Local Government
- Elections and Voting

STRUCTURE OF CONTEMPORARY JAPANESE GOVERNMENT

JUDICIARY **EXECUTIVE** **LEGISLATURE**

Emperor

↑ Advises

Appoints judges ←

Supreme Court ← Prime Minister --- Cabinet

Prime Minister — Responsible to → DIET: House of Representatives | House of Councillors

Cabinet — Responsible to →

↑ Decide policy

Lower Court

Decide cases

Bureaucracy

Administer and implement laws

VOTERS

Legend
- Parliament
- Executive branch of government consists of the Emperor and Prime Minister; responsible to the Diet
- Legislature called the Diet consists of an elected upper House of Councillors and a lower House of Representatives
- Judiciary consists of the Supreme Court
- Power (elects)

The Meiji Constitution (1890–1945)

Put into effect in 1890, the Meiji Constitution defined Japanese politics until 1945. The constitution made the Emperor the holder of all executive, legislative, and judicial power. Although a bicameral parliament was created, its political authority was limited. The government was responsible directly to the Emperor rather than to the parliament. The military was given a role in politics through the convention that all ministers of the army and navy had to be officers in active service. As a result, political power under the Meiji Constitution rested not in the parliament but in the bureaucracy and the military.

Naomi Wakan, Pacific-Rim Slide-Bank, LLHCE001

Bureaucracy

The Meiji Constitution gave the bureaucracy considerable power to formulate national policy. Though every law required the consent of the parliament, most were drafted within government ministries and the military. As well, decrees issued in the name of the Emperor were prepared by the bureaucracy, which allowed it to have direct control over wide areas of public policy making.

Military

The constitutional practice of appointing active officers to head the army and navy gave the military a powerful voice in Japanese politics in the 1920s and 1930s.

Political Independence. According to the Meiji Constitution, only the Emperor had the right to control the operations of the army and navy. The government was often not informed about military policies and was powerless to stop the military when it acted to change national policies. This lack of control was clearly demonstrated in September 1931, when young officers of the Japanese army who were stationed in Manchuria to protect the railway occupied all of Manchuria. The government could not stop the military occupation or force the military to withdraw from Manchuria.

The political independence of the military also encouraged the formation of radical right-wing factions within the army and navy that sought political power. The most important of the radical right-wing factions in the army were the Imperial Way and the Control Faction. The Imperial Way stressed the importance of the *samurai* (warrior) spirit and complete devotion to the Emperor. The faction's leaders supported a policy of expansion in China as a means of stopping the spread of Communism from the Soviet Union into East Asia. The Control Faction preferred a more cautious policy of expansion into China and Southeast Asia.

Military Takeover. In May 1932, young naval officers and army cadets assassinated Prime Minister Inukai Tsuyoshi. The army demanded and got a new government with an increased military influence. In February 1936, young officers of the Imperial Way faction attempted to seize control of the government. Though the uprising was suppressed, it marked the end of civilian government in Japan. The Control Faction filled all important posts in the government. Military influence led to the mobilization of the nation's resources to wage war on China. In July 1940, all political parties were forced to disband and become part of the Imperial Rule Assistance Association. For the next five years, during World War II, Japan was a one-party state.

Japanese Emperors
of the 20th Century

Meiji	1868–1912
Taisho	1912–1926
Showa	1926–1989
Heisei	1989–

LEFT: Emperor Meiji assumed the throne following the overthrow of the Tokugawa Shogunate in 1868. Under his reign (1868–1912), many political and economic reforms were introduced. Japan was transformed from a feudal society into a modern industrial state and emerged from isolation into the ranks of major world powers.

PHOTO: One duty of the Emperor is the opening of Parliament. Emperor Akihito is reading a statement to open a session of the National Diet.

The 1947 Constitution

One of the first important actions of the occupying American authorities following the surrender of Japan was the drafting of a new constitution for the country in 1946. The new constitution introduced a democratic system of government, which emphasized the rights and dignity of the individual. The role of the Emperor was reduced to that of a constitutional monarch with many ceremonial duties. The Diet (parliament) became the highest decision making body in the country. The judiciary was given independent status from the government, with power to judge the constitutionality of laws. A unique feature of the new constitution was the renunciation of war. Japan was forbidden to station military forces outside the country. The Diet enacted the new constitution as an amendment to the Meiji Constitution.

AP/Wide World Photos

Executive Power

Executive power resides in the Cabinet, which consists of the Prime Minister and ministers.

Emperor. The Emperor is the symbol of the state and of the unity of the people. He is a constitutional monarch, but not a head of state. His duties as monarch and "symbol of the state" include

- opening Parliament
- signing laws
- proclaiming general elections
- performing ceremonial duties
- receiving foreign ambassadors and ministers
- appointing the cabinet on advice of the Prime Minister
- dissolving the House of Representatives.

The current "symbol of the state" is Emperor Akihito. He became Emperor in January 1989 following the death of his father Emperor Hirohito, who ruled from 1926 to 1989. As a constitutional monarch, Akihito is expected to remain politically neutral.

Prime Minister. The constitution stipulates that the Prime Minister is the head of the government. The Prime Minister is chosen by members of the House of Representatives and is responsible to that body for policies and conduct. The Prime Minister can

- appoint and dismiss members of the cabinet
- submit bills to Parliament
- exercise control and supervision over ministries
- manage foreign affairs and conclude treaties
- prepare the budget and submit it to Parliament.

Preamble to 1947 Constitution (Excerpt)

We, the Japanese people, acting through our duly elected representatives in the National Diet, determined that we shall secure for ourselves and our posterity the fruits of peaceful cooperation with all nations and the blessings of liberty without the land, and resolved that never again shall we be visited with the horrors of war through the action of government, do proclaim that sovereign power resides with the people and do firmly establish this Constitution. Government is a sacred trust of the people, the authority for which is derived from the people, the powers of which are exercised by the representatives of the people, and the benefits of which are enjoyed by the people.

Japanese Prime Ministers Since 1945

Shidehara Kijuro	1945–1946	Sato Eisaku	1964–1972	Kaifu Toshiki	1989–1991
Yoshida Shigeru	1946–1947	Tanaka Kakuei	1972–1974	Miyazawa Kiichi	1991–1993
Katayama Tetsu	1947–1948	Miki Takeo	1974–1976	Hosokawa Morihiro	1993–1994
Ashida Hitoshi	1948	Fukuda Takeo	1976–1978	Hata Tsutomu	1994
Yoshida Shigeru	1948–1954	Ohira Masayoshi	1978–1980	Murayama Tomiichi	1994–1996
Hatoyama Ichiro	1954–1956	Suzuki Zenko	1980–1982	Hashimoto Ryutaro	1996–1998
Ishibashi Tanzan	1956–1957	Nakasone Yasuhiro	1982–1987	Obuchi Keizo	1998–
Kishi Nobusuke	1957–1960	Takeshita Noboru	1987–1989		
Ikeda Hayato	1960–1964	Uno Sosuke	1989		

Contemporary Japanese government is divided into three branches—executive, legislative, and judiciary.

LEFT: In Japan, China, Korea, and other Asian countries, family names precede the given name.

Legislative Power

The Diet is composed of two chambers, the upper chamber House of Councillors and the lower chamber House of Representatives.

House of Councillors. The 252-member House of Councillors is elected for six-year terms, with one-half of its members elected every three years. Of the 252 Councillors, 100 are elected by proportional representation from a single nationwide electoral district and 152 are elected in 47 constituencies, each returning 2 to 8 members. Though the House of Councillors can initiate some legislation and consider bills from the House of Representatives, its legislative power is weaker than that of the House of Representatives.

House of Representatives. The House of Representatives has complete authority to choose a Prime Minister, enact legislation, decide the budget, and approve treaties. All members of the House are elected for a term of four years, although the Emperor, acting on the advice of the Prime Minister, can dissolve the House for early general elections. Presently, the House has 500 members, of which 300 are elected in single-member constituencies and 200 chosen by proportional representation.

The leader of the largest political party in the House is generally selected to be the Prime Minister. The Prime Minister and Cabinet must be members of the House and are collectively responsible to it.

They must enjoy the support of the House in order to remain in power. If the Prime Minister and the government are removed from power through a vote of no confidence, leaders of other parties are invited to form a government. From 1993 to 1996, the government was a series of coalitions.

PHOTO: Completed in 1936, the Diet building contains the House of Representatives and House of Councillors.

Courtesy of House of Councillors/The National Diet of Japan

Judicial Power

Under the 1947 Constitution, the Supreme Court is the final court of appeal with the power to determine the constitutionality of any law or official act. Supreme Court justices are appointed by the Prime Minister, subject to acceptance by the House of Representatives. The House can also remove judges by majority vote for unprofessional conduct or involvement in criminal activities.

Policy Making and Legislation

Since 1947 much legislation has been enacted in the Diet. The bureaucracy helps set national policies and influences the decisions of business organizations and other groups.

Policy Making

Policy making in Japan is determined in large measure by the country's large bureaucracy and various powerful interest groups.

Bureaucracy. The Parliament is the highest law making body in Japan, but the bureaucracy, directed by the cabinet, formulates most bills that are submitted to parliament for enactment into law. A bureaucracy of over three million persons has significant influence on national policies.

The powerful ministries are the Ministry of Finance (MOF) and the Ministry of International Trade and Industry (MITI). These ministries maintain close ties with the country's most influential social, business, and professional groups. Many retired ministerial officials have entered politics and business, and influence the workings of political parties and business organizations.

Interest Groups. Interest groups have considerable influence in Japanese politics, especially large business organizations. When the government wants to introduce new bills, it often consults experts in the country's large network of business and professional groups. The most important business lobby group is the Keidanren (Federation of Economic Organizations), whose members have close ties with senior government officials.

Farmers' groups, environmentalists, consumer groups, trade unions, and women's associations are also influential. Most farmers' groups maintain close ties with the Liberal Democratic Party and have considerable influence over agricultural policies. Environmental and consumer groups often appear before parliamentary committees. Trade unions are allied with the Socialist Party (now Social Democratic Party) and the Communist Party.

Legislative Process

Once a bill has been drafted, it begins a lengthy process of passage through the two chambers of the Diet, as in the Canadian parliament. The Prime Minister submits bills to the Diet on behalf of the cabinet. The Speaker then refers the bills to a committee for study. For important bills like the budget, public hearings are held to consider the opinions of interested groups and experts. A committee may amend, shelve, or reject a bill. Once the bill has been studied, it is debated and put to a vote in the House of Representatives. If approved, it is sent to the House of Councillors for debate and approval.

After the House of Councillors approves the bill, it is sent to a joint committee that considers differences of opinion on the bill, a process similar to the conference committee in the American Congress. When a consensus is reached, the bill is sent to the Emperor for his signature and then proclaimed into law.

HOUSE OF REPRESENTATIVES

Introduction

↓

Committee Stage

↓

HOUSE OF COUNCILLORS

↓

Committee Stage

↓

Plenary Debate

↓

Joint Deliberation Committee

↓

Submitted to Emperor

↓

Enactment

↓

LAW

Adapted from *National Diet*. http://www.shugiin.go.jp

Local Government

Japan was and remains a unitary state. The central government has long controlled local government. In 1945, American authorities decentralized local government as part of their policy to democratize the country. Today, local government consists of prefectures and municipalities.

Division of Responsibilities

The division of responsibilities among levels of government is demonstrated in the diagram below. The central government is responsible for finance, national defence, foreign affairs, trade, economic development, education, taxation, labour standards, and social welfare.

Prefectures are one form of regional government in Japan. They are responsible for regional development, roads, bridges, police, and compulsory education standards. Each prefecture has a governor and a legislature elected for a term of four years.

Municipalities are the basic level of local government and closest to the daily lives of Japanese citizens. They are responsible for hospitals, utilities, local taxes, schools, parks, and transportation. Mayors and municipal assemblies are also elected for terms of four years.

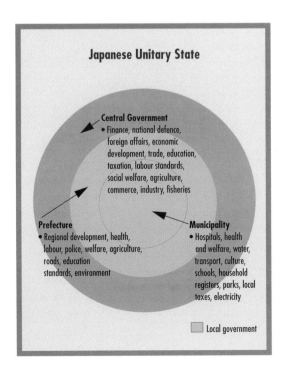

Citizen Participation

In recent years citizens have demanded greater accountability from local government. The Local Autonomy Act of 1947 grants local autonomy to prefectures and municipalities. It has provided citizens with various powers to repeal local laws, dissolve local assemblies, recall elected representatives, dismiss local government officials, and inspect local public finances.

Citizen petitions for the repeal of local laws must be signed by at least 2% of registered voters. Petitions for the dissolution of local assemblies and recall of elected representatives must be signed by at least one-third of an area's registered voters. The matter is then decided by a referendum. Public petitions for recalling elected officials have led in recent years to the resignation of several elected municipal officials.

Japan is not alone in having a mechanism for dismissing elected officials from office. In Canada, British Columbia has legislation to recall an elected Member of the Legislative Assembly (MLA) if at least 40% of registered voters in a provincial riding sign a petition calling for a new election. In April 1998, voters in a Vancouver Island riding submitted a petition to recall their MLA on the grounds that he misled voters. The MLA resigned from his seat two months later.

In Japan, elected local government officials can also be removed through petitions signed by at least one-third of registered voters. Following debate on the petition, the local official is dismissed if three-quarters of the local assembly votes in favour.

Japanese citizens have the right to inspect local public finances. Citizens can file claims in court against local governments. Other channels for citizen participation include public hearings, open sessions of local councils, and the publication of council meetings.

Though Japan is organized as a unitary state, local governments have considerable autonomy. This autonomy is strengthened by direct citizen participation.

Elections and Voting

Unlike their Canadian, American, and Swedish counterparts, Japanese political parties are organized more around personalities and factions, which in the past led to practices such as "pork barrelling" and "money politics."

Japanese political parties are organized more around personalities than is the case in Canada, the United States, and Sweden. Most Japanese political parties consist of factions that come together for reasons of personal loyalty, not necessarily for particular policies. Political parties based on personalities are usually weak and constantly in danger of splitting apart. From 1955 to 1993, the Liberal Democratic Party (LDP) successfully dominated Japanese politics by skilfully combining policies and personal loyalty to the leader.

Electoral Politics

All Japanese citizens who are 20 years and older can vote in general elections.

The political success of the LDP was due in large measure to its system of rewarding factions for supporting the leader. Loyal members were rewarded with well-paid positions in government ministries, big business, or local government. Party members who disagreed with their leader were sometimes forced to resign from the party, but more often they were excluded from powerful party posts and decision making.

Compared to other political parties, the LDP had a well organized and powerful network of financial backers in big business. Before 1995, most constituencies were large and elected more than one member to the National Diet, which required candidates to raise large sums of money (typically US$1–5 million) to win and to hold on to a seat. Because many forms of campaigning in Japan were illegal, including door-to-door canvassing and TV and radio commercials, politicians were compelled to devote considerable time and energy cultivating grass-root support in their ridings by attending weddings, funerals, and New Year's parties or by offering donations and gifts to local institutions. These activities continued year-round, not just during elections.

Candidates for election to the House of Representatives must be at least 25 years old and those for the House of Councillors must be at least 30 years old.

Japanese political commentators noted that these practices gave rise to extensive "pork barrelling" and manipulation of candidate nominations. It was not uncommon for many business firms to endorse candidates and press their employees to vote for the candidate. In exchange for company financial support, the candidate promised to act as the company's representative in getting government contracts. Other forms of "pork barrelling" included allocating government money for roads, bridges, and food subsidies.

All of this led to tight control over the nomination of party candidates. Candidates favoured by party factions were nominated and selected on the basis of past background and loyalty. The result was that many seats became controlled by powerful local families who passed representation of the seat from one generation of family members to another. On election day, voters were reminded to demonstrate their loyalty to the local candidate by electing him or her to represent their interests in the Diet.

In 1992, the power of the LDP was shaken when one party leader admitted to having accepted bribes from big business. In June 1993, several members of the LDP caucus quit to form a new political party, the Renewal Party, which promised to end bribe-taking and corruption in government.

Electoral Reform

In the July 1993 national elections, Japanese voters elected a seven-party coalition to power, ending 38 years of Liberal Democratic Party rule. The most important policy introduced by the new coalition government was a bill which proposed to change the country's electoral system of multi-member constituencies that had been established in 1925. Critics of multi-member constituencies argued that the system emphasized "money politics" and a lack of accountability to the voters.

The new electoral law went into effect in 1995, dividing the country into 300 single member constituencies in which the candidate with the greatest number of votes wins. The new law also created 200 seats elected by proportional representation according to party lists. Each Japanese voter now casts two ballots—one for a candidate in a single member constituency and another for a political party to determine the distribution of seats among parties.

Voting Patterns

The October 1996 general elections were the first held under the new electoral system. Voters returned the Liberal Democratic Party to power with 239 seats, although voter turnout was low (see chart "Japanese Election Results"). The New Frontier Party (renamed the Liberal Party in early 1998) became the country's second largest political party, with 156 seats in the House of Representatives. The Democratic Party, Communist Party, and Social Democrats, (formerly called the Socialist Party) also had members elected to Parliament. Popular support for the Communists rose sharply, while support for the Social Democrats, who for decades had been the country's main opposition party, collapsed (see chart below). An unprecedented 24 women were elected to the House of Representatives. In the July 1998 elections to the House of Councillors, a record 43 women were elected. Voter turnout rose to 58.8%.

AP/Wide World Photos

PHOTO: Since 1990, women have taken an increasing role in Japanese politics, as shown here with the election of Yoko Komiyama of the Democratic Party in the July 1998 elections to the House of Councillors.

Japanese Election Results (1986–1998)

	House of Representatives				House of Councillors				
	1986 Seats	1990 Seats	1993 Seats	1996 Seats	1986 Seats	1989 Seats	1992 Seats	1995 Seats	1998 Seats
Liberal Democratic Party	300	275	223	239	116	109	108	110	103
Social Democratic Party	85	136	70	15	55	66	72	38	13
Communist Party	26	16	15	26	15	14	11	14	23
Democratic Party	–	–	–	52	–	–	–	–	47
Liberal Party[1]	–	–	–	156	–	–	–	56	12
Sakigake Party	–	–	13	2	–	–	–	3	3
Others	100	84	190	1	66	63	61	31	51
	511	511	511	500	252	252	252	252	252
Voter turnout	71.4%	73.3%	67.3%	59.7%	71.4%	65.0%	50.7%	44.5%	58.8%
Women members	10	12	14	24	22	33	37	35	43

[1]Called the New Frontier Party in 1996.

Compiled from *Asian Survey*, various years and *National Diet* http://www.shugiin.go.jp

JAPANESE ECONOMIC SYSTEM

The Japanese economic system is based on private enterprise, with considerable government regulation of the domestic economy to promote exports and high economic growth.

Advance Organizer

The Japanese economic system today is based on private enterprise, with considerable government regulation of the domestic economy. For much of the 20th century, the government has managed the economy through regulations and protective trade measures. Since 1945, government regulation of the economy has been justified as necessary for promoting exports and encouraging the development of competitive industries.

SECTION OVERVIEW
- Economic Policies
- Private Sector
- Public Sector

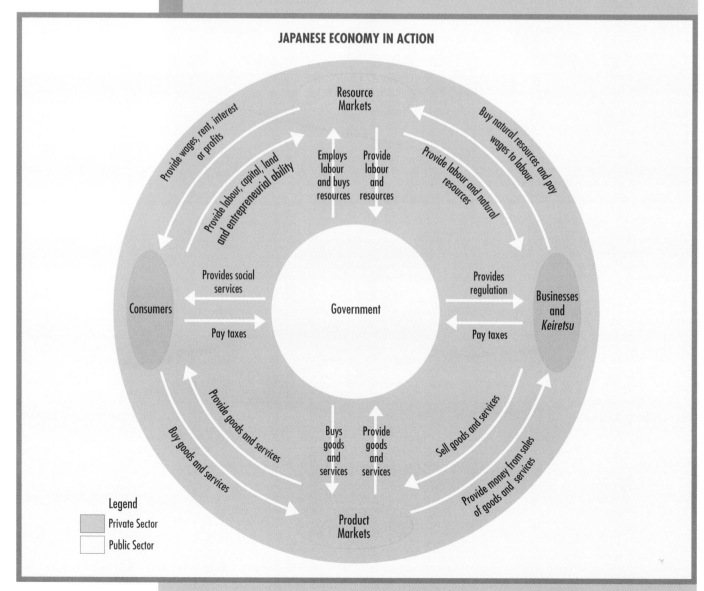

JAPANESE ECONOMY IN ACTION

Resource Markets

Provide wages, rent, interest or profits

Buy natural resources and pay wages to labour

Provide labour, capital, land and entrepreneurial ability

Employs labour and buys resources

Provide labour and resources

Provide labour and natural resources

Provides social services

Provides regulation

Consumers

Government

Businesses and *Keiretsu*

Pay taxes

Pay taxes

Provide goods and services

Sell goods and services

Buy goods and services

Buys goods and services

Provide goods and services

Provide money from sales of goods and services

Product Markets

Legend
- Private Sector
- Public Sector

264

Economic Policies

When Japan surrendered to American forces in August 1945, much of its industrial base lay in ruins. Since 1945, Japanese economic policy has focused on industrial development, exports of manufactured goods, and self-sufficiency in rice production. The main objective of this economic policy was to make Japan into a leading trading and industrial power.

Development of a Regulated Economy (1945–1984)

In the first years after Japan's surrender, the economy faced the problem of reconstruction. Millions of men who were released from the Japanese army could not find work. Much of the housing was in ruins, leaving millions of Japanese homeless. Massive sums of money were needed to rebuild the country's economy and housing stock.

In 1949, American authorities introduced an economic program to encourage the Japanese people to rebuild their own industries. The Japanese economy was reorganized as a private enterprise economy and exposed to international competition.

During the Korean War (1950–1953), Japanese exports and production of goods for American use in Korea greatly expanded. In 1955, the Japanese government introduced the first of several economic plans that emphasized full employment and a steady rise in living standards. These goals were achieved between 1955 and 1973, through a dramatic expansion of the country's industrial base and the promotion of exports. During these years, the Japanese economy became highly regulated.

The sudden rise in oil prices and a worldwide recession in 1973–1974 brought an end to the rapid expansion of the Japanese economy. The higher oil prices increased costs of production and affected the United States, the country's largest export market. The response of the government was to encourage industries to cut their costs and make their production more efficient by adopting less energy intensive methods. Greater emphasis was placed on automation, computerization, and the use of robots in production.

Boom and Speculation (1985–1990)

The government's policy to make Japanese industry more competitive was successful. By 1985, the country was exporting more than it was importing and had large trade surpluses with its main trading partners, especially with the United States. In late 1985, the Japanese government agreed to raise the value of the Japanese yen against the US dollar in order to decrease the country's growing trade surpluses. The value of the yen soared from 260 yen to the dollar in 1985, to 120 yen to the dollar in 1991. Instead of lowering the trade surplus, exports grew. Japanese exporters increased their productivity and efficiency by adopting more technical innovations in their production. Many exporters shifted their production from making basic industrial products like steel and machinery to high technology products such as computer chips, electronic goods, and luxury cars. Others moved their production overseas to the United States, Canada, Southeast Asia, and the European Union to maintain a competitive edge.

Export promotion and high economic growth have been two objectives of Japanese economic policies since 1945.

August 1945	1949	1950–1953	1952	1955	1963	1973–1974	1974–1975	1979–1981
Surrender to American forces; World War II ends in Pacific	American plan for reconstruction of Japanese economy; *zaibatsu* banned	Korean War; Japanese economy expands	*Keiretsu* allowed to form; MITI policy of administrative guidance over the economy begins	First plan for economy unveiled; promotion of exports stressed	Law for Welfare for the Aged passed; personal responsibility for care of older family members	First world oil price rise	First major postwar recession in Japan	Second world oil price rise

1985
Japan allows value of yen to rise to reduce trade surpluses

1987–1989
Speculation; stock market and real estate boom

December 1989
Record trading at Tokyo Stock Exchange

Development of a Regulated Economy 1945–1984

Boom and Speculation 1985–1990

Note: Timeline is not to scale

As Japanese companies improved their competitiveness, the government in 1986 lowered interest rates. This encouraged the country's major banks to increase lending for investment in the stock market and land. As prices of shares on the stock market rose, many companies issued new shares to meet the demand, while other companies borrowed against their real estate and invested the loans in the stock market. The banks increased their lending to real estate companies in the belief that land prices would continue to rise in the future. The stock market boom generated huge profits for the banks and permitted them to increase lending. Between May 1986 and December 1989, land prices doubled and the Tokyo Nikkei stock market index rose almost 300%. Japanese began to call their economy a "bubble economy."

In early 1989, the government began to raise interest rates, which touched off a collapse in stock prices. By the end of 1990, the Tokyo stock market had fallen 38% from its peak on December 29, 1989, wiping out 300 trillion yen (US$2.3 trillion) in value. The stock market decline forced several major firms into bankruptcy. The "bubble" had popped.

Slump and Deregulation (since 1991)

In the early 1990s, the stock market decline began to affect land prices. Several banks failed when borrowers could not repay their loans. This provoked a crisis in consumer confidence and consumers decreased their spending. In 1992–1995, the economy went into a steep recession (see chart below). In 1993, the government increased spending to raise economic growth, but this policy failed to lift the economy out of its recession or improve profits for the country's major banks.

As the economy struggled with recession and financial problems, the United States, the European Union, and various Japanese business groups began to express concern about excessive government regulation of the economy. In 1997–1998, the government introduced numerous plans to deregulate and improve the economy.

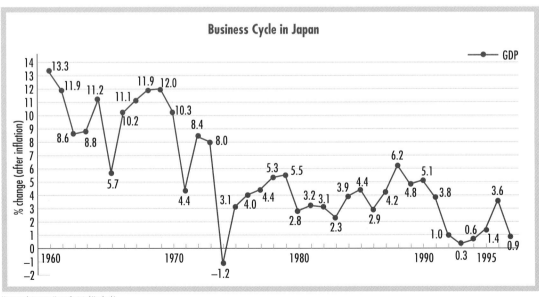

Business Cycle in Japan

— GDP

% change (after inflation)

13.3, 11.9, 11.2, 11.1, 11.9, 12.0, 10.2, 10.3, 8.6, 8.8, 5.7, 8.4, 8.0, 4.4, 3.1, 4.0, 4.4, 5.3, 5.5, 2.8, 3.2, 3.1, 2.3, 3.9, 4.4, 2.9, 6.2, 4.2, 4.8, 5.1, 3.8, 1.0, 0.3, 0.6, 1.4, 3.6, 0.9, −1.2

1960   1970   1980   1990   1995

Nippon toukei nenran (Japan Statistical Yearbook)

1991
Economic recession begins; shares and real estate fall sharply

1993
Coalition government pledges to revitalize economy

1997
Plans to deregulate economy and increase economic growth; ban on *zaibatsu* removed; several banks and brokerage companies fail

1998
Parliament passes bill to close bankrupt banks and protect savings

Private Sector

Japan's postwar economic reconstruction and its rapid growth from 1955 to 1990 were the result of many factors: government policies promoted rapid economic growth, Japanese big business was very powerful, and international economic conditions were favourable. All these factors allowed Japan to increase its exports.

Domestic Economy

As in Canada, the United States, Sweden, and other countries with market economies, in the Japanese economy consumers and businesses are the main decision makers.

Consumers. As shown in the graphs of total domestic spending and income, consumer sovereignty is the main form of decision making in the Japanese economy. Purchases of goods and services by businesses account for about 30% of all spending in the economy. Government purchases are much smaller, less than 10%. Wages and salaries are the main source of domestic income, accounting for over 72% of total income earned in Japan. Other types of domestic income are from self-employment (11.1%), interest and investment (8.5%), and business profits (7.5%).

Businesses. In 1997, there were 6.6 million private business enterprises in Japan. As in Canada, Japanese businesses are organized as sole proprietorships, corporations, or partnerships.

Most Japanese sole proprietorships are small and family-owned. There are over 3.7 million sole proprietorships in Japan, most of which employ fewer than 50 workers. About 20% of the Japanese labour force is employed in family-owned businesses. These small businesses are common in retail trade, food services, transport, and general services.

Japanese corporations vary greatly in size, from those that employ one or two workers to giant companies that employ over 100 000 people. The overwhelming majority of the estimated 2.5 million Japanese corporations employ fewer than 100 workers each. Only about 50 000 corporations are classified as big businesses, with an average work force of 260 people. Corporations are the most common form of business enterprise in manufacturing, construction, finance, and real estate. These industries require the large amounts of capital and access to bank credit that are more easily obtained by corporations. About 1700 Japanese corporations have their shares listed on the Tokyo Stock Exchange, the country's largest stock exchange.

As in Canada, partnerships are not a common form of business organization. There are an estimated 400 000 partnerships. They are common in specialized services such as accounting, medicine, advertising, and law.

Corporate Japan

Big business in Japan is organized differently from big business in Canada, the United States, and Sweden. Japan has a unique type of big business called the *keiretsu*, which is a large group composed of several different companies.

The chart "Japan's Top Companies" (see page 268) shows several interesting features of Japanese big business. The first is the importance of the trading company. Many Japanese manufacturing companies rely on trading companies to sell their output. The five largest companies listed are trading companies. They not only buy and sell goods, but also participate in overseas investments, negotiate with other firms, and advise companies in the *keiretsu* about new markets.

A second feature of big business is that most of Japan's largest industrial companies, such as Toyota, Mitsui, Mitsubishi, Sumitomo, Matsushita, Marubeni, and Hitachi, belong to *keiretsu*. Even independent companies like Sony and Honda Motors maintain ties with companies belonging to *keiretsu*. These large business groups also have close ties with bureaucrats and politicians who advise them on government policies.

The financial power of *keiretsu* is clearly seen in the size of the country's largest banks (see chart "Japan's Top Banks"). Collectively, these banks are an

TOTAL DOMESTIC SPENDING

1997

- ☐ Personal 58.8%
- ☐ Government 9.1%
- ☐ Business 30.4%
- ☐ Foreign trade 1.7%

TOTAL DOMESTIC INCOME

1997

- ☐ Wages and salaries 72.0%
- ☐ Business profits 7.5%
- ☐ Interest and investment 8.5%
- ☐ Self-employment 11.1%
- ☐ Farming income 0.9%

Nippon toukei nenan (Japan Statistical Yearbook)

immense source of capital for the *keiretsu*, possessing assets totalling US$4.08 trillion. They control a large share of domestic savings, though many Japanese savers prefer to deposit their savings in the government-owned postal savings offices. In spite of their great financial power, Japan's top banks in March 1998 lost collectively over US$13.8 billion, the result of writing off billions of dollars of loans held by bankrupt companies and speculation in real estate in the 1980s. Recent projections show they will be profitable again.

Japan's Top Companies (March 1998)
(in millions of US$)

	Industry	Sales	Profits	Employees
Mitsui & Company	Trading	$142 688.3	$268.7	40 000
Mitsubishi Corporation	Trading	128 922.3	388.1	36 000
Itochu Corporation	Trading	126 631.9	(773.9)	6675
Marubeni Corporation	Trading	111 121.2	140.4	64 000
Sumitomo Corporation	Trading	102 395.2	209.8	29 500
Toyota Motor Corporation	Automobiles	97 137.0	3701.3	159 035
Nissho Iwai Corporation	Trading	81 893.8	24.7	18 158
Nippon Telegraph	Telephones	76 983.7	2361.3	226 000
Hitachi	Electronics	68 567.0	28.3	331 494
Matsushita Electric	Electronics	64 280.6	762.5	275 962
Sony Corporation	Electronics	55 033.0	1809.1	173 000
Nissan Motor	Automobiles	53 478.2	(114.1)	137 201
Honda Motor	Automobiles	48 876.3	2123.2	109 400
Toshiba Corporation	Electronics	44 467.2	59.8	186 000
Tomen Corporation	Trading	43 399.7	(179.1)	10 920

Japan's Top Banks (March 1998)
(in millions of US$)

	Assets	Sales	Profits	Employees
Bank of Tokyo-Mitsubishi	$690 461.7	$34 749.8	$(4271.6)	18 386
Sumitomo Bank	482 797.2	21 007.9	(2047.2)	15 111
Dai-Ichi Kangyo Bank	432 189.5	19 712.7	(586.7)	16 965
Sanwa Bank	427 077.4	22 805.5	(1485.6)	19 745
Fuji Bank	413 296.2	22 912.0	(2813.0)	14 615
Sakura Bank	398 649.3	21 292.3	(719.3)	17 420
Norinchukin Bank	391 726.0	14 582.6	1092.0	3 000
Industrial Bank of Japan	369 174.2	26 917.8	(1651.0)	4 971
Tokai Bank	261 870.5	12 103.8	116.1	11 407
Asahi Bank	212 714.0	8 292.0	(1500.0)	12 700

Losses appear in brackets.

Compiled from *Fortune*, August 3, 1998, and *Forbes*, July 27, 1998

Zaibatsu. Before World War II, large business groups called *zaibatsu* owned by wealthy families played a dominant role in industrializing Japan. Some, such as Mitsui and Sumitomo, were founded in the 16th and 17th centuries, while others like Mitsubishi were founded in the 19th century. Most expanded into industry, trading, and banking in the 1920s. The major *zaibatsu* of those years were Mitsui, Mitsubishi, Sumitomo, and Yasuda. In key industries like steelmaking, heavy machinery, mining, and cement, the *zaibatsu* established large-scale factories, used modern technology, and employed thousands of workers.

By 1929, the *zaibatsu* reached the height of their power and influence. They controlled about a quarter of all domestic industrial production. Their influence in politics was enhanced by financial contributions to the main political parties. Mitsui and Mitsubishi, the two largest *zaibatsu*, actively used financial contributions to get officials to change government economic policy.

In the 1930s, the *zaibatsu* aligned themselves with various factions in the military, with the view of becoming military suppliers. As well, they became strong supporters of military expansion into China and Southeast Asia as a means of acquiring new markets for their goods and sources of raw materials for production.

Keiretsu. Under American occupation (1945–1952), the family-owned *zaibatsu* were broken up into smaller companies to encourage competition and prevent monopolies. The *zaibatsu* were forbidden by a 1949 law from reestablishing themselves. However, after 1952 many companies that once belonged to the *zaibatsu* reunited to form *keiretsu*. The main difference lay in the fact that *keiretsu* were not owned or controlled by families but by individual shareholders and other investors.

A *keiretsu* generally includes a bank, manufacturing companies, and a general trading company (see chart below). Within the *keiretsu* these companies are linked together directly through the ownership of shares or indirectly by informal agreements to form a web of interests. The bank lends money at low interest rates set by the government to the manfacturing company and trading company. The manufacturing company uses the money to buy raw materials and equipment, and pay workers. The trading company borrows from the bank to buy the manufacturing company's production for sale locally or abroad.

Keiretsu companies share information about products, demand and supply, research and product development, and government guidelines. Decision making is conducted through regular meetings of top management (presidents' club) and generally based on achieving a consensus of opinion and commitment to long-range plans. Though this process requires considerable time and discussion before all decision makers agree on shared goals and objectives, once decisions are made they are implemented without question.

Reestablishing the *Zaibatsu*. In 1997, the government announced that it would lift the official ban on the *zaibatsu*. The government hopes that the reestablishment of the *zaibatsu*, with its concentration of ownership, will force businesses to be more accountable to shareholders. In the *keiretsu*, even large shareholders could not successfully demand that directors be accountable for their decisions. Often directors invested company funds in risky ventures that did not improve profits of the whole business group.

The origin of many present-day Japanese *keiretsu* is the prewar *zaibatsu*, family-owned industrial and financial business groups that dominated the Japanese economy between 1912 and 1941.

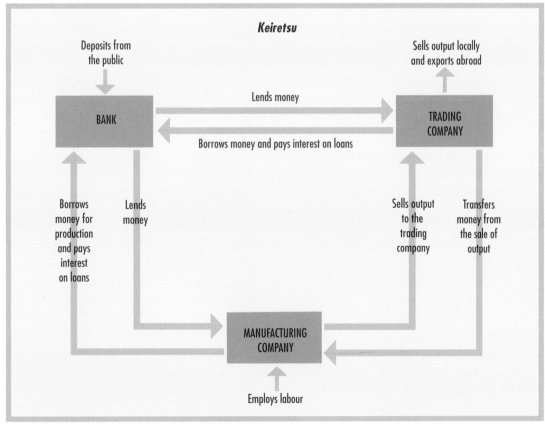

Adapted from Kenichi Miyashita and David W. Russell. *Keiretsu: Inside the Hidden Japanese Conglomerates.*

Toyota Keiretsu

Toyota is the largest automobile manufacturer and most powerful *keiretsu* in Japan, after Mitsui, Mitsubishi, Itochu, Marubeni, and Sumitomo (see chart on page 268). In 1997, Toyota had sales of US$112.6 billion and earned profits of more than US$3.5 billion, making it one of the most profitable *keiretsu*.

The original Toyota company was the textile company, Toyoda Automatic Loom Works, located in Toyota City, midway between Tokyo and Osaka. Today, this company makes engines and is one of 12 directly controlled group companies. Others produce electronic components, automotive parts, and materials (see chart).

Besides the directly controlled companies, several companies operate as suppliers to Toyota of automotive parts, equipment, and materials. Most of these companies are located close to Toyota's main automotive assembly plants and work closely with the company, using its internationally known "just-in-time" production methods.

The basic idea behind Toyota's "just-in-time" production is that car plants should not keep unnecessary supplies of parts and materials. The company plans the production of its *keiretsu* companies so that they supply parts and materials only when they are needed in production.

Toyota first applied its "just-in-time" production method in 1963, after studying how American supermarket chains were able to distribute their goods efficiently and profitably. "Just-in-time" production

methods require close links and cooperation between suppliers and manufacturers. This has forced affiliated companies in the *keiretsu* to reduce production costs. "Just-in-time" production methods have made it possible for Toyota to produce high quality cars at low prices.

Toyota's success in selling cars abroad has often singled it out for criticism from non-Japanese car makers. They claim that the *keiretsu* system of close management and production ties

among companies protects Toyota from foreign competition. Non-Japanese car makers argue that these practices make it expensive and unprofitable for foreign businesses to start up operations in Japan.

Since the mid-1980s, Toyota has expanded its operations worldwide. Today, the company is the third largest producer of cars, trucks, and vans in the world.

ORGANIZATIONAL CHART OF TOYOTA MOTOR CORPORATION

Directly Controlled Companies

Toyota Central R & D Laboratories — R & D	Kanto Auto Works — Car assembly	Toyota Auto Body — Car assembly	Toyoda Machine Works — Machine tools
Toyoda Automatic Loom Works — Engines	Aichi Steel Works — Special steels	Toyoda Gosei — Resin, rubber parts	Toyoda Boshoku — Air Filters
Toyota Tsusho Corp. — Wholesaler	Towa Real Estate — Real estate	Nippondenso — Electronics	Aisin Seiki — Parts

Koito Manufacturing — Lighting

Shiroki Corporation — Interior components

Independent group

- Nippon Wiperblade
- Tsuda Industries
- Anjo Denki
- Asmo

- Aisin-AW
- Aichi Giken
- Aisin Takaoka

Company Suppliers

		Chuo Spring — Suspensions	Maruyasu Inds. — Rubber parts	
Owari Precise Prods. — Parts	Taiho Kogyo — Metal	Horie Metal — Fuel parts	Araco Corporation — Car assembly	
Tokai Rika — Switches	Aisan Ind. — Fuel injectors	Futaba Industrial — Silencers	Kyowa Leather Cloth — Upholstery	Trinity Industrial — Paint equipment
JECO — Clocks	Koyo Seiko — Bearings	Tokyo Sintered Metal — Metal parts	Kyoho Mach. Wks. — Pressed parts	Chuo Malleable Iron — Metal parts

Adapted from *Charting Japanese Industry* by Tomokazu Ohsono. London: Cassell, 1995, p.18

Inside the *Keiretsu*

Since the late 1950s, the *keiretsu* have enjoyed significant economic power and have influenced the working and living conditions of millions of Japanese workers. The corporate power and influence of Japanese big business exceed anything large companies have in Canada and other industrial countries.

Labour Relations. The *keiretsu* employ about 25% of the Japanese labour force, while government employs about 15% and small businesses 60% of all workers. A distinguishing feature of the *keiretsu* has been the use of lifetime employment, seniority-based wages, and company unions to promote worker loyalty and to reward hard work. This gave rise to a type of worker whose identity was strongly connected with that of the company.

This system of relations between employee and employer appeared after World War II when the economy was growing rapidly and profits were rising. Large companies introduced lifetime employment and seniority-based wages to obtain a supply of skilled workers and to protect the company's investment in training workers. At graduation from university, students were hired by large companies and trained for a few years. The employee was expected to work long hours, including voluntary overtime without pay. Initially, wages were low, but in recognition of long-term loyalty and performance wages increased until retirement at age 55. Most smaller companies could not afford to offer the same benefits.

Since the early 1990s, economic recession and industrial restructuring have prompted the *keiretsu* to rethink lifetime employment and seniority-based wages. Many large companies are laying off older workers or transferring them to subsidiaries. Wage levels based on length of employment are changing because of a growing shortage of labour. It is becoming more common for younger workers at smaller companies to be paid more than their counterparts in larger companies. Younger workers are leaving larger companies to work in smaller companies where personal initiative receives greater recognition.

Another aspect of labour–management relations in Japan is the presence of company unions. In Canada, the United States, and elsewhere, labour unions are organized according to occupation and have members in many different companies. In Japan, most labour unions are organized within the company. Regardless of their occupation, all employees belong to the same union. This has strengthened company loyalty among employees.

Company loyalty and commitment are also expressed by reciting company rules or singing the company song. This encourages employees to work together and strengthens group identity. Becoming a member of such an organization may provide for benefits such as a person's wedding, his or her children's schooling and job hunting, and family funerals.

Diego Goldberg/SYGMA

PHOTO: Company loyalty and commitment are expressed by morning exercises, reciting company rules or singing the company song.

Company Benefits. The *keiretsu* provide their workers with many benefits. These are used to reward loyalty and compensate workers in part for the high cost of living. Company benefits include housing allowances, retirement allowances, and employment security.

The cost of owning a house is very high in Japan. The average price is several times higher than in Canada. Yet more than 60% of all Japanese families own a house,

JAPANESE WOMEN AT WORK

1997

Nippon toukei nenrian (Japan Statistical Yearbook)

By occupation:
- Professional 13.5%
- Managerial 0.8%
- Clerical 29.3%
- Sales 13.4%
- Service 12.9%
- Agricultural 6.1%
- Industrial 17.8%
- Labourers 5.3%
- Other 0.9%

The average unemployment rate among Japanese youth aged 15–24 years exceeded 10.1% in 1997.

making Japan second only to the United States in the rate of house ownership. Workers of *keiretsu* companies receive a housing allowance and low interest loans to buy a house. Workers in smaller companies can qualify for special government allowances to buy a house. The typical Japanese house is small by North American standards and located far from the city centre, where land prices are lower. Japanese workers spend on average two to three hours a day travelling to and from work.

Until recently, workers did not receive company pensions at retirement (usually at 55). Instead, they received a retirement allowance equalling two to four years' income, based on years of employment and the size of the company. In many cases, the retirement allowance was sufficient to start a small business, buy a farm or house, or pay off debts. Because government pensions begin at age 65, most retired people must work after age 55, and many even after age 65. Government pensions are low and do not provide enough to pay for living costs, thus many Japanese families need to save large sums for retirement.

Unlike in Canada, people in Japan do not change jobs very often. Companies usually do not hire workers who quit a job at another company, because this indicates that the worker is disloyal and unreliable. Before 1990, the trend was for workers to stay with their employers until retirement at age 55. If a company went bankrupt, the government tried to find another company to take the firm over and restore it to profitability, saving workers from becoming unemployed.

Since the early 1990s, poor economic conditions have created many bankruptcies and large lay-offs of workers. However, many *keiretsu* companies still prefer not to lay workers off, keeping the surplus workers on the payroll even though they may do very little work. There are an estimated three to four million surplus workers, or what the Japanese call the "tribe by the window." Smaller companies cannot afford to keep surplus workers when the economy is poor.

Despite the constitutional guarantee of equality of employment, wages, and promotion opportunities, Japanese women have lagged behind their male counterparts in these areas. Many *keiretsu* companies have employed women in clerical, sales, and service jobs that require little training, and expected their female workers to leave the labour force once they were married and raising children. Women returning to work have been paid less and often offered only part-time employment. Consequently, women have had few opportunities for promotion.

The chart "Japanese Women at Work" shows that few women held managerial positions in 1997, but this situation is changing rapidly. Changing social conditions, a weak economy, and rapid aging of the population are forcing many *keiretsu* companies to change their traditional views that women should devote themselves to the home after marriage. Young Japanese women today are more interested in pursuing careers than in becoming housewives. Many have university or technical education. Increased competition and low profits resulting from a weak domestic economy are making companies realize the contribution women employees can make to increasing profits. The aging population has important consequences for many *keiretsu* companies. Companies now realize that the number of young people entering the labour force is smaller than older workers leaving the labour force because of retirement. This means that companies must consider young women for long-term employment to replace the large numbers retiring, to avoid future labour shortages.

Taken together, these factors largely explain the low unemployment rate in Japan, which in 1998 averaged 4.0% compared to 8.7% in Canada. The low unemployment rate hides the fact that large numbers of discouraged workers, mostly women, have left the labour force.

Critique of the *Keiretsu*

The original purpose of the *keiretsu* was to mobilize resources for rapid industrial development. In less than three decades, the *keiretsu* turned Japan into a global industrial power, and raised living standards of ordinary Japanese to among the highest in the world. However, the question remains whether the *keiretsu* are efficient forms of business for streamlining the Japanese economy.

Advantages

1 Stable corporate performance. Member firms of the *keiretsu* help one another in times of serious business hardship. When a member company encounters financial difficulties, it can be assured of financial and sometimes managerial assistance from other member companies. This prevents large lay-offs and numerous bankruptcies.

2 Long-term contracting. Long-term contracting between suppliers and manufacturers lowers production costs, improves product quality, and provides management of member firms with greater flexibility to adjust production when demand changes.

3 Cooperative research. Member firms of the *keiretsu* work together to share the costs of research and to carry out the development of technology. Member firms are then encouraged to compete with each other to create innovations using the new technology.

Disadvantages

1 Concentration of power. By their nature the *keiretsu* encourage concentration of economic power in the hands of a few. Most firms join the *keiretsu* because together they have greater economic strength and a greater ability to influence government economic policies. Over the years, many *keiretsu* have used their influence to convince government bureaucrats of the need for regulations and measures that protect them from foreign competition in the domestic market.

2 Inflexible management. Because many corporate decisions are made by consensus, managerial decision making tends to be slow and cumbersome. However, once a decision is made, all concerned are expected to carry it out without question. This poses problems when unfavourable economic conditions demand quick decisions on changes in production costs and methods.

3 Technology and production driven. Most *keiretsu* companies devote considerable resources to research and development, especially in technical design and innovation. This has enabled them to become major producers and exporters of consumer electronics, automobiles, and computer hardware, but has not led to much success in areas where creativity and decentralized decision making are necessary, such as information technology, telecommunications, and aerospace.

PHOTO: *Keiretsu* companies have long valued technological innovation and developed new technologies such as DVD (digital video disc) recording systems.

AP/Wide World Photos

Public Sector

There is significant government participation in the Japanese economy. Bureaucrats in the trade and finance ministries set economic policy and develop regulations for economic growth. Business is expected to cooperate. In social policy, the government enacts laws to reinforce cultural values about family responsibilities and self-reliance.

Regulation

The Japanese government uses regulation to influence the direction of the economy. The ministries charged with regulating business are the Ministry of International Trade and Industry (MITI) and the Ministry of Finance (MOF).

Ministry of International Trade and Industry. In 1952, MITI began to use a policy of administrative guidance to encourage textile firms to become more innovative and competitive. Over time, the temporary regulation of the textile industry became a model for regulation of other industries.

In the late 1950s and early 1960s, MITI introduced policies to protect certain industries to enable them to build up their international competitiveness. Steel, shipbuilding, petrochemicals, and machinery were designated as industries for expansion. In the 1970s, automobiles, tires, electronics, and precision instruments were added to this list. These industries were protected from foreign competition by tariffs and other means. In exchange for this protection, firms were forced to comply with MITI instructions on product standards and investment. Firms under MITI guidance received low-cost loans and favourable tax treatment on profits. When a firm overexpanded production and encountered some financial difficulty, it received temporary financial assistance from MITI.

Administrative guidance by MITI was accompanied by economic forecasts on the overall economy. These forecasts were drawn up to provide information on economic trends and guidelines for business. Business used the forecasts to identify areas for future growth. In the 1980s, firms began to rely more on their own sources of information.

Ministry of Finance. The Ministry of Finance (MOF) policies kept corporate taxes low, expanded government spending on ports and transportation, and promoted exports. The major concerns of the MOF were to ensure a balanced budget and a stable exchange rate for the yen. The Ministry fixed interest rates and ordered banks to provide low-cost loans for business investment to industries under MITI guidance. In more recent years, fiscal policy has been geared to stimulating the economy by running large budget deficits.

Results of Regulation. Overall, these measures have brought great prosperity, but they have also made Japan a very expensive place for ordinary people to live. Laws that promote self-sufficiency in rice by restricting imports of cheaper foreign rice also restrict the construction of housing on farmland. This makes land and house prices, as well as prices for rice and other basic foods, very high because demand is always greater than supply. Other laws restrict business activity and raise the cost of domestically produced consumer goods.

PHOTO: Since the late 1950s, Japanese government policy has focussed on promoting exports and protecting some domestic industries from foreign competition.

Phyllis A. Arnold

Social Services

Government social services are organized to reinforce the obligations of family members as caregivers. Social services such as home health care, lunch services, and nursing care are generally provided for elderly people who are deemed needy because of low income, disability, or lack of close family members.

Public Assistance. The Daily Life Security Law demands that those who apply for public assistance programs must first exhaust their personal resources, including family resources and personal savings, before they can be considered eligible. This explains in part why the Japanese are some of the world's largest savers.

Another condition of the Law requires family members to care for their parents and close family relations. The Law declares that family members have a financial and moral responsibility to support older family relatives and maintain family ties. By stressing the importance of family responsibility for, and obligation to, its own members, the government is able to keep its spending on social services at a much lower level than other industrial countries, such as Canada, the United States, and Sweden.

Social policy for the aged is similarly guided by expectations about family obligations and responsibility. For example, the following excerpt from the Law for Welfare for the Aged written in 1963 expresses the expectation that the elderly will modify their behaviour in ways appropriate to their age:

The aged shall be loved and respected as those who have for many years contributed toward the development of society and a wholesome and peaceful life shall be guaranteed to them.

The aged shall be conscious of their mental and physical changes due to aging, and shall always endeavour to maintain their mental and physical health to participate in society with their knowledge and experience. In accordance with their desire and ability, the aged shall be given opportunities to engage in suitable work or to participate in social activities.

In early 1997, legislation was introduced to establish a compulsory universal nursing care insurance program. The initial annual premium for the program was set at 30 000 yen (US$220), but the program was to be limited only to those who had no family members to care for them.

In late 1998, the government announced that it would increase spending on the care of elderly people. However, a shortage of suitable locations for nursing and retirement homes hinders the construction of more facilities for the country's growing numbers of retired people. For most Japanese families, there are presently few nursing homes which can provide reasonably priced accommodation for elderly people with special needs.

Aging Population. In the 21st century, some economists argue, the government will be compelled to reconsider its past emphasis on making families responsible for the care of elderly members. Demographers estimate that by the year 2020 over 26% of the country's population will be over 65 years of age, which could become a serious financial drain on the country's resources. The number of workers supporting each retired person, demographers predict, will fall from 4.5 workers in 1996 to 2.2 by 2020.

Phyllis A. Arnold

In 1996 the number of people aged 65 years and older exceeded the number of people aged 14 years and younger.

PHOTO: The effects of aging of the country's population are expected to be felt most strongly in rural areas.

JAPANESE POLITICAL ECONOMY

Advance Organizer

Since the early 1950s, Japanese society has focussed almost exclusively on making their country a global economic power. Policy making was concentrated in the hands of three groups, big business (*keiretsu*), the bureaucracy, and the government, what the Japanese call the "iron triangle." In the 1990s, corruption scandals, bank failures, and huge government budget deficits threatened the authority of the iron triangle. These events have stimulated discussion in Japan on the need for deregulation of business, greater accountability of politicians and bureaucrats to the people, and more open trading practices with other nations. This has also meant a reexamination of Japanese values and how Japanese society should respond to the challenges of the 21st century.

SECTION OVERVIEW
• Growth of Government
• The Iron Triangle
• Trade and Deregulation

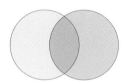

Japanese Political System
Japanese Economic System
Japanese Political Economy

Growth of Government

The chart "Growth of Japanese Government" illustrates clearly the rapid growth in the size of all levels of government in Japan from 1960 to 1997. In 1960, total government revenue as a percentage of Gross Domestic Product (GDP) was 18.8%, while spending by all levels of government accounted for 17.5% of GDP. The government had a small surplus. In 1960, the country had one of the lowest levels of public debt among industrial countries. For the next 30 years,

up to 1990, government revenues and spending grew more rapidly than the economy. Public debt also grew, but growth slowed in the 1980s. After 1990, all levels of government increased spending on housing and public works projects to stimulate a weak economy. These efforts have not been very successful. Instead, the increased government spending led to growing budget deficits and an exploding public debt. In 1997, the budget deficit was 5.0% of the GDP, the largest among major industrial countries. Public debt reached 95.7% of the GDP.

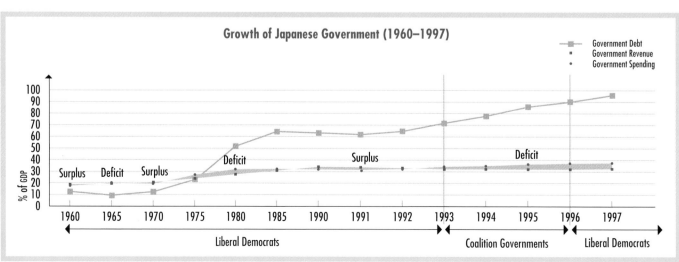

Growth of Japanese Government (1960–1997)

Nippon toukei nenran (Japan Statistical Yearbook)

276

Government Spending

In the 1990s, the Japanese economy entered a period of weak growth. The response of the government to the weak economy was to increase its spending on public works projects to stimulate the economy.

In August 1992, the Liberal Democratic government announced the first of several government spending programs to stimulate the economy and increase consumer spending. Most of the government spending was slated for new housing and roads. The spending package failed to revive the economy and restore consumer confidence.

In 1993, the Liberal Democratic government was replaced by a coalition government. One of the first measures the new government introduced was a massive program of new spending and some tax cuts to stabilize the economy. Two years later, the coalition government introduced another economic stimulus package which, like previous ones, failed to revive the economy and consumer confidence.

When the Liberal Democrats returned to power in 1996, they increased government spending to spur economic recovery and revive public confidence in the economy. Consumers and businesses, however, continued to be pessimistic about the economy. The results of the various government spending programs undertaken to stabilize the economy were deepening the budget deficit and public debt grew rapidly.

The chart "Growth of Japanese Government" on page 276 shows that the debt of all levels of government in Japan grew from 63.2% of GDP in 1990 to 95.7% of GDP in 1997. The level of public debt as a percentage of GDP in Japan in 1997 was higher than that in the United States and Sweden, and almost the same as that in Canada (see chart below).

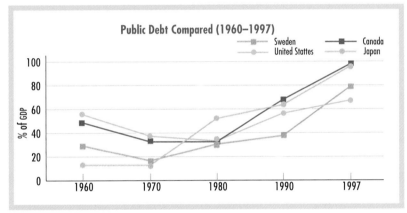

Public Debt Compared (1960–1997)

Sweden · Canada · United Stattes · Japan

% of GDP

Compiled from Organization for Economic Cooperation and Development.

ついうまうまと入った道は〝実刑〟行き止まりの袋小路だった　　山田　紳

Asahi Shimbun 1997.10.2 Yamada Shin

Glen BonBernard

LEFT: "Guilty—The road which was embarked upon confidently and without a thought has turned out to be a dead end alley named 'Conviction.'" [translated by Sinh Vinh]

PHOTO: To spur economic growth, the Japanese government in the 1990s increased public spending on roads, railroads, and housing.

The Iron Triangle

At the same time as the government tried to stimulate the economy by spending on public works, the Japanese public began to lose confidence in their government and the business elites. For decades, the public had had high respect for the ability of the bureaucracy, the *keiretsu*, and the government to lead the country. They considered their bureaucrats to be the best and brightest minds in the country. The *keiretsu* were admired for transforming Japan into a global industrial power and raising people's living standards. The government led by the Liberal Democratic Party was respected for its sensible and forward-looking leadership.

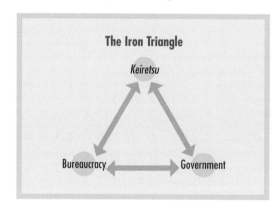

The Iron Triangle

Keiretsu

Bureaucracy

Government

Conflicts of Interest

The first cracks in the public's respect for the iron triangle appeared in the late 1980s, when the country's media revealed that many government politicians were receiving bribes from big business. It was also revealed that bribe taking and other illegal activities were common among top leaders in the bureaucracy and *keiretsu*.

Further disclosures by the press in the early 1990s made it clear to the public that some top politicians, bureaucrats, and business leaders had been working together with no regard for the needs of the people. It was reported that several politicians received campaign funds from big business in exchange for favours such as government contracts. Several big business leaders were reported by the media to have bribed top bureaucrats to change regulations or introduce new ones to protect them from competition. Many top bureaucrats were given comfortable jobs in business after retirement so that they could continue to influence regulations and laws in favour of big business.

The extent of these close relationships was revealed when the government announced in early 1996 that it would spend 685 billion yen (US$5.7 billion) to close the country's bankrupt mortgage companies. The Ministry of Finance was accused of negligence for allowing these companies to continue their lending to real estate companies long after other financial institutions had been ordered to reduce their lending.

Bank Failures

On November 18, 1997, the country's tenth largest bank, the Hokkaido Takushoku Bank, failed. One week later, the fourth largest brokerage firm, Yamaichi Securities, went bankrupt. The reason cited for these spectacular financial failures was the sharp decline in the value of the Tokyo Stock Exchange, which had witnessed a tremendous boom in stock prices in the 1980s.

Another reason cited by many economists was the lax regulation of the country's banking system. For years government policy had encouraged banks to lend money to industry at low interest rates. In exchange for this, the banks were protected from foreign competition and given favourable tax rates. Regulators in the Ministry of International Trade and Industry (MITI) and Ministry of Finance (MOF) also allowed banks to own shares in business firms, creating a conflict of interest between banks and their borrowers. Several financial analysts estimated in 1997 that 45% of all shares of Japanese companies listed on the Tokyo Stock Exchange were held by banks and *keiretsu* companies.

During the 1980s, the banks made loans worth billions of dollars to construction companies and real estate firms on the assumption that land and property prices would rise indefinitely. The banks did not anticipate that real estate prices would suddenly level out, then decline more than 70% by 1997. Many Japanese also believed that the rise in property values would make them rich and provide them with financial security in their retirement.

Government regulators did not believe that such an event could bankrupt the country's powerful banking sector. When it became apparent that the banks' loans to real estate companies would never be repaid, the regulators did not force the banks to write off the bad loans. In January 1998, under public pressure, the Ministry of Finance disclosed that bad loans at Japan's banks totalled 76.7 trillion yen (US$595 billion).

Just as the country's banks were beginning to write off their large bad loans, a new crisis threatened the Japanese banking sector. In late 1997, a financial crisis shook South Korea, Thailand, and Indonesia. From the early 1980s to the mid-1990s, the economies of these countries had grown rapidly and attracted investors, giving high rates of return on investment capital. All major Japanese banks had loaned money for investment in factories, office buildings, and mines in the region. Many loans were made on the assumption that high economic growth in South Korea and Southeast Asia would continue for several more years. In 1998, borrowers in these countries began to default on their loans, estimated by some financial analysts at 25 trillion yen (US$195 billion), from Japanese banks.

Japanese savers reacted to this news by transferring their savings to the government-owned postal savings bank and the country's largest banks, assuming they were safer. In early 1998, the government proposed a rescue package worth US$325 billion for the country's largest banks and a reform of banking laws that would allow foreign banks to offer savings accounts to the public.

In October 1998, after heated debate, the parliament passed a government bill to rescue the country's largest banks from financial collapse. The bill offered 60 trillion yen (US$500 billion) in assistance to the banking sector. In addition to financial assistance, the bill would merge, nationalize, or close down any insolvent bank. Financial analysts in Japan and abroad applauded the new legislation but remarked that the task of restoring the country's banking system to financial health could take up to ten years to accomplish.

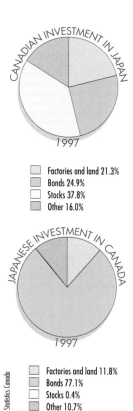

CANADIAN INVESTMENT IN JAPAN

1997

☐ Factories and land 21.3%
☐ Bonds 24.9%
☐ Stocks 37.8%
☐ Other 16.0%

JAPANESE INVESTMENT IN CANADA

1997

☐ Factories and land 11.8%
☐ Bonds 77.1%
☐ Stocks 0.4%
☐ Other 10.7%

Statistics Canada

PHOTO: Trade has been the lifeblood of the Japanese economy since the early 1950s. Today, Japan is the world's third largest trading nation.

Trade and Deregulation

Trade has been the lifeblood of the Japanese economy since the 1950s, when MITI formulated a policy of export promotion and restriction of imports. From 1960 to 1985, Japanese exporters relied on a low exchange rate for the yen to make their products competitive in international markets. However, in 1985, at the insistence of American and various European governments, Japan introduced measures to raise the value of the yen in order to reduce Japan's growing trade surpluses. The rise of the yen from 260 per US dollar in 1985 to less than 90 per US dollar in April 1995 did not initially reduce Japan's trade surpluses (see chart "Japanese Foreign Trade").

Increasing the value of the yen was not the only measure needed to reduce the country's large trade surpluses. For decades, government regulations of all kinds protected Japanese producers and *keiretsu* companies from foreign competition and investment. Many sectors of the economy were closed to foreign companies. The US government argued that the Japanese economy had to be opened up to foreign competition or else it would impose quotas and tariffs on Japanese exports entering the United States. In the early 1980s, the United States and Canada introduced quotas on imported Japanese cars.

The Japanese government was at first reluctant to deregulate the economy. However, international pressure forced the government to deregulate the retail trade, allowing American stores such as The Gap and Walmart to open large stores in Japan. Regulations were reduced in the banking sector to give more freedom to foreign banks and brokerage houses.

To maintain their competitive edge and avoid further American criticism, Japanese firms responded by investing more of their profits outside the country. The main destinations of this investment were the United States, the European Union, and East Asia. Total Japanese investment abroad in 1985 was US$83.7 billion, but by 1995 it had grown to US$463.6 billion, of which 41.9% was in the United States.

Investment between Canada and Japan has grown significantly in recent years. In 1997, the total value of Canadian investment in Japan was C$12.8 billion and included factories, bonds, stocks, and land. The total value of Japanese investment in Canada was over C$60.6 billion and consisted mainly of bonds, factories, and land (see pie charts, left).

Phyllis A. Arnold

Japanese Foreign Trade (1988–1997)									
(in billions of US$)									
	1988	1989	1990	1991	1992	1993	1994	1995	1996	1997
Exports	264.9	273.9	287.6	314.8	339.9	362.2	397.0	443.1	411.3	421.1
Imports	187.4	209.7	235.4	237.0	233.2	241.6	275.2	336.0	349.6	338.6
Surplus	77.5	64.2	52.2	77.8	106.7	120.6	121.8	107.1	61.7	82.5

Direction of Trade Statistics Yearbook.

The leader of one main opposition party, Ichiro Ozawa, wrote *Blueprint for a New Japan* in 1994. In it, he remarked that Japan did not behave as a "normal nation." To become "normal," it needed a government accountable to the people and an economy based on more freedom, competition, and risk taking. He further noted that the future of Japanese society depended on giving people freedom from urban overcrowding, domination by companies, overwork, ageism and sexism, and regulation.

Blueprint for a New Japan: The Rethinking of a Nation

(Excerpts) by Ichiro Ozawa. Tokyo: Kodansha International Ltd., 1994.

If we can achieve these five freedoms, we will release our citizens from their social and political shackles and begin to build a society that truly values the individual. Japan must become a society in which individuals can act freely, based on their own judgment. Respect for the individual does not refer only to oneself, but to a society that enables mutual self-respect and coexistence among individuals. Individual freedom will mean a society that offers many choices, a society that not only permits but encourages diversity.

Unnecessary regulations must be recognized as such and eliminated as quickly as possible. Companies and individuals must act more autonomously. The power that has been concentrated in the capital must be decentralized; local areas must make their own decisions and turn Japan into a society that embraces diversity. We must put all our effort into rectifying our extreme Tokyo-centrism, whose distorted form of efficiency has hampered improvements in ordinary life. Senior citizens and women, who are today bound by too many social restrictions to participate to their full potential in society, must be accorded greater freedom. We must also contain the excesses of corporate behavior that today so distort individual lives.

The release of people from what is effectively a protective but confining social incubator is long overdue. This will, of course, require that people take responsibility for themselves, but this should not be considered undesirable. There should be no freedom of choice without a sense of responsibility for self. We must make available whatever information will allow individuals to make their own choices and take responsibility for their own lives. That is the meaning of a free society.

What kind of society will Japan be if we liberate people from their tethers and proclaim these five freedoms? It will depend on the choices each individual citizen makes. When diversity flourishes, the content of a gratifying and prosperous life will differ according to the individual.

Government should have little to say about individual choice. What is required of government is not that it offer citizens a ready-made "affluent life." It should instead eliminate the barriers to individual action and provide an environment in which people can use their own power as they see fit to construct the kind of lives they want. This is the intent of the five freedoms I am calling for. If we can attain these freedoms, the appropriate course toward rich and meaningful lives will open before us of its own accord. The question is how to do it.

Japanese Beliefs and Attitudes

Between November 1996 and January 1997 the Japanese advertising firm Dentsu interviewed Japanese in Tokyo on their beliefs and attitudes.

Beliefs (% who agree with the statement)

Parents should not rely on their children	39%
Men work, women should stay at home	21
Children should look after aged parents	15

Top five concerns (% agree)

Health and welfare	68%
Cost of living	56
Economic development	48
Pollution	46
Employment	37

Image as a nation (% agree)

Hard-working	65%
Bad at negotiating	45
Loyal to company	42
Closed society	36
Polite	30

What the state must do (% agree)

Adopt policies according to public opinion	68%
Grant full social benefits	65
Promote competition based on ability	25
Regulate individual rights for greater good	11
Adopt Western systems	8
Have a strong leader push social reform	5

Adapted from "A Peep into Asia's Soul." *Asiaweek.* September 26, 1997, p. 78.

REVIEW

Summary

In the 20th century, Japan has experienced considerable political and economic change. Following its defeat in World War II and postwar occupation by the United States, Japanese political institutions were democratized but many prewar characteristics were retained. Legislative power was granted to the National Diet, and the Emperor's role was reduced to that of "symbol of the nation."

Though Japan had begun to industrialize before World War II, at the end of the war its industrial base lay in ruins. After 1950, Japanese industry organized as *keiretsu*. Under the guidance of economic ministries, the economy grew rapidly by exporting manufactured goods to the United States and elsewhere. By 1985, the Japanese economy had become the world's second largest industrial and financial power.

Since 1990, Japanese society has experienced several painful adjustments. One of the most painful has been the realization that the country's business, political, and government elites have not always recognized people's concerns about health, welfare, cost of living, economic development, pollution, and employment.

Japanese Values and Political Philosophy

1. Briefly describe in what way each of the following factors has influenced the development of Japanese values.
   A. its geographical position as a chain of islands
   B. its largest geographical neighbour
   C. the code of ethics called *bushido*
   D. the Shogun period
   E. the Meiji restoration

2. The text identifies seven core Japanese values. Pick the two you think we should **most** consider adopting, and explain the reasons for your choices.

3. Japanese politics have been dominated by the Liberal Democratic Party since 1955.
   a) Which core values would help explain why the Japanese people gave power to this party for most of the latter part of the 20th century?
   b) Where do the Japanese political parties fit on the left–right political continuum?

   Left   Right

4. Japanese faith in their dominant party was shattered in the early 1990s. They moved their votes to some of the new parties that had been formed.
   a) What two things happened to destroy some of the faith in the Liberal Democratic Party?
   b) What are some of the programs and platforms of the parties that emerged in the early 1990s?
   c) Indicate on the political continuum where these new parties are positioned in comparison to the Liberal Democrats.

   Left   Right

5. Which Japanese core values help explain why left-wing parties have not gained large-scale support in Japan?

Japanese Political System

1. Outline, in point form, information you could use to defend the following position: Under the Meiji Constitution, the lack of democracy resulted in disaster for the Japanese nation.
Use the following questions as a guide.
   a) What two groups had political power under the Meiji Constitution?
   b) Under the Meiji Constitution, who drafted the laws to be passed by parliament?
   c) Decrees were issued in the name of the Emperor. What is a decree, and how is it undemocratic?
   d) Who controlled the military, and how was this a problem?
   e) Using a timeline, trace the independent actions taken by the military that ultimately led to World War II.

2. What are the five key characteristics of the 1947 Constitution drafted by the Americans that make it democratic?

3. a) What is the position of the Emperor in contemporary Japanese politics?
   b) How is his role similar to that of the Governor-General in Canadian politics?

4. How is the Japanese method of choosing the Prime Minister different from the Canadian method?

5. Members of both the upper and lower houses of parliament (called the Diet) are elected in a particular fashion.
Describe the distinguishing features of the different means by which members are elected.

6. In all modern governments the bureaucracy plays a significant role. In Japan it is even more so. What is the bureaucracy's role in law making?

7. During the 1970s and 80s, Japan was often referred to as "Japan Incorporated" because of the close relationship between corporations and government. This relationship was often seen as one of the main reasons for Japan's phenomenal economic and export success.
   a) What are the two most powerful ministries of the government?
   b) What does the power of these two ministries indicate about the focus or emphasis of the government?
   c) What interest group has the most influence in Japanese politics?

8. Consensus is very important in Japanese society. Which elements of the legislative process before a bill becomes law are examples of this desire for consensus?

9. Japan is a unitary state, with local government responsibility divided between prefectures and municipalities. Draw a web of the division of responsibilities from the national government on down.

10. The Japanese constitution encourages people to participate in government at the local level. In fact, they have been given a fair amount of power to ensure accountability from local government, and may recall or even remove local officials.
Take and defend a position on the issue: Should voters be able to recall elected officials between elections?
Use the following questions as a guide.
   a) What are the elements in the process by which Japanese citizens attempt to dismiss a local assembly?
   b) How may voters in British Columbia recall elected officials?
   c) What are some of the advantages and disadvantages of recalling elected officials between elections?

11. Japan's elections and voting procedures have been fairly unusual. This was particularly so before 1995, when changes were

implemented. Determine what lessons may be learned from the Japanese experience for the political process in our own country. Use the following questions as guides for your answer.

a) Personalities play an important role in Japanese politics. What are the possible strengths and weaknesses of this system?

b) How are factions, loyalty and rewards significant elements of Japanese politics?

c) How were "money politics," "pork-barrelling," and powerful local families problems in the Japanese system?

d) Describe elements mentioned in the above three questions that are present in our political system.

e) How did the electoral reform of 1995 change the old system of money politics in Japan?

12. Which of the following core values **best** explains the dominance of Japanese politics by one party for most of the second half of the 20th century?

A. personal allegiance
B. social harmony
C. egalitarianism
D. group affiliation

Japanese Economic System

1. From 1945–1984, the economy was highly regulated by the government. It was characterized by a considerable degree of cooperation between government and corporations in order to achieve national economic goals. Take and defend a position on the issue: Should the Japanese example of a highly regulated economy be used as a model by other nations?

Use the following questions as a guide.

a) What did the first economic plan of 1955 emphasize?

b) What did the government emphasize after the 1973 rise in energy costs, and what was the effect of this emphasis by 1985?

c) Because of its huge trade surpluses, Japan agreed to raise the value of its money, following the theory that Japanese exports would be made more expensive, thus reducing the surplus. How did "Japan Incorporated" meet this challenge.

d) During the slump of the 1990s, what changes have been advocated by the United States, Europe, and various Japanese business groups?

e) Who has resisted the changes?

2. Examine the Business Cycle in Japan graph on page 266. How would you describe what has happened to the Japanese economy in the period 1960–1995? Provide evidence from the graph to support your conclusions.

3. Identify three elements of private enterprise in the Japanese economy.

4. a) From the chart, Japan's Top Companies, how many of the largest seven companies in terms of sales in 1997 were trading companies?

b) What generalizations can be made about the importance of these trading companies to Japan's economy?

5. A unique characteristic of the Japanese economy is the existence of huge associations of companies and banks called *keiretsu* and *zaibatsu*. Prepare notes for use in a discussion on **one** of the following positions: Japanese *keiretsu* and *zaibatsu* organizations should be used as models by other nations.

OR

Japanese *keiretsu* and *zaibatsu* give Japan unfair advantages in world trade and should be abolished.

Use the following questions as a guide.

a) What are *keiretsu* and *zaibatsu*? How are they similar, and how are they different?

b) Mitsubishi and Sumitomo are important companies belonging to *keiretsu*. From the list of Japan's top banks, note the assets of these two companies' banks and their rank on the list. Should industrial companies be able to own banks? Why or why not?

c) Business organizations similar to *keiretsu* are illegal in most industrial nations. (Refer to antitrust and anticombine legislation in Chapter 3.) Why are similar organizations illegal in many other states?

d) The *zaibatsu* were abolished by the Americans after the war. What did the *zaibatsu* do in the 1930s that led to their being broken up?

e) What three elements do a *keiretsu* include, and how do these form a web of interests?

f) How do *keiretsu* companies share and cooperate?

g) Why is the government lifting the ban on *zaibatsu*?

h) The Toyota *keiretsu* development of the "just-in-time" production method that has been copied around the world was made easier by the type of organization it is. Describe the method, and why it was used by Toyota.

i) Why have foreign car manufacturers criticized the *keiretsu*?

j) What are some of the benefits workers receive, not just for belonging to a *keiretsu*, but also for their loyalty?

k) What examples are there that women have not been treated equally by the *keiretsu*?

l) Chart the strengths and weaknesses of the *keiretsu*.

6. In chart form, identify the strengths and weaknesses of the government's regulation of the economy.

7. Japan's social services costs are much lower per capita than other industrialized states. In some other countries, particularly those with aging populations, political parties that want to cut social services costs sometimes cite the Japanese example as a model to be copied.

a) In Japan, who has the primary responsibility for family welfare?

b) How do government social services, the Daily Life Security Law, the Law for Welfare for the Aged, and the universal nursing care insurance program reinforce this primary responsibility?

c) In a one-page essay, take and defend a position on the issue: Should our country develop a social services system based on the Japanese model?

Japanese Political Economy

1. The Japanese economy suffered a recession in the early 1990s. The government tried the traditional Keynesian approach in order to stimulate the economy. What did the government do, and what was the effect on both the economy and government debt? Use the line graph on page 276 to provide evidence where appropriate.

2. Japan's economic troubles in the 1990s are being blamed by some on the iron triangle. What exactly is meant by the iron triangle?

3. The key problem with the iron triangle has been corruption, resulting from the lack of accountability within the Japanese political–economic system.

a) Draw the iron triangle and create a web to indicate the flow of campaign funds, bribes, and comfortable jobs for bureaucrats, in return for low tax rates, low interest loans, and protective tariffs.

b) To whom is there no accountability in this relationship, considering the fact that Japan is a democracy?

4. How did the banks, the iron triangle, the stock market, and the Asian financial crisis contribute to Japan's economic problems in the 1990s?

5. a) What is the significance of the cartoon on page 279?
   b) What series of events are represented by the wave?

6. Examine the chart at the bottom of page 280.
   a) What has been the general trend of foreign trade between 1988–1997?
   b) What does the fact that Japan has enjoyed a trade surplus mean for Japan's trading partners? How might this affect the political relationship between Japan and its trading partners?

7. Japan's industries were aided in their development at home and in their pursuit of foreign markets by government protection and regulation. In the 1980s and 1990s, there has been pressure to deregulate the economy and reduce protection.
   a) Why did the European and American governments want these changes?
   b) How have both the Japanese government and industry responded to these demands? Find evidence in the text to support your conclusions.

8. In his book *Blueprint for a New Japan*, Ichiro Ozawa claims Japan is not a normal nation. What changes does he recommend for Japan to achieve "normal" status? After reading the section on Changing Japan, which of Japan's core values (page 253) will be most changed if Ozawa's ideas become reality? Provide evidence to support your choices.

Chapter Consolidation

1. This chapter began with a quotation by Masao Miyamoto.
   a) What evidence is there in this chapter to demonstrate the validity of his comments?
   b) To what extent do you think that the efforts of ordinary people in any society go largely unrecognized? Provide arguments and evidence to support your views.

2. a) On what values were the political and economic systems of Japan based?
   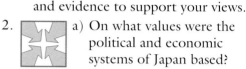 b) Whose ideas were influential in the development of the political and economic systems of Japan? Briefly explain the ideas and how they were applied in Japan.
   c) Create a chart, identifying the type of political system and economic system in Japan and the strengths and weaknesses of those systems.

CHAPTER 8

NAZI GERMANY

"The man who is born to be a dictator is not compelled; he wills it. . . . The man who feels called upon to govern a people has no right to say, If you want me or summon me, I will cooperate. No, it is his duty to step forward."
—Adolf Hitler, speech at his trial for treason in Munich, March 22, 1924

European politics went through a period of instability in the years following World War I (1914–1918), as governments and peoples struggled to rebuild their societies in the aftermath of war. In Italy, the Fascist movement led by Benito Mussolini seized power. His success provided inspiration for a small fascist movement in Germany led by Adolf Hitler, which sought and eventually took power in that country.

As a political system, fascism embodied a vision of government and society in which a single political party ruled and controlled aspects of political, economic, cultural, and social life. Its leaders believed in creating a powerful nation, promoting extreme nationalism and using military force to establish control over other nations.

Private enterprise played an important role in the fascist economic system. However, the government regulated and controlled private enterprise in activities that it considered important for expanding national power, such as heavy industry and the production of weapons. In these sectors the government made decisions about production and distribution of goods and services, including the allocation of resources for the production of weapons.

Key Concepts/Vocabulary

Aryan	concentration camp
Reichstag	corporate state
Enabling Act	Four Year Plan
Fuehrer	anti-semitism
Fuehrerprinzip	pogrom
propaganda	*Kristallnacht*
Sturmabteilungen	Holocaust
Schutzstaffeln	de-Nazification
Gestapo	

Focus On Issues

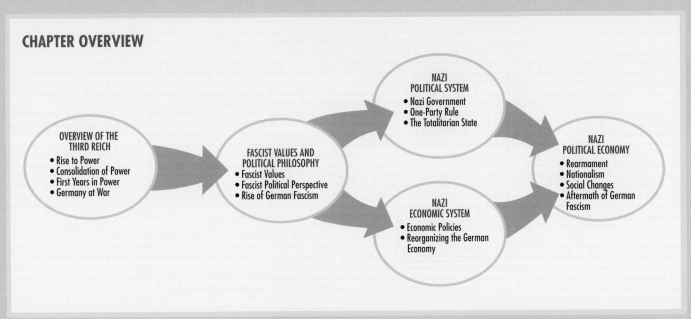

CHAPTER OVERVIEW

OVERVIEW OF THE THIRD REICH
- Rise to Power
- Consolidation of Power
- First Years in Power
- Germany at War

FASCIST VALUES AND POLITICAL PHILOSOPHY
- Fascist Values
- Fascist Political Perspective
- Rise of German Fascism

NAZI POLITICAL SYSTEM
- Nazi Government
- One-Party Rule
- The Totalitarian State

NAZI ECONOMIC SYSTEM
- Economic Policies
- Reorganizing the German Economy

NAZI POLITICAL ECONOMY
- Rearmament
- Nationalism
- Social Changes
- Aftermath of German Fascism

OVERVIEW OF THE THIRD REICH (1933–1945)

Canapress

Bundesarchiv, Koblenz, Germany. Foto Bild 102/14381.

Rise to Power (1919–1932)

1919—Adolf Hitler joins the German Workers' Party (DAP), which is renamed the National Socialist German Workers' Party (NSDAP, or Nazi Party) in 1920.

1921—Hitler becomes leader of NSDAP.

1923—November 9, Munich Beer Hall *putsch* (attack) fails; Hitler arrested and later sentenced to prison, where he writes *Mein Kampf (My Struggle)*.

1925—After release from prison, Hitler reorganizes the NSDAP.

1928—Reichstag elections; Nazis win 12 seats with 2.6% of the vote.

1930—Reichstag elections; Nazis win 107 seats with 18.3% of the vote.

1932—Hitler a presidential candidate; loses to President Hindenburg, who is re-elected. (In the year's two elections, the Nazi Party emerged as the largest party in the Reichstag.)

Consolidation of Power (1933)

January 30—President Hindenburg appoints Hitler Chancellor.

February 28—President Hindenburg signs emergency decree suspending the constitution following the Reichstag fire.

March 5—Reichstag elections; Nazis win 288 seats with 43.9% of the vote.

March 23—Enabling Act passed; Hitler granted dictatorial powers until 1937.

April 1—Nationwide boycott of Jewish businesses; Hitler signs decree removing judges and civil servants who disagree with Nazi ideology.

May 6—German Labour Front (DAF) replaces all trade unions.

May 10—Nazis carry out nationwide book burning to "purify German culture."

July 14—NSDAP becomes only legal party; Germany a one-party state.

November 12—Reichstag elections; only Nazi candidates on the ballot; NSDAP wins all seats and 95.4% of the vote. In a plebiscite, voters confirm Germany's withdrawal from the League of Nations.

December 1—Germany becomes a totalitarian state.

HUGO JAEGER, COPYRIGHT TIME INC.

First Years in Power (1934–1939)

1934

May 3, 1934—All legal traditions and civil rights abandoned; opponents of Nazi regime often held without trial.

June 30—"Night of the Long Knives"; Hitler purges Storm Troops (SA) and removes all opposition within NSDAP.

August 2—President Hindenburg dies.

August 19—Hitler proclaims himself Fuehrer and Chancellor.

September 4–10—Leni Riefenstahl films *Triumph of the Will* at Nazi Party Congress.

1935

March 17—Military service reintroduced, in violation of Treaty of Versailles.

September 15—Nuremberg Laws restrict citizenship to those of "German or kindred blood." (Germany's 500 000 Jews lost their citizenship rights and were deprived of political and civil rights, such as the right to vote and hold public office. Marriages between Jews and non-Jews were declared illegal; those involved were forced to divorce or face prison. Many Jews left Germany.)

Archive Photos

1936

March 7—Germany occupies the Rhineland; Great Britain, France, and League of Nations protest violation of Treaty of Versailles.

August 1—Olympic Games open in Berlin; anti-Jewish signs removed until Games are over. (Jesse Owens, an African–American, won four gold medals and set a world long jump record, discrediting Hitler's claim of Aryan supremacy.)

October 19—Four Year Plan is announced; marks beginning of Germany's rearmament.

November 25—Germany and Japan sign the Anti-Comintern Pact pledging mutual support against the Soviet Union.

1937

January 30—Enabling Act extended for further four years.

November 13—Italy joins Anti-Comintern Pact with Germany and Japan against international communist movement and the Soviet Union.

Gerd Ruehle, *Das Dritte Reich.* 1935 (p. 408)

ABOVE: National military flag of Nazi Germany

LEFT: Crowd participating at the November 1938 Nazi Party Congress in Nuremberg.

RIGHT: African–American athlete Jesse Owens set a world long jump record at the 1936 Summer Olympic Games in Berlin.

289

© Hulton-Deutsch Collection/Corbis

Archive Photos

LEFT: The arrest of Jewish families by Nazi troops in Warsaw.

RIGHT: Men and women arriving at Auschwitz extermination camp in Poland.

Sinti–Roma peoples, once called Gypsies, were peoples who originally came from India to Europe in the 14th century and lived a migratory way of life.

1938

March 13—German troops march into Austria.

March 29—In a plebiscite, German and Austrian voters overwhelmingly approve (99.8%) Austria's unification with Germany (*Anschluss*).

September 29—Leaders of Great Britain, France, Italy, and Germany agree to permit German annexation of Sudetenland in western Czechoslovakia.

October 1—Germany occupies Sudetenland.

November 9—Night of the Broken Glass (*Kristallnacht*) pogrom against Jews; SS troops burn and loot Jewish homes, shops, and synagogues, killing 100 Jews and sending thousands to concentration camps. (The event marked the beginning of a more violent Nazi persecution of Jews, political opponents such as Communists, Social Democrats, and trade unionists, Sinti–Roma peoples, Jehovah's Witnesses, homosexuals, and clergy who spoke out against Nazi policies.)

Germany at War (1939–1945)

1939

August 23—Germany and Soviet Union sign Non-aggression Pact permitting the invasion of Poland and Soviet occupation of Baltic States and Bessarabia.

September 1—Germany invades Poland.

September 3—Great Britain and France declare war on Germany.

September 10—Canada declares war on Germany.

September 17—Soviet Union invades eastern Poland.

October—Hitler orders mentally and physically disabled people put to death.

1940

April 9—Germany invades Denmark and Norway.

May 10—Germany invades Belgium, France, Luxembourg, and Netherlands.

June 10—Italy enters war.

June 17—Soviet Union occupies Baltic States.

June 22—France surrenders to Germany.

July 10—Battle of Britain begins.

Sovfoto

1941

April 6—Germany invades Yugoslavia and Greece.

June 22—Germany invades Soviet Union; Jews segregated in ghettos. (Starvation, overcrowding, and disease were commonplace in these restricted areas. Signed passes were required to enter and leave area.)

September 1—All Jews ordered to wear yellow Star of David and confined to ghettos; Soviet and Polish prisoners of war killed at Nazi death camp at Auschwitz, Poland; gas chamber executions at "extermination camps" throughout occupied Poland.

December 11—Hitler declares war on United States following Japanese attack on Pearl Harbour December 7.

1942

January 20—Wannsee Conference; plans for "Final Solution" for Europe's Jews confirmed. (It is estimated that millions of European Jews were sent to extermination camps in Poland from 1942 to 1945. The extermination program was later extended to Europe's Sinti–Roma peoples.)

August 19—First Allied attempt to invade France fails; over 3000 soldiers, including many Canadians, die at Dieppe.

1943

February 2—German 6th Army surrenders at Stalingrad. (The event marked a turning point in the war in Europe; from this time on German forces began to retreat.)

Archive Photos

1944

June 6—D-Day; Allied forces successfully invade France.

July 20—Failed assassination attempt on Hitler by General Stauffenberg and other military officers.

1945

January 1—Soviet troops enter German concentration camp at Auschwitz in Poland.

April 12–30—American troops enter concentration camps in Germany.

April 25—American and Soviet troops meet on the Elbe River.

April 28—Mussolini shot fleeing to Switzerland.

April 30—Hitler commits suicide.

May 2—Soviet troops enter Berlin.

May 7—Germany surrenders to Allied forces.

May 8—Victory in Europe (VE) Day celebrated.

May 9—Victory Day celebrated in the Soviet Union.

TOP: A view of the barracks of the Birkenau camp located at Auschwitz in Poland.

LOWER RIGHT: Victory in Europe (VE) celebrations in Times Square, New York City, May 8, 1945.

FASCIST VALUES AND POLITICAL PHILOSOPHY

Advance Organizer

As an ideology, fascism owes much to the personalities of Mussolini in Italy and Hitler in Germany. Both leaders believed that elitism, a powerful state, extreme nationalism, organized violence, war, and loyalty were necessary for achieving and maintaining their power.

SECTION OVERVIEW
- Fascist Values
- Fascist Political Perspective
- Rise of German Fascism

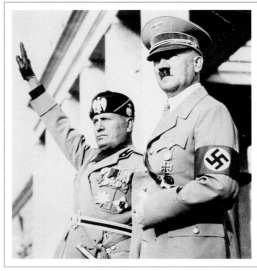

Archive Photos

PHOTO: Benito Mussolini and Adolf Hitler at an official meeting in Berlin.

In Ancient Rome, the Consuls were chosen by civic and military leaders to represent Rome in diplomatic matters and to represent Rome to its citizenry.

Fascist Values

The word "fascism" is derived from the Latin word *fasces*, referring to the bundle of rods carried by Consuls in Ancient Rome to signify their authority. In the 1890s, the word *fascio* was used in Italy to refer to a small political group or band. In 1919, Mussolini used the terms "fascist" and "fascism" to describe his armed squads and political views. Over time, the term "fascism" acquired a certain ideological meaning and, for some, became a way of life.

Leaders of Fascism

The rise of fascism in Italy and Germany owes much to the force of personality of its leaders. In Italy, Benito Mussolini was a charismatic leader, while in Germany Adolf Hitler's public speaking skills captivated his audiences.

Benito Mussolini (1883–1945). Born in Romagna, Italy in 1883, Mussolini was deeply involved in the Italian socialist movement prior to World War I as an organizer and editor of the official newspaper of the Italian Socialist Party. In 1915, Mussolini broke with the socialists over their opposition to Italy's participation in the war.

In March 1919, Mussolini assembled about 100 ex-socialists and former military men to found a new political movement called the Fascio italiano di combattimento (Italian Combat Group). Their program included several radical measures to solve the country's political, social, and economic problems in the aftermath of World War I, including the formation of national militias, councils for labour and management, the nationalization of all munitions factories, heavy taxation of wealth, and the confiscation of all property belonging to the Catholic Church.

The Fascist movement developed rapidly. In the early 1920s, armed black-shirt action squads fought socialists in the streets. By the autumn of 1922, the Fascists controlled many northern towns. On September 20, 1922, Mussolini called on the Italian king to allow his movement (renamed the National Fascist Party in November 1921) to govern Italy. The king refused. Mussolini mobilized his action squads and threatened to march on Rome and seize control of the government. Unwilling to risk a confrontation, the government resigned. The king called on Mussolini to become Prime Minister and form a new government.

Adolf Hitler (1889–1945). Born in Linz, Austria in 1889, Hitler's early years before World War I were spent in Linz and Vienna, where he became acquainted with antisemitic and racial ideas. At the outbreak of World War I, Hitler volunteered for service in the German Army. He was an able and loyal soldier during the war, rising to the rank of corporal.

Following his demobilization from the German Army in early 1919, Hitler was attracted to the political activities of a small nationalist group called the *Deutsche Arbeiterpartei* (DAP—German Workers' Party). On September 12, 1919, Hitler attended a party meeting and impressed the members with his oratory. Soon after, he was admitted into the party as propaganda chairman.

Core Fascist Values

Much has been written about the fascist movements led by Mussolini and Hitler. Political scientists Ebenstein, Ebenstein, and Fogelman have identified the following beliefs as core fascist values.[1]

Human inequality. Fascists believe that there is no equality among individuals; men are superior to women, soldiers to civilians, party members to nonparty members, one's own nation to others, and the strong to the weak. Fascists argue that human beings should not be treated equally nor should they have equal rights.

Cult of the leader (hero worship). Fascists have an image of their leader as a saviour of the nation and a father figure who understands the ways of the world. The leader is considered to be an all-powerful and all-knowing person whose authority is based on a natural superiority and charisma and who demands unquestioning loyalty from followers.

Government by an elite group. Fascists believe that only a select minority is capable of forming a government, because this elite alone understands what is necessary for the people and this entitles them to make decisions. This elite informs people about what is necessary and demands their obedience in implementing government policies.

Extreme nationalism. Fascists believe in the ideal that individuals must be totally dedicated to the nation and be willing to subordinate personal interests to the greater glory of the nation. Individuals, they believe, exist only to serve the nation and the state. To do otherwise would be considered an act of treason.

Racial purity and superiority. Fascists believe that all individuals are not equal, and thus also that there is no equality among nationalities and nations. Hitler's beliefs on this issue were extreme. His followers accepted the belief that some nationalities, ethnic groups, and nations were inferior and should be eliminated or enslaved, while others were superior and destined to rule the world.

Hitler's beliefs about racial purity and the existence of an Aryan master race consisting of Germanic peoples was based on the racist belief that all non-Germanic peoples were inferior.

Organized violence. Fascists are prepared to use mass murder, torture, and other forms of organized violence to destroy enemies and others who dare to question the leader's wishes. They justify the use of organized violence on the grounds that if they do not eliminate their enemies (socialists and communists among others), their enemies will destroy them.

War and military force. Military preparedness, discipline, and combat with other nations and peoples are the highest ideals to which every fascist must aspire. It is believed that this will strengthen an individual's character and give the person a sense of purpose in life.

[1]See Alan Ebenstein, William Ebenstein, and Edwin Fogelman, *Today's Isms: Socialism, Capitalism, Fascism, Communism*, Tenth edition. Englewood Cliffs: Prentice-Hall, 1994. Chapter 3, pp. 79–109.

Fascist Political Perspective

Mussolini and Hitler attempted over time to develop a body of political thought to inspire their followers. They wrote several works that outlined principles to be adopted and followed by all fascists.

Mussolini's Beliefs

The most comprehensive statement of Mussolini's fascist beliefs appeared in his book *La dottrina del fascismo* (*The Doctrine of Fascism*) published in 1932, ten years after his political movement had taken power in Rome in late October 1922. Mussolini's beliefs spanned many topics.

On human inequality. *The concept of freedom is not absolute because nothing is ever in life. Freedom is not a right, it is a duty. It is not a gift, it is a conquest; it is not equality, it is a privilege. The concept of freedom changes with the passing of time.*

Fascism denies that numbers, as such, can be the determining factor in human society; it denies the right of numbers to govern by means of periodical consultations; it asserts the irremediable and fertile and beneficent inequality of men who cannot be levelled by any such mechanical and extrinsic device as universal suffrage.

On the state. *The keystone of the Fascist doctrine is its conception of the State, of its essence, its functions, and its aims. For Fascism the State is absolute, individuals and groups relative. Individuals and groups are admissible insofar as they come within the State.*

The Fascist State lays claim to rule in the economic field no less than in others; it makes its actions felt throughout the length and breadth of the country by means of its corporative, social, and educational institutions, and all the political, economic, and spiritual forces of the nation, organised in their respective associations, circulate within the State.

On nationalism. *A nation exists inasmuch as it is a people. A people rise inasmuch as they are numerous, hard-working and well-regulated. Power is the outcome of this threefold principle.*

I believe that if a people wish to live they should develop a will to power, otherwise they vegetate, live miserably and become a prey to a stronger people, in whom this will to power is developed to a higher degree.

On national superiority. *Fascism sees in the imperialistic spirit—i.e., in the tendency of nations to expand—a manifestation of their vitality. In the opposite tendency, which would limit their interests to the home country, it sees a symptom of decadence. Peoples who rise or rise again are imperialistic; renunciation is characteristic of dying peoples. The Fascist doctrine is that best suited to the tendencies and feelings of a people, which like the Italian, after lying fallow during centuries of foreign servitude, is now reasserting itself in the world.*

On violence. *Comrades this is our programme: fight. Life for the Fascist is a continuous, ceaseless fight, which we accept with ease, with great courage, with the necessary intrepidity.*

On war. *First of all, as regards the future development of mankind,—and quite apart from all present political considerations—Fascism does not, generally speaking, believe in the possibility or utility of perpetual peace. It therefore discards pacifism as a cloak for cowardly supine renunciation in contra-distinction to self-sacrifice. War alone keys up all human energies to their maximum tension and sets the seal of nobility on those people who have the courage to face it.*

Hitler's Beliefs

Hitler's beliefs are outlined in *Mein Kampf* (*My Struggle*), which he wrote in 1924–1925. Published in two volumes, *Mein Kampf* became the official statement of the principles of national socialism after 1933. Hitler's book covered many topics.

On human inequality. *It is therefore not to be regretted if a number of men set out to attain the same objective, it is thus that we recognize the strongest and swiftest and the man who conquers.*

On leadership. *The young Movement [National Socialist] is in its essence and organisation anti-parliamentarian, i.e., it* rejects, in principle and in its composition, any theory of the majority vote, implying that the leader is degraded to merely being there to carry out the orders and opinions of others. In small things and great, the Movement stands for the principle of unquestioned authority of the leader, combined with fullest responsibility.

On the state. *The national State must work untiringly to set all government, especially the highest (that is the political leadership), free from the principle of control by majorities—i.e., the multitude—so as to secure the undisputed authority of the individual in its stead.*

The best form of State and Constitution is that which with natural sureness of hand raises the best brains of the community to a position of leadership and predominant influence.

On nationalism. *For myself and all other true National-Socialists there is only one doctrine: Nation and Fatherland.*

What we have to fight for is security for the existence and increase of our race and our nation, nourishment of its children and purity of its blood, freedom and independence for the Fatherland, and that our nation may be able to [fulfil] the mission appointed for them by the Creator of the Universe.

On national superiority. *If we divide the human race into three categories—founders, maintainers, and destroyers of culture—the Aryan [Germanic peoples] stock alone can be considered as representing the first category.*

On violence. *The lack of a new and great idea is at all times a sign of lack of fighting force. The conviction that there is a right to use weapons, even the most brutal, ever goes hand in hand with fanatical belief that a new and revolutionizing order of things must be victorious in the world.*

A Movement that fails to fight for such high ideals and aims will never fight to the very last.

What we needed then, and need now, was and is not a hundred or two wrong-headed conspirators, but a hundred thousand, and again a hundred thousand, fanatical fighters for our world-theory. The work must be done, not in secret . . . but by powerful

massed strokes; the road cannot be cleared for the movement by dagger or poison or pistol, but by conquering the man in the street. We have to destroy Marxism, so that future control of the street may be in the hands of National Socialism—now, just as it will be in the future.

On war. *No nation on earth holds a square yard of territory by any right derived from heaven. Frontiers are made and altered by human agency alone.*

The fact that a nation succeeds in acquiring an unfair share of territory is no superior reason for its being respected. It merely proves the strength of the conqueror and the weakness of those who lose by it. This strength solely constitutes the right to possess.

Gerd Ruehle, *Das Dritte Reich.* 1936. (p. 398)

PHOTO: Official Nazi announcement advertizing Hitler's *Mein Kampf (My Struggle).*

Collapse of the German
Currency (1920–1923)
(Average number of
marks to us$)

Jan 1920	64.8
Jul 1920	39.5
Jan 1921	64.9
Jul 1921	76.7
Jan 1922	191.8
Jul 1922	493.2
Jan 1923	17 972.0
Jul 1923	353 412.0
Aug 1923	4 620 455.0
Sep 1923	98 860 000.0
Oct 1923	25 260 208 000.0
Nov 1923	4 200 000 000 000.0

Statistiches Jahrbuch für das Deutsche Reich
[Statistical Yearbook for the German Reich]

PHOTO: Children playing
with worthless German
currency during the
hyperinflation of 1923.

Rise of German Fascism

Hitler's exceptional organizational and
public speaking skills, and the numerous
political and economic crises that beset
Germany, contributed to the growth of
German fascism between 1919 and 1933.

Early Years (1919–1924)

From 1919 to the end of 1924, the Nazi
Party was a small party committed to
nationalist and socialist goals. In party-
organized public rallies, Hitler denounced
the Treaty of Versailles as an unjust and
intentional attempt by Allied Powers to
make Germany weak. The Treaty articles
cited below restricted the size of Germany's
armed forces and ended the production of
military weapons. It obligated Germany to
accept its war guilt and pay for damages it
caused in World War I.

Article 159. *The German military forces
shall be demobilized and reduced. . . .*

Article 170. *Importation into Germany
of arms, munitions, and war material of
every kind shall be strictly prohibited. The
same applies to the manufacture for, and
export to, foreign countries of arms,
munitions and war material of every kind.*

Article 231. *The Allied and Associated
Governments affirm and Germany accepts
the responsibility of Germany and her allies
for causing all loss and damage to which the
Allied and Associated Governments and
their nationals have been subjected as a
consequence of the war imposed upon them
by the aggression of Germany and her allies.*

In January 1923, France occupied the
Ruhr Valley when the German government
refused to make reparation payments. The
German government organized a campaign
of passive resistance among workers in the
Ruhr. Industrial output fell, consumer
prices skyrocketed, and the value of the

German currency collapsed when the
German government resorted to printing
money to deal with the crisis.

On November 9, 1923, Hitler
announced from a platform in a Munich
beer hall, that his party was seizing power
from the ruling government. The Munich
Beer Hall uprising was suppressed by the
army. Hitler and other party leaders were
arrested. In April 1924, he was sentenced
to five years' imprisonment for treason.
While in prison, he devoted his time to
reading, meeting party members, and
writing the first volume of *Mein Kampf.*
In December 1924, Hitler was released on
the condition that he refrain from any
public speaking until 1928.

AKG London

November 11, 1918	January 1919	June 1919	September 1919	April 1920	July 1921	January 1923	August 1923	November 1923	April 1924	December 1924
Germany signs ceasefire	Reichstag elections; German Workers' Party formed	Germany signs Treaty of Versailles	Hitler joins DAP	DAP renamed NSDAP	Hitler becomes leader of NSDAP	French occupy Ruhr	Hyperinflation in Germany begins	Munich Beer Hall *putsch*	Hitler jailed	Hitler released

Rise of German Fascism

Note: Timeline is not to scale

296

Campaigning for Votes (1925–1932)

While in prison, Hitler grew convinced that he must gain power through legitimate means by actively seeking voter support in elections. He remarked to a party worker:

Instead of working to achieve power by an armed coup, we shall have to hold our noses and enter the Reichstag against the Catholic and Marxist deputies. If outvoting them takes longer than outshooting them, at least the result will be guaranteed by their own constitution. Any lawful process is slow. . . . Sooner or later we shall have a majority—and after that, Germany.

In February 1925, the Nazi Party was reorganized, with Hitler as its undisputed leader. The Nazi Party was redesigned as a political organization which could be identified by its party salute (the outstretched right arm), banners, insignia, and uniforms. The paramilitary wing, the Storm Troops (SA), were used to distribute party literature (newspapers, pamphlets, and *Mein Kampf*), to recruit new members, and to support their leader at rallies.

A series of unstable coalition governments that split into factions and fell meant that Reichstag elections were held several times during this period. The Nazi Party participated for the first time in national elections in May 1928. They campaigned on a nationalist platform and won 12 seats, with 2.6% of the vote. Representation in the Reichstag gave the party a forum to publicize its views throughout the country. In the September 1930 national elections, the Nazi Party campaigned for policies to improve the plight of the country's growing numbers of unemployed. The party won 107 seats, with 18.3% of the vote.

Hitler was a candidate in the March 1932 presidential elections. Although he came second to President von Hindenberg, he received widespread publicity and support. In the July 1932 national elections, Hitler promised policies to reduce unemployment and restore prosperity to the country. The Nazi Party won 230 seats, with 37.3% of the vote, and became the largest party in the Reichstag. However, it did not have enough seats to form a government. In the November 1932 elections, their support was reduced slightly to 196 seats and 33.1% of the vote.

> Because of proportional representation, the number of seats in the Reichstag varied. This ensured that each party received the same percentage of seats as the votes they received.

Reichstag Election Results (1928–1933)

	May 20, 1928 Vote	May 20, 1928 Seats	September 14, 1930 Vote	September 14, 1930 Seats	July 31, 1932 Vote	July 31, 1932 Seats	November 6, 1932 Vote	November 6, 1932 Seats	March 5, 1933 Vote	March 5, 1933 Seats
Right-wing Parties										
National Socialists	2.6%	12	18.3%	107	37.3%	230	33.1%	196	43.9%	288
Nationalists	14.3	73	7.0	41	5.9	37	8.5	52	8.0	52
People's Party	8.7	45	4.9	30	1.2	7	1.9	11	1.1	2
Centrist Parties										
Centre Party	15.2%	78	14.8%	87	15.7%	97	15.1%	90	14.0%	92
Democrats	4.8	25	3.5	20	1.0	4	1.0	2	0.8	5
Small Parties	14.1	51	13.9	72	3.0	11	3.1	12	1.6	7
Left-wing Parties										
Social Democrats	29.8%	153	24.5%	143	21.6%	133	20.4%	121	18.3%	120
Communists	10.6	54	13.1	77	14.3	89	16.9	100	12.3	81
Totals	100.0%	491	100.0%	577	100.0%	608	100.0%	584	100.0%	647
Voter Turnout	74.6%		81.3%		83.4%		79.9%		88.1%	

Biographisches Handbuch der Reichstage [Biographical Handbook of the Reichstag]

February 1925	April 1925	July 1925	May 1928	October 1929	September 1930	July 1931	January 1932	April 1932	July 1932	November 1932
NSDAP reorganized	Hindenberg elected President	*Mein Kampf* published	Reichstag elections; 12 Nazis elected	Stock Market Crash; beginning of Great Depression	Reichstag elections; 107 Nazis elected	Banking crisis; unemployment hits 4.8 million	Unemployment reaches 6.1 million	President Hindenberg reelected; Hitler presidential candidate reelected	Reichstag elections; 230 Nazis elected	Reichstag elections; 196 Nazis elected

Rise of German Fascism

Consolidation of Power (1933)

In January 1933, the chief conservative spokesman, Franz von Papen, who was Chancellor from June to December 1932, concluded an agreement in which Hitler would become Chancellor and form a right-wing coalition government. On January 30, President Hindenburg called on Hitler to form a government.

Once in power Hitler quickly out-manoeuvred his opponents and called for new elections to be held on March 5. On February 27, the Reichstag was set on fire. Hitler claimed the Communists were responsible for the fire and manipulated President Hindenburg into declaring a state of emergency. The decree suspended civil liberties (freedom of speech, assembly, press, privacy, freedom from home searches without a warrant, and right to fair trial). On March 5, German voters, some frightened by Hitler's claims of a coming Communist revolution and others intimidated by Nazi violence during the campaign, elected 288 National Socialists to the Reichstag, with 43.9% of the popular vote. The following day, offices of the Social Democrats and Communists were ordered closed. Thousands of Social Democrat and Communist members were arrested and sent to a concentration camp set up in a munitions factory at Dachau.

On March 23, with support from the Nationalist Party and Centre Party, the Nazis were able to pass the Enabling Act, granting Hitler dictatorial powers until 1937. The Social Democrats voted against the bill and Communist deputies were prevented from voting. Hitler promptly used his power to remove all political opponents and consolidate his power over the country.

On April 1, Hitler called for a national boycott of Jewish businesses. Storm Troops and members of the SS blocked entry to Jewish shops and posted signs such as: "Don't buy from Jews—Defend Your-selves!" The reaction of Germans was mixed. Some continued as usual, others attacked Jews. Jewish reactions also varied: some prepared to leave Germany, but most stayed. The British and French governments protested German treatment of Jews. A week later, Hitler signed the Civil Service Law which removed judges and lawyers who disagreed with Nazi beliefs. Jewish civil servants, teachers, professors, and lawyers were fired. Communists were removed from all government posts.

On May 6, the Nazi government set up the German Labour Front (DAF) to replace all trade unions. A few days later, Nazis carried out a nationwide campaign of book burning in an attempt to "purify German culture" of Jewish influence. Most books burned were written by non-Jewish authors. Some Germans protested the action, but many remained silent.

On July 14, the Law Against the Formation of Political Parties was passed, legalizing one-party rule by the Nazi Party and banning all other political parties. Another law, allowing forced sterilization of physically and mentally disabled people, Sinti–Roma peoples, and African–Germans, was also passed.

In the November 12 elections to the Reichstag, only Nazi candidates appeared on the ballots. The Nazi Party received 95.4% of the vote and all seats in the Reichstag. German voters also approved in a plebiscite the country's decision to withdraw from the League of Nations.

The Law Safeguarding the Unity of Party and State was passed December 1, 1933. The law declared the Nazi Party to be part of the government and above all laws. Germany became known as the Third Reich.

Many Germans did not support the Nazi Party and its political platform. Hitler was compelled to consolidate his power by gradually eliminating political opponents and then introducing Nazi policies.

PHOTO: Book burning rally held in Berlin in May 1933.

Archive Photos

298

Why German Democracy Failed (1919–1933)

Between 1919 and 1933, Germany had the most democratic constitution in Europe. Initially, the new constitution appeared to be successful, but ultimately it failed to provide Germany with a stable government. The following are some of the key reasons for the collapse.

Proportional representation. The 1919 German constitution established an electoral system based on proportional representation. As long as a political party received at least 0.5% of the popular vote, it was given representation in the Reichstag. This allowed many small parties to exist and enabled the Nazis, with only 2.6% of the vote in 1928, to be represented in the Reichstag, giving them a forum to express their political and economic policies.

Weak governments. Between February 1919 and January 1933, Germany had 20 coalition governments. Each government lasted on average eight months and consisted of three or four parties. Disputes frequently broke out over policies and the division of cabinet positions, which led one or more parties to withdraw from the government, depriving it of a majority in the Reichstag. These unstable governments were often unable to pass important legislation to deal with the country's many economic problems, especially unemployment, which grew rapidly between 1930–1932.

Political polarization. The failure of the country's main parties to form stable governments dismayed many German voters, who concluded after 1930 that the Communists and Nazis alone seemed capable of dealing with the country's problems. In the 1932 national elections, the Nazis on the right and Communists on the left won a majority of the seats in the Reichstag. Though hostile to each other, the Communists and Nazis blocked every effort by other parties to form a stable government and pass needed legislation. Faced with political deadlock in the Reichstag from March 1930 to January 1933, President Hindenburg used his presidential powers to govern and pass legislation.

Disunity among the left. Before World War I, the German left had been unified under the leadership of the Social Democratic Party. In 1919, the Social Democratic Party split into two groups following the formation of the German Communist Party. Initially an independent-minded party, in the 1920s the Communists increasingly came under Soviet control and rejected all forms of cooperation with the Social Democrats and other parties that might support German democracy. In the early 1930s, the Communists resisted all initiatives by the Social Democrats to create a coalition government to keep the Nazis from taking power.

Hostility to parliamentary democracy. When Germany became a parliamentary democracy in 1919, the military and nationalists, as well as many citizens rejected it as a foreign political system imposed on them by the victorious Allied Powers. Many longed for the restoration of the monarchy. Many Communists and workers regarded parliamentary democracy as bourgeois and conspired to overthrow it in favour of a workers' government. Hitler viewed Germany's parliamentary democracy as symbolic of the country's defeat in World War I and its acceptance of the Treaty of Versailles.

Great Depression. The collapse of the New York stock market in October 1929 was a shock to the German economy. Foreign capital was removed from the country and demand for German goods fell. Unemployment rose and social distress increased. In January 1932, over six million Germans were unemployed and the government seemed to be powerless to resolve the mass unemployment. The German people began to look to more extreme political parties for solutions. In the July 1932 elections, Hitler campaigned on a platform of economic recovery, which appealed to many unemployed workers. The Nazi Party became the largest party in the Reichstag.

Between 1919 and 1933, Germany was often called the Weimar Republic because its new constitution was wrtten in the city of Weimar in January 1919.

NAZI POLITICAL SYSTEM

All political power resided in the Fuehrer (see chart "Structure of Nazi Government" below).

Advance Organizer

The Nazi political system that arose in Germany from 1933 to 1945 was based on the centralization of political power in the Nazi Party led by Adolf Hitler. Its political power was maintained and strengthened by propaganda, indoctrination, and periodic use of plebiscites and other forms of controlled participation to mobilize popular support for the party. Local government became subservient to officials acting in the name of the party. The secret police sought out, arrested, and imprisoned or executed those persons who opposed the policies of the Nazi Party and Hitler.

SECTION OVERVIEW
- Nazi Government
- One-Party Rule
- The Totalitarian State

Nazi Government

The 1919 Weimar constitution was never formally abolished when the Reichstag passed the Enabling Act granting Hitler dictatorial powers on March 23, 1933. After March 1933, Hitler decreed other laws to amend the constitution and concentrate power in the executive branch of government.

Executive Power

Prior to Hitler's appointment as Chancellor on January 30, 1933, executive power under the 1919 Constitution was divided between the elected Office of the President and the Office of the Chancellor. The President was the official head of state. The Chancellor was the head of government and relied on majority support in the Reichstag. Following President Hindenburg's death on August 2, 1934, Hitler merged the position of President with that of Chancellor, creating a single position, the Fuehrer. By doing so he assumed various executive, legislative, and judicial powers.

Fuehrer. Hitler intended the post of Fuehrer to be more than just leader of the state. As Fuehrer, Hitler was viewed as the head of the German people and nation and represented the spirit of the people. He believed that he gave the people

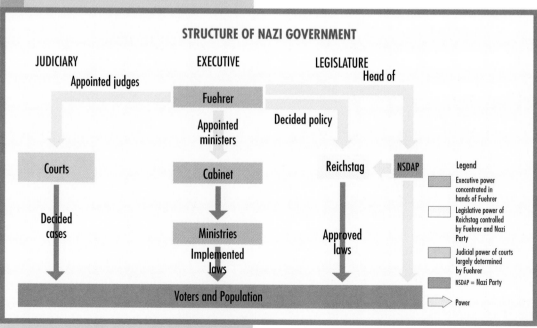

STRUCTURE OF NAZI GOVERNMENT

JUDICIARY	EXECUTIVE	LEGISLATURE
Appointed judges		Head of
	Fuehrer	
	Appointed ministers	Decided policy
Courts	**Cabinet**	**Reichstag** ← **NSDAP**
Decided cases	Ministries	Approved laws
	Implemented laws	
Voters and Population		

Legend
- Executive power concentrated in hands of Fuehrer
- Legislative power of Reichstag controlled by Fuehrer and Nazi Party
- Judicial power of courts largely determined by Fuehrer
- NSDAP = Nazi Party
- ⇨ Power

purpose in life. Nazis also believed that as Fuehrer, Hitler was accountable to no one but God.

Through the principle of *Fuehrer-prinzip* (the absolute right to lead the people and demand absolute loyalty and obedience from the people), all state functions were carried out by Hitler. As the President of the country, Hitler had the executive authority to officially represent the country, be commander-in-chief of the country's armed forces, decide all questions of foreign policy, peace, and war, and determine leading political aims as well as policies of the country. As Chancellor, he had the legislative authority to initiate and enact all laws that met his approval. As party leader, he had the authority to make all decisions relating to the activities of the party and its place in German society.

The entire power of the State, internal and external, was united in the hands of the Fuehrer. As the holder of this power Hitler was above the law and was not required to be accountable to the people. This made him one of the most powerful executives in Europe at that time. Under portraits of Hitler in Germany were his words: "Nothing happens in this Movement, except what I wish."

Legislative Power

Prior to 1933, the German constitution divided the parliament into two chambers, the Reichsrat and the Reichstag.

Reichsrat. Under the 1919 constitution, the Reichsrat was the upper chamber of parliament and represented the states of the country. Its function was to consider legislation initiated in the Reichstag that could affect the administrative powers of the states.

In 1934, Hitler abolished the Reichsrat and centralized the powers of the states in Berlin, making Germany a unitary state. The governments of the states were placed under the authority of the Minister of the Interior. All state assemblies were dissolved and their legislative powers transferred to central authorities. Hitler appointed governors to administer the states and ensure that all legislation enacted in Berlin was faithfully carried out.

Reichstag. Under the 1919 constitution, the Reichstag was the lower chamber of parliament and elected directly by the population under a system of proportional representation. The passage of the Enabling Act in March 1933 stripped the chamber of its power to initiate and enact legislation.

In 1937, the emergency powers to govern by decree given to the Chancellor under the Enabling Act were extended for another four years. The Reichstag was transformed into a chamber of little real power. At the Fuehrer's discretion it was dissolved and reopened. It did not discuss proposed legislation but passed laws drafted by the Nazi Party and reasserted, without debate, its confidence in the Fuehrer's policies.

After the November 12, 1933 national elections, which were contested and won solely by the Nazis, the Reichstag lost all power as an independent legislature. It became, as one observer of the day commented, "the highest paid male chorus in the world."

Judicial Power

In April 1933, Hitler signed a decree to remove what he called all "politically unreliable" judges and lawyers. In their place, loyal Nazis were appointed. The judiciary was gradually stripped of its independence and made subservient to the Nazi Party and therefore Hitler.

The Fuehrer was declared to be the supreme source of law in Nazi Germany, binding judges and courts to him. The law was the "order of the Fuehrer," and the "order of the Fuehrer" was the law. Law was no longer an impartial concept of justice, but an instrument to subjugate the German people to Hitler's will and the Nazi Party. Judges and judicial officers were to serve the interests of the regime. When they questioned the validity of government policies, the government had them removed.

As Fuehrer, Hitler held undisputed power and control over the legislative and judicial branches of German government.

Nazi Party Membership (1930–1940)

1930	389 000
1932	920 000
1934	2 100 000
1936	2 610 000
1938	4 985 400
1940	5 340 000

Nationalsozialistische Jahrbuch [National Socialist Yearbook]

One-Party Rule

The concentration of political power and authority in the hands of the Fuehrer, Adolf Hitler, was not enough to ensure Nazi control over German politics. The Nazi Party was the instrument through which the Fuehrer could influence and control all levels of government, society, and the economy. Following the consolidation of power in 1933, the Nazi Party developed into a mass political organization involved in every government agency and ministry, cultural organization, educational institution, communications medium, factory, and neighbourhood. Membership in the Nazi Party grew from less than one million in 1932 to 5.34 million in 1940.

Party Organization

The organization of the Nazi Party was hierarchical and resembled in many ways that of the Communist Party of the Soviet Union under Stalin (see page 342 in Chapter 9). The Nazis often borrowed tactics and strategies from the Communists

for their own purposes. Power in the Party flowed from the Fuehrer downward through the Executive Committee and the party organization to the block and cell groups at the bottom (see chart "Organization of the Nazi Party"). The Fuehrer was the highest authority in the party organization. On joining the party, all members took a pledge of loyalty to support Hitler, accept his decisions, and carry out any task he asked of them:

I pledge allegiance to my Fuehrer, Adolf Hitler. I promise at all times to respect and obey him and the leaders whom he appoints over me.

The Executive Committee met to formulate policies and approve the decisions of the Fuehrer. It performed the role of a party cabinet. Each member of the Executive Committee was a leader in the Nazi movement and acted as the head of one or more of the party's organizations and affiliated groups. All important party leaders were men, though the party had a separate department for women.

Below the Executive Committee, the Party was organized into district, county, and municipal units. The district leader was appointed directly by Hitler and responsible to him for all party matters in the district. Below the district leader there were county and municipal officials who had specific responsibilities. Municipal units were subdivided into cells and blocks, consisting of about 50 party members. The cells and blocks acted as the "eyes and ears" of the Nazi Party, reporting to party leaders any unauthorized political activity, dissent, and opposition.

Each party official was responsible to the official directly above and had complete authority over those below. All aspects of party work were coordinated by municipal and county leaders. However, in practice, district leaders had the greatest influence in the party organization and used it to control party activities in their districts.

The party was formally organized as a parallel state, with its own leaders and network of administrators. However, in practice, party leaders occupied all important positions of power in the government (see chart "Organization of the Nazi Party").

Organization of the Nazi Party

NATIONAL SOCIALIST ORGANIZATION		GOVERNMENT
Policy Making Arm of Party	Decision Making Arm of Party	Policy Implementation
	Fuehrer	Chancellor
Party Congress	Executive Committee	Government Ministries
District Party Congress	District Party Leader Organization	District Government Offices
County Party Congress	County Party Leader Organization	County Government Offices
	Municipal Party Leader Organization	Municipal Government Offices
	Block and Cell Leaders	Civil Service
POPULATION		

Legend
→ Power

Adapted from *Organisationsbuch der NSDAP [Organization Manual of the NSDAP]*

Gerd Ruehle, *Das Dritte Reich.* 1934. (p. 474)

PHOTO: An official photograph of the September 1934 Party Congress held at Nuremberg.

The head of the Nazi Party was the head of the country. Members of the Executive Committee were ministers of the government. District party leaders held district government offices. County and municipal party leaders served as party agents to county and municipal government leaders. These people were empowered to nominate candidates for mayor, appoint municipal councillors, and approve city laws. At the bottom, cell and block leaders occupied positions in the civil service and experienced considerable authority over neighbourhood committees, labour unions, and business groups.

Party Congress

The Party Congress (Parteitag) was the main policy making body of the Nazi Party. It met every September at Nuremberg to demonstrate the strength, activity, and organization of the Party. After 1933, the Party Congress became a national political event. The last Party Congress was held in 1938.

The Party Congress was a convenient forum for Hitler to announce new policies and generate mass enthusiasm for the Nazi Party. Well-orchestrated pageants, mass rallies of party faithful, and personal speeches and addresses by Hitler all contributed to an atmosphere of great excitement and support for the leader and the Nazi Party. The most well-known example of the mass enthusiasm generated at a party rally was

the 1934 Party Congress, which was filmed by Leni Riefenstahl and released as *Triumph of the Will*.

Duties of Party Comrades

The Fuehrer is always right!

Never go against discipline!

Do not waste your time in idle talk or in self-satisfying criticism, but take hold and work!

Be proud, but not arrogant!

Let the program be your dogma; it asks of you the greatest devotion to the movement!

You are a representative of the party; control your bearing and your manner accordingly!

Let loyalty and unselfishness be your highest principles!

Practise true comradeship and you will be a true socialist!

Treat your racial comrades as you wish to be treated by them!

In battle be hard and silent!

Spirit is not unruliness!

What promotes the movement, Germany, and your people is right!

If you act according to these principles, you are a true soldier of your Fuehrer.

Organisationsbuch der NSDAP [*Organization Manual of the NSDAP*]. Translated from German by David Rees.

Mass assemblies are necessary because whilst attending them the individual who feels on the point of joining a young movement and takes alarm if left by himself receives his first impression of a larger community, and this has a strengthening and encouraging effect on most people. He submits himself to the magic influence of what we call "mass-suggestion."
—Mein Kampf

Consequences of One-Party Rule

The establishment of one-party rule by Hitler had consequences for German politics.

Authoritarianism. The Nazi Party was the sole source of political power and authority. Any political organization that existed without authorization from the Nazi Party was suppressed or forced to operate secretly to avoid detection by the secret police. Candidates for government positions were chosen and approved by the Party and Hitler, from the Reichstag at the national level down to local assemblies.

Nazi Party control over German social, political, and economic organizations had a positive result. It brought stability and order throughout the country, following a period of weak governments and economic difficulty. The German people could rely on firm leadership to defend the country and clearly express national interests.

Centralized Decision Making. Because most important political decisions were made by the Fuehrer and the Executive Committee, official party decisions and statements had the force of law and were imposed on party members and the people.

At the 1946 Nuremberg Trial held after World War II, a study of Nazi administrative practices revealed that Hitler's centralized decision making led to considerable administrative confusion. Instead of promoting efficient decision making, the report noted that the centralization of decision making in Hitler's hands led to considerable infighting among party and government leaders for his personal favour. It often led to poor decisions and inefficiency. Many officials were appointed to high positions on the basis of their personal loyalty to the Fuehrer rather than their ability.

However, centralized decision making allowed the Nazi government to formulate policies for the whole country. Laws and standards were applied to all regions of Germany, which helped the Nazis to develop a consensus for National Socialism among all Germans.

Limited Accountability. Since there were no checks on the use of power by Nazi leaders, corruption became rampant in the Party and government. Many top party leaders lived in luxury. Local party officials became known for their high living, favouritism, inefficiency, and willingness to break party rules of conduct. Party leaders were not accountable to the people or party members for their actions.

Nazi leaders argued that public debate and discussion of policies were unnecessary in Germany. When the country had a parliamentary democracy, they claimed, Germany was beset by political divisions, social unrest, and economic chaos. With firm leadership, the country would have steady direction, political stability, and national unity.

Little Dissent. Nazi Party members were expected to carry out all party decisions without question or debate. Dissenters were generally expelled from the Nazi Party and arrested. Also, party members were arrested for not having a pure German background and for any past association with Social Democrats and Communists. Occasionally, the Nazi Party conducted a purge of its membership and a detailed examination of the ethnic, social, and political history of its members. In discouraging dissent, the party encouraged secrecy and compelled party members to withhold important information out of fear that it would be used against them.

To the Nazi leadership, it was important for the country that Nazi Party members were loyal and prepared to carry out party policies. The country, they argued, was surrounded by hostile countries, and it needed people who were known for following orders and steadfastness in leadership.

The Totalitarian State

Under Hitler, the Nazi Party controlled the political process. Elections and plebiscites were conducted to increase popular support for Hitler, the Nazi Party, and its policies. Propaganda was used to glorify the accomplishments of Hitler and his government. The education system was used to indoctrinate youth with the values and principles of National Socialism. A national security apparatus sought out and eliminated dissent among the population.

Controlled Participation: Elections and Plebiscites

Between 1933 and 1939, Hitler held two national elections and three plebiscites. The purpose of these elections and plebiscites was to mobilize the people in a show of support for his policies and government.

Elections were organized with great fanfare, numerous public rallies, and military style parades of Nazi Party members. Public buildings, businesses, and houses were draped in Nazi flags and banners. Nazi party literature was posted in public places, urging voters to mark their ballots for Hitler. The speeches of top party leaders were broadcast throughout the country. All of this gave the appearance of great public excitement and enthusiasm for the government; the outcome of the elections was never in doubt.

The Nazi Party chose all the candidates who would appear on the voting list. Once chosen by party officials, the candidate list was submitted to Hitler for final approval and then released to the public. On voting day, if voters approved the candidate list they placed a mark in the box opposite the list. If voters disapproved of the candidate list, they had no choice but to cross out the candidate's name on the ballot and the ballot was counted as spoiled. In the November 1933 national elections, 7.9% of voters spoiled their ballots. In later elections, the number of spoiled ballots declined to just over 1% of the total number of votes cast.

Gerd Ruehle, *Das Dritte Reich*. 1936. (p. 387)

Gerd Ruehle, *Das Dritte Reich*. 1936. (p. 386)

Besides national elections, the German people were asked to vote in a number of plebiscites on specific government policies.

- On November 12, 1933, German voters confirmed Hitler's decision to withdraw Germany from the League of Nations.
- On August 19, 1934, German voters approved Hitler's decision to combine the offices of President and Chancellor into one post and confirmed him as the country's leader.
- On March 29, 1938, German voters approved Austria's unification with Germany (called the *Anschluss*).

The plebiscites were well-crafted propaganda exercises to show to the world that Hitler had widespread support among the German people for his policies. The government had actually made its decision weeks earlier.

TOP: Ballot used in the March 29, 1936, Reichstag elections. The text reads:

"Reichstag for Freedom and Liberty

Electoral District . . .

National Socialist German Workers' Party

Adolf Hitler

Hess Frick Goering Goebbels"

MIDDLE: Public poster directing voters to mark their ballots for Hitler in the March 29, 1936, Reichstag elections.

In fascist Italy, voters were given two ballots—one for yes and one for no. Voters elected their members of parliament by handing the ballot openly to the electoral officer who recorded it.

Propaganda

Propaganda was highly effective in controlling people's participation in the political process and in enhancing the power of the Nazi Party and Hitler. Hitler understood the psychology of large groups and the capacity of propaganda to influence their thoughts. In *Mein Kampf*, Hitler wrote:

The receptive ability of the masses is very limited, their understanding small; on the other hand, they have a great power of forgetting. This being so, all effective propaganda must be confined to very few points, which must be brought out in the form of slogans, until the very last man is enabled to comprehend what is meant by any slogan.

Both in subject and form, propaganda should be framed so as to reach the mass of the people; the only means of measuring its correctness is success in practice. In a large popular assemblage the most effective speaker is not he who most resembles the educated section of his audience, but he who captures the hearts of the crowd.

In March 1933, the Ministry of Public Enlightenment and Propaganda was established and headed by Josef Goebbels. The Ministry was responsible for initiating and administering propaganda campaigns for the purpose of mobilizing support for the Nazi Party and Hitler's policies.

The *Voelkischer Beobachter [People's Observer]*, the chief newspaper of the Nazi Party, praised every word and action Hitler made. It attempted to create a "cult of the leader" among the people. This campaign was successful in generating considerable support among Germans for Hitler. Many ordinary citizens believed that Hitler was their country's saviour and great leader. The following excerpts from *Voelkischer Beobachter* provide examples of propaganda expressed in the press at the time.

July 3, 1934
The whole German people and the National Socialist movement, together in one unique union, are solemnly dedicated to one idea, the idea of one sole leader, the Fuehrer.

July 14, 1934
Adolf Hitler knows he can trust his people more than ever. He rules not merely to lead but to inspire. It is satisfaction enough for him to forgive the past and gives him new strength for the future's great work. Heil Hitler!

August 20, 1934
Germany is Hitler and Hitler is Germany! One People! One Nation! One Fuehrer!

January 4, 1935
The National Socialist movement, all Germany, and loyal followers salute Adolf Hitler, not as a ruler of the nation but as the true genuine Fuehrer of Germany. Heil Hitler!

April 20, 1936
Hitler is the genius of all Germany, and through him we receive purpose and oneness. Hitler is the greatest genius the German has ever had. Long life to Adolf Hitler! Heil Hitler!

Other Uses. Besides creating a positive image of the Fuehrer, Goebbel's Ministry promoted popular culture, sports, and social welfare. It funded films, theatrical works, operas, and the visual arts with the expressed purpose of showing to Germans and foreigners alike the talent, diversity, and greatness of German culture.

It supported German participation in numerous international sporting events. The Ministry gave the 1936 Summer Olympic Games in Berlin considerable radio and press coverage to show that German athletes were superior to all others. The accomplishments of African–American Jesse Owens in several track and field events embarrassed the Ministry, because they showed that the Nazi idea of German racial superiority was false.

In the field of social welfare, the Ministry conducted various social help and public relief campaigns such as the Winter Help to emphasize the Nazi slogan of "the common good before personal interest."

Indoctrination

Under Hitler, indoctrination was considered necessary. Schools were important instruments for creating citizens who supported the policies of the Nazi Party, Hitler's leadership, and the principles of National Socialism.

Hitler's *Mein Kampf* was studied extensively in the classroom. On the subject of education, Hitler wrote in *Mein Kampf*:

The National Socialist state will have to take care that it obtains, through an appropriate education of youth, a generation which is ready for the final and greatest decisions on this globe. Moreover, the people that first start on this road will be victorious.

To achieve this objective, school textbooks were rewritten and new courses were offered that promoted the teachings of the party leadership. Courses in history, biology, and German were revised to include Nazi ideas about race, heredity, and the past. Exercises in mathematics, physics, and chemistry used questions about military operations and bombs. All teachers were required to join the National Socialist Teachers' Organization. Teachers who disagreed with the new course curriculum were dismissed and replaced by more ideologically loyal ones.

National Socialist Values. High school students in the Third Reich were required to take courses on the history of the Nazi Party and the "German race." Students were taught the values of loyalty, sacrifice, vigilance, and duty.

- All Nazis were expected to be loyal to the nation, the party, and the Fuehrer, who represented the people and demanded complete loyalty from them.
- Sacrificing one's own personal interests for the group was one of the highest goals to which all Nazis were expected to aspire. Only by placing the interests of the German nation before personal desires could individual interests be realized.
- All Nazis were expected to be alert and prepared to protect and unearth enemies and people who were hostile to the nation, the ruling political party, and the Fuehrer.
- Duty and work were important virtues for every Nazi. They were believed to strengthen an individual's character for carrying out any unpleasant tasks demanded of him or her by the party and the Fuehrer.

Youth Organizations. Political control over the country's young people was an important goal for Nazis. On December 1, 1936, Hitler Youth (Hitlerjugend) became a state agency to bring together all of Germany's young people between the ages of 10 and 18. In 1939, membership in Hitler Youth totalled about eight million. Programs of Hitler Youth were divided between outdoor pursuits, military training, and political indoctrination. The declared principle of Hitler Youth was "Youth must be led by youth."

Young people were admitted to Hitler Youth at the age of ten. They joined on April 20, Hitler's birthday, and made the following pledge: *I promise to do my duty always within Hitler Youth, full of love and faithfulness to the Fueher and our banner.*

©UPI/Corbis-Bettmann

For the first four years (ages 10 to 14) boys and girls belonged to the Young People (Jungvolk) group. At age 14, again on Hitler's birthday, boys joined the Hitler Youth group and girls joined the League of German Girls (Bund deutscher Madel). At age 18, boys were accepted into the Nazi Party if they had a good record. Girls became party members at age 21. The motto of Hitler Youth was "Fuehrer commands—we obey!"

Education of German youth was regarded by Hitler as important to creating citizens who supported the Nazi Party and its policies.

In fascist Italy, Mussolini set up the Balilla (National Youth Movement) to teach young people between the ages of 8 and 18 fascist values.

PHOTO: A Hitler Youth rally held in Berlin in February 1934.

Hitler Youth

Statement from von Schirach, Hitler Youth Leader, December 1936

(Excerpts) *Hitlerjugend [Hitler Youth]*, 1937. Translated by David J. Rees.

Germany has once again a youth that does not seek for selfish gain but is prepared to sacrifice itself in the service of the community. That is the idea dominating the Hitler Youth. A fellowship of Germans who asks nothing for themselves. And because they ask nothing for themselves, they are able to serve their great nation to the utmost of their powers. No youth with new rights, but a generation pledged to fulfil a bounden duty.

. . . My mission has been entrusted to me by the German Reich. I am responsible to the Reich for seeing that the entire Youth is physically, mentally, and morally trained and schooled in the sense of a National Socialist conception of the State. A certain service has been introduced for enabling this educational mission to be carried out. And I have not the slightest objection to make if, outside this service, every youth is given religious instruction at the place chosen by his parents or by himself.

Letter From a Teacher, May 1939

(Excerpt) German Freedom Party, *Uncensored Germany*. London: Sidgwick and Jackson Ltd., 1940

A regime which so frequently and so emphatically proclaims itself to be authoritarian, which glorifies its leadership principle as the greatest of modern achievements, and which puts forward its claim to have saved Europe, has proved itself *incapable* of educating our youths to be decent human beings who think,

feel, and act in a moral way. [It was recently reported] that the number of minors condemned by courts is continually on the up-grade, having almost *doubled* itself in the course of four years. (In 1934 there were 10 250; in 1937 there were 19 094.) This is a queer achievement to be put to the credit of National Socialist youth training! It is surely a striking proof of the complete failure of the system! The system has, indeed, favoured the demoralization of our youth, and it is the Nazi youth leaders—apart from the consequences of the regime itself—who bear the responsibility for the present situation.

. . . A further aggravating factor is that the number of youths sent to prison in 1937 was the highest for nine years. The crimes have become more serious, not less. The Government announces daily that Germany has become a better and finer country, that life is now easier and more joyous; but more reformatories are being provided and the regime itself is contributing to the backsliding of our young people by its approval of moral depravity, by the deterioration of social conditions, by the dissolution of family ties, and by violent propaganda against religion and morals. Crime springs from social circumstances and is a measure of the value of a system of government.

Statement from Bernhard Rust, Reich Minister of Science, Education, and Popular Enlightenment, May 1938

(Excerpt) *Germany Speaks*, London: Thornton Butterworth Ltd., 1938

The third educational factor, in addition to the home and the school, is the Hitler Youth. It

has been commissioned by the Fuehrer to train German boys—in close collaboration with the home and the school—for their great tasks in the future. The schools have to devote the major part of their time to intellectual education; and although, they do exercise an important influence in the direction named, they have but few opportunities for enabling their pupils to cultivate the corporate spirit beyond their own limits. This drawback is . . . overcome by the Hitler Youth. The youth of all classes and all vocations is initiated by it in the practical working of a national community and is to be prepared for that achievement by physical, ethical, and political training.

Letter From a Parent, February 1939

(Excerpt) German Freedom Party, *Hitler Calls This Living!* London: Sidgwick and Jackson Ltd., 1939

I cannot, for many reasons, put on paper what comes to our eyes and ears, nor could I tell you verbally. The children are learning absolutely nothing. It is of course good that they are no longer being crammed with dreary and useless knowledge as we were, and I realise that, but their education in the most elementary matters is being neglected. . . . We hear so much about the authority and order prevailing in Germany to-day, but when one speaks with teachers and Party functionaries about the dreadful conditions, they shrug their shoulders and have no advice to offer.

Nazi Constitutional Law

Under Hitler, the 1919 Weimar constitution was never formally abolished. Instead, it was superseded by certain laws which provided Hitler with the legal justification and means to impose Nazi Party control over the government and society. Listed below are four laws which suspended civil liberties, granted dictatorial powers to Hitler, abolished all political parties except the Nazi Party, and established totalitarian rule in Germany, led by the Nazi Party.

The Enabling Act passed on March 24, 1933, granted Hitler dictatorial powers until 1937. In 1937 the Enabling Act was renewed for another four years. Hitler held this power until his death in April 1945.

Decree of the Reich President on Protecting the People and State (February 28, 1933).

This decree suspended all civil liberties and gave the government unlimited power to restrict people's freedom, invade personal privacy, and seize private property without compensation.

In accordance with Article 48, paragraph 2 of the constitution as a measure against Communist acts of violence endangering the state the following is decreed:

1. Articles 114, 115, 117, 118, 123, 124, and 153 of the constitution of the German Reich are until further notice suspended. This means restrictions on personal liberty, the right of free expression, including freedom of the press, the right of assembly and association, and violations of the privacy of postal, telegraphic, and telephone communications; warrants for house searches and for the confiscation as well as restriction of private property are also allowed beyond legal limits otherwise prescribed.

Law Against the Formation of Political Parties (July 14, 1933).

This law legalized one-party rule by the Nazi Party and banned all other political parties.

The Reichstag has resolved the following law, herewith promulgated:

1. In Germany exists only one political party, the National Socialist German Workers' Party.
2. Whoever undertakes to maintain the organization of another political party or a new political party will be punished . . . with forced labour up to three years or with a term of six months to three years in prison.

Reichsgesetzblatt [German Law Gazette] Translated from German by David Rees.

Law on Removing the Distress of People and State (March 24, 1933).

Known as the Enabling Act, this law stripped parliament of its power to initiate and enact laws. The power to enact laws was given to Hitler and his cabinet.

The Enabling Act declared that the cabinet did not have to seek approval from parliament to adopt a budget and borrow money for government spending.

The law also allowed the cabinet to enact any law it desired, even if the law contravened the constitution. The Chancellor was given the power to initiate and enact laws on behalf of the cabinet without approval of parliament. Laws were declared in effect once they had been printed. The cabinet had the power to sign treaties with foreign powers without parliamentary consent. Lastly, the Enabling Act was valid for four years and could be renewed for additional years.

Law on Safeguarding the Unity of Party and State (December 1, 1933).

This law granted the Nazi Party all political power in the country and declared the Party to be part of the government and above all laws.

1. Following the victory of the National Socialist revolution, the National Socialist German Workers' Party is the bearer of the German state and indissolubly joined to the state.
2. It is a public organization with rights. The Fuehrer determines its statutes. . . .

Agents of Political Control

To suppress political opposition to Nazi one-party rule and the Fuehrer, an extensive national security apparatus was set up. This included the Sturmabteilungen, or Storm Troops (SA), the Schutzstaffeln, or Protection Service (SS), and the Gestapo, or Secret Police. These three organizations together employed thousands of people and operated a network of concentration camps.

Sturmabteilungen (SA). The Storm Troops (SA) were formed in October 1921 as the paramilitary wing of the Nazi Party. Following the Munich Beer Hall *putsch* in November 1923, the SA was disbanded by the German government. After his release from prison in early 1925, Hitler reestablished the SA with Ernst Roehm as its commander. The SA became responsible for protecting the party leadership, distributing party literature, recruiting new party members, participating in rallies and demonstrations, and using violence in the streets against political enemies. Members of the SA were recognized by their uniforms and became known as the "Brown Shirts."

After Hitler became chancellor in January 1933, Roehm and other leaders of the SA pushed for the achievement of a real socialist "second revolution" in Germany. Roehm wished to bring the German army under his command to create a powerful people's militia. This was perceived as a threat to Hitler's power in the Nazi Party and the independence of the army.

On June 30, 1934, in what has become known as the "Night of the Long Knives," Hitler ordered the arrest and execution of Roehm and other top leaders of the SA. Hitler's dominant position in the Nazi Party was preserved and enhanced, and army leaders took a personal oath to Hitler out of gratitude. Thousands of SA members were detained and hundreds sent to concentration camps. The role of the SA was reduced to that of providing basic military education to young German men and participating in party rallies.

Schutzstaffeln (SS). Formed in February 1925 and led by Heinrich Himmler, the SS was responsible for protecting Hitler and other top party leaders, and for gathering confidential information about suspect party members. Dressed in black uniforms to distinguish themselves from the SA's brown shirts, SS members were selected on the basis of their German background, physical appearance, and dedication to Hitler. On entering the SS, each man made the following oath:

I swear to you, Adolf Hitler, as Fuehrer and Chancellor of the German Reich, loyalty and valour. I pledge to you and to the superiors whom you will appoint obedience unto death.

Under Himmler's leadership, the SS expanded quickly to become the main agent of political control in Nazi Germany. The purpose of the SS, defined by Himmler, was "to find out, to fight, and to destroy all open and secret enemies of the Fuehrer, the National Socialist movement, and our racial resurrection."

In 1939, the SS numbered about 240 000 men, organized in divisions and regiments. It was responsible for national security and the country's concentration camp system. In November 1939, Himmler organized Armed SS units (Waffen-SS) as autonomous military corps for action in Eastern Europe.

Gestapo (Secret Police). In late March 1933, Hermann Goering established the Gestapo as an instrument of state terror. The duties of the Gestapo were to arrest and imprison all opponents of the Nazi Party and perceived enemies of the state. The Gestapo launched a nationwide campaign, arresting and imprisoning over 150 000 Communists and Social Democrats. To house these political prisoners, concentration camps were set up. The first one was opened in an old munitions factory at Dachau near Munich in April 1933. Initially, the camp at Dachau was meant to confine and reeducate political prisoners, however, confinement and reeducation soon gave way to forced labour. Dachau became the model for all later concentration camps.

By the end of 1933 several new camps were established to incarcerate trade union leaders, writers, university professors, publishers, lawyers, and others who openly disagreed with Nazi policies. Camps were set up to house women political prisoners. After 1934, new camps were set up to house homosexuals, Jehovah's Witnesses, Jews, and Sinti–Roma peoples (formerly called Gypsies), whom the Nazis believed were inferior and should be separated from the rest of German society.

Following the purge of the SA on June 30, 1934, the Gestapo and the concentration camps were placed under the control of Himmler's SS. The Gestapo became responsible for the management and operation of the system of concentration camps for political opponents. Under Himmler's authority, camp prisoners were subjected to harsher treatment and forced labour.

In April 1939, the Gestapo reported that 300 000 people were imprisoned in 100 concentration camps. Over one-half of these people were held under "protective custody" without trial, with sentences varying from a few weeks to life. A great many people incarcerated in the camps were victims of denunciation by colleagues, neighbours, or family. The repression relied on a great deal of self-policing by society, as pressure was imposed on individuals to conform.

© The National Archives/Corbis

During World War II, the concentration camp system was extended to German-occupied parts of Europe. The SS and Gestapo supervised the operation of concentration camps for Jews, Sinti–Roma peoples, and other nationalities in German-occupied Europe.

The first concentration camps were set up by the British during the Boer War (1901) in South Africa to intern civilian captives. In Nazi Germany they served to confine and reeducate enemies such as Communists, Socialists and Centrists, as well as to provide forced labour.

During World War II, these camps were used to detain Jews and other peoples for execution, as part of the Nazi's "Final Solution."

BOTTOM LEFT: The motto "Work Makes You Free" on the gates of the Dachau concentration camp.

TOP: A procession at the 1935 Nazi Party Congress rally in Nuremberg.

BOTTOM RIGHT: A view of the barracks at the Flossenberg concentration camp.

MGJ

Imperial War Museum/Archive Photos

Official Views of Nazi Control

Both politics and life changed in many unforeseen ways in Germany under the Nazis. The following official views were published in the book *Germany Speaks* in London in early 1938, to show British readers aspects of life in Germany under Adolf Hitler.[1]

Wilhelm Frick, Reich Minister of the Interior

It was . . . not until the advent of the National Socialist regime under the leadership of Herr Hitler (1933) that the authority still wielded by the then-existing seventeen federal States was so severely curtailed that it became subordinated to that exercised by the National Government.

Seventeen parliamentary bodies, each of which nullified the will of the German people by creating artificial antagonisms and fomenting party dissension, were swept away by the fervour of the National Socialist movement. Before that, the supreme authority of the Central Government was constantly weakened by its own instability, by its dependence upon shifting parliamentary majorities, and by the resulting civil disturbances. These conditions vanished as if by magic as soon as the triumph of Herr Hitler and the National Socialist movement became a reality. Party strife and class war came to an end. The menace of a Bolshevist revolution was overcome at the eleventh hour. Communism was suppressed, and the last traces of the always smouldering civil war were eradicated. A regime that was shaken by one crisis after the

other, that lacked the confidence of the nation, and wearily continued its precarious existence from day to day, had to give way to that of Herr Hitler, which enjoys the support of the great majority of the German people. Since then, order and security prevail again, and economic conditions are continually improving. . . .

Four years have elapsed since Herr Hitler's assumption of power on January 30, 1933. Anyone visiting the country can personally convince himself of the immense improvement wrought in that short time. Within a few months, supreme power throughout the country was concentrated in the hands of the Leader. Since then, systematic steps have been taken to rebuild the State. The measures introduced to that end no longer depend for their success upon political accidents or the intrigues of political opponents. Recent elections and plebiscites have shown that not a mere majority, but actually 99 per cent of the electorate, support the Government and endorse its decisions, so that the Reichstag is now more fully representative of the nation's will than it has ever been before.

The victory of National Socialism has thus created the political conditions indispensable to the complete unification of Germany.

Franz Guertner, Reich Minister of Justice

National Socialism looks upon the community of the nation as an organisation which has its own rights and duties and whose interests come before those of the individual. When we speak of the nation, we do not confine

ourselves to the generation to which we happen to belong, but extend that term so as to comprise the sum total of the generations that have preceded us and those that will succeed us. This view has found expression in the National Socialist doctrine asserting that "the needs of the commonwealth take precedence of those of the individual." It dominates National Socialist policy, and its natural corollary is that the rights of the individual must be subordinated to those of the community. The protection enjoyed by individuals is not based on the assumption that their particular rights are sacrosanct and inviolable, but rather on the fact that all of them are regarded as valuable members of the national community, and therefore deserve protection. The reason, therefore, why the National Socialist State can justly claim to be called a constitutional State is that its laws are intended to promote the interests of the community, that—in pursuance of the confidence that forms a connecting link between the rules and the ruled—every citizen can rest assured that his claim to justice will be satisfied, and that everyone who loyally fulfils his duties towards the community can look forward to receiving an equal measure of loyalty from the organs of the State. The political and economic development of the past four years has convincingly shown that we are doing our utmost to provide a secure basis of existence for everyone.

[1] *Germany Speaks*. London: Thornton Butter-worth Ltd., 1938

Personal Accounts of Nazi Control

The following excerpts are taken from letters published anonymously by the German Freedom Party in London under the title *Hitler Calls This Living!*[1]

From a Worker, March 1938

The law does not exist for us any longer. We have no right to change our place of work in order to try and obtain better wages. We have no right to lead our family life and bring up our children decently. You are not even allowed to discuss the fact that things are going badly with you, that you cannot give your child enough to eat, and that your wages are too low to buy the barest essentials, in view of the great increase in the cost of living which has taken place since Hitler came into power. We haven't the right, therefore, to live like human beings. What we have to fight for, in the first place, are the elementary rights of man, which are nowadays being trampled under the boots of the SA. . . .

From a Young Employee, January 1939

. . .The lives of all of us are continually threatened and we are under observation all the time. At home we are ruled by the Block Warden, and besides him there are the Air Raid Precautions Warden and people whom we do not even know. They keep a record of every one of us in a card index, and on it they write whether we give anything for the Winter Help, whether we put out flags, how big the flags are, and how we hang them. They know what we eat, who comes to visit us, they know what kind of [radio] set we use, and whether it can get programmes on the short waves. They keep an eye on our mail and know where our relatives live, whom we go about with, and what we say. They even note the tone of voice in which we ask for the 125 grammes of butter which are allowed us every week. I have never occupied myself with politics and I do not know anything about political parties, but suddenly everything has become political, whatever I say or do, or whatever I don't say or don't do. All I want is to live in peace, to be able to lead my own life, to go for a walk in the woods on Sunday with a friend if I want to, or to paddle a canoe. But none of these things is possible.

And whom can I trust, whom is it possible to trust? I should like for once to say everything I feel, but I do not dare. . . . One spies on the other and tries to trap him. Every spy has somebody else spying on him. We all know we are continually being watched and our lives are being made intolerable.

. . . I do not want to have anything to do with politics, I do not understand anything about politics, and I can only see that they make people bad. But just because I want to be free and honest again, because I should like to say what I think and do as I want to, I am exposing myself to the danger of being denounced. I can be asked to go to the police station, arrested, locked up, and then disappear never to return. Such cases have happened. I can be dismissed from my job, they will write in my employment book that I was sacked for "political" reasons, then I shall never find a post again or even receive relief. I shall be an outlaw. The only thing left for me will be to wait until I am sent to do compulsory labour somewhere.

From a Teacher, December 1938

. . . Party functionaries train their children to be spies and *agents provocateurs*. The relationship of trust between youth and adult has broken down. A further factor in this demoralization is the progressive shattering of family life. Divorce is on the increase, a growing number of married couples are living apart, parents are being forcibly separated because the father has to work in a different town for months at a time. . . .

The youth organizations, particularly the Hitler Youth, have been accorded powers of control which enable every boy and girl to exercise authority backed up by threats. This has its repercussions in the relations between children and parents, and contributes to the conflict and discord in the family. . . . A mere denunciation, with the basest of motives and the slightest justification, is often sufficient to brand a man or woman as "hostile to the State." The refusal of parents to "allow their young children to join the youth organization" is regarded as an adequate reason for taking the children away.

---

[1] *Hitler Calls This Living!* London: Sidgwick and Jackson Ltd., 1939

Dissent and Opposition

There were voices of dissent in Nazi Germany, but none was strong or committed enough to provide much opposition, let alone attempt to overthrow the Nazi regime. Many Germans supported the Nazis to varying degrees and did not publicly object to the suppression of political opponents. Others opposed the regime and were quickly silenced.

Social Democrats and Communists. The Social Democrats smuggled anti-government literature into the country and began to organize an underground movement. In many ways the Communists were better organized to operate underground than the Social Democrats, but their opposition was ineffective. Some Communists were able to pass information about German industry and government to Soviet authorities, until their activities were discovered in 1942 by the Gestapo. The inability of the Social Democrats and Communists to work together greatly hampered their oppositional activities.

Student Groups. A small but active student group, the White Rose movement, appeared at Munich University in the winter of 1938–1939. Its original members consisted of Hans and Sophie Scholl, Alex Schmorell, Christoph Probst, and George Wittenstein. Later Willi Graf and Professor Kurt Huber joined the movement. The movement began writing and publishing leaflets in 1942. In its leaflets, the White Rose first urged youth to engage in passive resistance to Hitler,

Nothing is so unworthy of a civilized people as allowing itself to be governed without opposition by an irresponsible clique that has yielded to base instincts.

Every people deserves the government it is willing to endure.
—White Rose

PHOTO: A photograph of Hans Scholl, Sophie Scholl, and Christoph Probst, leaders of the White Rose student resistance movement, taken in summer 1942.

George J. Wittenstein, Santa Barbara, California, United States

and later informed them about the killing of Jews, Poles, and Sinti–Roma peoples in Eastern Europe. In addition, during the night, slogans such as "Down With Hitler" and "Hitler, Mass Murderer" were painted in huge letters on the walls of important buildings.

On February 18, 1943, Hans and Sophie Scholl were arrested at Munich University. More arrests followed, a total of around 85 people. A hastily convened Volksgerichtshof (People's Court) condemned all of them to death in two trials. Members of the movement made no attempt to hide and maintained their convictions to the very end.

Catholic Church. Fearful that the Church would be attacked by Hitler in the same way it had been sixty years earlier by Chancellor Bismarck, the Roman Catholic Church signed a Concordat agreement in July 1933 with Hitler's government. Hitler feared that the Church would become a threat to his government by discouraging Catholics from supporting him. He wanted the Church to be neutral in political affairs. The Concordat guaranteed Catholic rights such as freedom of worship, protection of Church property, and religious education. In return for these rights, Catholic bishops were required to swear loyalty to the German state, and the Church was ordered to dismantle its Catholic trade unions, permit the dissolution of the Centre Party, which was affiliated with the Church, and promise that the clergy would not participate in politics. Almost immediately following the signing of the Concordat, the Nazi government announced a sterilization law, which the Church opposed, and began to interfere in church and school matters. By the end of 1936, numerous bishops and priests were speaking out against policies of the government from their pulpits. In 1937, Pope Pius XI attacked Nazi principles in a papal encyclical (letter). Hitler responded by intensifying government control of the church and arresting dissenting priests. By 1939, hundreds of priests were in concentration camps.

Protestant Churches. The Protestant churches were no more successful than the Catholic Church at maintaining their independence, though some managed to survive Hitler's attempt to control them. When Hitler took power in January 1933, a group within the Lutheran Church called German Christians wished to fuse Christian and Nazi principles in a new national church.

The idea of a national church was widely supported and the Evangelical Church came into being in May 1933. Non-German pastors were excluded and other German Christians called for the removal of the Old Testament from the Christian Bible on the grounds that it was a "Jewish book." Martin Niemoeller and others formed the Confessional Church within the Evangelical Church as an opposition organization. They defended the Church's right to be free of political interference and to work with youth. In 1937, Niemoeller was arrested and sent to a concentration camp. Hundreds of pastors were arrested and the Confessional Church was made illegal.

Other religious groups such as Jehovah's Witnesses refused to cooperate with Hitler and his government. As a result, the Gestapo arrested about 5000 Jehovah's Witnesses and deported them to concentration camps.

Other Opposition. Opposition to Hitler came from conservatives among traditional elites in the civil service and the German army. In the 1930s, these people did not realize that Hitler's policies would bring great hardship on the German people. During World War II, several conservatives and top officials in the military became convinced that Hitler was leading the country to destruction. Several assassination plans were discussed and in July 1944 one almost succeeded. A bomb placed in a meeting room by Colonel von Stauffenberg exploded but did not kill Hitler. The conspirators, many of whom belonged to the country's military corps, were executed by the Gestapo. Ultimately, all opposition, dissent, and resistance against the Nazis failed and Germany had to await defeat in May 1945 to end rule by Hitler and the Nazi government.

Niemoeller in his own words

Martin Niemoeller was released from a concentration camp in early 1945, after eight and one-half years of imprisonment. He called on fellow Germans to admit their guilt for supporting the Nazi Party and its policies in October 1945.

When, in 1933, Goering publicly boasted that all active Communists had been imprisoned and rendered harmless— that was when we forgot our responsibility, that was when we should have warned our parishioners. Many a man from my own parish who went and joined the National Socialist Party and who is now to do penance for his act could rise up against me today and say that he would have acted differently if I had not kept silence at that time. . . . I know that I made my contribution towards the enslavement of the German people.

Dietmar Schmidt, *Pastor Niemöller*, London: Odhams Press Limited, 1959. p. 151

The following poem was based on Niemoeller's October 1945 statement about his personal responsibility for not having opposed Nazi rule between 1933 and 1937.

First they came for the Communists
and I did not speak out—
because I was not a Communist.
Then they came for the Socialists
and I did not speak out—
because I was not a Socialist.
Then they came for the trade unionists
and I did not speak out—
because I was not a trade unionist.
Then they came for the Jews
and I did not speak out—
because I was not a Jew.
Then they came for me—
and there was no one left
to speak for me.

From *The Six Days of Destruction: Meditations toward Hope*, by Elie Wiesel and Albert H. Friedlander. New York: Paulist Press, 1988. pp. 93–94

NAZI ECONOMIC SYSTEM

From 1933 to 1936, the Nazis justified government intervention in the German economy by the need to reduce mass unemployment and raise national income. After 1936, the German economy came under increasing government control for the purposes of building up the country's military capacity.

Advance Organizer

As the Nazis consolidated their political power, they gradually expanded government control over the German economy. After 1936, the German economy was controlled from above by a comprehensive system of regulation. Private ownership of the means of production was only accepted insofar as it served the interest of the state.

SECTION OVERVIEW
- Economic Policies
- Reorganizing the German Economy

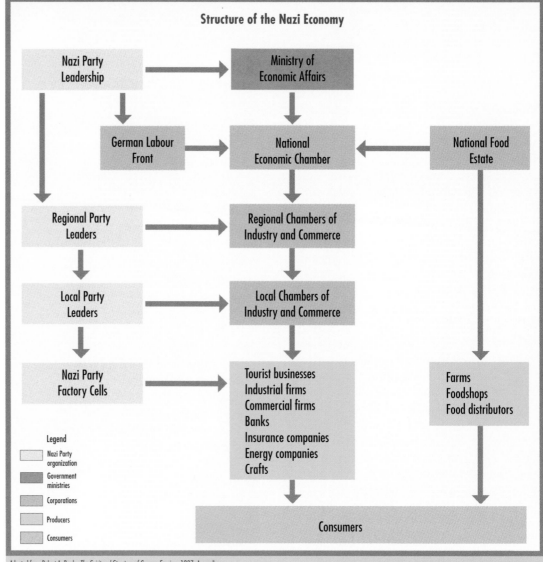

Structure of the Nazi Economy

Legend
- Nazi Party organization
- Government ministries
- Corporations
- Producers
- Consumers

Adapted from Robert A. Brady. *The Spirit and Structure of German Fascism*, 1937. Appendices.

Economic Policies

Economic policies in Nazi Germany were guided by Hitler's political objectives of reducing unemployment in order to gain the support of workers, and making Germany strong. To achieve these objectives, Hitler stressed an active role for government in the economy. The economy was to serve the political interests of the Nazi Party. There were precedents for Hitler to draw on in the Soviet Union and Fascist Italy. The Soviet Union had completed its First Five Year Plan in 1933 and created worldwide interest in how the state could rapidly industrialize a country's economy. In Italy the corporate state offered a solution to labour unrest and low productivity. The extent to which Hitler drew on both remains unclear, but his decision to create an economy based on state control of private enterprise is closer in concept to Fascist Italy's idea of a corporate state.

Italian Corporate State (1926–1940)

Mussolini's attempts to establish a corporate state in Italy began in 1926 with the creation of syndicates to represent the interests of employers and workers. The purpose of the syndicates was to regulate collective bargaining between workers and employers. Members of the syndicates were chosen for their loyalty to the Fascist Party and Mussolini.

Between 1919 and 1922, prior to Mussolini's assumption of power in October 1922, there was widespread labour strife caused by inflation and falling living standards of workers. Many workers, encouraged by Communist and Socialist activists, went on strike for higher wages. The Fascists hoped that by combining the interests of labour and business the syndicates would maintain labour peace, reduce support for the socialist movement among workers, and increase the productive capacity of the Italian economy. A Ministry of Corporations was also set up in 1926 to supervise and control the activities of the syndicates.

The syndicates were successful in reducing labour strife but did not increase economic growth. In 1927, the Italian government faced an economic crisis because of its high spending. When Mussolini took power, his government sharply increased public spending on the military, employed thousands of loyal Fascist Party members, and launched a large program of public works (railway stations, roads, and bridges) to convince the Italian people of fascist efficiency.

The financial crisis of 1927 was followed by the Great Depression in 1930. In early 1930, as unemployment was rising sharply, Mussolini's government set up the National Council of Corporations to act as a consultative body on the economy. This government body discussed all major questions of economic policy for the country and decided how economic policies could be implemented in accordance with directives made by Mussolini and the Fascist Party.

In early 1934, the Italian government established corporations for all leading sectors of the economy. The government announced that these corporations would exercise "organic and unitary control over the nation's productive forces with a view to furthering the growth of wealth, the political power and the well-being of the Italian people." Theoretically, the corporations were designed to be self-governing agents for planning and regulation of the Italian economy. In practice, they had little regulatory power and control over the economy. A major function of the corporations was to provide employment for thousands of Fascist Party members.

The real power in the Italian economy was held by the state-owned Instituto per la Reconstruzione Industriale (IRI), established in 1929 to take over bankrupt private companies. After 1930, the IRI expanded state ownership over industry to such an extent that, except for the Soviet Union, Italy had the greatest level of public ownership of the means of production in Europe. After 1936, state intervention in the Italian economy took the form of controls on prices and production, and regulation of the banking system.

Economic Recovery (1933–1936)

In a speech on May 1, 1933, Hitler announced measures to end unemployment and raise national income in Germany. To achieve this, he declared that his government would provide support to farmers and undertake a massive public works program for roadbuilding.

Nazi ideology stressed the importance of the peasantry and the land. Nazis believed that food production would be increased and the country would become self-sufficient in food if the small farmer was protected. In fact, guaranteeing the existence of small farms made development of large-scale farming difficult, so self-sufficiency was never achieved.

Nazi ideology was socialist and anti-business in outlook, yet Hitler needed big business to achieve his economic and political aims of reducing unemployment, creating economic self-sufficiency, and rearmament. Big business alone had the technology and expertise to build new factories and produce military weapons. A partnership developed between government and big business that allowed large companies to grow, although they were subservient to the Nazi Party and its economic policies.

Four Year Plan (1936–1940)

On September 12, 1936, at the annual Party Congress in Nuremberg, Hitler announced a Four Year Plan to mobilize the German economy for military rearmament of the country. The Plan aimed to make Germany self-sufficient in fuels, iron ore, zinc, copper, lead, and other materials needed in the production of weapons. He declared:

In four years Germany must be completely independent of foreign countries so far as concerns those materials which by any means through German skill, through our chemical and machine industry, or through our mining industry, we can ourselves produce. Further, the new development of this great German raw-material industry, within the national economy, usefully employs the supplies of labour which will be set free on the completion of our rearmament.

For goods that could not be produced domestically, Germany looked to East European suppliers. Through a system of special foreign exchange accounts and barter trade agreements, Germany obtained important raw materials. This strongly tied East European economies to Germany.

By 1939, Hitler's economic policies had transformed the German economy. Compared to the 1920s and early 1930s, industrial production expanded and unemployment fell. But this economic prosperity was achieved through increased controls over wages, employment, consumption, trade, finance, and investment. As well, economic power became concentrated in fewer large corporations, leading to monopoly power in some sectors of the economy, such as I.G. Farben and its subsidiaries in chemicals.

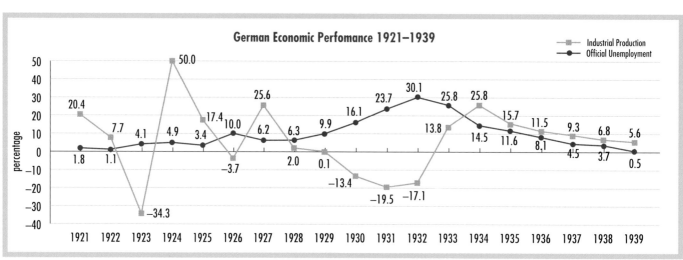

German Economic Performance 1921–1939

Statistical Yearbook of the League of Nations

Reorganizing the German Economy

Key to economic expansion under Hitler was the reorganization of labour unions, farming, and business under Nazi Party control. Although this reorganization of the German economy did not create a fully planned economy, as in the Soviet Union under Stalin, after 1933 it produced an economic system which German economists called a "managed economy," with high levels of state regulation and intervention. During World War II, the German economy came to rely increasingly on more coercive measures, including the use of forced labour in agriculture and industry.

German Labour Front

In early May 1933, labour union offices were shut down by the SA and SS. Labour unions were banned and replaced by the German Labour Front (DAF). Its leader, Robert Ley, called on labour to work as an industrial army for the state and to support the Nazi Party.

The Labour Front promoted Nazi labour policies such as vocational training programs for young and unskilled workers. It built model housing for workers. Under its "Beauty of Work" program, it introduced accident and safety protection, concerts during work breaks, and office beautification. Under its "Strength Through Joy" program, travel was made accessible to the ordinary worker. The program also offered low-interest loans to workers who wished to buy a "people's car" (*Volkswagen*), but the war occurred before any cars could be delivered.

Every May 1, the Labour Front organized mass demonstrations to show that Germany was "a workers' state." The Labour Front claimed to represent workers, but its overall aim was to control them. For example, all workers were issued a "labour book" which contained details about their occupation, employer, and reasons for dismissal. Without a "labour book," a worker could not be employed.

National Food Estate

In March 1933, the National Food Estate was set up to implement the government's agricultural policy. All persons and businesses involved in farming, food processing, and marketing of farm products were obliged to join the National Food Estate.

The Food Estate regulated all aspects of agriculture. It monitored the movement of peasants from the countryside to the cities, regulated land ownership and farm labour, and selected locations for new farming settlements. It implemented the government's program to make Germany self-sufficient in food. It restricted imported foodstuffs, introduced production quotas, and controlled profit margins on the sale of foodstuffs. The goal of self-sufficiency in foodstuffs was never achieved.

National Economic Chamber

In 1934, the National Economic Chamber was created to organize German business into seven groups: crafts, tourism, industry, commerce, banking, insurance, and energy. The National Economic Chamber operated under the formal control of the Ministry of Economic Affairs, which administered the overall direction of the economy. The main functions of the National Economic Chamber were to provide the Ministry with economic reports and proposals and transmit policy from the Ministry to the Chambers of Industry and Commerce.

These Chambers were established as corporations and controlled by the Ministry of Economic Affairs. They had complete control over local business because all businesses had to belong to them. They regulated production, marketing, and prices.

The Chambers were important also for ensuring business loyalty to the state. They selected and recommended businesses for government contracts. Businesses whose owners did not display sufficient enthusiasm for the Nazi cause were disciplined either through the threat of expropriation or loss of government contracts. Businesses which did not contribute their officially allotted share of investment capital in government-sponsored enterprises to promote national self-sufficiency in raw materials and foodstuffs were similarly disciplined.

Official Views on Nazi Economic Policies

The following official views of German economic policies appeared in *Germany Speaks*, which was published in London in early 1938.[1]

Fritz Reinhardt, Secretary of State in the National Ministry of Finance

In 1932, there were about 26 000 000 unemployed throughout the world. At present [1937] the figure stands at about 19 000 000, a decrease of 7 000 000. Out of this decrease, 5 000 000 persons fall to the share of Germany. During the same period in which the rest of the world succeeded in reducing the number of its unemployed from 20 000 000 to 18 000 000 . . . National Socialist Germany was able to provide work for 5 000 000 of her unemployed population. When National Socialism came into power, mass unemployment was higher in Germany than anywhere else. . . . To-day, Germany no longer ranks among countries in which mass unemployment exists.

The above figures prove that Germany's fight against the scourge of unemployment has actually been a complete success. Without the elimination of the exaggerated party system by the Hitler Government, and without the resulting substitution of National Socialist discipline for the Liberalistic absence of systematic efforts, such success would have been unthinkable.

R. Walther Darré, Head of the National Food Estate

What was considered impossible a short while ago has been achieved—the price of butter has, for instance, remained unchanged for two years and a half, and the same applies to most of the other kinds of agricultural produce. The interference of speculators and vested interests has been eliminated, notably in the grain trade. Prices no longer fall to pieces when the harvest has been particularly abundant. . . . The number of middlemen in the process of distribution has been reduced to a minimum. During the preceding economic era, production was rationalised. To-day it has become necessary to organize the distribution—and therefore the supply—of goods in accordance with the dictates of common sense, without restricting production in any way. This makes it possible to effect enormous savings, which can then be utilised for the benefit of the producer or the consumer. The increase in the yield of agricultural production is mainly due to such savings.

Robert Ley, Leader of the German Labour Front

One of the first necessities with which the Hitler Government found itself faced was that of dissolving the organisations that kept alive the antagonism between employers and employees. They were replaced by the German Labour Front—a body comprising employers as well as employees. At the same time, preparations were made for the creation of an entirely new system of social order based on the following National Socialist principles: the solidarity of all persons working for their living; the idea of leadership; the recognition of the factory, etc., as a bond of union, and the ethical conceptions of honour and loyalty. All this preliminary work crystalized in the passing of the Act governing the regulation of national labour.

Dr. Fritz Todt, Inspector-General of the German Road and Highways System

In view of the vast amount of unemployment which prevailed in Germany before National Socialism came into power, it goes without saying that the tackling of this problem was a main consideration in the construction of Reich motor roads. Through their construction, 130 000 men were directly kept at work on the building sites. A further 130 000 men find additional work and their daily bread in the supplying and consuming industries, that is to say in stone quarries, bridge building plants, cement works, iron working shops, building-machine factories, etc. The increased consumption of foodstuffs and purchase of clothes by this host of workmen who are again able to earn their own living is a factor which carries considerable weight. . . .

In addition to the construction of the 7000 kilometres of new motor roads, a comprehensive road-construction programme will be put into effect for modernising the former long-distance roads of the various States and provinces, i.e., the present Reich roads. About 40 000 kilometres of such roads have been taken over by the Reich, and are either in course of reconstruction or

[1]*Germany Speaks*. London: Thornton Butterworth Ltd., 1938

extension. . . . Within the framework of other important measures undertaken by the National Socialist Government in its fight against unemployment, the construction of new roads was the first and foremost, and remains so up to the present day [1937].

Personal Views on Nazi Economic Policies

Government control over the economy affected big businesses less than small businesses, which were devastated by government regulations. By 1939, government restrictions were forcing thousands of small businesses to close and their owners to seek work in the factories of larger businesses.

The owner of Thyssen Steel Works, one of Germany's largest steel companies, supported the Nazi Party financially for years. In September 1939, he fled to Switzerland and his companies were nationalized without compensation. He later criticized Hitler's economic policy of controlling German business for national interests.

Fritz Thyssen, Thyssen Steel Works

(Excerpt) from Fritz Thyssen, *I Paid Hitler*. London: Hodder and Stoughton Ltd., 1941. p. 178

The pet enterprise of the regime was the famous Four-Year Plan. I have always wondered why it was called a "plan." Government regulation of commerce and industry in Germany had led to total state control; Hitler picked up the Russian idea of the Five-Year Plan. Yet the difference is considerable. The Russians desired to create large-scale industrial production in a country where it was as yet non-existent. . . . When Hitler announced the Four-Year Plan at Nuremberg, German industrialists were greatly surprised. He had consulted nobody and no one knew what he meant.

A Small Business Owner

(Excerpts from letters smuggled out of Germany) German Freedom Party, *Uncensored Germany*. London: Sidgwick and Jackson Ltd., 1940

"Now we have to keep our shops open even when there is nothing to sell, and our customers must be sent away empty-handed. That is the new decree. An agreement had been made by which we might close our shops as soon as we were sold out, but that is now prohibited." This was said to me by my butcher, whom I have known for years and with whom I talk frankly when there is nobody in the shop, as we used to do in former times.

He joined the Nazi Party during its early days and was very active both in the "cell" to which he belonged and in his [local Chamber of Industry and Commerce]. In 1933 he saw heaven opening before his eyes, but within a few months he began to grumble and has not stopped since. At first I did not trust him, and thought he was trying to find out what I really thought about the regime; but at last I realised from the agitated tone of his voice that he was in deadly earnest. He is still impressed by the successes in the field of foreign policy, though sometimes, especially since last spring, he has said anxiously, "If only things don't go wrong!"

His chief anxiety, however, is for his business and the difficulty he finds in obtaining supplies. A strict quota is allotted to him, and he receives just as much as the authorities reckon he requires, but no more. If he cannot give his customers the right kind of meat they stay away, though it is not his fault since there is always a shortage of one kind of meat or another. It is quite impossible for him to adjust his business to the changed conditions, and his relations with his customers are not always pleasant. He has, moreover, lost some of his best customers through the Jewish persecution. "It hasn't done us any good at all," he complained to me.

He used to do a splendid business, but now his sales have declined enormously. Prices are fixed, and in addition there is the irritation caused by the [tax] authorities, who examine every detail, check his books with a microscopic attention, and have other less obvious ways of controlling his sales. Every [cent] has to be accounted for and taxes are collected with ruthless severity, to say nothing of the various compulsory levies for the Party and its organisations. No comfort can be gained by airing his grievances, for nobody can be trusted and there is the risk of having his shop confiscated. "If you are finding things too difficult," he was once told, "why don't you close down? We've got enough butchers' shops, but not enough workers. Perhaps you would feel happier if you were to do a little digging in the Siegfried Line!" [August 1939]

NAZI POLITICAL ECONOMY

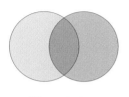

- Nazi Political System
- Nazi Economic System
- Nazi Political Economy

Advance Organizer

In 1933, Hitler declared Nazi rule in Germany would last 1000 years. As time passed, this rule began to rely increasingly on military rearmament and an extreme nationalism, all of which would eventually lead Germany to go to war. After it was defeated in 1945, Germany underwent several profound political and economic changes, which also transformed political and economic conditions in Europe.

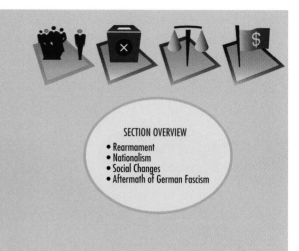

SECTION OVERVIEW
- Rearmament
- Nationalism
- Social Changes
- Aftermath of German Fascism

Rearmament

Under Hitler, most political and economic policies were dedicated to the objective of rearming Germany. To Nazis, rearmament would restore national pride and end the country's humiliation under the 1919 Treaty of Versailles. Thus, the government increased its spending as a percentage of GDP (see chart below).

Government Deficits. The chart illustrates the extent to which Nazi fiscal policy relied on deficit financing to fund government spending on work creation and rearmament. The budget deficit ballooned from 1.0% of GDP in 1932 to 24.6% of GDP in 1939.

Government debt as a percentage of GDP escalated from 27.4% in 1932 to 74.0% in 1939. The increase in government spending after 1932 was devoted largely to the military. In 1939, spending on military rearmament accounted for about 80% of all government spending.

How could the country continue to incur ever larger budget deficits without causing an inflationary spiral similar to that which occurred in 1923–1924? In 1934, the central bank developed the MEFO bill, a form of credit to businesses for the production of goods. From 1934 to 1938, the central bank issued over 12 billion marks (US$4.8 billion) in MEFO bills for military goods. In January 1939, Schacht, the head of the central bank, warned Hitler that his government's fiscal policy would lead the country to ruinous inflation if government spending on military weapons was not slowed. Schacht was dismissed and Hitler sharply increased government spending.

The effect of the government's rearmament program greatly affected German society and economy. By 1939, the sharp rise in government debt brought an end to the rise in living standards, as more resources were allocated to military spending. The increased production of military weapons led to greater government control over the economy, and further eroded the independence of private business.

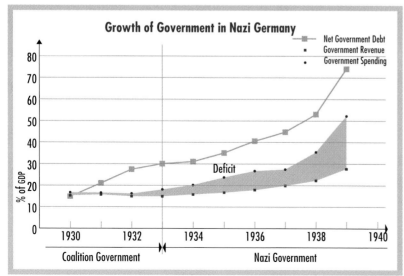

Growth of Government in Nazi Germany

- Net Government Debt
- Government Revenue
- Government Spending

Deficit

Coalition Government | Nazi Government

% of GDP

Compiled from *Statistical Yearbook of the League of Nations* and Rene Erbe. *Die nationalsozialistische Wirtschaftspolitik 1933–1939* [*National Socialist Economic Policy 1933–1939*]

Nationalism

Hitler's nationalist views included the glorification of the German people as a "superior" race.

Hitler's Racial Philosophy

According to Hitler, the German people belonged to a superior race called the Aryans, who were founders of culture and created the world's greatest civilizations. Other peoples merely passed culture on to others, according to Hitler's philosophy, because they did not have the physical, psychological, and intellectual capacity to create culture and great inventions. Hitler believed that the French, English, and other Western Europeans belonged to this second racial category. At the bottom of Hitler's racial hierarchy were the people he labelled destroyers of culture—the Jews, Slavic peoples, and Sinti–Roma peoples. Hitler believed these people should be segregated from other peoples because they were "subhuman." Hitler believed that the Germans, as the superior race, were destined to rule Europe and the world. All Germans were required to prove the racial purity of their family backgrounds, and those who had doubtful racial backgrounds were segregated, arrested, deported, or killed.

Gerd Ruehle, *Das Dritte Reich*. 1933. (p. 427)

Anti-Semitism

Anti-semitism had a long history in Germany and elsewhere in Europe. Various nationalist political parties in Europe were formed on a platform of anti-semitism. Following Germany's defeat in World War I, some German nationalists blamed the Jewish minority for the country's defeat (Jews numbered about 500 000, or less than 1% of the population in 1933). Jews were also blamed for the spread of communism in Germany because some Jews belonged to the communist movement.

Once in power, the Nazi government enacted laws to force Jews out of the civil service, professions, and business. The Nuremberg Laws of 1935 deprived all German Jews of their citizenship and legally classified them as a foreign "race," without political rights. They became outcasts in German society and subjected to public persecution. This persecution resulted in a nationwide pogrom carried out by SS and SA units on November 9, 1938, called the *Kristallnacht* (Night of the Broken Glass). In all, 177 synagogues and 7500 shops were destroyed. *Kristallnacht* signalled the beginning of a more violent phase in Nazi racial policy.

In reality, the majority of Germany's Jews had long been assimilated into mainstream German culture and society. Thousands had fought and died for Germany in World War I. Many had made significant contributions to German business, science, education, and culture. When the National Socialists introduced anti-semitic practices and laws, approximately 300 000 Jews emigrated, and the country lost their talents. Among those who emigrated were physicists Albert Einstein, Max Born, and James Franck, playwright Ernst Toller, and photo journalist Erich Salomon. The young diarist Anne Frank emigrated with her family to Holland, where they were later captured. Those who remained in Germany were so restricted in their activities that they could not function as productive citizens. Most of these German Jews were arrested and imprisoned in concentration camps, where they were subjected to inhuman treatment and millions died.

PHOTO: A poster in a department store window in Berlin in April 1933 advising Germans not to believe propaganda put out by British and French governments about Nazi treatment of German Jews and to buy goods only from stores owned by Germans.

The Holocaust

During World War II, millions of Jews in German-occupied countries were rounded up and sent to their deaths in extermination camps, in what has become known as the Holocaust. The following three primary sources document some scenes from that time.

My Testimony and Legacy: Survivor of the Nazi Holocaust

(Excerpts) by David Bergman, reprinted with permission.

I, David Bergman, survivor of Auschwitz, Dachau and other death camps, hereby sign my name below attesting to the horrors and brutalities that I personally witnessed and experienced during the Nazi reign of terror, known as The Nazi Holocaust.

Daniel Bergman

May 1997

In April 1944, at the age of 12, I, my mother, father, brother, sister, grandparents, relatives, friends and other Jewish people from our hometown in the Carpathian Mountains of Europe, travelled through this corridor, *Entering The Hell of Auschwitz*. As the freight train came to a stop, the guards unlocked the doors. After I stepped out of the train, I saw the darkest and most brutal side of humanity ever imagined. Instantly, I became a changed person. It felt like a new force took control over me. Instead of initially wanting to question why God was allowing this to happen, this new invisible force guided me to focus upon survival. . . .

In the end, I would be the only one from my family and the only youth my age from my hometown who would make it back alive.

After I stepped out of the freight train in Auschwitz, I heard shootings and shouting. I saw children being beaten and crying as they were being dragged away from their parents. I saw parents being beaten for trying to prevent the guards from taking their children away. No one expected anything like this. Before we were deported, the Nazis told us that we would be taken to a city in Hungary to help with the war effort. . . . Men were ordered to form one line, women and children another line. I was ordered to go into a children's line. Ahead of the line was the Gestapo. They were about to act as God, deciding who shall live and who shall die. Just the motion of a hand decided one's fate.

After the separations, I was placed in a children's line . . . . That new force within me prodded me to get out of the children's line because of the danger I faced. It urged me to attempt to get into the line where the male adults were standing. The question was how to do it when we were being guarded so closely.

Amidst the shooting and shouting and all of that confusion, I kept a close eye on the guard who was watching over us. When he turned around momentarily to look the other way, I quickly got out of the children's line and ran over to the adult line. Fortunately the guard did not see me. In the adult line, I also found my father. Both of us

would soon face a Nazi officer who would decide our fate either to be sent to a work camp or to the gas chamber. Those victims I was with, in the children's line, were soon taken to the gas chamber and within a few hours they were all dead.

All of those considered unfit for work were taken to a building under the pretense of taking a shower. Instead of water coming through the shower heads a poisonous gas came out. Within a span of about 15 minutes they would all be dead. A gas chamber could asphyxiate as many as 2000 victims at one time. From the gas chambers the bodies were then taken to crematoriums where they were turned into ashes. . . . As others were being judged in front of me whether to be sent to a work camp or the gas chamber, the Gestapo officer would generally just motion his hand, ordering the victim to go into one line or the other.

But when it came my turn to be judged, it was different. Before motioning his hand for me to go one way or the other, the Gestapo officer stopped and asked me how old I was. I wanted to tell him that I was 12, but my voice just froze and the words would not come out. The Gestapo officer was beginning to get irritated.

He was wondering how I got into this line in the first place. I was supposed to have been in a children's line. My father sensing the danger I faced, suddenly told the Gestapo officer that I was 14. I wanted to yell out loud to say that I was only 12 because I was taught to always tell the truth. But something held me back and I just could not speak. The

Gestapo officer was now deliberating which line I should be sent to. All of a sudden, the Gestapo officer motioned his hand for me to go into the line where those judged to be fit for work were sent. Fortunately, my father was also sent to the same line. Within a few minutes, my voice came back and I was able to speak again. As I was standing in the line waiting to be told what the next step will be, I happened to notice my mother, brother, and sister standing in another line. From everything that just happened, I was just too numb, too shocked, too dazed, and too scared to even say hello or goodbye to them. Little did I know at that time that the brief glance that I had of them during that moment was going to be the last. They all perished in Auschwitz. . . .

Only my father and I were allowed to stay together in Auschwitz. We did not know the fate of the rest of our family at that time.

Soon afterwards, we were taken to the barracks. We were ordered to remove all of our clothing and belongings and leave them on the floor. Afterwards, we were ordered to go into a different area to get our new striped cotton uniforms.

In Auschwitz we spent our time waiting to be sent to a work camp. After about seven days in Auschwitz (on May 3, 1944), a Gestapo guard entered our barracks and ordered me, my father and about fifteen others to get out. Once outside of the barracks, we were ordered to march to a freight train that was awaiting to take us to a work camp.

. . . After about three hours of travelling, we arrived in a camp called Plaszov. In Plaszov, my father worked as a tailor and I became a bricklayer. After about three months of being together we were forcibly separated. We had to say goodbye through a barbed wire fence. It was a very painful separation, which I have never gotten over. I never saw him again.

From Plaszov I was taken to Gross Rosen, a concentration camp in Germany. In Gross Rosen, I was just waiting to find out whether I would be taken to the gas chamber or a work camp. Luckily I was sent to Reichenbach, a work camp.

From Reichenbach, I was taken to Dachau and from Dachau to the Tyrolean Mountains of Austria, where I was finally liberated in May of 1945.

Letter from General Eisenhower

(Excerpt) Letter from Supreme Commander of the Allied Forces in Europe General Dwight D. Eisenhower to Chief of Staff George Marshall, April 12, 1945

The things I saw beggar description. . . The visual evidence and the verbal testimony of starvation, cruelty, and bestiality were so overpowering as to leave me a bit sick. In one room, where there were piled up twenty or thirty naked men killed by starvation, George Patton would not even enter. He said he would get sick if he did so. I made the visit deliberately, in order to be in a position to give firsthand evidence of these things if ever, in the future, there develops a tendency to charge these allegations merely to "propaganda."

Archive Photos

PHOTO: One of many mass graves found by American forces in early 1945 at the Belsen concentration camp.

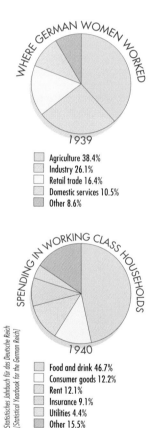

WHERE GERMAN WOMEN WORKED

1939

- ☐ Agriculture 38.4%
- ☐ Industry 26.1%
- ☐ Retail trade 16.4%
- ☐ Domestic services 10.5%
- ☐ Other 8.6%

SPENDING IN WORKING CLASS HOUSEHOLDS

1940

- ☐ Food and drink 46.7%
- ☐ Consumer goods 12.2%
- ☐ Rent 12.1%
- ☐ Insurance 9.1%
- ☐ Utilities 4.4%
- ☐ Other 15.5%

Statistisches Jahrbuch für das Deutsche Reich [Statistical Yearbook for the German Reich]

PHOTO: Members of a women's farm work team.

Social Changes

German society underwent some important changes under the Nazis. One influence was a campaign to promote and support traditional roles for men and women. Also, although the Nazis ended mass unemployment, their labour policies had significant effects on the living standards of many German workers.

Role of Men and Women

According to Nazi beliefs, men and women had traditional roles in society. The man's role was centred outside the home, in the labour force, while the woman's role was in the home, as a child-bearer. In 1934, the Nazi Party organized the National Socialist Women's Union (NSF) as a department responsible for the ideological, cultural, and economic leadership of women. It closed down women's groups and birth-control clinics. Abortion was made illegal. In collaboration with the Ministry of Public Enlightenment and Propaganda, the Women's Union organized public campaigns stressing the traditional roles of *Kinder, Kirche, Küche* (child, church, and kitchen). In practice, many women continued to work outside the home, though women in professions and management were forced by the Nazi government to give up their careers.

In March 1938, to ensure a larger supply of workers, a campaign was launched to encourage more women to enter the labour force. Women were to provide labour for agricultural work and household service. In 1939, it was officially reported that women constituted about 37% of the labour force. The main areas of work for women were agriculture, industry, retail trade, and domestic services (see chart "Where German Women Worked").

Living Conditions

Though mass unemployment had been eliminated by 1937, wages did not return to the levels of 1929. The abolition of trade unions and official controls on wage rates effectively kept workers from demanding higher wages. The only way for workers to earn higher incomes was to work more hours. The average work week increased from 46 hours in 1929 to 48 hours in 1939. In most heavy industries, the average work week exceeded 50 hours. During World War II, workers were ordered to work longer hours.

The chart "Spending in Working Class Households" shows that food was the largest single expense for the average working class household, accounting for 42.8% of the average wage. Insurance, rent, heating and lighting, and clothing together accounted for another 34.9%. Less than 25% remained for other expenses. This situation was not significantly different in many middle class households, as more and more of the country's national income and productive capacity was diverted to war production.

Friedrich Stieve, *Neues Deutschland [New Germany]*. Munich: Heinrich Hoffman-Verlag, 1939. (p. 41) Presse-Hoffmann, Berlin.

Aftermath of German Fascism

At 4:30 AM on September 1, 1939, German forces invaded Poland and began World War II. For the next five years and nine months Germany was at war. Hitler committed suicide on April 30, 1945. On May 7, Germany's leaders unconditionally surrendered to Allied forces at Rheims, France. The era of Nazi rule was officially closed, but its influence continued to be felt in the immediate postwar years, as Germany underwent political and economic reconstruction.

Political Reconstruction of Germany

The political reconstruction of Germany in the postwar period took the form of a massive deportation of most Germans living in Eastern Europe, the division of the country into two separate republics, a program of de-Nazification, and the establishment of new democratic institutions.

Deportation. From 1945 to 1948, an estimated 12 million Germans were expelled from Eastern Europe, from parts of Germany ceded to Poland, and from the Soviet Union. The campaign to deport Germans from Czechoslovakia was particularly ruthless. In the course of these deportations, an estimated 2.2 million Germans perished from hunger, disease, and exposure.

Division. In August 1945, Germany and the city of Berlin were divided into four zones of Allied occupation (American, British, French, and Soviet). In 1948, the American, British, and French zones were united, and in 1949 they became the Federal Republic of Germany (West Germany), with its capital at Bonn. The Soviet zone became the German Democratic Republic (East Germany), with its capital in East Berlin. For the next 40 years Germany and the city of Berlin (which lay within East Germany) remained divided. A thriving democracy was established in West Germany, but in East Germany, Soviet forces supported a Communist regime which finally collapsed in November 1989. On October 3, 1990, East Germany officially rejoined West Germany, ending 45 years of political division. Berlin was reunited and in 1999 became the capital of Germany once again.

De-Nazification. While under Allied occupation, Germans were subjected to a campaign of "de-Nazification." Under this campaign, all Germans who were members of the Nazi Party or collaborated with the Nazis were compelled officially to renounce their political past and accept guilt for their misdeeds. In 1946 at Nuremberg, several high ranking Nazi leaders were put on trial for war crimes. Some were hanged and others imprisoned. The Nuremberg Trial set a historical precedent, because for the first time a country's leaders could be held accountable to the international community for their policies.

Democratization. In 1949, West Germany received a new democratic constitution. In it, the powers of government were clearly defined and governed by a system of checks and balances. The powers of the President to suspend the constitution were greatly reduced. To prevent a dictatorship from reoccurring, the powers of the chancellor were reduced and the chancellor was made accountable to a bicameral parliament composed of a lower chamber, the Reichstag, and an upper chamber, the Reichsrat. Proportional representation was retained from the Weimar constitution, but political parties now had to obtain at least 5% of the popular vote to enter the Reichstag. West Germany became a federal state, with many powers granted to the states.

That same year, East Germany received a new constitution which centralized political power under the Communist Party. For the next 40 years the Communist Party held all political power in East Germany. In November 1989, the Communist Party voluntarily agreed to give up power. Democratic elections were held in March 1990. Six months later in October, the German Democratic Republic was united with the Federal Republic of Germany.

The Allied Powers in World War II were the United States, Soviet Union, Great Britain, and their allies.

The Axis Powers in World War II were Germany, Italy, Japan, and their allies.

The Federal Republic of Germany was established in 1949 following the unification of the American, British, and French zones of occupation. The flag of the Federal Republic of Germany is based on the flag of the Weimar Republic (1919–1933).

The German Democratic Republic (1949–1990) was set up in the Soviet zone of occupation. The flag of the German Democratic Republic above was adopted in 1973. In 1990, the German Democratic Republic became part of the Federal Republic of Germany.

The European Union officially replaced the European Economic Community on January 1, 1994. Germany was a founding member of the European Economic Community in 1957.

© European Communities, 1995–1998
(Source: www.europa.eu.int)

On January 1, 1999, the euro became the official currency of the European Union.

Economic Reconstruction and Integration

The political reconstruction of Germany after 1945 was accompanied by economic reconstruction. The reconstruction and integration of the West German economy began with the Marshall Plan in 1948, and was later furthered with the formation of the European Economic Community. In 1949, East Germany became a member of the Council for Mutual Economic Assistance (Comecon).

Marshall Plan. Named after United States Secretary of State George C. Marshall, the Marshall Plan was set up in 1948 as an economic assistance program to help Western Europe and West Germany rebuild their war-damaged economies. From 1948 to 1952, the Marshall Plan disbursed over $10 billion in grants for economic reconstruction. The Organization for European Economic Cooperation (OEEC) was set up in 1948 to administer the Marshall Plan. Its objective was to coordinate the economic and social policies of countries receiving assistance under the Plan. The Marshall Plan was a success. In 1961, the OEEC became the Organization for Economic Cooperation and Development (OECD), to coordinate economic policies of industrial countries.

Comecon. In 1949, in response to the Marshall Plan in Western Europe, the Soviet Union and five East European countries (Bulgaria, Czechoslovakia, Hungary, Poland, and Romania) formed the Council for Mutual Economic Assistance (Comecon) to promote economic growth and strengthen domestic industry. East Germany joined soon after. Comecon strengthened trading ties between Eastern Europe and the Soviet Union. Following the unification with West Germany in 1990, East Germany became part of the European Economic Community. In June 1991, Comecon was voluntarily disbanded.

Treaty of Paris. In April 1951, the first step toward European integration was made with the signing of the Treaty of Paris. It established the European Coal and Steel Community (ECSC) to administer the coal and steel industries of West Germany, France, Italy, Belgium, Netherlands, and Luxembourg for peaceful purposes.

Treaty of Rome. In March 1957, the six members of the ECSC signed the Treaty of Rome to create a common market called the European Economic Community (EEC). The aim of the EEC was "to promote throughout the Community a harmonious development of economic activities, a continuous and balanced expansion, an increased stability, an accelerated raising of the standard of living, and closer relations between its member states."

As a member of the EEC, West Germany's economy grew rapidly, prompting many Germans in the 1960s to refer to it as an "economic miracle." Since the 1970s, German economic growth has slowed, yet today Germany has the third largest economy in the world.

European Union. In December 1991 at Maastricht, member states of the European Community (the former European Economic Community) signed a treaty which proposed to create a European economic and monetary union. In this economic union, all member states pledged to coordinate their economic and fiscal policies to prevent large budget deficits. The monetary union proposed to replace national currencies by 1999 with new European currency called the euro. On November 1, 1993, Germany became the last member formally to ratify the Maastricht Treaty. Effective January 1, 1994, the European Community was renamed the European Union (EU) to signify the beginning of the transition to an economic and monetary union.

Five years later, the economic and monetary union began in Germany and ten other European Union member countries, with the introduction of the euro. In Germany, the euro will gradually replace the mark, which will continue to circulate until July 1, 2002, by which time all marks will be replaced by euros.

REVIEW

Summary

Fascism emerged as an ideology when the fascist movement, led by Benito Mussolini, gained power in Italy in 1922, and when the Nazi Party under Adolf Hitler took over Germany in 1933. The beliefs of Mussolini and Hitler emphasized human inequality, worship of the leader, government by elites, extreme nationalism, racial purity, organized violence, and glorification of war.

The Nazi political system in Germany was a totalitarian dictatorship characterized by centralization of political power and decision making in the hands of Hitler and the Nazi Party. Power was maintained through one-party rule of the Nazi Party. People's participation in the political process was tightly controlled through the use of carefully staged elections and plebiscites. Propaganda and indoctrination were used to persuade people to believe that Hitler and the Nazi Party governed the country for the common good. A secret police and armed guards were often used to arrest, imprison, and execute political opponents and dissenters to Nazi rule.

Under the Nazis, the German economy came under increasing government control, and regulation of private enterprise was achieved through the creation of separate corporations for industry, agriculture, and labour. Greater government intervention in the economy was necessary for rebuilding the country's capacity to produce military weapons and prepare it for war.

German society under the Nazi regime became increasingly concerned with rearming the country and promoting extreme nationalism. These changes brought Germany to war with its neighbours, then to a crushing defeat in 1945, followed by political and economic reconstruction in the immediate post-war years.

Fascist Values and Political Philosophy

1. Read the section on core fascist values and answer the following questions.
   a) Imagine that you are living in a society with a fascist government. What would your life be like as a young person in that society?
   b) Describe two or three possible consequences for people living in a society with a strong belief in human inequality.

2. a) Compare the beliefs of Mussolini and Hitler in chart form, showing similarities and differences.
   b) How would you describe fascism, based on these beliefs?

3. What post-World War I event angered and motivated the Nazis to action?

4. a) After 1925, the activities and goal of the Nazi Party changed. What event motivated the change?
   b) What does the text tell us about Hitler's views of democracy in 1925?
   c) What role did the SA play in the Nazi rise to power?
   d) After 1930, what problem did Hitler promise to solve?

5. The rise of fascism in Italy and Germany owed much to the strong personalities of its leaders.
   a) How did Mussolini take power in Italy?
   b) How did Hitler achieve power in Germany?

6. Examine the chart on page 297 and answer the following questions.
    a) Support for the Nazis rose dramatically between the May 1928 and September 1930 elections. What important event of the 20th century began between these two events? Why would one consequence of

this be a significant increase in votes for the Nazis?

b) Which other political party gained greater public support during this same period? Why did they receive greater support?

c) The Nazis did not win enough seats in July 1932 to form a majority government; however, only the Social Democrats had received a greater percentage of votes (37.9%) in the 1919 election. From 1919–1932, Germany only had coalition governments of two or more parties. To what extent do you think that the Nazis had earned the right to govern Germany by 1932?

7. Choose what you think is the correct answer to the question below. Explain why you think it is correct and the other three are incorrect.

Which of the following generalizations can **best** be supported from the information presented on the chart on page 297?

A. The Nazis increased their support by beating up their opponents in the streets.

B. There was a dramatic increase in support for left-wing parties during this time.

C. Moderate parties experienced no drop in support during these years.

D. As time passed, more and more people voted for extremist parties.

8. Read the Consolidation of Power on page 298. How important was the Enabling Act to Hitler becoming dictator of Germany? Explain your answer.

Nazi Political System

1. Explain how Hitler came to hold all the executive power in Germany by 1934.

2. Identify the features that characterized the Nazi political system.

3. Did the German judiciary remain independent after Hitler came to power?

4. The margin notes on page 302 indicate the growth in the membership of the Fascist Party in Italy and the Nazi Party in Germany. For what reasons do you think that millions of people would join these parties?

5. What does the chart on page 302 demonstrate about the nature of the government? Provide evidence from the chart to support your answer.

6. By what means did Hitler centralize political power? How was participation in the political process controlled?

7. What steps were taken by Hitler to ensure that he maintained control over the Nazi Party?

8. Read the section on Consequences of One-Party Rule. A common view suggests that dictatorships are run smoothly and efficiently and that decisions can be made quickly. What evidence is there on page 304 to suggest that this view is either correct or incorrect?

9. In the November 1933 national elections, 7.9% of voters spoiled their ballots. The number of spoiled ballots declined in later elections to just over 1% of the vote. What might have accounted for this change?

10.
a) In his own words, what was Hitler's view of the importance and nature of propaganda?

b) What methods were used by the Nazis to indoctrinate people?

c) Who in society were the special targets of Nazi propaganda?

d) What did the Nazi Party do to ensure control over education in Germany?

e) What type of young men and women were the Nazis hoping to create?

11. Read the Focus On Critical Thinking on page 308.

a) Briefly summarize the view expressed in each of the four excerpts.

b) What do you think was the situation for German youth during the 1930s? Provide evidence to support your opinion.

12. Describe the role the SA, SS, and Gestapo played in controlling the people of Germany. Include the role played by Heinrich Himmler.

13. a) Which peoples especially were targets of the Gestapo?

b) What happened to them?

14. What is the significance of the words *Arbeit Macht Frei* on the gate at Dachau (bottom left, page 311)?

15. Read the views expressed in the Focus On Critical Thinking section on pages 312 and 313. How would you describe life in Germany for ordinary people by 1939 on the eve of World War II?

16. Read the section on Dissent and Opposition (pages 314–315) and answer the following questions.

a) Briefly describe the nature of the opposition of each of the groups mentioned.

b) How successful was the opposition by each of these groups?

c) What lessons are to be drawn from Martin Niemoeller's own words about his lack of warning to his parishioners, and the words attributed to him about not speaking out?

d) To what extent does the White Rose serve as an example for students to follow when faced with a political system or situation which they oppose?

Nazi Economic System

1. Read the section on the Italian Corporate State on page 317. Identify the strengths and weaknesses of the Fascist approach to the economy.

2. a) When Hitler took power in January 1933, what were his immediate economic objectives?

b) How did he propose to deal with these problems?

c) Was his thinking about the role of big business ideological or practical? Explain your answer.

3. The first Four Year Plan began in 1936. Read the text, including Hitler's own words. What was the ultimate goal of this plan?

4. What were the political and economic goals of the German Labour Front, the National Food Estate, and the National Economic Chamber?

5. Read the Focus On Critical Thinking section on pages 320–321 and answer the following questions.

a) Briefly summarize the main idea of each of the four official views.

b) From the four statements, what generalizations can be made about the German economy by 1939?

c) What difficulties were faced by owners of small business by 1939?

d) From these personal narratives, what can be said about the relationship between the business community and the Nazi Party by 1939?

e) To what extent do the views of business contradict the official views?

6. What role did the Nazi state play in answering the four basic economic questions? (See page 77, Chapter 3)

Nazi Political Economy

1. a) By 1939, what were the most serious economic problems facing Germany?

   b) What success did they have in solving these economic problems?

2. Why did government spending increase after 1936?

3. Use the line graph on page 322 to answer the following questions.

    a) As a percentage of GDP, how much did government spending increase over government revenue by mid-1939, compared to 1936?

   b) To what extent were the Nazis successful in controlling budget deficits and the public debt? Cite statistics to support your conclusion.

   c) As an economic advisor to the Nazi Party, what arguments could you put forth in favour of war to solve the specific economic problems illustrated by this graph?

4. a) How widespread was anti-semitism in Europe in the early part of the 20th century?

   b) What were the political and economic effects of the Nuremberg laws and *Kristallnacht* on the Jewish population of Germany?

   c) Even without war, what was the harm done to German society because of the extreme anti-semitism of the Nazi regime?

5. Read the Focus On Critical Thinking section on pages 324 and 325.

   a) Summarize the experiences of Mr. Bergman in point form.

   b) How do you think you might react to an experience like this?

   c) What has likely been the effect of this experience on the author, David Bergman?

d) What lessons does the Holocaust teach all people, regardless of where they live, about how to deal with regimes like that of Adolf Hitler?

6. By 1949, what changes had occurred in Germany?

7. a) How much has the German economy been integrated into a general European economy (page 328)?

   b) How important do you think the German economy is to the overall strength of the European economy today?

Chapter Consolidation

1. This chapter began with a quotation by Adolf Hitler from his trial in 1924. Knowing what you do about the Nazi period in Germany, what would you say to a person who made a public statement like that today?

2. a) On what values were the political and economic systems of Nazi Germany based?

   b) Whose ideas were influential in the development of the political and economic systems in Nazi Germany?

   c) Create a chart, identifying the type of political system and economic system in Nazi Germany and the strengths and weaknesses of these systems.

9

SOVIET UNION

"Socialism is Soviet power plus the electrification of the whole country."
—Vladimir Lenin, Report to the Congress of Soviets, December 22, 1920

In the 20th century, communism was the first major ideology to seriously challenge the existing political and economic systems. It first appeared in Russia following the seizure of power by Vladimir Lenin in November 1917. Communism in the Soviet Union was based on rule by one political party which attempted to control all aspects of political, economic, and social life. Political power was concentrated in the hands of one leader or a small group, and power was preserved by a vast secret police network which attempted to silence all opposition. The Soviet Union became the first example of a 20th century totalitarian state.

As an economic system, communism was based on central planning, state ownership of the means of production, and the collectivization of agriculture. The five year plan was an important instrument for the rapid industrialization of the Soviet Union.

This chapter discusses the political and economic systems of the Soviet Union from 1917 to 1985. The last years of the Soviet Union, from 1986 to 1991, are examined in the chapter on the Russian Federation (see Chapter 10).

Chapter Concepts/Vocabulary

Marxism–Leninism	GULAG
Stalinism	*samizdat*
Presidium	War Communism
Council of Ministers	New Economic Policy
General Secretary	Five Year Plan
Supreme Soviet	collective farm
Party Congress	state farm
Politburo	GOSPLAN
Secretariat	collectivization
Central Committee	*kulak*
democratic centralism	de-Stalinization re-Stalinization
Komsomol	*sovnarkhozy*
"Great Purge"	*nomenklatura*

Focus On Issues

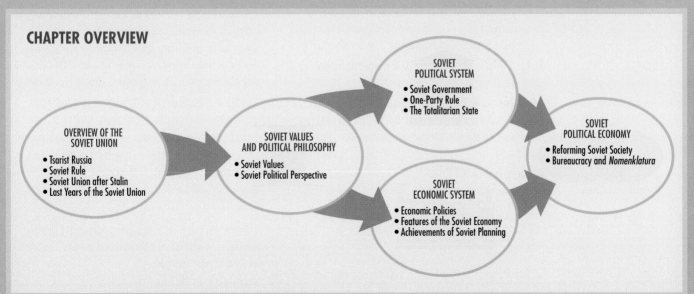

CHAPTER OVERVIEW

OVERVIEW OF THE SOVIET UNION
- Tsarist Russia
- Soviet Rule
- Soviet Union after Stalin
- Last Years of the Soviet Union

SOVIET VALUES AND POLITICAL PHILOSOPHY
- Soviet Values
- Soviet Political Perspective

SOVIET POLITICAL SYSTEM
- Soviet Government
- One-Party Rule
- The Totalitarian State

SOVIET ECONOMIC SYSTEM
- Economic Policies
- Features of the Soviet Economy
- Achievements of Soviet Planning

SOVIET POLITICAL ECONOMY
- Reforming Soviet Society
- Bureaucracy and *Nomenklatura*

OVERVIEW OF THE SOVIET UNION

Tsarist Russia

Under Nicholas II (1894–1917)

1894—Tsar Nicholas II (Nicholas Romanov) crowned; period of unprecedented political and economic change begins

1898—Russian Social Democratic Labour Party (RSDLP) founded in Minsk; meeting broken up by tsarist secret police

1903—RSDLP convenes in London; Lenin forces party to split into Bolshevik (majority) and Menshevik (minority) factions

1904–1905—Russo–Japanese War; Russia defeated

1905—Revolution in Russia; "Bloody Sunday"—police fire at peaceful demonstration of workers in St. Petersburg, killing more than 100; workers strike, peasants burn estates; tsar promises political reforms guaranteeing personal freedoms and establishing the first Duma (parliament)

1914–1917—Russia enters World War I; military setbacks and economic troubles

February–March 1917—Revolution; demonstrations and riots; Provisional Government formed; Tsar Nicholas II forced to abdicate

April 1917—Lenin returns to Russia; Provisional Government pledges to continue Russia's involvement in the war

July 1917—Bolshevik demonstrations against Provisional Government

October–November 1917—Bolshevik troops overthrow Provisional Government; Lenin proclaims Soviet government in Russia

December 1917—Soviet government nationalizes banks, establishes Cheka (secret police)

Prior to February 1918 Russia followed the Julian calendar, which was 13 days behind the Gregorian calendar used in the West. According to the Julian calendar, the Bolshevik Revolution occurred on October 25, 1917 (November 7, 1917, according to the Gregorian calendar).

Soviet Rule

Under Lenin (1917–1924)

1918–1921—Civil war; foreign intervention; Soviet government introduces War Communism; nationalization of industry, forced grain requisitions from peasants, abolition of money, mass terror against political opponents

March 1921—Peasant revolts and Kronstadt uprising; Lenin announces New Economic Policy (NEP)

1921–1928—New Economic Policy (NEP) creates mixed economy, allows private businesses and markets, ends forced grain requisitions from peasants

January 1924—Lenin dies; power struggle between Stalin and Trotsky begins

Under Stalin (1924–1953)

1924–1927—Power struggle between Stalin and Trotsky; Trotsky forced from power and expelled from Communist Party

1928–1941—Rapid industrialization; NEP ended; Five Year Plan, October 1928; industrial development continues under Second Five Year Plan (1933–1937) and Third Five Year Plan (1938–1941)

1929–1933—Stalin launches forced collectivization; millions of peasants arrested, executed, or deported to Siberia; millions die in famine in Ukraine and Kazakhstan

1936–1939—"Great Purge"—campaign of mass terror; secret police arrest and imprison millions in forced labour camps in Siberia; prominent party leaders tried and executed; Stalin becomes absolute leader

1936—"Stalin Constitution" adopted; guarantees people's human rights

1941–1945—Germany invades June 1941; Soviet Union enters World War II (Great Patriotic War); Soviet forces occupy Berlin May 1945; Germany surrenders

1946–1950—Reconstruction of economy

1946—Cold War begins; Soviet Union helps to establish Communist governments in Eastern Europe

March 1953—Stalin dies

Soviet Union after Stalin (1953–1985)

Under Khrushchev (1953–1964)

1953—Khrushchev becomes Party leader

1954—Khrushchev relaxes controls on literature and people's lives

February 1956—Khrushchev denounces Stalin in secret speech to Communist Party; "de-Stalinization" begins; uprisings in Poland and Hungary; Hungarian revolt crushed by Soviet troops

1957—Soviet Union launches first space satellite; Khrushchev abolishes planning ministries and establishes economic councils (*sovnarkhozy*)

October 1964—Khrushchev removed from power for poor harvests and economic problems

Under Brezhnev (1964–1982)

October 1964—Brezhnev becomes Party leader

1965—Economic reforms reestablish planning ministries

1966—Brezhnev halts "de-Stalinization"; "re-Stalinization" begins

1973–1980—Government clamps down on dissidents; hundreds arrested and imprisoned in forced labour camps; writer Aleksandr Solzhenitsyn deported in 1973; physicist Andrei Sakharov exiled to Gorky in 1980

1977—"Brezhnev Constitution" replaces "Stalin Constitution"

1981—American President Reagan imposes economic sanctions on Soviet Union

November 1982—Brezhnev dies

Under Andropov and Chernenko (1982–1985)

November 1982—Andropov becomes Party leader; proposes to improve economy

February 1984—Andropov dies; succeeded by Chernenko, who dies March 1985

Last Years of the Soviet Union (1985–1991)

Under Gorbachev (1985–1991)

March 1985—Gorbachev becomes Party leader

February–March 1986—Communist Party approves Gorbachev's economic reforms of *perestroika* (restructuring) and *glasnost* (openness)

April 1986—Nuclear accident at Chernobyl contaminates large areas of Ukraine, Belorussia, and Eastern Europe

February 1988—Ethnic riots in Armenia and Azerbaidzhan

June–July 1988—Nineteenth Party Conference; Gorbachev calls for democratization of Soviet political system, proposes elected legislature, multi-candidate elections, and ban on interference in economy by local party organizations

March 1989—Elections to Congress of People's Deputies; many Communist candidates defeated; Yeltsin and Sakharov elected with large majorities

September–December 1989—Collapse of communism in Eastern Europe; Soviet Union does not intervene

March 1990—Lithuania declares independence from Soviet Union

June 1990—Cold War declared ended

August 1990—"500 Day Plan" to create market economy in Russian Republic announced; Gorbachev unveils his plan in October

June 1991—Yeltsin elected President of Russian Republic

August 1991—Attempted coup against Gorbachev; Gorbachev disbands Communist Party

December 1991—Ukrainians vote to leave Soviet Union; Commonwealth of Independent States (CIS) formed; Gorbachev resigns as President of Soviet Union

January 1, 1992—Soviet Union replaced by CIS

The last years of the Soviet Union, from 1986 to 1991, are examined in Chapter 10: Russian Federation

SOVIET VALUES AND POLITICAL PHILOSOPHY

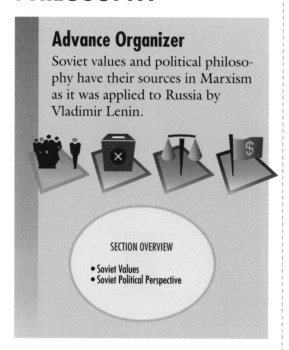

Advance Organizer

Soviet values and political philosophy have their sources in Marxism as it was applied to Russia by Vladimir Lenin.

SECTION OVERVIEW

• Soviet Values
• Soviet Political Perspective

Soviet Values

Before the 20th century, Russian society was ruled by a small aristocratic elite and the tsar. The country depended heavily on a large peasant class, which was involved in agriculture for its economic livelihood. In the early 20th century, Russian society experienced tremendous social change, with the growth of new industries, cities, and a working class. In 1905, a war with Japan and the effects of rapid social change led to a revolution, which forced the tsar to introduce some political and economic reforms. These limited reforms primarily benefited the country's small aristocracy and middle class. They had little effect on the lives of the country's peasants and working class.

When the Bolsheviks seized power in November 1917, they hoped to create a new society in Russia in which no individual or social class would exploit another. This new society, Bolsheviks believed, would eventually lead to the establishment of communism in Russia.

Leaders of Communism

Communism in the Soviet Union was the work of Vladimir Lenin, who applied Marx's views about socialism to Russia. His successor, Joseph Stalin, expanded Soviet rule over people's lives.

Popperfoto/Archive Photos

Vladimir Lenin (1870–1924). Born Vladimir Ilyich Ulyanov, Lenin became a follower of Karl Marx in the 1890s. In 1895 Lenin was imprisoned for revolutionary activities and in 1897 he was exiled to Siberia, where he wrote extensively about Marxism. When he returned from Siberia in 1900, he became an important leader of the newly founded Russian Social Democratic Labour Party (RSDLP). At the second congress of the RSDLP held in London, his opinions about how to carry out a revolution in Russia caused the party to split into the Bolshevik and Menshevik factions. The Bolsheviks believed in establishing a small disciplined party run by professional revolutionaries. The Mensheviks believed that the RSDLP should be a large mass party campaigning for social reforms and improved conditions for workers. Between 1904 and 1917, Lenin lived in Europe. He returned to Russia in April 1917, following the overthrow of Tsar Nicholas II. In November 1917, he initiated the Bolshevik seizure of power and became head of the first Soviet government. The first years of his government were

| 1894 Nicholas II crowned tsar | 1895 Lenin joins revolutionary movement | 1898 RSDLP formed; Stalin joins revolutionary movement | 1905 War with Japan; revolution in Russia | 1914–1917 World War I | 1917 November Revolution; Lenin in power | 1918–1920 Civil War in Russia | 1921 New Economic Policy | 1922 Stalin Party Secretary | 1924 Lenin dies | 1928–1932 First Five Year Plan; Collectivization | 1941–1945 World War II | 1953 Stalin dies |

Note: Timeline is not to scale

spent fighting a civil war and establishing a communist society in Russia. In January 1924, Lenin's death sparked a bitter power struggle among various party leaders.

Archive Photos

Joseph Stalin (1879–1953). Born Joseph Vissarionovich Dzhugashvili, Stalin joined the Georgian socialist movement in 1898 and became active in underground revolutionary activities. Stalin was arrested and exiled to Siberia in 1902. In 1917 he went to St. Petersburg, where he played an active role in the Bolshevik seizure of power and in Lenin's Soviet government. In 1922 he became General-Secretary of the Communist Party, a post he held until his death in March 1953. Following Lenin's death in 1924, Stalin became involved in a struggle for power. Gradually, he triumphed over his rivals, and by 1928 he was head of the party and the government. From 1928 to 1932, Stalin launched campaigns for the collectivization of agriculture and the rapid industrialization of the country. Under his leadership, a powerful political system was successfully created and the Soviet Union was transformed into a world power.

Core Soviet Values

Both Lenin and Stalin believed that if communism were to be successful in Russia, it was necessary to teach the people new values, including egalitarianism, collectivism, public ownership, and internationalism.

Egalitarianism. Communists believed that all people, men and women, and all nationalities should be treated equally. However, equality among people did not always occur.

Collectivism. Lenin and Stalin believed that the interests of the group should take precedence over individual interests. Attributes of individualism such as profit-seeking, private ownership, and competition were discouraged, because it was believed they did not promote the interests of the collective (group).

Self-sacrifice. They believed that all individuals should be encouraged to sacrifice personal interests in the interests of their collective (group). The spirit of self-sacrifice was viewed as necessary for the attainment of a communist society.

Public ownership. The public ownership of all means of production formed the basis of all economic activity under socialism. Private ownership of the means of production in industry, agriculture, banking, and transportation was forbidden by the Soviet constitution.

Economic planning. According to Lenin and Stalin, rapid industrialization and the management of a strong economy in the interests of society were possible only on the basis of economic plans. The goal of economic planning was the fullest possible satisfaction of people's material, cultural, and intellectual needs.

Classless society. According to Lenin and Stalin, the ultimate goal of communism was to create a classless society in which differences between class, between town and country, between mental and physical labour, and between nationalities would be eliminated.

Workers' government. During the transitional period from capitalism to communism, a workers' government would take the form of a "dictatorship of the proletariat" to defend the interests of the working class against bourgeois and capitalist counter-revolutionaries who might seek to restore capitalism in the Soviet Union. Once the classless society was attained, the "dictatorship of the proletariat" would cease to exist and the state would "wither away."

Internationalism. Communists believe in peace and international cooperation based on the principles of equality, in order to achieve international working class solidarity.

Soviet Political Perspective

Both Lenin and Stalin endeavoured to organize, direct, and inspire their followers through their writings and speeches. However, it was Lenin who created the most significant body of political philosophy.

Lenin's Beliefs

Lenin's political beliefs were formed during many years of studying Marx and other writers, and debating their ideas. The pamphlet *What Is to Be Done?* (published in 1902) argued for a highly disciplined and professional movement to carry out revolution in Russia. Lenin's book *Imperialism: The Highest Stage of Capitalism*, written in 1916, argued that imperialism was a stage of capitalist development. In *The State and Revolution*, written in 1917, he put forth new ideas about class struggle and the state in Russia. This body of political thought became known as Marxism–Leninism.

On political activity. *We must "go into all classes of the population" as theorists, as propagandists, as agitators, and as organizers. . . .*

. . . An agitator from among the workers who is at all talented and "promising" must not work in the factory eleven hours a day. We must take care to ensure that he is maintained by the party, that he should know how to go underground in time, that he should change the place of his activities, since otherwise he will not develop much experience, will not widen his horizon, will not be able to continue the struggle against the [police] for at least a few years without being arrested. [From *What Is to Be Done?*]

On revolution. *. . . revolution itself must not be imagined at all as a single act . . . but as several rapid changes from more or less powerful explosions to greater or lesser calm.* [From *What Is to Be Done?*]

On capitalism. *The enormous development of industry and the extremely rapid concentration of production in ever larger enterprises constitute one of the most characteristic peculiarities of capitalism. . . .*

Imperialism is capitalism in that phase of its development in which the domination of monopolies and finance-capital has established itself; in which the export of capital has acquired very great importance; in which the division of the world among the big international trusts has begun; in which the partition of all territories of the earth amongst the great capitalist powers has been completed. [From *Imperialism: The Highest State of Capitalism*]

On the economy. *As long as the "highest" phase of Communism has not arrived, the Socialists demand the strictest control, by society and by the state, of the quantity of labour and the quantity of consumption; only this control must start with the expropriation of the capitalists, with the control of the workers over the capitalists, and must be carried out, not by a government of bureaucrats, but by a government of the armed workers.* [From *The State and Revolution*]

On Communist society. *The whole of society will have become one office and one factory, with equal work and equal pay. But this "factory" discipline, which the proletariat will extend to the whole of society on the defeat of capitalism and the overthrow of the exploiters, is by no means our ideal, and is far from our final aim. It is but a foothold as we press on to the radical cleansing of society from all the brutality and foulness of capitalist exploitation: we leave it behind as we move on.* [From *The State and Revolution*]

On the state. *Again, during the transition from capitalism to Communism, suppression is still necessary; but in this case it is suppression of the minority of exploiters by the majority of exploited. . . .*

The State will be able to wither away completely when society has realized the formula: "From each according to his ability; to each according to his needs"; that is when people have become accustomed to observe the fundamental principles of social life, and their labour is so productive, that they will voluntarily work according to their ability. [From *The State and Revolution*]

Stalin's Beliefs

In early 1924, Stalin delivered a series of lectures to university students on his interpretation of Leninism. These ideas were published in 1924 in the book *Foundations of Leninism* and later formed the basis of what has become known as Stalinism.

On Leninism. *Leninism is Marxism of the era of imperialism and the proletarian revolution. To be more exact, Leninism is the theory and tactics of the proletarian revolution in general, the theory and tactics of the dictatorship of the proletariat in particular. Marx and Engels pursued their activities in the pre-revolutionary period (we have the proletarian revolution in mind), when developed imperialism did not yet exist, in the period of the proletarian's preparation for revolution, in the period when the proletarian revolution was not yet an immediate practical inevitability. But Lenin, the disciple of Marx and Engels, pursued his activities in the period of developed imperialism, in the period of the unfolding proletarian revolution, when the proletarian revolution had already triumphed in one country [Russia], had smashed bourgeois democracy and had ushered in the era of proletarian democracy, the era of the Soviets.*

That is why Leninism is the further development of Marxism.

On seizure of power. *"The fundamental question of every revolution is the question of power."* *Does this mean that all that is required is to assume power, to seize it? No, it does not. The seizure of power is only the beginning. For many reasons, the bourgeoisie that is overthrown in one country remains for a long time stronger than the proletariat which has overthrown it. Therefore, the whole point is to retain power, to consolidate it, to make it invincible.*

On state power. *. . . Soviet power is a new form of state organisation different in principle from the old bourgeois-democratic and parliamentary form, a new type of state, adapted not to the task of exploiting and oppressing the labouring masses, but to the task of completely emancipating them from all oppression and exploitation, to the*

tasks facing the dictatorship of the proletariat.

. . . Soviet power, by combining the legislative and executive power in a single state organisation and replacing territorial electoral constituencies by industrial units, factories and mills, thereby directly links the workers and the labouring masses in general with the apparatus of state administration, teaches them how to govern the country.

On the Communist Party. *The Party is the highest form of organisation of the proletariat. The Party is the principal guiding force within the class of the proletarians and among the organizations of that class. But it does not by any means follow from this that the Party can be regarded as an end in itself, as a self-sufficient force. The Party is not only the highest form of class association of the proletarians; it is at the same time an* instrument *in the hands of the proletariat for achieving the dictatorship when that has not yet been achieved and for consolidating and expanding the dictatorship when it has already been achieved. . . .*

The proletariat needs the Party for the purpose of achieving and maintaining the dictatorship. The Party is an instrument of the dictatorship of the proletariat. But from this it follows that when classes disappear and the dictatorship of the proletariat withers away, the Party also will wither away.

. . .The achievement and maintenance of the dictatorship of the proletariat is impossible without a party which is strong by reason of its solidarity and iron discipline. But iron discipline in the Party is inconceivable without unity of will, without complete and absolute unity of action on the part of all members of the Party.

On the worker. *The combination of Russian revolutionary sweep with American efficiency is the essence of Leninism in Party and state work.*

This combination alone produces the finished type of Leninist worker, the style of Leninism in work.

Stalin's beliefs about Leninism and the role of the state and the Communist Party formed the basis of his policy of "socialism in one country." Socialism in one country meant developing the Soviet Union into a country which was self-sufficient and could protect itself politically and militarily from external threats.

SOVIET POLITICAL SYSTEM

Advance Organizer

Following the seizure of power the Bolsheviks, led by Lenin, set up a Communist government. After Lenin's death in 1924, a totalitarian state was established in the Soviet Union under Stalin in which all political power and authority was centralized in the Communist Party. The political power and authority of the Communist Party was maintained by a large secret police force that suppressed political opposition and frightened potential opponents into silence.

Following Stalin's death in 1953, totalitarian controls were gradually relaxed but never completely removed. The Communist Party and its leadership continued to control all aspects of the country's political system, society, and economy.

> **SECTION OVERVIEW**
>
> • Soviet Government
> • One-Party Rule
> • The Totalitarian State

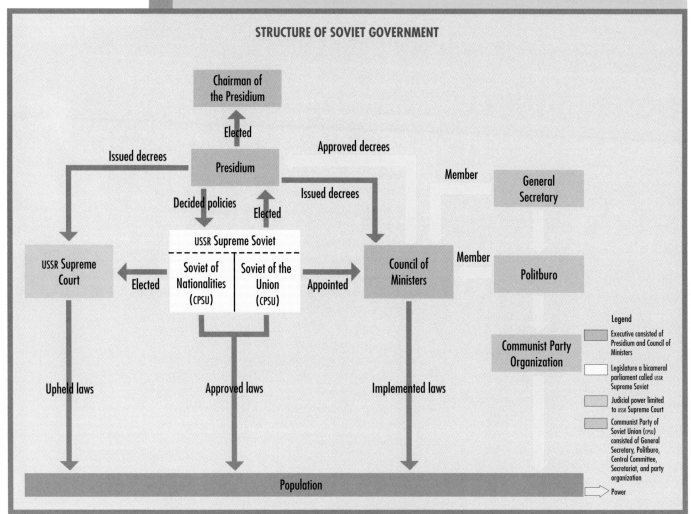

STRUCTURE OF SOVIET GOVERNMENT

Chairman of the Presidium

↑ Elected

Presidium

Issued decrees → (to USSR Supreme Court)

Approved decrees

Decided policies ↓   Issued decrees → (to Council of Ministers)

Elected ↑

Member — General Secretary

USSR Supreme Soviet
Soviet of Nationalities (CPSU) | Soviet of the Union (CPSU)

USSR Supreme Court ← Elected

Appointed → Council of Ministers

Member — Politburo

Communist Party Organization

Upheld laws   Approved laws   Implemented laws

Population

Legend
- Executive consisted of Presidium and Council of Ministers
- Legislature a bicameral parliament called USSR Supreme Soviet
- Judicial power limited to USSR Supreme Court
- Communist Party of Soviet Union (CPSU) consisted of General Secretary, Politburo, Central Committee, Secretariat, and party organization
- ⇨ Power

Adapted from *Konstitutsiia soiuza sovetskikh sotsialisticheskikh respublik [Constitution of the Union of Soviet Socialist Republics]*, 1977.

Soviet Government

The Soviet system of government was based on the principle that all power belonged in the hands of the soviets (elected councils), of workers', peasants', and soldiers' deputies. The 1977 Soviet constitution declared the Soviet Union to be "a socialist state of the whole people, expressing the will and interests of the workers, peasants, and intelligentsia." In practice, the real power was held by the Communist Party, as indicated in the diagram on page 340 and the following discussion of the political system.

Executive Power

Executive power in Soviet government was held by the Chairman of the Presidium, acting as the head of state, and the Chairman of the Council of Ministers, acting as the head of government.

Presidium. A 30-member body elected by the Supreme Soviet, the Presidium had the power to open sessions of the Supreme Soviet, deal with foreign governments, supervise the military, and proclaim states of war or martial law. It issued decrees on taxation, economic policy, and law enforcement and had the power to interpret all Soviet laws.

Council of Ministers. The 1977 constitution made the Council of Ministers the highest executive and administrative body of the state. It was appointed by the Supreme Soviet to supervise the government bureaucracy, approve economic plans, draft the budget, and protect state security. Top Communist leaders, including the General Secretary, were members of the Council of Ministers.

General Secretary. Nowhere in the Soviet constitution were the powers and responsibilities of the General Secretary, who was the head of the Communist Party, mentioned or defined. The power of the General Secretary rested on the power given by the constitution to the Communist Party to be the country's sole legal political party. This effectively made the General Secretary the most powerful politician in the Soviet Union.

Legislative Power

Since the early days of Soviet rule, soviets (elected councils), existed at all levels of government. At the national level, legislative power resided in the 1500-member USSR Supreme Soviet. In December 1988, the Supreme Soviet was replaced by the USSR Congress of People's Deputies (see Chapter 10).

Supreme Soviet. The Supreme Soviet was divided into a 750-member Soviet of the Union and a 750-member Soviet of Nationalities, each having equal powers under the constitution. Deputies of both chambers were elected at the same time for five year terms. All deputies were approved by or members of the Communist Party. The Supreme Soviet met for about two weeks a year to elect the Presidium and the Supreme Court and to appoint the Council of Ministers. During the session, reports on the economy, important sociocultural questions, foreign affairs, and the state budget were approved.

The Supreme Soviet rarely initiated legislation or acted as a source of legislative authority. The Communist Party had this power. The Supreme Soviet largely accepted without discussion decrees issued in the name of the Presidium. Though the Council of Ministers was formally accountable to the Supreme Soviet, in reality ministers were responsible to the leadership of the Communist Party.

Judicial Power

The USSR Supreme Court was the country's main court of appeal but its power to review cases and Soviet laws was limited. Its main purpose was to uphold national laws. The Presidium had the constitutional power to interpret all Soviet laws.

Communist Party Membership (1917–1990)

1917	240 000
1930	1 972 483
1952	6 882 145
1961	9 716 005
1976	15 694 187
1986	19 004 768
1990	18 500 000

Knizhka partiinogo aktivista (Booklet of the Party Activist)

One-Party Rule

The constitutional basis for one-party rule first appeared in Article 126 of the 1936 Constitution. It declared the Communist Party of the Soviet Union (CPSU) to be the leading political organization of the working class. This power was broadened in the 1977 Constitution to read that the CPSU "is the leading and guiding force of Soviet society and the nucleus of its political system" and "exists for the people and serves the people." The Communist Party, the sole legal political party, became the country's most powerful political organization and came to control many aspects of Soviet government, society, and the economy. In 1986, total membership in the Communist Party reached 19 million people, over 7% of the total population. Party members came from every Soviet nationality, region, and occupational group.

Party Organization

The Communist Party was not organized to represent interest groups or to win popular elections but to formulate policies for the country, direct all political activity, and hold power. Power in the Communist Party flowed downward from the Politburo (Political Bureau) and the General Secretary at the top to primary party organizations (party cells) at the bottom (see chart below).

The constitution of the CPSU defined the Party Congress as its main policy making body. In practice, the Party Congress had little power and was subordinate to the Central Committee, Politburo, and Secretariat. The 5000 delegates of the Party Congress met about every five years to approve policy decisions made in the Politburo and to elect the members of the Central Committee.

Historically, the Party Congress witnessed spirited debates over leadership, policies, and organizational matters. Following Stalin's victory over his political rivals in 1927, the Party Congress became an outward expression of unanimous support for the General Secretary and his policies. The last Party Congress of the CPSU (28th Party Congress), held in June 1990, witnessed several dramatic disputes between

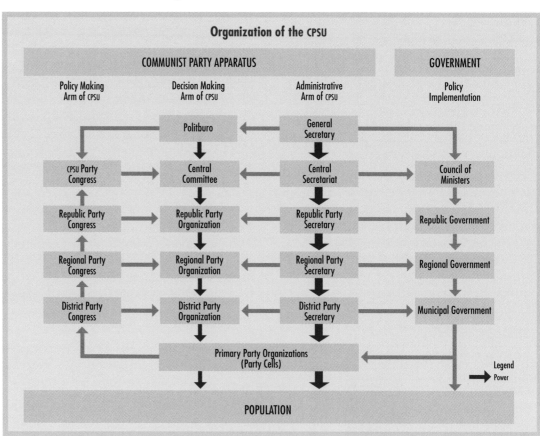

Adapted from *KPSS: Skhemy, tablitsy, diagrammy (CPSU in Charts, Tables, and Diagrams)*, 1989.

the General Secretary and some delegates (see Chapter 10).

The most powerful position in the CPSU was the General Secretary, who headed the Secretariat, the administrative arm of the Communist Party. The Secretariat supervised party affairs, managed party funds, selected party personnel, and directed party work in the government. This was achieved through a network of party secretaries that existed at all levels of the party organization, from republic down to regions and districts. Party secretaries were responsible to officials above them and had complete authority over those below. They were personally responsible for the performance and activities of party members under their authority.

The Politburo was the highest decision making body of the CPSU. Members of the Politburo included the General Secretary, the Chairman of the Council of Ministers, the Chairman of the Presidium of the Supreme Soviet, and several members from the Central Secretariat. The Politburo discussed policy, made decisions, and issued directives to government ministries and agencies.

The Central Committee formally directed activities and bodies of the CPSU between Party Congresses. It met for a few days twice a year to elect the Politburo and Central Secretariat to act in its name. The Central Committee consisted of over 300 voting and non-voting members, of which the largest group was party secretaries and officials. In reality, most party decisions were made in the Politburo and Central Secretariat.

General Secretaries of the CPSU (1922–1991)

Joseph V. Stalin (1922–1953)

Nikita S. Khrushchev (1953–1964)

Leonid I. Brezhnev (1964–1982)

Yuri V. Andropov (1982–1984)

Konstantin U. Chernenko (1984–1985)

Mikhail S. Gorbachev (1985–1991)

Decision Making

Decision making in the Soviet Union was governed by two principles. The first was the principle of democratic centralism, which guided all decision making within the Communist Party. The second principle was control of the government by the Communist Party.

Democratic Centralism. In 1919, Lenin formally defined democratic centralism to be the main decision making principle of the Communist Party. Democratic centralism meant that all lower bodies of the Communist Party had to follow decisions taken by higher bodies. In theory, the principle of democratic centralism allowed for internal party discussion. It permitted Communist Party members to discuss and debate party policy.

In early years of Soviet rule, the Communist Party witnessed many spirited debates over policy. In later years, especially under Stalin, much debate among members was silenced. Criticism of the Communist leadership and policies by party members came to be viewed as disloyalty, and was grounds for expulsion from the Communist Party.

Control of the Government. As the leading and guiding force of the Soviet society, the Communist Party enjoyed power over all government bodies. This meant that party decisions and resolutions had the force of law. The power of the Communist Party over government also meant that, while the party did not directly administer the government and economy, its members and leaders held important positions in all government ministries, agencies, and committees in the republics and various regions, districts, and municipalities of the country. By these means, party leaders were able to influence administrative affairs, the bureaucracy, and direction of the economy.

To become a member of the Communist Party, a person had to present to a local party cell a personal statement, recommendations from three Communist Party members, a short auto-biography, and an application. A general meeting of the party cell was then held to exchange views about the candidate. A vote was held and at least two-thirds of the party cell members had to approve the candidate.

Soviet Federalism

The power of the Communist Party over government also determined how political power was allocated between various levels of government. When the Soviet Union was formed on December 30, 1922, as a voluntary union of four republics (Belorussia, Russia, Transcaucasia, and Ukraine) each republic was granted the right of self-determination. This was a recognition of the fact that the Soviet Union was a multinational country. In later years, the right of self-determination was extended to new republics. However, as long as Communist governments ruled each republic, there was no question of a republic seceding from the Soviet Union.

In the early years of Soviet rule, the constitution allowed for considerable de-centralization of power between the central government in Moscow and the republics. Under Stalin, the decentralization of power was minimized by the constitutional right of the central government to override the republics in the interests of national unity.

Union Republics. According to the constitution, the Soviet Union was divided into 15 union republics, officially called a soviet socialist republic (SSR), as shown in the map below. The union republic was officially recognized as a homeland for a major Soviet nationality. In this respect, each union republic had the right to its own constitution and to secede from the Soviet Union. In reality, the union republic's constitution and right to leave the Soviet Union could be overridden by the Soviet leadership.

The union republic had exclusive control over justice, education, social welfare, and internal affairs. Areas such as transport, agriculture, labour, and finance were shared equally between the union republic and Moscow, with Moscow having the power to override the interests of the union republic. Moscow held exclusive jurisdiction over foreign affairs, national defence, communications, and industry.

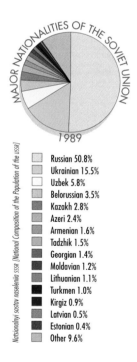

MAJOR NATIONALITIES OF THE SOVIET UNION

1989

Natsionalnyi sostav naseleniia SSR [National Composition of the Population of the USSR]

- Russian 50.8%
- Ukrainian 15.5%
- Uzbek 5.8%
- Belorussian 3.5%
- Kazakh 2.8%
- Azeri 2.4%
- Armenian 1.6%
- Tadzhik 1.5%
- Georgian 1.4%
- Moldavian 1.2%
- Lithuanian 1.1%
- Turkmen 1.0%
- Kirgiz 0.9%
- Latvian 0.5%
- Estonian 0.4%
- Other 9.6%

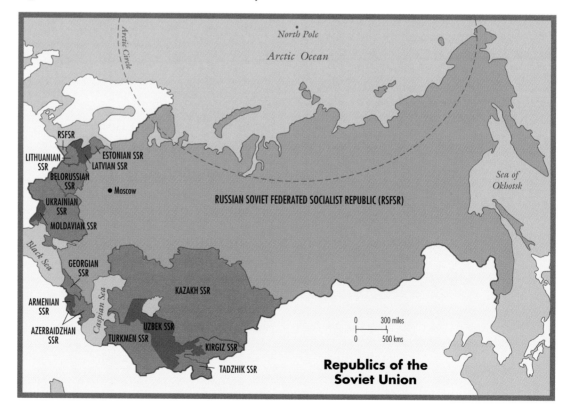

Republics of the Soviet Union

Consequences of One-Party Rule

The establishment of one-party rule by the Communist Party had important consequences for Soviet politics. They included authoritarianism, centralized decision making, limited accountability, and power struggles.

Authoritarianism. As the only legal political party, the Communist Party was the source of all political authority in the country. Only the Communist Party had the right to make policy decisions for the country. An individual or group of individuals was not allowed to establish any organization without approval from the Communist Party.

However, control over social, political, and economic organizations by the Communist Party did play a positive role in such a large multinational country as the Soviet Union. It ensured stability and order throughout the country. It also provided firm leadership on which the people could rely, which clearly expressed national interests and defended the country against foreign aggression.

Centralized Decision Making. Because the Politburo and Secretariat made most important decisions, the ability of the government to make laws for the country was greatly reduced. The result was that most official party statements had the force of law, compelling Communist Party members to carry them out without question. This led to considerable cynicism and apathy among Communist Party members and the population regarding their leaders.

Centralized decision making had a positive side for the Soviet Union. Top party leaders formulated policies in the interests of the whole country. Laws and standards applied equally to all social groups and nationalities in the country, which helped to strengthen national unity and developed commitment to a common purpose among the Soviet people, that of building socialism in the Soviet Union.

Limited Accountability. The centralization of political power in the Communist Party meant that there were few checks on the use of power by party leaders. The leadership was not always held accountable to the public for their actions and policies.

To Soviet leaders, the democratic principle of accountability to the people could not be applied to the Soviet Union. They argued that the country was surrounded by hostile powers which wanted to overthrow the Communist system. National survival was more important than public accountability. This meant that the country's leaders needed to have the ability to quickly determine national need and mobilize the people to implement policies.

Power Struggles. Because the leader of the Communist Party was the most powerful politician in the country, when the leader died there usually followed a struggle for power among top Communist leaders. After Lenin's death in 1924, a bitter power struggle between Stalin and other party leaders ensued. Following Stalin's death in 1953, Khrushchev competed with other party leaders for control of the Communist Party. Khrushchev was later removed by Brezhnev in a power struggle in 1964.

Although they were initially destabilizing for the Soviet political system, the power struggles were usually brief and intense. From the competition for power there emerged strong leaders who could rule the country for long periods. Also, the power struggles brought to the fore new ideas and policies which could lead the country forward.

David J. Rees

PHOTO: The political authority of the Communist Party was expressed throughout the Soviet Union by public monuments to Vladimir Lenin.

The Totalitarian State

For the Communist Party to maintain its power, it was necessary for it to control public participation in the Soviet political process. Elections were used to mobilize the people in a show of support for the policies of the Communist Party, its leadership, and government. Widespread use of propaganda praised the achievements of the Communist Party and, at times, the leader. Indoctrination of the population, especially the young, into the teachings of communism was intensive. The constitution guaranteed individual rights and freedom, but also limited people's civil and political rights in the interests of society and justified the Communist Party's control over the political process. To preserve the Party's domination of the political process, an extensive public security force suppressed unauthorized opposition and dissent.

Controlled Participation: Elections to the Soviets

The elected bodies in the Soviet Union were the soviets. Elections to the soviets were conducted on a regular basis and often depicted as examples of public support for the Communist Party. Candidates were chosen by local Communist Party secretaries on the basis of their membership in the Communist Party. Non-Communists could stand for election if they were approved by the Party.

In the 1920s and early 1930s, voters elected their deputies openly by the raising of hands and not by secret ballot. It was argued that in a period of class struggle and possible foreign invasion all voters should openly declare their views and sympathies. This often resulted in low voter turnout in elections to the soviets because many voters did not want to publicly reveal their choice and risk being arrested for anti-government views. Voting rights were restricted to people with a working class or peasant background.

In 1936, Soviet voters were allowed to elect deputies to the soviets by secret ballot. However, the ballot contained only one candidate, approved by the Communist

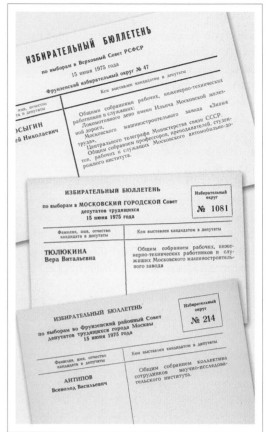

David J.Rees

Party. If voters approved of the choice, they simply dropped the ballot into the voting box without marking it. If voters disagreed with the choice of the candidate, they were required to mark the ballot, thereby publicly revealing their choice to polling officials who could report them to the secret police. The result was that most voters left their ballot unmarked and dropped it into the ballot box.

Officially, over 98% of the Soviet electorate went to the polls and voted for Communist Party-approved candidates. Unofficially, voter turnout was much lower and polling officials were compelled to manipulate vote counts to hide the low voter turnout. Manipulating vote counts was relatively easy to do because it was impossible to distinguish an unmarked ballot cast by a voter and one by a polling official. These practices became less common in early 1989, when Soviet voters were given some choice of candidates (see Chapter 10).

Propaganda

Since the earliest days of Soviet power, propaganda had been a useful way to encourage and control public participation in the political process.

The Communist Party used the media to convince the population about the superiority of communism over capitalism, the successes of the Soviet economy, the invincibility of the Red Army, and the morality of Soviet society. By the mid-1980s, a large segment of the Soviet population had begun to question the validity and accuracy of the official truths about their society. This skepticism would compel the Communist Party in 1987 to introduce a policy to encourage more accuracy and truth in the media's reporting on Soviet society (see Chapter 10).

Glorification of the Leader. In many instances, instead of promoting Soviet accomplishments, the media glorified the achievements of the leader. In the 1930s, the leading newspaper of the Communist Party, *Pravda* (Truth), praised Stalin as "the architect of the Soviet Union," "the great leader," and "the great teacher." In 1956, Khrushchev condemned the practice of praising the leader of the Communist Party. However, in the 1970s and early 1980s, the praise of Brezhnev grew, though it never reached that of Stalin in the 1930s and 1940s.

From the Pages of Pravda
(Translated from Russian by David Rees)

January 15, 1935
Stalin is the architect of the tremendous creation called the Union of Soviet Socialist Republics. He is the source of all life in the Soviet Union. His thoughts set the whole mechanism of Soviet life in motion.

May 21, 1935
We are strong by reason of our industrialization, our collective farming, our valiant Red Army, but our greatest strength, that makes our country impregnable and invincible, lies in the union of the people with its great leader, Joseph Stalin.

December 21, 1949
Comrade Stalin is the great continuer of Lenin's work.

Comrade Stalin is Lenin today.

Comrade Stalin is the genius of socialism.

Comrade Stalin is the great architect of communism.

March 5, 1953
The immortal name of STALIN will live forever in the hearts of the Soviet people and all progressive mankind.

Long live the great and all-conquering teachings of Marx, Engels, Lenin, and Stalin!

Long live our mighty socialist motherland!

Long live our heroic Soviet people!

Long live the great Communist Party of the Soviet Union!

February 26, 1976
His splendid qualities as a staunch Marxist–Leninist have earned Leonid Ilyich Brezhnev— the universally recognized leader of our Party—the deep respect of the Soviet people and all working people and have raised him to the ranks of the most outstanding figures of the world Communist and workers' movement and the most authoritative political and state leaders of our time.

April 23, 1977
Lenin lives in the . . . tireless and fruitful activity of our Party's Central Committee and its Politburo headed by an outstanding Marxist–Leninist—Comrade L.I. Brezhnev, General Secretary of the Central Committee.

November 5, 1982
Comrade L.I. Brezhnev, General Secretary of the CPSU Central Committee and Chairman of the Presidium of the USSR Supreme Soviet, is making an inestimable contribution to the creative development and implementation of our Party's policy, within the country and in the international arena.

In Soviet politics propaganda was a useful way to manipulate public participation in the political process. All forms of mass media were controlled and used by the Communist Party and government to indoctrinate and educate the population about the goals of the Communist Party and Soviet government.

Indoctrination

Communist leaders long believed in the importance of having a social program and education curriculum which could create citizens who supported the policies of the Communist Party and the principles of Marxism–Leninism. As Lenin said in 1920, to an assembly to youth leaders:

Only by radically remoulding the teaching, organisation, and training of the youth shall we be able to ensure that the efforts of the younger generation will result in the creation of a society that will be unlike the old society, the creation of a Communist society.

Communist Values. According to Lenin, the basic objectives of Soviet education should be to train young people to be productive citizens and teach them Communist values such as work discipline, patriotism, collectivism, and atheism.

- Discipline in work enables every Soviet citizen to be prepared to undertake any task the Communist Party demands.
- Love of the Soviet motherland and the Red Army is the duty of every Soviet citizen. Lenin noted that the Soviet Union was surrounded by hostile capitalist countries and every Soviet citizen should be ready to protect the nation from foreign aggression.
- Every Soviet citizen should work for the benefit of society and reject "selfish individualism" and personal gain.
- Every Soviet citizen should be an atheist and reject all religious beliefs and convince others to do the same. The citizen should understand that according to Marxism–Leninism, religion makes people passive and allows them to be exploited by capitalists.

Komsomol. To teach Communist values to youth and prepare them for work in Soviet society, the Communist Party established the Komsomol (Communist Youth League) in 1918. Initially, membership in Komsomol was restricted to young people aged 15–28 years. In the 1920s, the Young Pioneers organization was set up for students aged 10–14 years and the Little Octobrists movement for children aged 7–10 years. In the 1930s, the Komsomol became a mass organization and millions of young people participated in national campaigns such as collectivization and the building of cities in Siberia. The motto of the Komsomol was: "Always prepared!"

After 1945, the Komsomol mobilized "volunteer" labour for special projects in Central Asia and Siberia, and aided collective and state farms during harvest seasons. Membership in the Komsomol became a prerequisite for admission to a university and into the Communist Party.

On entering the movement as a Pioneer, every young person made the following pledge:

I, on joining the Pioneers, solemnly promise in the presence of my comrades

to warmly love my Motherland

to live, study, and struggle as the great Lenin willed, as the Communist Party teaches

to always carry out the rules of Pioneers of the Soviet Union.

Rules of Pioneers of the Soviet Union

A pioneer is devoted to the Motherland, the Communist Party, and Communism.

A pioneer is prepared to become a member of Komsomol.

A pioneer looks up to heroes of struggle and labour.

A pioneer reveres the memory of fallen fighters and is prepared to defend the Motherland.

A pioneer is diligent in study, work, and sports.

A pioneer is an honest and true comrade, always standing boldly for the truth.

A pioneer is a comrade and guide of the October Revolution.

A pioneer is a friend to other pioneers and children of all countries.

Trevozhnaia molodost [Restless Youth], translated from Russian by David Rees

Soviet Constitutions

From 1917 to 1985, the Soviet Union had four constitutions. Their purpose was not only to give constitutional power to the Communist Party but also to reflect changing political and economic realities in Soviet society.

- The 1918 constitution proclaimed "the dictatorship of the proletariat" and a new revolutionary order in Soviet Russia.
- The 1924 constitution created a federal socialist state, the Soviet Union.
- The 1936 constitution recognized the victory of socialism in the Soviet Union. Stalin declared it "the only thoroughly democratic constitution in the world" because of its guarantee of individual civil and political rights.
- The 1977 constitution proclaimed the Soviet Union to be a "developed socialist society" and retained all individual rights outlined in the 1936 constitution, but imposed responsibilities and duties on Soviet citizens.

Civil Rights. In theory, the 1936 and 1977 constitutions granted Soviet citizens numerous civil rights, such as the right to guaranteed employment, rest and leisure, health protection, maintenance in old age, housing, and education. Soviet citizens were granted equality of gender, freedom of conscience, freedom of religious worship, freedom of speech, freedom of the press, freedom of assembly, freedom of public demonstrations, and freedom to privacy.

The 1936 constitution stressed that every Soviet citizen had civil duties. The 1977 constitution further emphasized the importance of people's duties and obligations to the state. They were obligated to work hard and protect public property from theft. Young males had to perform military service and defend the "Socialist Motherland." Soviet citizens were obligated to "respect the rights and lawful interests of other persons, to be uncompromising toward anti-social behaviour, and to help maintain public order."

Political Rights. Theoretically, the 1936 and 1977 constitutions gave Soviet citizens many political rights, including the right to vote at age 18, to elect deputies by secret ballot, and to be nominated for elected office. However, both constitutions emphasized that people's actual political rights were determined by the Communist Party. The Communist Party was declared to be the basis of the entire Soviet political system.

Limits on Civil and Political Rights. Under Stalin, people's civil and political rights were suspended when they were convicted under Article 58 of the Criminal Code. In *The Gulag Archipelago*,[1] Aleksandr Solzhenitsyn wrote:

> *Who among us has not experienced its all-encompassing embrace? In all truth, there is no step, thought, action, or lack of action under the heavens which could not be punished by the heavy hand of Article 58.*
>
> *The article itself could not be worded in such broad terms, but it proved possible to interpret it this broadly.*
>
> *Article 58 was not in that division of the code dealing with political crimes; and nowhere was it categorized as "political." No. It was included, with crimes against public order and organized gangsterism, in a division of "crimes against the state." Thus the Criminal Code starts off by refusing anyone under its jurisdiction as a political offender. All are simply criminals.*

Anti-social behaviour in the Soviet Union was commonly called "hooliganism," which included disturbing the peace, petty theft, and public drunkenness.

PHOTO: This stamp souvenir sheet with a portrait of Leonid Brezhnev was issued in 1977 to commemorate the proclamation of a new Soviet constitution. Brezhnev was the first Soviet leader to have his image on a stamp in his lifetime. The other Soviet leader to appear on official stamps was Lenin, and only after his death.

David J. Rees

---

[1]Excerpts taken from pp. 60, 126–127, 128, from *The Gulag Archipelago 1918–1956: An Experiment in Literary Investigation III–IV* by Aleksandr Solzhenitsyn. ©1974 by Aleksandr Solzhenitsyn. English language translation ©1975 by Harper & Row Publishers, Inc. Reprinted with permission of HarperCollins Publishers, Inc.

Unspoken guidelines for living under Stalin:

Don't think!

If you think, don't speak!

If you speak, don't write!

If you write, don't publish!

If you publish, don't sign!

If you sign, recant!

—Roy Medvedev, *On Socialist Democracy*

Secret Police

One of the first acts by the Bolsheviks in December 1917 was to set up a secret police force, the Cheka, to assist the Communist Party to establish control over the country. The Cheka had the power to arrest, imprison, and execute political opponents of the Communist Party without trial. In the 1920s, the secret police were reorganized several times, each time acquiring greater powers to monitor the activities of the population and to arrest and imprison perceived "enemies of the state." In 1934, the secret police force, renamed the NKVD (People's Commissariat of Internal Affairs), became a massive public security apparatus, employing thousands of people as agents, informers, police officers, administrators, and guards in prisons and forced labour camps. In 1954, this vast police force became the Committee for State Security (KGB—Komitet Gosudarstvennoi Bezopasnosti).

Agents and Informants. From the 1930s, the Soviet secret police relied on an army of paid agents and volunteer informers. In the mid-1980s, it was estimated that the KGB had a paid staff of about 500 000 agents and two million volunteer informants. The paid agents belonged to various departments of the KGB, such as foreign espionage, counterintelligence, and political affairs. These agents investigated anti-Soviet activities, censored the mail, monitored telephone conversations, and guarded the Soviet leadership. Foreign journalists, tourists, diplomats, and students, and Soviet citizens who travelled abroad or had contact with foreigners in the country were kept under surveillance.

Militia. Besides the secret police, there was a large militia (armed police force) to enforce laws on the movement of people. The internal passport, introduced in 1932, became an effective means to monitor and control people's movements. Every citizen over the age of 16 was required to have an internal passport listing their name, place of birth, birth date, place of residence, and nationality. This document also recorded all changes of address and marital status.

People were required to carry their internal passport at all times or risk being arrested. The internal passport was also required for people to vote in elections to the soviets.

After 1938, every adult was issued a "labour book," used by the state to control the activities of workers. The "labour book" included the person's work history and current employment status. Without a "labour book," a person could not be employed. Once a person was employed, the "labour book" was kept with the employer. In this way, employees could not easily move from one employer to another.

The "Great Purge" (1936–1939). In December 1934, the Leningrad Communist leader Sergei Kirov was assassinated. The assassination escalated into a massive program of terror called the "Great Purge," which would leave deep psychological marks on millions of Soviet citizens who lived through it.

The first public manifestation of the "Great Purge" began in August 1936 in Moscow with the show trial of Kamenev and Zinoviev, who had shared power with Stalin in the mid-1920s. Both were forced to confess to various crimes against the people. They were accused of plotting with Leon Trotsky, who was exiled and living in Mexico, to kill Stalin and other top Communist leaders. No defence or material evidence was provided. They pleaded guilty and were immediately shot. Two more show trials were staged in 1937 and 1938, at which several respected Communist leaders confessed their guilt and were also shot.

In 1937, the secret police conducted a sweeping purge of government agencies, diplomatic corps, media, educational institutions, and cultural organizations. Millions were arrested and sent to forced labour camps. In 1938, most of the commanders of the Red Army and its officer corps were arrested and executed. Top officials in the secret police were also executed. In early 1939 Stalin ordered the end of the "Great Purge," but not before millions had been sent to the GULAG.

The first Soviet forced labour camp of the GULAG was set up in 1923 to confine non-Communist politicians, priests, monks, and other political opponents. In the early 1930s, other camps were established to receive millions of *kulaks* (wealthy, successful peasants) and placed under the control of the secret police (NKVD). During the Great Purge (1936–1939) the GULAG employed millions as labourers to mine gold, build roads, cut lumber, construct canals, or manufacture consumer goods. From 1936–1956 an estimated eight million people were imprisoned in the GULAG system, which stretched across the entire country. As late as 1985, the GULAG continued to house thousands of prisoners. In his novel *The Gulag Archipelago*,[1] Aleksandr Solzhenitsyn, a former prisoner of the GULAG, described the conditions that existed in the forced labour camps.

The Gulag Archipelago

(Excerpts) by Aleksandr Solzhenitsyn

According to the recollections of Ivan Semyonovich Karpunich–Braven (former commander of the 40th Division and of the XII Corps, who recently died with his notes incomplete and scattered), a most dreadfully cruel system of food, work, and punishment was established in the Kolyma [forced labour camps in the Soviet Far East]. The prisoners were so famished that at Zarosshy Spring they ate the corpse of a horse which had been lying dead for more than a week and which not only stank but was covered with flies and maggots. At Utiny Gold-fields the zeks [political prisoners; an abbreviation of z/k, meaning in Russian *zakliuchenny*] ate half a barrel of lubricating grease, brought there to grease the wheelbarrows. At Mylga they ate Iceland moss, like the deer. And when the [mountain] passes were shut by snowdrifts, they used to issue three and a half ounces of bread a day at the distant gold-fields, without ever making up for previous deficiencies. Multitudes of "goners," unable to walk by themselves, were dragged to work on sledges by other "goners" who had not yet become quite so weak. Those who lagged behind were beaten with clubs and torn by dogs. Working in 50° below zero Fahrenheit [−45°C], they were forbidden to build fires and warm themselves. (The thieves were allowed this.) Karpunich himself also tried "cold drilling by hand" with a steel drill six and a half feet [two metres] long, and hauling so-called "peat" (soil with broken stone and boulders) at 60° below zero [−50°C] on sledges to which four men were hitched (the sledges were made of raw lumber, and the boxes on top were made of raw slab); a fifth accompanied them, a thief-*expediter*, "responsible for fulfilment of the plan," who kept beating them with a stave. Those who did not fulfil the norm (and what does it mean—those who did not fulfil?—because, after all, the production of the 58's [people convicted under Article 58 of the Criminal Code for "crimes against the state"] was always "stolen" by the thieves). [They] were punished by the chief of the camp, Zeldin, in this way: In winter he ordered them to strip naked in the mine shaft, poured cold water over them, and in this state they had to run to the compound; in summer they were forced to strip naked, their hands were tied behind them to a common pole, and they were left out, tied there, under a cloud of mosquitoes. (The guard was covered by a mosquito net.) Then, finally, they were simply beaten with a rifle butt and tossed into an isolator. . . .

At Mylga (a subordinate camp of Elgen), under Chief Gavrik, the punishments for women who failed to fulfil the norm were lighter: simply an unheated tent in winter (but one was allowed to go outside and run around it), and at haying time under the mosquitoes—an unprotected wattle shack. . . .

At that point, they abolished the remaining days off for the 58's and lengthened the summer workday to 14 hours, came to consider 50° and 60° below zero Fahrenheit suitable for work; and allowed work to be cancelled only on those days when the temperature was lower than 65° below zero Fahrenheit. (And because of the caprices of individual chiefs, some took the prisoners out for work even at 75° below.) At the Gorny Gold-fields . . . those who refused to go out to work were tied to the sledges and hauled thus to the mine face. It was also accepted in the Kolyma that the convoy was not only present to guard the prisoners but was also answerable for their fulfilment of the plan, and therefore had to avoid dozing and continue slave-driving them eternally.

[1]Excerpts taken from pp. 60, 126–127, 128, from *The Gulag Archipelago 1918–1956: An Experiment in Literary Investigation III–IV* by Aleksandr Solzhenitsyn. ©1974 by Aleksandr Solzhenitsyn. English language translation ©1975 by Harper & Row Publishers, Inc. Reprinted with permission of HarperCollins Publishers, Inc.

"The inability to find the truth and then to say it, is a deficiency that can never be camouflaged by our ability to talk about lies."

—Boris Pasternak

Dissent

Criticism and dissent in the Communist Party and Soviet society were not always suppressed. In the 1920s, a lively and wide-ranging debate over industrialization appeared, but once the official policy line was decided and began to be implemented in the early 1930s, any debate on official policy was declared to be "anti-Soviet." In the late 1950s and early 1960s, the Communist Party leadership again encouraged some discussion and different views to emerge, but this ended in the mid-1960s when a new leadership initiated a crackdown on dissent, and in the 1970s it grew harsher. Although dissent and criticism might be allowed, challenging the basic principles and rights of the Communist Party to hold power and be the leading force in Soviet society was never permitted. The Communist Party's chief official for ideology, Leonid Ilyichev, noted in *Pravda* in December 1962:

We have complete freedom to fight for Communism. We do not have any freedom to fight against Communism and there can never be any such freedom.

Dissidents. After the death of Stalin, many dissenting intellectuals made their appearance. Two prominent ones were Aleksandr Solzhenitsyn and Andrei Sakharov.

Reuters/Alexander Natruskin/Archive Photos

The author Aleksandr Solzhenitsyn came to prominence in 1962 with the publication of a novel about life in a forced labour camp. The novel was well received by Soviet readers but not by the Soviet leadership. In the mid-1960s, Solzhenitsyn came under increasing secret police surveillance. In 1970, Solzhenitsyn received the Nobel Prize for literature for his novel about the Stalin years, *Cancer Ward*. In early 1974, he was arrested for treason, stripped of his Soviet citizenship, and deported from the country. He returned to Russia in 1994, after 20 years in the United States.

Archive France/Archive Photos

Andrei Sakharov, the physicist and inventor of the Soviet H-bomb, was not forced into foreign exile like Solzhenitsyn. The Soviet government declared that he knew too many state secrets. He was placed under house arrest in 1980 and sent to live in the city of Gorky, a city located 500 km east of Moscow which was closed to foreigners. His crime was campaigning for the protection of human rights in the Soviet Union and publishing in the Western press cases of human rights abuse in the Soviet Union. Sakharov was awarded the Nobel Peace Prize in 1975 but not allowed to leave the country to receive it in person. His wife Yelena Bonner received the award on his behalf.

Many thousands of other dissidents were not as fortunate as Solzhenitsyn and Sakharov. They were imprisoned, sent to forced labour camps, or sent to psychiatric hospitals.

Samizdat. As leading dissidents came under greater police surveillance in the 1960s and 1970s, numerous self-published bulletins (*samizdat*) began to circulate privately among the population. Many *samizdat* sought to inform the people about events happening around them and their legal rights. Other *samizdat* became forums for private discussion of important issues like political freedom, human rights, and environmental destruction. Although Communist officials attempted to suppress these unofficial bulletins, *samizdat* materials provided them with information about problems in Soviet society. However, a citizen caught possessing *samizdat* materials was immediately arrested and sentenced to 5–10 years of hard labour in prison.

Views from Samizdat

Most contributors writing in the *samizdat* literature did not advocate the overthrow of the Soviet system. Their views were meant to remind their leaders that the task of building socialism was far from finished. Many Soviet writers contributed to both the official press and to *samizdat*. The following viewpoints are taken from two *samizdat* publications, *Political Diary*, which appeared in the 1960s, and *Chronicle of Current Events*, which circulated in the 1970s and 1980s.

Political Diary[1]

No. 25, October 1966

The experience of the years since our revolution has shown that the chief danger in a young socialist society is the rise of "strong-willed" leaders who aspire to one-man rule and are intolerant of any criticism. Under a one-party system, with extremely strict party discipline, such leaders can easily eliminate those who get in their way and can become unlimited dictators. That's how it was not only with Stalin but also with Khrushchev. Shouldn't we draw the conclusion from this that more democratic procedures should be introduced in the countries where socialism has been victorious? I do not mean the introduction of a multi-party system but the democratization of the Communist Party itself, free and public discussion and debate, and the chance to criticize any Party leader openly, either in print or orally. There is no need for harsh, semimilitary discipline in the present circumstances; it is even harmful. The Soviet people have changed greatly, and we do not have any internal class enemies within the country—neither the bourgeoisie, the landlords, the *kulaks*, nor the aristocracy—against whom a bitter struggle has still to be waged.

No. 66, March 1970

Our country has made great strides in the development of production, in the fields of education and culture, in the basic improvement of the living conditions of the working class, and in the development of new socialist human relationships. Our achievements have universal historical significance. They have deeply affected events throughout the world and have laid a firm foundation for the further development of the cause of Communism. However, serious difficulties and shortcomings are also evident. . . .

. . . Defects in the system of planning, accounting, and incentives often cause contradictions between local and departmental interests and those of the state and nation. As a result, new means of developing production potential are not being discovered or properly put to use, and technical progress has slowed down abruptly. For these very reasons, the natural wealth of the country is often destroyed with impunity and without any supervision or controls: forests are leveled, reservoirs polluted, valuable agricultural land flooded, soil eroded or salinized, and so on.

Chronicle of Current Events

No. 26, July 5, 1972

Our society is infected by apathy, hypocrisy, petit-bourgeois egoism, and hidden cruelty. The majority of representatives of its upper stratum cling tenaciously to their open and concealed privileges and are profoundly indifferent to violations of human rights to the security and the future of mankind. Others, although deeply concerned in their hearts, cannot permit themselves any "freedom of thought" and are condemned to the torment of internal conflict. . . . The basic class, social, and ideological features of the regime did not undergo any essential changes. With pain and alarm I have to note that after a period of largely illusory liberalism there is once again an increase in restrictions on ideological freedom, efforts to suppress information which is not controlled by the state, persecution of people for political and ideological reasons, and a deliberate aggravation of the nationalities problem.

No. 42, October 8, 1976

In general, we must remember that the fight against religion leads only to the moral degradation of society, an increase in crime, and the reinforcement of anti-cultural tendencies among the people.

No. 56, April 30, 1980

I consider it my duty as a human being and a citizen to appeal to all Communists: defend our rights, demand that the CPSU must genuinely—not just in words—reestablish democratic institutions, and demand the annulment of the administrative exile . . . imposed on [Andrei] Sakharov . . . and the immediate release of the editors of the journal *Searches* who have been arrested.

I do not intend to request readmission to the ranks of the CPSU. Until the shameful persecution of free thinking ceases in my Motherland, I do not wish to remain in a party which sanctions this persecution.

[1]From *An End to Silence: Uncensored Opinion in the Soviet Union* by Stephen F. Cohen, editor, translated by George Sanders. Translation ©1982, by W. W. Norton & Company, Inc. Reprinted by permission of W.W. Norton & Company, Inc.

SOVIET ECONOMIC SYSTEM

Advance Organizer

The Soviet economic system developed in stages following the November 1917 Revolution. Its essential features were largely established under the First Five Year Plan for industrializing the country. From 1928 to 1990, the Soviet economy was based on the principles of central planning, state ownership and control of the means of production, and cooperative activity in the interest of the society.

SECTION OVERVIEW

- Economic Policies
- Features of the Soviet Economy
- Achievements of Soviet Planning

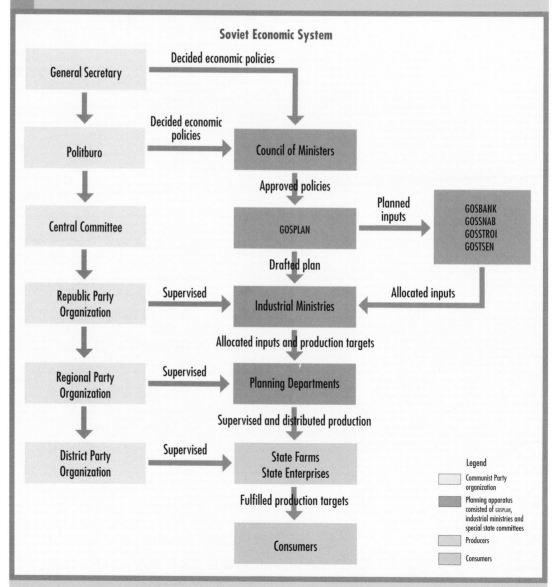

Soviet Economic System

General Secretary — Decided economic policies →

Politburo — Decided economic policies → Council of Ministers

Central Committee

Republic Party Organization — Supervised → Industrial Ministries

Regional Party Organization — Supervised → Planning Departments

District Party Organization — Supervised → State Farms State Enterprises

Council of Ministers — Approved policies → GOSPLAN

GOSPLAN — Planned inputs → GOSBANK GOSSNAB GOSSTROI GOSTSEN

GOSPLAN — Drafted plan → Industrial Ministries

GOSBANK GOSSNAB GOSSTROI GOSTSEN — Allocated inputs → Industrial Ministries

Industrial Ministries — Allocated inputs and production targets → Planning Departments

Planning Departments — Supervised and distributed production → State Farms State Enterprises

State Farms State Enterprises — Fulfilled production targets → Consumers

Legend

- Communist Party organization
- Planning apparatus consisted of GOSPLAN, industrial ministries and special state committees
- Producers
- Consumers

Economic Policies

In the first decade, Soviet economic policy was marked by sudden shifts. From June 1918 to March 1921, the government under Lenin worked towards establishing a state-controlled economy called War Communism, attempting to create a communist society. It was characterized by the nationalization of industry and natural resources, forced grain requisitions, the abolition of money and private trade, and centralized planning for production and distribution.

The policy failed for a number of reasons. When War Communism was introduced, civil war in Russia made it difficult for the government to implement the policy. Secondly, after three years of war with Germany, the Soviet Union lacked sufficient resources to support War Communism. More importantly, the new government did not have many people who were trained and experienced in administering and implementing policy. In March 1921, War Communism was abandoned for the New Economic Policy.

New Economic Policy (1921–1928)

The New Economic Policy (NEP) proposed to create a mixed economy in which the state controlled large-scale industry but left most small-scale enterprises and farming in private hands. The state accepted a limited role for the market in the economy. Forced grain requisitions were replaced by a tax on agricultural production. Many small businesses that had been nationalized under War Communism were returned to private ownership, but the government retained control of banking, transport, and heavy industry (called the "commanding heights of the economy"). By 1926, the economy had largely recovered to its prewar levels. In 1928, the First Five Year Plan and a centrally planned economy replaced the NEP.

The NEP was abandoned for economic and ideological reasons. Though rich in natural resources, the Soviet Union in 1928 had little capital for investment in industry, resource development, and improved transportation. The country's industrial base was too small; most of the population lived in the countryside and worked on their own farms. Agricultural production had increased; however, plots remained small and few farmers could afford machinery. The massive increases needed to feed people and create a large surplus to be sold abroad to finance new industrial production were still not possible. To encourage further private enterprise would be contrary to communist ideology. Increasing industrial production under the First Five Year Plan would satisfy both the economic and ideological objectives. The resulting growth in industrial production would lead to the development of a large urban working class, a necessary condition for creating a communist society in the Soviet Union.

Development of a Planned Economy (1928–1941)

Between 1928 and early 1941, the Soviet government inaugurated three five year plans. Their primary tasks, according to Stalin, were rapid industrialization, creation of a planned economy (public enterprise economy), collectivization of agriculture, and expansion of the country's defence capacity.

- **First Five Year Plan (1928–1932):** Heavy industry (steel-making, mining, and heavy machinery) was greatly expanded. An extensive planning apparatus was established to administer the plan. After much human suffering, private farming was eliminated. Collective farms and state farms were established.
- **Second Five Year Plan (1933–1937):** Heavy industry was further expanded at the expense of light industry (consumer goods), and development of the natural resources of Siberia and the Far East began.
- **Third Five Year Plan (1938–1941):** Heavy industry and defence spending were emphasized; Germany's invasion of the Soviet Union in June 1941 interrupted the plan.

From 1928 to 1985, the Soviet government implemented eleven Five Year Plans, which greatly expanded the country's industrial base.

Collective farms (*kolkhozy*) were formed as an association of people who came together to work the land and to share the results of their work. In 1985, there were 26 200 collective farms in the Soviet Union, with an average population of 485 people and area of 6500 ha.

State farms (*sovkhozy*) were owned and operated by the state. Every worker on the state farm was an employee and was paid a wage. In 1985, there were 22 700 state farms in the Soviet Union, with an average labour force of 530 people and area of 16 100 ha.

World War II and Reconstruction (1941–1950)

The war with Germany (1941–1945) devastated much of the Soviet economy, destroying 1710 cities, over 70 000 villages, 6 000 000 buildings, 65 000 kilometres of railway track, and 31 850 factories. Thousands of hospitals, schools, and libraries were burned. Property losses also included the slaughter of millions of farm animals. War damages were fixed at 679 billion rubles (US$110 billion). Human losses were officially estimated at 24 million people, or more than 12% of the 1940 population.

- **Fourth Five Year Plan (1946–1950):** Reconstruction of Soviet industry was accomplished in part by the transfer of considerable amounts of industrial equipment and machinery from Soviet-occupied Germany. Much of this equipment was viewed by the Soviet government as compensation for damages caused in Germany's invasion of the Soviet Union in 1941.

Postwar Growth and Stagnation (1951–1985)

From 1951 to 1985, the Soviet economy expanded but at ever-decreasing rates. Rapid economic growth during the 1950s gave away to slower growth in the 1960s. Poor harvests in the early 1960s affected industrial production, especially light industries that processed agricultural products for domestic consumption.

In the 1970s, the discovery of large oilfields in Western Siberia and the export of large amounts of oil and natural gas to Europe boosted economic growth and industrial production. Agriculture continued to experience problems resulting from poor harvests and inefficient production techniques.

In the early 1980s, the country's economic performance was blamed on poor planning techniques, obsolete and inefficient production methods, widespread waste, and low labour productivity.

Soviet Industrial Production Compared (1926–1952)
(as a percentage of world total production)

	1926	1939	1952
United States	42.2%	38.8%	43.9%
Germany	11.6	12.7	7.3
Great Britain	9.4	9.2	6.7
France	6.6	4.5	4.0
USSR	4.3	9.7	14.5

Compiled from *League of Nations* and *Narodnoe khoziaistvo SSSR [National Economy of the USSR]*

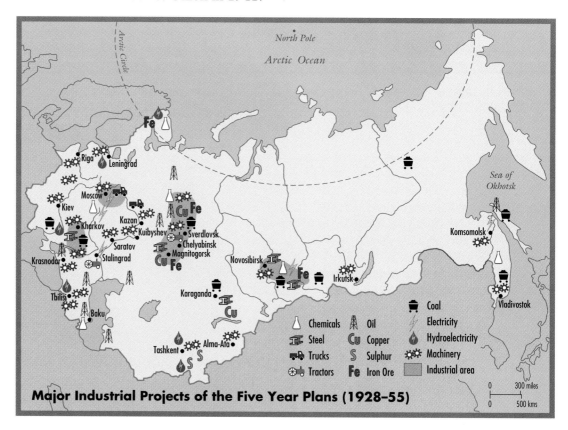

Major Industrial Projects of the Five Year Plans (1928–55)

Features of the Soviet Economy

From 1928 to 1985, the Soviet economy was regulated and controlled by centrally-administered plans to industrialize the country, raise living standards, and make the Soviet Union a major military power. Every Soviet citizen was expected to work for the common good of society. The state owned and controlled all means of production, but small-scale private enterprise was allowed under tight regulations.

Central Planning

The Soviet constitution declared that state plans formed the basis of the Soviet economy. These plans were based on Communist Party policy and implemented through central planning authorities.

Early Years (1920-1928). Economic planning began to be developed in the 1920s under the NEP. Economists in GOSPLAN (State Planning Commission) and the Supreme Council of the National Economy (VSNKh) prepared annual forecasts or indicative plans for the economy, called "Control Figures." These plans estimated future production trends, pointed out problems in the economy and suggested possible improvements. They were used by state enterprises in heavy industry, transportation, and communications but not by privately-owned businesses or in agriculture. After Stalin demanded in November 1927 that planners prepare more ambitious annual plans for the Soviet economy, GOSPLAN economists drafted the First Five Year Plan (1928–1932).

First Five Year Plan (1928-1932). A central planning system was set up to carry out the rapid industrialization of the Soviet Union during the First Five Year Plan (1928–1932). GOSPLAN (State Planning Commission), the industrial ministries, and the planning departments of the ministries became the main planning bodies. GOSPLAN took over VSNKh and became responsible for drafting the five year plan. Industrial ministries received production targets from GOSPLAN and distributed them to state farms, factories, and enterprises under their control. The ministries also regulated the activities of their enterprises to ensure fulfilment of all assigned production targets. The Communist Party organization supervised the creation and implementation of the five year plans.

Postwar Planning (1946–1985). After 1945, attempts were made to improve the quality and effectiveness of central planning. The Politburo and the Council of Ministers became responsible for developing economic policies for the country, which included full employment, universal availability of social services, and income equality.

GOSPLAN was given the sole responsibility of reviewing economic policies, and from them drafting an economic plan for the whole economy. The national economic plan contained production targets and instructions for their fulfilment. The production targets were developed to meet regional and national needs.

The production targets were prepared in close collaboration with GOSSNAB (State Committee for Material and Technical Supply), GOSBANK (State Bank), and GOSSTROI (State Committee for Construction). GOSSNAB allocated the necessary materials for production by factories and state farms. GOSBANK handled all sales transactions and payment of enterprise bills. GOSSTROI oversaw all major construction projects such as dams, railroads, and new factories. Two other state committees fixed prices for all goods and coordinated research and development in the country's technical institutes.

The industrial ministries were authorized to implement GOSPLAN production targets. Departments and regional offices within the industrial ministries allocated production targets among enterprises under their authority and supervised them. All enterprises were legally required to fulfil their production targets.

From 1928 to 1985 the Soviet economy was developed on the basis of centrally-administered plans, cooperation, group incentives, and public ownership of the means of production.

Central planning determined the overall direction of the Soviet economy. Its primary objective was to rapidly industrialize the country.

One Day in the Life of a Soviet Consumer

by Igor Djavrov

Shopping was pretty much the same everywhere in the Soviet Union. All shops and shopping centres were state-owned, except for some food markets where peasants sold their own home-grown produce. State shops looked very much the same. In Moscow, Leningrad and other large cities, there were big department stores called GUM, TsUM, and Detskii Mir (Children's World) and some shops which sold products from European socialist countries (East Germany, Poland, Czechoslovakia, and Yugoslavia).

In small and provincial towns there were no such large department stores and shopping areas. People usually did their shopping in small shops. These local shops were not well stocked. To buy goods like furniture, cars, carpets, and electronic goods, people had to travel to Moscow and other large centres.

Food in the Soviet Union was sold in state grocery stores and farmers' markets. In state food stores, prices were low but the quality was poor. The best quality food was sold in the farmers' markets, but the prices were very high. Farmers' markets in the northern parts of the country did not sell as large a variety of produce as those in the southern regions of the country.

Because most villages had poorly stocked food stores, people frequently travelled to the large cities to buy food. Every weekend one could see people going home in the countryside with large bags filled with food.

Buying foreign goods was always very difficult because of a shortage of high quality foreign goods in the country. "Beriozka" shops sold foreign goods and only for foreign currency. For Soviet citizens, owning foreign currency was illegal and one could be put into prison for just having foreign currency in one's pocket. Nevertheless, there were many people, called *fartsovshchiki* (black market dealers) who traded in foreign goods and currency. They bought dresses and other goods from foreigners and then sold them to Soviet citizens. They also traded in foreign currency, which was considered to be the most profitable business.

It was easy to buy clothes, but if one wanted a TV set or refrigerator, for example, you had to go to Moscow or another large city, stay there for some time, buy the item, and then transport it back home. If the item you bought was very heavy, like furniture or construction materials, you had to make arrangements yourself to ship it home, which was often difficult to do. Of course, not everyone could do this and so "black market people" offered their services, which were not cheap.

If you wanted to buy a car, it was another story. Cars were not sold in shops and were very expensive for the ordinary Soviet family. To buy a car, one had to be put on a waiting list for 2–6 years. Such lists were in enterprises where people worked. If the factory was not large enough to have such a list, people were put on a list in their local city administration. There were special lists for war veterans and privileged lists for deputies of the soviets and Communist Party workers.

The Soviet Union produced only two or three models for people to buy. No one could buy a foreign car or a vehicle such as a minivan, van, truck, or limousine; these were used only for state purposes. The price of an ordinary car was equivalent to 5–6 times the annual salary of a worker, engineer, or doctor. Salaries of most workers were low, just enough to buy basic necessities. Salaries were much the same all over the country.

Shopping was often an unpleasant experience. Sales clerks were generally not interested in serving people. There was no concept like "customer" and "serving the customer." Sales clerks were often rude to customers and vice versa.

When something you wanted was in short supply, you had to resort to buying it under the counter. The sales clerk kept the good separately and charged a higher price for it. If one had connections and influence (*blat*), one could get scarce goods. As the economy deteriorated and shortages of high quality goods appeared in the early 1980s, one had to use *blat* more often to get the better goods. Despite this, basic goods were available for most people to buy.

Cooperation

At factory meetings and through the press and poster campaigns, ordinary workers were encouraged to meet and exceed the planned production targets of the five year plans during and after the Stalin era. The Communist Party declared that workers should produce for the collective good of Soviet society and launched campaigns to promote "socialist competition" between enterprises. According to the Communist Party, the difference between "socialist competition" and competition that existed under capitalism was that "socialist com-petition" called on enterprises to compete for the honour of being the first to overfulfil the production target.

The consequences of "socialist competition" were serious. By the late 1970s and early 1980s, inefficient production practices such as "storming" and the production of low quality goods were common. "Storming" occurred when an enterprise had to make up for lost production time caused by shortages of materials. To fulfil monthly production targets, factory management increased the pace of work. This led to numerous industrial accidents and low quality goods. Soviet consumers learned not to buy goods made in the final week of the month, when pressure on workers from factory management to fulfil or overfulfil production quotas was most intense.

Workers who did not cooperate in meeting production targets were arrested. Strikes were illegal, and quickly suppressed when they did occur. Organizers of strikes were arrested and imprisoned for "anti-Soviet activity."

Factory managers were dismissed if their factory failed to meet planned pro-duction targets. As a result, many managers became cautious in reporting problems in their enterprises. Local party officials, who could be reprimanded and demoted if their district's enterprises failed to achieve production targets, also covered up problems in production.

Incentives

During the First Five Year Plan and Second Five Year Plan, incentives such as higher wages, better housing, and public recognition were used extensively to reward those who exceeded production targets. The Communist Party and Soviet government bestowed awards, honours, and publicity on workers and factories that performed exceptionally. The most famous example of this appeared in 1935 when Aleksei Stakhanov, a coal-miner, claimed to have mined 102 metric tonnes of coal in five hours and 45 minutes (the normal production per miner was 7 metric tonnes). Stalin proclaimed Stakhanov a "Hero of Labour" and a new type of Soviet worker, who represented a qualitative leap forward in human behaviour and level of service to society.

After 1955, these campaigns to create superhuman "heroes of labour" largely disappeared. Instead, Communist Party-controlled trade unions distributed material incentives such as cash bonuses, free vaca-tions, more consumer goods, and gifts of imported goods to motivate worker behaviour. Soviet trade unions, unlike Canadian trade unions, did not represent worker interests but rather acted to ensure that all members fulfilled production targets. They rewarded satisfactory performance and dismissed "troublemakers."

Cooperation was considered essential in meeting production targets and promoting collective spirit among workers.

After 1955, material incentives such as high wages, free vacations, and consumer goods became more important than non-material incentives such as awards, honours, and public recognition for fulfilling production targets.

"They pretend to pay us, we pretend to work" was a popular joke in the Soviet Union in the 1970s.

Monthly Work Schedule. "I order! Push! Fulfil! Complete!"

Krokodil/G. and V. Karaveavykh

State Ownership

State ownership of the means of production was the foundation of the Soviet economic system. All natural resources, industries, agriculture, transportation, banking, and most urban housing belonged to the state.

Collectivization (1930–1933).

The nationalization of natural resources and industrial enterprises was completed in the early years of Soviet rule. However, this was not the case in agriculture. Under the New Economic Policy of the 1920s, the Soviet government permitted private farming and markets in agricultural produce, because over 80% of the population lived in the countryside and the government needed their support to increase food production.

In 1927–1928, Communist Party leaders realized that an agricultural base of small peasant farms posed an obstacle to rapid industrialization. Most peasant farms were too small and their technology too inefficient to produce the high yields needed to supply the government with enough agricultural produce to supply industry, feed town workers, and sell abroad. Communist leaders also understood that the existence of private farms would prevent the creation of a communist society in the Soviet Union and would limit the government's ability to direct the economy.

The economic and ideological solution to the problem was the collectivization of peasant farms. Stalin declared in 1929 that all peasant farms should be reorganized into collective farms in order to contribute significantly to the country's industrialization through greatly increased production. It was believed that without collectivization the goal of rapid industrialization would have to be abandoned.

In 1930, the compulsory collectivization campaign was launched, against strong resistance. Many peasants killed their animals and burned their crops rather than give them up to the collective farms. Stalin ordered Red Army detachments, secret police units, and thousands of Communist Party members into the villages to end all peasant opposition to collectivization. Poorer peasants were encouraged to turn against better-off peasants, or *kulaks*, many of whom were executed or deported to Siberia and Central Asia.

The Soviet government imposed high grain delivery targets on the newly created collective farms. This grain was meant to feed the country's rapidly growing urban population, supply the Red Army, and buy foreign machinery for heavy industry. The delivery targets exceeded the total annual production of many collective farms. As a result, many collective farms were left with little food to feed their members after meeting the grain deliveries. Beginning in early 1932, millions of peasants throughout Ukraine, southern Russia, and Kazakhstan suffered starvation. When the famine ended an estimated ten million peasants had died and millions had abandoned their villages for the cities to find food and work.

Collectivization also served the purpose of consolidating Communist control over the countryside. Up to 1930, control over the peasantry was limited. By organizing the collective farms, the Communist Party was able to exercise more effective control.

A high price was paid for collectivizing the peasantry. It embittered them toward the Soviet system and deprived agriculture of its most productive people. Despite billions of rubles in investment between 1953 and 1985, agriculture remained the weakest sector of the Soviet economy. Had the peasants not been permitted to cultivate private plots, the country would have experienced serious shortages of basic foods such as milk, meat, eggs, fruits, vegetables, and potatoes (see chart "Distribution of Total Agricultural Output).

In 1985, private plots occupied about 3% of the agricultural land but produced 22.9% of all milk, 27.5% of the meat, 28.1% of the eggs, 50.2% of the fruit, 25.0% of the vegetables, and 61.0% of the potatoes of the USSR.

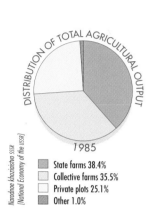

DISTRIBUTION OF TOTAL AGRICULTURAL OUTPUT

Narodnoe khoziastvo SSSR [National Economy of the USSR]

1985

- State farms 38.4%
- Collective farms 35.5%
- Private plots 25.1%
- Other 1.0%

PHOTO: While collectivization ended the existence of private farming in the Soviet Union, some private ownership was allowed in the form of farmers' markets for produce from private plots.

David J. Rees

Two Views of Collectivization

Collectivization of private farming had a profound impact on Soviet society. To those directly affected, collectivization changed a way of life forever. To the Soviet leadership, collectivization was claimed as a great achievement, the rescue of millions of peasants from poverty.

The following personal account describes the collectivization that took place in Ukraine between 1930 and 1933.

Execution by Hunger

(Excerpts) From *Execution by Hunger: The Hidden Holocaust* by Miron Dolot. ©1985 by Miron Dolot. Reprinted with permission of W.W. Norton & Company, Inc.

Our village was completely collectivized sometime at the beginning of 1931. But this early completion of collectivization did not mean that our villagers accepted the system of collectivized agriculture willingly. They never did. Our village was half ruined; more than one third of our entire population was physically exterminated or banished from the village. Any food we had was confiscated. By the end of 1931 we faced mass starvation. There was no way to survive but to stay in the collective farm where we had been promised some food for our daily work.

Yet the struggle of the farmers against collectivization did not terminate with our forced joining of the collectives. On the contrary, we became even more stubborn in the following years. During the harvest of 1930 and 1931, the government used the newly organized collective farms to expropriate as much of the grain and other agricultural products as it wanted. There was talk in our village that more than three quarters of the total crop of 1931 had been taken by the government. We heard that in some neighboring villages the whole crop had been taken. It was easily done, without any opposition. There was no bargaining over the price. It was the government who set the prices, not the farmers. . . .

In the collective farm, our personal existence became completely dependent upon the dictates of the Communist Party, and on the whims of the local officials. Every detail of our life was supervised. Our daily routine was subject to the strictest regimentation. We had to obey orders without any protest, and without giving any thought as to their sense or purpose. A vast system of secret police, spies, and *agents provocateurs* watched our every move. . . .

The battle for the Ukrainian wheat crop of 1932 started almost two months before the harvest.

At the end of May, some strangers appeared in our village, and little by little, we began finding out who they were. The Party had mobilized 112 000 of its most active and reliable members in order to organize a speedy harvest of the new crop, and to secure its swift and smooth requisitioning and final delivery to the State. Soon these members became known to us as the Hundred Thousanders, or just Thousanders. There were nine of them in our village, one for each Hundred, and one who was to become the village Thousander . . . In no time at all, these new Thousanders took over our entire village like tyrants, imposing their wills and their demands upon us.

The name of our new village Thousander was Livshitz. We called him Comrade Livshitz, or simply Comrade Thousander. Nobody knew where he came from . . . .

Comrade Thousander's announcement that in 1932 we had to deliver the same quota of grain as in 1931 was a hard blow to us. We simply could not fulfil his demands. The 1932 grain quota was not based on the actual amount of grain sown, cultivated, and harvested; it was based upon an unrealistic government plan.

The farmers were either unused to or not interested in working in the collective farms. There was a shortage of manpower and draft animals. Because of famine, many villagers were either too weak to work or had left the village altogether in search of food. As a result, much collective land stood idle. A great deal, if not half, of the grain crop was lost in fields during reaping; such losses occurred during the harvest of 1931, and even more losses were expected during the harvest in 1932. Their corn bins stood empty or had been used for firewood. Thus Moscow's demand to deliver the same grain quota in 1932 as in previous years was not only impossible, but promised to be catastrophic. . . .

The long-awaited harvest of 1932 finally arrived. Its beginning was loudly heralded by endless political speeches. . . .

From the very start of the harvest to the end, not a single pound of wheat had been distributed to the village inhabitants. Nothing was left for them. We were told that all the grain had to be transported to the railroad stations. We also learned that there it had been dumped on the ground, covered with tarpaulins, and left to rot. . . .

As 1932 neared its end, we often heard explanations of why the officials continued searching our homes for grain. They were very simple: since we were still alive, we must have been eating something to survive. We had not fulfilled the grain delivery quota, and yet we had been complaining that we had nothing to eat. But we were still alive! That meant that we had to have food—but where? It had to be somewhere. The officials felt that they had failed in their duties to find the hidden treasure of food. This made them frustrated, angry, and all the more vicious and cruel to us. . . .

We looked toward the approaching winter of 1932–1933 with great trepidation, as if awaiting the arrival of the Judgment Day. It came with nature's crushing wrath. The particularly severe winter con-spired with the Communists against the farmers. . . .

. . . Yet the members of the Bread Procurement Commission continued in their task, relent-lessly tramping from house to house, confiscating everything edible they could find in their attempt to meet the state quotas. Even the smallest amounts of grain and meat were forcibly seized from the villagers.

We had to do something. No one wanted to lie down passively and starve to death. One of the first steps undertaken by the villagers was a mass exodus to the neighboring cities where they hoped to find jobs and food. All—young and old—tried to reach the cities as they had tried before during the last

spring famine. Many did not make it, and their frozen bodies became roadmarkers for others on the snowed-in route to the county towns. Those who were strong enough to reach the cities failed to find a paradise of plenty, even though the food rationing there slowed down the onslaught of famine somewhat. The food rations were so small that the city dwellers could not help the starving farmers.

Official View of Collectivization

Speech by Joseph Stalin

Speech to collective farm activists and organizers, February 1933

One of our achievements is that we have helped millions of poor peasants to join the collective farms. It is an achievement of ours that by joining the collective farms, where they have at their disposal the best land and the finest implements of production, millions of poor peasants have risen to the level of middle peasants. It is an achievement of ours that millions of poor peasants who formerly lived in penury have now, in the collective farms, become middle peasants, have attained material security. It is an achievement of ours that we have put a stop to the differentiation of the peasants into poor peasants and *kulaks;* that we have routed the *kulaks* and have helped the poor peasants to become masters of their own labour in the collective farms, to become middle peasants.

What was the situation before collective-farm development was launched, about four years ago? The *kulaks* were growing rich and were on the upgrade. The

poor peasants were becoming poorer, were sinking into ruin and falling into bondage to the *kulaks.* The middle peasants were trying to make the grade and catch up with the *kulaks,* but they were continually losing their hold, tumbling down, and swelling the ranks of the poor peasants, to the amusement of the *kulaks.* It is not difficult to see that the only ones to profit by this scramble were the *kulaks,* and perhaps, here and there, some of the other well-to-do peasants. . . .

By developing collective-farm construction we have succeeded in abolishing this scramble and injustice; we have smashed the yoke of *kulak* bondage, brought this vast mass of poor peasants into the collective farms, given them material security there, and raised them to the level of middle peasants, having at their disposal collective-farm land, enjoying the privileges granted to collective farms and the use of tractors and agricultural machinery. And what does this mean? It means that no less than 20 000 000 of the peasant population, no less than 20 000 000 poor peasants have been rescued from destitution and ruin, have been rescued from *kulak* bondage, and have attained material security thanks to the collective farms.

This is a great achievement, comrades. It is an achievement such as has never been known in the world before, such as no other state in the world has yet scored.

These, then, are the practical, tangible results of collective-farm development, the results of the fact that the peasants have taken the collective-farm path.

Achievements of Soviet Planning

The achievements of Soviet planning were remarkable. In a relatively short time, Soviet planning accomplished four major national objectives—the creation of a modern society, industrialization, collectivization of agriculture, and the creation of a military establishment capable of protecting the country from foreign aggression.

Modernization

Central planning had profound social and cultural implications for Soviet society. It involved a massive educational effort, both to eliminate illiteracy and to develop the skilled labour force required by industry and government. Millions learned to read and write, and received training. An educational system centred on scientific research and development appeared.

Central planning enabled the government to establish a national system of social welfare in the Soviet Union. The government set up facilities for medical care, preschool education, child care, urban housing, and recreation. These facilities greatly reduced infant mortality, increased life expectancy, eliminated cases of contagious diseases among the population, and ended malnutrition.

Central planning changed the role of women in Soviet society. Millions of women were drawn into the labour force to work in factories, mines, hospitals, schools, scientific institutes, cultural organizations, stores, communications services, and government departments. Millions learned to read and write, and enrolled in institutions of higher learning. In 1985, women comprised over half the total Soviet labour force and many held important administrative and managerial posts in government and industry.

Industrialization

Central planning enabled the government to set ambitious goals for heavy industrial production and recruited millions of peasants as factory workers. It allowed the Soviet Union to establish new industries, such as machine-tools, automobile and tractor manufacturing, chemicals, and aircraft production; they also greatly expanded existing ones, such as steel-making, mining, oil, electricity generation, and consumer goods production. By 1950, the Soviet Union was the world's second largest industrial power, a rank it would hold until the early 1980s.

Industrialization under central planning changed Soviet society. Urbanization developed rapidly as peasants moved to cities seeking jobs and a higher standard of living. By 1980, the country had become highly urbanized. Industrialization also realized Lenin's dream of providing electricity to every community throughout the Soviet Union.

More importantly, the Soviet experience showed that high economic growth was possible under central planning. In the 1950s and 1960s, many developing countries in Africa, Asia, and Latin America adopted the Soviet model of central planning to industrialize their economies and raise living standards.

Collectivization

Under central planning small peasant farms were consolidated into large organizational structures. Collectivization of agriculture enabled the Communist Party and Soviet government to begin the task of teaching the peasant population a modern and socialist way of life and thinking. In this way, Communist control was consolidated over the whole country and national unity was maintained.

Military Capacity

With its emphasis on heavy industry, central planning spurred the production of tanks, airplanes, missiles, and other weapons. A large military-industrial complex situated deep inside the country was created, far from foreign attack. Central planning gave the Soviet Union the means to withstand invasion and defeat Nazi Germany in World War II, and to undertake national reconstruction after the war. In the 1960s and 1970s, central planning enabled the country to greatly expand its military capability as a superpower on par with that of the United States.

Women comprised 51.1% of the labour force in 1985, compared to 27.0% in 1928. The percentages of women in the following occupations in 1985 were

Sales clerks	99%
Librarians	91
Bookkeepers	89
Economists	87
Teachers	75
Artists	68
Doctors	67
Engineers	58
Researchers	52
Veterinarians	45
Farm workers	44

Trud v sssr [Labour in the ussr]

SOVIET POLITICAL ECONOMY

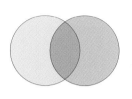

Advance Organizer

The establishment of socialism and a planned economy in the Soviet Union was made possible by the formation of a totalitarian political system under Stalin. After Stalin's death in 1953, his successors faced the issue of how to deal with the history of his regime and how to encourage Soviet society to adapt to changing circumstances.

SECTION OVERVIEW

• Reforming Soviet Society
• Bureaucracy and *Nomenklatura*

Historical events relating to reforms are outlined on pages 334–335.

Reforming Soviet Society

The first attempts at relaxing controls on Soviet society were made by Nikita Khrushchev in 1956. His objective was to make the Soviet political system and economy more responsive to the needs and aspirations of an increasingly urban society. Many of the political and economic controls that were relaxed by Khrushchev in the 1950s were reinstated by Brezhnev in the 1960s and 1970s.

Under Khrushchev (1953–1964)

Khrushchev's attempts to deal with Stalin's record and to make Soviet society somewhat freer produced many surprises.

De-Stalinization. In a secret speech to the 20th Party Congress of the CPSU in February 1956, Khrushchev condemned Stalin for his cruel repression of the Soviet people and flagrant abuse of power. He stated that Stalin had misinterpreted Lenin's beliefs on socialism and brought misery to the people. Khrushchev's speech stunned the Communist Party, and also the world after it was leaked into Western diplomatic hands.

Khrushchev used the speech to distance himself from the policies of Stalin, to be seen as more liberal at home and in the West, and to justify attempts to reform Soviet society. These attempts became known later as "de-Stalinization."

Numerous social controls on the Soviet people were relaxed and the powers of the secret police curbed. Thousands of people were released from forced labour camps. Restrictions on the movements of people were eased.

De-Stalinization became known as "the thaw" in literature and the arts. Writers were allowed to be more critical. Artists were given more freedom to be creative and expressive. Many of the country's intellectuals began to call for some change in the country's political and economic institutions.

The "thaw" was accompanied by the removal of Stalin's image from public places and the rewriting of history books to de-emphasize his role in Soviet history. In 1961, Stalin's body was removed from Lenin's tomb and placed in a simple grave inside the Kremlin. The city of Stalingrad on the Volga River was renamed Volgograd.

Excerpts from Khrushchev's Secret Speech (February 25, 1956)

At present we are concerned with a question which has immense importance for the Party now and in the future—with how the Stalin cult grew, the cult which became at a certain specific stage the source of a whole series of exceedingly serious and grave perversions of Party principles, of Party democracy, of revolutionary legality.

Because not all as yet realize fully the practical consequences resulting from the cult of the individual leader, the great harm caused by the violation of the principle of collective direction of the Party, and because immense and limitless power was gathered in the hands of one person, the Party Central Committee considers it absolutely necessary to make the material pertaining to this matter available to the 20th Congress of the Communist Party of the Soviet Union. . . .

Comrades! The cult of the individual leader caused the employment of faulty principles in Party work and in economic activity; it brought about gross violation of inner-Party and Soviet democracy, sterile administration by fiat, deviations of all sorts, covering up of shortcomings and varnishing of reality. Our country gave birth to many flatterers and specialists in false optimism and deceit.

We should also not forget that due to numerous arrests of Party, Soviet, and economic leaders, many workers began to work uncertainly, showed overcautiousness, feared everything that was new, feared their own shadows and began to show less initiative in their work. . . .

Comrades! In order not to repeat errors of the past, the Central Committee has declared itself resolutely against the cult of the individual leader. We consider that Stalin was excessively extolled. However, in the past Stalin undoubtedly performed great services to the Party, to the working class, and to the international workers' movement.

This question is complicated by the fact that all that we have just discussed was done during Stalin's life, under his leadership and with his concurrence; here Stalin was convinced that it was necessary for the defence of the interests of the working classes against the plotting of the enemies and against the attack of the imperialist camp. He saw this from the position of the interests of the working class, the interests of the working people, the interests of the victory of socialism and communism. We cannot say that these were the deeds of a giddy despot. He considered that this should be done in the interests of the Party, of the working masses, in the name of defence of the revolution's gains. In this lies the whole tragedy! . . .

We should consider the question of the cult of the individual leader quite seriously. We cannot let this matter get out of the Party, especially not to the press. It is for this reason that we are considering it here at a closed Congress session. We should know the limits; we should not give ammunition to the enemy; we should not wash our dirty linen before their eyes. I think that the delegates to the Congress will understand and assess all these proposals properly.

Economic Reforms. As part of his policy of de-Stalinization, in 1957 Khrushchev introduced a massive shake up of the Soviet planning system. The system of industrial ministries and planning departments was abolished and replaced with regional economic councils (*sovnarkhozy*). New plan indicators such as product quality and technical innovation were introduced and the importance of production targets downgraded. The overall goals of Khrushchev's economic reform were to improve production practices, end the waste of scarce resources, encourage technical innovation, and raise living standards.

In industry, the new economic councils developed rapidly. In agriculture, Khrushchev initiated several campaigns to increase production, including the Virgin Lands Project in Kazakhstan and the cultivation of corn in Ukraine. These projects at first significantly increased food production, but in 1963–1964, crop failures affected the economy and led to Khrushchev being ousted from power by Leonid Brezhnev in October 1964.

Under Brezhnev (1964–1982)

Brezhnev's removal of Khrushchev from power marked the return to more restrictive policies and controls over Soviet society. Khrushchev was removed on the grounds that the construction of communism "does not tolerate wild schemes, hasty decisions and actions, one-man decisions, and disregard for the practical experience of the masses."

Re-Stalinization. A return to more restrictive policies, similar to those under Stalin, appeared with Brezhnev's speech at the 23rd Party Congress in March 1966. He called for greater discipline and vigilance among Communist Party members against "bourgeois ideology, revisionism, dogmatism, and reformism."

This also brought an end to criticism of Stalin and his role in creating the Soviet Union. In later years, Stalin was presented more favourably in official Soviet history and textbooks.

In the late 1960s and 1970s, many writers and artists who criticized the government and Communist Party rule were arrested, tried, and sentenced to hard labour or sent to mental hospitals. Writer Aleksandr Solzhenitsyn and physicist Andrei Sakharov were two prominent critics of the Soviet system who were suppressed in the 1970s.

Restoration of Ministries. In 1965, Brezhnev abolished Khrushchev's system of regional economic councils and restored the system of industrial ministries and planning departments. By restoring central control over the economy, the leadership hoped to increase economic growth and living standards, encourage greater technical innovation, and reduce waste of natural resources and labour.

These hopes were not realized. Growth in national income and industry fell sharply in the 1970s, while agriculture suffered from a series of bad harvests (see chart "Soviet Economic Growth"). The years of Brezhnev's rule became known among Soviet citizens as "the years of stagnation."

At the 26th Party Congress held in February 1981, Brezhnev noted that the country's future economic development depended on ending the waste of scarce natural resources. As he remarked:

The urgency of these tasks is linked to the fact that they involve nonrenewable resources. We are responsible for their correct and economic utilization, not only to present but also to future generations. And no one has the right to forget this.

Under Andropov and Chernenko (1982–1985)

Imposing Discipline. In 1983, the new General Secretary Yuri Andropov announced a series of measures to reduce wasteful production practices and inefficient planning. One of his aides, Mikhail Gorbachev, was entrusted with administering the campaign against wasteful production practices. After Andropov's death in 1984, the new leader Konstantin Chernenko shelved the campaign. Chernenko's health problems made him unwilling to undertake a controversial challenge of the Party and government.

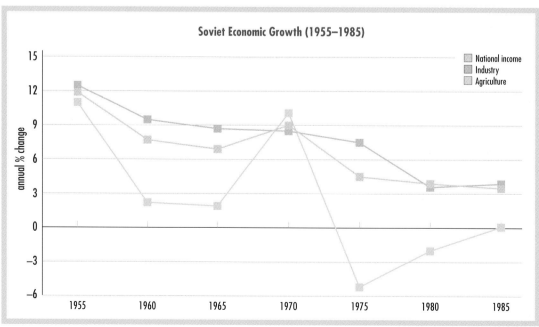

Narodnoe khoziaistvo SSSR [National Economy of the USSR]

Bureaucracy and *Nomenklatura*

The Communist Party and Soviet government were unable to eliminate waste and inefficiency in production and planning because of bureaucracy and powerful vested interest groups in Soviet society.

Bureaucracy

Under central planning, the objective of every Soviet state-owned enterprise was to meet its production targets or quotas. This required a great number of planning officials and personnel to administer, supervise, and inspect the activities of state-owned enterprises and their fulfilment of production targets.

This bureaucracy was responsible for determining resource allocation, scientific and technological development, the development of infrastructure, the environment, and many aspects of social policy.

Khrushchev attempted to reduce the bureaucracy's power over the economy by creating regional economic councils which would coordinate decision making among local enterprises. Under Brezhnev, the abolition of the regional economic councils and restoration of the industrial ministries greatly strengthened the power of bureaucracy to regulate agriculture and industry. In the 1970s, the bureaucracy grew and continued to introduce regulations and rules that controlled the daily operations of state-owned enterprises under its authority.

Nomenklatura

The power of the bureaucracy was enhanced and protected by the *nomenklatura* system of appointment. In the Soviet Union, *nomenklatura* referred to a list of people one was entitled to appoint. All important posts in government and society were filled from a list of candidates approved by the Communist Party. By this means, the Communist Party was able to impose its political priorities on Soviet society.

The *nomenklatura* system had three important consequences for Soviet society. First, the system was not accountable to the public. Ordinary Soviet citizens came to view their ruling elites as unresponsive and far removed from daily life, with

Krokodil/G. Iorsha

access to special stores, medical clinics, good housing, and imported goods.

Second, the *nomenklatura* system encouraged elites to withhold information from the general public. Information, no matter how minor, such as changes in bus routes and street names, was not disclosed to the people. Secrecy was officially excused on the basis that such information did not interest people or that people could not be trusted to act in a responsible manner if they were informed.

Third, the *nomenklatura* system created elite groups who appointed their own candidates to important posts. These groups owed their loyalty not to the Communist Party but to the person who got their names on the list. Such patronage-style appointments were based on "whom one knew" and not on "what one knew." It became rare to obtain a position on the basis of qualifications alone. Consequently, the power of these groups extended throughout all levels of government, the Communist Party, and society.

Two Years in the Soviet Union— A Personal Account

By Gerry Magennis

In September 1980 I set off for ten months in the Soviet Union as an exchange student from Great Britain.

When I arrived in Leningrad (St. Petersburg) after a three-day rail trip, I was tired, dirty, and anxious to see what my living conditions were like. I discovered that I was to live in a dormitory. The dorm was, by Soviet standards, luxurious, which meant that there was usually hot water in the showers, and the toilets were cleaned at least once a week, but toilet paper was something you had to provide yourself. It was a capitalist dorm; in other words students from capitalist countries (e.g., America and Western Europe) were housed here along with officially hand-picked Soviet students who were there as shining representatives of the Workers' state.

The reason why almost all students, Soviet and foreign alike, lived in dorms was because of a terrible housing shortage in the Soviet Union. Not only students but also workers from out of town had to live in these cramped and unpleasant conditions. Leningrad is an enormous city of five million people and, as in Moscow (a city of nine million), anyone who wanted to live there had to have a special document. This was extremely difficult to get, but millions of peasants moved to the cities every year. Their reason was simple—a tiny concrete cell of an apartment with electricity and running water, or even a shared room in a crowded dorm, was preferable to a wooden shack miles from anywhere.

Soviet shopping was not like in a modern western supermarket. In the Soviet Union each product had its own shop—if you wanted milk, you had to go to the milk shop, the same for meat and vegetables. Each shop had its own lineup, and, if you were lucky, there was something left to buy when your turn came. Standing in line for an hour for ten eggs (bring your own bag to put them in), then taking them home to find that they were rotten, was something I will never forget. If you wanted, you could complain about service and quality as every shop had a "Complaints Book" prominently displayed. I did once see an angry shopper request this book. The shop assistant took the book from the shelf and began beating the consumer about the head with it —so much for customer service Soviet-style.

Friends and contacts in the Soviet Union in 1980 were more important than anything else, even money. As a graduate, I received 200 rubles a month, more than the average salary, but what use was money if there was nothing to buy with it? However, average Soviet citizens had their own way of doing things, which made survival possible. Here's how it worked. Suppose citizen Popov sees toothpaste on sale— he buys as many tubes as he can, and passes them on to his friends who aren't at the sale. This was how people got their basic necessities. As soon as something appeared in the shops, it disappeared into people's homes. The Russians used to say that in the West there was everything in the shops, but nothing at home, whereas in the Soviet Union there was nothing in the shops,

but everything at home. Personal contacts and most-favoured-customer status, obtained through presents, meant that more goods went out the back door of a store than were sold and went out the front. The Russians had a word for it: *blat*, which means influence. You needed influence to put fresh meat on the table or to get a better job. Those lacking influence joined the ranks of the hungry and frustrated.

This means Soviet citizens could not easily have a lifestyle similar to their counterparts in the West. Let me illustrate by telling you about a family I knew. The father was head of a university department, the mother a professor, and the daughter a professional translator, a situation which, in Canada, would generate a combined annual salary of over $100 000, and as a result a good lifestyle. This Soviet family lived in a one-bedroom apartment with the living room becoming the parents' bedroom at night. The father's mother also lived with them. The family car was a seventeen-year-old Lada. They considered themselves lucky because the apartment was downtown, and they had a lot of influence in the local shops, so they didn't have too much trouble getting food.

Why didn't people attempt to change things? The Soviet Union in the period 1980–82 was in the final years of Brezhnev's leadership and of what came to be called the period of stagnation. The country was ruled by old and sick men who were unable and unwilling to change things, and refused to let anyone else change things. What this meant was that no one was not prepared to make any kind of effort, and so the living conditions did not improve.

The role of the military in Soviet life was obvious to anyone who visited the country at that time. This was especially so in Leningrad (St. Petersburg) with its many military training centres. Military uniforms were a common sight on the streets. Not only the Soviet army, but every regional army, from Polish to Mongolian, trained many of its officers in the city. Every male at age eighteen had to spend two years in the armed forces. If he was lucky he spent that two years repairing roads and working on construction for six dollars a month—if he was unlucky he found himself fighting in Afghanistan.

The Soviet war in Afghanistan was a major topic during my stay there. It was almost like America during the Vietnam war, only without the protests. The government pretended that the Afghanistan War wasn't very serious, but the stories were heard everywhere of how terrible it actually was. By 1984 there were even disabled soldiers appearing on the streets, begging for food. The KGB quickly removed these people, as they reminded everyone of a war the government would sooner forget.

It was the KGB more than any other organization, be it the Communist Party or the military, that was responsible for keeping things under control and ensuring that no one complained too loudly about Soviet lifestyles. The basic rule seemed to be that one could abuse the system as much as one wanted, by cheating, bribing, and refusing to work, but anyone

caught trying to change it was asking for trouble, and usually got it. In the end, the system continued, while the country was falling to pieces. The nation was in a mood of despair.

How was this mood reflected in the behaviour of ordinary Soviet citizens? Let's take three examples, one who fled, one who stayed, and one who played. The one who fled was a Lithuanian theatre director, Aivaras. He was fed up with the hundreds of government rules that stifled his talent. He was desperate to leave the country. Aivaras eventually left and now lives in the USA, earning his living by selling real estate. This situation was repeated hundreds of thousands of times in the 1960s, 1970s, and early 1980s, with the result that the country lost many talented and educated people.

My second example—the one who stayed in the Soviet Union—was an anti-communist dissident, Rostislav. He was a man who tried desperately to change the rules and the way things were done. This resulted in his arrest and interrogation by the KGB. They were anxious to expel him from the Soviet Union to the West (where many were longing to go), but Rostislav refused to leave, preferring a twelve-year jail sentence on his native soil to freedom in a foreign land.

My third example, and perhaps the most successful of the trio, was the one who played. Boris Grebenshchikov ignored the political situation entirely—it didn't bother him—he was a rock musician, and was only interested in his music, and in keeping his band "Aquarium" together. He played in private

apartments, passed the hat around afterwards so that he had enough money to buy bread and cheese. Boris ignored the system, and it left him alone. He was a poor but happy man. He and his music had status among a small and select group of fans. After Gorbachev came to power, Boris and his band became international rock stars, and his albums have been sold all over the world. In spite of his success, he still chooses to live in St. Petersburg rather than Los Angeles.

Shortly after I arrived in the Soviet Union in September 1980, someone who was to become a close friend made a remark that has since turned out to be all too true. She said, "The only thing that can give us freedom in the Soviet Union is an economic collapse." Everyone then and throughout the early 1980s could sense the coming economic collapse, but the mood was one of growing fear: fear that this might lead to the emergence of a new dictator.

REVIEW

Summary

The aim of the Bolsheviks' seizure of power in 1917 was to create a society based on group interests. In this new society, collectivism was more important than individualism. For the next 70 years Soviet political and economic systems reflected the values and beliefs about the group and collectivism.

The Soviet political system was established as a dictatorship of the proletariat, with all political power held by the Communist Party and its leaders. The political power and authority of the Communist Party to make policies for the country was protected and maintained by a large secret police. Any individuals who disagreed with the policies and decisions of the Communist Party leadership were arrested, imprisoned, or executed.

The Soviet economic system was established in 1928 as an economy based on public enterprise for the purpose of rapidly industrializing the country. The Soviet government controlled and regulated the economy in the interests of the working class and the Communist Party. Central planners made most decisions about production and distribution of goods and services as well as the allocation of resources. All means of production were owned or controlled by the state.

The establishment of a "socialist" society and planned economy was made possible by the formation of a totalitarian regime under Stalin. Following Stalin's death in 1953, Khrushchev introduced political reforms to encourage greater creative expression and some discussion of Communist policies, but many of his political reforms were reversed under Brezhnev. Economic reforms introduced by Khrushchev aimed to improve central planning, economic growth, and people's living standards. Most of these economic reforms were also reversed under Brezhnev. However, these political and economic reforms did force many Communist Party officials to be more accountable to Soviet society for their actions.

Soviet Values and Political Philosophy

1. From reading the short biographies of Lenin and Stalin on pages 336 and 337, what role did each man play in the development of the modern Soviet state?

2.
   a) Which of the core Soviet values do you think our society would benefit from implementing, at least to some degree?
   b) With which two of the core values would you most disagree? Provide reasons for your choices.

3. It is argued, by some, that Lenin created the theory and conditions that Stalin used to create his one-man dictatorship. From reading Lenin's beliefs on page 338, pick out statements that:
   a) could be used to support this view
   b) could be used to support arguments against this view.

4. What statements in Stalin's beliefs (page 339) indicate the type of dictatorship he would later create, and the role of the Communist Party in that dictatorship?

5. Use the Overview of the Soviet Union on pages 334–335 to answer the following questions.
   a) Select events which best characterize the type of leader that Stalin was. Explain your selections.
   b) Compare the leadership of Stalin, Brezhnev and Gorbachev, outlining the similarities and differences of events and policies from each era.

Soviet Political System

1. The Soviet government appeared to be democratic in both theory and principle, but the reality was quite different. Explain where power was based in both theory and practice in the Soviet system.

2. In the chart on page 340, how would the arrows need to be changed to make the Soviet government democratic?

3. Which was the most powerful position in the Soviet Union? Provide evidence from the text.

4. Using the broad definition of democracy to mean leaders chosen by and responsible to the citizens of the state, which of the elements of the Soviet government could be classified as: a) democratic; b) partially democratic; c) non-democratic? Be prepared to defend your decisions.

   President (Chairman of the Presidium)
   Prime Minister (Chairman of the Council of Ministers)
   Presidium
   Council of Ministers
   General Secretary of the Communist Party
   Supreme Soviet (made up of the Soviet of the Union and the Soviet of Nationalities)

5. Why was the General Secretary the most powerful person in the Soviet system when this position was never mentioned or defined in the constitution?

6. The Communist Party felt that they alone could develop a better political and economic system. How were they able to justify this one-party monopoly on power?

7. a) In what ways were elections, propaganda, indoctrination, and constitutions used to control the people's participation in the Soviet political process?

   b) To what extent are there similarities to other non-democratic states that you have studied?

8. a) Why do you think there was a fairly strict set of conditions and recommendations that had to be met before new members could join the Communist Party? (See page 343)

   b) By 1986 the CPSU had 19 million members, or 7% of the population. In Canada, only about 5% of the population belongs to political parties. What might explain the difference in the Soviet system, particularly considering that membership was limited?

9. The Soviet Union became a totalitarian dictatorship. All the following were used by the Communist Party to maintain power. Which one would be considered to be **least** characteristic of a dictatorship?

   A. controlled elections
   B. indoctrination
   C. a constitution
   D. propaganda

10. Your society is not a non-democratic state, however some of the methods used by the Communist Party to maintain power are also used, in some form or another, in our system.

    a) Which methods are used in our system, and how are they different from the way they were used in the Soviet system?

    b) Which methods are not used in our system? Explain your answer.

11. Using a Venn diagram, compare communist values, (page 348) with those of your society.

12. All societies try to mould the values, attitudes, and beliefs of their young people. Indicate which aspects of the Komsomol you find acceptable and unacceptable in a youth organization. Be prepared to explain your views.

13. Stalin claimed that his constitution of 1936 was the most democratic in the world because of its guarantee of individual rights. To what extent were individual rights guaranteed in the Soviet Union under Stalin?

14. Explain how the Gulag, the secret police, agents and informers, the militia, the internal pass, the labour book, and the Great Purge were used to limit rights and freedoms.

15. In small groups, discuss the apparent contradiction between the core Soviet values (page 337) and the methods the government used to hold power (see pages 349–351).

16. Read the Focus On Critical Thinking on page 351. Imagine that you are a prisoner. Write a one-page diary entry outlining what life is like on a typical winter day.

17. Why do you think the leaders of the USSR condemned people like Solzhenitsyn and Sakharov rather than use their ideas to reform and improve their society?

18. While the *samizdat* were illegal, they were also useful to Communist Party officials. Read page 352 of the text and the Focus On Critical Thinking on page 353. List arguments and evidence to support the assertion that the *samizdat* were a danger to communist society.

Soviet Economic System

1. Create a chart to summarize the economic developments during the following economic periods.
   a) War Communism
   b) New Economic Policy
   c) Planned Economy (Five Year Plans)
   d) Reconstruction
   e) Growth and Stagnation

2. What were the differences between state farms and collective farms?

3. a) In chart form, describe the role played by the Politburo, GOSPLAN, GOSSNAB, and GOSSTROI in Soviet Central Planning.
   b) In your view, how efficient does this system appear to be?

4. In the USSR, industry was regarded as successful if it fulfilled or exceeded its production quota. Managers would then receive awards and rewards.
   a) How does this differ from what generally occurs in a capitalist economy?
   b) What would be some of the problems with basing success and reward on meeting or exceeding a quota in the Soviet Union?

5. In Russia today there are people who would like to return to the safety of the communist type of planned economy. After reading the Focus On Critical Thinking by Igor Djavrov on page 358, draw up a list of advantages and disadvantages of life in a planned economy.

6. a) Two features of free enterprise, competition and incentives, were used throughout the entire Soviet period. How were they adapted for use in the Soviet Union? Provide three examples.
   b) If you were living in the Soviet Union, which incentive would you prefer? Explain your reasons.

c) What was socialist competition, and how was it different from capitalist competition?

d) What was storming, and what was the result of this practice?

e) What happened to people charged with not cooperating and not meeting production targets?

f) What types of incentives were used in the early years?

g) What incentives did the Communist Party controlled unions hand out after 1955?

7. a) Examine the cartoon on page 359. What does it say about factory managers' dedication to their work?

b) What people in Soviet society might agree with the cartoonist?

8. During the 1930s, the collectivization of agriculture was completed.

a) What was collectivization?

b) What was the practical reason for its implementation?

c) What was the ideological reason for its implementation?

d) How were the peasant farmers affected?

e) Who were the *kulaks*? Why do you think they were singled out for brutal treatment?

f) How did collectivization benefit the Communist Party?

9. Stalin was convinced that the capitalist nations would eventually wage war against the Soviet Union to destroy the threat of communism. The economic emphasis was on rapid industrialization, focussing on heavy industries to build military strength. Collectivization of agriculture to produce surpluses for export, would pay for industrialization. In a short essay, take and defend a position on the issue: To what extent were collectivization and the Five Year Plans necessary for the development of the Soviet Union in the years prior to World War II?

10. Read the Focus On Critical Thinking by Miron Dolot on page 361.

a) To what extent is the title of Dolot's book an accurate statement of what happened in Ukraine between 1930–1933? Provide evidence to support your position.

b) Why do you think Stalin's government took these actions in Ukraine?

c) To what extent is the Official View, as expressed by Stalin in February 1933, an accurate assessment of what occurred in Ukraine in 1932–1933?

11. Create a chart outlining the strengths and weaknesses of the Soviet system of central planning.

12. a) Review Soviet Values and Political Philosophy (pages 336–339) and list the economic rights of Soviet citizens in theory.

b) Review the Soviet Economic System and Soviet Political Economy sections on pages 354–369. To what extent were the economic rights in theory a reality in the 1980s and 1990s?

Soviet Political Economy

1. a) Why did Khrushchev feel there was a need to reform both the political and economic systems?

b) What are some examples from Khrushchev's period of reform that gave it the names "thaw" and "de-Stalinization"?

c) What types of economic reforms did Khrushchev make? What were his reasons for making them?

2. Brezhnev's period in power is characterized by a return to some Stalinist principles.

a) Briefly describe the Brezhnev era, focussing on examples of re-Stalinization, and the economic results.

b) Why did the Party and bureaucracy continue to support Brezhnev, or at least made no move to replace him, even when his health deteriorated and the economy stagnated?

3. Read pages 367–369. To what extent do you think that the systems of *nomenklatura* and the bureaucracy were responsible for the failure of the Soviet economy and the decline and fall of the Soviet Union?

4. Examine the cartoon on page 367. To what extent will the person on the left be able to "show initiative"? Why or why not?

5. Read the Focus On Critical Thinking by Gerry Magennis on pages 368–369.

a) Write down two or three words that come to mind about life in the Soviet Union. Be prepared to discuss why you chose those words.

b) What are three things that you would find most difficult to adjust to if you had gone to live in the Soviet Union in 1980–1982?

Chapter Consolidation

1.   The chapter began with a quotation by Lenin from 1920. What significance does this quotation have in describing the Soviet Union between the 1920s and 1985?

2. Answer the question below by choosing the best answer. Explain why your choice is the best answer and why the other three are incorrect. Which of the following statements **best** describes the difference between political and economic life under Stalin and under Krushchev?

A. The Soviet system became less bureaucratic and relied more on free enterprise.

B. Repression was relaxed and more consumer goods became available.

C. For the first time opposition parties were permitted to run for office.

D. The Soviet Union remained as repressive as ever but industry reached new heights of efficiency.

3. a) On what values were the political and economic systems of the Soviet Union based?

  b) Whose ideas were influential in the development of the political and economic systems of the Soviet Union? Briefly explain the ideas and how they were applied in the Soviet Union.

   c) Create a chart, identifying the type of political system and economic system in the Soviet Union and the strengths and weaknesses of those systems.

CHAPTER
10 RUSSIAN FEDERATION

"The presidential elections have taken place! They were free and honest. On July 3, you and I chose the country's future. I am proud of the fact that we passed this test. I am proud of Russia! I am proud of you, the people of Russia!"
—Boris N. Yeltsin, televised address to the nation, July 4, 1996

In 1985, the Communist Party chose a dynamic new leader named Mikhail Gorbachev, who in five short years would change forever the political, economic, and social structure of the Soviet Union. In his first years of rule Mikhail Gorbachev's government introduced several economic changes, in the hope of improving central planning, raising living standards, and ending widespread corruption. Soon other changes were launched to restructure the country's political institutions.

Gorbachev's changes released both positive and negative forces in Soviet society. One complex force was nationalism. The Soviet Union was a multinational entity containing over 100 different nationalities. The government of the Soviet Union was unable to control the demands from its numerous nationalities for greater autonomy. In 1991 the Soviet Union began to disintegrate, as its republics began to declare their independence. In December 1991, the Commonwealth of Independent States (CIS) was formed to replace the Soviet Union. The Russian Federation emerged as the dominant state in the CIS.

Like all members of the CIS, the Russian Federation was not prepared for independence. Its political transition from a non-democratic to a democratic political system and economic transformation from a centrally planned to a private enterprise economy has been difficult and painful.

Focus On Issues

Key Concepts/Vocabulary

cooperative
glasnost
perestroika
democratization
Congress of
  People's Deputies

State Duma
presidential decree
self-determination
hyperinflation

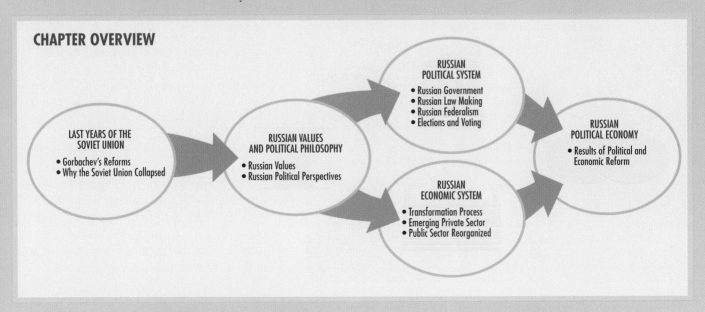

CHAPTER OVERVIEW

LAST YEARS OF THE SOVIET UNION
- Gorbachev's Reforms
- Why the Soviet Union Collapsed

RUSSIAN VALUES AND POLITICAL PHILOSOPHY
- Russian Values
- Russian Political Perspectives

RUSSIAN POLITICAL SYSTEM
- Russian Government
- Russian Law Making
- Russian Federalism
- Elections and Voting

RUSSIAN ECONOMIC SYSTEM
- Transformation Process
- Emerging Private Sector
- Public Sector Reorganized

RUSSIAN POLITICAL ECONOMY
- Results of Political and Economic Reform

LAST YEARS OF THE SOVIET UNION (1985–1991)

Historical events relating to the Soviet Union are shown in the chronology on pages 334–335.

Advance Organizer

On March 11, 1985, Mikhail Sergeevich Gorbachev, an energetic, university-educated party leader, was elected General Secretary of the Communist Party of the Soviet Union (CPSU) by the Politburo. His election opened a new chapter in the history of the Soviet Union. Few people knew much about Gorbachev or expected he would introduce numerous social, political, and economic changes. No one could have imagined that six years later he would resign from power, communism would collapse, and the Soviet Union break up.

SECTION OVERVIEW
- Gorbachev's Reforms
- Why the Soviet Union Collapsed

Gorbachev's Reforms

When Gorbachev became General Secretary in early March 1985, few people knew what he stood for. His earlier political work under General Secretaries Leonid Brezhnev (1964–1982) and Yuri Andropov (1982–1984) consisted largely of routine party work and gave no indication that Gorbachev desired to significantly change the country's existing social, political, and economic structures.

PHOTO: Mikhail Gorbachev (in centre of photo) during his brief tenure as General Secretary of the CPSU introduced numerous political and economic reforms which profoundly changed the Soviet Union.

His first speeches emphasized the continued importance of Communist ideology, one-party rule, and a centrally planned economy. In early 1986, his policy of *perestroika* (restructuring) was introduced as an attempt to eliminate bureaucracy, corruption, and the inertia of the Brezhnev era. In early 1987, the policy of *glasnost* (openness) had been introduced to ensure greater commitment by the Soviet people to *perestroika*. In 1988, *perestroika* and *glasnost* were followed by democratization of Soviet politics.

Perestroika (Restructuring)

For decades, the ruling elite made little effort to satisfy the basic needs of the Soviet people but had focussed their energies on heavy industry. By 1985 the Soviet economy had practically stopped growing. Gorbachev's policy of *perestroika* was intended to increase economic growth through better planning, the introduction of new technologies, and the production of better quality consumer goods. At the outset, most Soviet citizens found the policies of *perestroika* to be unclear and contradictory. In time, the Soviet government approved a series of laws that became part of *perestroika*.

Reuters/Stringer/Archive Photos

Law on Individual Labour. Before 1987, it was illegal in the Soviet Union to carry on a private business or to hire workers. On May 1, 1987, the Law on Individual Labour legalized a wide variety of private business activities which earlier had been conducted secretly. The newly legalized private businesses were allowed to hire only family members and were restricted to retail trade, car repair, writing, and services such as typing and private tutoring. They were not allowed to compete with state-owned enterprises or buy goods and services from state enterprises.

Law on State Enterprises. On January 1, 1988, the Law on State Enterprises gave state enterprises and farms greater freedom to manage their own costs, salaries, and sales. After satisfying the orders of their ministries, enterprises were free to produce goods according to supply and demand, reward increased productivity with wage increases, and introduce new products. Successful enterprises could share profits among workers and managers. Unprofitable enterprises were allowed to go bankrupt and be closed down. In practice, state enterprises could still be penalized for not fulfilling production targets.

Law on Cooperatives. On May 1, 1988, the Law on Cooperatives allowed cooperatives to hire as many workers as they wanted, own private property, and contract out work to private businesses. However, they faced new restrictions in the form of high taxes, interference from local party officials, and shortages of materials. Despite these difficulties, by 1991 cooperatives employed over six million workers.

Glasnost (Openness)

Gorbachev's policy of *glasnost* was introduced early in 1987. Gorbachev believed that the Soviet people needed to have a greater awareness of reality and of the results of previous government decisions before they would be willing to commit themselves to *perestroika*. *Glasnost* was meant to facilitate communication between the state and society and to change the beliefs Soviet citizens held about their society.

Soviet Society. Once the media were allowed to report on social problems in Soviet society, people became more aware of their existence. Television programs that unearthed inefficiency and corruption in government drew huge audiences of television watchers. The official view of a harmonious and progressive Soviet society building communism together was revealed to be false.

Glasnost (openness) was a policy initiated by Soviet General Secretary Mikhail Gorbachev in 1986 to improve communication between the state and society and to change the beliefs Soviet citizens held about their society.

"Perestroika! Perestroika!"

Krokodil/V. Til'man

Soviet Past. For decades, the Communist Party proclaimed the Soviet Union to be a voluntary federation of nationalities based on equality. This official version was challenged in 1988 when Estonian, Latvian, Lithuanian, and Moldavian nationalists asserted that their republics did not join the Soviet Union willingly but were occupied by Soviet forces and became Soviet republics under Stalin's orders. Information about Soviet treatment of peasants during the 1929–1932 collectivization drives, wartime deportations of small nationalities to Siberia and Central Asia, and brutality against ordinary citizens during the "Great Purge" also became public.

Democratization

Gorbachev introduced a series of political reforms, known as "democratization," to encourage greater public participation in politics and to force the Communist Party to be more responsive to people's needs. To achieve these goals, Gorbachev convened a special conference of the Communist Party in June 1988 to reorganize the government and allow national elections.

Law on Electoral Reform. On December 1, 1988, the Law on Electoral Reform created an elected legislative body called the USSR Congress of People's Deputies. It was composed of 2250 deputies, of which 1500 deputies would be directly elected by the population and 750 deputies elected by trade unions, intellectual groups, the Communist Party, and other public organizations. Although the Congress would meet only periodically, it would be the country's national parliament with the power to formulate laws, elect a full-time Supreme Soviet, and represent the interests of the population.

To be elected to the Congress, a candidate would have to obtain at least 50% of the support of all registered voters of a district or public organization. If no candidate received more than 50% of the vote, a second or runoff election between the leading two candidates would be held two weeks later. Voters had the option of striking off the name of all candidates on the ballot as a sign of disapproval.

On March 26, almost 90% of Soviet voters went to the polls to elect deputies to the USSR Congress. Prominent critics of the Communist Party such as Boris Yeltsin and Andrei Sakharov were elected by large majorities. In several districts candidates received less than the required 50% support and were forced into runoff elections.

USSR Congress of People's Deputies. The first session of the USSR Congress of People's Deputies (May 25–June 9, 1989) was televised live throughout the Soviet Union. Gorbachev presented a detailed analysis of the country's economic and social problems, and called for the election of new governments in the republics.

Elections in the republics took place in early 1990, at the same time as the Congress abolished the Communist Party's leading role in government and society and allowed other political parties to exist. The Congress elected Gorbachev to be the first President of the USSR, with the power to appoint the Prime Minister, sign laws, and dissolve the Supreme Soviet for new elections.

In December 1990, the USSR Congress granted President Gorbachev extensive emergency powers to issue decrees. These powers were granted to deal with civil disorder, ethnic unrest, growing food shortages, and falling industrial production.

Growth of Nationalism

In allowing the Soviet people greater freedom to express ideas and participate in politics, *glasnost* and democratization gave the country's numerous nationalities opportunities to express their grievances and concerns about Soviet rule.

Calls for Sovereignty. In 1988, Estonians, Latvians, and Lithuanians pressed the Soviet government to accept that its occupation of their lands in June 1940 had been illegal and that the Baltic republics had a right to secede from the Soviet Union, a right guaranteed by the Soviet constitution. In March 1990, President Landsbergis declared Lithuania's independence from the Soviet Union, which President Gorbachev declared illegal.

In June 1990, Boris Yeltsin, the head of the government of the Russian Republic, declared that the republic's laws took precedence over Soviet ones. This declaration by the largest Soviet republic quickly led to similar declarations by all fifteen republics. Gorbachev was freed in 1991 to put forth various proposals to make the Soviet Union a decentralized and voluntary union of republics.

Attempted Overthrow. On August 19, 1991, a group of officials of the central government, KGB, Communist Party, and military attempted to seize power. Gorbachev was placed under house arrest while on holiday in the Crimea. The leaders of the coup moved to control the press, ban public meetings, and restore central authority over the country. Boris Yeltsin of the Russian Republic, elements in the Soviet army, and Baltic leaders opposed the coup. On August 21, the coup collapsed and its leaders were arrested. Gorbachev returned to power, but his authority was greatly reduced.

Collapse of the Soviet Union. On August 24, Gorbachev resigned as the General Secretary of the Communist Party and ordered the party to end its political activity in government agencies, state enterprises, the military, and KGB.

When voters in Ukraine chose independence for their republic on December 1, 1991, the Soviet Union crumbled. On December 25, 1991, Gorbachev resigned as President of the USSR just as the Soviet flag over the Kremlin was lowered and replaced by the red, white, and blue flag of the Russian Federation. On January 1, 1992, the Commonwealth of Independent States (CIS), a loose grouping of eleven former Soviet republics with no central decision making authority, replaced the Soviet Union.

Commonwealth of Independent States, 1992

* Joined CIS in 1993

Member of the Commonwealth of Independent States
Non-member of the Commonwealth of Independent States

Why the Soviet Union Collapsed

The collapse of the Soviet Union in late 1991 was astonishing, and it dramatically changed the political map of the world, but it was not completely unexpected. In the early 1980s, there had been growing awareness among some Soviet leaders and citizens of the country's increasing problems. The reasons for the breakup of the Soviet Union can be traced to economic, political, ideological, social, and ethnic problems that had been gradually growing in importance since the death of Stalin in 1953.

Economic Decline. Central planning succeeded in industrializing the Soviet Union and in making it the world's second largest industrial power, a position it held up to the early 1980s, when Japan's economy became second largest. However, central planning also created an economy that became more and more difficult for planners and top Communist leaders in Moscow to manage and direct. Instead of individuals answering most economic questions about production and distribution of goods and services and the allocation of resources through the mechanism of the marketplace, the Soviet economy employed an army of government bureaucrats, directors, and planners to direct the economy.

This group, part of the *nomenklatura*, evolved into a powerful interest group which gradually began to run the Soviet economy in a way that enhanced their power and privilege. Whenever top leadership introduced policies to raise economic growth and improve the living standards of ordinary Soviet citizens, the *nomenklatura* resisted the changes. They considered reform policies to be a threat to their positions and their power to manage the economy. Like his predecessors Khrushchev, Brezhnev, Andropov, and Chernenko, Gorbachev could not significantly change the behaviour of the *nomenklatura*.

The failure of Communist leaders to reform the economy had serious long-term effects. Economic growth and living standards of the people were not raised.

The Soviet economy continued to waste scarce natural resources and produce low quality goods. By 1990, industrial production was falling and the country was faced with shortages of all kinds.

Political Inertia. As the only legal political party with the constitutional right to hold political power, the Communist Party did not develop into a democratic party. Under Stalin and later leaders, the Communist Party grew into a giant political organization with millions of members. By 1986, the membership of the Communist Party exceeded 19.4 million. Many of these members did not join the Communist Party to support the Communist cause but to further personal interests and careers. Inside the Communist Party, party officials established networks of friends and trusted members and enjoyed very comfortable lives. The power of these party officials grew after Stalin's death, especially under Brezhnev, who did not challenge government and party officials to improve their performance. As General Secretary, Gorbachev attempted to introduce policies to democratize the Soviet political system in the hope that this would force party officials to become more accountable to Communist Party members and leaders, as well as to the ordinary Soviet citizen. Instead of becoming more accountable, party officials began to use the new political institutions to prevent more political change from reducing their power and privileges.

Ideological Stagnation. In the early years of the Soviet Union, Marxism–Leninism inspired the Soviet people to support great national projects such as industrialization, collectivization, and the building of socialism. After Stalin's death, instead of inspiring the people with Marxist–Leninist ideology, Communist Party leaders gradually adapted it to justify the slowdown of economic growth and their failure to achieve the goal of communism.

In reality, Marxism–Leninism could not offer any creative solutions to new problems. Marx's main work, *Das Kapital*, was a critique of 19th century capitalism and did not provide a blueprint for creating and governing a socialist society in the 20th century. Following Lenin's death in 1924, this task was left largely to Stalin to carry out. Stalin's conception of a socialist society was based on developing heavy industry and subordinating the working class to the Communist Party.

Under Khrushchev, the Soviet Union opened up to the outside world. Foreign ideas, many of them hostile to Marxism–Leninism, began to enter the country. Many people discovered that living standards in the Soviet Union were lower than in the capitalist West. In the late 1960s and early 1970s, controls on people's lives began to produce apathy. By the 1980s, most Soviet citizens were disillusioned with Marxism–Leninism and believed that their leaders were too isolated from the ordinary citizen to offer any practical solutions to their daily problems.

Social Inequality. For decades, Soviet society was proclaimed to be a classless society in which everyone was treated equally. Though Stalin introduced policies to ensure that people had more or less equal incomes and access to goods, he also introduced ranks, distinctions, and differential rewards. This, plus industrialization, created social differences and inequality. Social inequality continued to increase under Khrushchev and Brezhnev. By the time Gorbachev came to power, Soviet society could no longer claim to be free of social inequality. Communist Party officials, top government bureaucrats, factory directors, and planners, all part of the *nomenklatura*, lived very comfortably and had access to scarce imported goods and foreign currency, special health clinics and schools, and spacious apartments. Though the media were forbidden to report on the lifestyles and privileges of the *nomenklatura*, most Soviet citizens knew about them. This created widespread cynicism among the population about the Communist Party and its leaders.

By allowing the media greater freedom to report on Soviet society, Gorbachev undermined the legitimacy of the Communist Party and its leaders. What many Soviet citizens had known privately about the lifestyles of Communist leaders became openly acknowledged—that Soviet society was divided into two classes, a small privileged ruling class and a large class of citizens living very modestly. Furthermore, the media exposed widespread corruption among their Communist leaders. This further brought into question the legitimacy of the Communist Party's right to rule the country, and it discouraged people from supporting Gorbachev and economic reforms of the Soviet economy.

Ethnic Nationalism. Like the Russian Empire it replaced, the Soviet Union was a multinational entity. For decades, Russians were a majority of the population. By 1989, about 49% of the population was non-Russian, with the likelihood that non-Russians would be a majority by 2000.

Theoretically, the Soviet Union was designed in 1922 to be a federation of republics, each having the right to secede from the Soviet Union. Each republic was set up to be an ethnic homeland, as an attempt to control nationalism. In reality, this created conditions that would later foster nationalism.

In the 1970s, nationalism began to emerge in several republics, but as long as the Communist Party ruled the republics it was held in check. Once Gorbachev allowed people to learn about past Soviet treatment of the country's non-Russian nationalities and to participate in the political process, nationalism became a powerful political force. In 1990–1991, nationalist parties were elected to power in several republics. These non-Communist governments called on the Soviet government to allow their republics to exercise their constitutional right to secede from the Soviet Union.

RUSSIAN VALUES AND POLITICAL PHILOSOPHY

Advance Organizer

The breakup of the Soviet Union presented the Russian Federation with a new reality. Today, the country faces the challenge of building new political and economic systems on entirely different principles.

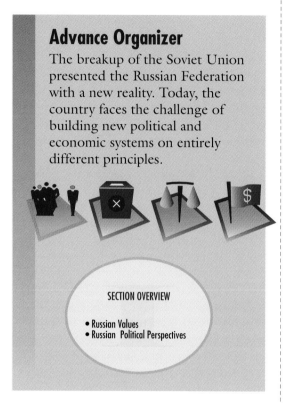

SECTION OVERVIEW

- Russian Values
- Russian Political Perspectives

Russian Values

The collapse of Communism in the Soviet Union has disoriented many Russians, who now feel lost in the world in which they live and unsure of how to relate to others. Changing the values and principles that underlie an ideology is slow and difficult. Time is needed for Russians to understand the principles that underlie many of the new values imported from the West, as they attempt to replace communist values with those more common in the West. Still, many Russians are changing their society in ways they never before thought possible.

New Values

A recent study of Russian society and culture, edited by Dmitri Shalin, called *Russian Culture at the Crossroads*[1] noted that Russian values today are a complex mixture of traditional Russian values, former Communist values, and newly adopted Western values.

Personal freedom. While most Russians believe that personal freedom is important, Western principles of individualism such as equality before the law, acceptance of differing opinions, self-reliance, and personal responsibility for one's decisions remain undeveloped. In many ways, the desire of many Russians for personal freedom is a reaction to having lived in a society that was once tightly controlled and regimented.

Democracy. Many Russians believe that periodic elections and an elected assembly are needed to represent people's views, but to many others democracy as practised in the West is a foreign concept and should not be accepted. Since 1992, Russian voters have participated in numerous elections to choose national, regional, and local leaders. At the end of 1997, Russians could proudly claim that for the first time in their country's long history the leaders of all levels of government were elected by the people.

Private enterprise. Since 1992, many Russians have become owners of their apartments and shareholders in private companies. While many have accepted private ownership of property as a fundamental principle of private enterprise, millions of others believe that public ownership of the means of production is essential for ensuring that all social groups can afford the basic necessities of life.

Strong central authority. Throughout its long history, Russia has endured periods of considerable social, political, and economic change. Whenever the country was beset with tremendous change, the people looked to a leader who could govern them with a strong and sure hand. A strong leader, to many Russian citizens, represents stability in an unstable world. A strong leader is also important to maintain national unity, defend the country's independence from foreign aggression, and define national interests.

---

[1]Dmitri Shalin, ed. *Russian Culture at the Crossroads: Paradoxes of Postcommunist Consciousness.* Boulder: Westview Press, 1996.

Russian Political Perspectives

Before the Bolsheviks took power in November 1917, Russia had more than 100 political parties. The political continuum ranged from Bolsheviks, Mensheviks, and Social Revolutionaries on the left, to Constitutional Democrats and Octobrists in the centre, to monarchists and nationalists on the right. After 1917, all political parties except the Bolsheviks (later renamed Communists) were banned. Political parties did not reappear until 1990, when the Communist Party's monopoly on political power was abolished. New political parties appeared, but they lacked organization, well-defined platforms, and financing. Their leaders were inexperienced in politics. Most voters did not identify with any party. Anti-party sentiments strongly outweighed pro-party feelings.

New Political Parties

Since the early 1990s, many Russian political parties have appeared. Some of them, such as the Communist Party, are well organized and have established electoral support. Other parties are not as well organized as the Communist Party but are quickly establishing party organizations throughout the country and gaining voter support. Since 1993, four main political blocs have appeared—Communist, centrist, democratic, and nationalist (see "Russian Political Continuum" below).

Communist Bloc. The largest and best organized party in the Communist bloc is the Communist Party of the Russian Federation. The party was formed in early 1993 from the former Communist Party of the Soviet Union (CPSU). Another party, the Agrarian Party, was formed from regional branches of the Communist Party. In 1995, the movement called Communists for the USSR was formed on a platform of restoring the former Soviet Union. All these parties receive their greatest support from older voters who remember Soviet times for its law and order.

Centrist Bloc. The main centrist party is Our Home Is Russia, which has strong ties with political leaders in Moscow and the regions. Its electoral support is concentrated among government workers and professionals. Another centrist party is the Women of Russia movement, formed in 1993 by various women's organizations.

Democratic Bloc. The parties of the democratic bloc are supported by many urban professionals. These parties were established in 1993. The best known are the Yavlinsky Bloc (Yabloko) and Russia's Democratic Choice.

Nationalist Bloc. The best known of the nationalist parties are the Congress of Russian Communities and the Liberal Democratic Party led by Vladimir Zhirinovsky. Many Western political analysts consider Zhirinovsky to be a fascist because of his right-wing nationalist views. Most nationalist parties have strong appeal among young and working class voters.

> Russian political parties today are divided into four main groups—Communist, centrist, democratic, and nationalist.

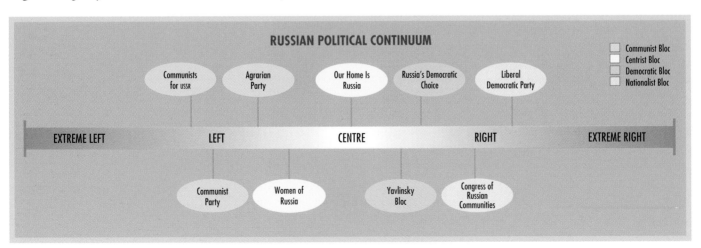

RUSSIAN POLITICAL CONTINUUM

- ☐ Communist Bloc
- ☐ Centrist Bloc
- ☐ Democratic Bloc
- ☐ Nationalist Bloc

Communists for USSR — Agrarian Party — Our Home Is Russia — Russia's Democratic Choice — Liberal Democratic Party

EXTREME LEFT — LEFT — CENTRE — RIGHT — EXTREME RIGHT

Communist Party — Women of Russia — Yavlinsky Bloc — Congress of Russian Communities

RUSSIAN POLITICAL SYSTEM

Advance Organizer

Since the breakup of the Soviet Union in December 1991, the Russian Federation has struggled to build a political system based on democratic principles in a society that has only experienced the centralized authoritarian rule of the tsars and the Communist Party. The country has often looked to other countries for ideas about how to establish democratic institutions. The 1993 Russian constitution declares the Russian Federation to be a "democratic and federal state based on the rule of law."

SECTION OVERVIEW

- Russian Government
- Russian Law Making
- Russian Federalism
- Elections and Voting

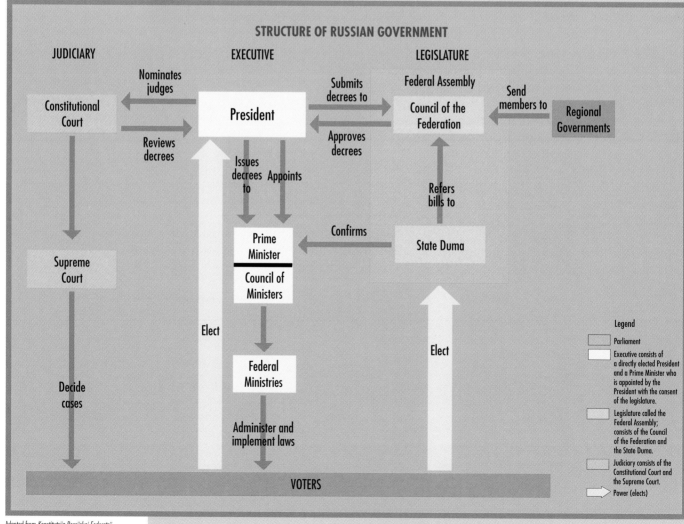

STRUCTURE OF RUSSIAN GOVERNMENT

| JUDICIARY | EXECUTIVE | LEGISLATURE |

Nominates judges

Constitutional Court

Reviews decrees

President

Submits decrees to

Approves decrees

Federal Assembly

Council of the Federation

Send members to

Regional Governments

Issues decrees to   Appoints

Refers bills to

Supreme Court

Prime Minister

Council of Ministers

Confirms

State Duma

Elect

Elect

Federal Ministries

Decide cases

Administer and implement laws

VOTERS

Legend

- Parliament
- Executive consists of a directly elected President and a Prime Minister who is appointed by the President with the consent of the legislature.
- Legislature called the Federal Assembly; consists of the Council of the Federation and the State Duma.
- Judiciary consists of the Constitutional Court and the Supreme Court.
- Power (elects)

Adapted from *Konstitutsiia Rossiiskoi Federatsii*
[Constitution of the Russian Federation], 1993

Russian Government

Russian government today combines features of a presidential and a parliamentary system, as in France.

Executive Power

Executive power in the Russian Federation is exercised by the President and the Chairman of the Council of Ministers (Prime Minister). The President is the head of state while the Prime Minister is the head of government.

President. The President is directly elected by the people for a five-year term. Any citizen over 35 years old can run for the position of President. To be elected, a candidate must receive at least 50% of the popular vote or face a second or runoff election. The President has the power to appoint the Prime Minister, with the consent of the State Duma, to dismiss the government, and to appoint government ministers and nominate judges of the Constitutional Court. The President can dissolve the State Duma for elections, sign and proclaim laws, veto legislation, and issue decrees. The President is the Supreme Commander-in-Chief of the Russian armed forces and can declare states of emergency.

Prime Minister. The Prime Minister is appointed by the President with the consent of the State Duma. As the head of the government, the Prime Minister is responsible for submitting the federal budget to the State Duma for approval and implementing government policies. The Prime Minister must have majority support in the State Duma. The President can dismiss the Prime Minister if the State Duma expresses no confidence in the government. The President can disagree with the State Duma and maintain the government in power. If the State Duma expresses no confidence in the government three times, the President can dissolve the Duma for new elections. This is another example of the extensive powers of the President.

Legislative Power

Legislative power at the national level rests in the Federal Assembly, a bicameral parliament composed of the Council of the Federation and the State Duma.

Council of the Federation. The Council of the Federation is the 178-member upper chamber of the Federal Assembly and represents the country's republics and regions. Like the American Senate, each of the country's republics, provinces, cities, and regions sends two representatives. The Council deals with regional issues and relations between the country's nationalities. It approves presidential decrees on martial law and states of emergency and schedules presidential elections. It approves the President's appointment of judges to the Constitutional Court and Supreme Court. It can remove the President from office through impeachment.

State Duma. The State Duma is the lower chamber of the Federal Assembly and represents all the people of Russia. It consists of 450 deputies, elected for a term of four years. Any Russian citizen 21 years and older is eligible to be elected as a deputy of the State Duma. The State Duma has the power (by majority vote) to initiate legislation, approve federal laws, and confirm the President's choice of Prime Minister. As well, it can vote no confidence in the government and begin impeachment against the President.

Judicial Power

Judicial power rests in the Constitutional Court and the Supreme Court. The Constitutional Court resolves disputes over jurisdictions between levels and branches of government. It reviews the constitutionality of decrees issued by the President. The Supreme Court is responsible for reviewing civil and criminal cases and providing interpretations of the law.

State Duma, the lower chamber of the Russian parliament, which has 450 deputies, holds the power to initiate legislation.

Russian Prime Ministers

Yegor Gaidar
1991–1992

Victor Chernomyrdin
1992–1998

Sergei Kiriyenko
1998

Yevgeny Primakov
1998–

Russian Law Making

The President, Prime Minister, Council of the Federation, and State Duma can all initiate legislation. The President signs bills into law and has the power to issue decrees on his or her own.

Presidential Decrees

Unlike the Canadian constitution, which gives the Parliament supreme power to make laws, the Russian constitution gives the President considerable power to issue decrees on his or her own. However, the Council of the Federation and the Duma can override a presidential decree if two-thirds of the members and deputies in the two chambers vote against it.

The President's ability to issue decrees is assisted by an extensive presidential administration composed of a Security Council and the Council of Ministers. The Security Council is responsible for drafting basic policy guidelines and prioritizing issues facing the President.

The Council of Ministers headed by the Prime Minister is the most important body under the President's control. The Council of Ministers resembles the cabinet in Canada. Members of the Council are appointed by and responsible to the President. This means that the ministries of foreign affairs, national defence, internal security, and home affairs, often called the "power ministries," are under the direct control of the President.

The many powers of the President have attracted much criticism from Russian political observers. Some have argued that the leadership role of the Communist Party has been replaced by the one-man rule of the President. Others have said that the 1993 constitution gave legal form to the seizure of power when President Yeltsin dissolved the Parliament in September 1993 and used military force in early October 1993 to prevent the dissolved Parliament from meeting. However, many Russians believe that a strong executive is needed to govern the large multinational Russian Federation.

A presidential decree is a law initiated directly by a President that does not require introduction in a legislative assembly. In the Russian Federation, presidential decrees can be overridden by a two-thirds vote in both chambers of the parliament.

Between 1993 and 1998, almost 50% of all Russian laws were enacted by presidential decree. During the same period, the President vetoed more than 250 bills passed by the State Duma.

Parliamentary Legislation

Law making in the Federal Assembly is shared by the Council of the Federation and the Duma. In some respects the process of law making in the Federal Assembly resembles that in the American Congress. Most bills are introduced in the State Duma, where they are sent to committees for examination and changes. Once this is completed, a final draft is sent to the whole Duma for debate and discussion, then passed. The bill is then sent to the Council of the Federation for debate, then passed. If the versions of the same bill passed by the two chambers differ, a committee is set up to achieve a compromise version, which is then sent to the President to sign. The President can veto the bill and send it back to the parliament. A bill can be passed into law without the President's signature if two-thirds of the deputies in both chambers vote to override the President's veto.

Checks and Balances

The 1993 Russian constitution does not have a well-defined system of checks and balances. It gives the President considerable power to make laws and to override legislation passed in the State Duma. This has led to several political crises in which the State Duma attempted to curb the law making powers of the President.

In March 1998, President Yeltsin suddenly dismissed Prime Minister Chernomyrdin. The State Duma did not initially approve the President's new Prime Minister, Sergei Kiriyenko. Kiriyenko was approved only after the President threatened to dissolve the Duma for new elections if it did not approve him.

Five months later in August, another political crisis was created when President Yeltsin dismissed Prime Minister Kiriyenko and nominated former Prime Minister Chernomyrdin as head of the government. The Duma did not confirm Chernomyrdin. The President was forced to find another candidate that the Duma would find more suitable. Foreign Minister Yevgeny Primakov was chosen and approved by the Duma as Prime Minister.

Russian Federalism

The Russian Federation is a federal state of 21 republics, 6 territories, 49 provinces, 2 federal cities, 1 autonomous province, and 10 autonomous regions. All these levels of governments are declared by the constitution to be equal members of the Russian Federation.

Division of Power

Division of power between various levels of government is outlined in the 1993 Russian constitution. The federal government is charged with upholding the constitution, individual rights and liberties, and the rights of national minorities. It has exclusive jurisdiction over customs, money, federal taxes, nuclear power, transportation, and communications, as well as foreign policy, foreign trade, and national defence.

The constitution outlines jurisdictions shared by the federal and regional governments. Shared responsibilities include law and order, public safety, natural resources, environmental protection, education, social security, science, and sports. Regional governments are solely responsible for roads and local housing.

Sovereignty and Self-Determination

Although Russians account for 81.5% of the total population, about 80 other nationalities live within the borders of the Russian Federation. The 1993 constitution recognizes that all peoples have the right to national and cultural development. However, no nationality has the right to secede from the Russian Federation. This has not stopped some ethnic groups from attempting to acquire greater independence, and others from attempting to leave the federation.

Tatarstan. In early 1992, voters in Tatarstan approved in a referendum a proposal for the independence of their republic. The Tatarstan government understood that the republic could never secede from the Russian Federation because it was surrounded on all sides by the Russian Federation and had a very large Russian minority. The Tatarstan government negotiated and, in February 1994, signed a treaty of union with the Russian Federation that allowed the republic to have a separate constitution, tax system, foreign policy, and foreign trade policy. Tatar and Russian became the official languages of the republic.

Chechnya. In Chechnya, geography and history were powerful motivating factors for that republic's drive for self-determination and secession from the Russian Federation. Unlike Tatarstan, Chechnya is not surrounded on all sides by Russia. The Chechens have a long history of unsatisfactory relations with Russia. In the 19th century they were subdued by Russia after a long war. In the 20th century, there were numerous attempts to suppress Chechen nationalism and culture. In 1944, Stalin ordered all Chechens deported to Central Asia. Under Khrushchev, they were allowed to return home. However, many Chechens could not return because their homes and land were occupied by Russians.

In October 1991, a Chechen force led by Dzhokhar Dudayev overthrew the government in Grozny, Chechnya's capital, and declared Chechnya's independence from the Russian Federation. Boris Yeltsin was concerned that Chechnyan independence threatened the Russian Federation with disintegration if other republics also seceded. Numerous efforts were made by Russia's federal government to remove Dudayev from power and force Chechnya to cancel its unilateral declaration of independence. In December 1994, Russian military forces invaded Chechnya and removed Dudayev from power.

When Russian forces withdrew in September 1996, the question of whether Chechnya had the right to secede was not resolved. According to the terms of the peace pact, Chechnya was given "special status" in the Russian Federation until 2001 when the issue of independence would be settled.

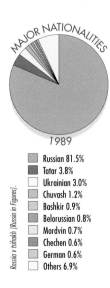

MAJOR NATIONALITIES

1989

Russian 81.5%
Tatar 3.8%
Ukrainian 3.0%
Chuvash 1.2%
Bashkir 0.9%
Belorussian 0.8%
Mordvin 0.7%
Chechen 0.6%
German 0.6%
Others 6.9%

Rossiia v tsifrakh (Russia in Figures).

Elections and Voting

The selection of government leaders in truly competitive elections is a recent practice in the Russian Federation. Before 1917, the tsar governed the country as he saw fit without approval from the people. This tradition of ruling without popular consent continued after Lenin and the Bolsheviks took power in November 1917. The 1989 elections of the Congress of People's Deputies were semi-competitive, and the 1990 elections in Russia were fully competitive. On June 12, 1991, Russian voters went to the polls to fill the newly established position of President of the Russian Republic from eight possible candidates.

Electoral Campaigning

The 1993 Russian constitution requires that elections of deputies to the State Duma and regional legislatures be held every four years. The President sets the date for Duma elections. In the republics and regions, Presidents and Governors set the date for elections to the regional legislatures. Presidential elections occur every four years, in a year when there are no elections to the State Duma.

When elections to the State Duma are announced, in order to be placed on the ballot political parties and independent candidates are required to collect signatures of eligible voters. The number of signatures required for a political party to be placed on the ballot is 200 000. Candidates running as independents in elections to the State Duma must collect at least 1% of eligible voters in a constituency.

The procedure for political parties and candidates to be listed on ballots for regional legislatures is similar. In presidential elections, to be listed on the ballot, candidates must collect at least 1 000 000 signatures of eligible voters.

Once political parties and candidates collect the required number of signatures of eligible voters and are officially approved by the Central Electoral Commission, they receive free advertising on state television. Limits on campaign spending for parties and candidates are set by law and monitored by the Central Electoral Commission. As well, parties and candidates use a variety of techniques to gain the support of voters, including door-to-door canvassing, rallies, distributing literature, and participating in debating forums. In the 1996 presidential campaign, the main candidates staged various public events such as rock concerts to capture voters' attention.

RIGHT: The poster from the 1996 presidential elections reads:

"Elections for President of Russia June 16

If you do not vote— others will choose your future.

Choose with the heart. Boris Yeltsin"

A candidate for election to the State Duma must be 21 years old or older.

A candidate for election to the Office of President must be at least 35 years old and a citizen of Russia for 10 years.

PHOTO: During the 1996 Russian presidential elections, the main presidential candidates used TV advertising, printed brochures, booklets, newspapers, and leaflets to inform voters about their platforms.

Voting

All Russian citizens aged 18 and older are permitted to vote by secret ballot. In elections to the Duma, voters cast two ballots, one for a political party and one for a candidate in their constituency. In presidential elections, voters cast one ballot for a candidate. On all ballots, voters can vote against all listed candidates by marking a box labelled "against all candidates." For an election result to be valid, more than 25% of registered voters must cast a ballot.

State Duma Elections. Since 1992, Russian voters have participated in two national elections. In the December 1993 State Duma elections, about 23% voted for the Liberal Democratic Party. The Communist Party and its ally, the Agrarian Party, together received about 20% of the popular vote. Voter turnout was only 54.8% of all eligible voters (see chart below).

In the December 1995 elections, voters were asked to choose deputies from a list of 43 political parties and movements. Only the Communists, Liberal Democrats, Our Home Is Russia party, and Yabloko were successful in obtaining more than the required 5% share of the popular vote to enter the State Duma. Voter turnout was 64.7%. The number of women deputies fell from 58 elected in 1993 to 46, largely because the Women of Russia movement failed to receive more than the required 5% of the popular vote to enter the State Duma on the party list.

Presidential Elections. In June 1991, Boris Yeltsin was elected president of the Russian Republic. His great popularity as a critic of the Communist Party and Gorbachev's economic policies enabled him to win easily on the first ballot.

In the 1996 presidential elections, Yeltsin was forced to campaign on his past record as president. He also faced Gennady Zyuganov, the leader of the Communist Party, the most popular political party among voters. During the electoral campaign Zyuganov accused Yeltsin of reducing the living standards of ordinary Russians. Yeltsin in turn warned voters that, if elected, Zyuganov would re-introduce a Communist dictatorship and controls on the economy.

On June 16, 1996, Russian voters chose their next President from a list of ten candidates. Yeltsin received 35.3% of the popular vote and Zyuganov 32%. Turnout was 69.8%. Because no candidate received the required 50% of the popular vote to win, voters returned to the polls on July 3, and Yeltsin was reelected President with 53.8% of the vote. Turnout was 68.9%.

State Duma Elections

	December 12, 1993		December 17, 1995	
	Popular Vote	Seats	Popular Vote	Seats
Liberal Democrats	22.9%	64	11.2%	51
Russia's Choice/Democratic Choice	15.4	66	3.9	9
Communist Party	12.4	48	22.3	157
Women of Russia	8.1	23	4.6	3
Agrarian Party	8.0	33	3.8	20
Yavlinsky Bloc (Yabloko)	7.9	27	6.9	45
Russian Unity & Accord	6.7	19	0.4	1
Democratic Party	5.5	14	—	—
Our Home Is Russia	—	—	10.1	55
Communists for USSR	—	—	4.5	1
Congress of Russian Communities	—	—	4.3	5
Other parties	13.0	156	28.0	103
	100.0	450	100.0	450
Voter turnout	54.8%		64.7%	
Women deputies		58		46

TsIK. *Vybory deputatov gosudarstvennoi dumy 1995. Elektoralnaia statistika* [Elections of Deputies of the State Duma 1995: Electoral Statistics].

RUSSIAN ECONOMIC SYSTEM

Advance Organizer

At the same time as Russia's leaders attempted to create a political system based on democratic principles, they introduced numerous reforms to transform the Russian economy into one based on private enterprise. Creating a private enterprise economy in place of a public enterprise centrally planned economy in the Russian Federation has been called one of the most dramatic economic events of the 1990s. The present Russian economy is classified by World Bank economists as a transitional economy, or economy in transition. Many Russians feel the development of private enterprise has brought unprecedented economic changes in their country.

The public enterprise economy of the Soviet Union is discussed on pages 354–363, the transformation process on page 391, and private enterprise economy of the Russian Federation on pages 392–395.

SECTION OVERVIEW

- Transformation Process
- Emerging Private Sector
- Public Sector Reorganized

RUSSIAN ECONOMY IN TRANSITION

Public Enterprise
(Centrally Planned Economy)
1928–1991

- Politburo
- ↓
- GOSPLAN
- ↓
- Ministries
- ↓
- State Farms and Factories
- ↓
- Consumers

Transformation Process
Since 1992

- Raise prices
- Privatize state property
- Create stable banks
- Retrain workers
- Develop business laws
- Reduce government spending

Private Enterprise
(Market Economy)
Emerging

- Resource Markets
- Consumers
- Government
- Business
- Product Markets

Legend

- ☐ Centrally planned economy
- ☐ Transformation process
- ☐ Market economy

Adapted from David Rees, *Troubles Escalate in the New World.*

Transformation Process

The first step to establishing a private enterprise economy in the Russian Federation occurred with the raising of prices on January 2, 1992.

Establishing Private Enterprise

In 1992, the Russian government announced that it would replace the country's centrally planned economy with a market economy. The two main objectives of this policy were to create a well-functioning private sector of consumers and businesses who would decide most questions about the production and distribution of goods and services; and to reorganize the government to regulate business activities, protect consumers, and encourage private ownership. To achieve these objectives it was necessary to raise prices, privatize state property, create stable banks, retrain workers, develop business laws, and reduce government spending. Refer to the chart "Russian Economy in Transition" on page 390.

Raise prices. Under central planning, basic goods and services were heavily subsidized by the government so that every citizen could afford them. Ending price controls on goods and services was necessary in creating a market economy; however, it meant that the prices of basic goods and services such as food, electricity, and apartment rents rose beyond many people's ability to pay for them. People's incomes were not protected from the effects of inflation.

Privatize state property. Privatizing state-owned property was complicated by the fact that no market for property existed to help establish how much the property was worth. As well, most state-owned businesses did not maintain accurate records of sales, expenses, and customer lists to help investors determine whether the state-owned business was worth buying.

Create stable banks. Under central planning, banks were state-owned, and they provided state-owned factories with interest-free loans for production. The losses of state-owned factories were paid by the government, so factories were not encouraged to be profitable. Consumers could not borrow and were expected to pay cash, except when purchasing a house. A market economy requires a stable and efficient banking system which provides loans to consumers and businesses.

Retrain workers. Under central planning, most factory and service work was done manually. As Gorbachev observed, the Soviet Union had missed out on the computer revolution. A market economy requires skills that may differ from those in a centrally planned economy. Computer and business skills are now in great demand.

Develop business laws. Laws to promote private businesses, protect the consumer, and safeguard the rights of property owners are necessary for a market economy. Under central planning, such laws did not exist.

Reduce government spending. Under central planning, government spending on the military, subsidies on basic goods, and social programs generally exceeded tax revenues. To cover these budget deficits, the government sold bonds at low interest rates or printed new currency. There was no efficient system of tax collection. A market economy requires an efficient system of tax collection and careful accounting of government spending.

> The general objectives of the transformation of the Russian economy since 1992 have been to create a well-functioning private sector and a public sector that could effectively regulate business activities and encourage private ownership.

Russian Economic Reforms Since 1992

January 2, 1992	Prices of goods and services are raised
January 29, 1992	Private trading is allowed
April 27, 1992	Russia joins IMF and the World Bank
August 1, 1992	Campaign for mass privatization begins with issuance of privatization vouchers
March 1, 1993	Law on bankruptcy goes into effect
June 30, 1994	Mass privatization campaign ends
April 26, 1995	Central Bank introduces "tight money" policy
November 30, 1995	Financial-industrial groups are allowed
March 1, 1996	New civil code regulating business activity goes into effect
January 1, 1997	New criminal code goes into effect
January 1, 1998	New ruble is introduced

Emerging Private Sector

Since 1992, the establishment of a well-functioning private sector has been the ultimate goal of the economic reforms launched by the Russian government. The private sector has grown rapidly, following the ending of price controls, privatization of state-owned property, and new laws on banking. By the end of 1997, over 58% of the labour force was employed in the private sector. Today, private individuals and businesses make most decisions about consumption, production, and distribution of goods and services.

Challenges

The private sector in the Russian Federation faces four challenges—developing new markets, encouraging competition, improving profits, and strengthening private ownership.

Developing New Markets. Many Russian businesses and consumers face undeveloped and weak markets. Russian producers lack expertise in advertising, customer relations, and distribution of goods for domestic and export markets. Many foreign firms have been successful in advertising their products to Russian customers and have established factories in Russia to manufacture their products for sale to Russian consumers. There has been a sharp decline in the production of consumer and industrial goods by Russian firms in this competitive market. Since 1991, Russian industrial production has fallen almost 50%. In 1997, industrial production registered its first increase in seven years as a result of higher sales of goods abroad and increases in consumer spending.

Russian companies that produce petroleum, natural gas, minerals, diamonds, and forest products have found markets abroad. Over 80% of all Russian exports consist of petroleum, natural gas, metals, chemicals, and forest products, while most imports are machinery, foodstuffs, and chemicals (see charts, left). Total Russian exports in 1997 were US$87.4 billion and imports US$67.6 billion.

Encouraging Competition. Weak competition among producers continues to affect many industries. Under central planning, most of Russian industry was organized as monopolies. The breakup of large state enterprises did not lead to strong competition among the new companies. Lack of investment capital and poor management skills meant most businesses could not significantly improve their efficiency and competitiveness. To help businesses compete and to encourage new investment, in 1995 the government allowed private banks to establish financial industrial groups. The result has not been increased competitiveness but the emergence of new monopolies, which attempt to reduce competition and raise prices in order to increase profits. These types of business groups now control the production of oil, natural gas, minerals, chemicals, steel, and heavy equipment.

Improving Profits. Weak domestic markets and domination of markets by large enterprises have greatly affected the profitability of many businesses. Various levels of government also impose numerous taxes on business. For most small businesses, high production costs and low sales mean low profits. Although more than 60% of all new businesses close their doors after two to three years of operation, the number of new businesses continues to exceed the number that close. This failure rate is not unusual in a market economy. In Canada, about 70% of new businesses fail within five years of operation.

Strengthening Private Ownership. The privatization of state-owned factories has brought fundamental changes to the Russian economy and businesses. From 1993 to 1997, the federal and regional governments sold over 100 000 state enterprises that had been operating in all sectors of the economy. In August 1992, the federal government issued free to all Russians a voucher valued at 10 000 rubles (US$50), which they could exchange for shares in a state enterprise of their choice. When the voucher campaign ended in June 1994, millions of Russians had

RUSSIAN EXPORTS

1997

- Petroleum and natural gas 47.7%
- Metals 20.0%
- Chemicals 8.2%
- Forest products 4.1%
- Machinery 10.6%
- Foodstuffs 2.9%
- Other 6.5%

RUSSIAN IMPORTS

1997

- Machinery 34.9%
- Foodstuffs 25.3%
- Chemicals 14.5%
- Metals 7.1%
- Petroleum 5.7%
- Other 12.5%

Rossiia v tsifrakh (Russia in Figures)

> Russia's emerging private sector faces the challenges of developing new markets, encouraging competition, improving profits, and strengthening private property ownership rights.

become shareholders, an unprecedented accomplishment for Russian society. Privatization also meant monopolies and many large state enterprises were broken up into smaller companies. For example, Aeroflot, the state airline, was broken up into about 400 companies. The oil and gas industry was divided into about 35 firms.

Since 1994, the mass privatization of state enterprises and apartments has created a need for real estate agents, banks, and lawyers. Today, the government faces the urgent task of developing laws that protect private property and a court system to enforce these laws.

Corporate Russia

The privatization of state enterprises created several large privately-owned companies. The majority of the companies listed below are producers of petroleum and natural gas. These companies are among the most profitable in the country because of their ability to find markets for their products abroad. The shares of most of these large companies trade on the Moscow and St. Petersburg Stock Exchanges, as well as on stock exchanges in Western Europe and the United States.

Another sign of the rapid growth of the Russian private sector since 1992 has been the emergence of the banking sector. By 1998, over 1500 private banks were operating in the country. The largest and most profitable bank, Savings Bank of Russia, is government-owned.

Irina Shchegoleva

TOP RIGHT: This retail operation is an example of almost two million privately-owned businesses active in Russia in 1998.

MIDDLE RIGHT: The German sportswear firm Adidas, like many foreign companies, has expanded into Russia in recent years.

David J. Rees

Top Russian Companies (1996–1997) (in millions of usS)				
Company	Industry	Sales	Profits	Employees
Gazprom	Natural gas	$ 23 528.8	$ 3869.5	362 225
EES Rossii	Electricity	22 782.1	1634.8	49 854
Lukoil	Petroleum	9429.2	317.3	83 043
Siberia Far East Oil	Petroleum	5183.8	133.5	100 556
Yukos Oil	Petroleum	4604.9	84.0	114 900
Surgutneftegaz Oil	Petroleum	4589.1	802.8	80 200
Avtovaz	Trucks	3884.1	197.7	n.a.
Tatneft	Petroleum	3660.1	311.2	71 800
Sibneft Oil	Petroleum	3414.6	152.3	36 171
Bashneftekhim	Chemicals	3400.7	882.8	n.a.

n.a.—not available

Compiled from *Finansovye izvestiia* [*Financial News*]

Public Sector Reorganized

Economic reforms in Russia since 1992 have not only created a private sector but also completely reorganized the public sector. A new role was established in the economy for government that included sound fiscal and monetary policies, new social security policies, and educational and retraining programs for the labour force.

Fiscal and Monetary Policies

Fiscal Policy. During the period of Soviet rule, there was no real functioning fiscal policy. All matters pertaining to taxation, expenditures, and regulation of the economy were decided by GOSPLAN and the Communist Party. Following the collapse of the Soviet Union in late 1991, the Russian government asked experts from World Bank and the International Monetary Fund (IMF) to help develop procedures for drafting realistic budgets, implementing new taxes, and dealing with a growing budget deficit (see graph below).

Since 1993, the Russian government has introduced numerous measures to collect taxes. The Russian government continues to have considerable difficulty in collecting taxes and social security contributions from businesses. In 1997, the State Tax Service reported that up to one-third of registered businesses did not pay their taxes in full or on time. It also reported that hundreds of tax inspectors and officers have been injured or physically threatened in the course of their work.

Faced with shortfalls in tax collection, the federal government has cut spending or delayed paying its expenses. Delaying payment has been practised on a vast scale in the case of pensions, family allowances, and wages to military personnel and government workers. In early 1998, the Ministry of Finance reported that the government owed more than 49 trillion rubles (US$8.3 billion) to pensioners, suppliers, military personnel, and government staff. Of this amount, the government owed pensioners more than 25 trillion rubles (US$4.2 billion). Pensioners on average received their pensions three months late.

Monetary Policy. During the period of Soviet rule there was no real functioning monetary policy. The USSR State Bank supplied interest-free loans to state enterprises for production. This practice greatly expanded the money supply; however the high inflation that this expansion would have caused in Western countries was prevented by state price controls on all goods and services. In 1992, the Russian government raised prices of many goods and services, but kept in force controls on important goods and services such as food, housing, energy, and minerals. Nevertheless, prices skyrocketed. To offset the effect of inflation on people's incomes, the Russian government greatly increased subsidies and other types of assistance, which resulted in the government running huge budget deficits. The Russian Central Bank financed these large deficits by printing money. This action quickly led to hyper-inflation in 1992–1994. In those three years, consumer prices increased by more than 30 000%. In contrast, during those same three years, consumer prices in Canada rose by less than 5%.

In April 1995, the Russian Central Bank introduced a "tight money" policy to lower inflation by reducing the rate of increase in the money supply. The policy successfully reduced the inflation rate to 14.5% in 1997, from over 300% in 1993–94.

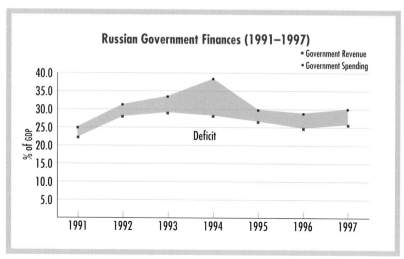

Russian Government Finances (1991–1997)

- ■ Government Revenue
- ● Government Spending

Deficit

Rossiiskii statisticheskii ezhegodnik [Russian Statistical Yearbook]

Social Security

Under central planning, state enterprises and local governments administered most social programs and services such as child care, health care, and pensions. State factories provided housing to their workers and operated cafeterias, day care centres, kindergartens, and health clinics for a small monthly charge. Income support and unemployment insurance programs did not exist because the state provided all citizens of working age with employment. With privatization, many enterprises transferred the ownership of their day care centres, kindergartens, and health clinics to local governments or closed them down altogether.

Following the introduction of economic reforms in 1992, the Russian government recognized the need to increase pension benefits, establish social programs for the disabled, and set up an unemployment insurance plan. To finance this spending on social security, businesses have been required to make contributions to the state pension fund, social insurance fund, and medical insurance.

Since 1992, the government has allowed the establishment and growth of private charities to provide social services to the population. In 1991 Russia had only a few private charities. In early 1998, the Ministry of Social Services reported that over 1000 private charities, ranging in size from small rural self-help groups to large urban charitable foundations, were operating. The Ministry noted that these charities offered a wide variety of social services, such as family counselling, child care, food aid, teenage counselling, and disaster relief.

Education and Retraining

Under Soviet rule, every Russian citizen was provided with basic education and access to free higher education. Students in higher educational institutions were required to take courses on communist political theory, philosophy, and planning. Courses on economics, accounting, marketing, law, business administration, banking, and management were rare or non-existent. The task confronting the Russian government after 1992 was to reorganize the curriculum to include such courses. New private universities and colleges were allowed to operate and offer programs in business administration, marketing, law, foreign languages, social sciences, and computing technology.

The emerging Russian private sector also requires a labour force trained and experienced in the use of modern technology. The task of retraining several million workers is enormous. As a result, the government is focussing many of its scarce resources on the training of young people and is allowing many higher educational institutions to establish links with foreign universities and colleges.

Changing Labour Force

Since the collapse of the Soviet Union in late 1991, the Russian labour force has experienced two profound changes. The first has been the change in employment status. Before 1991, over 90% of Russian workers worked in state-owned enterprises. This changed with the mass privatization of most state enterprises in 1993–1994. In 1997, 36.2% of the labour force were employees of state-owned enterprises and 62.3% were employees of private and mixed private–state firms (see chart "Where Russians Work").

The second change has been in employment. Before 1991, over 40% of all workers were employed in industry and construction, 14% in agriculture, 8% in transportation, and 37% in services. With mass privatization, employment in industry and construction dropped by over 25%, in agriculture by 10% , and in transportation by 9%, but in services employment rose by 11%. In 1997, about 32% of workers were employed in industry and construction, 14.2% in agriculture, and almost 46% in services (see chart "Distribution of Employment").

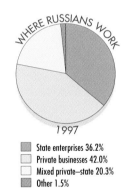

WHERE RUSSIANS WORK

1997

- State enterprises 36.2%
- Private businesses 42.0%
- Mixed private–state 20.3%
- Other 1.5%

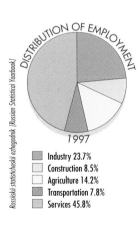

DISTRIBUTION OF EMPLOYMENT

1997

- Industry 23.7%
- Construction 8.5%
- Agriculture 14.2%
- Transportation 7.8%
- Services 45.8%

Rossiiskii statisticheskii ezhegodnik (Russian Statistical Yearbook)

RUSSIAN POLITICAL ECONOMY

SECTION OVERVIEW

• Results of Political and Economic Reform

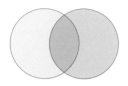

☐ Russian Political System
☐ Russian Economic System
☐ Russian Political Economy

Results of Political and Economic Reform

The political and economic transformation of the Russian Federation has produced both positive and negative results for Russian society.

New Business–Political Elite

One result of the transformation of the Russian economy has been the rise of a new business–political elite. With Gorbachev's economic reforms in the 1980s, the *nomenklatura* split into a new political elite and a new economic elite. The new political elite consisted primarily of Communist Party and Soviet government personnel, while the new economic elite recruited its members from the ranks of the planning ministries and factory directors. As the Russian government privatized state property in 1992, the new economic elite began to acquire great wealth.

The early stages of privatization began with the abolition of planning ministries. New companies were formed to take over the ministries' assets and enterprises. They were often located in the same building, with the same furniture and personnel. The company issued shares to the government (usually a majority of shares) and to the former ministry's top officials and directors.

Sometimes a commercial bank was created from a ministry's financial department, with the former director becoming the new bank's chief executive. Other banks were formed from the division of state banks.

When large-scale privatization of state enterprises began in 1993, directors took control of their enterprises. They began to make decisions about production and the operation of their enterprises. For some, this control resulted in great personal financial benefit.

A small number of Russian business people were also amassing wealth through the political and economic changes in Russia. Through connections in the government some business people bought state enterprises in resource industries such as oil and natural gas. These people were allowed to establish holding companies and links with banks, which were used to acquire other businesses and create monopolies.

During the June 1996 presidential election, the new business elite backed Yeltsin in his bid for reelection and urged Russian voters to return Yeltsin to power. Politically, this elite favoured a strong central government to protect their investments from foreign competitors and monopolies to keep prices and profits high. Some Russian political observers have noted that this powerful business elite has been able to turn national economic policies to their advantage.

Growing Income Inequality

Falling industrial production and rapidly increasing consumer prices since 1990, both consequences of economic reforms, have caused a pronounced fall in people's spending. In 1990, Russian consumers spent an average of 36% of their wage on food, 47% on consumer goods, 10% on services, 2% on housing, and 5% on other goods. In 1997, they spent 50% on food, 31% on consumer goods, 10% on services, 6% on housing, and 3% on other goods. In contrast, the average Canadian family in 1997 spent 9.6% on food, 22.8% on housing, 11.0% on recreation, 17.3% on transportation, 2.8% on education, and 36.5% on other goods and services.

Some groups are better off and others worse off as a result of economic reforms. Surveys of Russian household income in late 1997 revealed that the population fell into four main income classes (see chart "Russian Households by Income"). About 26.8% of all Russian households lived on an income below the official poverty level and were classified as needy. The majority of people in this income group were pensioners and unemployed individuals. Another 28.7% of households had modest incomes and were able to buy food and other basic essentials of life. About 36.1% of households earned enough income to live with some material comfort. The remaining 8.4% of households had an income that supported a standard of living similar to that of the lower middle class in industrial countries.

Irina Shchegoleva

Krokodil/V. Sumarokov

Though income distribution has become more unequal in Russia as a result of economic reforms, it is not significantly different from that in Canada. According to government statistical sources, the richest 10% of the Russian population in 1997 controlled about 26% of the country's total income, while the poorest 10% had only 2%. Statistics Canada estimated that in 1997 the richest 10% of the Canadian population had about 28% of the country's total income and the poorest 10% about 4%.

Unemployment

Unemployment in recent years has emerged as a serious concern for many Russians. Most state-owned enterprises are now privatized and are beginning to reduce their labour forces to cut production costs. Other enterprises have gone bankrupt or closed their doors. As a consequence, unemployment has risen from less than 1% in 1991 to almost 9% in 1997.

Wide differences in unemployment rates exist in the country. Unemployment is highest in the North Caucasus where ethnic strife has shut down most industry and affected agriculture. It is lowest in Moscow, St. Petersburg, and other large cities where the new Russian business class and foreigners are investing in the service sector. The majority of unemployed Russians are between 30 and 49 years old. The unemployment rate among those aged 16–24 years was about 17% in 1997, similar to the same age group in Canada.

"It's not an amoeba, it's our wage."

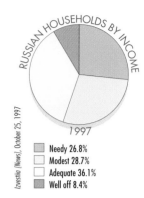

Izvestiia (News), October 25, 1997

RUSSIAN HOUSEHOLDS BY INCOME

1997

- ▨ Needy 26.8%
- ☐ Modest 28.7%
- ☐ Adequate 36.1%
- ▨ Well off 8.4%

In 1997, private plots occupied 2.6% of all agricultural land but produced 47.0% of all milk, 55.2% of the meat, 30.4% of the eggs, 80.2% of the fruit, 76.3% of the vegetables, and 91.3% of the potatoes in Russia.

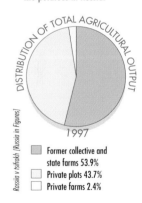

Rossiia v tsifrakh (Russia in Figures)

DISTRIBUTION OF TOTAL AGRICULTURAL OUTPUT

1997

- ▨ Former collective and state farms 53.9%
- ☐ Private plots 43.7%
- ☐ Private farms 2.4%

PHOTO: Many segments of Russian society cope with changing economic circumstances by selling produce grown on their private plots. About 58% of the population has access to a private plot.

Generational Differences

Economic and political reforms have also created some profound changes in how Russians view their society. Public opinion surveys in recent years have revealed fundamental ideological differences between young people and older people.

The survey below shows that young people aged 18–24 years prefer capitalism. Many young people do not want to see their country return to the conditions that existed in the Soviet Union before 1985. The preference for socialism and a return to the Soviet Union is more pronounced among people of 40 years and older, who remember life under Communist rule.

The survey also revealed that many Russian citizens prefer to work in privately-owned enterprises. Many believe that pay, job satisfaction, and management are better in privately-owned enterprises than in state-owned enterprises. Young people aged 18–24 years show the greatest willingness to establish their own businesses.

In contrast, many Russians prefer to buy goods and services at state-owned enterprises. This preference is strongest among people 40 years and older who remember the low prices for goods and services in Soviet times.

David J. Rees

Generational Differences

Attitude Toward Capitalism
"Are you pleased that Russia has embarked on the path of capitalism?"

Age Groups	Yes	No	Do Not Know	Total
18–24	45%	30%	25%	100%
25–39	22	48	30	100
40–55	17	63	20	100
56+	6	82	12	100
All age groups	20	58	22	100

Attitude Toward Return to USSR
"If it were possible, would you want life in Russia to return to what it was in the USSR before 1985?"

Age Groups	Yes	No	Do Not Know	Total
18–24	34%	39%	27%	100%
25–39	52	30	18	100
40–55	62	26	12	100
56+	75	15	10	100
All age groups	59	26	15	100

Preferred Workplace
"At which enterprise would you personally like to work?"

Age Groups	State Enterprise	Private Russian	Foreign Business	Own Personal Business	Do Not Know	Total
18–24	16%	20%	29%	20%	15%	100%
25–39	22	10	32	10	26	100
40–55	38	13	18	6	25	100
56+	46	4	3	6	41	100
All age groups	30	12	23	9	26	100

Preferred Sources of Consumer Goods and Services
"At which enterprise would you buy consumer goods and services?"

Age Groups	State-Owned	Privately-Owned	Do Not Know	Total
18–24	32%	33%	35%	100%
25–39	38	25	37	100
40–55	46	20	34	100
56+	58	7	35	100
All age groups	45	20	35	100

Compiled from *Segodnia* [*Today*], June 7, 1996, and Vserossiiskii tsentr po izucheniiu obshchego mneniia [All-Russian Center for the Study of Public Opinion]

Lena Sjöblom

New Realities of Russian Capitalism

By Irina Shchegoleva, ITAR-TASS Agency correspondent

The file of people stretched for 30 metres from the small stall in St. Peterburg's food market. People's faces were strained and gloomy. In the past three days, food prices had risen over 100% and showed no signs of stopping. Salaries and pensions had not risen. My mother, a pensioner, spent four hours in the line-up to buy five kilograms of macaroni.

I could not convince her that it was unnecessary to waste time in such lines. Like many people in Leningrad, Mother had been in the Leningrad blockade (1941–1944) during World War II. Since then, she has always worried about hunger. But there was no war in August 1998. What made people recall hunger?

In recent years in Russia, President Boris Yeltsin had tried to implement economic reforms, but a severe financial and political crisis erupted. August 17 became a "black day" for the Russian economy when the government declared bankruptcy and stopped paying Russian and foreign investors their money in government bonds (called GKOs). At first it seemed that nothing bad had happened for ordinary people who did not have government bonds. However, most had savings in the State Savings Bank and private banks, and the banks had put money into government bonds that had turned into meaningless paper in one day. Depositors panicked and rushed to the banks, but the banks could not pay back their money immediately.

At the same time, the government of Prime Minister Sergei Kiriyenko was dismissed. The crisis became not only economic but also political. The value of the ruble fell 75% in two weeks. Prices rose higher and higher. It was impossible to buy US dollars, and people tried to buy everything in the shops, especially basic goods such as flour, macaroni, cereals, salt, and sugar, in case there were food shortages.

I am a journalist working in Sochi, a southern Russian resort city on the Black Sea. I took a month's holiday in August 1998 to visit my mother in St. Petersburg. I did not take much cash with me, and it became impossible for me to withdraw any money from my savings account at the State Savings Bank. Every day the bank asked everyone to wait a few days because of a shortage of cash. After three weeks, I still could not get money from my bank. I cut my spending on entertainment and even simple things like newspapers and city transport.

I had planned to pay my son's tuition fees at university, but university officials asked me to pay cash because they also could not get money from the bank. I was not able to transfer money from my bank to pay the fees.

Our family had been glad in 1991 when Russia started economic reforms and rejected old Communist methods. Like my husband, I greeted the "construction of capitalism" in our country with enthusiasm and pleasure. My husband, a civil engineer, created one of the first private construction companies in Sochi in 1991. He built houses for individual customers and made a good profit at first. He used his profit to buy building equipment, trucks, and tools. We were glad to be among the first entrepreneurs, the so-called "new Russians."

After two years our belief in Russian capitalism began to sink rapidly. My husband tried to work honestly—pay all taxes, receive all licenses, and so on— but it was becoming less profitable. Entrepreneurs who did not pay taxes, only bribes, were successful. Those who preferred straight dealing in their businesses failed because of high taxation and corruption among government officials.

A sharp social division among Russians now exists. There are either very rich or extremely poor people. There is no middle class. The poor only have money for food. Of course, they do not plan to build new houses. We have no system of credit in our country to use to buy anything, only cash. The rich have stopped building because of the uncertain future and possible nationalization of private property. They know history and remember the lessons of the October 1917 Russian revolution . . .

In mid-September 1998, the political situation improved somewhat. The new Prime Minister, Yevgeny Primakov, was a compromise between the Communists and democrats. The situation is unstable. Inflation continues and the Communists are seeking power.

Evidently, we have only one exit from the blind alley, the way of continued reforms. A return to the past means a threat of civil war. We must find an exit from the impasse.

REVIEW

Summary

When Mikhail Gorbachev became leader of the Soviet Union in 1985, the country was in need of new policies. Gorbachev introduced *perestroika* (restructuring), *glasnost* (openness), and democratization in an attempt to modernize the Soviet economy, society, and political system. These policies, however, shook the social, political, and economic foundations of the Soviet Union. In late 1991, the Soviet Union collapsed and several independent states emerged, of which the Russian Federation was the largest.

Since 1992, Russian society has attempted to adopt new values about the role of the individual in society, but many Soviet values about collectivism and public ownership remain strong among the people. Russian society today is deeply divided and beset with many social problems.

Many of the current problems of the Russian political system are related to the country's transition from a non-democratic system to a democratic one. The Russian political system today consists of a directly elected President, an elected State Duma, and an appointed judiciary. However, the political system has few checks and balances to prevent the President from dominating the other branches of government, to allow all groups in society to participate in determining policies, or to protect minority rights.

Since 1992, the Russian Federation has attempted to transform its economy into one based on private enterprise. This has meant raising prices, selling state property, creating stable banks, retraining workers, developing business laws, and reducing government spending. Though consumers and businesses are now the main decision makers in the economy, the government still has considerable power to intervene in the economy.

The political and economic transformation of Russia since 1992 has not been without its problems. Corruption, income inequality, unemployment, and inter-generational differences have appeared.

Russian Values and Political Philosophy

1. The new values that are emerging in Russia are creating divisions in society and new problems. Which values, or lack of agreement on values, pose the greatest threat to the development of a democratic–capitalist Russia? Explain your choices.

2. Briefly describe the political perspectives of the new political parties on page 383.

Russian Political System

1. Following the collapse of the Soviet Union in December 1991, what aspects of Russia's past made it difficult to establish a political system based on democratic principles?

2. Compare the similarities and differences of the Russian executive, legislative, and judiciary with that of Canada in a chart.

3. The Russian President has the ability to create laws by decree, without the agreement of the Duma. To what extent do you agree that the Russian President should have this power? Be prepared to defend your position.

4. How successful has Russia been in dealing peacefully with demands for independence within its borders?

5. After reading pages 385 and 386, identify and explain the checks and balances in the Russian system that prevent the abuse of power.

6. Why do you think that the Russian system requires parties, independent candidates, and presidential candidates to get a certain number of signatures of supporters before being placed on the ballot?

7. How similar are Russian and Canadian election campaigns?

8. a) Why must a party receive 5% of the vote for its list of candidates before the party has representatives in the Duma?

   b) What are the strengths and weaknesses of this requirement?

9. a) What causes a second vote to take place in a presidential election?

   b) To what extent do you agree with this system? Be prepared to defend your position.

Russian Economic System

1. Identify the problems encountered as the government attempted to make the transformation from a planned to a market economy. (See page 391.)

2. Chart the strengths and weaknesses of the Russian economy in the 1990s (pages 392–393). Use the following questions as a guide.
   a) What types of products formed the bulk of Russian imports and exports?
   b) What do the types of imports and exports say about the Russian manufacturing industry's ability to compete on the world market?
   c) What generalizations can be made about the Russian economy from the list of top Russian companies on page 393?

3. The Russian government had all of the following problems with its fiscal policies in the 1990s except one. Choose the **exception**. Explain the effect of these problems.
   A. the collection of taxes
   B. the delaying of social security payments, often for months
   C. tax officials threatened and injured
   D. government forced to spend less than it earned

4. Hyperinflation, where prices increased by over 30 000%, was a problem in the early 1990s. This was primarily caused by
   A. government taking price controls off important goods and services
   B. the printing of money to offset the rising deficit
   C. the new privately-owned businesses trying to increase profits
   D. corruption and the increased power of the mafia

Russian Political Economy

1. a) From what elements of Russian society does the elite in the new Russia come?

   b) What is the significance of this development for Russian society?

2. a) Which commodity had the greatest proportionate increase in price for Russian citizens between 1990 and 1997?
   b) What was the effect of this on the Russian people?

3. Which of the following statements is (are) supported by the chart on page 398?
   a) A minority wants to work for privately-owned businesses, but a majority wants to buy from state-owned businesses.
   b) A majority of older Russians want a return to the Soviet system, and would prefer to work in state-owned businesses.
   c) A minority of the youngest group would prefer to work in state-owned businesses, but a majority of this group support the move to capitalism.
   d) A majority of Russians would prefer a return to the Soviet system, however they don't want to work for state-owned businesses.

4. Read the Focus On Critical Thinking on page 399. Why did Irina Shchegoleva and her husband first welcome the change to a capitalist economy, but later become disillusioned?

Chapter Consolidation

1. This chapter begins with a quotation by Boris Yeltsin from 1996. Given the political and economic developments since then, to what extent has Yeltsin's optimism been justified?

2. Examine the cartoon on page 377. What does it indicate about what is happening within Russian society?

3.

   a) On what values were the political and economic systems of the Russian Federation based?

   b) Whose ideas were influential in the development of the political and economic systems of the Russian Federation? Briefly explain the ideas and how they were applied in the Russian Federation.

   c) Create a chart, identifying the type of political system and economic system in the Russian Federation and the strengths and weaknesses of these systems.

11 CHINA

"Hold high the great banner of Deng Xiaoping Theory and push forward the cause of building socialism with Chinese characteristics to the 21st century in all spheres."
—Jiang Zemin, report to the 15th Party Congress, September 12, 1997

China is the world's third largest country in area and has the largest population. Although these factors make it a world power, for much of the 20th century China was weak and divided. In October 1949, the country was united under the Communists led by Mao Zedong. Under Mao, China developed a political and economic system based on socialism, revolutionary enthusiasm, and isolation.

Under Deng Xiaoping, economic reforms were introduced to modernize the country. The reforms improved the living standards of millions of ordinary Chinese citizens, encouraged personal initiative and creativity, and expanded the economy and the country's links with the rest of the world.

This economic prosperity has led to somewhat greater political freedom than under Mao Zedong. The country's political system continues to be dominated and controlled by the Communist Party, which does not allow criticism of its policies.

Key Concepts/Vocabulary

Long March
mass campaign
Great Leap Forward
Cultural Revolution
Four Modernizations
"one country, two systems"
Four Cardinal Principles
socialism with Chinese characteristics
National People's Congress
autonomous region
special administrative region

neighbourhood committee
one-child family policy
work unit
socialist market economy
contract responsibility system
township and village enterprise
special economic zone
open door policy
iron rice bowl

Focus On Issues

CHAPTER OVERVIEW

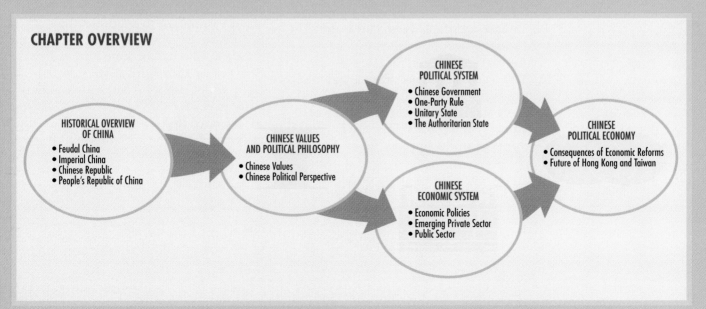

HISTORICAL OVERVIEW OF CHINA
- Feudal China
- Imperial China
- Chinese Republic
- People's Republic of China

CHINESE VALUES AND POLITICAL PHILOSOPHY
- Chinese Values
- Chinese Political Perspective

CHINESE POLITICAL SYSTEM
- Chinese Government
- One-Party Rule
- Unitary State
- The Authoritarian State

CHINESE ECONOMIC SYSTEM
- Economic Policies
- Emerging Private Sector
- Public Sector

CHINESE POLITICAL ECONOMY
- Consequences of Economic Reforms
- Future of Hong Kong and Taiwan

HISTORICAL OVERVIEW

The following dates for China's dynasties are cited by the government of People's Republic of China. Dates in other sources may differ.

Feudal China	
Xia	2205–1766 BCE
Shang	1766–1122 BCE
Zhou	1122–221 BCE
Imperial China	
Qin	221–206 BCE
Han	206 BCE–220
Three Kingdoms and Six Dynasties	220–589
Sui	589–618
Tang	618–907
Five Dynasties and Ten Kingdoms	907–960
Song	960–1279
Yuan (Mongol)	1279–1368
Ming	1368–1644
Qing (Manchu)	1644–1912

Feudal China (2205–221 BCE)

Chinese civilization is said to have begun with the Xia dynasty in north central China in 2205 BCE. Under the Shang dynasty, farming, metal working, and a written language appeared. During the Zhou dynasty, Chinese culture and economy flourished and the works of Lao Zi and Confucius were written. The Zhou dynasty ended in social and political instability.

Imperial China (221 BCE–1912)

In 221 BCE, China's first Emperor Qin Shi Huang unified the country. Under his rule, a centralized bureaucracy was created, written language standardized, opposition controlled, and the Great Wall consolidated to protect the country from invasion. After his death, the country entered periods of political instability and division. Despite this, Chinese culture attained a high level of development in the arts, technology, and administration.

Political contact with European powers came in the late 17th century when China signed a treaty with Russia. Contacts with European powers grew in the 18th century, and trade relations expanded in the 19th century. After the Opium War (1840–1842), Great Britain forced the rulers of China to open the country to outside influences. Treaties were signed with France and the United States, and what some writers have called China's "century of humiliation" began.

Weakened by internal division and mismanagement, the Qing dynasty ceded lands to Russia and Japan. In 1898, China was forced to grant territorial leases to France, Germany, Great Britain, and Russia. These concessions led to rebellions against foreign intervention in Chinese domestic affairs.

Chinese Republic (1912–1949)

In late 1911, the Qing dynasty collapsed. On January 1, 1912, Sun Yat-sen proclaimed the Republic of China. From the beginning, the new government in Beijing was unable to exercise its authority over the whole country. In the south at Guangzhou, Sun Yat-sen formed a rival government led by the Nationalist Party.

When the Versailles peace conference awarded rights over German territories in China to Japan in 1919, Beijing students demonstrated. A mass movement against the government began. The May Fourth Movement sparked an intellectual revolution and became a source of inspiration for the formation of the Chinese Communist Party in July 1921.

In the early 1920s, Soviet agents were active in China assisting revolutionary activity. In 1923, Soviet agents agreed to help strengthen the Nationalist Party to achieve the goals of national reunification and social change. The newly-formed Communist Party was encouraged to cooperate with the Nationalists in a united front. In 1926, the united front began a military campaign to overthrow the Republican government in Beijing. Chiang Kai-shek, who had become Nationalist Party leader after Sun Yat-sen's death in 1925, conducted a violent anti-communist purge in April 1927. In early 1928, Chiang consolidated his control over China, with the surrender of the government in Beijing.

221 BCE Unification of China under Emperor Qin	**220–589** Political division of China	**1839–1842** Opium War; beginning of European penetration into China
25 Buddhism enters China from India	**1644** Qing dynasty begins	**1912** Chinese Republic ends Qing dynasty; Sun Yat-sen forms Nationalist Party
2205 BCE Xia dynasty established	**551 BCE** Confucius born	

Feudal China 2205–221 BCE

Imperial China 221 BCE–1912

Note: Timeline is not to scale

LEFT: Mao Zedong addresses Communist followers at Yan'an.

RIGHT: Chinese Red Army soldiers in late 1936 crossing the Chiachin Mountains on the Long March from Jiangxi to Yan'an.

Following their expulsion from the Nationalist Party in 1927, Mao Zedong and other communist leaders fled to southern China, where they established a rural base in Jiangxi.

Mao was born in Hunan province in 1893, and became a follower of Marxism while working at Beijing University. As a member of the Chinese Communist Party, he participated in organizing peasant associations, initiating strikes, and conducting propaganda work. In Jiangxi, Mao formulated the dogma of "revolutionary war."

January 1934
The revolutionary war is a war of the masses; it can be waged only by mobilizing the masses and relying on them.

January 1934
Rallying millions upon millions of people round the revolutionary government and expanding our revolutionary war, we shall wipe out all counter-revolution and take over the whole of China.

December 1936
A revolutionary war is a mass undertaking.

November 1938
Every Communist must grasp the truth, "Political power grows out of the barrel of a gun."

In October 1934, Mao led a communist force estimated at 100 000 people on the Long March from Jiangxi in south China to Yan'an in northwest China to escape encirclement by Chiang's Nationalist forces. The Long March ended over a year later. Fewer than 8000 people arrived at a communist base in Yan'an.

In July 1937, Japan attacked China from Manchuria, which it had occupied in 1931. The Nationalists, led by Chiang, were unable to repel the Japanese invasion. The invasion brought the Communists and Nationalists together again to defend the country. After Japan's surrender in 1945, the united front broke up and the country was engulfed in a civil war between the Communists and Nationalists. On October 1, 1949, Mao Zedong declared a Communist government in Beijing. Nationalist forces fled to Taiwan, where Chiang maintained a government of the Republic of China.

Official sources estimate that up to 40 million people may have died from the effects of civil war, war with Japan, and political instability between 1919 and 1949.

1919	1924–1927	1928	1934–1935	1946–1949
May Fourth Movement	First united front between Nationalists and Communists	Communists set up government in Jiangxi	Long March from Jiangxi to Yan'an; Mao becomes leader of CCP	Civil war between Nationalists and Communists
1921				**1949**
Communist Party formed	**1927**	**1931**	**1937–1945**	Communists proclaim People's Republic of China in Beijing; Nationalists retreat to Taiwan
	Power struggle between Nationalists and Communists begins	Japan seizes Manchuria	Nationalists and Communists form united front against Japanese invasion	

Chinese Republic 1912–1949

PHOTO: Portrait of Mao Zedong above Tiananmen Gate. Mao Zedong announced the formation of the People's Republic of China from Tiananmen Square in Beijing on October 1, 1949.

Between 1950 and 1959, over 12 000 Soviet technical experts, specialists, and instructors worked in China.

Phyllis A. Arnold

People's Republic of China (Since 1949)

Under Mao Zedong (1949–1976)

On October 1, 1949, Mao proclaimed the People's Republic of China. The proclamation began a new era in Chinese history, Mao noted:

From now on our nation will belong to the community of the peace-loving and freedom-loving nations of the world and work courageously and industriously to foster its own civilization and well-being and at the same time to promote world peace and freedom. Ours will no longer be a nation subject to insult and humiliation. We have stood up. Our revolution has won the sympathy and acclaim of the people of all countries. We have friends all over the world.

Consolidation and Reconstruction (1949–1952). In the first years of power, the Communist government moved to restore order, rebuild the economy, and consolidate its control over the country. Land was redistributed among peasant households. A new currency was introduced to end inflation. The written language was simplified to promote literacy. Basic health care programs were implemented to combat common diseases. People were given the right to elect and participate in councils, led by the Communist Party. Government bodies were modelled on Soviet ones.

Our present task is to strengthen the people's state apparatus—mainly the people's army, the people's police, and the people's courts—in order to consolidate national defence and protect the people's interests.

First Five Year Plan. Once reconstruction was completed in 1953, the First Five Year Plan was introduced. It nationalized most private businesses and collectivized agriculture. These measures were introduced to prevent the reemergence of private farming and to increase food production and exports. The goal of the First Five Year Plan was to double industrial production by 1957, creating an industrial base for future increases in living standards.

To assist China in building up its heavy industry and to strengthen the world communist movement, the Soviet Union sent thousands of technical advisors. With their assistance, many industrial plants were built and new industries created.

The change-over from individual to socialist, collective ownership in agriculture and handicrafts and from capitalist to socialist ownership in private industry and commerce is bound to bring about a tremendous liberation of the productive forces. Thus the social conditions are being created for a tremendous expansion of industrial and agricultural production.

● October 1949
People's Republic of China proclaimed

● November 1949
Land redistribution to peasant households begins

● 1950
Policy of reconstruction announced; first Soviet technical advisors arrive

● 1953
First Five Year Plan implemented; nationalization of private business and collectivization of agriculture

Note: Timeline is not to scale

Phyllis A. Arnold

Archive Photos

LEFT: Statue of Mao Zedong on top of an office building in downtown Chengdu.

RIGHT: Communes, which replaced the collective farms in 1958, were organized as large administrative production units. They were responsible for local industrial development, the provision of education, welfare, public health, and the militia, as well as farming. The communes were disbanded between 1979 and 1982.

Hundred Flowers Campaign (1956–1957).

Spurred by Khrushchev's criticism of Stalin in February 1956, Mao announced the Hundred Flowers campaign in May, with the following statement:

Let a hundred flowers bloom, and a hundred schools of thought contend.

People were encouraged to submit opinions on the direction of the country. Writers complained about press censorship. Peasants demanded the end of collective farms and the return of their land. Workers protested low wages and poor working conditions.

The campaign ended suddenly in June 1957, when Mao felt the critics went too far in criticizing his leadership and the Communist Party. An Anti-Rightist campaign was launched against scientists, professionals, and skilled workers. Thousands were labelled "rightists" and imprisoned, and thousands more sent to live in the countryside to learn from the peasants the value of struggle and hardship.

January 1958

Rightists are oppositionists; those on the right of centre also oppose us, the middle-of-the-roaders are doubters. The masses at large and the leftists among the bourgeoisie and bourgeois intellectuals support us.

Great Leap Forward (1958–1959).

The disappointing results of the First Five Year Plan and the Hundred Flowers Campaign inspired Mao in May 1958 to officially launch the Great Leap Forward. The Great Leap Forward was a plan to achieve communism in China. It promised to build socialism by relying on mass mobilization, drawing on local initiative, and striving for more balanced development. Mao called the policy one of "walking on two legs and not on one-and-a-half-legs." During the Great Leap Forward, tens of millions of Chinese were mobilized to build dams and double the production of steel and grain. Collective farms were transformed into communes.

Backyard furnaces were set up in the villages to teach peasants how to make steel. Private property was abolished and personal belongings like watches, cookware, and jewellery were collected or seized. Most were voluntarily relinquished in an atmosphere of mass enthusiasm.

August 1958

... Imperialism oppresses us; and so within three, five, or seven years we must build our country into a great industrial power. For this goal we must concentrate our strength on building up our large-scale industrial base. ...

We must go all out for the next two years on the production of iron, steel, copper, aluminum, molybdenum, and other nonferrous metals. It won't do not to go all out. Steel targets must be fully met; iron can be a little less, but we must also strive to fulfil that target.

1956
Hundred Flowers campaign begins

1957
Anti-Rightist campaign ends
Hundred Flowers campaign

1958
Great Leap Forward
announced

People's Republic of China—Since 1949

407

PHOTO: A detachment of Red
Guards marching in
Guangzhou in January 1967.

Grain Production (1957–1965)

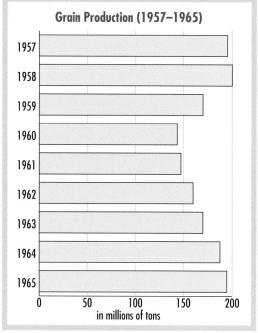

in millions of tons

Zhongguo tongji ninanjian [*China Statistical Yearbook*]

Express Newspapers/E 593/Archive Photos

The steep drop in grain
production due to the
Great Leap Forward and
droughts created famine
conditions in the country.

Retrenchment (1960–1965).

By 1960, the Great Leap Forward had created numerous shortages of foodstuffs and metal goods. The frenzy to make steel kept millions of peasants from tending their fields. Crop production fell and livestock died. Floods and droughts further reduced food production, creating famine conditions throughout the country. Disagreements between China and the Soviet Union over the direction of the international communist movement prompted Khrushchev to suddenly recall all Soviet technical advisors from China in July 1960.

In 1961, the government was forced to reintroduce some elements of private enterprise to save the economy from total collapse and lessen the effects of famine. Years later, the Chinese government admitted that eight million people had died following the Great Leap Forward. Unofficial sources, mainly Soviet, estimate that more than 20 million people died.

Cultural Revolution (1966–1976).

By the end of 1965, the economy had recovered from the effects of the Great Leap Forward. In May 1966, Mao announced the beginning of a new mass campaign called the Great Proletarian Cultural Revolution, or the Cultural Revolution, which aimed to end all forms of private enterprise and change Chinese society permanently. In his speech, Mao stated that the people still believed in private property and personal gain, and declared that Chinese society needed to be radically transformed. He felt that people had to become more accepting of physical hardship and be revolutionary-minded, like Communist fighters during the Long March in 1934–1935, if a communist society was ever to be established in China.

Mao called on all Chinese youth to form detachments of Red Guards. He told them to attack the "four olds"—old ideas, culture, habits, and customs. Schools and universities were closed. The Red Guards were encouraged to ransack museums, destroy valuable historical objects, and round up government and party officials and denounce them as "capitalist roaders." Top Communist leaders like Liu Shaoqi and Deng Xiaoping were labelled "Number One and Number Two capitalist roaders." Like thousands of others they were subjected to intense questioning, verbal abuse, and beatings to make them confess their "mistakes."

1958–1960
Crop failures and shortages
appear; sudden recall of Soviet
technical advisors from China

1961
Chinese–Soviet ideological break

1962
Government stabilizes the
economy with policies favouring
some private enterprise

People's Republic of China—Since 1949

Robert Philippe, *Political Graphics Art As A Weapon.* Oxford: Phaidon Press Ltd., 1982, p. 268.

The Red Guards were also expected to study the thoughts of Mao Zedong and carry out the revolution. Every Red Guard possessed a little red book, called *Quotations From Chairman Mao Zedong*, which contained selected quotations from Mao's speeches and writings. They wore a button embossed with the image of Mao. Every Red Guard was expected by Mao to dress the same, rejecting all public display of individual preference.

At Mao's urging, Jiang Qing, his wife, became a prominent organizer of the Red Guard Movement. She represented him in her travels throughout the country. Mao made few public appearances, but when he did thousands of Red Guards assembled in Tiananmen Square.

In 1969, Mao declared that all Red Guards should go to the countryside and live among the peasants to endure physical hardship and deepen their commitment to revolution. Millions of Red Guards went to work as labourers in the fields, mines,

and forests, where most remained until Mao's death in 1976. The Cultural Revolution left deep psychological scars on the population and deprived an entire generation of young people of opportunities to complete their education.

During the Cultural Revolution, Mao was glorified as "the Great Helmsman" and as "the great leader and teacher." The campaign to create a cult of Mao was directed by *Renmin ribao* (*People's Daily*), the main newspaper of the Communist Party.

December 26, 1966
Worker comrades throughout the country, as long as we are good at studying and applying Chairman Mao's works creatively, and at mastering the invincible ideological weapon that is Mao Zedong Thought, we can undoubtedly march from victory to victory.

October 1, 1967
Long live the great leader and teacher Chairman Mao! Long live the invincible Mao Zedong Thought!

April 28, 1969
Let the whole Party unite, let the whole nation unite, hold high the great banner of Mao Zedong Thought, be resolute, fear no sacrifice, and surmount every difficulty to win victory. Long live the dictatorship of the proletariat! Long live the great, glorious, and correct Communist Party of China! Long live great Marxism–Leninism–Mao Zedong Thought!

April 22, 1970
Long live great Marxism! Long live great Leninism! Long live great Mao Zedong thought!

October 1, 1973
Under the guidance and leadership of the Central Committee of the Party headed by our great leader Chairman Mao, let us go all out and continue to advance!

May 16, 1976
Chairman Mao's proletarian revolutionary line is invincible, and our advance cannot be stopped! The Great Proletarian Cultural Revolution will shine forever!

"Everyone reads the works of Chairman Mao," a Chinese poster, 1967.

Some historical sources estimate that up to 100 million Chinese suffered persecution and imprisonment for their personal beliefs. Many of these people recall the Cultural Revolution as a period of lost opportunity.

1966
Cultural Revolution begins; Red Guard Movement formed

1969
Mao calls for Red guards to go to the countryside

1976
Mao dies; end of Cultural Revolution

Under Deng Xiaoping (1978–1997)

In the weeks following Mao's death in September 1976, Jiang Qing and three other party leaders who comprised the "Gang of Four" were arrested. There ensued a brief but intense struggle between Mao's chosen successor, Hua Guofeng, and Deng Xiaoping for control of the Communist Party and the government.

Canapress/Mark Avery

Born in Sichuan province in 1904, Deng Xiaoping joined the Communist Party as a work-study student in France. In 1925, he returned to China and worked with Mao in Jiangxi. He accompanied Mao on the Long March to Yan'an in 1934–1935. After 1949 he held several high-level government and party positions. In the early 1960s, he worked to restore the national economy. However, during the Cultural Revolution, Deng was denounced and imprisoned, and then sent to work in the countryside.

In 1977, Deng returned to his previous high posts in the party and government. He had a broad base of support in the Communist Party, and in 1980–1981 Hua was forced to surrender leading positions to Deng's supporters. For the next 17 years Deng carried out his own policies for the economic development of China, which helped repair harm done during the Cultural Revolution.

Phyllis A. Arnold

Glen BonBernard

Four Modernizations. The objective of the Four Modernizations policy, announced by Deng in December 1978, was to modernize agriculture, industry, science and technology, and national defence. The goal of the new policy, Deng remarked, was to achieve a comfortable standard of living for the country's huge population by the end of the 20th century.

The modernization of agriculture meant abolition of the communes established under Mao. Peasant farmers were given individual control over and responsibility for their production and profits.

The modernization of industry would be accomplished by freeing industrial enterprises from the control and supervision of the central government. Factory managers were given the authority to determine production and to pursue profits for their enterprises. Enterprises were opened to foreign investment.

1976
Hua Guofeng takes over leadership; "Gang of Four" led by Jiang Qing arrested

1977
Deng returns to Beijing

1978
Deng emerges as top party leader and announces Four Modernizations

1979
Beginning of "open door" policy; communes begin to be disbanded

1980
First special economic zone established at Shenzhen near Hong Kong

1981
Hua Guofeng removed from party leadership

People's Republic of China—Since 1949

Marcey Andrews/Arnold Publishing Ltd.

Reuters/Will Burgess/Archive Photos

The modernization of science and technology was to be accomplished by thousands of well-educated technicians and managers who were to spearhead the country's development. Developing trade and cultural ties with the West, encouraging enterprises to form partnerships with foreigners and import modern technology for use in raising production and improving the quality of goods produced, and sending students abroad were also part of the modernization plan.

The modernization of national defence was to be achieved through upgrading the defence industry, training officers better, and improving strategic military planning. At the same time, China sought to further develop peaceful relations with neighbouring countries and heighten international awareness of China's dedication to maintaining peace and cooperation. The adoption of the "one country, two systems" policy in 1982 promised to reduce tensions between

China and Taiwan, with the goal of reunifying Taiwan with China by allowing it to maintain its economic system while under China's authority. The policy paved the way for an agreement between Great Britain and China, signed in 1984, for the handover of Hong Kong in 1997.

In 1987, Deng retired from politics, but he did not lose his ability to influence the direction of the country because of the support he received from the military. This was clearly demonstrated when he urged the military to suppress a student protest movement in Tiananmen Square on June 3–4, 1989. Although Deng introduced policies that allowed elements of private enterprise in the economy, the democratization of Chinese politics was not part of his agenda. Since his death in February 1997, the Party leadership, headed by Jiang Zemin, has affirmed Deng's economic policies, but has made few changes to the political system.

LEFT: Modernization of science aimed to increase technological innovation, computer literacy, and research.

RIGHT: Modernization of the military aimed for better officer training and improved military planning.

1982	1987	1989	1993	1997	1998	1999
Policy of "one country, two systems" announced	Deng retires from politics but remains supreme leader	Tiananmen Square incident; Jiang Zemin becomes party leader	Jiang Zemin becomes President of the People's Republic	Deng dies; Hong Kong reverts to Chinese sovereignty; Jiang calls for privatization of state enterprises	Jiang Zemin reelected President of People's Republic	Macau reverts to Chinese sovereignty

People's Republic of China—Since 1949

CHINESE VALUES AND POLITICAL PHILOSOPHY

Advance Organizer

As contemporary Chinese society changes, there has been a shift in emphasis from group to individual values. However, political philosophy continues to emphasize group over individual interests and the need to preserve national unity.

SECTION OVERVIEW

- Chinese Values
- Chinese Political Perspective

Chinese Values

For centuries, a comprehensive system of values and beliefs underpinned Chinese civilization and defined Chinese identity. The values held by the Chinese people today are the result of their country's geography, long history, culture, and economic development.

Sources of Values

Roughly the size of Canada, China is situated in the eastern part of Asia, stretching about 5100 kilometres from the Amur River in the northeast to Hainan Island in the southwest, and about 5200 kilometres from the Pamir mountains in the west to the Pacific Ocean in the east. This means China is a land of great geographical diversity and important regional differences in customs, religious beliefs, spoken language, and livelihoods. This geographical diversity has long presented a challenge to the country's rulers in maintaining national unity.

China is one of the few modern countries with a recorded history that stretches back almost 4000 years. In 221 BCE, Qin Shi Huang unified China and established the first centralized, unified, multinational state in Chinese history, the Qin dynasty. For the next 2000 years, the concepts of a strong ruler, centralized power, and national unity formed the framework of the Chinese political system.

In the 6th and 5th centuries BCE, thinkers such as Lao Zi (604–531 BCE) and Confucius (551–479 BCE) influenced Chinese culture. Their ideas spread in later centuries to cultures in Korea, Japan, and Southeast Asia. Lao Zi formulated a philosophy in which human beings were part of the universe, and the path (*dao*) to wisdom was a matter of living in harmony with nature and the universe. Confucius developed a code of ethics and morals in which everyone had a place in society, with duties and responsibilities. Social harmony was achieved when everyone observed the "Three Cardinal Principles" of obedience to the ruler, parents, and husband.

Ancient China was fairly well developed economically. During the Han and Tang dynasties, agriculture, handicrafts, weaving, metalworking, and shipbuilding were advanced. Transportation by land and water were well developed and the country established extensive economic and cultural relations with Japan, Korea, India, Persia, and Arabia.

Papermaking, printing, gunpowder, and the compass were major creations of Chinese science and technology which profoundly influenced world history. Other examples of Chinese scientific advances were the first star charts, the invention of the seismograph, the calculation of *pi*, and acupuncture.

In the 20th century, Chinese society has experienced great social, political, and economic changes. The most important is the country's continuing industrialization. With 21% of the world's population, China holds economic power that influences the world economy.

EARTH'S FARMLAND

- China 7%
- Rest of Earth 93%

WORLD'S POPULATION

- China 21%
- Rest of World 79%

World Bank. *World Development Indicators 1998.*

Core Values

A survey of 2000 individuals in the greater Shanghai area conducted by Godwin Chu and Ju Yanan in the late 1980s and early 1990s revealed that Chinese values today are a complex mixture of traditional, communist, and imported Western values.[1]

Close family ties. In spite of the political turmoil of the Cultural Revolution from 1966 to 1976, which saw many families separated for years, family ties remain close. Most Chinese today regard the family as a source of stability, personal safety, financial security, and emotional comfort in times of rapid social, political, economic, and technological change. Many adult children continue to live with their parents. They often consult their parents about personal matters and show them considerable respect. Ties with relatives and respect for older family members remain strong.

Discipline and resourcefulness. These traditional values continue to be highly praised by most Chinese. Discipline and hard work are considered important to success in one's work, career, and business. Resourcefulness with money and savings is viewed as a practical way of overcoming poverty and preparing oneself and one's family for unexpected emergencies.

Education. Chinese place great importance on education because traditionally an educated person earned high respect in the community. Most educated persons were employed in the state bureaucracy, which gave their families privileges and prestige. Many families are willing to support their children through college or university.

Loyalty to the state. This value is often expressed in the desire for strong central authority and leaders who can rally the people for common purposes. For centuries, Chinese governments, including the current Communist one, have relied on this political value to maintain national unity and preserve national identity.

Collectivism. Placing public interest above personal interest remains a deeply held value in Chinese society. The spirit of individualism is highest among those exposed to Western influences, many of whom are reluctant to place public interest above individual interest unless the public interest is formulated in consultation with them.

Private enterprise. From the early 1950s until the 1980s, the government did not allow private businesses. In the early 1980s, as a result of Deng's policies, individual private businesses began to appear. Today, setting up their own business is the goal of many Chinese.

Materialism. Under Mao, Chinese citizens were encouraged to be less materialistic, have empathy for others, cooperate, and engage in self-sacrifice so that a communist society would emerge in China. Since the early 1980s, Deng's slogan, "To be rich is glorious," has sparked a revolution among the population about the virtues of wealth and consumption. Many people seek the good life of new homes, imported vehicles, luxurious meals, and foreign travel, but this good life is available to a very small percentage of the population.

PHOTO: Foreign influences are increasingly modifying the landscape of China's cities.

Phyllis A. Arnold

[1]While Shanghai is not typical of all of China this survey shows an overall impression of trends in China during the 1990s. For a more detailed examination of survey results see Goodwin Chu and Ju Yanan, *The Great Wall in Ruins: Communication and Cultural Change in China*. Albany: State University of New York Press, 1993.

Chinese Political Perspective

The political principles of Chinese communism were developed and put into practice by Mao Zedong (1949–1976). In the 1980s, Deng modified some of Mao's doctrines by repudiating ideological purity and stressing the need for pragmatism in implementing policies. In September 1997, Jiang Zemin declared Deng's political beliefs important for China in the 21st century.

Four Cardinal Principles

The political beliefs of the ruling Communist Party remain largely based on the application of Marxism–Leninism in China. In 1979, Deng Xiaoping outlined the principles of Communist Party doctrine in the form of the Four Cardinal Principles—building socialism, maintaining the people's democratic dictatorship, upholding leadership by the Communist Party, and upholding Marxism–Leninism–Mao Zedong Thought.

Building Socialism. Building socialism in China is the long-term goal of the Communist Party. Under Deng, the goal evolved into the policy of building socialism with Chinese characteristics. This involves maintaining public and collective ownership and control of the means of production (land, labour, and capital) and central planning of key industries, such as steel, coal, and electricity. It means accepting some elements of private enterprise in agriculture and sectors not considered important to overall national development, such as services and consumer goods.

According to Deng, socialism with Chinese characteristics developed from the fact that China is a big country with a large population and an economy largely based on agriculture. The overall goal of building socialism in China is to increase people's living standards.

Building socialism in China, according to Deng, means rejecting Mao's insistence on ideological purity and strict egalitarianism of everyone "eating from the same big pot." It should be pragmatic and realistic. Characteristic of Deng's approach were statements that he popularized, such as, "To be rich is glorious" and "It doesn't matter whether it's a black cat or white cat as long as it catches mice!"

At the 15th Party Congress, held in September 1997 six months after Deng's death, Jiang Zemin reaffirmed the need to build socialism in China:

Socialism is the primary stage of communism and China is in the primary stage of socialism, that is, the stage of underdevelopment. . . . We are destined to go through a rather long primary stage of socialism. During this stage we shall accomplish industrialization and the socialization, market-orientation, and modernization of the economy. This is a historical stage we cannot jump over.

Maintaining the People's Democratic Dictatorship. The Communist Party holds steadfastly to the principle of the dictatorship of the proletariat, now called the "people's democratic dictatorship." This means that political rights and civil liberties, though constitutionally guaranteed, are limited and must not challenge the role of the Communist Party to determine national policies. Any public display of opposition and dissent, which may be tolerated for brief periods, must be under the control of the Communist Party and can be suppressed when necessary.

Deng remarked in December 1986 that China could not do without dictatorship and should exercise it when necessary to maintain national unity. In September 1997, Jiang added that the people's democratic dictatorship was a fundamental feature of the Chinese political system:

The essence of socialist democracy is that the people are the masters of the country. All power of the state belongs to the people. China's state system, featuring people's democratic dictatorship, and its system of government, featuring people's congresses, are the result of the struggle waged by the people and the choice of history. It is imperative that we should uphold and improve this fundamental political system, instead of copying any western models. This is of decisive importance in upholding leadership by the Party and the socialist system and realizing people's democracy.

Upholding Leadership by the Communist Party. The principle of leadership by the Communist Party gives the Party the right to hold the reins of power and to control the government and society. This ensures that when top leaders of the Communist Party make a decision it can be promptly implemented without question. Deng strongly supported this principle and dismissed any need for the division of power among the branches of government. In September 1997, Jiang Zemin, Deng's successor, reaffirmed the leadership of the Communist Party.

The Communist Party is the core of leadership of the people of all nationalities in China. The leading role of the Party is determined by its nature of being the vanguard of the working class and secured after going through ordeals in long years of struggle.

Upholding Marxism–Leninism–Mao Zedong Thought. The thoughts of Mao Zedong are part of the political heritage of the Communist Party of China. Mao's contributions to the development of Marxism–Leninism in China included the development of revolutionary strategy and tactics, the exercise of the dictatorship of the proletariat, and the promotion of socialism. Deng Xiaoping noted in 1978 that the "fundamental point of Mao Zedong Thought is seeking truth from facts and integrating the universal truth of Marxism–Leninism with the concrete practice of Chinese revolution."

In 1979–1980, the Communist Party admitted that Mao had made several serious mistakes during the Great Leap Forward and Cultural Revolution, but his successes, such as the founding of the People's Republic and the implementation of the First Five Year Plan, outweighed his mistakes. The Communist Party declared that overall Mao's policies were 70% correct and 30% incorrect.

After 1980, all further discussion and appraisal of Mao Zedong was carefully controlled. Mao Zedong Thought came to be used to justify changes in policies and as a source of authority to legitimize the Communist Party's rule over the country.

In September 1997, Jiang Zemin, Deng's successor, proclaimed at the 15th Party Congress that the principle of upholding Mao Zedong Thought should include upholding Deng Xiaoping Theory:

Practice proves that Deng Xiaoping Theory, a continuation and development of Mao Zedong Thought, is a correct theory guiding the Chinese people in successfully accomplishing their socialist modernization in the process of reform and opening to the outside world. In China, today, it is Deng Xiaoping Theory, which integrates Marxism with the practice of present-day China and the features of the times, and this theory alone, that can settle issues concerning the future and destiny of socialism. Deng Xiaoping Theory is Marxism of present-day China, representing a new stage of development of Marxism in China.

方向転換なんてとんでもない　ついていくだけで精いっぱい
山田　紳

Asahi Shimbun 1997.9.15 Yamada Shin

"A change in direction is out of the question. There is enough to do right now."

CHINESE POLITICAL SYSTEM

Advance Organizer

Since 1949, political power in China has been centralized in the Communist Party and its leadership. The Communist Party retains power through one-party rule. Its political authority has been maintained through control of the political process, the use of propaganda and indoctrination, constitutional limitations on human rights, and the use of force to suppress opposition and dissent. In recent years, China's leaders have introduced some elements of democracy but at the same time have insisted on the right of the Communist Party to rule the country and determine the development of the political system.

SECTION OVERVIEW
- Chinese Government
- One-Party Rule
- Unitary State
- The Authoritarian State

STRUCTURE OF CHINESE GOVERNMENT

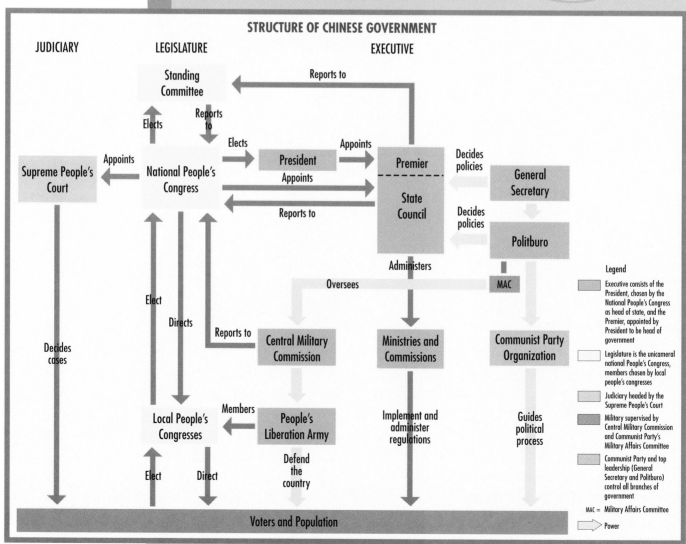

JUDICIARY   LEGISLATURE   EXECUTIVE

Standing Committee — Reports to

Reports to

Elects

Supreme People's Court — Appoints — National People's Congress — Elects — President — Appoints — Premier — Decides policies — General Secretary

Appoints

Reports to

State Council — Decides policies — Politburo

Administers

Oversees — MAC

Elect

Directs

Reports to

Central Military Commission   Ministries and Commissions   Communist Party Organization

Decides cases

Members

Local People's Congresses — People's Liberation Army

Implement and administer regulations   Guides political process

Defend the country

Elect   Direct

Voters and Population

Legend

- Executive consists of the President, chosen by the National People's Congress as head of state, and the Premier, appointed by President to be head of government
- Legislature is the unicameral national People's Congress, members chosen by local people's congresses
- Judiciary headed by the Supreme People's Court
- Military supervised by Central Military Commission and Communist Party's Military Affairs Committee
- Communist Party and top leadership (General Secretary and Politburo) control all branches of government

MAC = Military Affairs Committee

⟹ Power

Adapted from *The Constitution of the People's Republic of China*

Chinese Government

According to the constitution, China is a socialist state under the people's democratic dictatorship led by the working class in an alliance with peasants. All power belongs to the people and is exercised by people's congresses under the leadership of the Communist Party of China.

Executive Power

Executive power in the Chinese government is held by the President acting as the head of state and the Premier of the State Council as the head of government. The President and Premier are also top leaders in the Communist Party.

Reuters/Win McNamee/Archive Photos

President. The President is elected by the National People's Congress for a term of five years. The President announces laws passed by the National People's Congress, appoints and removes members of the State Council with approval from the National People's Congress, confers awards, and receives foreign diplomats.

Premier. The Premier is appointed by the President upon ratification by the National People's Congress and heads the State Council. The Premier and members of the State Council serve until a new National People's Congress is elected, once every five years. The Premier's duties include formulating policies, administering government ministries, and exercising leadership over regional and local governments, as well as drafting the state budget and administering public security.

Legislative Power

In theory, legislative power is currently exercised by the National People's Congress and the smaller Standing Committee. In reality, over 85% of the members of these two bodies are Communist Party members.

National People's Congress (NPC). Members of the NPC are elected by members of local people's congresses in the provinces and regions, and from the People's Liberation Army for a term of five years. The NPC meets once a year for about two weeks, mainly to hear and discuss reports of the State Council. Its other functions include enforcing the constitution, enacting laws, electing the President, approving appointments to the State Council, appointing the head of the People's Supreme Court, and approving five year plans and the state budget. Most of these decisions are approved unanimously with little debate, although debate has grown significantly in recent years.

Standing Committee. The NPC also elects the Standing Committee to exercise power when the NPC is not in session. The Standing Committee interprets laws passed by the NPC, supervises the work of the State Council, ratifies foreign treaties, and can declare martial law.

Judicial Power

Judicial power is exercised by the Supreme People's Court, but its power is limited and largely confined to supervising justice in lower people's courts.

Military

The constitution provides the military with a role in Chinese politics. The Central Military Commission directs the activities of the People's Liberation Army (PLA) and reports to the National People's Congress. The Communist Party's Military Affairs Committee exercises leadership over the Central Military Commission. Deng's rise to power in the late 1970s and leadership over the country in the 1980s was based on close ties with the military. He headed the Military Affairs Committee and for a time chaired the Central Military Commission. In 1989 he resigned as head of the Military Affairs Committee. His successor was General Secretary Jiang Zemin.

In theory, the Chinese system of government is based on the principle that all power belongs to the people. In practice, Communist Party members hold most important positions in the executive, legislative, and judicial branches of the government. There is no clear separation of powers among the branches of government.

PHOTO: Jiang Zemin was elected President in 1993 and reelected to a second five-year term in March 1998.

The number of members of the NPC may not exceed 3000. The number of citizens represented by each rural deputy is four times that represented by each urban deputy (880 000 people to 220 000).

One-Party Rule

The source of all political power and authority in the People's Republic of China is the Communist Party of China (CPC). The Communist Party determines the social, political, and economic goals of society. Its members ensure the attainment of these goals by supervising and controlling institutions and groups in society. In 1997, the membership of the Communist Party reached 58 million people, almost 10% of the total adult population. Communist Party members come from every nationality, region, and occupational group in the country.

Communist Party Organization

Like the former Communist Party of the Soviet Union (CPSU), the Communist Party of China is organized to formulate policies for the country, direct all political activity, and hold power. The main bodies of the Communist Party are the National Party Congress, Standing Committee, Politburo, and Central Secretariat. Political power in the Communist Party flows downward. At the top are the Standing Committee, Politburo, Central Committee, and Central Secretariat headed by the General Secretary, and at the bottom are primary party organizations (party cells) (see chart on page 419).

In theory, the National Party Congress is the Communist Party's main policy making body, but in practice it has little real power. The National Party Congress meets every five years to discuss major questions concerning the Communist Party, approve policy decisions, and elect members to the Communist Party's Central Committee. Congresses are held at the provincial, county, and district levels to choose delegates for the National Party Congress.

The proceedings of the National Party Congress are accompanied by great fanfare and televised to the population. The National Party Congress serves as a rallying point for party members and for Communist Party leaders to announce new policies.

- In September 1982, the 12th Party Congress approved Deng Xiaoping's policy of modernization under the slogan of "building socialism with Chinese characteristics."
- In October 1987, the 13th Party Congress confirmed the policy of building socialism with Chinese characteristics.
- In October 1992, the 14th Party Congress established Deng Xiaoping's theory of building socialism with Chinese characteristics as the basic thought of the Party and declared the aim of Deng's economic reforms was to establish a socialist market economy.
- In September 1997, the 15th Party Congress overwhelmingly endorsed Jiang Zemin's policy of reforming the country's state sector and affirmed the late Deng's economic reform policy.

The Standing Committee and the Politburo are the highest decision making bodies in the Communist Party. Both bodies are elected by the Central Committee. In theory, the Central Committee has the power to make decisions for the whole party and country; in practice this power is delegated to the Standing Committee and Politburo. The Standing Committee, which includes the General Secretary and Premier, meets regularly and is the most powerful decision making body in the country. The Politburo holds frequent meetings and discussions on policy but it is considered to be too large to make the most important decisions.

The most powerful position in the Communist Party is that of the General Secretary, who heads the Central Secretariat, the administrative arm of the Party. The Central Secretariat implements Communist Party policies and manages the Communist Party's organization. It selects and assigns party personnel for specific tasks and directs the work of the government. All these tasks are accomplished through a network of Communist Party secretaries, existing at all levels of the party organization. These secretaries, who report to top Communist Party leaders, are responsible for the performance and activities of all Communist Party officials under their authority.

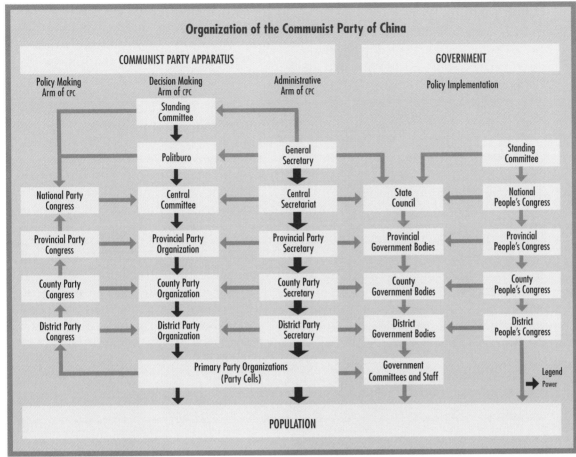

Organization of the Communist Party of China

COMMUNIST PARTY APPARATUS			GOVERNMENT
Policy Making Arm of CPC	Decision Making Arm of CPC	Administrative Arm of CPC	Policy Implementation

Standing Committee

Politburo — General Secretary — Standing Committee

National Party Congress — Central Committee — Central Secretariat — State Council — National People's Congress

Provincial Party Congress — Provincial Party Organization — Provincial Party Secretary — Provincial Government Bodies — Provincial People's Congress

County Party Congress — County Party Organization — County Party Secretary — County Government Bodies — County People's Congress

District Party Congress — District Party Organization — District Party Secretary — District Government Bodies — District People's Congress

Primary Party Organizations (Party Cells) — Government Committees and Staff

Legend → Power

POPULATION

Adapted from *The Constitution of the Communist Party of China*

Decision Making

Decision making in China is governed by two principles. The first is Lenin's principle of democratic centralism to guide all decision making in the Communist Party. The second principle is the control of the government by the Communist Party.

Democratic Centralism. Decision making in the Communist Party is conducted on the principle of democratic centralism. Its basic features are the subordination of the minority to the majority and obedience by Communist Party members to decisions made by party leaders. In theory, democratic centralism allows for internal party discussion and debate. However, in practice, it has been used to ensure party discipline and suppress dissent among Communist Party members. Party leaders have tried to encourage internal party debate on issues, but once the top leadership makes a decision all party members are expected to support and implement it without question.

Control of the Government. According to the constitution, the Communist Party is the leading political organization in the country, guiding the government and people toward the ultimate goal of creating a communist social system (see chart "Organization of the Communist Party of China").

At the 15th Party Congress in September 1997, General Secretary Jiang Zemin called on the Communist Party to establish a rule of law to ensure more effective government.

In ruling the country by law, we can unify the adherence to Party leadership, development of people's democracy and doing things in strict accordance with the law, thus ensuring, institutionally and legally, that the Party's basic line and basic policies are carried out without fail, and that the Party plays the role of the core of leadership at all times, commanding the whole situation and coordinating the efforts of all quarters.

Unitary State

Another feature of the Chinese political system is the centralization of power in Beijing. The country is officially declared to be a unitary state. The central government holds all power and may delegate power to local governments.

Local Governments

China is divided into provinces, autonomous regions, and municipalities.

Provinces. The provinces are the most common form of local government. Their powers are determined by the central government in Beijing in accordance with national policies. The country's 22 provinces range in size from Sichuan, with over 100 million people, to Qinghai, with fewer than five million people.

Autonomous Regions. Five autonomous regions, located in border regions of China, are inhabited mainly by non-Han peoples. (Han are the majority nationality of China.) The largest non-Han groups in China are the Zhuang, Hui, Uigher, Yi, Miao, and Tibetan peoples. Altogether, minority nationalities comprise about eight percent of the country's total population, but inhabit almost 60 percent of the country's territory. Autonomous regions were created in 1949 to consolidate Communist control over minority groups. In recent years there have been clashes between local minorities and Chinese in two autonomous regions, Tibet and Xinjiang.

Municipalities. The country's four municipalities of Beijing, Tianjin, Shanghai, and Chongqing are important urban centres that perform special functions. Beijing is the national capital and seat of the central government, Tianjin the main seaport for Beijing, Shanghai the country's largest city, and Chongqing a major industrial centre in south China.

There are 55 officially recognized national minorities in China. Two (Hui and Manchu) speak Chinese and the other 53 ethnic groups use their own spoken language.

The constitution declares that all autonomous regions are inalienable parts of China and have no right to secede from the country.

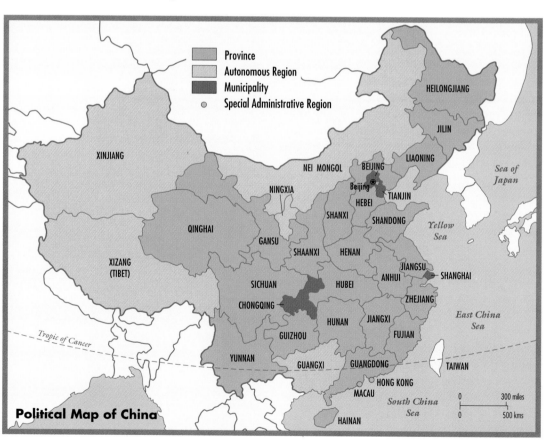

Political Map of China

Special Administrative Regions

China has two special administrative regions (SAR), Hong Kong and Macau. They were created to fulfil the policy of "one country, two systems," reuniting Hong Kong, Macau, and Taiwan under Chinese sovereignty. Special administrative regions are granted considerable power to decide local policies and maintain their own distinctive economic systems for a period of 50 years after reunification, but the central government in Beijing has final say in any decisions which affect its authority over them.

Hong Kong. On July 1, 1997, Hong Kong, a city of 6.3 million located on the southeast coast, returned to Chinese sovereignty as a Special Administrative Region. China ceded Hong Kong Island to Great Britain in 1842, then it was enlarged in 1860 and in 1898, when China leased an additional tract of land north of Hong Kong to Great Britain for 99 years. In 1949, thousands of business and professional people fled from Shanghai to Hong Kong and expanded the colony's manufacturing and financial sectors. In 1984, an agreement between Great Britain and China granted Hong Kong considerable local autonomy and the right to maintain its private enterprise economy for 50 years after returning to China in 1997.

The SAR is governed by a Chief Executive appointed by the government in Beijing, who serves a term of five years. The Chief Executive's duties include signing bills, appointing various officials, and implementing directives issued by Beijing. Of the 60 members of the Legislative Council, 20 are directly elected by voters, 30 are elected by occupational and professional groups, and 10 are chosen by an election committee. The Legislative Council can enact laws, approve budgets, and debate questions on government work.

Macau. A special administrative region has been established for Macau, which returns to Chinese control on December 20, 1999. Macau was originally set up as a trading port by the Portuguese in 1557.

Taiwan. A special administrative region has yet to be created for Taiwan, an island situated about 160 kilometres from the Chinese mainland.

From 1895 to 1945, Taiwan was part of the Japanese empire. It returned to Chinese control at the end of World War II. Chiang Kai-shek and his Nationalist forces fled to Taiwan in 1949, and established a dictatorship.

Until his death in 1975, Chiang claimed that his government on Taiwan represented all of China and vowed to return eventually to the mainland. Taiwan, known at the time as the Republic of China, held China's seat in the United Nations until 1971, when the United Nations revoked Taiwan's membership and gave it to the People's Republic of China.

In the 1980s, the island's economy developed rapidly, becoming one of the world's largest exporting countries. By 1998, Taiwan had become an urban industrial country, and its 21.5 million citizens enjoyed a high standard of living.

During the 1980s and 1990s, Taiwan's political system evolved into a democracy. In 1996, the country held its first democratic presidential elections. The newly-elected president Lee Teng-hui had openly campaigned for Taiwan's readmission into the United Nations and increased relations with the People's Republic.

The objective of China's special administrative regions is to reunite Hong Kong, Macau, and Taiwan with China under the policy of "one country, two systems."

Flag of Hong Kong SAR

Flag of Republic of China (Taiwan)

Presidents of Taiwan
Chiang Kai-shek
(1949–1975)
C.K. Yen
(1975–1978)
Chiang Ching-kuo
(1978–1988)
Lee Teng–hui
(1988–)

PHOTO: A stamp souvenir sheet with the portrait of Deng Xiaoping was issued in 1997 to commemorate the July 1, 1997, handover of Hong Kong to Chinese control.

The Authoritarian State

The political authority of the Communist Party in Chinese politics has long been maintained through controls over the political process, propaganda, indoctrination, constitutional limits on human rights, and the use of force. In the 1990s, many of these controls were relaxed but did not disappear.

Controlled Participation: Elections to the People's Congresses

All citizens over 18 years of age are permitted to vote. The main elected bodies in China are the people's congresses. The election process in China differs from that in Canada and other democracies in several important ways.

First, although all elections are multi-candidate, the Communist Party manages the electoral process at all levels. It controls election committees, which approve slates of candidates for all elected positions. Local Communist Party secretaries can disqualify from running for office any candidates whom they consider unacceptable to the Communist Party. However, internal negotiation and compromise are often used in selecting candidates. Generally, most candidates who run for office are Communist Party members.

Secondly, there are no direct nationwide elections in China. At the village and neighbourhood level, people directly elect representatives to their local committee. People elect their representatives of the district and county people's congresses for a term of three years. Above the county level, congresses elect members to congresses above them, in a system of indirect elections. At the highest level, provincial and regional congresses elect the members of the National People's Congress (see chart "China's System of People's Congresses").

Thirdly, elections by secret ballot are now conducted on a regular basis for congresses at the municipal and provincial levels, but this was not always the case before 1982.

Fourthly, the electoral campaign at the village level follows strict rules. Information about the candidates is printed and distributed among voters, posted on public bulletin boards, and broadcast on the radio. Public campaign rallies are prohibited by law. Candidates who publicly criticize political leaders can be arrested and imprisoned. On election day, voters choose their candidates by crossing out the names of candidates on the ballot they do not want.

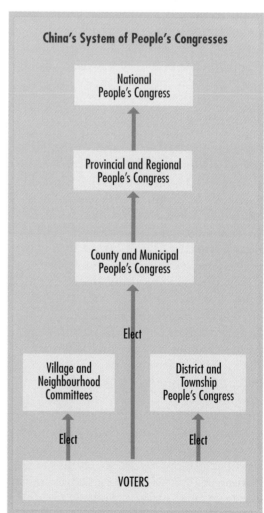

China's System of People's Congresses

National People's Congress

Provincial and Regional People's Congress

County and Municipal People's Congress

Elect

Village and Neighbourhood Committees — District and Township People's Congress

Elect — Elect — Elect

VOTERS

Adapted from *The Constitution of the People's Republic of China*

Propaganda

All media (press, television and radio, cinema and the arts, and the internet) in China are under government control.

Press. All newspapers in China are licenced by the government. The Communist Party sets direction for the press through statements sent from its propaganda authorities. The government can close down any newspaper that violates directives on news reporting. For example, stories on crime, natural disasters such as earthquakes and floods, airplane crashes, government mismanagement, and corruption must receive approval from the Central Propaganda Department before publication. When foreign correspondents write stories that portray the government and Communist Party in a negative light, they can be expelled from the country.

Television and radio. Television and radio are the most popular media in China, where there are over 200 million television sets and 350 million radios. Government control of televised news is tight, especially when considered to be politically sensitive. State-owned China Central Television issues a carefully selected edition of prime-time domestic and international news for the entire nation each day. Generally, news stories are broadcast that feature successes of the government and the Communist Party, such as the opening sessions of the National People's Congress and speeches by top Communist leaders.

On the other hand, media coverage of natural and human-made disasters is severely restricted. When floods inundated large areas of China in August 1998, foreign reporters were forbidden to enter the disaster areas, and even Chinese reporters were ordered out of these regions. Foreign news radio signals, such as the BBC and the Voice of America, are frequently jammed.

Cinema and the arts. Cinema and the arts have long been useful to the Communist Party as means of creating enthusiasm for Communist policies. Under Mao, the cinema and the arts popularized the victory of communism and the superiority of socialism over capitalism.

In the 1980s, the government relaxed controls on the arts and the production of films. Works of popular entertainment were encouraged and foreign films were allowed to be shown.

Since the early 1990s, the government has urged film producers to make films and television programs that promote greater patriotic sentiment among the general public. Large audiences have watched documentary films on the lives of past leaders like Mao Zedong, Chou En-lai, and Deng Xiaoping, and historical events such as the establishment of diplomatic relations between China and the United States.

Internet. Until 1996, access to the internet was not tightly controlled. The central government now orders service providers who offer telephone access to the global computer network to go through a government-run service. By controlling access to the internet, the government hopes to block access to some worldwide sites that it considers offensive, such as pornography, forums for discussions about Taiwan and Tibetan independence, and the electronic versions of some Western news media.

The Chinese Internet Centre reported that in June 1998 the number of internet users in China had reached 1 175 000. Over 80% of the internet users were graduates of college and vocational schools.

PHOTO: A billboard in Guangzhou publicizes Deng's Four Modernizations.

Marcey Andrews/Arnold Publishing Ltd.

Indoctrination

The Communist Party considers indoctrination through the educational system and its youth organizations an important means of promoting loyalty to the policies of the Communist Party, the country's leaders, and the principles of Marxism–Leninism and Mao Zedong Thought. The constitution affirms the importance of "the civic virtues of love for the motherland, for the people, for labour, for science, and for socialism," and calls on the state to educate people in patriotism, collectivism, internationalism, and communism.

Education. The educational system in China is an important vehicle for teaching values and needed skills to the people. In the first years of the People's Republic, the Communist Party worked hard to increase the country's rate of literacy, an effort that won them considerable support from the people. The Cultural Revolution (1966–1976) set back the country's educational system. Schools were closed and millions of students were urged to give up education, study the thoughts of Mao Zedong, and take part in revolutionary action. Consequently, millions of students never completed their education.

Since 1980, in keeping with the policy of modernization, the emphasis on teaching communist values such as collectivism, patriotism, vigilance, and atheism in the schools has been reduced because of the need to train students for technical and professional jobs. Courses on Mao Zedong Thought, Marxism–Leninism, and the history of the Communist Party have been emphasized less, in favour of a new school curriculum of mathematics, physics, chemistry, biology, economics, and foreign languages. In some institutes of higher education, courses such as the history of the Communist Party and Marxism–Leninism have been cancelled and replaced by more popular courses on economics and business administration.

Youth Organizations. To prepare young people for work in a socialist society, the Communist Party established the Communist Youth League in 1949. Today, the youth organization has about 60 million members, most of whom live in urban areas. It has two branches—Young Pioneers, for students aged 9–14 years, and Young Communists, for students aged 14–25 years.

The Young Pioneers learn the history of the Communist Party of China, elementary principles of Marxism–Leninism–Mao Zedong Thought, and the importance of discipline. At age 14 the Young Pioneer becomes a member of the Communist Youth League. Members study the principles of Mao Zedong Thought, undergo some military training, learn civil responsibilities, and perform duties for the local party organization.

At age 26, Young Communists can become members of the Communist Party if their references, work history, and school achievement are satisfactory. Candidates have to demonstrate that they have the correct attitudes about the Communist Party and will obey party instructions.

Since the mid-1980s, young people have become less enthusiastic about joining the Communist Youth League. Many students are more interested in expressing their individuality and personal views than in adopting a spirit of selflessness and desire to "serve the people." Forums and conferences sponsored by the Communist Youth League have revealed that a majority of youth expressed a lack of confidence in the "superiority of socialism," Marxism, and Mao Zedong Thought. Today, many young people wish to pursue goals like going into business, getting a good job, and buying expensive clothing and consumer goods. However, many other young people still join the CYL for the educational and work opportunities provided.

In the late 1980s, forums sponsored by the Communist Youth League revealed that a majority of young people expressed a lack of confidence in Marxism, Mao's thought, and socialism. Since the early 1990s, most teenagers have been reluctant to join the Communist Youth League to become party activists.

In 1998, the Ministry of Education reported that in 1997 the enrolment rate of school-age children reached 98.7% nationwide.

Surveys by the State Statistical Bureau in 1990 and 1995 showed that the number of people without literacy skills over 15 years of age had decreased from 182 million to 145 million—a drop in the rate from 22.3% to 16.5%.

Chinese Constitutions

Since 1949, China has adopted four constitutions. Their purpose has been to grant constitutional power to the Communist Party and to reflect changes in Chinese society.

- The first constitution, adopted in 1954, declared a dictatorship of the proletariat led by the Communist Party in China.
- In 1975, a new constitution recognized the revolutionary order created by the Cultural Revolution.
- In 1978, the constitution was amended to reflect Deng's program of modernization and included a section on the fundamental rights and duties of citizens.
- The fourth (current) constitution, adopted in 1982, recognized China's opening up to the world and policy of building "socialism with Chinese characteristics." It declared family planning and birth control to be an important national policy.

Civil Liberties. The 1982 constitution grants Chinese citizens numerous civil liberties. In theory, they have the rights to work, education, rest and leisure, financial support in old age, gender equality, freedom of religious belief, freedom of the press, freedom of assembly, freedom of public demonstration, and privacy. However, in practice, these civil liberties are limited and the constitution states that to enjoy these liberties citizens must perform duties to the state and society.

For example, every citizen must work hard and is encouraged to participate in voluntary labour. Parents have the duty to practise family planning and birth control so that population growth may fit plans for economic and social development. On becoming adults, children are required to support and assist their parents. Every citizen is required to "safeguard the security, honour, and interests of the motherland" and to "defend the motherland" from foreign aggression. Every citizen is obligated to perform military service.

The constitution also grants powers to the state to restrict civil liberties. For example, the state has the power, in the interest of protecting national security, to invade people's privacy, censor personal letters coming from abroad, and monitor telephone conversations. The state can prohibit a citizen's right to criticize government officials if this criticism challenges current policies of the Communist Party and government.

Political Rights. The 1982 constitution grants all citizens the right to vote and stand for election, criticize state officials, be equal before the law, and be free from unlawful arrest. Citizens can be deprived of the right to vote and stand for election if they do not support the Four Cardinal Principles —socialism, the people's democratic dictatorship, leadership by the Communist Party, and upholding Marxism–Leninism–Mao Zedong Thought. Other activities leading to the restriction of a person's political rights include those that threaten national unity, create disharmony among minorities, directly threaten public security, and create social unrest. A person caught organizing a political group without authorization from the Communist Party can be sentenced to 10–15 years in prison or a labour camp.

Human Rights Violations. In the 1990s, one source of considerable tension in relations between China and various western countries has been the country's violations of its citizens' human rights. International human rights organizations estimate that up to 20 million people are held in labour camps and prisons for activities the government considers to be "counter-revolutionary," which include the desire for religious freedom, as well as calling for changes in the country's political system and establishment of multi-party elections. In recent years, the government has allowed several prominent dissidents to leave the country.

The government does not consider the issue of human rights and the guarantee of individual civil liberties and political rights to be of highest importance. It believes that food self-sufficiency and political stability are more important goals for Chinese society.

Public Security

The Ministry of Public Security is responsible for maintaining public order and ensuring obedience to the policies of the Communist Party. It supervises a large secret police force and an extensive system of urban and rural committees and work units that monitor, and at times control, people's activities.

Secret Police. The Ministry of Public Security employs a large network of agents and informants to monitor and report on people's activities. The activities of dissidents are routinely watched and in some cases tightly controlled. Foreign journalists, tourists, diplomats, students, and Chinese citizens who have close contact with foreigners in the country are frequently under surveillance.

Neighbourhood Committees. Urban neighbourhood and village committees are responsible for registrations of local households and detecting suspicious behaviour. Every citizen in China is issued a residency permit and identity card which contain personal information such as name, place of birth, marital status, record of military service, and place of work. These documents are used to control and monitor population movements. All people must register with the local committee to enter school, gain employment, participate in elections, serve in the armed forces, marry, and obtain housing, or they face arrest and deportation out of the area. People registered in rural areas are prohibited from moving permanently into the cities, and people registered in the cities are prevented from moving from one city to another without a formal change in urban registration. For example, a person cannot move from Shanghai to Beijing before receiving permission to live in Beijing.

These committees are also responsible for enforcing the government's official policy of population control in the form of "one-child families." The basic demands of family planning are late marriage and late childbirth. In the cities, families who have only one child receive more pay at work, better housing, free health care, and access to day care, kindergarten, and schooling for their one child. Families with more than one child can be forced to wait longer for housing and a placement in school for their children. These families can be fined and ordered to pay for health care. Other measures ordered by local committees to enforce population control in their districts have included forced sterilization and abortions.

In rural areas, population control measures are less strictly enforced. Peasant families are strongly urged to have no more than one child. However, when the first child is a girl, the peasant family is allowed to have another child. Families from national minority groups living in the autonomous regions (see map on page 420) are allowed to have more than one child.

Work Units. Work units exist in most places of employment and schools. They allocate housing, school, and work assignments to their members. They also keep information on the work and family history, education, travel in China and abroad, and political and ideological correctness of their members. Local Communist Party committees associated with the work units maintain these files and use them to reward or punish individual behaviour.

Challenges to Public Order. Since the 1980s, economic reforms have weakened the ability of neighbourhood and village committees and work units to monitor and control Chinese citizens. The government estimates today that up to 200 million workers belong to neither a work unit nor a neighbourhood committee. The vast majority of these people are rural labourers who have left their villages to find work in the cities, often without official authorization and registration. Another 30 million or so are self-employed and not affiliated with work units. Restructuring to state-owned enterprises promises to further increase the number of workers no longer belonging to work units.

People's Liberation Army

According to Mao, the military was an essential component of political power in China. As he remarked, "political power grows out of the barrel of a gun." The constitution entrusts to the People's Liberation Army (PLA) several important tasks: "to strengthen national defence, resist aggression, defend the motherland, safeguard the people's peaceful labour, participate in national reconstruction, and work hard to serve the people." The more important of these are serving the people, being a model for society, and defending the country.

Serving the People. One aspect of service to the people by the PLA is its participation in national reconstruction and development. In the early years of Communist rule, the PLA helped to distribute land among the peasants. It supported the establishment of collective farms and provided labour for the construction of key industrial projects. In the 1980s and 1990s, PLA labour corps built railways, tunnels, bridges, highways, airports, and water conservation projects.

Another aspect of the PLA's service to the people is its participation in emergency rescues and disaster relief work. In 1976, when a powerful earthquake destroyed the city of Tangshan, killing over 240 000 people, the PLA provided badly needed food and shelter to the survivors, and helped to rebuild the city. In 1998, when floods inundated large areas of China, the PLA gave emergency assistance to homeless peasants and sent troops to build and maintain dikes to contain the flood waters. The 1998 flood control effort was considered to be the largest military mobilization since 1949, with almost one million troops deployed.

Model for Society. In the early years of Communist rule, the PLA was seen as a model of the new communist society. Members of the PLA were trained to treat the people with honesty and respect in accordance with Mao's 1947 code of conduct. Each soldier was expected to follow three main rules for discipline and eight points for attention (see margin note).

Since 1980, the need to raise the professional training of the PLA officer corps has to some extent supplanted Mao's code of conduct. The PLA soldier still serves as a model for young Chinese men, but more for patriotic reasons and to promote national development.

Defending the Country. In the early years of Communist rule, the PLA played an important role in preserving national unity from threats such as the return of Nationalist forces from Taiwan. In November 1950, when American forces advanced deep into North Korea, close to the Chinese border, China sent the PLA into Korea. The government feared an invasion by American forces in support of Chiang and his Nationalist forces.

During the Cultural Revolution, when chaos and violence caused by power struggles among Red Guard factions was widespread, the Communist Party placed the country under military control to maintain law and order. PLA leaders took prominent positions in the Communist Party and government.

Following Mao's death, PLA involvement in politics remained important, especially in the support it gave to Deng in his rise to power in the late 1970s. In 1978, Deng called for the modernization of and increased spending on the armed forces, a policy which pleased top PLA commanders. In exchange for this, Deng obtained military support for his reform policies and leadership over the country.

In 1989, the PLA was drawn into the political arena, when student demonstrations in Tiananmen Square threatened Deng's political authority and sparked a power struggle among top Communist Party leaders. In May 1989, Deng convened an emergency meeting of top PLA commanders to enforce martial law, which was imposed in Beijing shortly thereafter.

Tiananmen Square Incident

When necessary, the Communist Party has used military force to suppress opposition to its political power. The most dramatic illustration of this was in Tiananmen Square on June 3–4, 1989, when the People's Liberation Army (PLA) used force to clear the Square of university student demonstrators who had occupied it since late April to protest government corruption, inflation, and economic mismanagement. Soon the students added demands for greater democracy in China. Estimates of the number of students killed varied widely. Official sources reported 23 students and 300 soldiers killed. Many newspapers and human rights groups put the figure at between 2600 and 3500.

Official View

Excerpts from *People's Daily*, June 8 and June 21; *China Central Television Station*, June 7; *Beijing Daily*, June 10; published in *Beijing Review*, September 11–17, 1989, pp. 22–23.

The details of the process of clearing Tiananmen Square are these: At 1:30 AM on June 4, the martial law enforcement troops moved close to Tiananmen and took up positions surrounding the square.

At 1:50 AM, an emergency notice issued by the Beijing Municipal People's Government and the headquarters of the martial law enforcement troops was broadcast on the square, saying that a counter-revolutionary riot had taken place in Beijing on June 3 and demanding students and onlookers on the square leave as soon as possible.

This emergency notice was broadcasted repeatedly for two hours through loud speakers. Most of the people quickly left the square. The remaining students, now numbering several thousands, massed around the Monument to the People's Heroes.

Then Hou Dejian, who had participated in a 72-hour hunger strike, went up to negotiate with an officer of the martial law enforcement troops. Hou said that the students were willing to withdraw from the square, but there were different points of view. It would take them some time to reach a unanimous opinion. The headquarters of the martial law enforcement troops in a broadcast announcement agreed with the students' demand to be allowed to withdraw from the square voluntarily and said that there was a way out at the southeastern end of the square.

About 4:40 AM, the students began to leave in an orderly way, lining up and carrying their own banners. Before they left, some of the demonstrators made a fire of the cotton clothes, quilts, and woollen blankets left on the square, in case the military vehicles ran over them. This was the reason for the first fires seen on the square.

After most of the students had withdrawn, there were still a few at the southeastern end of the square who refused to leave, and armed police and the martial law enforcement troops compelled them to do so. At 5:30 AM, the clearance was completed.

In the process of the clearance, a few rioters vainly attempted to take soldiers' rifles and the soldiers fired in the air to give a warning. In order to eliminate the loudspeakers hung by the "Beijing college students' autonomous federation" on the southeast corner of the Monument to the People's Heroes, soldiers shot at them to silence them. After the demonstrators withdrew, when someone shot at the troops from a high-rise

Reuters/Stringer/Archive Photos

PHOTO: A Beijing resident stops a tank column near Tiananmen Square on June 4, 1989.

building in the southeast of the square the solders shot back at the roof of the building to give a warning. But no person was killed or run over by military vehicles.

At dawn, in order to clear away the garbage, boxes and rickety tents on the square, the soldiers set a fire to them. This was the reason for the second fire in the square.

Personal Account

(Excerpt) *Massacre in Beijing*, published by the International League for Human Rights, August 4, 1989.

At 10 PM on 3 June, on the other side of Nanchizi near the Beijing Hotel, a convoy of military vehicles was coming towards us. A woman student from the Beijing Teachers' University stopped them and spoke to the vanguard. She said, "PLA soldiers, you are the people's army. We students have nothing against you. We are compatriots. Please do not aim your rifles at the people. We are not mobsters. We are university students who love peace and freedom . . . ." Before she could finish, a burst of sub-machine gun killed her there and then . . . . Several of my other schoolmates had rushed to Xidan. Assault rifles had started firing; tanks were approaching. What did the civilians there use to stop the troops?

They stood there hand in hand, unarmed—the student pickets, the civilian pickets, elderly women and men and the zealous workers. All these people who sent us food in the daytime, who comforted us, encouraged us and voiced their support for us, formed layer after layer of human barricades. Tanks were closing in, the vanguard were emerging from both sides, all wearing helmets and camouflaged uniforms—they were their death squads.

The tanks moved forward, then paused and soldiers immediately dashed out, apparently with their guns aimed at us. Many of the students swore not to give way and shouted slogans like "Down with fascists!" "Down with autocrats!" At this instant, the machine guns on top of the tanks were tilted down and started strafing the crowd. All the people in the first row were instantly killed. Then followed the assault troops who raked the crowd with their assault rifles. The tanks then savagely rolled over the first row of the crowd, leaving a paste of human flesh behind its trail. I heard gunshots from assault rifles and machine guns. I heard screams. I did not quite gather what was going on. As I led my colleagues to join the nearby crowd, the crowd in front had already dispersed to the sides . . . .

The assault troops kept firing at the crowd. They raked places where the loudest noise came from, the loudest chanting of slogans and the loudest shouting. Furious people on the street who threw stones and bricks or those who might be in the convoy's way were swept with bullets and then rolled over by tanks. . . .

When I arrived at Jianguomen, I saw that many students were killed, some were crushed by tanks and could no longer be recognized as human beings. . . . I spotted a woman university student with long hair who was bayonetted in the chest by a soldier. As the girl fell, the soldier delivered a few more strokes on her back. She was stabbed to death on the spot. The killing was most severe opposite Xidan and the Military Museum. Some of the students were trying to escape; some tripped and were crushed by the tanks tailing after them while others were fired at indiscriminately by assault rifles. . . . A few individuals who survived the first shot were given a second or even a third to make sure that there would be no survivors.

On the outskirts [of the Square], the massacre continued for several hours. At 2 AM on 4 June, it was the height of the slaughter. Sitting at Tiananmen Square, one could hear gunshots, machine gun bursts, noise from the tanks and screams of the people.

To the south and north of the People's Monument, the sky was brightly lit by tracers. By 3 AM or 4 AM, the outskirts were cleared, most of the students had been slaughtered.

Reuters/Pat Benic/Archive Photos

PHOTO: The Goddess of Democracy, erected in Tiananmen Square by students in late May 1989.

CHINESE ECONOMIC SYSTEM

The Chinese economy was ranked seventh largest in 1997.

Gross Domestic Product at current prices and exchange rates (in billions of USS)

United States 7819.3
Japan   4223.4
Germany   2115.4
France   1393.8
Great Britain 1278.4
Italy   1146.2
China   917.7
Brazil   803.3
Canada   599.0
Spain   533.4

Compiled from OECD and World Bank

Advance Organizer

China today is undergoing two profound transformations. The first is the development of an urban industrial society. Currently, about 70% of the population lives in the countryside and about 50% of the labour force is employed in agriculture. Per capita GDP in 1998 was estimated at US$800, compared to US$18 870 for Canada. The second is the transformation of the centrally planned economy into one that is partially market-based. Since 1978, the Chinese government has implemented many economic reforms to spur economic growth. The result is an economic system which the Chinese government calls a socialist market economy. World Bank economists classify the Chinese economy as a transitional economy because it has more features of a developing private enterprise, market economy.

SECTION OVERVIEW

• Economic Policies
• Emerging Private Sector
• Public Sector

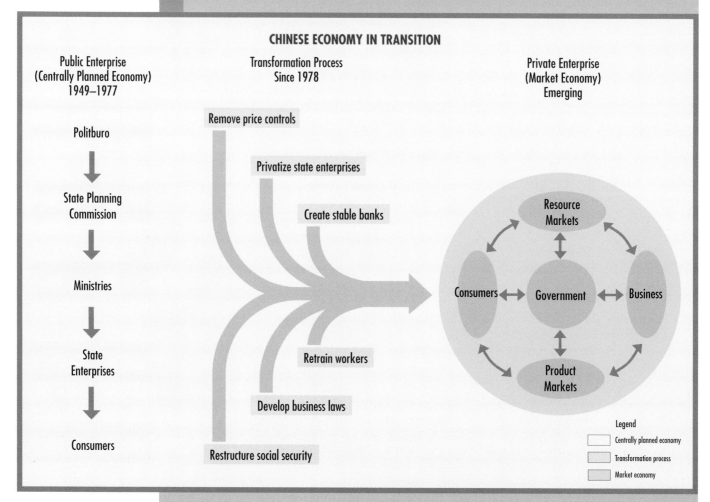

CHINESE ECONOMY IN TRANSITION

Public Enterprise
(Centrally Planned Economy)
1949–1977

Transformation Process
Since 1978

Private Enterprise
(Market Economy)
Emerging

Politburo

↓

State Planning
Commission

↓

Ministries

↓

State
Enterprises

↓

Consumers

Remove price controls

Privatize state enterprises

Create stable banks

Retrain workers

Develop business laws

Restructure social security

Resource Markets

Consumers ↔ Government ↔ Business

Product Markets

Legend

☐ Centrally planned economy
☐ Transformation process
☐ Market economy

Economic Policies

Since 1949, China has experienced two significant changes in economic policy. From 1949 to 1976, economic policy focussed on central planning and on government ownership and control of the economy. Since 1978, government control of the economy has been greatly reduced.

Centrally Planned Economy (1949–1976)

Under Mao's leadership, the Chinese economy was transformed into a centrally planned economy with public ownership of the means of production. Mass campaigns were launched to rapidly industrialize the economy and promote social equality, but the economy that these campaigns had produced by 1976 was inefficient.

Economic Transformation (Since 1978)

Under Deng Xiaoping's leadership (1978–1997), economic reforms were introduced to revitalize the economy and increase people's living standards. Unlike reforms introduced in Russia in the early 1990s following the collapse of the Soviet Union, Deng's economic reforms were implemented gradually, beginning first in agriculture and the countryside where the majority of the population lived. Once productivity in agriculture had been raised, his government introduced reforms in other areas of the economy.

Four Modernizations (1978–1992). The objectives of the Four Modernizations policy in 1978 were to modernize agriculture, industry, science and technology, and national defence. The policy introduced some elements of private enterprise while the government retained overall control over the economy. In 1982, the Four Modernizations became known as "building socialism with Chinese characteristics."

The first measure of the Four Modernizations was the disbanding of communes in agriculture. Peasant households were allowed to farm the land as they wished under the household responsibility system. In exchange for the right to farm the land, peasant households signed contracts to sell to the government a portion of their grain at fixed prices. The remaining portion of their grain could be sold privately in village markets. Profits from these private sales could be invested in private businesses.

In early 1984, private businesses were permitted in cities. Individuals were allowed to set up small private businesses such as restaurants, beauty parlors, taxicab operations, bicycle repair shops, and food stands.

In 1988, state-owned enterprises in industry were given greater freedom to make decisions about production. Planning was decentralized and production quotas lowered. State-owned enterprises were encouraged to operate profitably and allowed to keep more of their after-tax profits.

The government also implemented a reform of centrally-administered prices. Price controls on many goods and services were removed. To prevent inflation, a transitional two-price system was set up, in which prices of raw materials needed in the five year plan were fixed while those of other goods not important in the five year plan could change according to supply and demand.

In 1979, the government announced an "open door" policy. Its objective was to

December 1978	September 1979	September 1982	April 1984	October 1987
Four Modernizations launched	Communes begin to be disbanded; peasant households allowed to farm the land	12th Party Congress; "building socialism with Chinese characteristics" and "one country, two systems" endorsed	Economic development zones established in 14 coastal cities	13th Party Congress; economic reforms speed up
July 1979 Law on foreign investment enacted; beginning of "open-door" policy	**May 1980** First special economic zone (SEZ) established at Shenzhen	**February 1984** Regulations for rural private businesses issued	**May 1984** First banking reform announced	**July 1988** Regulations on private enterprises introduced; law on State Enterprise enacted
			May 1985 Price controls on agricultural products lifted	

Economic Transformation—Since 1978

Note: Timeline is not to scale

encourage Chinese enterprises to establish joint ventures with foreign investors, import foreign technology, and increase trade with other countries. After 1980, special economic zones and development areas were established to attract foreign investment. To create a large pool of skilled people to work in industry, education, scientific research, and technology, many Chinese students were sent to foreign universities to study economics, business management, engineering, science, foreign languages, and other subjects.

In the field of national defence, the government introduced measures to improve the quality of domestically-produced armaments. In 1982, the policy of "one country, two systems" was launched to reduce tensions between China and Taiwan. The policy helped make possible an agreement between China and Great Britain in 1984 on a peaceful return of Hong Kong to Chinese control in 1997.

Socialist Market Economy (Since 1992).

In October 1992, Deng announced the goal of establishing a "socialist market economy" in China for the 21st century. In a "socialist market economy," supply and demand would play the primary role in determining answers to the basic economic questions. State-owned and privately-owned enterprises would compete for sales and produce only goods and services that customers want. Enterprises would maximize profit and be efficient. The government would no longer manage most state-owned enterprises but would be involved only in the overall planning and regulation of the economy. The major difference between a market economy and a socialist market economy in China would be the degree of government control and ownership of factors of production (land, labour, and capital).

In September 1997, six months after Deng's death, General Secretary Jiang Zemin proposed new economic reforms. They included proposals to privatize most state-owned enterprises, restructure the central planning system, create a stable banking system, and implement new codes for business practices and property ownership. In the future the government would own enterprises only in key industries such as steel, coal, electricity, transportation, and telecommunications.

LEFT: A shopping mall in Shenzhen special economic zone.

RIGHT: A billboard in Shanghai advertises the sale of personal computers.

Phyllis A. Arnold

Glen BonBernard

A Point of View of Two Transformations

China's transition from a centrally planned economy to a market-based one has been quite successful, especially when compared to the transition from central planning to private enterprise in Russia (see chart below). World Bank economists in a report called *China 2020* offered six reasons for the differences between China and Russia.

1. Political stability. China benefited from a stable political system. The Chinese Communist Party remained in charge of the government, economy, and society. In the Soviet Union, Mikhail Gorbachev introduced political reforms to give the people greater say in decision making and the Communist Party gave up its constitutional right to hold power. These changes destabilized the Soviet political system and led to the collapse of the Soviet Union in late 1991. The breakup into fifteen new countries disrupted trading links among the Soviet republics.

2. High savings rate. Between 1979 and 1997, China's savings rate averaged around one-third of GDP, one of the highest in the world. As the economy grew and personal incomes rose, people began to save for housing, consumer goods, retirement, and education. In Russia after the collapse of the Soviet Union, hyperinflation and lower living standards caused the savings rate to fall sharply.

3. Record of gradual and pragmatic reforms. Aware of the fact that the country had endured much hardship during the Cultural Revolution, Deng believed that the best approach to modernizing the country and raising living standards was to implement reforms gradually. Growth was important, but not at the expense of stability. Russia, on the other hand, introduced a radical reform program—"shock therapy"—to quickly transform the economy into a market-based one. This policy destabilized the economy and brought hardship to millions of Russians.

4. Disciplined labour force. Mao's campaigns to introduce socialist values among the population were not very successful in the villages, where most Chinese continued to hold in high esteem the traditional value of personal initiative. When trading and small-scale businesses were legalized in the early 1980s, Chinese entrepreneurs needed little encouragement to expand. After more than 70 years of communism in Russia, workers had learned to be submissive and depend on the government. When private enterprise was legalized, many Russians had to develop the values of personal initiative, hard work, and profit-making.

5. Supportive overseas Chinese community. When reforms began, China could rely on a large community of approximately 50 million Chinese living in Hong Kong, Macau, Taiwan, Southeast Asia, North America, and elsewhere. Many of these Chinese were experienced and wealthy business people. After 1985, they began to invest heavily in labour-intensive industries in China. Russia, in contrast, had a very small overseas Russian community of about two million people on which to draw for business experience and capital.

6. Strong administrative capacity. Over the centuries, China had developed a strong system of local government, which became stronger under Communist rule. When reforms were introduced, local governments were able to take on new responsibilities. In Russia, the tradition of strong central government was further strengthened under Communist rule. Lack of expertise at the local government level slowed the implementation of economic reforms in the early 1990s.

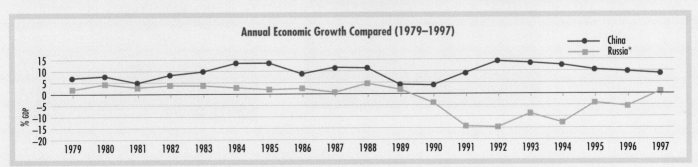

Annual Economic Growth Compared (1979–1997)

Compiled from *Zhongguo tongji nianjian* [Chinese Statistical Yearbook] and *Rossiiskii statisticheskii ezhegodnik* [Russian Statistical Yearbook]
*Refers to the Russian SFSR in the Soviet Union before 1991 and Russian Federation after 1992

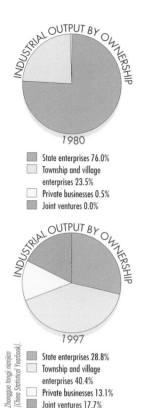

INDUSTRIAL OUTPUT BY OWNERSHIP

1980

- ■ State enterprises 76.0%
- ☐ Township and village enterprises 23.5%
- ☐ Private businesses 0.5%
- ■ Joint ventures 0.0%

INDUSTRIAL OUTPUT BY OWNERSHIP

1997

- ■ State enterprises 28.8%
- ☐ Township and village enterprises 40.4%
- ☐ Private businesses 13.1%
- ■ Joint ventures 17.7%

Zhongguo tongji nianjian (China Statistical Yearbook).

China's emerging private sector consists of privately-owned businesses, collectively-owned township and village enterprises, peasant households, and joint ventures between foreign companies and domestic Chinese firms.

LEFT: A woman entrepreneur selling clothing in the Chongqing market.

RIGHT: A logging truck owned by a township and village enterprise near Wuhan.

Emerging Private Sector

Since the announcement of the Four Modernizations by Deng in 1978, the government has initiated various policies to build up the private sector in the economy. The private sector is the most rapidly growing sector of the Chinese economy. It is diverse and includes privately-owned businesses, collectively-owned township and village enterprises, peasant households, and foreign joint ventures. All are allowed to make decisions about production and distribution, sell goods and services, and keep the profits. In 1997, the private sector accounted for 71.2% of total industrial output, compared to 24% in 1980 (see charts, left).

Private Businesses

In China, private businesses are defined as businesses owned by a household or an individual and employing no more than seven people. They are generally located in urban areas and operate in the service sector. The most common types of private businesses are restaurants, hair salons, retail stores, and small-scale manufacturing. In 1997, individually-owned businesses employed an estimated 60 million people and accounted for 13.1% of total industrial output.

Phyllis A. Arnold

Township and Village Enterprises

Township and village enterprises were established in 1979–81, when peasant communes were disbanded. These enterprises were allowed to sell their product at market prices, retain profits, and set wages based on productivity. They were not required to follow planned production targets and were to operate according to market conditions. They were not obliged to provide social support services and could employ workers according to need. Many have been organized to operate as partnerships between private individuals and the local community.

Today, township and village enterprises are an important part of the national economy and the mainstay of the rural economy. In 1997, there were more than 23.4 million township and village enterprises. They employed almost 140 million people and produced 40.4% of total industrial output. Enterprises produce consumer goods and construction materials, provide transport and communication services, and export consumer goods overseas. To the government, these enterprises are important sources of employment in rural areas.

However, these enterprises do face problems. Every year, thousands of them go bankrupt, largely because of lack of capital. They also encounter difficulties in transporting their goods because of lack of good roads, poor communication services, and restrictions on the movement of goods between regions. They often lack expertise and capital to become major players in overseas trade.

Glen BonBernard

Peasant Households

The largest segment of the private sector is the more than 250 million peasant households that farm the land under the contract responsibility system introduced in 1979. Under this system, the household is given the right to use the land for a specified period of time, usually 49 years. For the use of the land, the household sells to the government a fixed portion of its harvest at low prices set by the state. The remaining portion can be sold in village markets or to private businesses for profit. All land is collectively owned and cannot be sold to individuals. However, households can transfer the right to use the land to others.

Since 1979, the contract responsibility system has raised household incomes in the villages. Between 1979 and 1985, agricultural output increased by 55%, an unprecedented rise. Many peasant households also specialized in the production of vegetables and fruits and the raising of fish, cattle, and pigs for sale to city dwellers with higher incomes.

Many peasant households were able to use their increased incomes to buy cosumer goods like bicycles and television sets for the first time. Some prosperous households built new houses, while others invested their profits in small manufacturing businesses. However, many peasant households continued to face economic hardship.

After a brief period of slow growth in the late 1980s because of falling production and grain prices, farm incomes have risen since 1990, although not as rapidly as in the early 1980s. One factor cited by government officials is the reduction of good farmland. Millions of hectares of farmland have been taken out of production for the construction of new housing and village factories. This has made it difficult for rural areas to feed and employ their growing populations. Consequently, over 120 million peasants have abandoned farming and moved to the cities to get work and a wage to support their families in rural areas.

Phyllis A. Arnold

Joint Ventures

A joint venture is a business owned by a foreign firm and a domestic Chinese firm. Foreign companies like McDonald's, Pizza Hut, Sony, Toshiba, and IBM participate in joint ventures. Many joint ventures are set up to export manufactured goods abroad. They enjoy various tax breaks and other incentives to import technology and equipment. Most are located in the special economic zones and development districts in large cities. Joint ventures employ over 17 million people. In 1997, they produced 17.7% of total industrial output and over 35% of total exports.

Unlike in China, economic reforms in Russia did not significantly change the agricultural sector. Collective and state farms became enterprises and private farms were encouraged. However, collective and state farms in many regions of Russia are quite resistant to the reestablishment of private farms.

RIGHT: Annually, several million workers migrate from their villages to Shanghai and other urban centres to work in construction, manufacturing, and services.

LEFT: Peasant homes in Sichuan province.

The State Statistical Bureau reported in early 1998 that, of the top 500 foreign firms operating in China, 241 were from Hong Kong SAR, 71 from Japan, 52 from the United States, 36 from the European Union, and 100 from other countries. Guangdong province is home to 173 of these firms. The largest Canadian firm in China is Nortel, manufacturing cellular phones.

Phyllis A. Arnold

Special Economic Zones

When the government adopted a policy of "open-door" to open up China to the world, it created special economic zones (SEZ). Officially, their objectives were to import foreign technology, attract foreign capital, and develop Chinese trade with the outside world. To accomplish these goals, the government introduced low taxes on the profits of foreign-owned companies in the SEZ and special treatment for the import of equipment and raw materials used in producing goods for exports. The SEZ were given special administrative powers to regulate business and received funding from Beijing. Today, almost 25% of the country's total export trade comes from the six special economic zones.

Shenzhen. The first special economic zone was established at Shenzhen, bordering on Hong Kong. A collection of small villages in 1980, by 1998 Shenzhen had become a large sprawling modern city of over 2.6 million people, containing thousands of factories manufacturing a wide range of consumer goods for export. Today Shenzhen is a leading manufacturing and export centre, and home of one of the country's largest stock exchanges.

Zhuhai. Established near Macau in 1980 to attract investment from Macau and Hong Kong, Zhuhai has become an important manufacturing and service centre for offshore oil exploration.

Xiamen. Created in Fujian province in August 1980 to attract foreign investment from Taiwan, the Xiamen SEZ today is a major manufacturing centre for the production of shoes and clothing, which were once produced in Taiwan. The main export markets of goods from Xiamen are in North America.

Shantou. Shantou SEZ was created in August 1980 to develop an export processing industry in northeastern Guangdong province and a supply base for offshore oil exploration.

Hainan Island. In April 1988, Hainan province was made a special economic zone in order to develop one of the country's poorest regions.

Pudong. Plans for the development of the Pudong SEZ, established outside Shanghai in 1990, included the creation of the country's largest stock exchange and an international banking centre which can compete with Hong Kong, Singapore, and Tokyo.

Before 1949, Shanghai was China's financial centre and a major banking centre in East Asia. When the Communists took over in 1949, thousands of Shanghai business people fled to Hong Kong, which they developed into a major financial centre. Under Communist rule, Shanghai's stock exchange was closed and its banks nationalized. The Shanghai Stock Exchange was reopened in December 1990.

Economic Development Zones. In 1984, the government established economic development zones in fourteen coastal cities. The objective of those development zones was initially to attract capital from foreigners and overseas Chinese investors for upgrading existing facilities rather than to build new ones. The development zones were given special incentives similar to the SEZ to attract foreign capital, but they had to support themselves without funding from Beijing. They also did not get the special administrative powers of the SEZ but could make their own policies to attract foreign investment. Since 1990, the role of economic development zones has expanded to promoting industrial development in non-coastal regions of the country.

PHOTO: A view of the Shenzhen International Trade Center.

Phyllis A. Arnold

Foreign Trade

In 1997, China was the world's tenth largest exporter and twelfth largest importer of goods. The country's exports totalled US$182.9 billion and imports US$142.2 billion in 1997, an unprecedented increase since 1950.

Trading Partners. In the 1950s, foreign trade had been confined largely to the Soviet Union and Eastern Europe, because few Western countries had diplomatic relations with China. The establishment of diplomatic relations with Canada, Japan, the United States, and other Western countries in the 1970s opened up new markets for Chinese goods. The country's main trading partners in 1997 were Japan, Hong Kong SAR, the United States, and the European Union (see chart "China's Top Trading Partners"). Hong Kong SAR is China's main outlet for trade with the rest of the world.

Exports and Imports. For decades, China exported mainly raw materials, textiles, and foodstuffs, and imported machinery, equipment, metal products, and occasionally grain. This began to change in the late 1980s and early 1990s. The main exports in 1997 were manufactured consumer goods, textiles, and semi-processed raw materials. Imports mainly consisted of industrial equipment, semi-processed metals, chemicals, paper, lumber, and foodstuffs.

Role in the Economy. Despite China's emergence as a major trading nation, international economists have noted that roughly half of the country's foreign trade has little effect on the domestic economy. Joint ventures between foreign firms and domestic Chinese enterprises in the special economic zones import raw materials, then process them into finished goods for export. If trade figures are adjusted to exclude the processing of imports, the country's economy is shown to be less dependent on foreign trade for economic growth.

Human Rights Issue. Since 1990, the issue of human rights has complicated China's relations with some of its trading partners. American, Canadian, and some European governments have protested publicly about China's harsh treatment of dissidents and violations of its citizens' human rights. The American and Canadian governments have from time to time exerted economic and political pressure on China to improve its human rights record. However, these disagreements have not stopped the United States, Canada, and other countries from trading with China.

Phyllis A. Arnold

Foreign Investment

When the first special economic zones were created in 1980, foreign investment was almost non-existent and confined to a few small joint ventures. Since then, foreign capital has flowed into China, attracted by special tax incentives, cheap labour, and the prospect of producing goods for the world's largest developing market. In 1997, China was the most popular destination for foreign investors. The State Statistical Bureau announced in August 1998 that at the end of June 1998 the total value of foreign investment in China had reached US$242.3 billion, making the country the second largest recipient of international investment after the United States. Over 50% of this foreign capital came from overseas Chinese living in Hong Kong SAR, Taiwan, and Singapore (see charts "Source of Foreign Investment").

CHINA'S TOP TRADING PARTNERS
1997

Direction of Trade Statistics, June 1998

- Japan 18.8%
- Hong Kong SAR 15.5%
- United States 15.1%
- European Union 13.2%
- Southeast Asia 7.5%
- South Korea 7.3%
- Taiwan 6.2%
- Canada 1.2%
- Other countries 15.2%

PHOTO: In 1997, China exported to Canada goods worth C$5.7 billion, mainly clothing, footwear and other consumer goods, and imported C$2.45 billion from Canada, consisting of foodstuffs, equipment, and minerals.

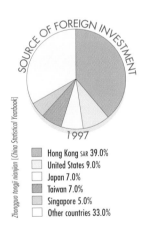

SOURCE OF FOREIGN INVESTMENT
1997

Zhongguo tongji nianjian [China Statistical Yearbook]

- Hong Kong SAR 39.0%
- United States 9.0%
- Japan 7.0%
- Taiwan 7.0%
- Singapore 5.0%
- Other countries 33.0%

State-owned enterprises dominate many industries. The following are percentage shares of state-owned enterprises in output by industry recorded in 1996.

Oil	95%
Tobacco	92
Refining	83
Water supply	78
Coal	65
Electricity	64
Natural gas	63
Steel making	62
Mining	53
Vehicle production	51
Pharmaceuticals	50
Chemicals	48
Food processing	45
Textiles	37
Electronics	30

Zhongguo tongji nianjian [China Statistical Yearbook]

Public Sector

Deng's economic reforms also meant significant changes in the public sector. They included the decentralization of central planning, reform of state-owned enterprises, and a restructuring of the social security system.

Central Planning

Central planning was introduced in China with the First Five Year Plan (1953–1957) under Mao. It closely resembled the Soviet system. The basic questions of production and distribution of goods and services and the allocation of resources were decided by central planners in Beijing. A State Planning Commission (SPC) set production quotas for every major industry and region of the country. Industrial ministries allocated these production quotas to planning departments, which administered state-owned enterprises under their control.

Since 1978, the role of central planning has been largely limited to heavy industry. Where private enterprise is extensive, production quotas have been replaced by state purchases of goods and services. Overall, planning is now decentralized and state-owned enterprises have some control over production and distribution of their goods.

In Beijing, the State Planning Commission still drafts plans for the overall economy, but production quotas are prepared only for heavy industry and some key sectors of the economy, such as banking, telecommunications, and railroads. Planners now consider current economic conditions and changes in supply and demand when drawing up their plans. In the provinces, plans are prepared and production targets are allocated to provincially-supervised state-owned enterprises.

Since 1988, all state-owned enterprises have been given specific targets to fulfil. Production over the specified quota can be sold in the marketplace. The introduction of this contract responsibility system for state-owned enterprises has led to less direct government intervention and more reliance on market prices. By 1997, there was state control over only 30 types of industrial goods and price controls on 7.2% of state-produced goods.

State Enterprises

China has 305 000 state-owned enterprises, and of these about 118 000 are industrial enterprises. Some are profitable but most are inefficient and unprofitable. Improving the efficiency and profitability of state enterprises has been a long and difficult task for the government.

In 1988, the government enacted the Law on State Enterprises to transform its state-owned enterprises into independent organizations responsible for their own profits and losses. Enterprises were allowed to keep any after-tax profits. Management was given more freedom to determine what goods and services to produce and how to produce them. Prior to the reforms, state-owned enterprises had little control over their production. They were forced to transfer profits to the state and relied on the government for subsidies to cover losses and grants for investment. Central planners set wages, and management was mainly responsible for fulfilling production quotas.

The Law on State Enterprises did not end all price controls. Production quotas for the sale of output to the government continued to be an important part of most contracts. As well, state-owned enterprises continued to have access to low-priced raw materials, low-interest bank credit, and government subsidies.

In the early 1990s, the number of unprofitable state-owned enterprises rose significantly. In 1997, nearly two-thirds of them operated at a loss. Many of these troubled firms remained in business by borrowing from state-owned banks. Very few state-owned enterprises were successful in cutting production costs, increasing sales, and improving their efficiency. The government estimated in early 1998 that these enterprises owed four state-owned banks 1.5 trillion renminbi (US$180 billion), much of which may never be repaid. This amount, roughly one-fifth of GDP, forced the central government in early 1998 to provide

US$35 billion in subsidies to prevent a collapse of the banking sector, which might have seriously destabilized the economy.

The government is faced with a dilemma. To protect people's savings and the banking sector, it may have to lay off several million workers to increase the efficiency of state-owned enterprises. This measure could lead to massive unemployment and worker unrest, and damage the economy. If state enterprises do not lay off workers and continue to rely on bank loans to stay in business, the government will face giving additional subsidies to the banking sector to save it from collapse. The result could be high inflation, falling living standards, and a weak economy.

In early 1998, the government announced a policy to reduce the number of state employees by one-half and privatize most state-owned enterprises in the early years of the 21st century. The government hopes that the economy will continue to grow rapidly and will create enough jobs for the estimated 40 million workers who will be laid off. The problem of revitalizing the country's failing state-owned enterprises is particularly felt in northeast China, where much of the country's heavy industry is located.

Social Security

The restructuring of state-owned enterprises is complicated by the fact that these enterprises are responsible for providing social security to workers. The country's social security system was set up in 1951 and modelled on that of the former Soviet Union. All social security expenditures are funded by the government and state-owned enterprises. State-owned enterprises provide housing, education, and medical care for their employees and families for a small monthly charge. An estimated 250 million people are covered under this comprehensive social security scheme. These benefits are supplemented by job security, paid vacations, and old-age pensions for seniors. Chinese refer to these benefits and guarantees as the "iron rice bowl."

However, the iron rice bowl does not extend to over one billion people who live in the countryside or are employed in private businesses. Before 1978, the communes offered peasants a package of basic social services, known as the "five guarantees"—food, clothing, fuel, primary education, and decent burial for the elderly. They also gave some financial assistance to the elderly, widows, orphans, and the destitute. "Barefoot doctors" provided basic medical attention and traditional herbal medicines. When the communes were disbanded between 1979 and 1981, the social security net shrank dramatically. By 1990, less than two percent of the rural population was covered by any form of social security.

The present dilemma facing the government is how to establish a social security system that can cover the country's 800 million peasants fairly and inexpensively. The government does not have the financial resources to implement a nationwide social security system for many years to come. In the meantime, peasants are forced to rely on their personal savings and family during times of need. These new realities have had a dramatic impact on the lives of those affected by the changes.

Another issue that complicates the social security question is the long-term problem of an aging population. China's population is aging rapidly, a process accelerated by the one-child family policy of the late 1970s and the 1980s, and increased life expectancy. About 9.8% of the population was older than 60 years in 1997. Demographers predict that the percentage of elderly in the population by 2020 will reach 16%. Life expectancy is forecast to rise from 69 years in 1995 to 73 years by 2020. By the year 2050, there will be about 400 million people over the age of 60 and 160 million over 80. Taken together, the public sector faces a challenge of how to develop a self-supporting pension program that can provide the country's growing numbers of elderly with sufficient income, a problem that faces most richer industrial nations today.

The Chinese government estimated the number of people receiving state pensions at 33.2 million in 1997 (total Canadian population was 30.1 million). The age of retirement in China is 55 years for women and 60 years for men (in Canada 65 years for both sexes).

CHINESE POLITICAL ECONOMY

Advance Organizer

From 1949 to 1978, all political and economic matters were decided by the Communist Party, which worked to build a communist society in China. Since 1978, the Communist leadership has launched moderate pragmatic reforms to modernize Chinese society. These reforms have greatly improved the lives of millions of ordinary Chinese citizens, encouraged personal initiative and creativity, and expanded foreign relations with the rest of the world. However, the reforms have also brought corruption, growing income inequality, unemployment, inflation, and mounting environmental problems.

SECTION OVERVIEW

- Consequences of Economic Reforms
- Future of Hong Kong and Taiwan

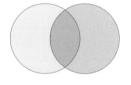

☐ Chinese Political System
☐ Chinese Economic System
▨ Chinese Political Economy

Consequences of Economic Reforms

Deng's economic reforms, despite their many benefits, have raised new and unexpected issues for the country. Corruption, rising income inequality, unemployment, inflation, and a deteriorating environment, in many cases associated with industrialization and urbanization, have accompanied the more positive changes in China.

Corruption

When the Communists took power in 1949, they arrested, imprisoned, and even executed some corrupt officials for their misdeeds. The country's new leaders attempted to project an image of honesty, dedication, and sacrifice.

In the 1980s, economic reforms provided opportunities for Communist Party and government officials to enrich themselves through personal connections and influence. At the 15th Party Congress in September 1997, General Secretary Jiang Zemin said that the continued existence of the Communist Party depended on ending corruption among party leaders, in the government, and throughout the country.

The fight against corruption is a grave political struggle vital to the very existence of the Party and state. Our Party can never be daunted and vanquished by an enemy. But the easiest way to capture a fortress is from within, so in no way should we destroy ourselves. If corruption cannot be punished effectively, our Party will lose the confidence and support of the people. We should fight corruption and continuously heed the warning throughout the process of reform and opening to the outside world. We should be mentally prepared to fight a protracted war against corruption, and we should win battles one by one and stage by stage. We should continue to make sure that leading cadres are clean, honest, and self-disciplined, investigate and deal with major cases, and rectify unsound practices in departments and trades. Party committees at all levels must take a clear-cut stand and firmly persevere in this work.

People's Liberation Army in Business.
In July 1998, Jiang Zemin ordered the People's Liberation Army (PLA) to confine its activities to military matters and end its involvement in business.

The army and armed police forces must earnestly carry out checks on all kinds of commercial companies set up by subsidiary units, and without exception from today must not engage in their operation.

The PLA has long been China's most powerful institution and interest group. Since 1949, it has been a dominant force in maintaining Communist rule over the country. All Communist leaders have depended on the PLA for support. Deng's close ties with the PLA and the support he received helped him attain his position in the Communist Party. At the beginning of the Four Modernizations in 1979, Deng allowed the military to open up businesses to finance its operations. By 1997, the military owned or controlled between 10 000 and 20 000 companies that earned an estimated US$9.5 billion annually from the production of cars, pharmaceuticals, chemicals, and electrical goods and from tourism and hotel management, real estate, and finance.

The closing down of PLA companies was in line with Jiang Zemin's anti-corruption policy announced in September 1997. Several high ranking government officials noted that the PLA risked becoming a source of corruption because of its involvement in commercial activities. As well, the PLA risked serious conflicts of interest when it devoted more of its attention to deal-making than to the task of national defence. By pulling the PLA out of business, the government hopes to reduce the size of the armed forces and create a more professional fighting force.

Glen BonBernard

Income Inequality

Income inequality was present in China before 1978, but the government attempted to keep income differences between occupations, regions, and city and countryside low. It spread the growth of industry throughout all regions of the country so that differences in living standards among social groups and between the rural and and urban workers remained small.

Under Deng, this policy was abandoned in favour of promoting economic growth and development by private businesses. Since 1979, income distribution has become more concentrated in the hands of the richest 20% of the population. In 1995, this group controlled 47.5% of total income in the country, while the poorest 40% had 15.3%, a decline from 18.4% in 1979 (see chart "Income Distribution in China").

Income Distribution in China (1979–1995)		
Income Group	1979	1995
Top 20%	39.3%	47.5%
Second 20%	24.8	22.3
Middle 20%	17.5	14.9
Fourth 20%	11.0	9.8
Lowest 20%	7.4	5.5
Totals	100.0	100.0

Compiled from *World Bank Development Indicators*

More importantly, the government noted that although living standards of Chinese citizens have improved as their incomes rose, significant differences in incomes exist between urban and rural areas. The State Statistical Bureau reported that in 1997 the average disposable income was 5160 yuan (US$625) for urban residents and 2090 yuan (US$255) for people in rural areas. Surveys of spending by urban households reveal that, while most households have a TV set, refrigerator, and washing machine, a growing number now also own a VCR, microwave oven, and pager (see chart "Household Ownership").

The establishment of special economic zones and the opening of coastal cities to foreign trade have widened income differences between coastal provinces and the

World Bank estimated that the number of Chinese people in poverty (less than US$1 a day per capita) fell from 568.9 million, or 59.5% of the population in 1978, to 269.3 million, or 22.2% of the population in 1995.

In a survey of urban households in 12 cities, the State Statistical Bureau reported that many households in 1998 had increased their ownership of consumer goods.

Household Ownership
(% of total)
TV	97%
Refrigerator	88
Washing machine	87
Hot water heater	60
Pager	36
Air conditioner	34
VCR	28
Microwave oven	23
Mobile telephone	12
Motorcycle	9
Personal computer	8
Private car	3

Compiled from Wei Bian, "City Dwellers Surveyed on Consumption." *Beijing Review*. September 7–13,1998. p. 23.

PHOTO: A small but growing class of affluent Chinese now enjoys a "Western lifestyle" and access to a wide range of services, such as automated banking.

interior. Today, China is characterized by wide income inequality among regions. The richest regions of the country are located along the coast (see map below) and the poorest regions are situated in the interior.

The coastal area contains a high percentage of the country's arable land and so has long had higher population density. It was industrialized early and had access to internal trade along China's rivers and overseas from the coast. In Shanghai, a coastal city, the average per capita income is 10 times greater than that in Guizhou, a southern province. By comparison, in Canada the difference in incomes between the highest (Ontario) and the lowest (Newfoundland) does not exceed two times.

Provincial incomes above national average
Provincial incomes at national average
Provincial incomes below national average

Regional Income Inequality, 1997

Zhongguo tongji nianjian [China Statistical Yearbook]

Unemployment

Officially, in 1997 over fifteen million people in the cities were classified as unemployed. In reality, the number of unemployed is much higher. The official figures do not take into consideration persons who work in occupations unrelated to their training and education, which may number several million more. Also, the official statistics do not count the number of unemployed in rural areas. The government estimated that in 1997 almost 35% of the rural labour force, or 175 million people, were subsisting on seasonal work or unemployed. Since 1994, the government also estimated that as many as 120 million peasants have left their villages for the cities and coastal provinces in search of work and a steady wage as construction labourers, restaurant help, and street vendors.

Women suffer disproportionately from unemployment. Government studies in 1997 found that in Shanghai and several provinces up to one-half of all eligible female workers were jobless. These women, as in many other countries, also faced discrimination by employers when seeking new jobs. In a survey of Chinese employers, the main reason for not employing women was the cost of maternity leave. Many employers did not want to be responsible for paying this benefit.

Inflation

For decades, the government proclaimed that inflation did not exist in China because the state set all prices. Inflation did not appear in the form of price increases but as shortages and long line-ups in the stores. Following the gradual removal of price controls and the establishment of market prices for most goods and services in the 1980s and early 1990s, inflation appeared. For most Chinese families, basic necessities such as food, clothing, and shelter are the main expenses and any increase in their price has an immediate impact on standard of living. The government reintroduced price controls on some basic goods following large price increases in 1988–1989. They were relaxed again in 1991–1992, but high demand and a booming economy in 1993–1995 caused them to be reintroduced. In 1997, the inflation rate fell to less than 1% from 6.1% in 1996 because of a slowing economy and measures by the government to prevent the prices of basic foods from escalating beyond the reach of ordinary Chinese citizens.

Deteriorating Environment

Since the early 1990s, the government has been confronted with finding a solution to the country's rapidly deteriorating environment. As in most other nations that have industrialized, industrial development has had a great impact on the environment. China's water and air have become heavily polluted as a result of industrial development and population pressures. Valuable renewable resources such as forests and soil have become depleted through overuse. Urbanization is using up scarce farmland and threatening the country's capacity to feed its population.

China's National Environmental Protection Agency recognizes that the country has some of most polluted places in the world. Annually, industry dumps hundreds of millions of tonnes of toxic waste and untreated water into the country's major rivers. It has been officially reported that up to one-fifth of the country's river water can no longer be used to irrigate farmland. About 75% of China's energy needs are met by coal, which is generally of low quality, untreated, and burned from relatively low smokestacks. Most cities are shrouded in smog, which contributes to respiratory ailments like bronchitis among a large portion of urban residents. Measures to clean up emissions and shut down polluting factories were introduced by the government in 1998 in response to public complaints about environmental degradation.

Soil erosion and desertification are serious environmental problems. The main cause is deforestation. Much of the country's forest has been cut down to supply industry and provide wood for new homes. Most forests are now located in remote areas and on the tops of mountains. Loss of forest cover has contributed to increased soil erosion, more floods, and droughts. Other causes for soil erosion are the intensive use of agricultural land and overgrazing of pasturelands. Efforts to plant more trees were announced in late 1998 after preliminary reports by the National Environmental Protection Agency indicated that much of the country's widespread flooding in August 1998 was caused by poor forest and land conservation practices.

In 1992, the government approved the construction of the Three Gorges Dam on the Chang Jiang (Yangtze River), but not without considerable debate. Supporters of the project argued that the dam will increase the supply of non-polluting hydroelectrical power, improve transportation, and control flooding downstream. After wide areas were inundated downstream in August 1998, supporters claimed that the dam would prevent such flooding from occurring in the future. Critics countered that the project could have potentially catastrophic effects on the environment. They charged that, besides forcing the resettlement of some 1.6 million people, the project would destroy rare plants and animals, as well as flood several million hectares of fertile farmland.

Urbanization and industrialization have had a tremendous impact on the country's scarce farmland. Since 1979, several million hectares of fertile farmland have been taken out of production for housing, factories, office buildings, and roads, reducing total farmland for food production, although the country has been able to increase grain production to 492.5 million tons in 1997 (see chart "Grain Production"). In a country where population grows annually by 13.5 million people, any reduction in scarce farmland will weaken the country's future capacity to feed its people and mean greater dependence on imported foodstuffs.

Deserts and desertified areas cover 2.62 million square kilometres or one-third of China's total land area.

Grain Production
(1980–1997)
(in million of tons)

1980	320.56
1982	354.50
1984	407.31
1987	402.98
1990	404.00
1995	455.50
1997	492.50

Zhongguo tongji nianjian [China Statistical Yearbook].

Phyllis A. Arnold

PHOTO: A view of the Three Gorges Dam under construction on the Chang Jiang river.

Future of Hong Kong and Taiwan

On July 1, 1998, Jiang Zemin visited Hong Kong to celebrate the first anniversary of its return to Chinese control. He remarked:

The developments in the year since Hong Kong's return have fully demonstrated that adherence to the policies of "one country, two systems," "Hong Kong people administering Hong Kong," and a high degree of autonomy and strict compliance with the Basic Law of the HKSAR [Hong Kong Special Administrative Region] *constitute the fundamental guarantee for long-term prosperity and stability in Hong Kong. Practice will continue to prove that the policy of "one country, two systems" will not only help safeguard the interests of people of different social strata in Hong Kong, but also maintain Hong Kong's status as the international financial, trading, and shipping centre. There is every reason to believe that as long as this correct policy is consistently followed, Hong Kong will be able to create a better future with the support of the mainland. There is also every reason to believe that the successful implementation of the policy of "one country, two systems" will serve as an example for Macau's smooth return to the motherland and for the final settlement of the Taiwan question.*

Since China announced its policy of "one country, two systems" in 1982, the country has benefited economically. Between 1982 and 1998, the wealthy business communities of Hong Kong, Macau, and Taiwan invested an estimated US$120 billion (almost one-half of total foreign investment) in equipment and new businesses in China.

In 1998, an international financial crisis and recession in East Asia threatened to sharply reduce the flow of capital from Hong Kong and Taiwanese investors to China.

Hong Kong

A financial crisis began in Thailand with devaluation of its currency in early July 1997 and quickly spread throughout Southeast Asia. In November 1997, the crisis hit South Korea. One contributing factor was the heavy indebtedness of many East Asian businesses. In the early 1990s, many firms borrowed heavily to build new factories, assuming that the East Asian economy would continue to grow rapidly well into the 21st century. In 1997, economic growth in the region slowed as consumers reduced their spending. Firms began to have difficulties selling their production and repaying bank loans. North American, European, and Japanese investors reacted to the unfavourable news by withdrawing their money from the region, which deepened the crisis.

In 1998, the financial crisis pushed Hong Kong into a recession, its first since 1975. The Hong Kong stock market fell and some financial companies went bankrupt. The stock market drop prompted many Hong Kong citizens to become pessimistic and cut their spending on goods and services. This forced businesses to lay off workers to cut costs and reduce investment plans in China. The Hong Kong SAR government, headed by Tung Chee-hwa, announced that they would increase public spending to bolster consumer confidence and attract foreign capital.

Taiwan

The Taiwanese economy did not escape the effects of the financial crisis in East Asia. Exports to Japan, South Korea, and Southeast Asia fell sharply. Domestic consumer and business spending slowed, prompting the government to announce an economic stimulus package of public spending on roads, housing, and rapid transit. Government economists forecast that the economy would grow about 5% in 1998, largely due to its stronger banking sector and lower business debt.

In October 1998, high-level talks on Taiwan's reunification with China resumed after a three year hiatus. Though the Chinese government welcomed this positive development, not all Taiwanese find China's policy of "one country, two systems" very persuasive or reassuring. Many believe that Taiwan will remain separate from China well into the 21st century.

REVIEW

Summary

In the 20th century, China has experienced considerable political instability, wars, and revolutions. In 1949, communist forces led by Mao Zedong took Beijing, proclaimed the People's Republic of China, and began to implement policies to build a communist society in China.

Since 1949, Chinese politics has been dominated by the Communist Party. It controls all branches of government and all political organizations in the country. Its political power and authority is maintained by controls on public participation in the political process, propaganda, and indoctrination, as well as constitutional means. When necessary, the government has used public security agencies and the People's Liberation Army to suppress dissent and opposition to communist one-party rule.

From 1949 to 1976, Mao Zedong attempted to create a centrally planned economy in which all economic questions about production and distribution of goods and allocation of resources would be decided in the interests of workers and peasants. Mao's economic policies were successful in promoting a fair distribution of incomes among the people, but disastrous for long-term economic growth, productivity, and living standards.

Mao's successor, Deng Xiaoping, understood that the country needed to transform its economic system and raise living standards of the ordinary Chinese citizen. From 1979 to 1997, Deng implemented numerous economic reforms, allowing individuals more freedom to decide questions of production and distribution. The government continued to make decisions about the allocation of resources in the country. Deng's economic reforms brought an unprecedented rise in the Chinese people's living standards.

However, this prosperity has brought considerable change to Chinese society. The country today faces many serious social and economic problems such as corruption, income inequality, unemployment, inflation, and the deteriorating environment.

Chinese Values and Political Philosophy

1. Do the core values (pages 412–413) seem to indicate that China will remain a dictatorship or will it move toward being a democracy? Provide evidence to support your opinion.

2. a) How were the "Four Cardinal Principles" of Deng Xiaoping a radical departure from Mao's attacks on the "four olds" (page 408)?

   b) What was the main goal that Deng's policies were intended to achieve?

3. What is meant by the phrase "building socialism with Chinese characteristics"?

4. When Jiang Zemin says that "Socialism is the primary stage of communism and China is in the primary stage of socialism," (page 414) he is saying that China
   A. does not need or want communism
   B. should be a socialist, not a communist state
   C. must be a socialist state before it can achieve communism
   D. needs to have a market-oriented dictatorship, not communism

5. Explain the concept of the "people's democratic dictatorship." Where on the following continuum would you place the People's Republic of China in 1998?

   democracy ⊢――――――⊢――――――⊣ dictatorship

6. How does the Communist Party justify its continued leadership?

7. a) Explain the link between Marxism and Mao Zedong Thought.
   b) In the words of Jiang Zemin, how is Deng Xiaoping Theory a continuation of Mao Zedong Thought?

8. Examine the cartoon on page 415. To what extent does the cartoonist see Jiang Zemin as an innovative thinker?

Chinese Political System

1. a) Which powers make the President the most powerful person in the government?

   b) How would the balance of power change if the same person held the top positions in the government and the party?

2. How powerful is the legislative branch in China compared to Canada? Provide evidence from the text to support your view.

3. a) Why has it been important for the Chinese Communist Party to include the military in the government?

   b) How does the relationship between the military and the government differ in a democracy?

4. Explain the differences between the roles of the political parties in Canada and the role of the Communist Party in China.

5. What does the chart on page 416 tell us about the position of the Chinese people in the Chinese political system?

6. Explain the theory of "democratic centralism." How is the practice different from the theory?

7. Compare party discipline in Canadian politics (page 137) with the kind of discipline that is exercised within the Chinese Communist Party.

8. Both Canada and the United States have chosen the federal system of government, giving provincial and state governments some powers over local matters. Given the diverse nature of China, why would the Chinese choose a unitary system instead?

9. Compare the status of Hong Kong, Macau, and Taiwan.

10. Explain why, in reality, the National People's Congress and the National Party Congress have very little law making power. What are the advantages for the Communist Party of having controlled participation in the electoral process?

11. What generalizations can you make about the control of the media in China?

12. The SARs[1], the internet, and increased foreign trade and travel are making it more difficult for the government to control the flow of information. Why is this a problem for a dictatorship?

13. The Chinese Communist Party has believed that the youth are important in creating a communist society and in China becoming a world power. How important have the Red Guards, the Young Pioneers, Young Communists, and the new school curricula been to the attainment of these goals?

14. China has a constitution that gives its people rights and liberties, as does the Canadian constitution.

    a) What must Chinese citizens do to enjoy these rights?

    b) In reality, do Chinese citizens enjoy the same rights as Canadians?

15. Briefly describe the system of public security. Which core values (page 413) does this system reflect?

16. a) Describe the various roles of the People's Liberation Army (PLA).

[1] Special Administrative Regions

b) How is the role of the Canadian Armed Forces both similar to and different from that of the PLA?

17. Read the Focus On Critical Thinking on pages 428–429. Compare the Official View with the Personal Account.

a) To what extent are the two accounts in agreement? Provide examples.

b) In what important ways do the accounts differ? Provide examples.

c) As the Prime Minister of Canada, which of the following actions would you have taken? Provide arguments to support your choice.

A. Take no action because this was an internal matter.

B. Send a formal complaint and remind the Chinese government of the importance of human rights.

C. Publicly condemn the Chinese government and demand the release of student demonstrators from prison.

D. Suspend trade and diplomatic relations with China until they agree to respect human rights.

Chinese Economic System

1. 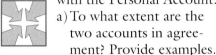 Examine the chart on page 430.

a) To what extent will the role of the consumer change under private enterprise compared to the 1949–1977 period?

b) How will job security be affected once the transformation is complete?

2. Why did the Deng Xiaoping government decide to move away from centralized planning?

3. Explain each of the following and describe how each contributes to the development of the Chinese economy:

a) Four Modernizations/building socialism with Chinese characteristics

b) socialist market economy

c) Special Economic Zones

d) open door policy/joint ventures

4. Read the Focus On Critical Thinking on page 433.

a) Briefly summarize the reasons why the World Bank feels that China's economic transformation has been more successful than that of Russia.

b) To what extent do you agree that China was wise not to introduce democratic reforms?

c) Examine the graph on page 433. What effects do you think these different growth rates have had on workers and consumers? Be prepared to discuss your answers.

5. a) On a chart, describe and show the importance of the following to the evolving Chinese economy: private businesses, township and village enterprises, peasant households, joint ventures, Special Economic Zones

b) What benefits and problems have these developments created?

6. a) What have been the advantages and disadvantages of increased foreign trade in recent years?

b) To what extent has increased foreign trade between China and other countries been beneficial economically and in other ways? Be prepared to discuss your ideas with others.

7. What percentage of China's foreign trade is with Asian countries (pie chart, page 437)? To what extent is China overly dependent on Asian markets?

8. a) Central planning on the Soviet model existed from 1953 until the late 1970s. What changes have been made to central planning since then?

b) How have the importance and operation of state enterprises changed since 1988?

c) What was the iron rice bowl and to whom did it apply?

d) What difficulties are faced by the Chinese government in providing for adequate social security?

e) Provide two or three generalizations describing how the role of government in the economy has changed since the late 1970s.

Chinese Political Economy

1. a) Explain the consequences of corruption for China.

   b) Why did the PLA become involved in business? To what extent do you think the armed forces should be in private business?

   c) To what extent are income inequality and unemployment a problem? Why do women suffer from unemployment more than men?

   d) To what extent is a deteriorating environment a serious problem? Provide examples to support your answer.

2. How might each of the following feel about the changes that have and are taking place in the Chinese economy?

   A. a worker in a state-owned factory

   B. the owner of the only bicycle shop in a small town

   C. a young man with university degrees in economics and computers

   D. a family that farms land on the edge of a large industrial city

Chapter Consolidation

1.   This chapter began with a quotation by Jiang Zemin spoken in September 1997. To what extent does socialism with Chinese characteristics reflect the ideas of Marx, Lenin, Stalin, and Mao Zedong?

2. 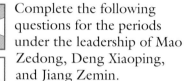 Complete the following questions for the periods under the leadership of Mao Zedong, Deng Xiaoping, and Jiang Zemin.

   a) On what values were/are the political and economic systems of China based?

   b) Whose ideas were/are influential in the development of the political and economic systems of China? Briefly explain the ideas and how they were/are applied in China.

   c) Create a chart, identifying the type of political system and economic system in China and the strengths and weaknesses of these systems.

PART

III

CHALLENGES
OF THE
21ST CENTURY

CONTEMPORARY ISSUES AND IDEAS

The 21st century, like the 20th, will be a time of great political and economic change. This section examines six possible challenges to be faced in the 21st century and how they may affect the world's political and economic systems.

Nationalism

Nationalism has been a source of considerable conflict in many parts of the world for much of the 20th century. In the first half of the century, the world witnessed the rise of various forms of extreme nationalism in Europe that resulted in the loss of millions of lives.

In the decades following 1945, as colonies of Great Britain, France, Netherlands, Germany, and Portugal became independent, nationalist sentiment grew in these and other areas and led to hundreds of ethnic conflicts throughout Africa and Asia. Many countries in Africa have populations composed of several ethnic groups, some of which have had little contact with other groups. This has led to a great deal of political turmoil in recent years.

Since the 1980s, nationalist feeling has found an outlet in the rise of fundamentalist religious movements in several countries in North Africa, the Middle East, and South Asia. Many people in these movements advocate a greater role for religious institutions in society and government. A small minority in these movements believe that the use of violence is necessary to achieve this goal.

In the early 1990s, following the collapse of communism, nationalism reemerged in the countries of Central and Eastern Europe. This led to the breakup of Czechoslovakia, Yugoslavia, and the Soviet Union. While Czechoslovakia divided itself peacefully, this was not the case for Yugoslavia. Conflict between several ethnic groups in regions of Yugoslavia resulted in the deaths of thousands of people and forced thousands more from their homes. The breakup of the Soviet Union into fifteen newly independent countries led to several conflicts and disputes among nationalities over borders and natural resources. In some of these conflicts, thousands of people died and thousands more were forced to flee the fighting. In Western Europe and Canada, nationalist movements have goals that call for greater autonomy, and in some cases for outright secession.

At the end of the 20th century, ethnic disputes have continued in many regions of the world. The challenge in the 21st century is for peoples to peaceably settle their differences, and for international agencies such as the United Nations to assist countries in finding peaceful settlements to ethnic disputes, while respecting people's rights and aspirations to self-determination. Recent international efforts to curb racism aim to promote greater inter-ethnic harmony through education and wider involvement of the global community.

Globalization

During the 20th century, the world became economically and politically interdependent. The lives of millions of people became dependent on what others did elsewhere. This led not only to an unprecedented growth in the movement of goods, capital, people, and ideas among countries, it also created opportunities for employment within countries, provided people with new types of goods, and raised living standards. Conflicts among countries became international, affecting not only the countries involved, but the entire world. World War I and World War II in the first half of the 20th century were examples of such conflicts.

In the 20th century, various international organizations were set up to resolve political and economic disputes. Some, such as the League of Nations, were not successful in ending wars and were later replaced. Since 1945, although international organizations like the United Nations have not been able to prevent conflicts from arising between nation states, they have helped prevent war from recurring on a global scale.

Economic interdependence among countries in the 20th century led to the development and growth of multinational corporations. Multinational corporations such as General Motors, Daimler Chrysler, Toyota, Hitachi, Hyundai, Alcan Aluminum, Electrolux, and others operate in many countries, producing and distributing goods for domestic consumption and international sales. These corporations make decisions about investment and employment that can influence the direction of a country's economy and policies. Often workers and regions have found themselves negatively affected as global corporations seek new opportunities, and abandon or reduce their activities in other areas.

At the end of the 20th century, no country or region could claim to be able to function independently of what was happening elsewhere in the world. The impact of global interdependence was clearly demonstrated in 1997–1998 when a financial crisis hit Thailand and then quickly spread throughout East Asia and into Eastern Europe. The crisis created an international flight of capital, which affected currencies, banking systems, and stock markets around the world. It also led to political changes in several countries in East Asia and in Russia.

As globalization draws systems, regions, and countries more tightly together, it also strengthens the power and influence of international organizations such as the World Bank and the International Monetary Fund (IMF). During the financial crisis of 1997–1998, the IMF was asked to provide loans to save the affected countries from economic collapse. In exchange for the loans, the IMF ordered these countries to restructure their banking systems, cut government spending, and reduce government controls over the economy.

The challenge in the 21st century will be for governments, the IMF, and the international investment community to work together to ensure that economic crises do not adversely affect countries elsewhere, while at the same time allowing goods, capital, people, and ideas to move freely between countries. The creation of the European Union and a pan-European currency, the euro, offers hope that the trend toward globalization and economic interdependence among countries will continue to benefit societies in the 21st century.

Technology and Information

During the 20th century, the growth of technology and information has been remarkable. It has drawn individuals, societies, systems, and countries together. Current electronic technology and information systems are bringing people together in a very personal way. It is changing the way many people perceive the world and their place in it. People no longer view the world only through the lens of their local communities, but also through global networks. This change in perception has important implications for all political and economic systems.

Public access to large amounts of information has made it more difficult for political elites to mobilize people to support particular policies. People are more aware of what is going on around the world and the impact of various policy choices. The rapid speed of electronic transmission of information means that people are quickly informed about events and can take appropriate action if they wish.

Technology is rapidly shaping all economic activities and systems. More information provides consumers with more choices. The internet and the development of electronic commerce is creating new products and markets and changing the way businesses and consumers interact. The internet has changed how people make financial transactions such as depositing and withdrawing money, travel, process and store data, communicate with others, and spend their leisure time. At the same time, the technology poses some threats to privacy, and has altered many people's activities and ways of working.

At the end of the 20th century the challenge will be to use technology and information to improve human existence. The development of new technologies in fields such as genetics, medicine, and biology creates not only political and economic issues but also ethical ones for societies.

Global Disparities

Industrialization in the 20th century has given rise to considerable disparity in global wealth. The World Bank reported in 1997 that about 56% of the world's population lived in countries whose annual income did not exceed US$785, and 28% lived in countries with an annual income between US$786 and US$9636. About 16% of the world's population enjoyed an annual income of over US$9636.

Important economic and social gaps between low and high income countries remain. These gaps are predicted to persist well into the 21st century. Although China and India, where as much as 60% of the world's poor live, have introduced measures that since the 1980s have lifted several hundred million people out of poverty, the World Bank predicts that income differences between low and high income countries may widen over time. Governments are recognizing that these income differences between countries may depend very much on how income is distributed among people within countries.

The World Bank predicts that some social differences between low and high income countries will narrow. As low income countries develop their economies, and as their people have greater access to education and healthcare, differences in social measures such adult literacy, life expectancy, the birth rate, infant mortality, and urbanization will decrease.

The challenge in the 21st century will be for governments and international agencies to design policies that can reduce some economic gaps between low and high income countries. Governments are now recognizing the importance of having policies that can promote better income distribution, such as giving priority to rural development, asset redistribution, education for all people, and employment.

Population Growth and Aging

In 1900, the world's population was estimated at 1.6 billion people, which by 1997 had grown to 5.82 billion, an unprecedented increase in human population. The World Bank estimates that world population will grow to 8.12 billion in 2025. This has profound implications for societies around the world.

The World Bank predicts that the population of South Asia, the Middle East, and Africa will rise much more rapidly than elsewhere. This rapid population growth poses major challenges for the governments of these regions to provide more housing, employment, and education for their people. International development organizations like the World Bank have come to recognize the long-term effects of rapid population growth and the need to establish programs that improve living conditions. For this reason, policies have been introduced to promote more home building, education, and self-employment.

At the same time as world population increases, more people will live longer. The World Bank forecasts that the percentage of the world's population aged 60 years and older will increase from 9.6% in 1997 to 14.4% by 2025. In countries like Canada, China, Japan, Russia, Sweden, and the United States the number of people over 60 years of age will grow dramatically, eventually becoming the largest population group.

The challenge in these and other countries with aging populations will be to design policies that can provide sufficient healthcare and income support for older people, without dramatically raising taxes to be paid by the young who will be supporting the growing numbers of retired people. Recent trends suggest that many people over 60 years of age will be encouraged to continue working in some capacity, using their experience and wisdom for the common good, the training of the young, and to provide themselves with sufficient income to live.

Environmental Protection

For much of the 20th century, people believed that the planet's natural resources were unlimited. Deposits of minerals, oil, and natural gas were exploited for industry and energy. Forests were logged for timber and materials for papermaking. Wildlife was killed or captured for food, sport, science, and medicines. As the planet's natural resources were developed, industrial and household wastes accumulated on the land, in the water, and in the air.

Beginning in the 1970s, environmental protection became a major political issue in North America and Europe. Environmental movements emerged, and a new way of thinking called environmentalism challenged the conventional wisdom of unrestrained economic development and government policies that promoted rapid economic growth.

Throughout Asia and Latin America industrial development has been proceeding on a grand scale. Hundreds of millions of Asians and Latin Americans are acquiring living standards that Europeans and North Americans have enjoyed for a long time. The effect of global industrialization is beginning to affect the planet's natural capacity to cleanse its oceans and atmosphere of pollutants.

The spread of pollution is no longer confined to the country or region where it is produced. Pollution created in one country adversely affects neighbouring countries. Even uninhabited regions of the world are now contaminated. These problems will grow as Asia and other regions industrialize.

The challenge will be to provide all people with a decent standard of living without further contaminating the planet. Recent global agreements on pollution control have been encouraging, but it will take a concerted effort by all governments to protect the environment. For industrial societies such as Canada, the United States, Sweden, and Japan, the introduction of measures to protect the environment may require people to make changes in their lifestyles that are more environmentally appropriate. For countries with developing economies, the challenge will be to learn from the mistakes of others; to continue to develop economically without further degrading the environment.

All of these challenges will affect humankind in more profound ways than ever before, because of their global nature. Now more than ever, all peoples, governments, and international agencies will need to show greater resolve and cooperate to a greater degree in order to meet these challenges.

REVIEW

1. Create a chart summarizing the possible positive and negative effects of events related to nationalism, globalization, technology/information, global disparities, population growth/aging, and environmental protection.

2. Choose one of these challenges to study in greater detail. While no one can predict the future with any accuracy, based on your knowledge and available primary and secondary sources, take and defend a position that suggests whether the situation will either improve or become worse in the 21st century.

3. Which of the six issues presented here, in your view, is the most important challenge for the 21st century? Provide supporting arguments for your point of view.

4. In addition to the six issues presented here, what other challenges would you predict for the 21st century? Be prepared to discuss your ideas.

APPENDIX

SKIMM™ (*Learning How to Learn*)

On the following pages you will find a variety of ideas for studying, making notes, critical thinking, analysing sources, essay writing, and preparing for and writing exams. Some graphic organizers are provided as sample formats for organizing and learning new material.

Study Skills

To be confident about your preparation for examinations, it is important to have good study skills and apply them regularly—as you learn new material, in your ongoing review, and as pre-examination preparation.

Learning Style

Know your learning style and use an appropriate set of studying techniques. A visual learner may need to see information, and will benefit from charting the relationships between ideas in graphic organizers, or using other visual note making techniques, such as sketches and colour underlining. An auditory learner may benefit from reciting, tape recording notes and playing them back, or team studying using questioning techniques. Some people study best by reading over notes, writing out lists, and creating summaries. A combination of techniques suitable for the type of information being studied is recommended.

Environment

Think about your study environment. A quiet comfortable place with good lighting is ideal, although some people feel they work well in noise or visual distraction without losing too much efficiency. If you have trouble concentrating, consider changing your environment.

Planning Ahead

Approach studying in a planned, organized, and effective manner.
- Identify the task.
- Limit the task according to the time available.
- Understand what is expected.
- Why is the information important?
- Where does it fit in the course?

Notes

Your note taking style and your study methods are related. It helps to record information in a way you can easily work with it in order to store it in your long-term memory. (*See also* Organizing Effective Notes)
- Review your notes. Decide what information is significant. Condense and summarize. Make lists of important terms, people, dates, events. Do this as an ongoing activity.
- Understand the table of contents and the title hierarchy in your textbook. Use them to outline the content of each section for a quick review.
- Use webs, mind maps, or outlines to make difficult concepts or knowledge clearer. (*See* diagrams, page 456)
- Put into words or use diagram connections to understand how information is related.
- Diagram comparisons using charts. Show similarities and differences in related information. When developing an idea for an essay exam, it is often valuable to describe something by comparing it to a related or opposite concept. (*See* diagrams, page 458–459)
- Develop a vocabulary of meaningful terms. Use a variety of techniques to learn new vocabulary besides defining. Try sketching, using colour, or using the word in context. (*See* diagrams, page 457)
- Use highlighting or underlining effectively. Focus your notes on the critical or main ideas. Show supporting examples or facts.
- Understand the sequence of related information. Identify cause and effect relationships.
- Timeline chronological events. Use pictures, colour, or other visual information to assist remembering.
- Use file cards, posters, or charts to record information. File cards are portable. Wall charts and posters are large-scale organizers and visual reminders.
- Use other media, such as video or audio recording or computers, for note recording and organizing information for review.

- Reading skills are particularly critical to success in multiple choice examinations. Develop a vocabulary of meaningful terms. Do not assume that you fully understand unfamiliar words just from the context. Confirm the definition in a dictionary or other resource, then practise the use of unfamiliar vocabulary. (*See also* Answering Multiple Choice Questions.)

Other Methods of Studying

- Learn by teaching to a friend or parent.
- Team study. Question each other. Read each other's notes—someone else's way of expressing an idea may stick with you. Get them to explain notes you do not understand. This will help you both.
- Use interviewing and role playing to understand and be able to explain the point of view of significant characters. Essay questions may ask you to write from someone's point of view.
- Use practice tests. Review old exams, forecast the types of questions you may face and practise sample answers.
- Make up your own exam and essay questions and share them with others.

Studying for an Examination

- What questions might be asked on an examination? Do you need to have broad understanding or a narrowly focussed knowledge of information? Do you need to know details, relationships, trends, points of view, comparisons? Will you need to take a stand and defend it with evidence?
- For an essay exam where the theme is known, decide what topics might be asked and how you might approach them. What general arguments and evidence can you prepare in advance? (*See also* Essay Writing)
- For an essay exam where the topic is known, what will your thesis be, and what arguments and evidence can be used to support it? (*See also* Essay Writing)
- For a multiple choice exam, what sorts of questions do you think will be asked? (*See also* Answering Multiple Choice Questions)

Organizing Effective Notes

Recording important ideas and information for concept understanding, for later referral, and for study can be done in a variety of ways. Writing, drawing, diagramming, graphing, and even recording on audio or videotape or in a computer are all ways of making notes. Using methods that suit both the information being learned and your learning style will make learning, understanding, and studying easier and more effective. (*See also* Study Skills)

To be useful, notes must be used, not stored. Come back to them often, add to them, organize and summarize them. Review them at the end of the day, the end of the week, and the end of the unit you are studying.

Sources of notes

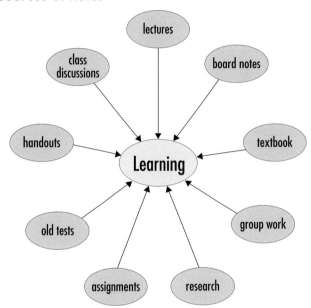

Organize your notes

In order for you to find and review material in your notes, they need to be organized.

- Keep notes in sequence, either by date or sorted and sequenced by theme or topic using dividers in a binder.
- Make bold or highlight headings and topics, and highlight important information.

Reuse your notes

Adding to your notes to clarify points and make connections between ideas increases their usefulness for studying.

- Leave wide margins or write only on one side of the page to allow for later annotations.
- When you review or study, use the margins to add diagrams, list key words, write out definitions,

refer to other sections of your notes, or add page numbers from the textbook.

- Recopy your notes if necessary to make them legible.
- If you don't remember or do not understand something you have written, mark it and look it up. Add an annotation.

Graphic Notes

- Create charts, diagrams, or timelines from the information in your notes.
- Show comparisons visually.
- Be creative in helping yourself see relationships between ideas; for example, use arrows, mind maps, colour coding.
- **If important material stands out on the page it will be recalled more easily.**

Following are examples of different types of charts and graphic organizers.

For organizing main ideas and supporting details:

a)

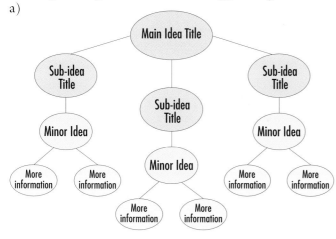

b)

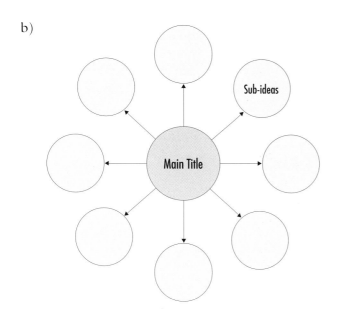

c)

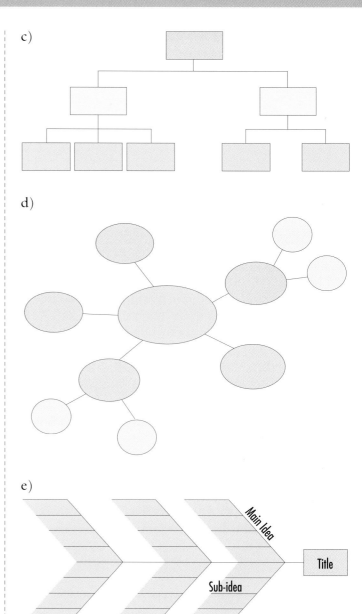

d)

e)

For showing the combining of ideas to form a new whole:

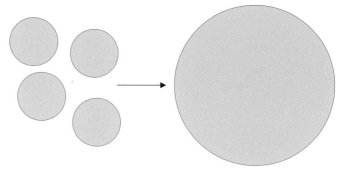

For separating a whole into parts or components:

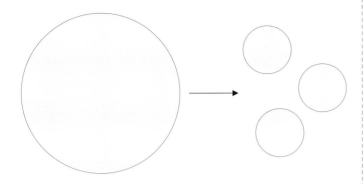

For recording definitions or new vocabulary:

a)

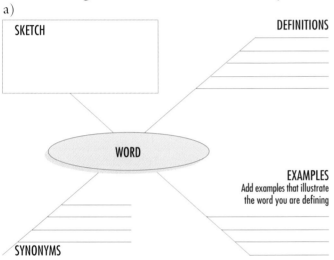

SKETCH

DEFINITIONS

WORD

EXAMPLES
Add examples that illustrate
the word you are defining

SYNONYMS

b)

Word		Picture
		Draw a simple sketch of the word and colour it. You are not expected to create something artistic. The activity of drawing aids memory.
Definition Write a definition in your own words. Use the information in the textbook, the glossary, or from a dictionary.	**Example** Write examples using the word in context.	

c)

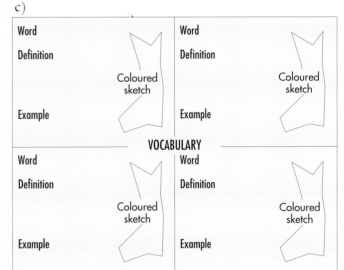

| Word Definition | Coloured sketch | Word Definition | Coloured sketch |
| Example | | Example | |

VOCABULARY

| Word Definition | Coloured sketch | Word Definition | Coloured sketch |
| Example | | Example | |

Critical Thinking

Critical thinking means not accepting information as presented without questioning. All published material contains opinion and bias, if only because the author and editor have selected some material to include and have left other material out. Information may be presented accurately, or it may be questionable. Judgments and generalizations are made from a certain point of view. Comparing more than one point of view or source of information regarding an event helps you confirm or check the validity of information. It is important to be able to correctly identify factual information and separate it from interpretation or opinion.

Bias

Critical thinking includes detection of bias. Bias literally means angle, a slanting line. It reflects the point of view or perspective from which information is presented. Bias in published material may be obvious, if judgments and expressions of opinion are stated or shown directly or strongly, or it can be subtle and more difficult to detect.

A fact is something that really happened and is verifiable. There is wide agreement about it, and the supporting evidence demonstrates or confirms it. There is no significant evidence that contradicts or denies it.

Opinion is something believed to be so. It can be detected by examining judgments and generalizations that are made. Opinion may be based on fact, but unless confirming evidence is present it must be considered questionable and lacking in validity.

Writer's Bias

Interpretation of events or ideas, even when supported by evidence, represents a point of view. Reports from different points of view of the same event may be contradictory because of the interpretation each person puts on events.

- Who is speaking/writing?
- Who is being addressed?
- What problem or issue is being dealt with?
- What is the speaker/writer's purpose, intention, or objective ?
- Does he/she identify with one side of the conflict or issue?
- Is the speaker/writer's attitude (bias) regarding the subject critical or approving?
- What facts are being presented? For example, Who? What? When? Where?
- If "Why?" is presented as part of the information, it reflects either the author's opinion or the reported opinion of someone else. Is the opinion supported by credible evidence?
- What facts are or might be missing? Information that is left out can tell you much about bias or opinion in an article. For example, is well-known contradictory evidence missing?
- How does the report make you feel? Does it appeal to your emotions or try to persuade you in some way?
- Are there unsupported judgments?
- Are supporting "facts" interpreted accurately in a balanced way? For example, have statistics been manipulated to form evidence?
- Some significant information about the author includes the time period when the report is written, the nationality or origins of the author, and any affiliation of the author that may affect his/her objectivity.

Reader's Bias

The reader/listener also brings his or her own bias to the communication process. What personal background or history, beliefs, values, or opinions may bias your understanding of subject matter? Always consider your own bias when you analyse reported material.

To Detect Bias

To detect bias, examine presented material carefully and identify choices that have been made in the presentation.

- choices of photographs, illustrations, visual style
- adjectives and adverbs, descriptions, emotional content
- facts presented; facts not included; facts given greater weight

- caricature—visual or verbal exaggeration of a person, idea, institution, or event with the purpose of exposing weakness, mocking, criticizing, or drawing attention to something
- general impression, either from the design, or the writing style (for example, powerful, delicate, sparse, cramped, richly textured, sketchy, intense, cool, angry)

Comparison

Comparison involves analysis of two or more items to determine similarities and differences, strengths and weaknesses, or advantages and disadvantages.

There are a variety of strategies or types of graphic organizers that can be used to organize the process of comparison.

Venn Diagrams

Compare A and B, showing characteristics that are unique to each (not shared) and characteristics that are shared by both.

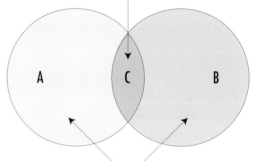

Similarities (shared characteristics)

Differences (not shared)

Criteria Comparison Chart

Organize comparable information about A and B according to specified criteria. This is a useful way to study features of systems for essay-type questions.

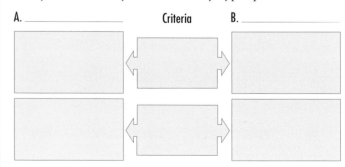

Criteria	System A	System B	System C
Strengths			
Weaknesses			

Other Comparison Charts

List key characteristics of comparable systems in chart form to sort out similarities and differences or strengths and weaknesses. Create a master chart to summarize all of the important points about political and economic systems that you may need to compare or analyse in an essay.

COUNTRY A (characteristics)	Political	Economic	Strengths (Advantages)	Weaknesses (Disadvantages)
Values				
Ideas				
Experience				
COUNTRY B (characteristics)				
COUNTRY C (characteristics)				

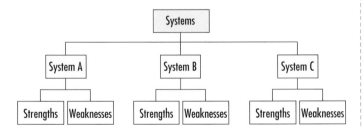

Thinking/Writing from Another's Perspective

Empathy is the ability to understand, emotionally or intellectually, the feelings of another person. Being able to empathize is essential to carrying on negotiations and solving problems between people.

Some essay and exam questions require you to write or think from someone else's perspective; for example, "Explain communism from the point of view of a wealthy Russian landowner after his land was confiscated by the government in 1919."

Understand the Person and the Issue

To understand another's point of view in order to be able to report from his/her perspective, ask yourself the following questions:

- Who is it? What background does the person have that is relevant to the issue? (For example, national, ethnic, cultural, political, racial, economic, occupational, religious, generational, gender, and so on.)
- What ideology does the person support? What are his/her values and beliefs?
- What is at stake for the person in this issue?
- What understanding does the person have of the opposing viewpoints? For example, what do detractors or enemies say about the issue? How would the person counter these arguments?

Prepare Your Argument

Practise preparing arguments and counter-arguments from a point of view:

- Identify an issue or conflict and the principal points of view to be represented.
- Summarize the facts.
- List the characteristics of the person(s) whose points of view are represented.
- Use a graphic organizer such as the one below to diagram opposing points of view about the facts.
- Interpret the facts in relation to the vested interests of the character(s).
- Defend the person's position, giving supporting evidence. **Anticipate and understand the opposing point of view so that you can effectively counter it**.

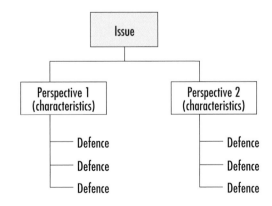

Cartoon Analysis

Cartoons are succinct visual expressions that convey information of several kinds in a small space. They may or may not be amusing. They usually express the values of the author and view an event from a particular perspective. Even cartoons whose primary objective is to amuse do so because they present an observation of human life that surprises us in some way.

Many cartoons use humour for serious purposes. Satire is intended to be persuasive. Public people, institutions, and events are portrayed in ways that cause viewers to observe them more closely, question them, take a different perspective on them, and possibly change their opinion of them.

Cartoons present some literal information (recognizably factual or accurate), and some implied information. This is sometimes referred to as the text and the subtext. Identifying and interpreting the implied information, or subtext, is a useful skill.

Irony, or saying the opposite of what is meant, is a common device in cartoons.

Interpreting Political Cartoons

- Identify recognizable elements—the setting, the characters (public buildings, geographical locations, public characters).
- Identify the contemporary reference (the news story) to which it relates. Even if you can't identify the reference, you can understand and describe much of the cartoonist's message.
- All visual detail is significant. It has been included for a literal or a symbolic reason.
- Identify symbols: flags, logos, animals, objects
- Position and other compositional elements are significant. What is in the foreground? What is in the centre? What is largest? What stands out because of contrast (light against dark, dark against light, detailed against vague)?
- Identify significant details to describe the character(s). Is the character an official, a worker, a member of an identifiable group, or is it the "everyman" or "everywoman" viewpoint? For example, a plaid-shirted, TV-watching, snack-eating, opinionated character is often caricatured in Canadian cartoons to represent the person-on-the-street observing the events of the day. (This is a negative stereotype. Stereotypes are commonly used in political cartoons, so it is good to learn to recognize them because they reflect bias.)
- Caricature, or exaggeration, may be used as a visual shorthand to identify public figures: for example, Stalin's huge moustache, Gorbachev's birthmark, General de Gaulle's nose.

- All text is significant. It may be a label, a quote or reference to a quote from the news, or a comment or observation from either an identifiable interest group, or else from a character that represents the "everyman" viewpoint.
- Understatement is often used ironically in captions to give the impression that something is less or more important than it is.
- A cartoonist's style is individual, like a voice or a signature. Notice how the style of drawing affects your interpretation of the content. How does the cartoonist convey his or her message and opinion through style?
- When and where was the cartoon published? You may need to research and do a critical analysis of the period and place. Find out about common opinions and attitudes of the time towards issues in order to understand the message of the cartoon in its contemporary context.

Analysis of Sources

Anything that gives you information about something you are studying or researching is a source.

Primary sources come from the time being studied. Contemporary newspapers, articles, books, speeches, coins, gravestones, paintings, posters, photographs, maps, local records, radio and television news or documentaries, diaries and memoirs, cartoons, and statistics are all primary sources if they were created at the time of the events studied. Interviews with people alive at the time are also primary sources.

Secondary sources provide an analysis of events, and are usually written after the events have taken place. They present a broader context and interpret events in the light of further developments. This textbook is an example of a secondary source, although it contains examples of primary sources. Analytical books, articles, films, documentaries, or radio programs created at a later time are all secondary sources.

To evaluate the credibility of a source, learn as much as possible about its origins.

Who? (Author)

- Who wrote (created) it—a man or woman, member of a group, social class, occupation, religious affiliation, and so on?
- What were the author's associations or affiliations? Has the author argued from a certain point of view? What is the political perspective?
- Is the author in an active or passive role, a leader, a follower, a participant, an observer?
- What is the level of education of the author?

- To what extent do the personal characteristics of the creator appear to have influenced what has been produced?

Who? (Audience)
- Who was the intended audience?
- Was it originally a private communication, or for use within a family, or for remembrance in coming generations of a family?
- Was it created for a wide audience, to educate, guide, convince, or entertain?

What?
- What type of source is it? For example, was it a primary or secondary source, a legal document, a personal diary, a newspaper, a textbook?

When and Where?
- When and where did it originate? What was the context of the time? Is a date provided or do you need to guess from evidence and inference? What had happened or was going on in the place and society when the source was created?

Why?
- Why was the source created? What was its purpose, intention, or objective? Was it intended to attack, defend, or describe? To persuade people to take a course of action? To entertain or inform? To be part of an historical record?
- Was it created to explain or justify the actions of a group, institution, or leader?
- Was it intended to be unbiased, or was a particular point of view being presented? Can you identify bias in the source? Was it intended to be a piece of propaganda, or was bias unintentional? Did it appeal to the emotions or the intellect?

Data Sources
When looking at primary sources that are principally statistical or factual, such as statistics, maps, or other data, some of the same questions about their reliability should be asked:
- Where did the information come from? Was it from a source likely to be unbiased or from a source with a vested interest in "looking good" or concealing information from either the public of the time or their opponents? Is the source credible?
- Can the information be confirmed or verified by checking other sources?
- Are there omissions or exaggerations?
- What was the context in which these data were published?

Essay Writing

An essay may be written out of class, in class, or in an essay examination. As with any assignment or examination, the purpose of the essay is to demonstrate your knowledge and understanding of a topic. Knowledge is shown by presenting accurate, relevant, and comprehensive information about the topic; that is, to sufficient depth and breadth. Understanding is shown by taking a thesis and defending it logically, systematically, and persuasively.

Position Paper
The most common type of essay to be written in a study of political and economic systems is the position paper. A position paper is a form of persuasive writing. For example,
- take and defend a position on an important issue
- explain why a particular event occurred
- explain why some regime or program was successful or unsuccessful
- compare systems, showing the advantages of one and disadvantages of the other.

The **topic** will take the form of a question that will likely begin with "Why," "Should," or "To what extent." Your position, opinion, point of view, or your answer to the question will be your **thesis**.

The **length** of a position paper will vary according to the time you have available and the complexity of the subject. Even in a short essay, a minimum of three important ideas should be developed in the body. Do not restrict yourself by an arbitrary paragraph count. Supporting your thesis in order to demonstrate your knowledge and understanding is the goal, not how many paragraphs you have.

The **format** for a position paper, regardless of length or the context in which it is written, should include an introduction, a body, and a conclusion.

Introduction
- set the broad context
- explain the problem to be examined
- state the range of opinion that exists on the issue
- state your specific thesis

The thesis is the most important element of the introduction because it provides the focus or direction of the essay. Your thesis may need to contain more than one idea if the issue is complex. It provides the limits to your exploration of the issue. Return to it regularly as you write. It will help you avoid
- extra detail that does not support your argument
- answering a different question than you started out to answer
- missing your conclusion

Body

The arguments and evidence that you provide to support your thesis can be presented in different ways. Each argument can be presented, one at a time, supported by relevant evidence, or argument and evidence can be woven together in a forceful defence of your thesis.

It is important that each paragraph and the entire body be organized logically, with each point leading to the next without confusion, backtracking, or irrelevance. Each sentence of a paragraph must relate to the topic sentence; each paragraph of the body must develop the thesis.

Correct **transitions** are essential. Accurately use such words as furthermore, consequently, then, as well as, on the other hand, in contrast. Transitions

- point the direction from one idea to the next (e.g., with this in mind)
- assert cause and effect relationships between ideas (e.g., as a result)
- label chronology, when the correct sequence of events or ideas is important to the development of an idea (e.g., subsequently)
- link related ideas (e.g., in a similar way)
- contrast opposing ideas (e.g., however)

Evidence comes from a variety of sources, both primary and secondary. Support your argument with a discussion of relevant values, theory as written by the thinkers you have studied, and case evidence from the case studies. Identify your sources. Be specific—general details dilute an argument.

When you refer to a source that may be biased, acknowledge the bias and show reasons why the opposing viewpoints may be incorrect. Use caution with such material—the intention is to strengthen, not weaken, your argument. You will need to make judgments about the worth and validity of values and perspectives, the ideas of philosophers, historians, and economists, and provide evidence to support your judgments. (*See also* Analysis of Sources)

Conclusion

Restate the main arguments in support of your thesis. If possible, tie them together in your final statement in order to summarize the logic of your argument in a convincing way.

Other considerations

- Read the topic or question carefully. Doing good work that doesn't answer the question will not satisfy an examiner that you have the knowledge and understanding being asked for.
- Brainstorm ideas about a possible thesis and supporting evidence and arguments before beginning to write.

- Create an outline of your evidence and arguments. Getting them in an appropriate order will help you remember to cover them all. Change the outline if you add new ideas as you write.
- Use clear language, and write concisely in order to make your point clearly. Make your words count, particularly if time is limited. Extra words will not convince an examiner of your knowledge—extra evidence will. Use vocabulary correctly in order to be specific and accurate when presenting your arguments and evidence.

Answering Multiple Choice Questions

Examinations are designed to allow you to demonstrate your knowledge and understanding of the subject you are studying. Multiple choice questions, while appearing to be a simple matter of choosing the correct answer, test complex ideas. Success in these examinations is a matter of both knowledge and skill.

A multiple choice question is composed of a stem and a series of distractors (possible answers) to choose from. In some questions, a source (e.g., a quotation) or set of sources is provided for you to read or analyse first, before answering a question or questions.

The stem may be in the form of a question or a statement to be completed. You select the distractor that answers the question or completes the thought correctly or most correctly.

Reading Multiple Choice Questions

Accurate reading and clear understanding of the questions being posed are essential to providing correct answers in multiple choice questions, where complex issues are phrased in very concise terms. You will need

- a good understanding of sentence structure, particularly interrogative (question) forms
- a good knowledge of the vocabulary of the subject
- attention to conditional verb tenses, particularly forms like *would*, *could*, and *might*
- attention to cues like *not, most, greatest difficulty, mainly, choose the exception, most closely, primarily, differ most*.

Sentence Structure

In order to create a question that fits the stem/distractor format, normal sentence structure may be reversed or a phrase used in an unusual way. If necessary, reword the sentence to confirm that you know what is being asked. For example, the following three stems mean the same and use the same words:

"The data in the graphs fail to provide an answer to which essential question?"

"To which essential question do the data in the graphs fail to provide an answer?"
"Which essential question do the data in the graphs fail to provide an answer to?"

Vocabulary

As well as content-related vocabulary, there are many phrases commonly used in multiple choice questions that you will need to understand. This list is just a sample. If you have access to old examinations, study terms such as these to confirm that you understand them.

categorize	underlying tenet of
reinforce the view that	context
consequently	specifically
departure from	validate the implication
neglected to	dilemma
apparent from	cumulative
characterized by	seriously challenge
ultimately	ironic
unique	infer from
assumption	implied by
alludes to	contradict
compatible with	assertion

Source Questions

Source questions provide a variety of materials for you to analyse, including quotations (from speeches, books, articles, headlines, and so on), cartoons, charts, graphs, maps, statistics, and others. When working with sources

- read the source to find the main point and understand the issue
- determine by whom and when it was created
- read the question for understanding, and read the alternatives (distractors)
- for multiple sources, read and determine the message, author, and contemporary context of each source separately; identify the common issue or link in the sources; then read the question and alternatives.

All Questions

- underline or highlight key words in the stem
- make sure you understand each key word or concept
- make sure you understand the question
- read each distractor carefully; eliminate any that are obviously wrong (put a stroke through the letter); choose and mark the correct one
- distractors that use terms such as "never," "always," "no one," and "all" are often wrong choices; read and consider them carefully
- compare distractors; you need to be able to determine whether or "to what extent" something is true or false, present or absent
- all distractors may be somewhat correct when you are asked to choose the best answer
- do not spend too much time on any one question; mark and come back to difficult questions after finishing the other questions (you may have recalled more information, or you may read it differently the second time)
- answer all questions; you have a minimum 25% chance of being right on a "best guess" answer.

Global Systems Homepage

Arnold Publishing invites you to visit our website at http://www.arnold.ca/ on the internet. For additional information, key in the **Global Systems** five number access code located on the inside front cover of this textbook. This will take you to Arnold Publishing's SKIMM™ **(Learning How to Learn)** web page.

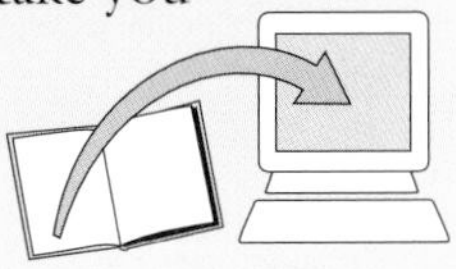

GLOSSARY

A

absolute monarchy—a form of authoritarian government in which a ruling family whose political authority rests on tradition, religion, or divine right controls the government; sometimes referred to as an autocracy

accountability—the requirement for government officials (elected and non-elected) to disclose their performance to the public

administrative guidance—in Japan, a policy of cooperation between government and business for national economic objectives, conducted primarily through the Ministry of International Trade and Industry (MITI), which guides industries in the selection of investment, production, and research

affirmative action—a set of voluntary policies enacted by the United States Congress in 1964 to correct past practices of discrimination against racial minorities, women, the disabled, and other historically disadvantaged groups

anarchism—a political belief where government and law are replaced by mutual agreement between people

anticombine legislation—legislation preventing companies from joining together for business or political advantage, such as price fixing

anti-semitism—a term first applied to a movement of opposition to Jews in the 19th century; prejudice or discrimination against Jews or anything Jewish

apartheid—a political system developed in South Africa in which white South Africans controlled the political process and introduced policies that separated people by race

Aryan—a descendant of the people who spoke Aryan, the parent language of India and Europe; according to Hitler's racial philosophy, considered to be a superior race

authoritarianism—a political principle or belief that all major decisions in society should be decided by one person or a small group of people

autocracy—a form of authoritarian government in which the ruler's power to make decisions for society is unlimited; *see also* absolute monarchy

autonomous region—a form of local government in the People's Republic of China, originally set up to preserve the customs and languages of minority groups in Inner Mongolia, Tibet, Xinjiang, Guangxi, and Ningxia

B

backbencher—a member of a political party who is not a member of the cabinet; an ordinary member of the legislature

bank rate—the interest rate set by the Bank of Canada and used in regulating the money supply to other banks

bourgeoisie—a social class that, according to Karl Marx, owns the means of production and does not work

bureaucracy—in any political system, a group of non-elected officials that controls the administration and implementation of decisions made by political leaders

business cycle—fluctuations in the level of economic activity, alternating between periods of depression and boom conditions

C

cabinet—a group of advisors chosen by the Prime Minister or President to formulate policies and propose measures required for the implementation of policies

capital—an economic resource that includes buildings, equipment, machinery, tools, and money to produce goods and services

capitalism—an economic system in which the means of production are controlled and owned by individuals for personal profit; often called market economy, free enterprise, private enterprise, *laissez faire*

Central Committee—a decision making body of a Communist Party elected by the Party Congress; *see also* Party Congress

centrally planned economy—an economy in which the state owns and controls the means of production, and all major economic decisions about production and distribution are made by a small group of planners

centre—the middle ground on the political left–right continuum; favouring the status quo or minor changes

checks and balances—a fundamental principle of presidential democracy in which political power is distributed among the executive, legislative, and judicial branches of a government

civil liberties—the freedoms of individuals to develop values, views, and personal ideas independent of government; includes the freedoms of expression, worship, assembly, and demonstration, association in political groups, equality under the law, protection from terror, and respect for personal property, gender, race, movement, and choice of residence; *see also* political rights

class struggle—a concept developed by Karl Marx referring to the driving force of social change; a fundamental belief of socialism and communism

classical economics—a body of economic theory, first developed by Adam Smith in the late 18th century and elaborated in the 19th century by Thomas Malthus, David Ricardo, and others; private ownership, self-interest, and competition are fundamental aspects of an economy; *see also* capitalism, invisible hand, private enterprise

closure—a measure by government to end debate on a bill by imposing limits on opposition party members' time to speak

coalition—a temporary alliance of political parties for some specific purpose

co-determination—a policy approved by the Swedish government in 1976 to give employees and their trade union representatives the right to participate in decision making in the workplace

collective bargaining—in Sweden, refers to nationwide negotiations conducted between employers and trade unions over wages and working conditions; in Canada and the United States, refers to negotiations between an employer and a trade union

collective farm—an association of people who come together to work the land and to share the results of their work; existed in the Soviet Union and, between 1950 and 1958, in China

collective ownership—a form of public property in which some property rights are granted to individuals and other rights are held by the state

collectivism—an ideology in which the interests of the group are more important than those of the individual

collectivization—the reorganization and concentration of peasant agriculture into larger production units under government control and supervision; the campaign of peasant suppression carried out in the Soviet Union from 1927 to 1933

command economy—*see* centrally planned economy

commune—in China, a type of production unit set up in 1958 to replace collective farms; abolished between 1979 and 1981 with the introduction of the contract responsibility system for peasant households; *see also* contract responsibility system

communism—a political and economic system based on community or state ownership of wealth, property, and the means of production, with each person working for the common good according to ability and receiving in return according to need

company union—in Japan, a labour union organized within a company rather than along occupational lines; officials of a company union are usually junior managers of the company

competition—individuals vying with one another to gain recognition for their achievements or to secure customers for their goods and services

concentration camp—a collection of barracks set up to hold prisoners of war, political opponents, and others; first used in 1900–1902 by the British in South Africa to intern civilians for helping Boer guerrillas; widely used in Nazi Germany for imprisoning political opponents

Congress—the bicameral, national legislature of the United States, consisting of an elected upper chamber, the Senate, and an elected lower chamber, the House of Representatives

Congress of People's Deputies—an elected legislative body created in the Soviet Union in 1988, with powers to formulate laws, elect a full-time Supreme Soviet, and represent the interests of the Soviet population; abolished in early 1992 following the breakup of the Soviet Union

consensus—general agreement among all people consulted

conservatism—the belief that social change should take place slowly and in accordance with established traditions

conservative—a political attitude or person supportive of the status quo based on traditional values

constituency—an area or territory whose voters elect a representative to a legislative body or assembly

constitution—the fundamental principles and rules according to which political power is allocated in a government, divided among various levels of government, and between a government and the people

constitutional monarchy—a form of government in which the head of state is a member of a traditional ruling family but whose functions are largely ceremonial, who acts on the advice of elected ministers

consumer sovereignty—an economic concept which describes the power of consumers to determine production

through their purchases of goods and services; sometimes referred to as dollar voting

contract responsibility system—a package of reforms in agriculture and industry in China which gave greater independence to producers in order to increase production; private plots, profit, and raises in wages were allowed and producers were freed from following production targets and quotas

controlled participation—a method used in a non-democratic system to give people a sense of participation in government

cooperation—individuals deciding to work together to realize mutual goals

cooperative—an organization or business which is collectively owned by its users, through which they realize mutually agreed-on goals

corporate state—organization of the economy based on grouping the labour force according to occupation, profession, and work; first developed in Italy under Mussolini in the 1920s; source of inspiration for some measures undertaken by Hitler to reorganize the German economy in the 1930s

corporation—a form of business organization that is created by law and has the right to sell shares to individuals, commonly referred to as a limited company

Council of Ministers—an executive and administrative body which directed most day-to-day activity of the Soviet government; the chairman of the Council of Ministers was the head of the government, roughly equivalent to a Prime Minister

Cultural Revolution—officially called the "Great Proletarian Cultural Revolution," the objective was to eliminate old ideas, culture, habits, and customs; people were to be able to endure physical hardship and accept the idea of permanent revolution; education and other fields of endeavour were damaged through loss of their leaders and young people

culture—a learned way of life shared by a group of people, including values, beliefs, customs, traditions, roles, knowledge, institutions; sometimes used to refer to the arts and artifacts of a society

D

demand—the quantity of goods and services people are willing to buy

demand-side economics—the body of economic analysis concerned with the capability of the economy to adjust to fluctuations in consumption and investment, with policies designed to increase total demand for goods and services in the economy

democracy—a political system whose origins lie in ancient Athens; rests on the fundamental principle of rule by the people; characterized by free competition for political power, political equality for all, and rule by the many

democratic centralism—a doctrine developed by Lenin in which discussion of issues by members of the Communist Party was allowed until a decision was made; once a decision was made, all party members were expected to follow it and no further discussion was tolerated

democratic socialism—*see* social democracy

democratization—a process that leads to increased public participation in the decision making process and the creation of democratically elected institutions

de-Nazification—a campaign undertaken by Allied forces to eliminate Nazism in Germany between 1946 and 1949; directed against Germans who were members of, or collaborated with, the Nazi Party; such individuals were compelled officially to renounce their political past and accept guilt for their misdeeds

depression—a sharp contraction in levels of production and employment

de-Stalinization—criticism of some of Stalin's actions and rejection of some of his practices, especially of the use of terror against the people; initiated by Khrushchev's secret speech in February 1956

dictatorship—a political system whose fundamental principle is authoritarianism and rule by one leader or a small group of people; *see* non-democratic system

dictatorship of the proletariat—a term developed by Karl Marx to refer to a form of society in which the workers seize the property of the rich classes, abolish private property, and establish a workers' government

Diet—the Parliament and major law making body in Japan, composed of an upper chamber, the House of Councillors, and a lower chamber, the House of Representatives; *see also* House of Councillors, House of Representatives

direct action—methods and practices used by interest groups to influence public opinion and exert pressure on leaders; includes mass demonstrations, organized boycotts, strikes, advertising, press conferences, and publications

direct democracy—a form of democracy without representation in which all eligible adult members of society participate in making decisions and passing laws

dissident—a person who criticizes the government and disagrees with the policies of the leadership

E

economic system—a set of institutions and practices that determine the production and distribution of goods and services

egalitarianism—the belief that all people should have equal political, economic, and social rights

electoral college—in the United States, a 538-member assembly that elects the President and Vice President

elitism—belief that some people are more capable than others of making decisions for society

Emperor—the hereditary head of state and symbol of Japan, who before 1945 was worshipped as a god by the Japanese people

Enabling Act—passed by the German Reichstag on March 23, 1933, temporarily suspending the constitution and granting the Chancellor power to enact laws by decree

equilibrium—an economic concept in which demand and supply are in balance and prices do not change

executive—a branch of government concerned with the execution of policy and leadership in society

F

faction—a grouping within a political party based on relations between the leader and supporters

factors of production—the economic resources needed for the production of goods and services to take place; *see also* land, labour, and capital

fascism—political belief developed by Mussolini in 1922 to establish authoritarian rule in Italy and after 1933 by Germany; characterized by extreme nationalism, reliance on military power to achieve national goals, and a state-controlled private enterprise economy; *see also* national socialism

Federal Reserve System—the central bank in the United States, comprised of 12 regional federal Reserve Banks and private commercial banks; commonly called the Fed

federal state—an organization and division of power among various levels of government wherein the central government cannot overrule or usurp the jurisdictions of other governments; *see also* unitary state

filibuster—an attempt to obstruct parliamentary proceedings by prolonging debate; common in the United States Senate where senators enjoy the right to unlimited debate

fiscal policy—a set of measures concerned with the overall effects of government spending and taxation on the economy

Five Year Plan—mechanism for facilitating and promoting the rapid expansion of heavy industry, first instituted in 1928–1929 in the Soviet Union; *see also* GOSPLAN

Four Cardinal Principles—a modification of the political doctrines of the Chinese Communist Party by Deng Xiaoping to assist the task of modernizing China; the principles were socialism, people's democratic dictatorship, leadership by the Communist Party, and Marxism–Leninism–Mao Zedong Thought

Four Modernizations—a policy announced by Deng Xiaoping in 1978 to modernize agriculture, industry, science and technology, and national defence, through increased foreign investment, trade, and cultural exchanges with the outside world; *see also* socialism with Chinese characteristics

Four Year Plan—a form of central planning devised by Hitler in 1936 to promote Germany's economic self-sufficiency and rapid rearmament

Fuehrer—title used by Hitler to signify his role as supreme head of National Socialist Germany and as the head of the German people and nation

Fuehrerprinzip—(German) leadership principle; term used by Nazis to signify absolute loyalty to the leader, who had the power to decide, enact, and implement all policies

G

General Secretary—head of the administrative arm of a Communist Party and member of the Politburo

gerrymandering—the drawing of constituency boundaries by the party in power to gain undue advantage in future elections

Gestapo—German abbreviation for GEheime STAatsPOlizei (Secret State Police); secret police force formed in 1933 to arrest and imprison political opponents of the Nazi Party and Hitler; sought to track down and eliminate all dissidents, complainers, and opponents of National Socialism

glasnost—(Russian) openness; a policy initiated by Soviet General Secretary Mikhail Gorbachev in 1986 to improve communication between the state and society and to change the beliefs Soviet citizens held about their society

GOSPLAN—Russian abbreviation for GOSudarstvennaia PLANovaia komissiia (State Planning Commission); the main planning agency for the drafting and administration of five year plans after 1932

government—the exercise of authority over and the performance of functions for a political unit

Governor-General—the head of state in Canada, who acts in the name of the British monarch

Great Leap Forward—a mass campaign directed by Mao in 1958–1959 to industrialize China and establish communes in the countryside, which promised a "leap" into socialism; *see also* mass campaign

"Great Purge"—the period of 1936–1939 when Stalin conducted a campaign to destroy all opposition to his rule in the Communist Party, government bureaucracy, military, and secret police

gross domestic product (GDP)—the value of all goods and services produced by the population of a country

GULAG—Russian abbreviation for Glavnoe Upravlenie LAGerei (Main Administration of Labour Camps); system of forced labour camps used for holding political prisoners in the Soviet Union

H

head of government—a person who holds the responsibility for carrying out the decisions of government and for leading a team of ministers or cabinet that controls the departments or ministries of government

head of state—a person who represents the interests of the nation by carrying out ceremonial functions in the country and abroad; in a parliamentary democracy the head of state and the head of government are different positions; in a presidential democracy they are combined in one position; *see also* parliamentary democracy, presidential democracy

Holocaust—the attempt by Nazis to systematically destroy all Jews in Germany and Europe.

House of Commons—the elected 301-member chamber of the Canadian parliament modelled after the British House of Commons

House of Councillors—the elected 252-member upper chamber of the Japanese parliament

House of Representatives—the elected 500-member lower chamber of the Japanese parliament; the elected 435-member lower chamber of the American Congress

hyperinflation—a condition of very high inflation, usually caused by excessive printing of money by the government to finance its spending

I

ideology—a set of beliefs about human nature, society, and patterns of interaction between human beings.

impeachment—a formal accusation of wrongdoing and formal removal of an elected leader of government

incentives—rewards, benefits, or any positive result that encourages a person to do something; may be material or non-material

indicative planning—a form of planning practised in Sweden, France, and other Western European countries which, unlike central planning, does not set legally binding production quotas on private businesses; generally takes the form of economic forecasts about the overall direction of the economy

individualism—the belief that the interests of the individual are more important than those of the group

indoctrination—the process of forcing people to adopt certain ideas, principles, and views; used to enhance the support and image of a leader or political system

inflation—an increase in the general level of prices in an economy over a period of time

interest group—a group of people who come together to influence government policies for their own purposes; commonly referred to as pressure groups

intervention—an action of government to influence a political or economic system

invisible hand—an economic concept developed by Adam Smith in which individuals acting in their own interest contribute to the common good

iron rice bowl—a term in China referring to the guarantees of employment, housing, clothing, and medical care provided by work units; *see also* work unit

iron triangle—a popular description in Japan of the determination of policies by big business, the bureaucracy, and the government, which has characterized policy making since 1955

J

joint venture—cooperative efforts between foreign investors and domestic enterprises

judiciary—a branch of government responsible for settling disputes, upholding the rule of law, and interpreting the constitution

junta—(Spanish) a council of military officers formed following the overthrow of a government to control the executive and legislative branches of government; *see also* military dictatorship

K

keiretsu—(Japanese) a group of affiliated private business enterprises in present day Japan; often, a loose grouping of former subsidiaries of industrial and financial empires that existed in Japan before World War II; *see also zaibatsu*

Keynesian economics—a branch of economic theory developed by John Maynard Keynes, which argues that government spending can be used to stabilize the economy

Komsomol—(Russian) the Communist Youth League; youth organization of the Communist Party of the Soviet Union; established in October 1918 to promote the teaching of Communist values to Soviet youth

Kristallnacht—(German) "Night of the Broken Glass"; a nationwide program of official violence directed against all Jews living in Germany on November 9, 1938; *see also* pogrom

kulak—(Russian) "tight fist"; a term applied by Communists to better-off peasants during the collectivization of agriculture between 1927 and 1933 in the Soviet Union; *see also* collectivization

L

labour—an economic resource composed of individuals in the population who are employed or looking for employment

laissez-faire—(French) a 19th century economic concept that advocated little or no government intrusion in the economy and argued that individual initiative was necessary for social and economic progress

land—an economic resource that includes real estate, minerals, vegetation, animals, and water

left—a position on the political left–right continuum characterized by demands for changes in new directions

legislature—a branch of government and body of representatives elected by the people to make laws for society

liberal—a political attitude or person supportive of reform and progress

liberalism—the belief that individuals are able to use their reason to undertake social reforms, that change is desirable, and that greater individual freedom is beneficial

lifetime employment—the practice of regularly promoting workers according to seniority, then finding positions for them in subsidiaries upon retirement; the foundation of management–labour relations in many large Japanese companies; *see also* seniority-based wages

lobbying—acting on behalf of clients or advising clients on how to exert influence on government policies

Long March—a 10 000 km trek made by 100 000 Chinese Communists led by Mao Zedong from Jiangxi to Yan'an between October 1934 and October 1935

M

majority rule—an electoral procedure by which a candidate with more than 50 per cent of all ballots cast wins; widely used as a synonym for universal suffrage

majority tyranny—a situation in which the majority disregards the rights and views of minorities and dissenters

market—a mechanism for decentralized decision making, occurring when people wanting to buy goods or services meet freely with others who want to sell them goods or services; also called the marketplace

market socialism—a set of economic policies to allow for the emergence of markets, competition, and profit in an economy characterized by central planning and public ownership of the means of production

Marxism—a set of ideas and beliefs about change, history, revolution, class struggle, and capitalism developed by Karl Marx and Friedrich Engels

Marxism–Leninism—also called Leninism; the body of Marxist thought developed and applied to Russia by Vladimir Lenin; advocated a revolutionary party composed of professional revolutionaries, a strong central state, and a planned economy

mass campaign—mobilization of the general population for political and economic purposes in China; *see also* Cultural Revolution, Great Leap Forward

mass media—several modes of popular communication such as radio, television, and newspapers

means of production—*see* factors of production

mercantilism—a school of thought that believes in promoting exports and limiting imports as the means for a nation to accumulate wealth

military dictatorship—a form of authoritarian government in which the military, through the use of direct rule or "state of emergency" and a council of military officers, controls all important posts of government; *see also junta*

military-industrial complex—a term coined by United States President Dwight D. Eisenhower to describe the powerful alliance of the military, government agencies, and corporations involved in the defence industry

ministerial responsibility—an aspect of responsible government whereby ministers or members of the cabinet are expected to explain and defend to the House of Commons policies and actions carried out in their names

minority rights—recognition of a minority's rights to existence, identity, and self-expression

minority tyranny—a form of authoritarian government controlled by a minority that enjoys full political rights and restricts the political rights of the majority; *see also* apartheid

mixed economy—an economic system that contains various elements of private enterprise and public enterprise; *see also* private enterprise, public enterprise

moderate—a political attitude or person supportive of gradual changes and minor reforms of the existing political and economic order

monetarism—the belief that control of the money supply is the most important tool for administering economic policy and preventing inflation

monetary policy—a set of measures used to control the supply of money and credit in the economy

monopoly—a single seller or producer of a good or service that controls an industry

multi-party system—three or more political parties compete to dominate the political process; no single political party is able to completely dominate the political agenda and decision making process

N

National People's Congress—the national parliament in China, which is indirectly elected and approves all decisions made by top Communist Party leaders

nationalism—an ideology that proclaims the uniqueness of one's language, culture, and ethnicity

nationalization—the transfer of ownership of private property to public ownership

national socialism—a political ideology developed from fascism by Hitler, which emphasized authoritarian rule, extreme nationalism, and racism

neighbourhood committee—a local administrative unit in China that is responsible for registration of local households and monitoring of people's behaviour

neoconservatism—an economic belief appearing in the 1970s and 1980s that rejected most principles of Keynesian economics in favour of classical economic ideas, such as little government regulation of private businesses, free competition, low taxes, and a balanced government budget; *see also* classical economics, supply-side economics

New Deal—a set of economic policies initiated by United States President Franklin D. Roosevelt in March 1933, to lessen the effects of the Great Depression (1929–1939) and provide relief, economic recovery, and social reform

New Economic Policy (NEP)—a policy introduced in 1921 by Lenin creating a mixed economy in the Soviet Union from 1921 to 1928; *see also* War Communism

nomenklatura—(Russian) a list of names; a system of appointment in which all important positions in the government and social organizations were filled from a list of approved candidates

non-democratic system—a political system characterized by rule of one person or a small group of people, the lack of free political competition, and the absence of political equality

O

oligarchy—a government by the few; a form of authoritarian government in which an elite (e.g., landowners, merchants, professionals, an ethnic minority, or a family) controls the government and makes decisions for society; a common form of dictatorship in Latin America

oligopoly—a few producers controlling an industry

ombudsperson (originally ombudsman)—an office of the Swedish parliament first established in 1809, responsible for monitoring the performance of the civil service and protecting the interests of ordinary citizens against arbitrary treatment by the civil service; since 1960, the Swedish system of ombudspersons has spread to other countries, including Canada

one-child family policy—a Chinese government policy to control population growth by limiting family size to one child

"one country, two systems"—a foreign policy announced by Deng Xiaoping in 1982 which stated that Hong Kong, Macau, and Taiwan could retain their capitalist systems when they reunited with China; this policy was part of foreign policy, not economic policy; *see also* special administrative region

one-party system—only one political party allowed to exist, which controls the government

open door policy—a policy imposed on China in the 19th century by foreign powers to open it up to trade; policy introduced by Deng Xiaoping in the early 1980s to increase trade, investment, and cultural contacts between China and the outside world; *see also* Four Modernizations, socialism with Chinese characteristics

opportunity cost—the value of an alternative that is sacrificed when a decision is made to use resources for a specific purpose

P

paramilitary—a private, sometimes secret, semi-military organization

parliament—a legislative (decision making) body of government; the most important political institution of a parliamentary democracy; in Canada, Parliament is the Governor-General, the Senate, and House of Commons, all three of which must consent to legislation

parliamentary democracy—a political system in which the legislature is the highest decision making body

partnership—a form of business organization owned and operated by two or more individuals who share financial resources, risk, management, and profits

Party Congress—the policy making body of a Communist Party, elected every five years to decide and approve party policies

party list—a form of ballot used under proportional representation that lists the main candidates of a political party

party platform—statement of policies of a political party

party whip—member of a political party chosen to ensure that all party members in the House of Commons vote on important party resolutions and follow party policies; ensures party discipline

patronage—rewards given to supporters as favours or encouragement

perestroika—(Russian) restructuring; a set of economic policies initiated by Soviet General Secretary Mikhail Gorbachev in April 1985 to improve the performance of the Soviet economy through increased labour productivity, more efficient production methods, better planning techniques, and more consumer goods

philosophy—a set of ideas and principles underlying knowledge of the universe, life, and morals

physiocrats—followers of a school of thought that appeared in France in the late 18th century that regarded agriculture as the sole source of a country's wealth

plan—a conscious effort by a person or group of people to set goals, assess the availability of resources, organize and implement activities, and evaluate results

pluralism—a condition in which there exists a diversity of opinions, views, and ideas, all competing for dominance; a theory that states that reality is composed of many differing parts

plurality—a type of electoral system in which the candidate with the most votes wins; sometimes referred to as "first past the post"

pogrom—organized violence directed against an ethnic group, religion, or culture

polarization—a situation in politics in which extremist views attract significant voter support

Politburo—the most powerful policy and decision making body of a Communist Party, which controlled the government

political culture—a society's values, beliefs, customs, roles, and institutions dealing with power and decision making

political party—a political group of people who come together voluntarily to represent certain views, including how to govern the country

political process—interaction among political groups, commonly referred to as politics; includes the nomination and selection of political leaders and other decision makers in government and society

political rights—the rights that enable people to participate freely in making political decisions; includes the rights of individuals to organize and participate in political groups, to vote and elect government leaders and representatives, and to participate in government; *see also* civil liberties

political system—an organized way of allocating power and making decisions in a society; composed of institutions and practices that make binding decisions for a society; includes the system of government, political groups, the political process, and the policies and goals of the government

pork barrelling—the appropriation of money or the passage of bills that benefit a politician's electoral district

preferential voting—a type of electoral system in which voters are required to select candidates in order of preference, from highest to lowest

presidential decree—a law initiated directly by a President that does not require introduction in a legislative assembly; in the Russian Federation, presidential decrees can be overridden by a two-thirds vote in both chambers of the parliament

presidential democracy—a political system in which voters directly elect the leader of the country

presidential veto—in a presidential democracy, the President is given the right to reject legislation passed by the legislature; in the United States a presidential veto can be overridden by a two-thirds majority vote in both chambers

Presidium—an executive committee of the Supreme Soviet serving primarily as the main legislative body between sessions; chairman of the Presidium was the official head of the Soviet Union

pressure group—*see* interest group

primary—in the United States, an election in which registered party supporters participate in the selection of a party candidate

Prime Minister—the head of government in a parliamentary democracy; in Canada, Japan, Sweden, and other parliamentary democracies, the leader of the political party that can command a majority of the members in the legislature; in Germany and Austria referred to as Chancellor

private enterprise—an economic system characterized largely by private ownership of the means of production and the existence of markets and competition; *see also* capitalism

private ownership—a form of property ownership under which all property rights are held by individuals and private organizations; private property

private sector—the part of the economy that is not owned or controlled by the government and is concerned with the activities of private individuals, businesses, and organizations; the private sector, together with the public sector, make up the national economy; *see also* public sector

privatization—transfer of ownership from government to private individuals

production target—*see* quota

profit—the gain received from the sale of a good or service; the difference resulting from the deduction of costs from sales

proletariat—a term coined by Karl Marx to refer to people who belong to the working class and do not own factories or businesses but must work for others to earn their income

propaganda—statements, printed material, posters, radio and television broadcasts, cinema, and films designed to win people over to some official point of view

property rights—a collection of rights that an individual or organization has over objects; include the right of use, disposal, and income

proportional representation—an electoral system in which candidates of a political party are elected on the basis of share of the popular vote

public enterprise—an economic system characterized largely by public ownership of the means of production and central planning of production

public ownership—a form of ownership under which all property rights are held by the state or government; public property

public sector—the part of the economy that is not privately-owned or controlled; includes all levels of government, government agencies, and organizations, as well as the policies of government that influence and regulate the working of the economy; the public sector, together with the private sector, make up the national economy; sometimes called government sector or state sector; *see also* private sector, fiscal policy, monetary policy

Q

quota—the portion or share of production allotted to any individual or group; also referred to as production target

R

radical—a person committed to making fundamental changes in society and government

reactionary—a political attitude or person supportive of returning to traditions and conventions that existed before they were changed

Reaganomics—a popular name given to the economic policies of United States President Ronald Reagan (1981–1989), which emphasized reducing government spending and reducing taxation of incomes and profits; *see also* supply-side economics

recession—a mild contraction in the levels of production and employment, expected to last for a short period of time

Reichstag—the main law making body and lower chamber of the German parliament elected by proportional representation

reparations—payment by a defeated nation for damages against, and expenses incurred by, a victorious nation

representative democracy—a form of democracy in which voters choose other individuals to act in their place in making decisions; sometimes called indirect democracy

republic—a state that does not have a monarch as the head of state

responsible government—a principle of parliamentary democracy whereby the head of government is accountable to the legislature and must have the confidence of a majority of the members of the legislature to remain in power

re-Stalinization—a return to more restrictive policies and practices in the Soviet Union from 1964 to 1982 under Brezhnev

Riksdag—the unicameral parliament in Sweden that has the sole power to discuss and enact laws

right—a position on the political left–right continuum characterized by demands for maintaining traditions or by a call to return to former values and traditions

rule of law—acceptance of laws as a guarantor of individual rights and equality of individuals before the law; the supremacy of law over arbitrary executive action

S

samizdat—(Russian) self-publishing; illegal hand-published bulletins and literature that appeared from the mid-1950s to the mid-1980s, expressing independent opinions and providing information about human rights, and which circulated privately among the Soviet population

scarcity—a limited quantity of available economic resources when demand is high

Schutzstaffeln (ss)—(German) Protective Service; formed in February 1925 as a bodyguard service for Hitler and other top Nazi Party leaders; after 1934, the main force responsible for arresting political opponents to the Nazi Party; after 1939 responsible for rounding up Jews and Sinti–Roma peoples for imprisonment in concentration and extermination camps

Secretariat—the administrative arm of a Communist Party, responsible for governing the party organization, recruiting members, and implementing party policies

self-determination—the right of a people to determine its own policies and government

self-government—government of a group or nation by its own people or members; independence

Senate—the upper chamber of the Canadian parliament whose members are appointed by the Governor-General on the advice of the Prime Minister; the elected upper chamber of the American Congress

seniority-based wages—in Japan, a system of wage increases and promotions based on an employee's age and length of service with a company

separation of powers—the principle that political power should be divided among several bodies as a precaution against power becoming centralized in the hands of one individual

Sinti–Roma peoples—peoples coming originally from India to Europe in the 14th or 15th century, living a migratory way of life, chiefly in Europe; once called Gypsies

Social Darwinism—a belief developed by Herbert Spencer and others in the 19th century that relations among human beings are characterized by competition and that the "survival of the fittest" is the source of economic and social progress

social democracy—a variant of socialist thought that does not believe in armed struggle by the workers; promotes peaceful change in the social conditions of workers and advocates people's participation in government, which governs in the interests of all

social welfare—a system of government-funded social policies that seek to enhance the well-being of citizens

socialism—a political and economic system in which the community owns and controls all means of production and distribution; contemporary socialists accept the existence of private enterprise while advocating some state control, ownership, and management of the economy in the interests of the people

socialism with Chinese characteristics—a policy announced by Deng Xiaoping in September 1982 which aimed to open up China to the outside world through increased foreign investment, trade, and cultural exchange; *see also* special economic zone

socialist market economy—a policy announced by Deng Xiaoping in October 1992 which would allow market forces to determine prices, production, and distribution, but the means of production would continue to be owned or controlled by the state

sole proprietorship—a business owned and operated by one individual; in Sweden, a family business

solidarity—agreement and unity in opinion, interests, and efforts

sovereignty—independent political power; power or right of self-government

sovereignty-association—a policy pursued by the Parti Québécois to reorganize Canada as two nation-states linked together in close economic union

sovnarkhozy—(Russian) regional economic committees set up by Khrushchev in 1957 to replace central planning with a system of decentralized planning agencies; abolished in 1965 after Brezhnev ousted Khrushchev from power

special administrative region—a form of limited local autonomy offered to Hong Kong, Macau, and Taiwan allowing these areas to retain their capitalist economies, while China would administer foreign policy and national defence

special economic zone—in China, designated areas where foreign businesses may operate joint ventures and enjoy special tax rates, investment incentives, and cheap labour

stagflation—a term developed in the 1970s to describe a situation characterized by economic stagnation and inflation

Stalinism—a body of political thought developed by Joseph Stalin, who ruled the Soviet Union from 1927–1953; an interpretation of Lenin's thought and set of policies for building a powerful centralized state in the Soviet Union; *see also* Marxism–Leninism

State Duma—the lower chamber of the Russian parliament, consisting of 450 deputies, with the power to initiate legislation

state farm—a farm owned and operated by the state in the Soviet Union

status quo—the state of things as they are or have been

Sturmabteilungen (SA)—(German) Storm Troops, formed in October 1921 as the armed wing of the Nazi Party; in 1934, placed under the control of the SS; *see also* Schutzstaffeln (SS)

supply—the quantity of goods and services available for sale by producers

supply-side economics—a body of economic analysis concerned with the productive capability of the economy and with policies designed to improve the efficiency and flexibility of markets

Supreme Soviet—the bicameral Soviet parliament composed of the Soviet of Nationalities and the Soviet of the Union

surplus value—a concept developed by Karl Marx referring to profit that results from the exploitation of workers by the bourgeoisie or capitalists

T

Thatcherism—a set of economic policies initiated by British Prime Minister Margaret Thatcher (1979–1990) to reduce the role and size of government and amount of government intervention in the economy; characterized by deregulation of the economy, privatization of government-owned companies, and decentralization of government departments

theory—a generalization or principle about an aspect of the world, based on observations or data

totalitarianism—a political system in which government has complete control over all areas of human life and society; often used to classify the political system of the Soviet Union under Stalin and Germany under Hitler

township and village enterprise—collectively-owned enterprises established when peasant communes were disbanded in China (1979–1981)

tradition—the passage of beliefs, customs, and practices from generation to generation

transitional economy—a term used by the World Bank to describe public enterprise economies that are in the process of conversion to private enterprise

two-party system—two political parties of roughly equal strength dominating the political process (although other parties exist), often alternating in power

U

union republic—officially called a soviet socialist republic (SSR), one of 15 main administrative subdivisions in the Soviet Union that served as homelands for non-Russian nationalities

unitary state—a central government that determines the allocation and division of power among lower levels of government; *see also* federal state

universal suffrage—a system of voting that grants the right to vote to all adults, without regard to political and religious beliefs, race, gender, and ethnicity

V

values—deeply held beliefs or convictions people have about the nature of the world, their relationship to it, and the basic qualities of human beings

W

War Communism—a set of policies introduced by the Bolshevik government in 1918 to create a communist society in Soviet Russia, ending March 1921; *see also* New Economic Policy

welfare capitalism—a policy of active government intervention in a private enterprise economy to address social injustices, promote economic growth and employment, and lessen the effects of the business cycle on overall production in the economy

welfare state—a system in which the government provides the population with pensions, social security benefits, free health care, and other benefits

work unit—a group through which housing, health care, and food rations were distributed to workers in China; played a key role in enforcing birth control policies and monitoring the activities of workers

Z

zaibatsu—(Japanese) family-owned industrial and financial empires that existed in Japan between 1912 and 1941

INDEX

Legend: ▪ chart • map

479

Legend: ■ chart • map

Legend: ▪ chart • map

Legend: ■ chart • map

Legend: ■ chart   ● map

Legend: ■ chart ● map

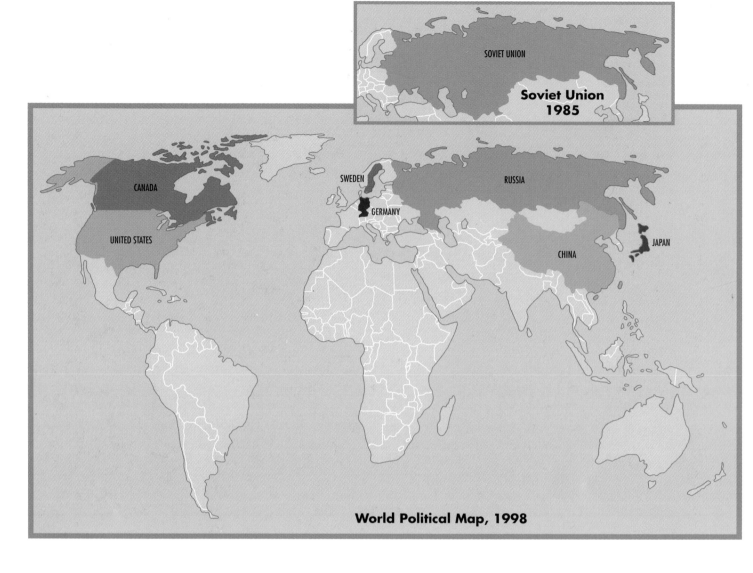

Soviet Union 1985

World Political Map, 1998

		Capital	Currency	Area (000 sq km)	Population (000)	Adult Literacy (percentage)	GDP (billions US$)
Canada (1997)		Ottawa	dollar	9976.1	29 989	96.0	599.0
United States (1997)		Washington, DC	dollar	9372.6	267 955	95.0	7819.3
Sweden (1997)		Stockholm	krona	450.0	8946	99.0	229.5
Japan (1997)		Tokyo	yen	377.8	125 717	99.0	4223.4
Nazi Germany (1938)		Berlin	reichsmark	470.9	68 560	95.0	39.2
Germany (1997)		Berlin	deutsche mark	356.9	84 068	98.0	2115.4
Soviet Union (1990)		Moscow	ruble	22 402.2	288 624	98.0	1530.0
Russia (1997)		Moscow	ruble	17 075.4	147 137	98.0	448.7
China (1997)		Beijing	yuan	9597.0	1 228 005	83.5	917.7

Compiled from *League of Nations*, *United Nations*, OECD, and *World Bank*.